AMNESTY INTERNATIONAL
REPORT 2000

UNITED STATES OF AMERICA

CANADA

ICELAND

UNITED STATES OF AMERICA

IRELAND

MEXICO

BAHAMAS

CUBA

PORTUGAL

MOROCCO

WESTERN
SAHARA

HAITI

DOMINICAN REP.

GUATEMALA
BELIZE

JAMAICA

MAURITANIA

HONDURAS

SAINT KITTS AND NEVIS

ANTIGUA AND BARBUDA

EL SALVADOR

NICARAGUA

DOMINICA

CAPE VERDE

SENEGAL

SAINT VINCENT AND
THE GRENADINES

SAINT LUCIA

GAMBIA

BARBADOS

GUINEA-BISSAU

GUINEA

COSTA RICA

GRENADA

SIERRA LEONE

CÔTE
D'IVOIRE

PANAMA

TRINIDAD AND TOBAGO

LIBERIA

VENEZUELA

ATLANTIC OCEAN

COLOMBIA

GUYANA

SURINAME

KIRIBATI

ECUADOR

PACIFIC OCEAN

PERU

BRAZIL

BOLIVIA

SAMOA

PARAGUAY

URUGUAY

TONGA

CHILE

ARGENTINA

AMNESTY INTERNATIONAL
REPORT 2000

This report covers the period January to December 1999

First published in 2000 by
Amnesty International Publications
1 Easton Street
London WC1X ODW
United Kingdom

www.amnesty.org

© Copyright
Amnesty International Publications 2000
ISBN: 1-887204-21-0
AI index: POL 10/001/00
Original language: English

Printed by:
John D. Lucas Printing Company
Baltimore, MD

Cover design by Synergy

CONTENTS

CONTENTS

PREFACE

Amnesty International (AI) is a worldwide movement of people who campaign for human rights. AI's work is based on careful research and on the standards agreed by the international community. AI is independent of any government, political ideology, economic interest or religion. AI mobilizes volunteer activists in more than 140 countries and territories in every part of the world.

This report documents human rights issues of concern to AI worldwide during 1999. It also reflects the activities AI has undertaken during the year to promote human rights and to campaign against specific human rights abuses.

The core of this report is made up of entries on individual countries and territories, listed alphabetically. Each of these entries gives a summary of the human rights situation in the country or territory and describes AI's specific human rights concerns there. The absence of an entry on a particular country or territory does not imply that no human rights abuses of concern to AI took place there during the year. Nor is the length of individual entries any basis for a comparison of the extent and depth of AI's concerns.

A world map has been included in this report to indicate the location of countries and territories, and each individual country entry begins with some basic information about the country during 1999. Neither the map nor the country information may be interpreted as AI's view on questions such as the status of disputed territory, population size or language. AI takes no position on issues other than human rights concerns which fall within its mandate (outlined in Part 3).

The later sections of the report contain information about AI and its work during the year. The final section focuses on AI's work with intergovernmental organizations and includes information about which states are bound by key international and regional human rights treaties.

AI'S APPEALS FOR ACTION

The country entries in this report include numerous examples of human rights abuses that AI is dedicated to oppose under its mandate. In response to these human rights abuses, AI urges those in authority in all countries where violations occur to take the steps recommended below. More detailed additional recommendations relevant to particular situations are included where necessary in the specific country entry.

Recommendations to governments
Prisoners of conscience
AI calls for the immediate and unconditional release of all prisoners of conscience. According to AI's Statute, prisoners of conscience are people detained anywhere for their political, religious or other conscientiously held beliefs or because of their ethnic origin, sex, colour, language, national or social origin, economic status, birth or other status — who have not used or advocated violence.
Political prisoners
AI calls for all prisoners whose cases have a political aspect to be given a prompt and fair trial on recognizably criminal charges, or released.

AI calls for trials to meet minimum international standards of fairness. These include, for example, the right to a fair hearing before a competent, independent and impartial tribunal, the right to have adequate time and facilities to prepare a defence, and the right to appeal to a higher tribunal.
Torture and ill-treatment
AI calls on governments to take steps to prevent torture and ill-treatment. Such steps include initiating impartial, prompt and effective investigations into all allegations of torture and bringing to justice those responsible for torture.

Further safeguards against torture and ill-treatment which AI promotes include:
- clear policies that torture and ill-treatment will not be tolerated;
- an end to incommunicado detention, including giving detainees access to independent medical examination and legal counsel;
- outlawing the use of confessions extracted under torture as evidence in courts of law;
- independent inspection of places of detention;
- informing detainees of their rights;
- human rights training for law enforcement personnel;
- compensation for the victims of torture;
- medical treatment and rehabilitation for the victims of torture.
Prison conditions
AI calls on governments to ensure that prison conditions do not amount to cruel, inhuman or degrading treatment or punishment, in line with international human rights standards for the treatment of prisoners.
Death penalty
AI calls on governments to abolish the death penalty in law and practice.

Pending abolition, AI calls on governments to commute death sentences, to introduce a moratorium on executions, to respect international standards restricting the scope of the death penalty and to ensure the most rigorous standards for fair trial in capital cases.
Political killings and 'disappearances'
AI calls on governments to end extrajudicial executions and "disappearances". It calls for prompt, independent and effective investigations into such violations and for those responsible to be brought to justice.

AI calls on governments to:
- demonstrate their total opposition to extrajudicial executions and "disappearances" and make clear to security forces that these abuses will not be tolerated in any circumstances;
- end secret or incommunicado detention and introduce measures to locate and protect prisoners;
- provide effective protection to anyone in danger of extrajudicial execution or "disappearance", including those who have received threats;
- ensure that law enforcement officials use force only when strictly required and to the minimum extent necessary — lethal force should be used only when unavoidable to protect life;
- ensure strict chain-of-command control of all security forces;
- ban "death squads", private armies and paramilitary forces acting outside the official chain of command.
Unlawful killings in armed conflict
AI calls on governments engaged in armed conflict to adhere to provisions of international humanitarian law, including the prohibition of direct attacks on civilians and of indiscriminate attacks.
Asylum-seekers
AI calls on governments to ensure that no asylum-seekers are returned to a country where they might suffer violations of their fundamental human rights.

AI calls on governments to ensure that all asylum-seekers have access to a fair and impartial individual asylum determination, and to ensure that they are not arbitrarily detained or otherwise put under undue pressure.
Promote and respect human rights
AI calls on states to ratify international and regional human rights instruments without reservations, and calls on all governments to respect and promote the provisions of these instruments.

Recommendations to armed political groups
AI calls on armed political groups to respect fundamental standards of human rights and international humanitarian law, and to halt abuses such as the detention of prisoners of conscience, hostage-taking, torture and unlawful killings.

AI REPORT 2000
PART 1

© Jane Bown

FOREWORD

by Pierre Sané, AI Secretary General

SOLDIERS IN THE NAME OF HUMAN RIGHTS

Are invasion and bombardment by foreign forces justifiable in the name of human rights? And have external military interventions succeeded in winning respect for human rights?

These issues are at the heart of the debate within the human rights community and the UN over the use of external armed force to counter massive human rights abuses. The debate has intensified in the light of last year's interventions in Kosovo and in East Timor, justified explicitly in terms of protecting civilians from the brutality of the authorities, and in the context of the international community's muted response to the Russian bombing of Chechnya.

We welcome this debate. At stake are the lives and futures of millions of people.

While we welcome the debate, we do not accept the terms in which it is generally posed. Invasion or inaction should never be the only options. Ethnic cleansing or bombing — this is not a choice that human rights activists should ever have to make.

I want to use this opportunity to clarify AI's position on humanitarian intervention — external military intervention in the name of human rights. AI has long refused to take a position on whether or not foreign armed forces should be deployed in human rights crises. We neither support nor oppose such interventions. Instead, we argue that human rights crises can, and should, be prevented. They are never inevitable.

AI does not reject the use of force: laws have to be enforced. When AI calls on governments to protect people from human rights violations and to bring perpetrators to justice, we understand that this may require the use of force, even lethal force. When we address those who have turned to armed struggle to achieve their aims, we do not call on them to lay down their arms, but to respect the basic rights of civilians and their opponents. We are not opposed to the use of force in order to gain justice. But we question whether justice is the driving factor in the international community's decision-making.

Supporters of intervention

Governments who support foreign intervention argue in terms of morality and universal values. US President Bill Clinton justified the NATO bombing of Belgrade on the grounds that to turn away from ethnic cleansing would be a "moral and strategic disaster". Prime Minister Tony Blair of the United Kingdom (UK) said, "This is a just war, based not on territorial ambitions but on values." French President Jacques Chirac called the intervention "a battle for the rule of law and for human dignity" and said, "What is at stake today is peace on our soil, peace in Europe..." .

Supporters of external intervention also cite the development of international law to back their arguments. They point to the Charter of the UN, which allows the UN Security Council to take coercive measures, including military action, if it determines that there is a threat to "international peace and security". The Genocide Convention, which emerged from the ashes of the Holocaust, allows states to call for action by the UN under its Charter to prevent and suppress genocide.

As someone who grew up in Africa, there have certainly been times where I personally would have welcomed intervention to save people's lives.

Opponents of intervention

Governments opposed to foreign intervention base their position on the principles of national sovereignty and non-interference in the internal affairs of a state. The same UN Charter says: "Nothing contained in the present Charter shall authorize the United Nations to intervene in matters which are essentially within the domestic jurisdiction of any state...".

China has long contended that human rights should not be subject to international scrutiny. "We are resolutely opposed to such an act of interference in another country's internal affairs under the pretext of human rights", said a government spokesman in response to criticism of China's human rights record. Russia claims that its bombing of civilians in Chechnya is an internal affair.

The President of Algeria, and Chairman of the Organization of African Unity, Abdelaziz Bouteflika, has argued similarly. He compared international intervention with breaking into a neighbour's house because a child had allegedly been beaten by his parents. "That would be a very serious violation of freedom. New theories [are] being invented solely to deprive peoples and states of their national sovereignty."

Opponents of foreign intervention claim the moral high ground in terms of protecting smaller nations from greater powers, and Algeria, China and Russia all have a history of colonialism or foreign invasion.

Having been born and spent my youth in a former colony, Senegal, I fully understand and support the desire to be free of foreign domination.

States' rights and victims' rights

Both sides of this debate therefore have legitimate arguments. Both sides can justify their positions in terms of internationally accepted principles.

For most individuals who engage in the debate, the issue is the need to react to human tragedies such as mass killings and amputations in Sierra Leone, ethnic killings in Afghanistan or forced mass displacement in the former Yugoslavia and East Timor. For members of AI, the debate is triggered by distress at the suffering in states torn apart by armed conflict or by the collapse of governmental structures. It is fuelled by frustration that AI's traditional techniques of focusing on individual victims seem to be ineffective in chaotic situations and in the face of mass abuses.

The motivation of the individuals and non-governmental organizations who engage in humanitarian interventions is not in question. There is no doubting their commitment to human rights and their personal courage in defending those rights.

Dubious motives

There is grave doubt, however, about the motives of governments. And at the end of the day it is governments who take the decisions about whether to intervene or not, and governments who send and finance military forces.

If government decisions to intervene are motivated by the quest for **justice**, why do they allow situations to deteriorate into such unspeakable injustice?

The NATO governments which bombed Belgrade are the same governments that were willing to deal with Slobodan Miloević's government during the break-up of Yugoslavia and unwilling to address repeated warnings about the growing human rights crisis in Kosovo. Thousands of lives might have been saved if the international community had responded to appeals like that issued by AI in 1993: "If action is not taken soon to break the cycle of unchecked abuses and escalating tensions in Kosovo, the world may again find itself staring impotently at a new conflagration."

Similarly, western governments supported Saddam Hussain's government in Iraq during the Iran-Iraq war, and turned a blind eye to reports of widespread human rights violations. AI called for international pressure on Iraq again and again, especially after the 1988 chemical weapons attack on Halabja which killed an estimated 5,000 unarmed Kurdish civilians. Nothing was done until Iraq invaded Kuwait in 1990.

And isn't it ironic that the state chosen to lead the intervention in East Timor, Australia, is one of the few states that formally recognized Indonesia's illegal occupation of East Timor.

If the motivation of governments is the protection of **universal values**, why is the international community so selective in its actions? The imposition of UN sanctions on Libya or Iraq, for example, stands in stark contrast to the non-imposition of sanctions on Israel for refusing to comply with UN Security Council resolutions. The actions over Kosovo and East Timor invite comparison with the international community's inaction over Chechnya or Rwanda.

In Turkey, an estimated 3,000 Kurdish villages have been destroyed, three million people internally displaced and thousands of Kurdish civilians killed by the Turkish security forces in the context of the 15-year armed conflict with the PKK. There have been no threats of action by the international community, Turkey has been accepted as a candidate for European Union membership and western arms supplies have continued unabated.

If the motivation of governments is **peace**, why do they fuel conflicts by supplying arms? There are at least 10 international wars and 25 civil wars being fought around the globe, many in sub-Saharan Africa, yet arms exports to the region nearly doubled last year. While international attention focuses on nuclear, chemical and biological weapons, the proliferation of small arms (assault rifles and sub-machine guns) has been virtually ignored.

In the case of East Timor, two of the major powers who argued for international intervention — the USA and the UK — were also the two major suppliers of arms to the Indonesian government, whose security forces were responsible for widespread and systematic violations of human rights in East Timor.

If the motivation of governments is **human rights**, why do they send refugees back to danger? The very states that take a leading role in arguing for humanitarian intervention have undermined the fundamental principles of refugee protection. They obstruct access to their borders, send refugees to countries where their lives will be at risk, detain asylum-seekers and exploit xenophobia. Their response to refugee crises elsewhere is selective and inadequate. For example, the refugees from Kosovo have received far more international assistance than the many refugees in western and central Africa whose desperate plight has been virtually ignored by governments outside the region.

The motivation of the governments who oppose intervention is equally dubious. They oppose the use of force to counter mass abuses in other countries, but do not hesitate to use force unlawfully themselves against their own citizens. **National sovereignty** is not a licence to torture, imprison and kill. National sovereignty was won by people fighting for freedom and national liberation; they did not make their sacrifices only to succumb to oppression and violence at the hands of their own leaders.

These governments argue that foreign intervention is not legitimate, but what is the **legitimacy** of a government whose democratic credentials do not stand the test of Article 21 of the Universal Declaration of Human Rights: "The will of the people shall be the basis of the authority of government; this will shall be expressed in periodic and genuine elections…".

These governments cite **international law** to back their positions, but many break international human rights law by abusing their powers and committing human rights violations. They use the UN Charter to justify their arguments, but resist the scrutiny of international bodies established by the UN to promote and protect human rights.

Failed interventions

Besides the moral arguments for and against humanitarian intervention, there is the fundamental question: does the strategy work in the interests of the victims? For those who argue against intervention there is plenty of evidence of failure.

In Kosovo, six months after NATO air strikes, violence was being committed on a daily basis against Serbs, Roma and moderate Albanians. In December 1999, murder, abductions, violent attacks, intimidation, and house burning were reported at a rate almost as high as in June when KFOR troops were

> Ethnic cleansing or bombing – this is not a choice that human rights activists should ever have to make.

> If government decisions to intervene are motivated by the quest for justice, why do they allow situations to deteriorate into such unspeakable injustice?

> National sovereignty is not a licence to torture, imprison and kill.

first deployed. Some 200,000 Kosovan Serbs had been forced out of their homes. Serbs and Roma were almost all living in enclaves protected by KFOR troops, and Serbs in Pritina and other mixed communities needed a military escort to leave their homes and conduct daily tasks such as buying food.

In Somalia, seven years after a UN military intervention, there is no functioning government and no judiciary. Continued fighting, especially in the south of the country, imperils hundreds of thousands of people already at risk of famine. UN forces sent in to protect aid convoys in a country ravaged by civil war and famine themselves committed serious human rights abuses. Their unsuccessful attempts to arrest clan leader General Aideed diverted them from the ostensible purpose of their mission, and they killed and arbitrarily detained hundreds of Somali civilians, including children.

Angola, where the UN intervened in the 1990s, is again in the grip of full-scale armed conflict and civilians are losing their lives. Some are deliberately and arbitrarily killed in indiscriminate shelling of towns. Others are dying from disease and starvation. Last year people in besieged cities were reportedly eating seeds, roots, cats and dogs in order to survive.

The international community clearly does not have the political will to intervene militarily in all the countries where mass human rights abuses are being committed. It has withdrawn its troops from Somalia and Angola, and, as this report shows, there are dozens of other countries where armed conflicts rage or human rights are being abused on a mass scale.

In those situations where the international community has chosen to intervene, the world's governments have not been prepared to commit the necessary resources. Rebuilding strife-torn societies on a basis of respect for human rights is a long-term commitment. By failing to sustain its efforts, the international community has often frustrated the stated aims of its operations. In Haiti, where the USA led a multinational intervention in the name of restoring democracy, the failure to invest in substantive reform of the judicial system has undermined efforts to improve the human rights climate by rebuilding the police force. In Kosovo, where 6,000 international police officers are needed according to the UN, only 2,000 had been deployed by the end of last year.

Consequences of inaction
The supporters of intervention counter these examples with the appalling consequences of inaction. They point to the suffering of the victims in Rwanda, where the UN pulled out its forces as mass killings began and up to one million people died in the ensuing genocide. They point to the years of prevarication before the Second World War, when thousands of people were killed in Germany. Had Hitler confined himself to exterminating communists, gypsies and Jews within Germany, rather than invading neighbouring countries, it is highly unlikely that the Allied powers would have reacted. Similarly, Iraq's treatment of its own citizens was virtually ignored by the international community until Iraq invaded Kuwait.

Another powerful argument in support of humanitarian intervention is the assault on our own humanity. Can governments really expect that we will sit and watch images of unutterable misery and do nothing about it? We all, as human beings, share a responsibility for the fate of other human beings, wherever they live.

The risk to regional peace and security is also used to justify armed foreign intervention. This too is a valid consideration. The tragedy of Rwanda lies not only in the deaths of those slaughtered in the genocide, but in the continuing conflict in the Great Lakes area of Central Africa, where killings continue to this day.

Proposed criteria
At the UN, the debate on humanitarian intervention was advanced when UN Secretary-General Kofi Annan outlined some criteria which might guide the UN Security Council in authorizing interventions, whether by the UN or by a regional or multinational organization. These criteria include:
- the scale and nature of the breaches of human rights and international humanitarian law;
- the incapacity of local authorities to uphold order or their complicity in the violations;
- the exhaustion of peaceful means to address the situation;
- the ability of the UN Security Council to monitor the operation;
- and the limited and proportionate use of force, with attention to the repercussions upon civilian populations and the environment.

I think these criteria appear very sensible. Clearly, the gravity of the violations being perpetrated is the starting point. Concern for the rights of the victims must be central to the justification for any enforcement action. While a degree of politicization and national self-interest is inevitable, the humanitarian element must be credible, visible and override all other considerations.

Also, the use of force must be truly a last resort, and the force used must be proportionate and fully respect international standards.

Perhaps the most important criterion, and probably the most difficult to evaluate, is the last — the impact on the civilian population, the very people on whose behalf the action is being taken.

Outstanding issues
For AI, a movement committed to the impartial protection of human rights all over the world, there remain some difficult unresolved issues of principle and practice.

The UN is the principal source of authority for military interventions, whether carried out by the UN or by other states with some degree of UN authorization. But the UN is composed of governments acting in their own interests. Every military intervention, no matter how it is described, is linked to the strategic interests of the governments behind the

> Can governments really expect that we will sit and watch images of unutterable misery and do nothing about it?

> If the motivation of governments is the protection of universal values, why is the international community so selective in its actions?

troops. The UN Security Council is dominated by its five permanent members — the USA, Russia, China, France and the UK. Can they really claim to be objective guardians of the UN Charter, and fulfil the promises of peace and security for all, when they are the world's five largest arms exporters?

The disproportionate power of certain states in the current world order is reinforced by the actions of the intergovernmental organizations that they dominate. UN or regional military interventions inevitably reflect the interests of politically and militarily powerful states. Conversely, the economically and militarily impoverished states are the most vulnerable to intervention and the least able to resist. If AI supported particular military interventions, prompted by the suffering of the victims, it might, over the longer term, find that it had inadvertently supported a global or regional concentration of power and in the short term had backed action that itself contributed to human rights abuses. In Somalia, UN troops committed serious human rights abuses; in Bosnia they stood by as towns declared "safe areas" by the UN Security Council were devastated; in Kosovo, NATO air strikes breached internationally agreed rules on the conduct of hostilities.

What is best for the victims?

AI's stance in this debate is clear. Our starting point is always to ask what is best for the victims. And what is best for the victims is to prevent massive human rights violations.

None of the human rights tragedies of recent years were unpredictable or unavoidable. The UN Special Rapporteur on extrajudicial, summary or arbitrary executions warned publicly in 1993 that Rwanda was in danger of slipping into genocidal violence. AI has repeatedly exposed the Indonesian government's gross violations of human rights, not only in East Timor, but also in Aceh, Irian Jaya and the rest of Indonesia. We fear now that our pleas for action on certain other countries featured in this report are similarly being disregarded or downplayed. When some human rights catastrophe explodes, will we again be expected to see armed intervention as the only option?

Prevention work

Prevention work may be less newsworthy and more difficult to justify to the public than intervention in times of crisis. It requires the sustained investment of significant resources without the emotive media images of hardship and suffering. It means paying attention to the day-to-day work of protecting human rights. It means using diplomatic measures and other avenues of pressure to persuade governments to ratify human rights treaties, to amend their legislation in line with those treaties and to implement and enforce their provisions. It means ensuring that there is no impunity for human rights abuses, and that every time someone's rights are violated the incident is investigated, the truth established and those responsible brought to justice. It means ratifying and setting up speedily the International Criminal Court. It

means ending discrimination and working to ensure the promise of the Universal Declaration of Human Rights, that governments work towards a world without cruelty and injustice, a world without hunger and ignorance.

Prevention work requires governments to condemn violations of human rights by their allies as well as their foes. It means that arms sales to human rights violators must be stopped. It means ensuring that economic sanctions do not lead to violations of socio-economic rights. In Iraq, after years of draconian sanctions, infant mortality rates in 1999 were the highest in the world. The rights of Iraq's children deprived of food and basic medical supplies do not appear to carry weight on the international community's agenda. Prevention work requires a serious commitment to protecting the human rights of all, wherever they live and whoever they are.

The international community has begun to accept the need for intervention to bring an end to massive violations. It is still a long way from accepting "preventive" interventions. Yet these are more effective and far less costly in terms of human suffering and material destruction than intervention in a crisis.

Conduct of operations

AI's refusal to be drawn on whether military intervention is appropriate in a given situation does not mean that we have nothing to contribute. On the contrary, we lobby governments and the UN on a range of human rights issues related to international interventions. We do not call for military action, nor do we oppose it, but we do campaign on how such interventions should be conducted. We do not take a position on when to intervene or who should intervene (whether the UN, a regional coalition, a single state or even an armed group such as the RPF in Rwanda), but we focus on the conduct of the operation.

We call for human rights concerns to be central at all stages of conflict resolution, peace-keeping and peace-building.

We demand that all parties respect international law. The legal system governing a military operation which is in effect taking over a territory must be clarified at the outset and applied from day one. If the local law cannot be applied (because as in Kosovo much of the justice system was dismantled, or because as in East Timor it was unclear what law should apply), the UN should develop a basic code of criminal procedures, consistent with international human rights standards, to be applied as soon as the peace-keepers touch ground.

This is much more than rules of engagement. It means recognizing that peace-keeping operations are about law enforcement as well as military control, and that human rights standards are therefore central.

It is inappropriate for soldiers, and unfair to them, to expect them to conduct themselves as police officers, let alone judges. Peace-keeping operations have gradually expanded to include a multitude of actors, from humanitarian assistance components to police and human rights monitors. The time has come to

In those situations where the international community has chosen to intervene, the world's governments have not been prepared to commit the necessary resources.

We call for human rights concerns to be central at all stages of conflict resolution, peace-keeping and peace-building.

ensure that police, judges and other legal professionals are present from the outset of those operations which, for all practical purposes, amount to the taking over of a territory.

Also key is proper human rights monitoring of international forces, to ensure that those engaged in an intervention do not consider themselves above the standards for which they have intervened.

International responsibility

International responsibility for the universal protection of human rights has gained wider acceptance over the past half century, as reflected in the growth of the UN human rights machinery and of international institutions of justice. For all of us working to promote the universality of human rights, this is cause for optimism in a turbulent world.

Many individual AI members believe that armed intervention is the logical next step in this process and that there are circumstances where soldiers should be deployed to prevent or end human rights violations. However, as an organization, AI recognizes the danger that the term "human rights" might be usurped to justify the military ambitions of powerful states. Standing apart from the clamour for armed action is difficult in the face of immediate suffering. It means acknowledging our own, painful, limitations.

However, I believe it is a wise position, indeed the most sustainable position, for an organization dedicated to the impartial protection of human rights.

So, in summary, AI neither supports nor opposes armed intervention, but argues that action should be taken in time to prevent human rights problems becoming human rights catastrophes.

Both intervention and inaction represent the failure of the international community.

Why should we be forced to choose between two types of failure when the successful course of action is known? Why should we be expected to give our seal of approval to either unacceptable option? The best we can do is to ensure that whatever route is chosen, we do what we can to contain the suffering and to let the powerful know our anger. Prevention of human rights crises is the correct course. The problem is not lack of early warning, but lack of early action. Only by protecting all human rights everywhere, every day, will we render the debate over humanitarian intervention obsolete. And that is a worthy goal for the 21st century.

Both intervention and inaction represent the failure of the international community.

INTRODUCTION

For the majority of the world's population 1999 brought repression, poverty or war. In country after country, imprisonment, torture and political killings were used by governments to silence opposition and maintain their hold on power. In some countries the widening gap between rich and poor fuelled protests by the desperate and dispossessed which were met with brutality and violence. In other countries, political instability degenerated into open armed conflict in which countless men, women and children were maimed or slaughtered. The millions of people fleeing in search of safety bore witness to the extent of persecution and violence around the world.

Yet in country after country, individual human rights activists refused to be daunted by the scale of the problems or the personal risks they faced. They organized protests, they mobilized to increase pressure for change and they took action to defend the victims of violations. They continued to draw new people into the growing network of human rights defenders, building a worldwide human rights movement of which AI is proud to be part.

The pages of this report do not only document a grim catalogue of human rights abuses, they also show the creativity, determination and successes of the human rights movement.

Kosovo

In March the deteriorating human rights situation in Kosovo erupted into a full-scale international crisis.

NATO launched air strikes against Serbian targets in Yugoslavia after political efforts failed to end the armed conflict between Yugoslav government forces and the Kosovo Liberation Army (KLA). The bombing triggered an escalation of gross human rights violations as Serbian police and paramilitary units and the Yugoslav army drove around 850,000 ethnic Albanians out of their homes, creating a regional refugee crisis. The following weeks saw widespread and systematic killings, "disappearances", torture, ill-treatment and forcible expulsions. There were also reports of rape or other sexual violence against ethnic Albanian women.

AI responded to the crisis by publicizing abuses and calling for action to end them, by sending researchers to the region to document human rights violations and assess the quality of refugee protection, and by issuing a range of news releases and reports.

AI members worldwide called on their governments to give absolute priority to bringing to justice the perpetrators of violations in Kosovo and to providing unrestricted protection to Kosovan refugees. AI denounced human rights violations by the Yugoslav authorities and publicly expressed concern that NATO was not taking sufficient precautions to minimize civilian casualties and may have violated the rules of war. When events in Kosovo moved from war to negotiations, AI called for the peace plan to incorporate steps to ensure respect for human rights and international humanitarian law. As the peace agreement took shape, AI lobbied hard with a set of key post-conflict recommendations to the UN. These centred on building effective programs for human rights protection in Kosovo. In the second half of the year AI drew attention to new victims — Serbs, Roma

© UNHCR

Returned ethnic Albanian refugees start to move back into their ruined houses in Kosovo. More than 850,000 people fled between March and June. Most were able to return by August, many to damaged homes.

and ethnic Albanians accused of "collaboration" – highlighting the fact that more than half of the non-Albanian population of Kosovo had fled their homes by the end of 1999.

For more than a decade AI has been warning of the growing human rights crisis in Kosovo. Before, during and after the war, AI members have persisted in their efforts to win respect for human rights. A vast amount of evidence has emerged about human rights abuses committed in Kosovo. Establishing and recording what happened is only the first step in an AI agenda for action which seeks to bring justice to the victims, and to break the cycle of violence for all the communities of the region.

East Timor

"Rarely has a short crisis resulted in such extensive damage to such a large percentage of the total population. Virtually every family in East Timor has been affected; 75% of all East Timorese were displaced and 70% of private residences, public buildings and essential utilities were destroyed."

Spokesperson for the UN Office for the Coordination of Humanitarian Affairs

On 30 August 1999, an extraordinary 98 per cent of East Timor's voters turned out for a UN-organized ballot over the territory's future. Since 1975, when Indonesia invaded and illegally annexed East Timor, its people have faced brutal repression; at least one third of the population has been wiped out.

Despite sustained intimidation by pro-Indonesian forces, the people of East Timor voted overwhelmingly for independence. Their brave stand was met with a systematic wave of violence, as the human rights violations which had characterized the months preceding the ballot intensified during September. Hundreds of thousands of people were forced to flee their homes; many were forcibly expelled from East Timor to Indonesia. Unlawful killings, rape and torture were committed by pro-Indonesian militias acting with the direct and indirect support of the Indonesian military and police. Journalists and human rights activists were forced out of the territory, making information hard to obtain.

As the violence escalated, AI mobilized its million-strong worldwide membership, especially those in the Asia/Pacific region, to exert pressure on the Indonesian authorities. In countries with strong financial or military links with Indonesia, AI members took part in public protests. As the scale of human rights violations emerged, governments imposed arms embargoes and suspended military training, and in September the UN deployed an Australian-led multinational force. By the time the troops arrived the vast majority of the population had fled or had been forcibly expelled. Returning refugees were faced with the destruction of whole communities and the basic infrastructure.

AI then reassessed its priorities and concentrated on the issues of combating impunity, supporting East Timorese human rights defenders and providing protection for refugees. AI called for the establishment of a strong and credible international investigation process into crimes against humanity and war crimes committed in East Timor, and publicly criticized delays in the deployment of the UN's Commission of Inquiry. In October, AI called on the Indonesian government to protect East Timorese refugees and to guarantee full and unimpeded access by the UN's refugee agency UNHCR and other organizations. It repeated its demand that the militias should be disarmed and disbanded.

AI's longer-term goals include pressing for the best possible constitutional, legal and institutional protection for human rights in an independent East Timor.

'Hidden' victims

While Kosovo and East Timor dominated headlines around the world, massive suffering in other countries went virtually unnoticed.

In China, for example, 1999 saw the most serious and wide-ranging crackdown on peaceful dissent for a decade. Thousands of people were arbitrarily detained. Torture and ill-treatment of prisoners were widespread. Thousands of people were sentenced to death. In the autonomous regions of Tibet and Xinjiang suspected nationalists suffered particularly intense repression. An AI report, published in April, documented massive human rights violations in the Uighur Autonomous Region of Xinjiang in western China. The targets were primarily Uighurs, the majority ethnic group among the predominantly Muslim local population. Against a backdrop of economic marginalization, social disadvantage and curbs on political and religious freedoms, Uighur people were also the victims of state violence: arbitrary detention, unfair political trials, torture, and summary executions. At the UN Commission on Human Rights in Geneva, AI called on the international community not to remain silent in the face of these abuses. But China's political and economic importance ensured that it again escaped criticism.

After weeks of intensive bombing of Chechnya by Russian forces, the plight of the hundreds of thousands of refugees trying to escape received international attention. However, the systematic harassment and intimidation of Chechens in Moscow and other parts of the Russian Federation were virtually ignored. In an atmosphere of increasing anti-Chechen xenophobia encouraged by inflammatory government statements, police and other public officials have targeted Chechens, tearing up their identity documents, beating them up and arbitrarily detaining them. AI tried to draw attention to these abuses; it condemned the muted response of the international community to reported abuses during the war in Chechnya and the failure to provide adequate help and protection to Chechen refugees.

The Saudi Arabian government spares no effort to keep its appalling human rights record a secret, and other governments have shown themselves more than willing to help maintain the silence.

© Reuters

Hundreds defy monsoon rains to gather near the Indonesian Embassy in Dhaka, Bangladesh, for a protest meeting organized by AI Bangladesh against human rights violations in East Timor.

Secrecy and fear permeate every aspect of society in Saudi Arabia. There are no political parties, no elections, no independent legislature, no trade unions, no Bar Association, no independent judiciary, no human rights organizations. The government allows no international human rights organizations to carry out research in the country and it ignores requests by such organizations for information. It has effective control over all kinds of information: there is strict censorship of the news media within the country and strict control of access to the Internet, satellite television and other forms of communication with the outside world. Anyone living in Saudi Arabia who criticizes this system is harshly punished. Hundreds of people are detained indefinitely on political grounds, torture is endemic, and public executions, flogging and amputations are carried out with total disregard for the most basic fair trial safeguards. Particularly vulnerable to these abuses are members of religious minorities, women and migrant workers.

In Iraq, in addition to the effects of UN sanctions, US-led bombing raids resulted in the deaths of scores of civilians during 1999. The world's news media paid little or no attention to these killings.

Impunity

The crises in Kosovo and in East Timor were both rooted in long-term patterns of human rights violations committed with impunity. In both, AI called for those responsible to be held accountable in order to secure respect for fundamental human rights. In both, the authorities had failed to act and the international community had, for too long, ignored the suffering of the victims and its own responsibilities.

Impunity – the failure to bring to justice and punish those responsible for human rights violations – usually arises from a lack of political will. This often stems from the fact that the state itself, or an arm of the state such as the military, has committed or encouraged the violations. Impunity can also result from a government's failure to make the defence of human rights a central part of its domestic political agenda. Whatever the cause, impunity means a denial of justice for the victims and creates a climate where individuals can continue to commit violations without fear of arrest, prosecution or punishment.

Combating impunity goes hand in hand with key human rights principles of fairness, accountability and justice. AI therefore opposes any measures which grant an amnesty to perpetrators of crimes against humanity and war crimes before the truth of the crimes has been established and is known; before the victims have been provided with reparation; or before the judicial process has been completed with a clear verdict of guilt or acquittal.

One of the most positive developments of recent years has been the establishment of international institutions of justice, such as the international tribunals prosecuting crimes committed in Rwanda and the former Yugoslavia. The international community's 1998 decision to establish an International Criminal Court with jurisdiction over genocide, crimes against humanity and war crimes was rightly seen as a vital step forward in the fight against impunity. However, the Court has yet to begin its work. Only six countries had ratified the Rome Statute of the International Criminal Court by the end of 1999 (it requires 60 to enter into force). AI members continued their efforts to persuade governments to bring the Court into being.

International human rights treaties – such as the UN Convention against Torture and Other Cruel, Inhuman or Degrading Treatment or Punishment – have established that there can be no safe haven for people responsible for crimes against humanity such as torture. The French judicial authorities used the jurisdiction established by the Convention against Torture to arrest and investigate a Mauritanian army officer in France accused of torture in Mauritania in the early 1990s. In April, in the first trial of its kind, a Rwandese local government official was sentenced to life imprisonment by a military court in Switzerland, for murder, incitement to murder and war crimes during the 1994 genocide in Rwanda.

In Guatemala, where a bitter civil conflict led to the death or "disappearance" of more than 200,000 people, certain steps were taken towards establishing and acknowledging the truth. The 1996 Peace Accords — negotiated over several years under the aegis of the UN and agreed by the government and the former armed opposition, the National Guatemalan Revolutionary Unity — formally ended the conflict which had raged over a period of more than three decades.

A Commission of Inquiry, established under the 1996 Peace Accords, published a report which concluded unequivocally that the Guatemalan state had been responsible for acts of genocide against indigenous Mayan communities, as well as massive human rights violations and other atrocities. The Commission's 3,400-page report identified the sites of some 630 massacres carried out by government forces. It placed the overwhelming responsibility for violations on the Guatemalan military, although it included details of 32 massacres carried out by the armed opposition. The government of Guatemala failed to publicly acknowledge the abuses catalogued by the Commission of Inquiry, or to act on the majority of the Commission's recommendations. The report referred to the direct and indirect role of the US government's Central Intelligence Agency (CIA) in supporting illegal operations, and three weeks later US President Bill Clinton publicly apologized for the role the USA had played in backing brutal counter-insurgency campaigns in the region.

In Sri Lanka, where tens of thousands of people have died in a long and brutal civil war, the process of establishing what happened to the victims, a vital part of any future reconciliation, made some progress in 1999. The graves of 15 people who allegedly "disappeared" in mid-1996 were exhumed and investigations into the circumstances of their deaths continued.

The Pinochet case

The relatives of those who "disappeared" or were extrajudicially executed during the military government of General Augusto Pinochet are still waiting to find out what happened to their loved ones. Thousands of victims of arbitrary detention, torture and exile also await justice. The vast majority of those who abused their positions in the Chilean state apparatus to order and carry out human rights violations under the military government (1973 to 1990) remain unpunished.

Augusto Pinochet was arrested in the United Kingdom (UK) on 16 October 1998, and at the end of the year he was still in detention waiting for the UK courts to decide his future. His arrest led to a number of positive developments in the application and interpretation of international human rights law. Fundamental principles were reaffirmed, such as the scope of universal jurisdiction and the absence of immunity from prosecution for former heads of state accused of crimes such as crimes against humanity and torture.

Israel and the Occupied Territories

There was some good news from Israel and the Occupied Territories during 1999. In September the Israeli High Court ruled that various interrogation techniques previously used by the General Security Service (GSS) were unlawful.

In 1987, the global campaign to eradicate torture had suffered a setback when Israel sanctioned the use of torture by accepting the Landau Commission of Inquiry's recommendation that the GSS should be allowed to use "moderate physical pressure" when interrogating security suspects.

Methods routinely used during interrogations of Palestinians have included violent shaking, shackling detainees to low chairs in contorted positions for extended periods, prolonged squatting, excessive tightening of handcuffs, and sleep deprivation.

These methods were banned after the High Court ruling. However, draft new legislation by private members to allow the security service to use "physical force" during interrogation was before parliament at the end of the year.

© David Mizrahi/ *Ha'aretz*

Omar Ghanimat, a Palestinian, during a High Court hearing in 1997 displaying marks of torture on his body following interrogations which lasted 45 days.

On 11 September 1973 General Augusto Pinochet led a bloody coup in Chile, and his military junta immediately embarked on a program of repression: constitutional guarantees were suspended, Congress was dissolved and a country-wide state of siege was declared. Torture was systematic; "disappearance" became a state policy.

In November 1974 AI published its first report on the gross human rights violations in Chile, following a fact-finding mission to the country in the early months after the coup. Since then AI has published hundreds of documents and appeals on behalf of the victims and has supported the struggle of victims and their relatives seeking truth and justice. The fate of most of those who "disappeared" in Chile during the military government remains unknown. However, there is overwhelming evidence that the "disappeared" were victims of a government program to eliminate perceived opponents.

In the course of a long search by relatives, human remains have been discovered in clandestine graves and hundreds of former detainees have made statements confirming that the "disappeared" were held in detention centres.

Following the return to civilian rule in 1990, two institutions were created to contribute to establishing the truth about "disappearances", extrajudicial executions and deaths from torture by state agents. The National Commission on Truth and Reconciliation and its successor, the National Corporation on Reparation and Reconciliation, documented the cases of more than 3,000 victims of these human rights violations.

For more than 25 years, relatives of the victims in Chile have campaigned for justice and truth. They have been blocked by several mechanisms which guarantee impunity to those responsible and prevent effective judicial investigations within Chile. The government of President Eduardo Frei Ruiz-Tagle has pursued all possible avenues to secure the release of Augusto Pinochet, to obtain his return to Chile and to prevent his trial in Spain. The Chilean government has justified its endeavours in the name of national sovereignty, the right of the Chileans to deal with their own past, and national reconciliation.

While the Chilean authorities have repeatedly stated that Augusto Pinochet can be tried in Chile, no attempts have been made to remove the obstacles to such a trial. Chief among these are the fact that Augusto Pinochet, as a senator for life, enjoys parliamentary immunity; that cases involving members and former members of the armed forces accused of human rights violations come within the jurisdiction of military courts; and the application of the Amnesty Law by military and civilian courts.

Crimes committed in Chile between 11 September 1973 and 10 March 1978 fall within the scope of the Amnesty Law decreed in 1978 by General Augusto Pinochet, then President of Chile. Although the Amnesty Law was declared constitutional by the Chilean Supreme Court, the Inter-American Commission on Human Rights and the UN Human Rights Committee have stated that it is incompatible with Chile's obligations under international law. The Amnesty Law, which can only be annulled by Congress, effectively guarantees impunity to those responsible for systematic and widespread human rights violations and remains a major obstacle to bringing Augusto Pinochet to justice in Chile.

The crimes against humanity committed in Chile since 1973 are subject to universal jurisdiction. This principle has been recognized under international law since the establishment of the International Military Tribunal of Nuremberg with jurisdiction over crimes against humanity irrespective of where those crimes had been committed.

The principles articulated in the Nuremberg Charter and Judgment were recognized as international law principles by the UN General Assembly in 1946. Similarly, torture is a crime which under international law is subject to universal jurisdiction.

The judicial investigation initiated in Spain by the Spanish National Court at the request of victims and relatives, the Spanish government's submission of a formal request for the extradition of Augusto Pinochet, together with the UK House of Lords rulings against his immunity as a former head of state constitute some of the most important developments in human rights since the adoption of the Universal Declaration of Human Rights in 1948.

The ruling of UK Magistrate Ronald Bartle, of Bow Street (London) Magistrates' Court, that the extradition of Augusto Pinochet should be allowed to proceed represents another step towards the acceptance of universal jurisdiction in cases of human rights violations and the universality of international human rights standards. The Magistrate considered that the effects of "disappearances" can amount to mental torture for the relatives of the "disappeared" and left it to a trial in Spain to decide.

International human rights mechanisms have already provided this definition. Article 1(2) of the UN Declaration on the Protection of All Persons from Enforced Disappearance of December 1992, states: "Any act of enforced disappearance... inflicts severe suffering on them and their families. It constitutes a violation of the rules of international law guaranteeing, inter alia,... the right not to be subjected to torture and other cruel, inhuman or degrading treatment or punishment".

The Inter-American Court of Human Rights, the European Court of Human Rights, the UN Human Rights Committee and the Inter-American Commission on Human Rights have all stated that "disappearances" per se violate the right of the relatives of the "disappeared" not to be subjected to torture or ill-treatment.

The Pinochet case has shown that international law is not a set of agreements that can be ignored, but a vital mechanism for the protection of individuals. The rulings by the UK courts have created a very important precedent for the future of human rights. They have also opened a window of hope for all the victims and relatives still pursuing justice.

THE STRUGGLE AGAINST IMPUNITY: THE CASE OF AUGUSTO PINOCHET

July 1996	Initial criminal complaints against Augusto Pinochet on charges of genocide and terrorism are submitted to the Spanish National Court.
February 1997	Spanish judicial investigations are initiated centring on human rights violations against Spanish citizens in Chile under the military government of General Augusto Pinochet and violations committed as part of *Operación Condor*. The charges, which include "disappearances", torture and extrajudicial executions, amount to crimes against humanity.
October 1998	Spanish judges Manuel Garcia-Castellón and Baltasar Garzón Real file an official petition with the UK authorities to question Augusto Pinochet.
	Augusto Pinochet is served with provisional arrest warrants, issued by a UK magistrate, and is placed in police custody in London.
	Judge Baltasar Garzón issues an international warrant of arrest against Augusto Pinochet in order to prepare the request for extradition.
	Criminal proceedings are announced in Italy, Luxembourg, Norway, Sweden and the USA.
	Augusto Pinochet's lawyers submit an appeal against his detention to the UK High Court of Justice.
	The UK High Court rules that Augusto Pinochet is immune from extradition and prosecution for systematic murder, torture, "disappearance", illegal detention and forcible transfers because he is a former head of state.
	The UK prosecution authority appeals against the High Court decision and is granted leave to take the case to the House of Lords.
November 1998	The Spanish government files a formal request with the UK authorities for Augusto Pinochet to be extradited to Spain to face trial for genocide, terrorism, kidnapping, torture, and "disappearances" and for conspiracy to commit these crimes.
	The Swiss and French governments also file extradition requests with the UK authorities.
	The UN Committee against Torture recommends to the UK government that the case of Augusto Pinochet "be referred to the office of the public prosecutor, with a view to examining the feasibility of and if appropriate initiating criminal proceedings in England, in the event that the decision is made not to extradite him". It also calls for reform of UK law which is in direct conflict with the UN Convention against Torture and Other Cruel, Inhuman or Degrading Treatment or Punishment by effectively granting immunity to heads of state and allowing a defence of "lawful authority" in prosecutions of people accused of torture.
	The Judicial Committee of the House of Lords, the highest UK court, reverses the High Court judgment. By a majority of three to two, the Law Lords rule that Augusto Pinochet is not immune from prosecution because he is a former head of state. This ruling leaves the way open for Augusto Pinochet to be extradited to Spain on charges of mass murder, terrorism and torture. The final decision on whether to allow the extradition to proceed rests with the UK Home Secretary, Jack Straw.
December 1998	The Belgian government also files an extradition request with the UK authorities.
	On the eve of the 50th anniversary of the Universal Declaration of Human Rights, the Home Secretary decides to order the application for extradition to proceed.
	The Law Lords' ruling is set aside, following a challenge to the composition of the judicial panel, on the basis of links between one of the Law Lords and Amnesty International Charity Limited. A new panel of seven Law Lords is scheduled to reconsider the case in January 1999.
	Augusto Pinochet remains under police guard in the UK while the legal proceedings continue.

January 1999	New hearings start before the House of Lords. AI, the Medical Foundation for the Care of Victims of Torture, the Redress Trust, Mary Ann and Juana Francisca Beausire, British torture victim Sheila Cassidy and the Association of Relatives of the Disappeared in Chile are granted leave to participate as third parties, as is the Chilean government.
March 1999	By a majority of six to one, the Law Lords rule that Augusto Pinochet does not have immunity from prosecution for acts of torture committed when he was head of state and that he could be extradited, but only for the crimes of torture and conspiracy to torture alleged to have been committed after 8 December 1988 – the date on which the UN Convention against Torture and Other Cruel, Inhuman or Degrading Treatment or Punishment became binding on Chile, Spain and the UK. Although all the other charges were eliminated, in their ruling the Law Lords stated that under General Augusto Pinochet's government "appalling acts of barbarism were committed in Chile and elsewhere in the world: torture, murder and the unexplained disappearance of individuals all on a large scale".
	The Law Lords' ruling stated that the UK Home Secretary could permit the extradition proceedings against Augusto Pinochet to continue on the reduced number of charges.
	The UN Human Rights Committee states that the Chilean Amnesty Law of 1978 violates the right to have an effective remedy and is incompatible with the obligation of the state to investigate human rights violations.
April 1999	The UK Home Secretary gives authority for the extradition application to proceed for a second time. Extradition hearings are scheduled for September.
August 1999	The Chilean 5th Court of Appeals rejects the judicial request to include Augusto Pinochet in the investigation related to the killing of 72 people in the 1973 "Caravan of Death" operation. In its ruling the Court states that, according to Article 58 of the Chilean Constitution, Augusto Pinochet's parliamentary immunity excludes him from such investigation.
September 1999	In the year following his arrest, 40 lawsuits are filed against Augusto Pinochet before Chilean courts.
	Extradition hearings against Augusto Pinochet start in the UK, before Magistrate Ronald Bartle of Bow Street Magistrates' Court, to determine whether to authorize the extradition of Augusto Pinochet on 35 cases of torture or conspiracy to torture committed after 8 December 1988, and on cases of torture resulting from 1,198 "disappearances" submitted by Spanish judge Baltasar Garzón.
October 1999	Magistrate Bartle orders the procedures allowing extradition of Augusto Pinochet to continue. He emphasized that the proceedings were not to decide whether or not Augusto Pinochet was guilty, but to decide whether or not the conditions were in place to order the committal of the accused to await the decision of the Home Secretary. Magistrate Bartle found that the information submitted to him relating to allegations after 8 December 1988 "constitute a course of conduct amounting to torture and conspiracy to torture" for which Augusto Pinochet "enjoys no immunity". In relation to the "disappearance" cases he considered that the effect on the families "can amount to mental torture".
	The Chilean government requests the UK authorities to undertake medical tests on Augusto Pinochet in order to consider his release on humanitarian grounds.
	Augusto Pinochet's lawyers appeal against the Magistrate's decision through application for a writ of habeas corpus.
November 1999	The UK Home Office asks for Augusto Pinochet to undergo independent medical tests following a request from the Chilean government that he be released on health grounds.
	The Spanish National Court rejects, for the third time, attempts by the Spanish Public Prosecution Office and by the Public Prosecutor's Department to stop the proceedings against Augusto Pinochet in Spain. The Court reaffirms the jurisdiction of the Spanish courts and authorizes Judge Baltasar Garzón's investigations.
December 1999	Two High Court judges schedule the hearing for Augusto Pinochet's appeal against the ruling of Magistrate Bartle for March 2000.

Government action against AI

AI always tries to engage in dialogue with governments. Sometimes we succeed, and sometimes such discussion leads to genuine reform. However, many governments try to ignore AI's findings, while others flatly reject AI's conclusions. It is not particularly unusual for AI's reports to be treated as subversive, but it is rare for a government to take court action against the organization.

In May 1999 AI published a report entitled *Togo: Rule of terror* (AI Index: AFR 57/001/99), which described a persistent pattern of extrajudicial executions, "disappearances", torture and ill-treatment. In particular, it alleged that hundreds of people had been killed by the security forces around the time of elections in mid-1998, and that bodies had been dumped at sea by military aircraft. The Togolese authorities reacted angrily, calling the document "a tissue of untrue statements, false allegations and bias, inspired by the bad faith of its authors", and forbidding reports by the local press. A four-person delegation, led by AI's Secretary General Pierre Sané, which sought to meet the government, was prevented from entering the country. Instead of investigating the allegations raised by AI, the Togolese authorities clamped down on human rights defenders, arresting several, torturing at least two, and forcing several others to go into hiding or to flee the country. The Togolese government also decided to start legal proceedings against AI, and issued a summons to Pierre Sané to appear before an investigating magistrate in Togo. AI has repeatedly stressed that it remains open to dialogue, but that human rights are not negotiable.

International Council Meeting

AI is a democratic movement, controlled by its members. The International Council Meeting (ICM), held every two years, is the movement's supreme policy-making forum, where AI delegates from all over the world review policy and plan future directions.

AI planned to hold its 1999 ICM in Morocco, which would have been the first time this conference had been held in a North African or Middle Eastern country, and would have been a further boost to the work of AI's groups in Morocco. However, just weeks before the ICM was due to open, the Moroccan authorities withdrew their permission for the conference to take place in Rabat. No clear reason was provided to explain this refusal. AI described the government's decision as a missed opportunity for Morocco, for AI and for human rights. The Prime Minister of Morocco wrote to AI in July, expressing the hope that dialogue between AI and the Moroccan authorities would continue.

The 1999 ICM was moved to Portugal after the Moroccan authorities withdrew permission to hold it in Morocco. Portugal is a country of symbolic importance for AI; the imprisonment in 1961 of two Portuguese students who had raised their wine glasses in a toast to liberty moved British lawyer Peter Benenson to write a newspaper article which proved the genesis of AI.

The 400 delegates at the ICM displayed an unprecedented confidence in the organization's

© AI

Antoinette Chahin was arrested, tortured and sentenced to death (commuted to life imprisonment) in Lebanon, for a political murder she did not commit. Following her release she wrote to AI: "You were the light in the darkness of my jail, you were my hope that pushed me to survive. I thank you from the bottom of my heart for your support."

capacity to respond to the many and difficult challenges facing the movement. Delegates from parts of the world where AI is just beginning to grow spoke out, demonstrating the movement's growing self-assurance and roots in areas beyond our traditional areas of strength in the west.

This confidence was reflected in the ICM's decisions to turn outwards in defining new areas of work, in adopting new methods and techniques, and in approaching new members, especially the young. Areas of increased attention include: campaigning to reduce abuses based on the victim's identity; developing our work on the impact of economic relations on human rights; working to empower human rights defenders and strengthen the human rights movement; campaigning against impunity; enhancing our work to protect refugees; and strengthening our grassroots activism.

One of the factors contributing to AI's success in building a worldwide membership and raising public awareness of its human rights concerns has been its ability to focus clearly and consistently on a limited set of civil and political rights. However, AI has perhaps not been as active as many would wish in addressing human rights issues in the wider context of economic, social and cultural rights. Part of the strategy set out by the ICM for moving forward in this arena is to increase work on identity-based rights, on the arms trade, and on companies and human rights, and to integrate these areas into all aspects of AI's campaigning.

Children's rights

Almost all governments have paid lip service to children's need for special protection and care. However, not only do children around the world continue to suffer many of the same human rights abuses as adults, many children are actually targeted because they are dependent and vulnerable.

AI's 1999 campaign on children's rights ran under the slogan "Children's rights: the future starts here", and emphasized that children's rights are an essential building block for a solid human rights culture and the basis for securing human rights for future generations.

Celebrating the 10th anniversary of the groundbreaking Convention on the Rights of the Child (CRC), AI campaigned for its effective implementation. The CRC is the most widely ratified human rights treaty in the world, but it is a long way from universal acceptance to universal observance. Spelling out and confirming children's rights is no more than a first step; ensuring that these rights are enforced is the challenge ahead.

AI members called for children who come into contact with the justice system — especially children in custody — to be given special care and assistance. Moving beyond AI's traditional focus on abuses of state power, campaigners called on all governments to protect children from physical or mental violence, whether the abusers be parents, teachers or officials. In the light of the huge numbers of children growing up in armed conflict, AI members called for the rights of refugee and internally displaced children to be protected, and for an end to the use of child soldiers.

There are more than 300,000 children under the age of 18 taking part in hostilities around the world, more than 120,000 of them in the many conflicts across Africa. As part of a growing international movement against the use of child soldiers, AI joined a number of other human rights organizations in a coalition to raise public awareness of the scale and gravity of the problem and to press for a strong Optional Protocol to the CRC banning the use of child soldiers. AI members participated in a number of national and regional initiatives. In April the All Africa Conference on the Use of Children as Soldiers was held in Mozambique and was attended by more than 250 participants, including representatives of governments, non-governmental organizations, the UN and the Organization of African

Unity (OAU). The Conference adopted a Declaration which, among other things, called for an Optional Protocol to the CRC which would raise the minimum age of soldiers to 18. Similar conferences were held in Uruguay and Germany.

Women

AI's determination to strengthen its work against abuses based on identity, with particular emphasis on women and children, was reflected in many aspects of research and campaigning. This involved, for example, examining the way AI's existing mandate has been interpreted with a view to integrating women's experiences. For instance, AI condemned the restrictions on women in Afghanistan, where Taleban edicts ban women from seeking employment, education or leaving home unaccompanied by a male relative. This extended AI's interpretation of "imprisonment" on grounds of gender.

During 1999, AI continued to build partnerships and coalitions with the women's movement. AI worked with women's groups and networks to promote a strong and effective Optional Protocol to the UN Convention on the Elimination of All Forms of Discrimination against Women, to allow individual women access to a remedy against abuses. An Optional Protocol was adopted in March. Although AI welcomed it and pledged to work towards its ratification by governments, it expressed disappointment at the weakness of the mechanism finally adopted.

Women's rights issues were central to AI's country campaigning, including campaigns against human rights violations in the USA (see below), Pakistan and Brazil.

The lives of millions of women in Pakistan are circumscribed by traditions which enforce extreme seclusion and submission to men. Men virtually own their female relatives and punish contraventions of their proprietary control with violence. When women begin to assert their rights, however tentatively, the response is harsh and immediate: the number of "honour killings" has risen in line with women's growing awareness of their rights. Every year hundreds of women are known to die as a result of honour killings. Many more cases go unreported and almost all go unpunished. Police almost invariably take the man's side in honour killings or domestic murders, and rarely prosecute the killers. Even when the men are convicted, the judiciary ensures that they usually receive a light sentence, reinforcing the view that men can kill their female relatives with virtual impunity.

AI's campaign against honour killings in Pakistan focused primarily on the state's responsibility for the protection of women. It drew on developments in international human rights law which oblige states to prevent, investigate and punish acts of violence against women, whether perpetrated by state agents or private individuals. AI made specific recommendations to the government of Pakistan, calling on it to provide effective protection to women against violence perpetrated in the name of honour and to end the impunity currently enjoyed by the perpetrators.

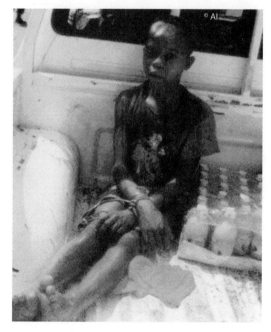

© AI

Sierra Leone: A child suspected of fighting with rebel forces arrested in Freetown in January 1999 by West African troops.

In June AI published *Brazil: "No one here sleeps safely" – Human rights violations against detainees* (AI Index: AMR 19/009/99), a report detailing the appalling conditions of detention in Brazil's prisons and police stations. The vast majority of people held in detention are adult males, but the report also highlighted the situation of women prisoners and juvenile offenders.

The relatively small number of female prisoners means that women's penal establishments are sometimes improvised and inadequate, and conditions vary widely. Police stations for women detainees are often severely overcrowded. Although both the Brazilian Prison Law and Constitution state that women's prisons should provide facilities for inmates to care for their children following childbirth, and for them to maintain regular contact with older children, provision is variable.

General health services for women in detention are inadequate and women held in police stations have virtually no access to medical care. Pregnant prisoners face a care lottery. Those who end up in a prison generally receive some pre- and post-natal care; those held in the police precincts and jails (about two thirds) receive none.

There is a general consensus in Brazil that prisons are facing a crisis and that widespread reform is needed. This report was a contribution to the debate in Brazil about the types of reforms needed. The main message of AI's action around this report was to expose and condemn the situation in Brazil's prisons while at the same time making constructive recommendations in support of existing good practice and initiatives for reform within Brazil.

Lesbian and gay rights

Sexual orientation is a fundamental aspect of the human personality. The rights to freely determine one's sexual orientation and to express it wiithout fear are therefore human rights in the fullest sense.Yet, despite their pledge to protect the human rights of all people without discrimination, governments around the world continue to deprive gay men and lesbians of their basic rights to life, security and equality before the law.

The AI Lesbian Gay Bisexual and Transgendered (LGBT) networks and groups represent one of the most dynamic growth areas of AI activism in the 1990s. By the end of 1999, there were networks, groups or other structures focusing on LGBT concerns in more than 20 countries.While working on the full range of AI mandate concerns, LGBT rights activists have played a central role in developing AI's capacity to combat violations based on sexual identity. They have assisted AI's International Secretariat with its research, provided decentralized coordination of actions and forged stronger links between AI and the global movement for lesbian and gay human rights.

A handbook on campaigning for LGBT rights was issued to help AI members, groups and networks become involved in promoting and defending lesbian and gay rights. It looked specifically at the ways in which AI can contribute to this campaigning and, by

Calvin Burdine's conviction and death sentence were overturned by a US court in September 1999. Calvin Burdine, an openly gay man, was defended at his trial by a lawyer who referred to gays as "queers", failed to interview a single witness in preparing the defence, and fell asleep during the trial. A retrial was ordered.

raising awareness about LGBT human rights within AI, it was hoped the handbook would play a part in facilitating greater cooperation between AI and the movement for LGBT rights.

Human rights defenders

Human rights defenders are a crucial link in the chain of human rights defence at all levels, from campaigning on behalf of the victims of human rights violations to lobbying at the highest levels for improved mechanisms for human rights protection. They are among the first to press for democratic freedoms and the right to peaceful dissent. They pioneer campaigns against impunity and fight for truth, justice and reparation, insisting that justice cannot be equated with vengeance, and that the independence and impartiality of the judiciary is one of the cornerstones of human rights protection and the rule of law.

Human rights defenders around the world have been targeted by governments. Human rights activists have been assassinated, "disappeared", tortured, arbitrarily detained, harassed and forced into exile for investigating and exposing human rights violations committed by agents of the state.

International concern for the difficulties faced by human rights defenders was reflected in the Declaration on the Right and Responsibility of Individuals, Groups and Organs of Society to Promote and Protect Universally Recognized Human Rights and Fundamental Freedoms (Declaration on Human Rights Defenders), adopted by the UN General Assembly on 9 December 1998. This Declaration set out a series of principles aimed at ensuring that states collaborate with human rights defenders by guaranteeing them the freedom to carry out their legitimate activities without hindrance or threat of reprisals.

The full and effective implementation of the principles contained in the UN Declaration on Human Rights Defenders could substantially help prevent human rights violations against individuals, groups, and organizations defending the rights of others. To this end, AI aimed to ensure that these principles were taken up by regional human rights systems and by governments. Human rights defenders in all regions of the world undertook initiatives in 1999 to protect and promote human rights.

In June, the Organization of American States (OAS) adopted a resolution on human rights defenders in the Americas in which the states of the Americas declared their intention to implement the UN Declaration on Human Rights Defenders. In particular, they agreed to "recognize and support the work carried out by Human Rights Defenders" and to provide "Human Rights Defenders with the necessary guarantees and facilities to continue freely carrying out their work of promoting and protecting human rights" as well as to adopt "the necessary steps to guarantee their life, liberty, and integrity".

International outrage at the ongoing repression of human rights defenders during 1999 was summed up in a resolution by the UN Sub-Commission on the Promotion and Protection of Human Rights which strongly condemned recent killings of human rights defenders in Colombia, Ecuador, Guatemala, Indonesia, Iran, Kosovo (Federal Republic of Yugoslavia) and Northern Ireland (UK), and called "upon governments concerned to ensure that crimes committed against human rights defenders do not go unpunished, to allow and facilitate all necessary

inquiry and to ensure judgment by a civil tribunal and punishment of the perpetrators as well as compensation of the families of the victims, including for the killings which occurred a long time ago".

In June AI published a report examining human rights violations faced by human rights defenders in Latin America between 1996 and 1999, *More protection, less persecution: Human rights defenders in Latin America* (AI Index: AMR 01/002/99). It showed how those struggling to protect the rights of others were often the first to suffer human rights violations such as killings, "disappearances", abduction, torture or ill-treatment. They, and sometimes their relatives, were also subjected to death threats, intimidation and harassment. Placing human rights defenders under suspicion by treating them as criminals or subversives, or by subjecting them to investigation on spurious charges, arbitrary detention, raids and surveillance, were just some of the ways in which state agents in some countries misused the judicial system to prevent defenders from carrying out their activities.

AI also showed how the extrajudicial execution of some human rights defenders might have been averted if the authorities had acted appropriately by investigating death threats, by providing adequate protection when requested, and by investigating the killing of other human rights defenders who died in similar circumstances.

"It is an unfortunate fact of life that one gets abandoned by friends when in prison even for a just cause. I never lost faith for I know that I have friends from AI. That is the magic of AI, its ability to gather a community of peoples all over the world for the common cause of humanity and dignity of man and woman ..."

Extract from the letter of Lim Guan Eng, sentenced to 18 months in prison for publicly criticizing the Malaysian government's handling of a rape charge against a minister. He was released in August.

© Reuters

Local human rights defenders working in small communities or conflict zones were especially vulnerable. Limited government attempts to provide protection to those at risk fell far short of the needs of those operating in areas outside the capital cities. Far from national and international networks that lend a degree of support and protection, they were frequently driven underground when their work brought them into confrontation with local state agents.

In collaboration with local and international organizations, AI set up protection mechanisms for human rights defenders at risk, as part of a special program to support human rights defenders in Latin America. AI also organized an electronic network to share information among defenders and generate immediate action for human rights defenders in danger.

Despite the difficulties they faced, human rights defenders in Latin America continued to break new ground and to gain in strength and determination.

In Brazil, human rights activists were involved in exposing the activities of a brutal "death squad" operating with the acquiescence of state officials in the Amazonian state of Acre. The "death squad" was

© Private

"Thank you for your letters. You are the only organization which throughout the whole two years has paid any attention to us."

Extract from a letter to AI from the father of a policeman in Kazakstan whose death sentence for murder was commuted to 25 years' imprisonment.

alleged to be responsible for dozens of killings of people from marginalized groups of society. Based on their experience in setting up and coordinating witness protection programs in some states, Brazilian defenders campaigned on the need for a national system of witness protection which would cover cases across the country that state governments are unable or unwilling to deal with. This was eventually approved by Congress in July.

In Peru, human rights organizations launched a nationwide campaign against torture to press for torture-free zones in which state agents would commit themselves to eliminating torture from their jurisdictions. They also pressed for full adherence to a new law reforming the Peruvian penal code and making torture a criminal offence. Between 1988 and 1998, Peruvian human rights organizations received more than 4,000 complaints regarding torture.

Building societies based on the rule of law and respect for human rights was a major focus. In Venezuela defenders made important recommendations on the drafting of the new Constitution, in respect of the right to life and personal integrity and the inclusion of the crimes of extrajudicial, summary and arbitrary execution, "disappearance", torture and other cruel, inhuman or degrading treatment. Other recommendations included provisions regarding the right to full investigations of human rights violations and an effective legal remedy and reparation, as well as the right to liberty and freedom of expression. In Paraguay, human rights activists continued to pressurize Congress on its, as yet unfulfilled, obligation under the 1992 Paraguayan Constitution to nominate a human rights Ombudsman.

The struggle against impunity for past and present human rights violations was central to many Latin American human rights defenders. Chilean activists campaigned on cases involving high-ranking military officials responsible for human rights violations committed during the military government (1973-1990). The fate and whereabouts of many of Latin America's "disappeared", many of whom were human rights defenders, remain unknown.

In Colombia, human rights defenders were often the only source of reliable information about human rights violations committed by the security forces and their paramilitary allies. As the conflict in Colombia intensified, and victims of human rights violations

THE DEATH PENALTY IN 1999

At least 1,813 people were executed in 31 countries. At least 3,857 people were sentenced to death in 63 countries. These figures include only cases known to AI; the true figures are certainly higher.

The vast majority of executions worldwide are carried out in a tiny handful of countries. In 1999, 85 per cent of all known executions took place in China, Iran, Saudi Arabia, the Democratic Republic of the Congo and the USA.

• In China, preliminary figures indicated that at least 1,077 people were executed, although the true number was believed to be much higher.

• At least 165 executions were carried out in Iran.

• Ninety-eight people were executed in the USA.

• In Saudi Arabia, 103 executions were reported, but the total may have been much higher.

• In Iraq, hundreds of executions were reported, but many of them may have been extrajudicial.

• As many as 100 people were executed in the Democratic Republic of the Congo.

Moves towards abolition

By the end of 1999, 73 countries had abolished the death penalty for all offences. A further 13 countries had abolished it for all but exceptional crimes, such as war crimes. At least 22 further countries were abolitionist in practice: they had not carried out an execution for 10 years and were believed to have an established practice of not carrying out executions.

During 1999 the death penalty was abolished for all crimes in Bermuda, East Timor, Turkmenistan and Ukraine, and Latvia abolished it for all but exceptional crimes.

were increasingly silenced by the fear of reprisals, human rights defenders played a crucial role in exposing atrocities perpetrated both by the security forces and the armed opposition. Since the beginning of 1997, more than 25 Colombian human rights defenders have been assassinated and at least as many have had to leave Colombia. The magnitude of the crisis was summed up by one woman who wrote: "We have always talked about our capacity as Colombians to put up with so much cruelty and tragedy, and the way we have tried to overcome such losses. But as the circle closes in and those who die become my closest, most loved friends and colleagues, I don't believe we have the same strength any more."

In May, human rights defenders from the Middle East and North Africa met in Beirut, Lebanon, to discuss how to reinforce soldiarity between human rights activists in the various countries of the region. They identified a need to improve methods of mutual protection, and to find ways of taking immediate action when a human rights defender comes under attack. They called for AI's support in capacity building and training, and adopted practical recommendations on enhancing communications links and exchanging information and experiences.

Disarming the killers

AI campaigns against the transfer of military, security and police equipment, weaponry, personnel and training to those likely to use such goods and services to abuse human rights. In 1999 the movement highlighted the links between unregulated movements of arms and human rights violations across Africa.

Throughout Africa, state repression and the arms and security trade have been inextricably linked. This can be seen in the past provision of electro-shock batons to torturers in Angola, the use of tear gas and water cannon against pro-democracy activists in Kenya, or the military training given to the Togolese security forces. Many other African countries, including Burundi, Liberia, Rwanda, Sudan and Somalia, show the devastation wrought by the abundance and misuse of small arms and related

military equipment and training. Even in countries ostensibly at peace, the availability and misuse of such equipment can facilitate the arbitrary detention, ill-treatment, torture or murder of anyone the governments deem a threat.

Using a mass-produced tabloid-style newspaper (the *Terror Trade Times*) and a poster to highlight the issue, AI members across the world, and especially in Africa, joined with other non-governmental organizations to press for greater regulation of the arms and security trade, campaigning to ensure that such weapons never reached the hands of those ready to use them for human rights violations.

Campaign on the USA – *Rights for All*

The *Rights for All* campaign on the USA, launched in October 1998, continued to be actively and imaginatively pursued by AI members in all parts of the world. The challenge was huge — to scrutinize and publicize injustices in the most powerful economy on earth.

The specific goals of the campaign were tightly drawn, and AI can point to several welcome improvements. The main goals included improving the treatment of women in custody. There were around 138,000 women in jails and prisons in the USA in 1999. The proportion of black and Latino female inmates greatly exceeded their representation in the general population. Rape and other forms of sexual abuse by male guards against female prisoners were widely reported, although victims were often reluctant to complain because they lacked confidence that the allegations would be dealt with effectively and because they feared retaliation by prison staff. Handcuffs and shackles were routinely used on sick and pregnant women in US prisons and jails both during transport and in hospital. The shackling of women in labour can seriously compromise the mother's and baby's health if there are complications during delivery.

Campaign goals included banning the routine use of restraints on pregnant women prisoners and all restraints during labour; and preventing sexual abuse by restricting and regulating the role of male

© AI Nepal

AI Nepal taking 40,000 signatures to the US Embassy in Kathmandu as part of the *USA: Rights for All* campaign.

correctional staff. Since the launch of the campaign, several states have amended their policies regarding use of restraints on pregnant female prisoners. During 1999 six states – Montana, Massachusetts, Virginia, West Virginia, Nebraska and Washington state – passed laws making sexual contact between prison staff and inmates a criminal offence, bringing the number of states offering legal protection for women prisoners against sexual abuse by staff to 43.

Police brutality was another focus of the campaign; the US Justice Department receives some 10,000 complaints of police abuse each year and systematic brutality by police has been uncovered by inquiries into some of the country's largest urban police departments. The majority of victims were members of racial or ethnic minorities. 1999 saw an unprecedented debate across the country on police brutality following a number of high-profile cases. Civil rights leaders demanded government action against police brutality and urged President Clinton to convene a summit on the issue.

In June, President Clinton attended a round-table discussion convened by the US Attorney General where he spoke out against certain racist police practices. As part of AIUSA's campaigning on this issue, a series of well-publicized hearings on police brutality were held in Los Angeles, Chicago and Pittsburgh.

Action against the death penalty generated worldwide activity. Although executions have continued despite tireless campaigning, there have been some successes. In Massachusetts, a bill to reintroduce the death penalty was defeated by seven votes – just 18 months earlier a similar bill had come within one vote of being passed. AI members in Ireland had worked with a Boston Committee – Irish Americans against the Death Penalty – to lobby members of Massachusetts' legislative council, more than half of whom have Irish connections. Nobel Laureate Seamus Heaney and the Roman Catholic Primate of All Ireland were among the many who faxed letters opposing the death penalty.

A number of individuals facing imminent execution received stays, including Larry Robison, who was already on his way to the lethal injection chamber when the stay was granted. Calvin Burdine, a gay man whose lawyer had slept through large parts of his trial and had been abusive towards homosexuals, was granted a retrial.

There were some 70 death row prisoners in 16 US states who were sentenced to death for crimes committed when they were under the age of 18, and efforts to achieve at least a moratorium on the execution of child offenders gathered momentum during the year. The urgency of the issue was highlighted by the execution in February of Sean Sellers, executed for a crime committed when he was just 16. In the cases of Derrick Lester in Oklahoma and Sean Dixon in Nevada, accused of crimes committed when they were 15 and 16 respectively, prosecutors dropped their intent to seek the death penalty after their offices were flooded with letters and faxes from AI members.

AI campaigners, dressed as US prisoners, protest against human rights abuses in the USA outside the US Embassy, Athens, Greece.

AI has called for an end to the use of the stun belt, which can deliver a 50,000-volt electric shock. The launch in June of AI's report *Cruelty in Control? The stun belt and other electro-shock equipment in law enforcement* (AI Index: AMR 51/054/99) received excellent media attention in the USA and internationally.

AIUSA's first ever International Week of Student Action focused on the US juvenile justice system and included a speakers' tour by AI representatives from Slovenia, Venezuela, Philippines and Ghana. Young people in countries around the world campaigned intensively for one week. Students at Birzeit University in the Palestinian Authority held a week-long action project on juvenile justice, which came up with a wide variety of campaigning ideas and produced, among other things, leaflets, posters, a petition, a radio program, a song, a play, a sketch, artwork and a visual installation.

The USA has been repeatedly challenged on its human rights record at international meetings during the campaign. In April AI organized a public meeting in Geneva at the UN Commission on Human Rights at which Pierre Sané chaired a panel on human rights in the USA. The event attracted considerable media interest and was attended by a large number of country delegates, including representatives from the USA. The US delegation subsequently asked for a meeting with AI. Among the wide range of issues discussed were the ratification and observance of international treaties, police brutality, abuses against women and refugee issues. With the help of the Ghanaian Section, AI launched a major report on race and the death penalty in the USA at the African-American Summit in Accra, Ghana, in May.

Sustained international mobilization for the *Rights for All* campaign has helped encourage and motivate the human rights constituency in the USA. One US human rights activist told AI: "It gives us a measure of hope to have our politicians and prison administrators receive many letters from all over the world in protest of their policies and actions. It makes our work more effective to have these people scolded appropriately by the international human rights community."

AI REPORT 2000
PART 2

AFGHANISTAN

TALEBAN's ISLAMIC EMIRATE OF AFGHANISTAN,
headed by Mullah Mohammad Omar, recognized as a
government by three countries
**ANTI-TALEBAN ALLIANCE's ISLAMIC STATE OF
AFGHANISTAN,**
headed by Burhanuddin Rabbani, recognized as a
government by other governments and the UN
Capital: Kabul
Population: 23.7 million
Official languages: Dari, Pushtu
Death penalty: retentionist

Human rights abuses by the warring factions against members of rival ethnic groups occurred throughout 1999. *Taleban* forces burned homes, destroyed orchards, wheat fields and irrigation systems and forcibly displaced more than 100,000 mainly Tajik people. The UN imposed financial and aviation sanctions on the *Taleban* for not surrendering Osama bin Laden to stand trial for his alleged involvement in US embassy bombings in August 1998. Women, children, human rights defenders, members of ethnic groups, people accused of homosexual activity, and refugees were systematically targeted by the *Taleban* and other warring factions on the basis of their identity. *Taleban* courts imposed sentences of death, amputation and flogging after apparently unfair trials.

Background
Hopes for a peaceful settlement of the conflict were dashed when military action by the *Taleban* escalated in August. In October, Lakhdar Brahimi, the UN Secretary-General's Special Envoy, suspended his activities saying the new fighting had undermined his peace efforts. Neighbouring countries continued to support their favoured warring factions, promoting shared ethnic or religious interests, but denied reports of military involvement in, or transfer of weapons to, Afghanistan.

UN sanctions
In October a UN Security Council resolution called on the *Taleban* to "cease the provision of sanctuary and training for international terrorists and cooperate with efforts to bring indicted terrorists to justice". It gave the *Taleban* one month to "turn over Osama bin Laden without further delay to appropriate authorities in a country where he has been indicted, or to appropriate authorities in a country where he will be returned to such a country, or to appropriate authorities in a country where he will be arrested and effectively brought to justice". The *Taleban* did not comply and on 14 November the Security Council imposed sanctions requiring all states to "deny permission for any aircraft to take off from or land in their territory if it is owned, leased or operated by or on behalf of the Taliban...

unless the particular flight has been approved in advance by [a monitoring] Committee on the grounds of humanitarian need, including religious obligation such as the performance of the Hajj", and to "freeze funds and other financial resources, including funds derived or generated from property owned or controlled directly or indirectly by the Taliban except as may be authorized by the Committee on a case-by-case basis on the grounds of humanitarian need".

Ethnic tension and forced displacement
Some minority groups continued to face harassment. According to reports, at *Taleban* checkpoints, non-Pushtun travellers could frequently only proceed at the behest of fellow Pushtun travellers or on payment of a bribe.

In August the *Taleban* systematically burned the houses and crops and destroyed the agricultural infrastructure of Tajik civilians living in areas north of Kabul as part of a policy of forcible displacement. Hundreds of children and young men were reportedly recruited by the *Taleban* from destitute families in Kabul and elsewhere to cut Tajik-owned vine trees and to seal their irrigation tunnels.

Among the tens of thousands of Tajiks from the Shamali plains forcibly displaced in August were some 8,000 children, women and elderly men reportedly separated by the *Taleban* from their male relatives and sent to the deserted Sarshahi camp near Jalalabad where they were effectively held prisoner by *Taleban* guards. Following international concern about their situation, the *Taleban* moved them to the bombed-out former Russian embassy in Kabul.

Tens of thousands of Tajik families who fled to the Panjshir valley received meagre assistance from the international community until late November when the *Taleban* agreed to the despatch of UN humanitarian aid from Kabul.

Systematic killings and house burnings in Bamiyan
As the *Taleban* moved into Bamiyan in April to capture the area from *Hezb-e Wahdat* — a party which draws its support from the Hazara minority — many who did not, or could not, flee were deliberately killed. Estimates varied widely, but hundreds of men, and some young women and children, who were separated from their families and taken away, remained unaccounted for at the end of 1999.

In addition, the *Taleban* burned more than 200 homes in villages along the road between Shiber and Bamiyan. Verbal condemnation of these house burnings by the *Taleban* leader, Mullah Mohammad Omar, did not prevent similar abuses by *Taleban* guards later in the year.

Abuses by other groups
Dozens of civilians suspected of collaborating with the *Taleban* on account of their ethnic origin were arbitrarily detained by factions opposing the *Taleban*. Abuses reported included severe beatings and the ill-treatment of other family members.

Women and children

As in previous years, women were forced to comply with the discriminatory policies of the *Taleban* who imposed severe restrictions on their education, employment and freedom of movement. Tens of thousands of women effectively remained prisoners in their homes, with no scope to seek the removal of these restrictions. Women who defied them were subjected to systematic ill-treatment. Reports that a number of local *Taleban* officials had agreed to education for young girls based on a strict religious curriculum, or to employment for a small number of women, were not backed by official statements from the *Taleban* leader.

The *Taleban* reportedly recruited Afghan children and deployed them as guards at checkpoints, as patrols in the streets, and as security guards in stadiums during the execution of cruel, inhuman or degrading punishments. Eyewitnesses testified to the presence of child combatants in *Taleban* military ranks.

Intellectuals

Fear of a new crack-down on non-*Taleban* educated Afghans in the country was heightened by a decree from the *Taleban* leader on 12 December ordering his supporters to identify government employees who won awards during the Soviet occupation of Afghanistan between 1979 and 1989. Hundreds of Afghan personalities were detained by the *Taleban* on account of their opposition to the continued war. Many were tortured, and more than a dozen were reportedly killed after arrest. Several Afghan personalities living as refugees in Pakistan were killed by gunmen believed to be close to the warring factions, especially the *Taleban*.
🗁 Abdul Ahad Karzai, a prominent Afghan politician engaged in efforts to bring about a negotiated peace, was gunned down by two assailants on 15 July during a visit to Pakistan.

Refugees

Asylum-seekers continued to flee Afghanistan, bringing the total number of Afghan refugees in Pakistan and Iran to around three million. Scores of Afghan refugees in the North West Frontier Province of Pakistan reported receiving death threats on account of their opposition to *Taleban* policies.

In Iran, hundreds of Afghan men were arrested by the Iranian security guards and forcibly deported to Afghanistan. Their families, who were often left with no other means of support, were given no news about their fate.

Unfair trials, cruel punishments and the death penalty

Taleban Shari'a courts, whose procedures fall short of international standards for fair trial, continued to impose cruel, inhuman or degrading punishments. At least a dozen people convicted of murder were executed by shooting — usually carried out by the victims' families. More than a dozen people were subjected to amputations and at least six were flogged. Thousands of people, among them children as young as

five years old, were either encouraged or forced to attend the public execution of these punishments in former sports stadiums. Children as young as 14 were assigned the task of displaying the severed limbs of victims to the spectators.

AI country reports

- Afghanistan: Detention and killing of political personalities (AI Index: ASA 11/005/99)
- Women in Afghanistan: Pawns in men's power struggle (AI Index: ASA 11/011/99)
- Human rights defenders in Afghanistan: Civil society destroyed (AI Index: ASA 11/012/99)
- Children devastated by war: Afghanistan's lost generations (AI Index: ASA 11/013/99)
- Afghanistan: The human rights of minorities (AI Index: ASA 11/014/99)
- Afghanistan: Cruel, inhuman or degrading treatment or punishment (AI Index: ASA 11/015/99)
- Refugees from Afghanistan: The world's largest single refugee group (AI Index: ASA 11/016/99)

ALGERIA

PEOPLE'S DEMOCRATIC REPUBLIC OF ALGERIA
Head of state: Abdelaziz Bouteflika (replaced Liamine Zéroual in April)
Head of government: Ahmed Benbitour (replaced Sma'il Hamdani in December)
Capital: Algiers
Population: 29.5 million
Official language: Arabic
Death penalty: retentionist
1999 treaty ratifications/signatures: African Charter on the Rights and Welfare of the Child

The level of violence and killings diminished considerably in 1999, but remained nonetheless high, especially towards the end of the year. Hundreds of civilians were killed in targeted and indiscriminate attacks by armed groups, which defined themselves as "Islamic groups". Hundreds of members of the security forces, paramilitary militias and armed groups were killed in attacks, ambushes and armed confrontations. More than 2,000 people convicted under "anti-terrorist" laws were released by presidential pardon in July and hundreds of others were released after receiving reduced sentences in new trials. Scores of other prisoners were released under the terms of a new law, the *Concorde Civile*, Law on Civil Harmony, which was promulgated in July. Under this Law, members of armed groups who surrendered within six months and who were not responsible for killings or rapes were exempt from prosecution and those who had committed such crimes would receive reduced sentences. The Law also ruled out the death penalty or life imprisonment for members of armed groups who surrendered within the six-month limit. The moratorium on executions imposed in 1994 remained in place. According to official sources more than 1,000 people, mostly members of the *Groupe islamique armé* (GIA), Armed Islamic Group, gave themselves up under the terms of the Law on Civil Harmony. Impunity remained a major concern as no concrete measures were taken by the authorities to shed light on the fate of the thousands of people who had "disappeared" or been killed since the beginning of the conflict in 1992, or to bring those responsible to justice. The Law on Civil Harmony raised further concerns that impunity, hitherto widely enjoyed by the military, the security forces and paramilitary militias, would be increasingly extended to members of armed groups responsible for killings and other grave human rights abuses.

Background

The campaign leading up to presidential elections in April marked a fundamental change in the approach to the conflict, with virtually all the candidates recognizing the political nature of the conflict and pledging to work for peace and national reconciliation. After his election, President Abdelaziz Bouteflika restated that his priority was to bring peace and in June he admitted that 100,000 people had died in the conflict since 1992; previously the government had put the figure at 26,000.

A secret agreement between the army and the *Armée islamique du salut* (AIS), Islamic Salvation Army, which had resulted in the AIS declaring a unilateral cease-fire in October 1997, was officially recognized in June, but its terms were not made public. In October the Interior Minister confirmed that the Law on Civil Harmony did not apply to AIS members; their cases would be dealt with by the authorities in a separate, undisclosed framework. Throughout the year AIS groups, reportedly numbering up to several thousand, retained their weapons and appeared to control certain villages and rural areas in the various parts of the country where they were based. Increasing reports were received of AIS cooperation with the army and the security forces in military operations against GIA groups and other armed groups which refused to surrender. The state of emergency imposed in 1992 remained in place.

Killings

Although 1999 saw a significant reduction in the level of violence, the number of killings nonetheless remained high and increased towards the end of the year. More than 1,000 civilians were killed by armed groups in both targeted attacks and indiscriminate bomb explosions. Often groups of up to 20 civilians, including women and children and entire families, were killed in their homes or at false checkpoints in rural areas by armed groups. The perpetrators were able to escape undisturbed on every occasion, even though at times these massacres were carried out near army and security force checkpoints or outposts. Hundreds of members of the security forces, paramilitary militias and armed groups were killed in ambushes and armed confrontations. However, often it was not possible to obtain precise details about the identity of the victims or the exact circumstances of their deaths. Some extrajudicial executions were reported.

In November Abdelkader Hachani, a key leading figure of the banned *Front islamique du salut* (FIS), Islamic Salvation Front, was shot dead in a dental surgery in Algiers. Shortly before his assassination he had complained of intimidation from the security forces and had expressed fears for his life. In December the authorities announced that they had arrested his murderer, who remained in detention awaiting trial at the end of the year. Abdelkader Hachani's family called for an independent investigation into his killing and for all those involved to be brought to justice.

'Disappearances'

The number of "disappearances" reported was considerably lower than in previous years, but cases continued to be reported. Despite promises made in 1998 by the government that it would carry out investigations into "disappearances", no concrete action was taken to this end. No information could be obtained about some 4,000 people who had "disappeared" after arrest by the security forces or paramilitary militias between 1993 and 1999.

During the election campaign and in the period following his election, President Bouteflika promised to take steps to ensure that the fate of the "disappeared" was clarified. However he later dismissed appeals from mothers of the "disappeared" and called on them to "turn the page". Relatives, especially mothers, of the "disappeared" continued to hold weekly demonstrations in the capital and other cities to call on the authorities to provide information about the fate and whereabouts of their relatives. Most of the time they were allowed to demonstrate but on some occasions, notably in January and March, the security forces broke up the demonstrations violently and ill-treated several women.

Torture and ill-treatment

Arrests of people accused under "anti-terrorist" laws diminished substantially in 1999, as did reports of illegally prolonged incommunicado detention, torture and ill-treatment. However, dozens of people arrested on suspicion of having links with armed groups, many of whom were released without charge or trial after a few days in secret detention, reported that they were tortured or ill-treated; some were held incommunicado beyond the 12-day maximum limit permitted by Algerian law.

In October Mohamed Zouaghi, Hacene Dimane, Abdelouahab Feroui and Nassima Fodail, whose husband was sought by the authorities, were arrested from their homes in the capital. They were held in secret detention for 10 days and allegedly tortured while being interrogated about possible contacts with members of armed groups. They reported that they were given electric shocks, burned with cigarettes, severely beaten, and forced to swallow large quantities of dirty water and chemicals while tied to a bench (known as the "*chiffon*" method). Some were subsequently released without charge and others were remanded in custody on charges of having links with armed groups.

Prison conditions

In October the International Committee of the Red Cross (ICRC) was allowed to resume prison visits for the first time since 1992. Conditions of detention were improved in some prisons, notably in the north of the country, prior to the resumption of ICRC visits. The release of thousands of prisoners through the presidential pardon and judicial reviews contributed to reducing overcrowding. However, families and lawyers reported that prisoners in Serkadji and Harrache Prisons in the capital were transferred from these prisons to Berrouaghia and other prisons inland prior to the ICRC visits. The exact number of prisoners who were transferred in these circumstances could not be established, but there were reports that dozens were beaten and ill-treated during the transfers.

Administration of justice

Hundreds of people tried on charges of "terrorism" were acquitted and hundreds of prisoners who had received death sentences or lengthy prison terms in previous years were retried and given more lenient sentences.

▭ In September a prison guard and 21 detainees had their convictions overturned by the Supreme Court. They had been tried in January 1998 in connection with a mutiny in Serkadji Prison in 1995 in which at least 96 detainees and five prison guards had been killed. The guard had been sentenced to death and the 21 detainees to up to 10 years' imprisonment after a trial in which the court had not sought to establish the causes or the circumstances of the deaths and defence lawyers had not been allowed to call key witnesses. The new trial had not taken place by the end of 1999.

However, trials continued to fall short of international standards for fair trial. Courts often convicted defendants of "complicity in terrorist activities" without establishing exactly what crimes the complicity referred to or who the perpetrators of the crimes were. Courts also continued to fail to investigate allegations of torture and ill-treatment by defendants and often refused to call defence witnesses or to allow defence lawyers to cross-examine prosecution witnesses.

▭ Rachid Mesli, a human rights lawyer and prisoner of conscience, was retried in June. In December 1998 the Supreme Court had quashed his conviction on charges of "encouraging terrorism" for which he had been sentenced to three years' imprisonment. Following his retrial, he was given the same sentence and the court again failed to investigate the circumstances of his abduction in July 1996 and his

allegations of ill-treatment during secret detention. He was released in July, four weeks before the end of his sentence.

Impunity

Impunity remained a source of major concern. With very few exceptions members of the security forces and paramilitary militias responsible for abuses including killings, torture, abductions and "disappearances" were not prosecuted. The few who were prosecuted tended to be lower-ranking officers.

▭ Two militia chiefs who were also mayors for the *Rassemblement national démocratique*, National Democratic Rally, the largest party in government, and who were briefly detained in 1998 on charges of grave abuses including murders, torture, abductions and racketeering, were not brought to trial.

Paramilitary militias armed by the state appeared to be less active than in previous years but no measures were announced or known to have been taken by the authorities to disband them or to bring them under the effective supervision of the regular security forces. These militias continued to carry out ambushes and military operations against the GIA and other armed groups either on their own or in conjunction with the army or security forces, in violation of the 1997 law regulating the activities of paramilitary militias, defined as *Groupes de légitime défense*, Legitimate Defence Groups.

The vast majority of members of the GIA and other armed groups who surrendered under the terms of the Law on Civil Harmony were declared exempt from prosecution within days of their surrender by probation committees, set up to implement the Law. Given that many of those who surrendered had been involved with armed groups for several years, the speed with which the probation committees concluded their investigations raised concerns that people who had been responsible for murders and other grave human rights abuses were granted immunity from prosecution.

The lack of clarity about the status of thousands of the AIS members, who were allowed to keep their weapons and who according to the authorities were being dealt with under the terms of a separate and secret deal, also raised concerns about impunity as AIS groups had also been responsible for murders and other grave abuses.

Intergovernmental organizations

The UN Special Rapporteurs on torture and on extrajudicial, summary or arbitrary executions were not granted access to Algeria.

In January the UN Committee on the Elimination of Discrimination against Women examined Algeria's initial report and recommended that Algeria take immediate steps to withdraw its reservations to essential articles of the UN Convention on the Elimination of All Forms of Discrimination against Women and take steps to amend the Family Code so as to bring it into conformity with the Convention and with the principle of equality set out in the Algerian Constitution. The Committee also expressed concern that a large number of the wives of "disappeared" persons could neither legally prove that their husbands were dead nor enjoy their status as married women. It called on the government to help this group of women by simplifying the legal procedures so that they could clarify their status, obtain custody of their children and legally dispose of property to which they are entitled.

Restrictions on human rights activities
In September President Bouteflika stated publicly that AI and other international human rights organizations, which had been refused access to the country for several years, would again be allowed entry. However, no visits could be arranged before the end of the year. Restrictions continued to be imposed on the activities of local non-governmental organizations and associations.

▭ In July the authorities banned a meeting of African human rights defenders organized by the *Ligue algérienne de défense des droits de l'homme*, Algerian League for the Defence of Human Rights, on the occasion of the Organization of African Unity summit in Algiers.

▭ The *Association nationale des familles des disparus*, National Association of Families of the Disappeared, set up in September 1998, continued to be refused legal registration by the authorities and was prevented on several occasions from holding public meetings and events as was the youth group *Rassemblement action jeunesse*, Rally for Youth Action.

AI country reports
- Algeria: "Disappearances": the wall of silence begins to crumble (AI Index: MDE 28/001/99)
- Algeria: Who are the "disappeared"? Case studies (AI Index: MDE 28/002/99)

ANGOLA

REPUBLIC OF ANGOLA
Head of state and government: José Eduardo dos Santos
Capital: Luanda
Population: 10.6 million
Official language: Portuguese
Death penalty: abolitionist for all crimes
1999 treaty ratifications/signatures: African Charter on the Rights and Welfare of the Child

A new round of large-scale human rights abuses were committed in the context of the return to full-scale armed conflict. The government restricted freedom of expression and launched an intimidatory campaign against journalists; many were threatened, others were assaulted and a few were detained. Five members of the National Assembly representing a non-violent faction of the *União Nacional para a Independência Total de Angola* (UNITA), National Union for the Total Independence of Angola, were detained. There were reports that civilians were deliberately and arbitrarily killed, both by the government and by UNITA, but these reports were hard to confirm. UNITA abducted hundreds of civilians and an armed opposition group in Cabinda took several hostages.

Background
The peace process unravelled during 1998 as it became apparent that the UNITA armed opposition would not comply with the 1994 Lusaka Protocol requirements to relinquish control of its territory and demobilize its troops. Heavy fighting broke out between UNITA and government forces in December 1998 and all contact between the two warring parties ceased.

In 1999 the peace process collapsed completely and the *Missão de Observação das Nações Unidas em Angola* (MONUA), UN Observer Mission in Angola, withdrew when its mandate ended in February. The government declared UNITA's leader, Jonas Savimbi, a war criminal in February and issued a warrant for his arrest in July.

The UN maintained a reduced human rights presence after its February withdrawal. In August it announced plans to open a new office to explore measures aimed at restoring peace. A Security Council resolution passed in October established the United Nations Office in Angola (UNOA) with 30 staff members. By the end of the year the staff had not reached the projected total of 12 human rights officers.

Fighting raged throughout the year, and was particularly intense in the centre of the country where UNITA encircled and shelled the cities of Huambo, Kuito and Malange. In October government forces took the UNITA strongholds of Andulo and Bailundo in the central highlands. By the end of the year the government controlled all the provincial capitals, all oil installations and the largest diamond mines.

The government concluded negotiations with international oil companies which would generate hundreds of millions of US dollars in return for the rights to operate offshore oil blocks. The projected revenue was expected to boost expenditure on the military campaign.

In an effort to stem the supply of arms to UNITA and to prevent the sales of diamonds which finance its war, the UN Security Council Sanctions Committee established two expert panels in August to monitor the implementation of the sanctions imposed in 1997.

The war took a heavy toll on the civilian population. Scores of people died in indiscriminate shelling by UNITA. People in the besieged cities of Huambo, Kuito and Malange were reportedly eating seeds, roots, cats and dogs in order to survive. The UN estimated in August that 200 people were losing their lives every day from disease and starvation. Church representatives and humanitarian workers called for the opening of humanitarian corridors through areas of fighting to allow supplies to reach people affected by hunger and disease, but neither the government nor UNITA responded to these requests. Aid agencies were unable to obtain permission to enter areas under UNITA's control. By the end of the year more than one million people had fled their homes to escape the fighting, bringing the total of those internally displaced since 1998 to 3,700,000.

Civil society groups coordinated their appeals for an end to the fighting. In July the *Grupo Angolano de Reflaxão para a Paz,* Angolan Group for Reflecting on Peace, published a Manifesto for Peace in Angola calling for a national dialogue to create a lasting peace. It was endorsed by prominent intellectuals, professionals, journalists, members of trade unions and representatives of religious groups. In October, several peace groups formed the *Fórum Nacional para a Paz,* National Forum for Peace.

The government continued to support President Laurent Kabila in the Democratic Republic of the Congo. In December Namibia agreed to allow Angolan troops to launch attacks against UNITA from Namibian soil. UNITA allegedly supported rebels in the Democratic Republic of the Congo and armed separatists in Caprivi, Namibia.

Freedom of expression
The rights to freedom of expression and association were restricted and the government resorted to legal procedures to stifle criticism. The government claimed that independent media reports relating to the war were endangering public order and security, while religious representatives complained that state media coverage did not accurately reflect the extent of suffering caused by the war.

Some 20 journalists, most of whom worked for privately owned radio stations and newspapers, were briefly held and questioned in connection with possible charges of defamation, slander and crimes against the security of the state. Another was detained for 41 days. Four were formally charged, and none was tried. No

state of emergency was declared and no exceptional measures to restrict the right to freedom of expression were imposed in law. The use of legal procedures to summon, question and intimidate journalists contravened constitutional guarantees on freedom of expression, as well as international treaties to which Angola is party.

Journalists critical of the government continued to receive death threats and several were assaulted. Violence against journalists was seemingly condoned by the government's failure to initiate investigations and to bring those responsible to justice. It was also encouraged by statements, such as that made by the Minister of Social Communication in June, that some journalists were acting as propagandists on behalf of UNITA.

UNITA leaders exerted overwhelming and complete control over freedom of expression in areas under their control.

▭ Rafael Marques, a freelance journalist, was arrested in October after he wrote an article for the independent newspaper *Agora* which was critical of President José Eduardo dos Santos. He was held incommunicado for 10 days at the *Laboratório Central de Criminalística,* Central Forensic Laboratory, where he went on hunger strike to protest against his detention.

In November he was formally charged with defamation of the President and released on bail. He appeared in court in December and requested that the case against him be dismissed. The request was submitted to the Supreme Court, but had not been decided by the end of 1999.

Rafael Marques was questioned for the first time in April together with William Tonet, the director of the biweekly newspaper *Folha 8,* after they published an article criticizing forcible recruitment and also draft evasion by young men with influential relatives.

▭ Josefa Lamberga, a correspondent for *Voice of America,* was slapped in the face twice and had her ear pulled by a soldier after she sought access to the military recruitment centre at the premises of the Transmissions Battalion in late April.

The assault appeared to be connected to an interview, broadcast five days earlier, in which interviewees alleged that white people and people of mixed race were exempt from the recruitment process.

Josefa Lamberga presented a complaint to the military court and attended an identity parade at the Transmissions Battalion, but the soldier who assaulted her was not present and the case remained unresolved at the end of the year.

UNITA officials
The five UNITA National Assembly deputies arrested in January were accused of crimes against state security; one was reported to be seriously ill. Their families and lawyers were not allowed to visit them for several months, and family members experienced difficulties in providing the detainees with food. One of the detainees was released in May and the remaining four were released in October, after a judge ruled that there was not enough evidence to

prove their alleged complicity in UNITA attacks.

Government forces, the militia and, in some cases, the police were responsible for the harassment, assault and detention of officials and others suspected of sympathizing with UNITA.

Ill-treatment
Small steps were taken to increase protection for human rights in police stations and detention centres, such as placing prosecutors in police stations to ensure the rights of detainees were respected, but there appeared to be little real political will to end human rights violations. Police, soldiers and other custodial authorities routinely abused their power, and there were numerous reports of police beating suspected criminals. There were also reports of police beating or otherwise ill-treating people in the streets with the intention of forcing them to hand over the goods they were carrying or selling. Reports of human rights violations by the police were seldom investigated and those responsible rarely held to account.

🗁 Father Leonardo Gaspar Chivanje was handcuffed and beaten on the head by a police officer in Humpata, Huila, after a minor traffic accident. The officer was subsequently reported to have been suspended from duty, but was not known to have been brought to justice.

Forcible recruitment
In addition to measures taken by the government to enforce the conscription laws between March and May, soldiers and police simultaneously conducted forcible recruitment. Men and boys were reportedly rounded up during raids by police and soldiers and sent to military bases throughout the country; many of those forcibly recruited were reportedly under 18 years of age. There were numerous reports that people were beaten in the course of the raids and some were reportedly killed.

UNITA also seized recruits, including some children. For instance, they reportedly abducted 80 children, aged between 12 and 18, from Mbanza Congo in January and February.

Violations of humanitarian law
Both parties to the conflict reported ambushes and attacks by their opponents in which civilians were killed; some may have amounted to wilful and indiscriminate killings. It was not always possible to confirm either the incidents or the identity of those responsible.

UNITA was responsible for most of the ambushes and attacks on civilians, as well as the majority of deliberate and arbitrary killings and incidents of indiscriminate shelling. More than 30 people were killed in Malange in January when UNITA forces shelled the city in broad daylight and more than 60 people reportedly died during an ambush on a clearly marked aid convoy in Uige in July.

UNITA abducted hundreds of civilians and UNITA soldiers reportedly raped women. Eight tribal chiefs were abducted from the villages of Quimozenguo and Quichiona in August allegedly because they had provided information to government forces and failed to recruit soldiers for UNITA. More than 300 people who escaped from UNITA captivity in August reported that they had been ill-treated while they were being held.

Government forces were implicated in scores of "disappearances" and extrajudicial executions, as well as indiscriminate attacks resulting in civilian deaths.

🗁 In December, soldiers were reported to have extrajudicially executed 11 civilians near Calai in Cuando Cubango province.

Cabinda
The government continued to face opposition from the two armed factions of the *Frente para a Libertação do Enclave de Cabinda* (FLEC), Front for the Liberation of the Cabinda Enclave. The Cabinda enclave is separated from the rest of Angola by a strip of territory belonging to the Democratic Republic of the Congo.

Two French men, two Portuguese men and an Angolan woman were taken hostage in March by the *FLEC-Renovda*, FLEC-Renewed. The woman was released within 24 hours but the four men, all of whom worked for foreign companies affiliated to the oil industry, were held until their release was negotiated for a ransom in July.

Maria Luisa Teresa Cuabo, Marta Macaia, Maria Cândida Mazissa and Maria Pemba were arrested outside the provincial government building in Cabinda City in April. The four women were among a small group of mothers staging a peaceful demonstration to protest against the conscription and forcible recruitment of their sons into the Angolan armed forces. They were released two days later without charge, after other women protested at their detention.

AI country reports
- Angola: Human rights – the gateway to peace (AI Index: AFR 12/001/99)
- Angola: Freedom of expression under threat (AI Index: AFR 12/016/99)

ARGENTINA

ARGENTINE REPUBLIC
Head of state and government: Fernando de la Rua
(replaced Carlos Saúl Menem in December)
Capital: Buenos Aires
Population: 35.4 million
Official language: Spanish
Death penalty: abolitionist for ordinary crimes
1999 treaty ratifications/signatures: Rome Statute of
the International Criminal Court

There were reports of ill-treatment and torture of
detainees in police stations and of killings by police
in circumstances suggesting possible extrajudicial
executions. Death threats and harassment against
human rights defenders continued. A prisoner of
conscience remained under house arrest. Human
rights violations committed during the period of
military government (1976 to 1983) were the subject
of legal proceedings within Argentina and abroad.

Elections

Elections were held in October for the President, for a
number of seats in the Chamber of Deputies, and for
some provincial governors. The new President,
Fernando de la Rua, of the centre-left coalition *Alianza*,
Alliance, was inaugurated in December.

Police brutality

Reports of torture and ill-treatment of detainees by
police officers continued. The authorities failed to
remedy the lack of effective measures to thoroughly
investigate allegations of torture. The non-
governmental organization *Coordinadora contra la
Represión Policial e Institucional*, Association against
Police and Institutional Repression, recorded more
than 80 killings by police during 1999.

▭ Juan Manuel Valdes was beaten and injured by
members of the police at South Police Station in Villa
Gessell, Buenos Aires Province, in January. His mother,
Lidia Abineme, a human rights activist who had been
pressing for a full investigation into the incident, was
knocked to the ground by unidentified men and
threatened with a gun following a human rights
gathering at the Plaza de Mayo Square in Buenos Aires
in November. It was alleged that a nearby police patrol
failed to intervene.

▭ In January, 18-year-old Fabián Manríquez was
arrested on suspicion of theft at his home, by members
of the Mendoza provincial police in Rincon del Medio.
He was reportedly severely beaten and shots were fired
at his feet. He was taken to the local police station
where his head was repeatedly submerged in water
until near asphyxiation. He was subsequently
transferred to a local hospital where medical personnel
lodged a formal complaint about his poor state of
health resulting from the torture. A judge dismissed the
charges of torture against the police officers and

charged them instead with unlawful coercion, which
allowed them to remain under provisional freedom.

Some members of the police force were brought to
trial and convicted of human rights violations.

▭ In May the Criminal Court in La Plata, Buenos Aires
Province, convicted four police officers of the torture
and "disappearance" of Miguel Bru in 1993. After years
of legal obstacles and repeated death threats against
Jorge Ruarte, the main witness in the case, the Criminal
Court sentenced two officers to life imprisonment and
two others to two years' imprisonment. Appeals against
the sentences were pending at the end of 1999.

Human rights defenders

In a new wave of threats and harassment against
human rights defenders, members and lawyers of the
non-governmental human rights organizations
Grandmothers of Plaza de Mayo and Mothers
Association of Plaza de Mayo were repeatedly
threatened during the year. The threats were related to
their work on behalf of their "disappeared" children
and the legal investigations and court rulings related to
past human rights violations.

Past human rights violations

Investigations and judicial proceedings in cases of
human rights violations committed during the period of
military government were initiated in Spain, Italy and
Germany. Investigations of cases of "disappeared"
children continued in Argentina. Investigations by the
Federal Court of La Plata, Buenos Aires Province, into
past "disappearances" continued during 1999 in
proceedings known as *Juicio por la Verdad* (the Truth
Trial), directed to uphold the right to the truth of the
relatives of the victims.

Spain

In November, Spanish judge Baltasar Garzón issued an
international arrest warrant against 98 members of the
Argentine armed forces in connection with
investigations initiated by the Spanish National Court
in 1996. Among the 98 were former members of the
military juntas.

The charges in the indictment included genocide,
torture and terrorism. However, the government of
President Carlos Menem consistently refused to
cooperate with the Spanish judiciary on the grounds
that human rights violations committed in Argentina
during the military period had already been dealt with
by the Argentine courts.

Italy

In July the Rome Tribunal was authorized by the Italian
Minister of Justice to initiate criminal proceedings
against five former Argentine military officers accused
of the homicide of three Italian citizens — Giovanni
Pegoraro, his daughter Susana Pegoraro, and Angela
Maria Aieta — during the period of military
government. The proceedings were the outcome of
investigations opened by the Italian judiciary in 1983
following complaints by relatives of Italians allegedly
held at the *Escuela de Mecánica de la Armada* (ESMA),
Navy Mechanics School in Buenos Aires, whose fate
remained unknown.

In a separate case, seven former Argentine military officers were committed for trial *in absentia* in connection with the abduction and murder of seven Italian citizens and the kidnapping of the child of one of them, during the years of military rule. The trial, scheduled to open in Rome in October, was postponed until December when, after one day, it was postponed until March 2000.

Other legal initiatives were under way in Italy into complaints of human rights violations committed against Italian citizens as a result of past collaboration between the Argentine security forces and the security forces in neighbouring countries.

Impunity

In January, Argentina signed the Rome Statute of the International Criminal Court.

For the first time a member of the military was ordered to pay damages for human rights violations. In August the Supreme Court ordered Emilio Massera, former leader of the military junta, to pay US$120,000 damages to Daniel Tarnopolsky whose family "disappeared" in ESMA in July 1976. The decision of the Supreme Court was unanimous. In the same ruling the Argentine state was ordered to pay US$1,250,000 damages.

In September the Federal Court confirmed the preventive detention of Jorge Rafael Videla and Emilio Massera and rejected the argument that the case had already been judged and that the statute of limitations had expired. The Federal Court's ruling set out important principles such as defining the kidnapping of children as a continuous crime and determining that the statute of limitations does not become effective while the whereabouts of the victim remain unknown. The Court also confirmed international legislation by ruling that "disappearance" is a crime against humanity and so comes within the scope of Article 118 of the Constitution which demands the application of international criminal law for crimes against humanity.

In November, within the framework of a friendly settlement sponsored by the Inter-American Commission on Human Rights of the Organization of American States, the Argentine government, in the case of Carmen Lapacó, acknowledged and guaranteed the right to the truth as a right unaffected by statutes of limitations. The government made a commitment to introduce legislation allowing national courts to uphold such a right. However, the relevant legislation had not been put forward by the end of 1999.

Prisoner of conscience

Fray Antonio Puigjane, a prisoner of conscience arrested in 1989, remained under house arrest serving a 20-year sentence. Fray Antonio Puigjane, a leading member of the *Movimiento Todos por la Patria*, All for the Fatherland Movement, was convicted of involvement in an armed attack in January 1989 on the basis of unsubstantiated allegations which he denied.

ARMENIA

REPUBLIC OF ARMENIA
Head of state: Robert Kocharian
Head of government: Aram Sarkisian (replaced Vazgen Sarkisian in November, who replaced Armen Darbinian in June)
Capital: Yerevan
Population: 3.8 million
Official language: Armenian
Death penalty: retentionist
1999 treaty ratifications/signatures: Rome Statute of the International Criminal Court

At least nine conscientious objectors to military service were imprisoned during the year. Allegations of torture and ill-treatment continued, and at least one person was said to have died in custody as a result of a severe beating. Three death sentences were passed during 1999, and 31 men were under sentence of death at the end of the year, although the moratorium on executions continued.

Background

A new government was formed following parliamentary elections in May. The elections were regarded as less seriously flawed than previous ones: the Council of Europe, which Armenia has applied to join, concluded that the vote was "an important step" towards meeting its standards. Further government changes occurred in October, after a group of five armed men opened fire on senior officials in the parliamentary chamber. A total of eight men died, including Prime Minister Vazgen Sarkisian, Speaker of Parliament Karen Demirchian, and the Speaker's two deputies.

Prisoners of conscience

Young men continued to face imprisonment because their conscience led them into conflict with the law that makes military service compulsory for young males, and offers them no civilian alternative. During 1999 at least six religious believers were sentenced to imprisonment, one of whom was given his second term for the same offence of refusing call-up papers. At least three others, including Karen Voskanian, continued serving terms imposed earlier.

Various officials mentioned moves towards drawing up plans for a civilian alternative service for conscientious objectors, but AI was not aware of any concrete proposals or timetable for a draft law in parliament.

In January 1998, knowing he was liable for call-up from the age of 18, Gagik Ohanian wrote to his local conscription office in Yerevan. He explained why, as a Jehovah's Witness, he was unable to carry out military service, but expressed his willingness to perform an alternative, civilian service. Gagik Ohanian was apprehended at his home in December 1998, reportedly by officials in civilian clothes who showed no documents, and was forcibly conscripted into a military unit in the Vajots region. There he was reportedly beaten by a senior officer when he refused to wear a military uniform. The visible injuries he sustained reportedly led military police in the city of Baik, into whose custody the military unit wished to transfer Gagik Ohanian, to refuse to accept him. In June 1999 Gagik Ohanian was sentenced to three years' imprisonment for evading military service, under Article 257 of the Criminal Code.

Torture and ill-treatment

Allegations of torture and ill-treatment in custody continued, including at least one case in which a detainee is said to have died as a result.

In February President Kocharian met a group of mothers whose sons had died as a result of violence in the army. He strongly condemned brutal hazing (bullying and humiliation) in the armed forces and pledged greater efforts to combat such crimes. At the same meeting the Military Procurator gave an assurance that many closed cases would be subject to review, and that 80 officers had been prosecuted the previous year for illegal actions. These included 34 convictions for abuse of power and two for causing suicides. Many families have complained that army deaths attributed to suicide have in fact been as a result of injuries inflicted during hazing, and that army officers and others have colluded in covering up the real cause of death.

▱ Senior military officer Artush Ghazarian was reportedly beaten so severely by law enforcement officials that he died in custody on the night of 30 September. He had been in detention since mid-September, charged with bribery. Artush Ghazarian was said to have been held at a civilian police station in the city of Vanadazor, but to have been taken from there for interrogation to a military police station where the beatings took place. An autopsy is said to have revealed injuries consistent with beatings, and a number of officials were detained.

Death penalty

Addressing the UN Human Rights Committee in October 1998, Armenia's representative stated that the death penalty would be abolished as of 1 January 1999, when a new criminal code was adopted. The death penalty would be replaced by a maximum sentence of life imprisonment. However, by the end of 1999 the draft code, which received its first parliamentary reading in April 1997, had still not received final approval from legislators. In February, speaking to an AI delegate in Yerevan, the Minister of the Interior reported that at that time there were around 30 men on death row. Three death sentences were passed during 1999, and 31 men were under sentence of death at the end of the year. No commutations by the President were reported, and no executions took place.

Among those who faced a possible death sentence during 1999 were those accused of planning or taking part in the October shootings in parliament. They included the five men who reportedly opened fire in the parliamentary chamber: Nairi Unanian, his brother Karen Unanian, their uncle Vram Galstian and two others named as Derenik Bezhdanian and Eduard Grigorian. These five were charged with terrorism (Article 61 of the criminal code) and premeditated murder (Article 99), both of which have a maximum sentence of death. AI welcomed President Kocharian's public assurances that the men would be given a fair trial, and urged the President to exercise his constitutional authority and commute to imprisonment all pending death sentences, as well as any future ones passed prior to abolition, in line with parliament's intention to remove the death penalty from the statute book.

Update on legislation

Failure to adopt the draft criminal code meant that, among other things, consensual homosexual acts between adult males remained criminalized, although no information on any prosecutions was available. A proposal to establish the office of ombudsperson in Armenia, put forward in 1998 by the newly-established presidential Human Rights Commission, also did not come to fruition.

AI country reports and visits
Report
• Armenia: "Respect my human dignity" – Imprisonment of conscientious objectors (AI Index: EUR 54/006/99)
Visit
An AI delegate visited Armenia in February and discussed issues of concern with various officials.

AUSTRALIA

AUSTRALIA

Head of state: Queen Elizabeth II, represented by William Deane
Head of government: John Howard
Capital: Canberra
Population: 18.5 million
Official language: English
Death penalty: abolitionist for all crimes

More than 4,000 refugee applicants and "boat people" were detained. Immigration reforms limited refugee rights and prohibited the national Human Rights Commission from initiating contact with immigration detainees. Continuing concerns about the detention of children and high rates of disputed deaths in custody led to inquiries by state Ombudsmen and other state authorities.

Background

There was considerable public debate about human rights throughout 1999, particularly focusing on the acceptance of refugees and UN intervention in East Timor. In March the UN Committee on the Elimination of Racial Discrimination found that a new Aboriginal land use law violated government treaty obligations to eliminate racial discrimination. The government rejected both the Committee's views and its request to visit Australia. In October, following a Federal Court finding that genocide is not a crime in Australian law, the Senate initiated an inquiry into Australia's implementation of the UN Convention on the Prevention and Punishment of the Crime of Genocide.

Refugees and asylum-seekers

Almost 4,000 people from Kosovo and another 1,500 from East Timor were granted temporary protection on condition that they did not seek refugee status in Australia.

Asylum-seekers arriving by boat increased in number, including 2,300 from Iraq and Afghanistan. A record 3,737 "boat people" arrived, among them at least 100 children. Detained under mandatory detention laws which prevent effective court review of the need for detention, at least 2,000 "boat people" were held in improvised accommodation.

A new law prohibited the Ombudsman and Human Rights Commission from initiating contact with immigration detainees, effectively restricting human rights monitoring of detention centres. Detainees may still contact the Commission in writing — if they are aware of its existence and their right to complain.

In May the Senate began an inquiry into the processing of applications for refugee status, judicial monitoring of asylum-related decisions, and procedures aimed at preventing the forcible removal of people to countries where they face torture or execution. Despite newly revised procedures to prevent such removals, only last-minute appeals to the Minister averted imminent deportation in several cases in 1999.

Sweeping reforms designed to target smugglers substantially limited the rights of asylum-seekers. New border protection legislation denies people the right to apply for asylum if the government considers they could have sought protection elsewhere. Those permitted to apply must show they have taken "all possible steps" to use any protection rights they may have in any other country. New visa conditions penalize accepted refugees if they arrived without valid travel documents. Unlike refugees resettled by the government, they must leave after three years or reapply; they are denied access to full health, welfare and education services; and family members are not allowed to join them.

◻ In May the UN Committee against Torture asked the government not to return a rejected asylum-seeker to Somalia where he risked torture. The government disputed the Committee's authority over the case partly on the grounds that in the absence of a central government in Somalia, there were no officials who could inflict torture. After 27 months in detention, the asylum-seeker was still awaiting a final decision about his status at the end of 1999.

◻ In September the Immigration Minister prohibited publication of the findings of a government inquiry into the case of a rejected Chinese asylum-seeker who had undergone an abortion after being deported to China when almost nine months pregnant. She claimed that Australian officials rejected her plea not to deport her until the baby was born, and that the abortion was involuntary.

Children in custody

In October AI registered concerns on the treatment of children in juvenile justice systems with a Senate inquiry into mandatory detention regimes. Under new sentencing laws in the Northern Territory and Western Australia, courts cannot take into account a child's circumstances or the severity of the offence, in violation of the UN Convention on the Rights of the Child. Many children were routinely held for brief periods in facilities for adults. In two states the ratio of Aboriginal children to non-Aboriginal children detained was reported to be 30 to one. In April, a Western Australia Aboriginal Legal Service submission to a state parliament inquiry claimed that 52 per cent of children in state police custody were physically abused and only one third informed of their rights.

Deaths in custody and ill-treatment

The findings of a number of coroner's inquests expressed growing concern about the circumstances of prisoner deaths and the care and treatment of inmates. The number of Aboriginal prisoners who died was again disproportionately high. Although estimates of the number of deaths in custody showed a slight decline over the previous year, Aborigines continued to make up a disproportionately large percentage of those who died in prison, and six Aborigines died in police custody.

🗁 In September a Sydney coroner criticized prison and police officers' lack of care in the case of Douglas Pitt, a 27-year-old Aboriginal man found dead in a court holding cell which the coroner described as "unsafe". Guards apparently ignored forms warning them that he was at risk of suicide. An ambulance officer, called after Douglas Pitt's body was found hanging in his cell, gave evidence at the inquest that she sensed hostility by prison officers and felt discouraged from trying resuscitation.

State Ombudsman inquiries in Tasmania and Western Australia into the circumstances of controversial prison deaths had not been completed by the end of 1999.

The Victoria state government prevented publication of a review of prison procedures. Among the facilities reviewed was a new privately-run prison where 10 people died within the first two years of operation.

A Northern Territory coroner's report criticized police treatment of 16-year-old Kwementye Ross who hanged himself when in "protective custody" on suspicion of drunkenness in Alice Springs in March 1998. Police had failed to check his condition or the video monitoring his cell for about 40 minutes after he was placed in a police cell for adult women.

In September a tribunal acquitted three officers of assault charges and commended them for using violent new restraint techniques. The officers had been accused of involvement in the beating of young Aborigines in Ipswich, Queensland, in March 1997. They had been filmed by a security video camera punching and kicking the victims, who were being held by other officers.

AUSTRIA

REPUBLIC OF AUSTRIA
Head of state: Thomas Klestil
Head of government: Viktor Klima
Capital: Vienna
Population: 8.1 million
Official language: German
Death penalty: abolitionist for all crimes

AI continued to receive allegations of ill-treatment of detainees by police officers. Most allegations involved non-Caucasian foreign and Austrian nationals. In some instances police officers were alleged to have used racist language. A foreign national died during his forced deportation after being gagged and bound by police officers.

Background
Austrian citizens voted for a new parliament on 3 October, resulting in a significant swing to the main party of the far right. The elections saw the use of openly xenophobic campaigning by the main far right party, which included the use of election posters calling for a stop to an alleged influx of foreigners and to alleged abuses of the asylum system. As a result of the electoral gains made by the main party of the far right, the traditional coalition between the Social Democratic Party and the People's Party appeared to be on the verge of collapse towards the end of 1999.

Intergovernmental organizations
In the period under review, Austria was scrutinized by both the European Committee for the Prevention of Torture and Inhuman or Degrading Treatment or Punishment (ECPT) and the UN Committee against Torture. In September the ECPT carried out a 12-day visit as part of its third periodic visit to the country, the findings of which had not been made public by the end of 1999. In November Austria came before the Committee against Torture, which expressed concern that "allegations of ill-treatment by the police are still reported". The Committee recommended that "clear instructions be given to the police by the competent authorities to avoid any incident of ill-treatment by police agents. Such instructions should emphasize that ill-treatment by law enforcement officials shall not be tolerated and shall be promptly investigated and punished in cases of violation according to law".

Allegations of police ill-treatment
AI continued to receive allegations of ill-treatment of detainees by police officers. The majority of complaints came from non-Caucasian foreign and Austrian nationals, who alleged they were ill-treated by police officers, often when being asked for identification. Most reported that they were subjected to repeated kicks, punches, kneeing, beatings with truncheons and spraying with pepper after being restrained. AI

expressed concern that investigations into allegations of police ill-treatment have not always been prompt or impartial, resulting in very few cases coming to trial.

⬜ On 1 November 1998 a black Austrian national, widely referred to in the Austrian media as Dr C., was stopped by the police after reversing his car into a one-way street and abusively asked for his identification. One of the police officers was alleged to have again racially abused Dr C. after he was unable to produce his passport, calling him names and saying that all black people were drug dealers. During the incident the police officers beat Dr C. unconscious. While he lay unconscious on the ground, the police handcuffed him, but continued to beat him after he regained consciousness. As a result of the attack, Dr C. spent 11 days in hospital suffering from injuries to his knees and elbows. After the incident Dr C. was charged with resisting arrest and physically injuring the police officers. In August a court rejected the counter-claim of the two police officers that Dr C. had physically assaulted them but upheld the charge that he had resisted arrest, sentencing him to a conditional four-month prison sentence. The judge found the two police officers guilty of intentionally injuring Dr C. and sentenced them to conditional six-month prison sentences. In October an Independent Administrative Tribunal found the police officers guilty of using excessive force against the detainee and reprimanded them for their use of racist language.

Racist police attitudes

In a number of cases of alleged ill-treatment, police officers were alleged to have verbally abused detainees, using racist language. AI also received information suggesting that racist attitudes among police officers were not confined to subordinate officers.

⬜ In October AI expressed concern about a senior police officer in the Vienna-Donaustadt Branch of Security who allegedly made racist comments to approximately 30 subordinate police officers during a training session at the end of August. He allegedly told police officers present at the training session that "Negroes deserve to be hit first, then asked their name".

Police counter-complaints

Detainees who lodged complaints of ill-treatment against police officers risked being threatened with criminal counter-charges such as resisting arrest, physical assault or defamation of the arresting police officers. In November the UN Committee against Torture stated "potential complaints of abuse committed by police authorities may be discouraged by the provisions enabling the police to accuse of defamation the person who lodges a complaint against them". Under Austrian law, conviction on a charge of defamation can result in a prison sentence or a fine, depending upon the severity of the allegations.

The threat of defamation was also used against witnesses, violating the principle that eyewitnesses should be protected against ill-treatment or intimidation.

⬜ In one case in March involving an alleged police assault on a French citizen of African origin, Mohammed Ali Visila, five people who had witnessed the incident were threatened by a leading police figure from the police trade union with being charged with defamation.

Death during deportation

Marcus Omofuma, a Nigerian citizen, died during his deportation from Vienna to Nigeria on 1 May. He allegedly suffocated on the airplane in the presence of three Austrian police officers after being gagged and bound. AI expressed concern that he may have died as a direct or indirect result of his treatment by the police. In November the UN Committee against Torture expressed its concern about "insufficient measures of protection in cases of individuals under an order of deportation".

The subsequent inquiry into the death revealed a considerable lack of clarity regarding the types of physical restraints which could permissibly be used during the expulsion of a deportee. AI was concerned that the Minister of the Interior, senior police officers and police officers of lower rank made contradictory statements about the permissibility of using mouth gags during forced deportations.

After the death of Marcus Omofuma the Austrian authorities created a Human Rights Advisory Council composed of representatives of both non-governmental organizations and the government to monitor and discuss a range of human rights issues in Austria. In its first report, published in October, the Council considered the human rights implications of forced deportations.

AI country visit

An AI delegate visited Austria in June and met representatives of non-governmental organizations, lawyers and victims of alleged police ill-treatment.

AZERBAIJAN

AZERBAIJANI REPUBLIC
Head of state: Heydar Aliyev
Head of government: Artur Rasizadeh
Capital: Baku
Population: 7.6 million
Official language: Azeri
Death penalty: abolitionist for all crimes
1999 treaty ratifications/signatures: Second
Optional Protocol to the International Covenant
on Civil and Political Rights, aiming at the abolition
of the death penalty

Several possible prisoners of conscience were
detained or prosecuted, apparently in connection
with their peaceful political or religious views.
Reports of torture and ill-treatment in custody
continued.

Background
The cease-fire continued to hold in the disputed
Karabakh region, which remained, along with adjacent
territories, outside the *de facto* control of the
Azerbaijani authorities. Discussions on resolving this
longstanding conflict moved into a new phase when the
Presidents of Armenia and Azerbaijan began a series of
one-to-one meetings, although no concrete proposals
had been made public by the end of the year. Hundreds
of thousands of people remained displaced by the
conflict.

Possible prisoners of conscience
Several possible prisoners of conscience were held
during 1999.
◻ Rasim Agayev, a political scientist and journalist,
was released early under a presidential pardon in July.
He had been sentenced to four years' imprisonment in
June 1998 for concealing a crime against the state.
Rasim Agayev had been detained by officials from the
Ministry of National Security in November 1996. His
lawyer was not permitted to see him until the fourth
day of his detention.
    Rasim Agayev reportedly confessed to one charge in
the indictment after officials threatened to prosecute
his daughter on a false charge of possessing drugs. He
later retracted this statement, but was found guilty; his
sentence reportedly could not be appealed as it had
been passed by the Supreme Court sitting as the court
of first instance.
    There were allegations that the charges against him,
which originally included the then capital offence of
treason, had been fabricated to punish him for his
known or imputed political views; he had been the
press secretary to former President Ayaz Mutalibov,
who remained in exile in Russia.
    Representatives of some Christian groups were
reportedly harassed; some were administratively
detained for short periods.

◻ In August Ibrahim Ikrameddin oglu Yuzbeyov, a
Jehovah's Witness from the village of Alekseyevka, was
summoned to the regional police headquarters in
Khachmas to discuss a complaint regarding his
proselytizing. Four police officers then accompanied
him to his home and reportedly searched it, without
obtaining a warrant, and confiscated a number of
items. Ibrahim Yuzbeyov was then returned to the
regional police headquarters where he was denied
access to a defence lawyer. The following day he was
sentenced to 15 days' administrative detention by
Khachmas district court for petty hooliganism. Ibrahim
Yuzbeyov denied the charge and alleged that he was
being prosecuted for his actions as a Jehovah's Witness.
He alleged that while in detention he was verbally
abused and beaten by officers to force him to renounce
his religion. Ibrahim Yuzbeyov was released at the end
of his term but the items confiscated during the search
were reportedly not returned to him. He also alleged
that after his release he was summoned by the regional
head of the Ministry of National Security in Khachmas
and warned that he would be forcibly expelled from
Azerbaijan within three days if he did not renounce
his faith.

Torture and ill-treatment
In November the UN Committee against Torture
reviewed Azerbaijan's initial report under the
Convention against Torture and Other Cruel, Inhuman
or Degrading Treatment or Punishment. AI had
submitted its own report to the Committee, expressing
concerns about continued and widespread allegations
of torture and ill-treatment. The Committee expressed
concern about the absence of a definition of torture in
the criminal code, as provided for by the Convention;
the numerous and continuing allegations of torture; the
apparent failure to initiate prompt, impartial and full
investigations into the numerous allegations of torture
reported to the Committee and to prosecute the alleged
perpetrators, where appropriate; the absence of
guarantees for the independence of the legal
profession, particularly the judiciary; and the use of
amnesty laws which might extend to the crime of
torture.

Deaths in custody
In January, 11 prisoners and two guards died during
disturbances at Gobustan prison, some 60 kilometres
outside Baku. According to official reports, two
prisoners attempting to escape managed to free other
prisoners and seize arms and hostages before guards
were alerted and sealed off the premises; two prisoners
and one guard were killed. The following day the
prisoners obtained a minibus, apparently intending to
drive to the airport. However, armed units opened fire
on the bus, killing nine prisoners and a guard who was
being held hostage.
    Reports of the incident varied and there were
allegations that the victims may have been
extrajudicially executed. An inquiry was initiated, but
the conclusions had not been publicly reported by the
end of the year.

Death penalty

In January Azerbaijan became a party to the Second Optional Protocol to the International Covenant on Civil and Political Rights (ICCPR), aiming at the abolition of the death penalty. However, it entered a reservation by which the death penalty could be applied for grave crimes committed in wartime or under threat of war. The criminal code was amended accordingly in October.

Legislative update

Measures outlined in the 1998 State program for the defence of human rights — including the ratification of the (first) Optional Protocol to the ICCPR and establishment of the institution of ombudsperson — had still not been fulfilled by the end of the year. There was no civilian alternative to compulsory military service for conscientious objectors; consensual homosexual acts between adult men were still punishable by up to three years' imprisonment; and concerns persisted that legislation punishing insult or slander directed against the President could be abused to punish the legitimate exercise of the right to freedom of expression.

Karabakh

Death penalty

The death penalty was retained in the disputed region of Karabakh. Death sentences continued to be passed, but no executions were carried out.

▢ Azerbaijani citizen Agil Ahmedov, who had been sentenced to death for subversive activities, was pardoned on health grounds and released in a prisoner exchange on 9 March.

Legislative issues

Military service remained compulsory, with no civilian alternative for those unable to perform this duty owing to religious, moral, ethical or other objections.

It was reported that the Karabakh Security Services were considering submitting a bill to parliament which would make "organizing illegal religious groups and sects" an offence punishable by 30 days' administrative detention or a fine. In the light of reported past harassment of some religious believers in Karabakh, there was concern that this could be used to imprison people solely for exercising their right to freedom of conscience and religion.

AI country report

• Azerbaijan: Comments on the Initial Report submitted to the United Nations Committee against Torture (AI Index: EUR 55/002/99)

BAHAMAS

COMMONWEALTH OF THE BAHAMAS
Head of state: Queen Elizabeth II, represented by Orville Turnquest
Head of government: Hubert Alexander Ingraham
Capital: Nassau
Population: 0.3 million
Official language: English
Death penalty: retentionist

Three people were scheduled to be hanged following a statement by Prime Minister Hubert Alexander Ingraham that hangings would be carried out; one received a stay of execution. Asylum-seekers continued to be denied access to a full and fair refugee determination procedure. Conditions of detention at the Carmichael Detention Centre and the Fox Hill Prison fell well below international standards.

Death penalty

In June the Prime Minister stated in an address to government leaders from Europe, the Caribbean and Latin America that he "looked forward to a day not long from now when the Bahamas may consider [abolishing the death penalty]". This statement received public criticism nationally and within days the Prime Minister issued another statement pledging that more hangings would be carried out "very soon".

There were 20 people under sentence of death at the end of 1999.

▢ John Higgs and David Mitchell — who were convicted of unrelated murders in 1996 and 1994 respectively — were scheduled to be hanged in August, even though the Inter-American Commission on Human Rights (IACHR) was still considering their petitions. The government scheduled the executions because both petitions had been pending before the IACHR for more than 18 months. The two men had petitioned the IACHR claiming that they were subjected to human rights abuses during the course of proceeding against them. For example, in his petition John Higgs claimed that he was subjected to a mock execution in 1997.

The men were granted stays of execution so that the Bahamas Supreme Court could consider motions filed by the men which challenged the constitutionality of executing them. The Court denied their motion, by a three-to-two majority verdict. Strongly worded dissenting judgments stated that the conditions under which the men had been held in prison were such as to amount to inhuman and degrading punishment and that the men's sentences should, therefore, be commuted. Both men were scheduled to be hanged on 6 January 2000.

American Convention on Human Rights

In June the Minister of Foreign Affairs stated that the government would not ratify the American Convention on Human Rights on the grounds that the government viewed one of the main purposes of the Convention to be the abolition of the death penalty.

Asylum-seekers

There were concerns that the treatment of asylum-seekers arriving in the Bahamas breached international standards.

Asylum-seekers were regularly denied access to lawyers, translators, or the UN High Commissioner for Refugees to assist in making an asylum claim; some alleged that they were denied access to any refugee determination procedure. There was no appeal process available to applicants to challenge a decision refusing asylum.

Asylum-seekers were arbitrarily detained at the Carmichael Detention Centre in Nassau where conditions were squalid and insanitary. There were insufficient beds and detainees were often forced to sleep on the floor. The quality of both food and water was very poor and the medical treatment available was inadequate.

Prison conditions

Conditions of detention at Fox Hill Prison were appalling and fell well below international standards. There were reports that prisoners were housed in cells which received no natural light and that they were only allowed out of these cells two or three times a week. Prisoners under sentence of death were further reported to be held in conditions amounting to solitary confinement. The cells were insanitary and contained little or no furniture, so that prisoners were forced to sleep on the floor. Access to washing facilities was limited. Food was of a very poor quality and access to medical treatment for sick prisoners was restricted.

BAHRAIN

STATE OF BAHRAIN
Head of state: Shaikh Hamad bin 'Issa Al Khalifa (replaced Shaikh 'Issa bin Salman Al Khalifa in March)
Head of government: Shaikh Khalifa bin Salman Al Khalifa
Capital: al-Manama
Population: 0.6 million
Official language: Arabic
Death penalty: retentionist

Several hundred anti-government protesters arrested in previous years continued to be held, the majority without charge or trial, and scores more were reportedly arrested and held for short periods during 1999. Some detainees arrested in previous years appeared before the State Security Court and received prison sentences of up to 10 years on charges including "violation of state security". The authorities continued to ban several Bahraini nationals from returning to the country. Hundreds of political prisoners and detainees, including prisoners of conscience, were released during 1999.

Background

The human rights situation started to deteriorate seriously in December 1994 following widespread demonstrations and protests calling on the government to restore the National Assembly, which had been dissolved in 1975. Thousands of people, including women and children, were arrested and hundreds were convicted after unfair trials. Torture and ill-treatment became widespread and a number of detainees died in custody. In March 1996 'Issa Ahmad Qambar was executed in what was the first execution in almost 20 years. He was arrested in connection with anti-government protests and convicted of the murder of a police official. However, a number of positive steps have been taken by the government in recent years. In 1996 the government signed an agreement which allowed the International Committee of the Red Cross (ICRC) to visit detainees, and in 1998 Bahrain acceded to the UN Convention against Torture and Other Cruel, Inhuman or Degrading Treatment or Punishment.

In March the Amir, Shaikh 'Issa bin Salman Al Khalifa, died of a heart attack at the age of 65. His son, the Crown Prince, Shaikh Hamad bin 'Issa Al Khalifa, officially acceded to the throne in June. Under the new Amir, several positive steps were undertaken. Hundreds of political detainees and prisoners were released. For the first time in 12 years, AI delegates visited Bahrain and the UN Working Group on Arbitrary Detention was invited to visit the country in 2000. In October the Amir issued a decree ordering the *Shura* (Consultative) Council to set up a committee to monitor human rights. The six-member committee was to "study all human rights legislation and regulations which apply in Bahrain" and "to raise awareness of human rights, take part in seminars and conduct studies and research in the field". In December the Amir announced that local elections would be held.

Release of political prisoners
In June the Amir ordered the release of 320 detainees and 41 convicted prisoners who had been held in connection with anti-government protests. The order also included 12 Bahraini nationals resident abroad who were allowed to return to the country. Among those who benefited from the Amir's order were young men and minors who had been detained without charge or trial for months or years.

Bahrain's longest serving political prisoner, al-Sayyid Ja'far al-'Alawi, was released in August after spending 18 years in prison. He and 72 other people were sentenced in 1981 for their alleged involvement in an attempt to topple the government. Al-Sayyid Ja'far al-'Alawi had received a 25-year prison sentence.

In June Muhammad 'Ali Muhammad al-'Ikri was released and in July prisoner of conscience Shaikh 'Ali bin Ahmad al-Jeddhafsi was released after spending more than three years in detention without charge or trial. It was not known whether his release was conditional.

In November the Amir ordered the release of a further 150 detainees and 50 prisoners all of whom were reportedly accused of "crimes against the state". Twenty Bahraini nationals living abroad were said to have been allowed to return to the country. In December the Amir ordered the release of another 195 political prisoners and detainees. By the end of 1999 it was not known whether all those who benefited from the Amir's orders had been released.

Prisoners of conscience
Six prisoners of conscience — Shaikh Hassan Sultan, Shaikh 'Ali 'Ashour, Shaikh Hussain al-Deihi, Sayyid Ibrahim 'Adnan al-'Alawi, Hassan 'Ali Mshaima' and 'Abd al-Wahab Hussain — remained held without charge or trial at the end of 1999.
Shaikh 'Abd al-Amir Mansur al-Jamri
Shaikh 'Abd al-Amir Mansur al-Jamri went on trial on 21 February before the State Security Court in Jaw, near al-Manama, on charges including incitement to acts of violence, sabotage and espionage. His trial violated international standards for fair trial. He was given access to a government-appointed lawyer only one hour before the court session. His family, however, appointed four other lawyers who defended him. Shaikh al-Jamri's family was allowed to attend the trial which was held *in camera*. The second court session did not take place until 4 July, and on 7 July he was convicted and sentenced to 10 years' imprisonment and a fine equivalent to $US 15 million. Defendants convicted by the State Security Court have no right of appeal. However, he was granted a pardon by the Amir and released on 8 July. His release was conditional on him refraining from any future anti-government activities and giving interviews to the media. Security forces were said to control access to his house in Bani Jamra and his movements were tightly controlled.

Political prisoners
During 1999 scores of anti-government protesters were reportedly arrested and hundreds of others arrested in previous years continued to be held without charge or trial. In January, five men were sentenced by the State Security Court to prison terms ranging from two to 10 years on charges including "violation of state security". Among them were 'Abd al-Ra'uf al-Shayib and Sayyid Ahmad al-Marzuq, who received prison terms of 10 and three years respectively. Details of their trial proceedings were not available.

Forcible exile
Bahraini nationals who had spent time living abroad continued to be banned from entering the country. In January 'Abd al-Majid Muhsin Muhammad al-'Usfur, his wife and their five children again attempted to enter Bahrain. They were held at al-Manama airport for two days, issued with new passports valid for one year and forcibly sent to Lebanon. Muhammad Ridha al-Nashit, his wife, Ma'suma Jad 'Abdullah, and their eight children were detained for 10 days in July at al-Manama airport and forcibly sent to the United Arab Emirates. At least five other families were banned from entering the country during the year.

Convention against Torture
In March 1998 Bahrain ratified the UN Convention against Torture and Other Cruel, Inhuman or Degrading Treatment or Punishment with a reservation to Article 20 and Article 30(1). Article 20 refers to a state party's obligation to cooperate with the Committee against Torture if the Committee receives "reliable information which appears to it to contain well-founded indications that torture is being systematically practised in the territory of a State Party". Article 30(1) refers to disputes between state parties concerning the interpretation or application of the Convention.

On 4 August 1999 Bahrain withdrew its reservation to Article 20. However, no investigations into past torture allegations were known to have been carried out.

Intergovernmental organizations
In April AI updated its previous submissions on Bahrain for review by the UN Commission on Human Rights under a procedure established by Economic and Social Council Resolutions 728F/1503, for confidential consideration of communications about human rights violations.

AI visit to Bahrain
For the first time since 1987, an AI delegation visited Bahrain in June and July and held talks with government ministers, senior judges and other officials. Several areas of concern were discussed including allegations of torture, trial procedures before the State Security Court, forcible exile and ratification of international human rights treaties. However, the delegates were not allowed to meet independently with non-governmental organizations, professional associations and others concerned with human rights protection and promotion. In November AI submitted a

memorandum of its findings and recommendations to the government. AI's recommendations included ratification of the International Covenant on Civil and Political Rights and its (first) Optional Protocol, the International Covenant on Economic, Social and Cultural Rights, the Convention on the Elimination of All Forms of Discrimination against Women and its Optional Protocol. AI also recommended amending the 1974 Decree Law on State Security Measures to ensure that it conforms with international human rights standards, as well as other practical measures for the promotion and protection of human rights.

BANGLADESH

PEOPLE'S REPUBLIC OF BANGLADESH
Head of state: Shahabuddin Ahmed
Head of government: Sheikh Hasina
Capital: Dhaka
Population: 125.3 million
Official language: Bangla
Death penalty: retentionist
1999 treaty ratifications/signatures: Rome Statute of the International Criminal Court

Institutional weakness, political instability and unchecked police brutality appeared to be the major factors in continued widespread human rights violations. Hundreds of people were injured and dozens killed, some as a result of police action, in nationwide strikes (*hartals*) called by opposition parties during 1999. Political party activists and student groups with links to the ruling and opposition parties continued to perpetrate acts of violence, including beating political opponents to death. Apparent corruption within the police and the lower judiciary, and burdensome bureaucracy, facilitated impunity for perpetrators of human rights violations and impeded access to justice for those without money or political influence.

Background
Political confrontations between the major opposition parties and the ruling Awami League, which were at times violent, dominated politics in Bangladesh. A coalition led by the largest opposition party, the Bangladesh Nationalist Party, accused the government of political and economic mismanagement, boycotted sessions of parliament and local elections and resorted to nationwide strikes which frequently brought the country to a standstill. Violent clashes between government and opposition supporters were a regular feature of the strikes. The government offered to enter into negotiations with the opposition, proposing to

hold early elections. It later accused the opposition of not responding and stated that it would complete its term of office.

Torture and ill-treatment by police
Disproportionate use of force by the police against demonstrators continued to be reported throughout 1999. Scores of people were injured when police indiscriminately beat anti-government protesters or journalists covering the *hartals*. Torture, consisting mostly of beatings by the police, was reportedly routine in all areas of the country. It was used to extract bribes or information, or to inflict punishment on detainees. At least three people were reported to have died in custody as a result of torture.

Violence against women
Women were subjected to an increasing number of violent attacks, highlighting the government's failure to take adequate measures to protect women and address underlying gender discrimination. Custodial violence against women continued to be reported, with at least three cases of women being raped by police. In the wider community, hundreds of women and girl children were scarred and maimed in acid attacks and scores of others were murdered in dowry-related incidents.

The failure of law enforcement officials to exercise due diligence to prevent, investigate and take legal action on acts of violence against women meant that perpetrators were rarely held to account. In one case, the police in Rajshahi were said to have demanded a large bribe before taking action to investigate the reported gang rape of a 12-year-old girl.

Legal and institutional reform
Although the government committed itself to a range of institutional reforms to improve human rights protection, implementation was unduly slow. Neither the proposed National Human Rights Commission nor the office of Ombudsman had been established by the end of 1999. Very few recommendations of the Public Administration Reform Commission, set up to examine ways of improving the effectiveness of public services, had been fully implemented. Despite calls by human rights activists for the Special Powers Act (SPA) to be withdrawn or amended, the law (which allows detention without charge or trial for an indefinite period) was still used to detain hundreds of people including political opponents. Although most people held under the SPA were released after short periods, others remained detained for prolonged periods. Some were released only after the High Court ruled their SPA detention orders to be unlawful.

Death penalty
The death penalty continued to be imposed with at least 19 people sentenced to death for murder. No executions were reported.

The Chittagong Hill Tracts
In May, tribal leader Shantu Larma finally took charge of the interim Chittagong Hill Tracts Regional Council,

after delays caused by disagreement over three government-nominated members. AI delegates who visited the area in May found that almost two years after the signing of a peace accord, some of its main provisions had not been implemented. These included the rehabilitation of all returned refugees, settlement of land confiscated from the tribal people, and withdrawal of non-permanent army camps from the Chittagong Hill Tracts.

Tension between pro- and anti-peace accord tribal groups and between tribal inhabitants and Bengali settlers often erupted into violence. At least six people were killed and dozens injured as the different groups clashed with each other.

AI country visit
AI delegates visited the Chittagong Hill Tracts in May to assess the human rights situation there.

BELARUS

REPUBLIC OF BELARUS
Head of state: Alyaksandr Lukashenka
Head of government: Sergey Ling
Capital: Minsk
Population: 10.4 million
Official languages: Belarusian, Russian
Death penalty: retentionist

The heightened protest activity by the opposition during 1999 was met by increasingly harsh measures on the part of President Alyaksandr Lukashenka's government. Prominent figures in the opposition who spoke out against President Lukashenka were imprisoned for exercising their rights to freedom of expression and peaceful assembly. There were several reports of possible "disappearances" of leading opposition figures. Political opponents of the President and human rights defenders were subjected to harassment and intimidation. The death penalty continued to be imposed on a frequent basis.

Background
During 1999 opposition groups staged a number of peaceful protests against President Lukashenka, questioning the legitimacy of his tenure in office. Several hundred people were arrested during the protests and given short prison sentences or fines. There were numerous allegations of police ill-treatment. In 1996 President Lukashenka held a referendum which led to the dissolution of parliament. This was followed later in the year by a referendum in which he secured a mandate to stay in office until 2001, even though an election was scheduled for 1999.

Opposition groups and a significant part of the international community argued that the second referendum was unfair and violated the Constitution and, therefore, that President Lukashenka's presidency expired in July 1999.

In protest against President Lukashenka's refusal to hold fresh elections, the opposition staged a series of high-profile, nationwide events, including unofficial presidential elections in May, in which around four million people reportedly participated, and several large-scale demonstrations in July and October, as well as numerous smaller protest actions, both in and outside Minsk.

Possible 'disappearances'
There was concern about the possible "disappearances" of leading opposition figures. The possible "disappearances" coincided with significant political events in the country and the authorities appeared reluctant to investigate.

In May the former Minister of the Interior, Yury Zakharenko, apparently "disappeared" in Minsk at the start of the unofficial presidential elections staged by the opposition; his whereabouts remained unknown at the end of the year. Viktor Gonchar — head of the unofficial electoral committee and first deputy chairman of the dissolved parliament — and his companion, Anatoly Krasovsky, apparently "disappeared" in Minsk on 16 September, three days before Viktor Gonchar was due to give an extensive report about the political situation in Belarus under President Lukashenka to members of the dissolved parliament.

Prisoners of conscience
The number of prisoners of conscience increased in 1999. Many leading opposition figures spent time in prison during the year for exercising their rights to peaceful assembly and freedom of expression. Hundreds of people were arrested during the various peaceful demonstrations and actions organized by the opposition. The majority of people were given administrative sentences of around 10 days' imprisonment, but some opponents of President Lukashenka were imprisoned for longer periods of time spanning months and even years.

The leader of the Belarusian Social Democratic Party, Nikolai Statkevich; human rights activist and deputy of the dissolved parliament, Valery Schukin; and the current deputy chairman of the dissolved parliament, Anatoly Lebedko, were arrested following opposition demonstrations during the year and served administrative sentences.

In March the former Prime Minister, Mikhail Chigir, was imprisoned for his opposition activities; he had intended to stand as a presidential candidate in the unofficial presidential elections scheduled for May. He was charged with financial impropriety relating to a position he held as head of a bank, a charge which he denied. After eight months' imprisonment, he was conditionally released at the end of November and was awaiting trial at the end of the year. Other prisoners of conscience — such as Andrey Klimov and Vladimir Koudinov, who were also imprisoned on charges relating to their businesses — had spent several years in detention.

Persecution of human rights defenders

Several prominent human rights defenders came under increased pressure in 1999 to cease their human rights work. There had been mounting concern in recent years about the intimidation by the authorities of a number of human rights defenders, including lawyers Vera Stremkovskaya, Nadezhda Dudareva and Gary Pogonyailo, who was also vice-president of the Belarusian Helsinki Committee.

In July Oleg Volchek was charged under Article 201(2) of the Belarusian Criminal Code with "malicious hooliganism". The charges related to his participation in a peaceful protest organized by the opposition during which he was arrested and ill-treated by police officers. Oleg Volchek is the head of the legal advice centre Legal Aid to the Population and head of a non-governmental committee which demanded an independent investigation into the possible "disappearance" of Yury Zakharenko.

Possible prisoners of conscience

The authorities attempted to curb the activities of a number of political activists and journalists. The independent media was the subject of considerable state attention in 1999 and a number of journalists were subjected to intimidation by the authorities. Article 128 of the Belarusian Criminal Code, which deals with defamation of a public official, continued to be used by the authorities to harass and silence outspoken members of the opposition and human rights defenders. Those convicted of charges under this Article can be sentenced to up to five years' imprisonment.

In July Irina Halip, editor of the independent newspaper *Imya*, was arrested at the Belarusian headquarters of the Russian television station, *ORT*, where she had been scheduled to give an interview. She was arrested on the charge that *Imya* had slandered the Belarusian Prosecutor General, Oleg Bozhelko, in a previous article. Although she was interviewed by the authorities on several occasions after her release, she had not been formally charged by the end of the year.

Prison conditions

Conditions in prisons and pre-trial detention centres fell well below international minimum standards and amounted to cruel, degrading or inhuman treatment. Prisoners were poorly fed, received inadequate medical care and were housed in poorly heated and ventilated conditions in overcrowded cells. Prisoners were often physically ill-treated by prison guards.

Aleksey Shidlovsky, a former prisoner of conscience released in February after 18 months in detention, alleged that during pre-trial detention in the town of Zhodino he and other detainees were made to leave their cells and stand in painful positions with their arms and legs stretched against a wall. Prison guards kicked them if they moved or fell. Meanwhile guards would fill their cells up with cold water and then force detainees to take off their shoes and socks and empty the cells using cups. He stated that if the cells were not emptied within 20 to 30 minutes, the whole exercise was repeated.

Death penalty

The death penalty continued to be imposed on a frequent basis. In August the Chairman of the Supreme Court of Belarus, Valyantsin Sukala, told a news conference that 29 people had been executed in the first seven months of 1999. There was continued concern about the veil of secrecy surrounding the death penalty. Information about the death penalty is classed as a state secret and even after a prisoner has been executed the relatives are not informed of the date or place of execution.

In July the mother of Anton Bondarenko, who was under sentence of death and whose appeal had failed, stated that the prison authorities refused to inform her of the exact date when her son would be executed. She had visited the prison where her son was being held on a daily basis for several weeks to see if her son was still alive. On 14 July she and a friend staged a picket near the Presidential Administration building to plead for Anton Bondarenko's sentence to be commuted. She was arrested by police officers and detained for three hours. Her son was executed 10 days later on 24 July.

Non-governmental organizations and the independent press

As a result of a presidential decree issued in January all political parties, trade unions and other non-governmental organizations were forced to re-register with the authorities. Members of the opposition maintained that the decree was a measure designed to silence more critical organizations. A number of non-governmental organizations were refused registration in the process.

Several prominent independent newspapers critical of the government also had their registered status revoked. In other instances, independent newspapers were closed down for alleged tax violations or after losing expensive libel cases for criticizing senior government figures. The harassment of the independent press aroused significant criticism abroad.

AI country reports

- Belarus: Vera Stremkovskaya — The continued persecution of a human rights lawyer (AI Index: EUR 49/005/99)
- Belarus: Torture and ill-treatment of peaceful demonstrators by the police, arbitrary arrests and prisoners of conscience (AI Index: EUR 49/012/99)
- Belarus: Possible prisoners of conscience (AI Index: EUR 49/024/99)
- Belarus: Possible prisoner of conscience — Professor Yury Bandazhevsky (AI Index: EUR 49/027/99)

BELGIUM

KINGDOM OF BELGIUM
Head of state: King Albert II
Head of government: Guy Verhhofstadt (replaced Jean-Luc Dehaene in July)
Capital: Brussels
Population: 10.2 million
Official languages: Dutch, French, German
Death penalty: abolitionist for all crimes
1999 treaty ratifications/signatures: UN Convention against Torture and Other Cruel, Inhuman or Degrading Treatment or Punishment

There were allegations that criminal suspects were ill-treated by law enforcement officers and that asylum-seekers were ill-treated during forcible deportations and in detention centres for aliens. A judicial investigation continued into the death in 1998 of an asylum-seeker following the use of a dangerous method of restraint during a forcible deportation. There was concern that the rounding-up, detention and collective repatriation in October of more than 70 Romani asylum-seekers from Slovakia, before appeals procedures had been exhausted in all the cases, indicated a discriminatory targeting of asylum-seekers on the basis of their ethnic identity, rather than an impartial application of the asylum procedure.

Background
In October, the new coalition government issued an outline of its policies on asylum and immigration, to be implemented over the period of a year. Among the measures announced were plans to accelerate and simplify refugee determination procedures; to draw up a "temporary protection" statute for people fleeing wars; to improve the situation of child asylum-seekers; to allow specific categories of immigrants residing illegally in the country to obtain permanent residency; to encourage voluntary deportation of rejected asylum-seekers by providing psychological and social support for those facing deportation; to maintain strict official limitations on the use of force by gendarmes performing escort duties during deportation operations; to allow a doctor and an observer from the human rights field to accompany deportees travelling under gendarme escort on special flights organized by the public authorities; and to establish an independent body mandated, among other things, to receive and examine complaints concerning the treatment of asylum-seekers.

Alleged ill-treatment and racism by law enforcement officers
In May the Centre for Equal Opportunities and Opposition to Racism, a body reporting to the prime minister and parliament, indicated that a significant percentage of formal complaints of racism made during

the six years of the Centre's existence related to ill-treatment by law enforcement officers. In October the Permanent Monitoring Committee of Police Services, a body examining the functioning of all law enforcement agencies, submitted its annual report to parliament and the government. It recorded dozens of complaints of unjustified use of violence by law enforcement officers.

In July the government stated that a working group had begun meeting in January to study certain recommendations of the European Committee for the Prevention of Torture and Inhuman or Degrading Treatment or Punishment and possible reforms. In 1998 the Committee had expressed serious concern that no progress had been made in introducing certain fundamental safeguards against ill-treatment in police custody which it had recommended to the government in previous years, such as the right of immediate access to a lawyer.

Alleged ill-treatment during forcible deportation
There were fresh allegations that foreign nationals being forcibly deported were physically assaulted and subjected to dangerous restraint techniques by gendarmes.

The use of a method of restraint known as the "cushion technique" — allowing gendarmes to press a cushion against the mouth, but not the nose, of a recalcitrant deportee to prevent biting and shouting — was suspended following the death of Semira Adamu, a Nigerian asylum-seeker, after a forcible deportation operation in September 1998 (see below). The government then asked an independent commission led by Professor Vermeersch, a moral philosopher, to evaluate the instructions and techniques relating to forcible deportations. The commission published its findings in January. It recommended, among other things, that certain restraint methods be definitively banned during forcible deportations, including "in particular, anything obstructing normal respiration (for example, adhesive tape, cushion on the mouth), and all forced administration of pharmacological products (except by doctors in urgent situations which would naturally mean the termination of the attempted deportation)". AI urged the government to adopt the commission's recommendation in its entirety. Basing its position on the expert opinions of internationally recognized forensic pathologists, AI underlined its own opposition to the use of materials and methods which could block the airways. New internal guidelines issued in July to gendarmes escorting deportees apparently largely reflected the commission's recommendations.

There were persistent claims in the course of 1999 that gendarmes used heavily padded gloves to cover the mouths of deportees, thus blocking the airway. There were also allegations that, in preparation for deportation, individuals were placed face down on the floor in restraints, with their hands and ankles bound together from behind — sometimes for prolonged periods — and then carried by the restraints. Such allegations described a restraint method reminiscent of "hog-tying", a highly dangerous procedure which can restrict breathing and lead to death from positional asphyxia, especially when applied to an individual who is agitated. In correspondence with the authorities, AI sought comments on the allegations concerning the use of padded gloves and "hog-tying" and information as to any steps taken to ascertain their veracity.

🗀 A judicial investigation was opened into allegations made by Matthew Selu, a Sierra Leonean national who was deported from Brussels-National airport to Dakar, Senegal, in November. He claimed that gendarmes used gloves to "choke" him; hit him, while handcuffed, on the chest, ribs and head; and placed him on "a kind of stretcher" on board the aircraft, with restraints placed around his shoulders, forearms, knees and ankles. He alleged that he briefly lost consciousness as a result of the blows inflicted.

A medical certificate issued by a doctor who examined him within a day of his arrival in Dakar recorded, among other things, a head wound some six centimetres long, a sprain to his left thumb, multiple contusions to his chest, neck and right shoulder, and bruising to his wrists and ankles. Matthew Selu said he was unable to recall precisely how he had incurred the head wound.

The Minister of the Interior stated that, according to gendarmerie reports, Matthew Selu had violently and vociferously resisted, tried to bite and head-butt the escorting gendarmes and had accidentally incurred a minor head wound when alighting from a gendarmerie vehicle transporting him to his flight. He indicated that Matthew Selu received first aid on board the aircraft, that he offered no further physical resistance once airborne, and that his handcuffs were removed for the rest of the flight, which was without incident.

Semira Adamu

A judicial investigation into the death in September 1998 of Nigerian national Semira Adamu following the use of the "cushion technique" had not concluded by the end of 1999. An initial autopsy had apparently concluded that she died of asphyxia. Three gendarmes remained under investigation in connection with possible manslaughter charges. In September the Belgian Human Rights League, which had lodged a criminal complaint against persons unknown and constituted itself as a civil party to the judicial proceedings opened after Semira Adamu's death, requested that two former Ministers of the Interior also be investigated in connection with possible manslaughter charges. The League held them responsible for the introduction and implementation of the "cushion technique" as an authorized method of restraint during forcible deportations and argued that they thereby also bore responsibility for Semira Adamu's death.

Alleged ill-treatment in detention centres for aliens

There were a number of allegations that detainees held in various detention centres were subjected to excessive use of force and ill-treatment. Several such allegations emanated from Steenokkerzeel detention centre 127-bis, located near Brussels-National airport.

🗀 An investigation was under way into a criminal complaint lodged in November 1998 by Blandine Kaniki, an asylum-seeker from the Democratic Republic of the Congo. She alleged that in October 1998, while accompanied by her five-year-old son, she and other inmates of detention centre 127-bis were subjected to an indiscriminate physical assault by helmeted gendarmes armed with batons and shields. Other inmates made written statements claiming to have been victims of, or witnesses to, the ill-treatment alleged. Blandine Kaniki was three months pregnant at the time and claimed that a miscarriage she suffered a few weeks later was the result of a blow to the stomach and subsequent inadequate medical assistance. The gendarmes had been called in to end an inmates' protest against an attempt to forcibly deport a Nigerian national earlier in the day; inmates claimed the man had been subjected to excessive force by members of the centre's personnel.

🗀 A judicial investigation was opened into a criminal complaint lodged by an Armenian national, Hovhannes Karapetyan, who alleged that, following his return to centre 127-bis after an attempt to deport him in June and pending transfer to another wing of the building, warders subjected him to an unprovoked assault, throwing him to the ground and beating him until he lost consciousness. He was then transferred to an isolation cell where he said he was held overnight without medical assistance. A doctor who examined him the following day ordered his hospitalization, and medical reports accompanying his complaint apparently recorded facial injuries and a fractured elbow. The Foreigners Office attached to the Ministry of the Interior, stated that warders intervened because Hovhannes Karapetyan had physically resisted his transfer to another section of the centre, had refused to see a doctor who went to visit him in the isolation cell during the night, and threw himself against one of the cell walls.

AI country report

• Belgium: Correspondence with the government concerning the alleged ill-treatment of detained asylum-seekers (AI Index: EUR 14/001/99)

BELIZE

BELIZE
Head of state: Queen Elizabeth II, represented by Colville Young
Head of government: Said Musa
Capital: Belmopan
Population: 0.2 million
Official language: English
Death penalty: retentionist

Three people were sentenced to death, but no one was executed. Reports of torture and shootings by police continued. One man was shot dead in disputed circumstances.

Death penalty

The Attorney General proposed to remove or limit criminal appeals to the Judicial Committee of the Privy Council (JCPC) in London, United Kingdom, with a view to speeding up the process of execution and pending the establishment of a Caribbean Court of Justice. AI wrote to the government expressing its concern that the proposal would lead to an immediate resumption of executions and a reduction in guarantees for fair trial. The proposal had not been adopted by the end of the year, and AI had not received a response to its inquiry.

Patrick Reyes, Alan Carl and Estevan Sho were convicted of murder and sentenced to death, bringing the number of people under sentence of death to 10. Seven people sentenced to death in previous years had appeals pending before the Court of Appeal in Belize or the JCPC. The JCPC quashed the conviction of Dean Tillett and passed his case back to the Court of Appeal to consider a retrial. The Court of Appeal ordered the retrial of Marco Tulio Ibañez, who subsequently pleaded guilty to manslaughter at the Supreme Court and was sentenced to 25 years' imprisonment.

Police use of excessive force and torture

Reports of torture continued. The government failed to submit its second and third reports to the UN Committee against Torture, in accordance with its obligations as State Party to the UN Convention against Torture and Other Cruel, Inhuman or Degrading Treatment or Punishment. The reports had been overdue since 1992 and 1996 respectively.

Belize's first Ombudsman was appointed in June to investigate alleged abuses of power by the authorities. He declared that he had received 25 reports of alleged police use of excessive force during the first two months of office, nine of which he forwarded to the police commissioner for further investigation.

☐ Hector Balcarcel alleged that he was repeatedly beaten and suffered burns to his genitals during detention in April. A medical examination identified abrasions on both his wrists and harm to his testicles and penis. AI received additional information from the government regarding Hector Balcarcel's allegations of torture, but it was still not clear if an independent and thorough investigation had taken place.

☐ Daniel Tillett was arrested in Independence Park on 21 September and died in the Belize Police Headquarters in Belmopan on the same day. A post-mortem examination reportedly revealed a ruptured liver, a fractured skull, and water in his lungs, and suggested that these injuries had been sustained in police custody. The Commissioner of Police was subsequently removed from office, a second police official was suspended and a third was charged with murder.

Police shootings

Reports of police shootings continued.

☐ Mateo Ramirez was shot dead in disputed circumstances by members of the Belize Defence Force in the village of Arenal in June. The police indicated that they had fired in self-defence, claiming that Mateo Ramirez had attacked them with a machete, but witnesses reported that the soldiers' lives had not been in danger. The Commission of Inquiry established to investigate Mateo Ramirez' death concluded that the shooting had been justified and was carried out in self-defence.

Children's rights

Minister for Youth Dolores Balderamos Garcia introduced legislation to Parliament in January regarding juvenile offenders, which provided for the separation of children from adults in prison.

The government submitted its initial report to the UN Committee on the Rights of the Child in January. The Committee expressed grave concern that corporal punishment was still widely practised in Belize and was not prohibited by law. It recommended that the authorities reform domestic legislation, in the spirit of the UN Convention on the Rights of the Child.

BENIN

REPUBLIC OF BENIN
Head of state: Mathieu Kérékou
Capital: Porto-Novo
Population: 5.6 million
Official language: French
Death penalty: retentionist
1999 treaty ratifications/signatures: Rome Statute of
the International Criminal Court

Ten people were sentenced to death, but no one was
executed. One person died as a result of excessive
use of force by the security forces, and another was
injured. Twenty-one asylum-seekers were held for
several days in January; they were released before an
official explanation was provided for their detention.
The trend towards greater respect for human rights
continued.

Background
A legislative election held in March, which appeared to
be fair and transparent, was won by the opposition, but
President Kérékou's new government, formed in June,
did not include opposition politicians.

Death penalty
Ten people were sentenced to death by a court in the
city of Cotonou after they were convicted of bank
robbery, but there were no executions for the 13th year
in succession.

Excessive use of force
One person died as a result of excessive use of force by
the security forces, and another was injured. Robert
Hodé was shot dead by the police in March after trying
to escape arrest, and Sacca Fikara, a member of
parliament, was beaten by five gendarmes during a visit
to a police station in May. President Kérékou
established a commission of enquiry, but it had not
reported by the end of the year.

Asylum-seekers
Twenty-one asylum-seekers from the Republic of the
Congo were arrested in January and held without
charge or trial. They were released several days later,
after protests from AI and several other human rights
organizations.

BHUTAN

KINGDOM OF BHUTAN
Head of state: King Jigme Singye Wangchuck
Head of government: Sangay Ngedup
Capital: Thimphu
Population: 0.6 million
Official language: Dzongkha
Death penalty: abolitionist in practice

Talks on the return of Nepali-speaking people from
southern Bhutan living in refugee camps in Nepal
resumed in September. Freedom of expression
continued to be restricted. Prisoner of conscience Tek
Nath Rizal, who had spent more than 10 years in
prison, was released in December following an
amnesty granted by the King.

Background
The National Assembly approved regulations governing
the devolution of executive power to an elected
Council of Ministers and a mechanism to register a vote
of confidence in the King. Several laws were passed,
strengthening the country's limited legal framework,
and a training program for judges and legal advisers
continued.

Nepali-speaking refugees
More than 90,000 Nepali-speaking people from
southern Bhutan continued to live in refugee camps in
eastern Nepal. The UN Sub-Commission on the
Promotion and Protection of Human Rights reiterated
its concern in August at the lack of progress in
negotiating a solution, and urged the governments of
Bhutan and Nepal to seek assistance from the UN High
Commissioner for Refugees and the UN High
Commissioner for Human Rights.

During the eighth round of bilateral talks in
September both governments made some progress in
defining the categories of people who would be eligible
for return, and reportedly discussed the mechanism for
the verification process.

AI submitted a memorandum to the governments of
Bhutan and Nepal outlining the application of
international standards governing nationality,
statelessness and repatriation. It called for the
resettlement programs to be carried out so as not to
jeopardize the refugees' return to land to which they
may have legitimate claim.

Several Bhutanese political organizations based in
Nepal and India, including the Druk National Congress
(DNC), continued to campaign for democracy and the
return of Nepali-speaking refugees. The leader of the
DNC, Rongthong Kunley Dorji, continued to face
extradition to Bhutan from India.

Nepali-speaking communities in Bhutan continued to
face discrimination when obtaining police clearance to
open a bank account, to travel abroad for training, to
work and to send their children to school.

Freedom of expression

More than 100 people were arrested in the border town of Phuntsholing during pro-democracy demonstrations organized by the DNC and other political organizations in exile. Several protesters reportedly required hospital treatment after they were beaten by members of the security forces, but all were subsequently released.

Royal amnesty

Prisoner of conscience Tek Nath Rizal, who had spent more than 10 years in prison, was released in December following an amnesty granted by the King. Thirty-nine political prisoners from eastern and southern Bhutan were also included in the amnesty, but 119 others continued to be held at the end of 1999.

Torture

The government did not respond to AI's calls to ratify the UN Convention against Torture and Other Cruel, Inhuman or Degrading Treatment or Punishment.
▭ Padam Lal Giri returned to Bhutan from the refugee camps in Nepal to investigate the reported resettlement of landless people on land previously occupied by people living in the refugee camps. He was arrested in June and taken to Geylegphug police station where he was allegedly beaten, kicked and punched, and stabbed in the head with a bayonet.

BOLIVIA

REPUBLIC OF BOLIVIA
Head of state and government: Hugo Bánzer Suárez
Capital: La Paz
Population: 7.8 million
Official language: Spanish
Death penalty: abolitionist for ordinary crimes
1999 Treaty ratifications/signatures: UN Convention against Torture and Other Cruel, Inhuman or Degrading Treatment or Punishment; Inter-American Convention on Forced Disappearance of Persons

There were reports of police brutality and at least one victim died of his injuries. Human rights defenders continued to be subjected to death threats and harassment, and the security forces reportedly committed human rights violations against coca-leaf growers and peasants in the El Chapare region. In most cases investigations into alleged human rights violations were unduly delayed or never initiated.

Police brutality

Freddy Cano López, a Peruvian citizen, was arrested in May and detained at the Interpol headquarters in La Paz. There were reports that the guards initially ignored his cries for help when a fire broke out in his cell. He was rescued eventually and taken to hospital, then transferred to Lima, Peru, where he died in June from his injuries. His death provoked a national and international outcry, prompting investigations into allegations that the fire had been started by guards. In June the Ombudsperson presented the conclusions of her investigation to the *Comisión de Derechos Humanos de la Cámara de Diputados*, Human Rights Commission of the Chamber of Deputies. She stated that the constitutional rights of Freddy Cano López had been violated and recommended, among other things, that the Interpol cells be closed. In July the Commission ordered the three police officers identified as criminally responsible for the incident to be tried before a civilian court, and ordered internal disciplinary proceedings to be brought against the National Director of Interpol. The case had not concluded by the end of the year.

At least 14 students were beaten by police after they were arrested while taking part in a demonstration in La Paz in June against the government's proposed reform of the education system. Journalists covering the demonstration were also reportedly beaten by police and attacked by police dogs. The Ombudsperson's office confirmed that the students had been ill-treated, but AI was unaware of any proceedings initiated by the authorities to bring those responsible to justice.

Peruvian immigrants and political refugees complained of discrimination, harassment and lack of protection by the police and security forces. Ten Peruvian inmates needed hospital treatment after they were attacked by some 200 Bolivian prisoners in El Abra prison, Cochabamba, in August. The Ombudsperson ordered an investigation into the role of prison guards in the incident.

Structural changes in the police force led to the discharge of several police officers who had been involved in corruption or accused of offences committed while on duty. However, most police officers accused of human rights violations remained on active service.

Human rights defenders

Human rights defenders continued to receive anonymous death threats and to face harassment from local authorities. Leading members of the *Asamblea Permanente de Derechos Humanos* (APDH), Permanent Human Rights Assembly, were threatened throughout the country in the course of their work. Adalberto Rojas, President of the APDH in Santa Cruz, was among those threatened after they complained about the ill-treatment of detainees in the cells of the *Fuerza Especial de Lucha contra el Narcotráfico* (FELCN), Special Anti-Narcotics Force. Arturo Alessandri, President of the APDH in Oruro, was threatened by a local judicial official with a criminal trial after he objected to the illegal detention of a minor.
▭ National APDH President Waldo Albarracin was abducted and tortured by members of the police in

January 1997. In 1999 he received anonymous death threats that were believed to be linked to the investigation and trial of four police officers by a civilian court, ordered in April by the *Comisión de Constitución de la Cámara de Diputados,* Constitution Commission of the Chamber of Deputies. Three of the officers remained on active service and by the end of the year the trial had not concluded.

El Chapare region

The security forces continued their program of eradicating coca-leaf crops in El Chapare, Cochabamba Department. There were fewer reports of human rights violations than in previous years, but the presence of the army contributed to the persistent climate of uncertainty and fear. The army maintained its presence alongside the *Policía Ecológica,* Ecological Police; the *Dirección de Reconversión de la Coca,* the government agency in charge of supervising coca-leaf eradication; and the *Unidad Móvil para el Patrullaje Rural* (UMOPAR), Mobile Rural Patrol Unit.

There were new complaints that the combined security forces had threatened and beaten peasants, taken part in violent incursions in El Chapare towns, confiscated personal belongings, and burned crops and dwellings. Non-governmental organizations demanded investigations into the incidents.

▭ In September UMOPAR members burned the homes of four peasants in Central Tacopaya and beat Sebastian Cuevas of the *Sindicato Villa Bolivar,* Villa Bolivar Union. They also arrested Guillermo Llaveta and beat him during interrogation.

BOSNIA-HERZEGOVINA

BOSNIA AND HERZEGOVINA
Head of state: three-member rotating presidency —
Živko Radišić, Ante Jelavić and Alija Izetbegović
President of the Muslim/Croat Federation of Bosnia and Herzegovina: Ivo Andrić Luzanski
President of the Republika Srpska: vacant since March 1999
Heads of national government: Haris Silajdzic, Svetozar Mihajlović, Neven Tomić
Capital: Sarajevo
Population: 3.1 million
Official languages: Bosnian, Croatian, Serbian
Death penalty: abolitionist for ordinary crimes

The 1995 General Framework Agreement for Peace (Framework Agreement) equipped the country with some of the world's most sophisticated human rights protection and monitoring institutions. Despite this, the majority of gross human rights violations committed during the 1991-1995 war remained unaddressed and more than 17,000 people remained unaccounted for. Some 1.2 million people were still internally displaced or living as refugees, and only 60,000 people returned to their pre-war homes during the year. More than 20 of the 53 suspects publicly indicted by the International Criminal Tribunal for former Yugoslavia (Tribunal) for violations of international humanitarian law in Bosnia-Herzegovina were still at liberty. They were believed to be in the country still, or in the neighbouring Federal Republic of Yugoslavia (FRY). Among them were Bosnian Serb suspects Radovan Karadžić and Ratko Mladić, who had been jointly indicted for genocide in the former UN enclave of Srebrenica in 1995.

Background

The 1995 Framework Agreement divided the sovereign republic of Bosnia-Herzegovina into two largely autonomous entities, the Federation of Bosnia-Herzegovina (Federation) and the Republika Srpska, and established a multi-ethnic government representing the three constituent national groups of Serbs, Croats and Bosniacs.

The Republika Srpska was seized by a political crisis for most of 1999, caused by the failure to form a new government after general and presidential elections in 1998. The High Representative for Bosnia-Herzegovina, Carlos Westendorp, removed President Nikola Poplašen from office in March on the grounds that he had failed to implement the Framework Agreement and had obstructed the formation of a new government. The president's post was still vacant at the end of the year.

The two entities failed to cooperate with one another, in particular with regard to the implementation of the human rights provisions of the Framework Agreement. In November Carlos Westendorp dismissed 22 officials throughout the country for this obstruction. The authorities also continued to withhold information which could shed light on past human rights violations, particularly on "disappearances" and abductions.

In October it was decided to reduce the Stabilization Force (SFOR), tasked to ensure compliance with the Framework Agreement and led by NATO, from 30,000 to 20,000 by April 2000.

'Minority returns'
The return of refugees and internally displaced persons to their pre-war communities, now administered and predominantly inhabited by a different nationality group, continued to be seen as an essential means of reversing the wartime attempt to create "ethnically pure" territories and a crucial test of the implementation of the Framework Agreement. Such "minority returns" have been declared an absolute priority by the international community, but the number of such returns registered by the Office of the UN High Commissioner for Refugees dropped from some 44,000 in 1998 to around 32,000 in 1999.

The presence of more than 50,000 Kosovar refugees, who fled the armed conflict in Kosovo and the NATO air campaign against the FRY (see Federal Republic of Yugoslavia entry), caused considerable stagnation in the overall return process. However, the largest obstacle was the lack of political will among the local authorities. Government officials in both entities were reluctant to enforce laws or implement judicial or administrative decisions on the return of property and the police did not adequately protect returnees.

There were virtually no Bosniac returns to Srebrenica municipality in the Republika Srpska in 1999. This compounded the severe human rights violations suffered by thousands of Bosniacs following the fall of the UN "safe haven" to the Bosnian Serb army in July 1995. The inaugural session of the multi-ethnic municipal council was held in July, almost two years after the first post-war municipal elections in the country, but none of the Bosniac councillors was able to live permanently in the municipality. Concerns for their personal safety increased after Munib Hasanović, the Bosniac deputy secretary of the municipal council, was beaten and stabbed by two masked assailants in October. He had apparently received threats before from a local Serb hard-line politician. Bosnian Serbs who publicly endorsed ethnic reconciliation and the return of Bosniacs to Srebrenica also suffered violence and intimidation. In September Milojko Andrić, the local representative of the multi-ethnic Social Democratic Party, was threatened by a local police officer a few days before his car was set on fire.

Bosnian Serbs continued to face serious administrative obstacles and physical violence while returning to Drvar municipality, now situated in the Federation and hosting a large Bosnian Croat internally displaced population. In September the High Representative and the Head of the Mission of the Organization for Security and Co-operation in Europe suspended the municipal council and dismissed a number of officials because they had been obstructing "minority returns". The Drvar Serb mayor, Mile Marfieta, was also dismissed out of concern for his security. He had been violently attacked in April 1998 in the wake of the murder of two elderly Serb returnees, Vojislav and Mileva Trninić, and no one had been brought to justice for either these murders or the ensuing attacks by the end of the year.

Political violence
There were a number of violent attacks on politicians, independent journalists and "minority returnees". In most cases investigations were launched immediately, often with the extensive support and supervision of the International Police Task Force (IPTF).

Zeljko Kopanja, editor of the Nezavisne Novine, lost both legs in a car bomb attack in Banja Luka in the Republika Srpska in October which was apparently motivated by a series of articles published in Nezavisne Novine in September and October. The articles alleged that the Republika Srpska authorities had destroyed evidence of paramilitary attacks on Bosniacs and Croats in 1992 and 1993 in the towns of Teslić and Doboj in an attempt to halt criminal proceedings or prevent future legal proceedings against the paramilitaries. Zeljko Kopanja had reportedly received death threats prior to the attack and reported them to the local police, but measures had not been taken to ensure his safety.

Steps to end impunity
Eight men indicted for violations of international humanitarian law came into the custody of the Tribunal. Dragan Kulundzija, Radomir Kovać, Radoslav Brdjanin and Damir Došen, all Bosnian Serbs, were arrested by SFOR troops. Momir Talić, a Bosnian Serb army general who had been secretly indicted for war crimes in the Prijedor and Sanski Most areas, was arrested by police in Vienna during a visit to Austria for an international conference in August. Bosnian Croat Vinko Martinović, who had been indicted for war crimes in the Mostar area, was extradited by Croatia in August, following intensive international pressure. In December SFOR arrested two more Bosnian Serb men, Stanislav Galić and Zoran Vuković, who had been indicted for crimes committed in Sarajevo and Fofia respectively.

Bosnian Serb Dragan Gagović was shot dead by SFOR soldiers during an attempted arrest in January. He had been publicly indicted for war crimes committed in the eastern town of Fofia, including the systematic rape of Bosniac women.

The Tribunal heard 11 defendants in five separate trials. Zlatko Aleksovski was convicted in June of violating the laws and customs of war but was acquitted of breaching the 1949 Geneva Conventions. He was sentenced to two and a half years' imprisonment but immediately released for time already spent in custody.

In October Goran Jeliić was convicted of war crimes and crimes against humanity; he was sentenced in December to 40 years' imprisonment.

Court proceedings against people accused of nationally-defined war crimes continued in local courts in both entities. The majority were affiliated with the wartime adversaries of the prosecuting authorities, and little effort was made to prosecute alleged perpetrators among the authorities' own supporters.

Unfair trials of political prisoners
In the Republika Srpska criminal proceedings continued against three Bosniac men from Srebrenica who had been sentenced in 1997 to lengthy prison terms for the murder of four Bosnian Serbs and retried in 1998, after a successful appeal to the Supreme Court. In January 1999 the Human Rights Ombudsperson reported that the Bijeljina District Court panel of judges presiding over the 1998 retrial could not be considered an independent and impartial tribunal. She also stated that the defendants' right to be presumed innocent and their right to be represented by a lawyer of choice had been violated and that incriminating statements extracted from the defendants by force had been used as evidence. The Ombudsperson also criticized the public prosecutor for failing to investigate allegations that the defendants had been ill-treated.

In May the Republika Srpska Supreme Court quashed the 1998 verdict, stating that the judges' reasoning had been contradictory and that the available evidence had not been used in accordance with domestic law. The case was again sent for a retrial, despite the lack of new evidence to support further criminal prosecution, and the three men were released from custody in June.

Ill-treatment by police
Reports of ill-treatment in custody continued despite the overwhelming level of international scrutiny that law enforcement officials were subjected to.

▭ Andrija Beljo, a Bosnian Croat businessman, was detained by police in Mostar on 26 August in connection with the alleged theft of cars in Croatia. He was reportedly punched in the face, beaten and kicked by three Bosnian Croat police officers, one of whom had been decertified by IPTF in 1997. When he left the police station on 27 August he was accosted by two of the three men and by a third man he did not recognize who forced him into a car at gunpoint and drove him to an open mine near Široki Brijeg. He was beaten and forced to participate in a mock execution before the three men received a mobile telephone call warning them that the IPTF were already inquiring into his whereabouts. The three then forced him to cross the Croatian border, where he was detained on the basis of a decision by the Split County Court investigating magistrate.

Andrija Beljo claimed that he had refused to pay a large sum of protection money to one of his assailants some months before his arrest. He stated that other local entrepreneurs had been forced to pay protection money to these police officers after they were physically intimidated and threatened with imprisonment.

AI Action
AI continued to call for SFOR to adhere to its mandate to seek out and arrest persons indicted by the Tribunal. It continued to call on the governments of Croatia, FRY and Bosnia-Herzegovina to live up to their obligations as UN member states to cooperate unconditionally with the Tribunal, to provide the Prosecutor's office with information, and to surrender any indicted suspects on their territory without delay. AI also called on the three governments to amend their domestic legislation in order to facilitate the surrender of indicted suspects.

During 1999 AI endeavoured to ensure that the fight against impunity for human rights abuses committed in the region was kept on the political agenda throughout the world. It stressed the crucial link between continued impunity and other unresolved human rights issues, such as "minority returns" and the resolution of the tens of thousands of persons still unaccounted for.

AI country reports and visits
Report
• Concerns in Europe, January – June 1999: Bosnia-Herzegovina (AI Index: EUR 01/002/99)
Visits
AI visited Bosnia-Herzegovina in February and March to collect further information related to "disappearances" and abductions, and to monitor trials against political prisoners.

BRAZIL

FEDERATIVE REPUBLIC OF BRAZIL
Head of state and government: Fernando Henrique Cardoso
Capital: Brasília
Population: 159.7 million
Official language: Portuguese
Death penalty: abolitionist for ordinary crimes

Conditions of detention for common prisoners, including juvenile offenders, constituted cruel, inhuman and degrading treatment. Torture and ill-treatment were reported to be common in many police stations, juvenile detention centres and prisons. Deaths in custody in these institutions were generally not documented or investigated. Police and "death squads" linked to the security forces continued to kill civilians, including children, in circumstances suggesting extrajudicial executions. Human rights defenders were threatened and attacked. Most of those responsible for human rights violations continued to benefit from impunity. Land reform activists in a number of states were harassed,

assaulted and murdered by gunmen hired by local landowners, with the apparent acquiescence of the police and authorities.

Violations against detainees

In 1999 approximately 170,000 common prisoners were incarcerated in more than 500 prisons and municipal jails, and in thousands of police stations. In June AI launched a campaign on the growing crisis in Brazil's penal system. In response, the authorities proposed a number of measures at federal and, in some cases, state level, which, if implemented, would improve the conditions of detention and the treatment of detainees. These included proposals to reduce the prison population by increasing the provision and application of non-custodial measures and by revising the penal code. The government also declared its intention to build smaller, decentralized prisons to relieve overcrowding and reduce the use of police stations for long-term detention.

Deaths in custody

As in previous years, scores of deaths in custody occurred as a result of violence on the part of police and prison officers, denial of medical care, or negligence on the part of the authorities in preventing violence between detainees. Military and civil police officers reacted to prison disturbances with excessive force and brutality; prisoners were injured, tortured and killed as a result.

In March John Robert Lamartine Soares was shot dead in the São Paulo House of Detention by a military police officer patrolling the perimeter wall who opened fire on prisoners and guards in the crowded yard following a verbal dispute with another prisoner. The police officer had not been charged by the end of the year.

Torture and ill-treatment

Civil police officers routinely resorted to torture and ill-treatment as a means of extracting confessions. Beatings and intimidation were also employed in prisons and police stations in order to control long-term detainees held in very overcrowded conditions. Prisoners who complained were often subjected to further abuse and reprisals.

In September public prosecutors, who are responsible for monitoring the police, paid a surprise visit to the Theft and Robbery police station, Belo Horizonte, Minas Gerais state. In a small bathroom they discovered instruments used for torture, including bare electrical wires for applying electric shocks, and a metal bar from which victims were suspended upside-down by their ankles and wrists, on the so-called "parrots perch". As the prosecutors were interviewing prisoners who had allegedly just been tortured, police forced them to leave, subjected them to abuse, and vandalized their car. The police chief and nine police officers were subsequently suspended from duty.

In January Jessé Correia de Oliveira Filho was allegedly tortured in the Cordeiro Police Station in Recife, Pernambuco state, because he refused to confess to involvement in a homicide. He was left stripped naked for several hours. His hands were tied behind his back and four police officers repeatedly placed a plastic bag over his head and stood on him. Eventually he agreed to confess. He subsequently lodged an official complaint and was shot dead in the street near his home the evening before he was due to attend an identification parade to identify his torturers.

Conditions of detention

Many pre-trial and convicted prisoners were held in extremely overcrowded, insanitary conditions in police stations and prisons. Health care was poor or non-existent.

AI delegates who visited the Roger Prison in João Pessoa, Paraíba state, in June found prisoners packed into dark airless cells which leaked rainwater. Broken sewer pipes were spilling sewage into the prison yard, where piles of decaying rubbish constituted a health hazard. The triage and isolation cells were small and windowless, with filthy and bloodstained walls and floors. The 600 prisoners had no work or educational facilities.

Children

Juvenile justice

Conditions of detention for many of Brazil's juvenile offenders were often no better and frequently violated the 1990 Children and Adolescents Statute.

By August the São Paulo state detention centre in Imigrantes, run by the Foundation for the Well-Being of Minors (FEBEM), held 1,648 juvenile offenders and suspected offenders in a complex designed for 364. In October AI delegates visiting this detention centre found boys sleeping on filthy mattresses on concrete floors. There were only eight showers and six toilets for 300 boys, most of whom suffered from skin problems. The majority had no access to work, education or exercise. These conditions resulted in a spate of riots and mass break-outs. After a riot in August, 69 boys were injured, allegedly by the military police riot squad. In September hooded warders were captured on film beating boys who had surrendered; riot police fired rubber bullets at relatives waiting outside. During a riot in October, four boys were brutally killed by fellow inmates.

Killings of children

Children continued to be the victims of "death squad" and police killings.

In February, 14-year-old Anderson Pereira dos Santos, 17-year-old Thiago Passos Ferreira, and 21-year-old Paulo Roberto da Silva were leaving a carnival party in São Vicente, São Paulo state, when they were stopped by members of the Military Police Mounted Regiment. Eyewitnesses saw them being beaten and driven off in a police car. Their bodies were found one week later dumped in an area of wasteland. They had been shot in the head at point-blank range with a high calibre pistol similar to those used by the military police. Four military police officers were awaiting trial at the end of the year.

There appeared to be a resurgence of killings of street children in Rio de Janeiro by individuals in civilian clothes with the apparent acquiescence or collusion of on-duty police officers in the area.

◻ In June a group of street children who were being rowdy on a bus were removed by a police officer. A man in civilian clothes then called over one of the children, 10-year-old Fabiano Teodoro Teixeira. As the boy ran away, he was shot dead by a man who was reportedly later identified as an off-duty military police corporal. The on-duty officer took no action to stop or detain him.

◻ João Fernando Caldeira da Silva, a 17-year-old paper recycler, was shot dead in June by a motorist near the Candelária church. A witness, Márcio Silva de Souza, ran away and was stopped and threatened by another man. Three military police officers nearby reportedly took no action. Márcio Silva de Souza is a survivor of the Candelária massacre of July 1993, when a group of off-duty military police officers killed eight people, seven of them children.

'Death squads'

"Death squads", acting with the participation or collusion of the police, continued to operate in a number of Brazilian states, including Acre, Bahia, Mato Grosso do Sul, Rio de Janeiro, Amazonas, and Rio Grande do Norte.

◻ In September the Brazilian Federal Congress removed from office a federal deputy for the western Amazonian state of Acre accused of international drug and arms trafficking and of running a "death squad" responsible for the deaths of at least 30 people whose bodies were often mutilated. Twenty-one civil and military police officers were also arrested in connection with these activities. At the end of the year, a federal Parliamentary Commission of Inquiry into drug trafficking was looking into similar allegations involving state officials in a number of other states, including Piauí and Espírito Santo.

Police
Eldorado de Carajás massacre
In August the trial began of the 153 Pará state military police officers indicted on a charge of aggravated homicide for the killing of 19 landless peasants in Eldorado de Carajás in April 1996. The three commanding officers, the first to be tried, were acquitted amid allegations of bias among the jurors and misconduct of the trial. The trial of the remaining accused was suspended pending a number of appeals in the state High Court. The governor of the state, the Secretary of Public Security and the Commander-in-Chief of the military police at the time of the massacre continued to enjoy immunity from investigation and prosecution, in contravention of the principle of chain-of-command responsibility in relation to extrajudicial executions.
Brasília's Urbanization Company
In December police in Brasília shot and killed José Ferreira da Silva while breaking up a demonstration in Brasília. Two men lost an eye, and some 30 others were wounded. Employees of Brasília's Urbanization Company (NOVACAP), responsible for the maintenance of public spaces, were negotiating an end to their occupation of the NOVACAP building when police from the Special Operations Battalion stormed the building firing rubber bullets and live ammunition.

Investigations into the incident were hampered by the failure to register firearms to users, and delays in handing over arms for ballistic tests. At the end of the year individual police responsible for the shootings had not been identified.

Human rights defenders and witness protection
In July, the government approved a new federal witness protection scheme which, if fully implemented and resourced, would enable witnesses and victims, including those with criminal convictions, to testify without fear of reprisals.

However, witnesses and human rights defenders frequently paid a high price during 1999 for their willingness to testify against the police and local politicians. Their vulnerability underscored the importance of federal government action to investigate serious human rights violations where the state authorities were unwilling or unable to do so promptly and impartially. At the end of the year a constitutional amendment was still under debate in Congress which would give the federal government additional powers to do so.

◻ Human rights defenders involved in investigating the "death squad" in Acre received death threats. In August Valdecir Nicásio Lima, a lawyer assisting investigations, left the country to ensure his and his family's safety. In September Maria de Nazaré Gadelha Ferreira Fernandes, a lawyer working with the Rio Branco Diocese Human Rights Defence Centre, suffered intimidation by known "death squad" members at her place of work and at home.

◻ In Rio Grande do Norte state, Antônio Lopes, a transvestite also known as "Carla", was shot dead outside his house in March. His death appeared to be linked to that of Francisco Gilson Nogueira, a lawyer at the Centre for Human Rights and Collective Memory, who was killed in 1996 while investigating a "death squad". Antônio Lopes uncovered and handed to the public prosecutor evidence which brought about the reopening in October 1998 of the police investigation into Francisco Gilson Nogueira's death.

Land-related violence
Land conflicts generated increasing tension and violence in Paraná state.

◻ In March Eduardo Anghinoni was shot dead by a gunman in Querência do Norte. He was visiting his brother, Celso Anghinoni, a well-known local leader of the Landless Rural Workers Movement (MST). One week later, Seno Staats, an MST regional coordinator, was abducted and tortured for five hours by armed men who told him that he and 10 other MST members, including Celso Anghinoni, were on a death list. While interrogating him about MST activities, they punched and kicked him, burned him with cigarettes, put a rope around his neck, placed a plastic bag over his head, and threatened to kill him, his family and other MST leaders. Some of those threatened were later arrested and placed under preventive detention on account of their MST activities.

AI country reports and visits
Report
• Brazil: "No one here sleeps safely" – Human rights violations against detainees (AI Index: AMR 19/009/99)

Visits
AI delegates visited Brazil in June and July, and again in October and visited prisons and youth detention centres. They launched the above report and discussed its recommendations with both state and federal authorities. An AI delegate visited Paraná state in July to discuss with the authorities a resolution to land-related violence.

BULGARIA

REPUBLIC OF BULGARIA
Head of state: Petar Stoyanov
Head of government: Ivan Kostov
Capital: Sofia
Population: 8.3 million
Official language: Bulgarian
Death penalty: abolitionist for all crimes
1999 treaty ratifications/signatures: Second Optional Protocol to the International Covenant on Civil and Political Rights, aiming at the abolition of the death penalty; Protocol No. 6 to the European Convention for the Protection of Human Rights and Fundamental Freedoms concerning the abolition of the death penalty; Rome Statute of the International Criminal Court

There continued to be widespread reports of ill-treatment and torture by law enforcement officials. Roma were frequently the target of such reported abuses, and often felt unable to pursue complaints, fearing retribution from law enforcement officials. Law enforcement officials continued to use firearms in circumstances prohibited by international standards, resulting in deaths and injuries.

Use of firearms by police
The Bulgarian Law on National Police, adopted in 1997, allows law enforcement officials to use firearms in circumstances far wider than those allowed by the UN Basic Principles on the Use of Force and Firearms by Law Enforcement Officials, which allow the use of firearms only in self-defence or the defence of others against the imminent threat of death or serious injury. The authorities made no move to reform the law during 1999 and new reports were received of fatal shootings by law enforcement officials in circumstances prohibited by international standards.
▢ In July Oleg Petrov Georgiev was shot dead by border police who fired shots into the lorry in which he was travelling near the border with Serbia. His father, Petar Lapatadov Georgiev, who was driving the lorry, was shot in the knee.

The actions of law enforcement officials who shot criminal suspects who were trying to escape were considered lawful if the officials were able to claim that they fired warning shots first, and that they had not intended to kill. In April the authorities replied to AI about fatal shootings by law enforcement officials in previous years and revealed a worrying lack of understanding of the international standards governing the use of firearms by law enforcement officials.
▢ Two Romani soldiers who had left their unit without permission, Kancho Angelov and Kiril Petkov, were shot dead by military police in their home village of Lesura in July 1996. The Ministry of Justice cited their previous convictions for petty crimes in order to claim that the two soldiers were "presenting serious danger" and stated that the use of firearms against them therefore complied with international standards, although the victims were unarmed and running away. The military police major who led the operation was reported to have shot about 20 bullets in automatic fire from a range of seven or eight metres. His actions were considered lawful by the authorities since "lethal use was not intentional". The investigation did not take account of the testimony of Romani witnesses to the shooting, who reported that the military police major had shouted racist abuse and threatened to kill them all shortly before he opened fire.

Ill-treatment and torture by police
There were reports of ill-treatment and torture by police, and of a death in police custody. There were also reports that people who complained about torture and ill-treatment by law enforcement officials were subjected to intimidation or further ill-treatment. Roma were reported to be particularly vulnerable to such abuses.
Death in police custody
▢ In September private security guards detained Kostadin Sherbetov at a Sofia school and took him to a police station, where he died the same day. Forensic examination recorded that he sustained several broken ribs, bruising all over his body, and that there were footprints on his clothes.
▢ Two police officers were tried and received prison sentences for beating Mincho Sartmachev to death in Dobrich police station in 1997, yet the authorities provided no information of any investigation into the alleged torture of his companion Stanimir Georgiev.
Police ill-treatment and intimidation
In July and August a special police detachment located at the training base of the Ministry of the Interior's Bureau for Operative Investigations, by the Iskar reservoir, reportedly ill-treated and threatened to shoot people.
▢ A detachment of about 15 armed special police beat with truncheons and threatened to shoot 46-year-old businessman Svetlyu Shishkov, his 20-year-old son Slaveiko Shishkov, and Slaveiko Shishkov's friends, Georgi Randev, Ivan Ivanov and Madlena Marinova, on

a beach by the reservoir. The police officers then shot at the Shishkovs' jet-ski, hitting it with 19 bullets and destroying it. The police action followed warnings the Shishkovs were given earlier in the day against observing from their jet-ski a private resort on the opposite shore where the Minister of the Interior was staying. The authorities failed to investigate the reported ill-treatment vigorously, but made public the addresses of the alleged victims, and past criminal offences committed by some of them and their relatives and friends. After filing a complaint, Svetlyu Shishkov was reportedly approached by a man claiming to represent his assailants, who allegedly threatened further violence against Svetlyu Shishkov and his sons if he did not drop his complaint and stop talking to the media. Slaveiko Shishkov and his friends were reportedly followed by a group of people in several cars.

Roma

There were numerous reports of law enforcement officials ill-treating Roma in a manner which suggested that many of them viewed such violent treatment of Roma as routine and necessary.

▢ In January a police officer at Pleven cooperative market reportedly verbally abused Stefka Ilieva Madjarova as she arrived to sell her goods at her stall, then kicked and dragged her into the police room at the market. Inside, he reportedly beat her with a truncheon.

▢ In October, four police officers reportedly beat Liliyan Yordanov Zanev and four other Romani men with truncheons. The Romani men had been waiting in a car on the outskirts of Pleven. The police officers accused them of intending to burgle nearby villas. After reportedly beating the Romani men for 30 minutes, the police officers departed in their cars.

There were reports of Roma being tortured in police custody to make them sign confessions.

▢ In November Dinio Stoyanov was arrested and detained in Stara Zagora Regional Police Department on suspicion of theft. Police officers reportedly forced him to kneel and crawl, trampled on his hands, handcuffed him to metal bars for several hours, beat him into unconsciousness with a wooden bat, beat him with a metal pipe and threatened to kill him with a knife, and later with a gun.

In some cases, police officers reportedly used violence against individual Roma in order to intimidate their communities.

▢ In February a police officer reportedly allowed his dog to savage Fanka Khristova on a hill outside Karnobat where she and two other Romani women had been collecting wood. When Fanka Khristova's companions pleaded with the officer to call off his dog, he refused and reportedly said that if at least one of the local Roma did not suffer, they would never stop taking wood from the hill.

There were reports of civilian guards hired by local mayors and field guards detaining and ill-treating Roma, and of police officers joining in.

▢ Three reports of ill-treatment of Roma in Beglej village in Lovesh region, perpetrated by the mayor's

guards and a named police officer, had been referred to the authorities by AI by the end of 1999. For example, in March, three mayor's guards forced their way into the house of 51-year-old Ivan Georgiev Ivanov and reportedly beat him and his wife, Antoineta Ivanova. They handcuffed Ivan Georgiev Ivanov and marched him towards the village centre, while continuing to beat him with their fists and a hose. The local police officer reportedly joined in the ill-treatment, kicking and thumping Ivan Georgiev Ivanov on his head, face and body. The police officer then freed Ivan Georgiev Ivanov and let him go home. The authorities maintained that, "[t]here is no evidence whatsoever... to conclude that physical maltreatment or any other unlawful acts against Roma citizens have occurred in the village."

The authorities' failure to protect Roma who complained about ill-treatment reportedly caused the victims of a police raid on Mechka village in July 1998, in which at least 15 people were reportedly injured, not to pursue their complaint to the appeal stage. There was a report that the father of a Romani teenager, who was reportedly beaten by police in Varna in May 1998, was ill-treated and interrogated by police about the action taken by AI on the case. Some victims of alleged ill-treatment were charged with offences by the police. Tanya Borissova, who was allegedly beaten by three police officers controlling a crowd of Roma in front of a Pazardjik labour office, was convicted of minor hooliganism on the evidence of two of the officers and a labour office employee.

Intergovernmental organizations

The UN Committee against Torture met in April and May to consider Bulgaria's second periodic report. The Committee found that Bulgarian law lacked a definition of torture and failed to ensure that all acts of torture are offences under criminal law. The Committee expressed concern about continuing reports of ill-treatment by public officials, particularly the police, especially of members of ethnic minorities. The Committee also expressed concern about deficiencies in the system of investigation of alleged cases of torture and the failure to bring those allegations before a judge or other appropriate judicial authority.

Conscientious objection

Krassimir Nikolov Savov, a conscientious objector to military service, was released from Plovdiv prison in the early part of the year on being granted a pardon by President Stoyanov. He had served half of a one-year sentence for failing to respond to military call-up. The Law on Alternative Service, which allows conscientious objectors to perform a civilian alternative to military service, albeit of double the duration, came into force on 1 January.

AI country report

• Bulgaria: Krassimir Nikolov Savov – prisoner of conscience (AI Index: EUR 15/001/99)

BURKINA FASO

BURKINA FASO
Head of state: Blaise Compaoré
Head of government: Kadré Désiré Ouédraogo
Capital: Ouagadougou
Population: 10.9 million
Official language: French
Death penalty: abolitionist in practice
1999 treaty ratifications/signatures: International
Covenant on Civil and Political Rights and its (first)
Optional Protocol; International Covenant on Economic,
Social and Cultural Rights; UN Convention against
Torture and Other Cruel, Inhuman or Degrading
Treatment or Punishment

Public outrage generated by the death of prominent
independent journalist Norbert Zongo and three
others in December 1998 resulted in social unrest
and calls for an end to impunity for human rights
violations. Widespread demonstrations led to arrests
and ill-treatment by the security forces. Leading
opposition political figures and human rights
defenders were intimidated and detained. Although
the government attempted to defuse the political
and social crisis, there was no effective action to end
impunity.

Background
Opposition political parties, human rights
organizations, trade unions, and journalists' and
students' organizations formed a coalition — the
*Collectif d'organisations démocratiques de masse et de
partis politiques* — which called for those responsible
for the death of Norbert Zongo to be brought to justice
and for an end to impunity. Demonstrations, some
violent, and strikes took place throughout the country
in the weeks following Norbert Zongo's death. There
was also unrest after a commission of inquiry into the
death published its findings in May. Women, young
people and intellectuals were among the many sectors
of Burkinabè society who joined the call for an end to
impunity. Scores of people were arrested and detained
briefly.

In June, faced with a deepening political and social
crisis, the government established a committee of
prominent people, the *Collège des sages,* to examine
the causes of the crisis and propose solutions. The
committee, which included former heads of state and
traditional and religious leaders, recommended the
formation of a government of national unity and early
legislative elections. The committee also called for
constitutional change, reform of the judiciary, and a
commission to investigate unresolved crimes.

Three members of smaller opposition parties were
brought into government in October. However, more
significant opposition parties, grouped together in the
Groupe du 14 février, 14 February Group, refused to
participate unless President Blaise Compaoré resigned

or suspects identified by the inquiry into Norbert
Zongo's death were arrested. In October the
government also announced the formation of two
consultative commissions, bringing together
government, opposition and civil society, to elaborate
political reforms and promote national reconciliation.
The 14 February Group, however, refused to participate,
claiming that the legislation establishing the
commissions did not guarantee genuine debate and
democratic decision-making.

Extrajudicial executions
Norbert Zongo, editor-in-chief of the newspaper
l'Indépendant, and President of the *Société des
éditeurs de la presse privée,* Association of
Independent Newspaper Editors, was killed with three
other people in December 1998. Norbert Zongo was
renowned for his independence and criticism of the
government. In particular, he had persistently pursued
the death in custody in January 1998 of R. David
Ouédraogo, the chauffeur of President Compaoré's
brother and presidential adviser, François Compaoré
(see below).

Independent Commission of Inquiry
The composition of the Independent Commission of
Inquiry, established in January, was modified after the
Collectif requested stronger representation for human
rights organizations. The *Mouvement burkinabè des
droits de l'homme et des peuples* (MBDHP), Burkinabè
Movement for Human and Peoples' Rights, a non-
governmental human rights organization, refused to
participate unless all those arrested in connection with
protests against Norbert Zongo's death were released,
no sanctions were taken against those who had
participated in strikes, and discussions began on
ending impunity for past human rights violations. Its
conditions met, the MBDHP agreed to participate, and
the judge appointed to head the Commission also
represented the MBDHP.

In late March the Commission ordered the *garde à
vue* detention of several members of the presidential
security force, the *Régiment de la sécurité
présidentielle.* The Public Prosecutor refused,
however, to extend the detention of a high-ranking
member and all were released shortly afterwards.

The Commission published its conclusions and
recommendations in early May. It concluded that
Norbert Zongo had been killed for purely political
reasons because of his work as an investigative
journalist, including his investigation into the death of
David Ouédraogo. The other three men who died with
him had been killed in order not to leave any witnesses.
The Commission named six members of the presidential
security force as suspects, although proof of their
culpability had not been established. It recommended
that judicial proceedings be brought against them and
that the judge assigned the case be provided with
adequate resources. Although a judge was
subsequently appointed, there had been no progress in
the case by the end of 1999. (However, three of the
suspects were subsequently arrested and charged in
connection with the death of David Ouédraogo.)

AI called for those responsible for Norbert Zongo's death to be brought to justice and for the judiciary to be allowed to act with complete independence.

The Commission's recommendations also included: compensation by the state for the dependants of those killed; respect for distinctions between military and police functions; limiting the role of the presidential security force to ensuring the security of the head of state; and resolution of all unexplained cases of "disappearances" and killings.

The Secretary General of *Reporters sans frontières*, a non-governmental human rights organization based in France, who had participated in the Commission, was arrested on 9 May and questioned for two hours before being taken to the airport by police. He had referred to the killers of Norbert Zongo as "thugs" in a radio interview. A delegation of *Reporters sans frontières* was refused permission to visit Burkina Faso in July.

Arrests of political opponents and ill-treatment

Intervention by police to disperse demonstrations in Ouagadougou in early January resulted in a three-day strike. Demonstrations also took place in other towns throughout the country, including Bobo Dioulasso and Koudougou, the home town of Norbert Zongo. Demonstrators clashed with police who used tear gas. As many as 100 people were reported to have been arrested but all were released after a few weeks. Some were reported to have been ill-treated while in custody by being beaten and having their heads shaved.

Members of the MBDHP were harassed and intimidated; some received death threats. Leading members of the *Collectif* were also arrested and detained during 1999.

▭ Halidou Ouédraogo, President of both the MBDHP and the *Collectif*, was arrested and detained for two hours on 17 May. A week earlier his home had been surrounded by a group of at least 100 people who threatened and insulted him, apparently at the instigation of the mayor of Ouagadougou, who was at that time Secretary General of the ruling party, the *Congrès pour la démocratie et le progrès*, Congress for Democracy and Progress. The police and gendarmerie reportedly took two hours to respond to requests for assistance. AI urged the government to take all possible measures to protect Halidou Ouédraogo and others defending human rights in Burkina Faso.

▭ A leading member of the opposition and member of parliament was also arrested on 17 May. Hermann Yaméogo was accused of being responsible for violent disturbances in his constituency of Koudougou but was released uncharged after three days. AI called for his immediate and unconditional release if, as it appeared, he had been arrested and detained solely because of his legitimate political activities and his demands for an end to impunity for human rights violations.

▭ Prominent members of the *Collectif*, including Halidou Ouédraogo, Tolé Sagnon, a leading trade unionist, Bénéwendé Sankara, a lawyer, and André Tibiri, a student leader, were arrested in early December after issuing a statement calling on the security forces to ensure the safety of demonstrators

during a protest against impunity. They were detained for three hours by the police State Security Department in Ouagadougou. They and two others were subsequently charged with undermining the morale of the armed forces and inciting disobedience within the army. They were, however, acquitted of all charges by a court on 27 December.

Two journalists, Boureïma Sigué of *Le Pays* newspaper and Paulin Yaméogo of *San Finna* newspaper, were also arrested for publishing the *Collectif*'s statement. Paulin Yaméogo's arrest was also apparently linked to the publication by *San Finna* of a photograph of Hamidou Ilboudo, who had been arrested with David Ouédraogo in 1997, which showed clear signs of torture. Boureïma Sigué was released the same day. Paulin Yaméogo was held for three days and later acquitted of inciting disobedience within the army.

Deaths in custody

At the centre of the case of Norbert Zongo was the death in custody as a result of torture of David Ouédraogo in 1998. A further death as a result of torture occurred in January 1999.

David Ouédraogo had been arrested in December 1997 with two others, accused of having stolen a large amount of money from their employer. He died the following month, apparently as a result of torture, in the custody of the presidential security force. No autopsy was carried out. Official investigations were obstructed during 1998 by the refusal of François Compaoré to cooperate with the judicial authorities.

François Compaoré was charged on 18 January 1999 with the murder of David Ouédraogo and with harbouring the body. He was not, however, arrested and the charges against him were not made public until 30 March. The following day, the Criminal Appeal Court in Ouagadougou ruled that it was not competent to hear the case and referred it to a military court. The judge of the military court was apparently obstructed in pursuing the case, which failed to advance.

Three members of the presidential security force suspected of being responsible for the death of David Ouédraogo were arrested in June at the request of the *Collège des sages* and charged. They remained in detention at a prison in Ouagadougou, the *Maison d'arrêt et de correction de Ouagadougou* (MACO) but had not been tried before the military court by the end of the year. All three were also among the suspects identified by the commission of inquiry into the death of Norbert Zongo.

▭ Auguste Pépin Ouédraogo, a trade unionist and employee at SONABEL, the national electricity company, was arrested on 11 January following an altercation with a gendarmerie commander in plain clothes in Bobo Dioulasso. He was severely beaten and died in hospital as a result of his injuries some 10 days later. Strikes demanding that those responsible be arrested followed. Six gendarmes, including the gendarmerie commander, were arrested on 24 June and imprisoned at the MACO. Five were convicted in December by a court in Ouagadougou of assault occasioning death and complicity in assault occasioning death and sentenced to prison terms of between two and five years.

Impunity
The government failed to respond effectively to the overwhelming public demand for an end to impunity for human rights violations. Although three suspects in the case of David Ouédraogo were arrested and charged, they had not been tried by the end of the year. There were no legal proceedings against those identified by the Commission of Inquiry into the death of Norbert Zongo.

No steps were taken to clarify past deaths in custody or in suspicious circumstances, such as those of university teacher Guillaume Sessouma in 1989, student Boukary Dabo in 1990 and opposition leader Clément Ouédraogo in 1991.

AI country reports
- Burkina Faso: Those responsible for the death of Norbert Zongo must be brought to justice (AI Index: AFR 60/002/99)
- Burkina Faso: a year after Norbert Zongo's death – still no justice (AI Index: AFR 60/004/99)

BURUNDI

REPUBLIC OF BURUNDI
Head of state and government: Pierre Buyoya
Capital: Bujumbura
Population: 6 million
Official languages: Kirundi, French
Death penalty: retentionist
1999 treaty ratifications/signatures: Rome Statute of the International Criminal Court

1999 saw a serious deterioration in the human rights situation. Grave human rights abuses were committed as the ongoing armed conflict escalated. These included the forcible displacement of hundreds of thousands of people and hundreds of unlawful killings of unarmed civilians by the armed forces or armed opposition groups. There was a dramatic increase in reports of "disappearances", and scores of people were arbitrarily detained. Thousands of people continued to be detained without charge or trial, many in very harsh conditions.

Background
The human rights situation continued to be dominated by abuses committed in the context of the armed conflict. Armed opposition groups continued to be involved in fighting in the provinces bordering Tanzania and escalated attacks around Bujumbura. On several occasions armed civilian patrols threatened violence in the face of the perceived weakness of the armed forces and a number of political parties made veiled calls for violence. Human rights defenders, humanitarian workers and journalists were threatened in the course of their work by members of the armed forces and of armed opposition groups. By September, Burundi was once again on the verge of a humanitarian and human rights crisis.

Peace process
Negotiations to find a settlement to the conflict continued in Arusha, Tanzania. There was little tangible progress on contentious issues. The talks were hampered by personal rivalry and internal divisions within most political parties and armed opposition groups. Armed opposition groups which did not attend the talks and political parties opposed to the negotiations exacerbated tensions and violence around the talks. The facilitator, former Tanzanian President Julius Nyerere, died in October. He was replaced in December by former South African President Nelson Mandela, who announced his intention to ensure that all armed opposition groups were involved in the talks.

Killings of civilians
Hundreds of unarmed civilians were killed by members of the armed forces and armed opposition groups, mainly in areas affected by conflict. As in the past, most killings by government soldiers of Hutu civilians appeared to take place in reprisal for insurgent activity or killings of Tutsi civilians by Hutu-dominated armed opposition groups. Unarmed civilians were killed on the pretext that they were believed to be armed combatants and scores of other civilians were killed by government soldiers who accused them of failing to provide information on armed opposition groups, or of having in some way protected or colluded with them. Virtually none of these killings was investigated. There were several reports of armed Tutsi civilians participating in military operations, some of which entailed serious human rights violations.

Armed opposition groups were also responsible for killing scores of unarmed civilians. In many cases these killings appeared to be reprisal or punishment killings of alleged collaborators or potential government informants. Both Hutu and Tutsi civilians were targeted. Armed opposition groups frequently attacked camps for the displaced and "regroupment" camps, deliberately and arbitrarily killing unarmed civilians.
More than 100 civilians were reported to have been killed by government soldiers accompanied by civilians, in the Busoro and Nkenga areas of Kanyosha commune in August. The killings followed an attack by an armed opposition group on a market in the vicinity. The area was closed off by the armed forces for several days after the killings were reported and members of parliament who attempted to visit the area on 12 August were not permitted to do so. It appeared that following

the attack on the market, soldiers who had been present but who had retreated, returned with reinforcements and attacked, burned and pillaged houses in the area, killing the people they found. No investigation had taken place into the killings by the end of the year.

🗁 In January, a series of attacks were carried out by members of the armed opposition, believed to be the *Conseil national pour la défense de la démocratie— Forces pour la défense de la démocratie* (CNDD-FDD), National Council for the Defence of Democracy— Forces for the Defence of Democracy, in the communes of Kibago, Mabanda, Kayogoro and Makamba in the southern province of Makamba. During the attacks more than 200 homes were burned in the Mabanda and Kibago areas and at least 36 civilians were killed, including nine children and a 75-year-old man.

Forcible 'regroupment'

In September, following weeks of repeated attacks on Bujumbura, military officials, together with the local administration, forcibly moved more than 260,000 people living in the surrounding province into camps, ostensibly as a counter-insurgency measure designed to remove potential support or cover from armed opposition groups. Conditions in the camps were appalling, with little or no sanitation. Freedom of movement was severely restricted and, as in the past, it was clear that the armed forces considered anyone outside the camps without authorization to be a military target. Cholera was reported to have broken out in the camps in December and nearly 400 people were reported to have died as a result of dehydration or lack of medical care by the end of the year. The camps were largely inaccessible and in some cases government authorities hindered or blocked efforts by humanitarian organizations to provide emergency assistance. Human rights violations committed by members of the armed forces — including rape, extrajudicial executions and "disappearances" — were reported from the camps, which were under military supervision. Some camps were also attacked by members of armed opposition groups who carried out unlawful killings of civilians. Elsewhere in the country, including the provinces of Rutana and Muramvya, thousands of other civilians were forcibly moved and thousands of people continued to flee the country. In October more than 7,000 refugees arrived in neighbouring Tanzania; many said they had fled to avoid being forcibly moved into camps.

Torture and 'disappearance'

As insurgency by Hutu-dominated armed opposition groups increased around the capital, hundreds of people were detained, many of them apparently arbitrarily. Scores of detainees were held in unauthorized detention centres or military barracks to which human rights groups and relatives were denied access. In some cases, authorities at the centres or barracks denied any knowledge of detainees, leading to fears that they may have "disappeared". Scores of detainees were secretly moved to different detention centres, further hindering access by human rights groups and relatives and making the detainees even more vulnerable to human rights violations. There were reports that the bodies found at an alleged secret burial ground in Kamenge were those of 15 people who had "disappeared" after their arrest by soldiers. No investigation was known to have taken place into these allegations.

Cases of torture continued to be reported throughout the year. People accused of collaboration with armed opposition groups were particularly at risk. Frequently reported torture methods included severe and prolonged beatings with electric cables, sticks, or with heavy implements on the joints, the soles of the feet and the genitals, and tying in excruciating positions. Death threats and other forms of psychological abuse were also reported.

🗁 Déo Nzeyimana, who was arrested in late September, was severely beaten during his detention at the *Brigade spéciale de recherche*, Special Investigation Unit — a gendarmerie unit responsible to the Ministry of Defence. He was accused of having passed information to people outside the country on human rights violations associated with the policy of forcible relocation after a document, widely available in Bujumbura, was found in his possession. Déo Nzeyimana was provisionally released on 12 November.

Children in detention

Several children were reported to have been detained for long periods without charge or trial and tortured. More than 150 children were held in prisons around the country, some accused of collaborating with armed opposition groups. Some had been held for months, even years, without trial. They were imprisoned together with adults, which put them at an increased risk of abuse. Some were tortured. Young girls were stripped and made to remain naked for hours in front of members of the security forces. Children as young as 12 arbitrarily accused of collaborating with armed groups were unlawfully detained, despite the fact that the law states that children under the age of 13 should not be detained.

Trials

The trials of scores of political prisoners accused of involvement in the massacres of Tutsi civilians in 1993, which followed the assassination of former President Melchior Ndadaye, continued to fall short of international standards for fairness. Most killings of Hutu civilians during the 1993 massacres had not been investigated.

🗁 The trial of 25 people charged with threatening state security after a failed attack in Cibitoke province in late 1998 took place at Bujumbura Court of Appeal. At least two of the defendants, both minors, claimed they had been tortured in the early stages of detention. A verdict had not been reached by the end of the year.

🗁 The trial by the Supreme Court of those accused of the murder of former President Ndadaye and of the attempted coup in October 1993 ended in May. Twenty-eight people, mostly low-ranking soldiers, were convicted for their roles in the assassination. Five death sentences were imposed, three *in absentia*. Thirty-eight other defendants, including the former head of the armed forces and the former commander of the Muha barracks where President Ndadaye was killed, were acquitted. The State Public Prosecutor appealed against the verdict. The trial had been marked by an apparent unwillingness to elucidate facts and responsibilities. The majority of those accused of participating in the assassination and attempted coup were never detained; of 81 defendants only 13 were in detention in May. During the trial, key defendants were appointed by the government to senior positions within the army, government and business or gained diplomatic postings abroad. The role of senior members of the armed forces was not investigated. Key witnesses did not testify in court. Several members of the armed forces rumoured to be able to provide evidence against senior government or military figures died in disputed circumstances suggesting they may have been assassinated. At least three other soldiers, also accused of involvement in the coup attempt, were shot and killed in December 1995. Official sources stated that they were killed trying to escape from Mpimba Central Prison. However, the exact circumstances of their deaths were not clear and they may have been the victims of extrajudicial executions.

Detention without trial

Thousands of people were held without trial. Some had been held for more than five years and had still not been informed of the charges against them. In a limited number of cases, attempts were made by the government to investigate whether there was a basis for continued detention, and more than 200 detainees were provisionally released. The majority of those held without trial were accused of participating in politically motivated violence since 1993.

Several political opponents of the government — including senior members of the *Parti pour le redressement national*, Party for National Renewal, the party of former President Jean-Baptiste Bagaza — had been held without trial since March 1997. They were charged with involvement in a plot to assassinate President Pierre Buyoya. In mid-1999 a ruling was made that the case would be tried by the Supreme Court, owing to the privileges enjoyed by some of the defendants. At least four of the defendants were reportedly tortured to extract incriminating statements and one defendant died in detention in 1997 after being denied medical care.

Death penalty

At least 85 people were sentenced to death in 1999. More than 280 people were under sentence of death at the end of the year, of whom at least 70 were awaiting the outcome of petitions for presidential clemency. The majority of those sentenced to death had received unfair trials. Prisoners under sentence of death in Mpimba Central Prison in Bujumbura were held in particularly harsh conditions. One execution was known to have taken place.

Corporal Bonaventure Ndikumana was executed on 29 July in Mabanda military camp, southern Burundi, just one day after being sentenced to death by a military court in Bujumbura and despite the fact that he had lodged an appeal. He had been convicted of the murder of another soldier on 21 July.

Intergovernmental organizations

Following its September session, the African Commission on Human and Peoples' Rights announced its intention to send a mission to Burundi to investigate the human rights situation. Several intergovernmental organizations — including the Organization of African Unity, the European Union and the UN — called for an end to the policy of forcible "regroupment" camps. The UN Special Rapporteur on the human rights situation in Burundi produced a highly critical report after visiting the country in October.

Following the killing in October of two expatriate UN personnel, the activities of the UN and international non-governmental organizations were dramatically reduced, and many international humanitarian workers were evacuated from Burundi. The killings of the UN personnel were attributed by members of the government to an armed opposition group, which denied the allegation. The government was reported to have initiated an investigation into the killings.

AI country reports and visits
Reports
- Burundi: Memorandum to the Government and National Assembly of Burundi on the proposed reform of the Code of Criminal Procedure (AI Index: AFR 16/006/99)
- Burundi: Memorandum to the African Commission on Human and Peoples' Rights (AI Index: AFR 16/007/99)
- Burundi: No respite without justice (AI Index: AFR 16/012/99)
- Burundi: Appeal to protect civilians (AI Index: AFR 16/026/99)
Visit
AI delegates visited the country in February.

CAMBODIA

KINGDOM OF CAMBODIA
Head of state: King Norodom Sihanouk
Head of government: Hun Sen
Capital: Phnom Penh
Population: 10.4 million
Official language: Khmer
Death penalty: abolitionist for all crimes

Impunity remained at the heart of Cambodia's human rights problems in 1999. A UN Group of Experts produced a report in March recommending the formation of a special international tribunal to bring to justice those suspected of responsibility for gross human rights violations during the period of Khmer Rouge rule (17 April 1975 to 7 January 1979). The Cambodian authorities rejected the report and stated their intention to hold trials in Cambodia under domestic law; there were concerns about standards of fairness and judicial independence. Two Khmer Rouge suspects were arrested and remained in pre-trial detention at the end of the year. Prime Minister Hun Sen ordered the rearrest of hundreds of people released by the courts. Two human rights workers were brought to trial on politically motivated criminal charges. Torture in police custody was reported, and excessive use of force during arrests caused a large number of deaths in police custody.

Background
The coalition government — formed by the Cambodian People's Party (CPP) and the National United Front for an Independent, Neutral, Peaceful and Cooperative Cambodia (FUNCINPEC) in November 1998 — remained in power, headed by CPP Prime Minister Hun Sen. Stated government priorities included a crack-down on crime, suppression of illegal firearms, military and police reform, judicial reform and poverty alleviation. Amendments to Cambodia's 1993 Constitution allowed the formation in March of an unelected Senate, as agreed in the 1998 coalition negotiations. Cambodia became a full member of the Association of South-East Asian Nations (ASEAN) in April.

The final collapse of the last remnants of the Khmer Rouge political movement brought an end to civil war, although there were reports of "armed bandits" launching attacks in remote rural areas. The proposed trials for former Khmer Rouge (see below) were a major focus of national and international attention.

Impunity
In the vast majority of cases where agents of the state were implicated in involvement in human rights violations — including extrajudicial executions, torture and ill-treatment — no action was taken against them. Numerous cases which were brought to the attention of the authorities throughout the year by local human rights workers were not investigated.

The governmental Cambodian Human Rights Committee, established in June 1998, was mandated to investigate UN reports of political killings during and after the July 1997 coup. Details of some investigations were made public, but no one was held to account for the vast majority of these crimes. The government reported that three people were tried, convicted and sentenced to terms of imprisonment for involvement in two cases of extrajudicial executions reported by the UN in 1998. No details were available about the conduct of these trials. Trials usually fell far short of international standards for fairness, undermining public confidence in the judicial system.

☐ Nuon Paet, a former Khmer Rouge commander accused of ordering the murder of three Western hostages in 1994, was tried in June. He was convicted after a one-day hearing, on a raft of charges, some under laws which were no longer in force and breached international standards. The judgment referred to facts and evidence which were not presented in the court. Two other former Khmer Rouge commanders gave evidence against Nuon Paet; they were then also charged with involvement in the murders, but had not been arrested or brought to trial by the end of 1999.

Khmer Rouge cases
There was widespread public disquiet at the official welcome to Phnom Penh of two senior members of the 1975 to 1979 Khmer Rouge administration who defected to the government side in December 1998 — Khieu Samphan and Nuon Chea. On 1 January, Prime Minister Hun Sen issued a statement saying that the government would wait for the views of the UN Group of Experts before deciding on whether the two men should be tried. Both men remained at liberty throughout 1999.

In March, Chhit Chhoeun (commonly known as Ta Mok), the last senior member of the Khmer Rouge still in opposition to the government, was arrested and detained at the Military Prosecution Detention Facility. The authorities announced that he would be tried by a Cambodian court. The UN Group of Experts report, made public in March, advised against such a trial and advocated the establishment of an *ad hoc* international tribunal, in order to ensure a fair hearing. The government rejected the report, arguing that Cambodian courts should hear any trials of Khmer Rouge leaders. In April Prime Minister Hun Sen wrote to the UN Secretary-General reiterating that any trial would take place in Cambodia in an existing court, but adding that the participation of foreign judges and prosecutors would be invited, to uphold standards for fairness, and that a law to allow for this would be drafted and presented to the National Assembly. In May former Khmer Rouge prison chief Kang Kek Ieu (also known as Duch) was arrested in Battambang province after giving interviews to Western journalists about his past. Detained in the same prison as Ta Mok, the two were assigned lawyers but were denied access to independent human rights workers and medical personnel.

Negotiations continued throughout 1999 between the government, the UN and other parties over the trials of these two men, and others suspected of involvement in grave human rights violations under the Khmer Rouge government. Senior delegates from the UN Office of Legal Affairs visited Cambodia in August for talks over the possible establishment of a mixed Cambodian and international tribunal. Significant differences remained between the two sides at the end of the talks, with the Cambodians undertaking to present a proposal to the UN for comment. In October the USA proposed a compromise plan whereby trials would take place in Cambodia under Cambodian law with a majority of Cambodian judges and a minority of international judges. In November, the government stated that a UN tribunal was unnecessary as the government was committed to bringing the Khmer Rouge to justice domestically.

A Working Group was established in August with responsibility for cooperating with international experts to organize the procedures under which Khmer Rouge cases should be tried. A draft law was made public in December.

Throughout the year Cambodian lawyers, human rights groups and opposition politicians all called for the establishment of an international tribunal, expressing concern about standards of fairness and judicial independence in Cambodia.

The Military Court
Following the arrests of Ta Mok and Duch and the assignment of their cases to the Military Court, a precedent was set whereby politically sensitive cases were automatically referred to the Military Court, regardless of its competence. The Military Court has legal jurisdiction only over military offences involving military personnel charged with breaches of military discipline or harm to military property. Judges in the Military Court retain military ranks and are accountable to the Ministry of Defence; the court is not independent of the executive branch of government.
⊟ Mong Davuth and Kong Bun Hean — members of the Sam Rainsy Party — were arrested in September and remained in detention at the end of the year in the Military Prosecution Detention Facility, under investigation by the Military Prosecutor on suspicion of plotting to kill Prime Minister Hun Sen in September 1998. Neither were serving members of the Royal Cambodian Armed Forces and the fact that the case was assigned to a court which was not competent to hear it underlined already serious concerns about the rule of law and political interference in the judicial system. Access to the Military Prosecution Detention Facility for human rights monitors, medical personnel and family members was severely restricted.

Legal developments
In August the National Assembly and the Senate adopted an amendment to the 1994 Law on Civil Servants. Article 51 of this law had effectively provided institutional impunity for agents of the state accused of committing crimes, as it required prosecutors to request permission from the relevant ministry — or in some cases the Council of Ministers — before bringing charges against a civil servant. In practice this rendered prosecutions of civil servants almost impossible. The new amendment requires the prosecutor to inform the relevant government department within 72 hours of deciding to bring charges against a civil servant, and to inform the senior official of a department immediately in the case of arrest or detention. Although the amendment was a step forward, ambiguities in the wording could still cause problems in upholding the law.

In August the National Assembly and the Senate adopted a law extending the maximum length of pre-trial detention from six months to three years, in cases of genocide, war crimes and crimes against humanity. This law raised serious concerns including that genocide, war crimes and crimes against humanity are not yet recognized criminal offences under Cambodian law. Such a long period of pre-trial detention also violates international standards for fair trial.

In December the Prime Minister issued an order for the rearrest of anyone released by the courts who had been charged with armed robbery, kidnapping or drug trafficking and the Minister of Justice suspended two senior court officials, effectively imposing executive authority over the judiciary. More than 50 people were rearrested in Phnom Penh within days of the order, including juveniles.

Intergovernmental organizations
At the UN Commission on Human Rights in April, AI highlighted ongoing impunity in Cambodia and government inaction on previous recommendations made by the UN. Cambodia's initial report to the UN Human Rights Committee was discussed in July. The Committee made a series of strong recommendations to the government to tackle impunity, a weak and corrupt judiciary, torture and ill-treatment. The government agreed to a two-year extension of the mandate of the Office of the High Commissioner for Human Rights in Cambodia, until March 2002. The Special Representative of the UN Secretary-General on Human Rights in Cambodia resigned his post in November; his report to the UN General Assembly identified ongoing serious human rights problems.

Torture and ill-treatment
Torture and ill-treatment in police custody — particularly during the first 48 hours of detention, when access to detainees was routinely denied — continued in 1999. Conditions in police cells and in prisons remained poor, with prisoners frequently being denied adequate food and medical care.
⊟ Three prisoners were killed following a mass escape from Sihanoukville prison in June. Available evidence suggested that at least two were extrajudicially executed by prison officers after being recaptured.

A growing trend of mob justice, sometimes facilitated by local police, became apparent. There were reports that police captured criminal suspects and then allowed them to be killed by angry bystanders. As many as 19 such cases were identified during 1999.

Human rights defenders

Prisoners of conscience Kim Sen and Meas Minear, employees of the local human rights group the Cambodian League for the Promotion and Defence of Human Rights (LICADHO), who were arrested in December 1998 following riots in Sihanoukville, were released on bail in January. They were brought to trial in July, on politically motivated criminal charges, but the case collapsed owing to lack of evidence against them. They and their co-defendants were released and all charges dropped.

AI country reports and visits
Reports
- Kingdom of Cambodia: No solution to impunity – the case of Ta Mok (AI Index: ASA 23/005/99)
- Kingdom of Cambodia: Open letter to the Royal Government on the jurisdiction of the Military Court (AI Index: ASA 23/015/99)
Visits
AI delegates visited Cambodia in March and observed the trial of Kim Sen and Meas Minear in July. In December an AI delegation held talks with representatives of the government.

CAMEROON

REPUBLIC OF CAMEROON
Head of state: Paul Biya
Head of government: Peter Mafany Musonge
Capital: Yaoundé
Population: 14.7 million
Official languages: French, English
Death penalty: retentionist
1999 treaty ratifications/signatures: African Charter on the Rights and Welfare of the Child

Large numbers of people were extrajudicially executed in the north of the country. Torture and ill-treatment by the security forces remained routine, and prison conditions amounted to cruel, inhuman and degrading treatment, resulting in a high mortality rate. Critics of the government, including supporters of opposition political parties, journalists and human rights activists, were harassed, arrested and imprisoned. Thirty-six people were convicted after an unfair trial before a military tribunal. Perpetrators of human rights violations continued to act with impunity.

Extrajudicial executions in the north
Extrajudicial executions of criminal suspects in North, Far-North and Adamawa Provinces continued during operations to combat armed robbery by a joint unit of the army and gendarmerie (the paramilitary police), known as the *brigade anti-gang*.

Since March 1998, when the unit was deployed, some 700 people were reported to have been extrajudicially executed.

In late April or early May 1999, 15 people were reported to have been extrajudicially executed by the *brigade anti-gang* on the road to Kossa, north of Maroua, Far-North Province, and their bodies abandoned by the roadside. While killings were reported to have continued throughout 1999, the practice of abandoning unburied bodies decreased and it became more difficult to establish the numbers killed.

The fate of Alioum Aminou, a photographer who had distributed photographs of victims of extrajudicial executions, remained unknown. He had been arrested by the *brigade anti-gang* in October 1998 in Maroua.

Human rights defenders
Members of a non-governmental organization, the *Mouvement pour la défense des droits de l'homme et des libertés* (MDDHL), Movement for the Defence of Human Rights and Liberties, were repeatedly threatened because of their exposure of extrajudicial executions by the *brigade anti-gang*. AI urged that those defending human rights be allowed to carry out their activities in safety.

◻ In early May 1999 the *brigade anti-gang* ambushed and threatened MDDHL members who were investigating the killings on the road to Kossa. Later that month they went to the homes of Abdoulaye Math, President of the MDDHL, and a colleague, Semdi Soulaye. Both men were away at the time. Abdoulaye Math's home was reported to have been surrounded by some 18 armed members of the *brigade anti-gang* who pointed guns at a member of his family. Abdoulaye Math and Semdi Soulaye fled to Yaoundé. Abdoulaye Math's house was surrounded and his family intimidated on subsequent nights.

Another MDDHL member, Maurice Tchambou, was arrested in November in Maroua by the gendarmerie. He was subsequently transferred to the custody of the *brigade anti-gang* and denied all visits. He remained held without charge at the end of the year.

Other killings by the security forces
Killings which appeared to be extrajudicial executions took place in other parts of the country.
◻ On 28 December 1998 a student, Guy Hervé Nwafo Diessé, was shot dead by a police inspector in Bafoussam, West Province, after a fight between the two men in a shop. The police inspector was subsequently arrested and on 2 August 1999 was convicted and sentenced to life imprisonment.
◻ On 4 February 1999, three men from the semi-nomadic pastoral Mbororo community were reported to have been killed on the orders of the traditional ruler, known as the *Fon*, of Bali, North-West Province, after a dispute about stolen cattle. The three men — Issa Adamaou, Salihou Jibo and Idrissou Kari Buba — were beaten and burned to death. An official investigation into the killing took place and an arrest

warrant was issued against the *Fon*, a prominent member of the ruling Cameroon People's Democratic Movement. He was not arrested and no further action was taken against him although several others were subsequently arrested in connection with the killings.

Torture and ill-treatment

Torture and ill-treatment of detainees in police stations and gendarmerie headquarters remained widespread and systematic; incidents were reported throughout 1999. Torture included severe beatings to the head, legs, feet, arms and back, and the *balançoire*, where victims were suspended from a rod between their hands tied behind their legs. Many victims were refused medical treatment for injuries sustained as a result of torture. Several people were also reported to have been injured in incidents where the security forces used excessive force.

◻ On 17 February an official of the Social Democratic Front (SDF), the main opposition party, was arrested in Bamenda, North-West Province, following an authorized SDF meeting and held at gendarmerie headquarters for nine days before being transferred to the Central Prison in Bamenda. While held by the gendarmerie he was reported to have been stripped, handcuffed and repeatedly beaten on the soles of his feet with a plastic truncheon. He was released after three weeks.

◻ A prisoner at the Central Prison, New Bell, in Douala was reported to have died on 25 March after being beaten with wooden truncheons by prison guards following an escape attempt. He had injuries to his head, shoulders and legs and had suffered a brain haemorrhage.

◻ On 17 March police officers forced their way into a children's home in Douala, apparently searching for a criminal suspect. They forced children to kneel and beat and kicked them. Two received bullet wounds and were refused medical assistance. Several children, including those with bullet wounds, were taken to a police station where they were beaten on their bodies and on the soles of their feet. The police eventually admitted that they had acted on incorrect information.

Legislation passed in January 1997 prohibiting torture was persistently violated by police and gendarmerie officers. Most enjoyed impunity, but in a few cases perpetrators were prosecuted. Two police officers, sentenced to 10 years and six years' imprisonment for the death in November 1997 of a young man in police custody in Yaoundé, had their sentences reduced on appeal to eight years and one year respectively in February 1999.

Conditions in prisons remained extremely harsh and amounted to cruel, inhuman and degrading treatment. In most prisons, prisoners under sentence of death were kept with their feet chained. Severe overcrowding, poor hygiene and ventilation, inadequate food and lack of medical care resulted in a high mortality rate. The Central Prison, Nkondengui, in Yaoundé, and New Bell prison in Douala, each designed to hold 800 prisoners, held some 2,700 and 2,500 prisoners respectively in mid-1999. At least 30 prisoners were reported to have died at New Bell prison during the first half of 1999.

Prisoners of conscience

Freedom of expression and association continued to be curtailed.

Journalists

Journalists were convicted of criminal offences such as criminal defamation, abuse, contempt or dissemination of false news.

◻ Séverin Tchounkeu, director of an independent newspaper, *La Nouvelle Expression*, journalist Henriette Ekwé and John Fru Ndi, leader of the SDF, had been charged with criminal defamation in 1998 following publication of allegations that a former SDF official had embezzled party funds. Both John Fru Ndi and Séverin Tchounkeu were convicted in February 1999 and received a suspended sentence of a fine; Henriette Ekwé was acquitted.

◻ Anselm Mballa, director of *Le Serment,* was convicted of defamation on 16 July 1999 and sentenced to six months' imprisonment following an article published in April which was considered to have criticized a government minister. He was serving his sentence in Nkondengui prison at the end of 1999.

◻ In May 1999 police went to the home of Aimé Mathurin Moussy, director of a weekly newspaper, *La Plume du Jour,* which had been suspended by the authorities in September 1997, and interrogated several members of his family. This followed an interview which was critical of the Cameroon government given by Aimé Mathurin Moussy, at that time in France, in May 1999 to a French radio station.

Political opponents

Members of opposition political parties, including the SDF, continued to be harassed, arrested and detained, usually for short periods. One prominent member of an opposition political party remained held throughout 1999.

◻ Nana Koulagna, a former National Assembly member of the *Union nationale pour la démocratie et le progrès* (UNDP), National Union for Democracy and Progress, continued to be held at Garoua Central Prison, North Province. He had conducted an election campaign on behalf of the UNDP in May 1997. He and other UNDP members were attacked by the private militia of the traditional ruler, known as the *lamido,* of Rey Bouba in North Province. Two UNDP members and three members of the militia died in the confrontation. While no member of the militia was arrested, Nana Koulagna and several other UNDP supporters were arrested and although the judicial authorities ordered Nana Koulagna's release, he remained in administrative detention. In October 1998 he and six other UNDP supporters were charged by a military tribunal with murder, arson, looting, illegal possession of arms and other offences. They were not, however, brought to trial. AI called for Nana Koulagna's immediate and unconditional release.

◻ Five men from Cameroon's English-speaking minority continued to be held without charge or trial in Nkondengui prison. Abel Acha Apong, Chrispus

Kenebie, John Kudi and Jack Njenta were arrested in September 1995 and Arrey Etchu Wilson in February 1997. In September 1995 they had collected signatures for an unofficial referendum on independence organized by the Southern Cameroons National Council (SCNC), a group supporting independence for the English-speaking North-West and South-West Provinces. AI called for their immediate and unconditional release unless they were to be charged with a criminal offence and given a fair trial.

Unfair trial before a military tribunal

In early October 1999 a military tribunal passed lengthy prison terms after an unfair trial. Those convicted, all civilians, had been charged with offences including murder, attempted murder, grievous bodily harm, illegal possession of firearms, arson and robbery, in connection with armed attacks in North-West Province in March 1997 during which 10 people, including three gendarmes, were killed. The authorities blamed the attacks on the SCNC and the affiliated Southern Cameroons Youth League (SCYL).

Fifty-three prisoners held in connection with these events at Nkondengui and Mfou prisons, most of them for more than two years, and another 15 who had been released on bail during 1998, were finally brought before a military tribunal in Yaoundé in April 1999 to be charged. A law passed in April 1998 extended the jurisdiction of military tribunals to offences involving firearms.

The trial began on 25 May 1999 and there were further hearings during the following months. Three defendants received life sentences and 33 others were sentenced to between one and 20 years' imprisonment; the others were acquitted. Those sentenced to two years or less were released. Eighteen prisoners remained imprisoned, serving sentences of eight years' to life imprisonment. Appeals against conviction and sentence had not been heard by the end of 1999.

The military tribunal was neither independent nor impartial. It operated under the authority of the Ministry of Defence and the prosecution was under the direction of the Minister of State in charge of Defence. The defendants had no access to defence lawyers during pre-trial detention, or to the indictment against them, and were therefore unable to prepare their defence adequately. Twelve lawyers represented all 68 defendants. Although prosecution witnesses referred to written evidence proving that SCNC and SCYL members had planned and coordinated the attacks, no such evidence was reportedly produced in court.

Members of the security forces who appeared as prosecution witnesses claimed that the defendants had confessed. Some of the defendants, however, said that they had been tortured and ill-treated during interrogation. At least 10 prisoners of this group had died since March 1997 as a result of torture and ill-treatment or inadequate medical care.

AI called for those convicted to be allowed a retrial before a civilian court in accordance with international standards of fair trial.

Intergovernmental organizations

In May 1999 the UN Special Rapporteur on torture visited Cameroon and travelled to Yaoundé, Douala, Bafoussam, Bamenda and Maroua. Findings and recommendations were expected to be published in early 2000.

In October the UN Human Rights Committee considered Cameroon's third periodic report under the International Covenant on Civil and Political Rights and expressed concern that rights guaranteed by the treaty were persistently violated. It criticized widespread extrajudicial executions, the imposition of death sentences, excessive use of lethal force, sometimes resulting in deaths, torture by police officials and the absence of an independent mechanism for investigation, and prison conditions characterized by severe overcrowding, inadequate food and medical care. The Committee expressed concern about indefinite administrative detention and the jurisdiction of military courts over civilians, and the prosecution of journalists for dissemination of false news. It also concluded that the National Commission on Human Rights and Freedoms lacked independence from the government.

In November, during the Commonwealth Heads of State and Government meeting in South Africa, AI called for Cameroon's human rights record to be scrutinized and for the recommendations of the UN Human Rights Committee to be reinforced by the Commonwealth. The organization specifically recommended that Cameroon be included in the mandate of the Commonwealth Ministerial Action Group on the Harare Declaration.

AI country reports and visits
Reports
- Cameroon's human rights record under scrutiny by the United Nations (AI Index: AFR 17/003/99)
- Cameroon fails to protect the fundamental human rights of its citizens (AI Index: AFR 17/006/99)
- Cameroon: Lengthy prison terms after unfair trial before military tribunal (AI Index: AFR 17/010/99)

Visit
An AI delegate visited Cameroon in July in order to observe the trial before the military tribunal in Yaoundé.

CHAD

REPUBLIC OF CHAD
Head of state: Idriss Déby
Head of government: Nagoum Yamassoum (replaced Nassour Guelengdouksia Ouaidou in December)
Capital: N'Djaména
Population: 7.2 million
Official languages: French, Arabic
Death penalty: retentionist
1999 treaty ratifications/signatures: Rome Statute of the International Criminal Court

Armed conflict continued during 1999, particularly in the north of the country. There were reports of torture, arbitrary arrest and extrajudicial executions, both in the north and elsewhere. Freedom of expression was once again threatened and human rights defenders came under attack. A number of prisoners of conscience were detained briefly; another prisoner of conscience who had been sentenced after an unfair trial in 1998 was released.

Background

The government of President Idriss Déby continued to be threatened by armed conflict. A number of armed opposition groups were active, but the most serious threat to the government appeared to come from the *Mouvement pour la Démocratie et la Justice au Tchad* (MDJT), Movement for Democracy and Justice, led by Youssouf Tougoumi, a former minister of defence and justice under President Déby. The MDJT carried out military operations throughout 1999 in the northern Borkou-Ennedi-Tibesti (BET) region, in which scores of soldiers were reported to be killed.

A number of other, sporadically operational, armed opposition groups split into factions, some of which allied themselves to the government. In July 1999, three members of the *Alliance nationale pour la Résistance* (ANR), National Alliance for Resistance, were reportedly arrested in Sudan and deported to Chad. They subsequently allied themselves to the government. Other factions of the ANR remained opposed to the government. Serious and widespread human rights abuses have been committed in Chad in recent years associated directly or indirectly with insurgency, and it was unclear what effect the changing alliances would have on the human rights situation or the political stability of the country.

Chad/Cameroon pipeline

In November, one person was killed in N'Djaména in a violent demonstration protesting at the announcement that the oil companies Elf Acquitaine and Shell, two of the major stakeholders in an oil development project in southern Chad, were to withdraw from the project. The project, which involves the construction of a pipeline through Cameroon, was opposed by human rights groups and environmental groups, on the grounds of the impact on local populations in terms of cultural, social and economic rights and because of environmental concerns, as well as concerns relating to the management of the project by the government.

Human rights defenders

Human rights defenders continued to be threatened because of their work, and several were arrested and briefly detained during 1999. In January and February, members of three regional offices of the *Ligue tchadienne des droits de l'homme* (LTDH), Chadian Human Rights League, received death threats or were detained for short periods of time, solely because of their human rights work, in particular the denunciation of human rights violations. Members of human rights groups who criticized the project to develop and transport oil from southern Chad were also reported to have been threatened.

Release of a prisoner of conscience

Ngarléjy Yorongar le Moïban was released on 5 February, after eight months in detention. In July 1998, Ngarléjy Yorongar was convicted of defaming President Déby and the President of the National Assembly and sentenced to three years' imprisonment. He had accused the President of the National Assembly of accepting money from a French oil company to finance his 1996 election campaign. The sentence was confirmed by the N'Djaména Court of Appeal in December 1998. Ngarléjy Yorongar's release was announced in a presidential decree which cited humanitarian reasons. AI had campaigned for the release of Ngarléjy Yorongar since his arrest, and in July 1998 sent an observer to his trial.

Torture

Cases of torture and ill-treatment, a longstanding concern, were reported throughout 1999, mainly in the early stages of detention. AI received information on detainees being beaten in detention and suffering broken bones as a result, of detainees being suspended by ropes by their feet as a form of torture, and of detainees being humiliated by interrogating officers. Many of the cases were reported to have been carried out by members of the gendarmerie.

Detention without trial

One person of a group of 12 people arrested in February 1998 remained in detention without charge. They had been detained after four French nationals were taken hostage by an armed opposition group in southern Chad. Ten of this group were reportedly released "for humanitarian reasons" during 1998, and one other died in detention in April 1998, possibly as a result of denial of medical care. All had reportedly been tortured. The motive for their arrests appeared to be solely that they came from the same area as the leader of the armed opposition group.

Three members of a new armed opposition group, the Action Committee for Freedom and Democracy (ACFD), were arrested in July 1999 in Logone oriental province, southern Chad. They were held without charge in N'Djaména. The group had been meeting local government officials. During the meeting, in circumstances which remained not entirely clear, there was an exchange of fire in which an ACFD bodyguard was killed and some members of the state delegation injured.

Intergovernmental organizations

In April, despite persistent serious human rights abuses in Chad, the UN Commission on Human Rights took the decision to stop consideration of the human rights situation of Chad under the confidential procedure established by UN Economic and Social Council resolutions 728F/1503. In May, the UN Committee on the Rights of the Child considered the initial report of Chad. Among other things, the Committee urged the government to strengthen its measures to combat the practice of female genital mutilation. The Committee also expressed concern at the lack of resources available to support the rehabilitation and social reintegration of demobilized child soldiers. In its April session, the African Commission on Human and Peoples' Rights considered the initial report of Chad.

CHILE

REPUBLIC OF CHILE
Head of state and government: Eduardo Frei Ruiz-Tagle
Capital: Santiago
Population: 14.6 million
Official language: Spanish
Death penalty: retentionist

There were reports of ill-treatment of detainees by prison guards and of excessive use of force by the police against demonstrators. Legal proceedings concerning past human rights violations continued in Chile and abroad. Human rights defenders were subjected to death threats. Three people were sentenced to death.

Background

Presidential elections were held in December, but none of the candidates obtained the number of votes required by the Political Constitution to become president. The two candidates with the highest number of votes — Ricardo Lagos of the Coalition for Democracy party and Joaquin Lavín of the Alliance for Chile — were due to contest a second round in January 2000.

In July a law decriminalizing homosexuality was passed. In September Congress approved the State Prosecutor's Organic Constitutional Law providing for the creation of a State Prosecutor's Office. The law is part of the Criminal Procedure Reforms, aimed at replacing the current inquisitorial system with an adversarial one, which were due to take effect gradually with a pilot plan to be implemented in the regions of Coquimbo and La Araucanía in December 2000.

Torture and ill-treatment

There were reports of ill-treatment of detainees by prison guards.

⌂ In February there were reports that political prisoners were ill-treated by prison guards during the transfer of 56 prisoners from the Colina I prison to Colina II prison. Inmates were reportedly thrown to the ground, beaten with fists and rifle butts, and doused with water and tear gas. There were reports that at least two were tortured with an electric prod and some others had their heads forced under water; all were handcuffed at the time. There was particular concern for the health of Marcelo Gaete Mancilla and Dante Ramirez Soto who suffered serious head injuries. Lawyers acting for the families of the prisoners filed a habeas corpus writ and a criminal complaint before the courts in Santiago. A request filed before the Appeal Court for the appointment of a special judge was rejected.

Demonstrations

There were reports of excessive use of force by police in the context of demonstrations.

⌂ In May Daniel Nicolas Menco Prieto, a student, died as a result of gunshot wounds. He had been shot by a police officer during a student demonstration in the city of Arica. Three other students were also injured in the same incident. Reports indicated that the officer who fired the shot was suspended from active duty. The case was transferred to the military justice system.

⌂ Demonstrators and police officers were injured and two people killed in disputed circumstances in separate incidents in September during demonstrations in Santiago to mark the 26th anniversary of the military coup led by General Augusto Pinochet. At least four demonstrators sustained bullet wounds and a baby died, allegedly as a result of inhaling tear gas from canisters thrown by police officers to disperse the demonstration.

Past human rights violations

The Chilean authorities continued their efforts to obtain the release of former General Augusto Pinochet. He had been arrested in London, United Kingdom (UK), in October 1998 following a request for his extradition by the Spanish government in connection with human rights violations committed under his government (1973 to 1990). (See pages 14 to 17 for further details.) In July a communication from the Chilean Foreign Minister to his Spanish counterpart proposed an agreement to send the Pinochet case to international arbitration through the International Court of Justice. At the end of June, the US administration declassified and made public over 5,000 documents related to human rights violations committed in Chile between 1973 and 1978. In Chile, judicial proceedings continued and an increasing number of lawsuits were filed against Augusto Pinochet in relation to human rights violations committed during his military government. A number of high-ranking officers were placed under arrest in connection with individual cases reopened by the courts relating to killings and "disappearances" during the same period.

Legal proceedings in the UK

International legislation was put to the test during the legal proceedings against Augusto Pinochet in the UK. In March, seven Law Lords ruled by a majority of six to one that Augusto Pinochet did not have immunity from prosecution for acts of torture committed when he was head of state and that he could be extradited, on the reduced charges of torture and conspiracy to torture alleged to have been committed after 8 December 1988. Extradition hearings started in September, and in October the magistrate hearing the case ordered the committal allowing for the extradition of Augusto Pinochet to proceed on 35 cases of torture or conspiracy to torture after 8 December 1988 and the continuing cases of torture resulting from 1,198 "disappearances" submitted by the Spanish judge Baltasar Garzón. Augusto Pinochet's lawyers filed an appeal against this decision which was scheduled to be heard in the High Court in March 2000. In November the UK Home Office asked for Augusto Pinochet to undergo independent medical tests following a request by the Chilean government that he be released on health grounds; these were scheduled to take place in January 2000.

Legal proceedings in Chile

Following his arrest in the UK, 40 lawsuits were filed in the Chilean courts against Augusto Pinochet in relation to cases of past human rights violations. Investigations into these lawsuits were initiated. However, in August the Fifth Court of Appeals rejected the judicial request to include Augusto Pinochet in the investigation into the case of 72 people killed during a military operation in 1973 in the north of the country known as the "Caravan of Death". In its ruling the Fifth Court of Appeals stated that, according to the Constitution, Augusto Pinochet's parliamentary immunity excluded him from such an investigation.

Amnesty Law

In July the Supreme Court reinterpreted the 1978 Amnesty Law, ruling that it could not be applied in cases of 19 people who "disappeared" during the "Caravan of Death" operation. The ruling established that, because the 19 bodies were never recovered, their deaths could not be legally certified. Under Chilean law kidnapping is an ongoing offence until such time as the person is found. The Supreme Court, therefore, ruled that none of the accused could benefit from the Amnesty Law. Five army officers were arrested and charged with "aggravated kidnapping".

Intergovernmental organizations

In March the UN Human Rights Committee included in its concluding observations that the constitutional arrangements made as part of the political agreements for the transition to civilian rule hindered full implementation of the International Covenant on Civil and Political Rights by Chile. The Committee stressed that internal political constraints cannot serve as a justification for a state's non-compliance with its international obligations under the Covenant. The Committee also underlined other areas of concern including: the 1978 Amnesty Law, reiterating that such a law was incompatible with the duties of a State party; continuing reports of torture; and the wide jurisdiction of the military courts.

In September, Chile withdrew its reservations under Article 30 of the UN Convention against Torture and Other Cruel, Inhuman or Degrading Treatment or Punishment, thus allowing international arbitration to be contemplated.

In November, the Inter-American Commission on Human Rights of the Organization of American States concluded that Chile had violated the rights to personal freedom and to life and integrity of Carmelo Soria, a UN official who had been kidnapped, tortured and killed in 1976. The Commission reiterated that Chile had violated its international obligations by applying the Amnesty Law in this case and recommended that, if the Chilean state could not fulfil its obligation to punish those found responsible, it should allow universal jurisdiction to be implemented.

Human rights defenders

Death threats against human rights defenders, particularly members of organizations established by relatives of victims of past human rights violations, became a regular pattern. Members of the *Agrupación de Familiares de Detenidos Desaparecidos*, Association of Relatives of the Disappeared, and of the *Corporación de Promoción y Defensa de los Derechos del Pueblo*, Committee for the Defence of the Rights of the People, were repeatedly subjected to anonymous threats. In some cases police protection was provided by the authorities, but there was no progress in investigations into complaints about these threats.

Death penalty

Three men were sentenced to death during 1999. Two of them, Hugo Gómez Padua and Rubén Millatureo Vargas, had their sentences commuted to life imprisonment in November and December respectively, and one was awaiting the outcome of his appeal at the end of the year.

AI country reports

- United Kingdom: The Pinochet case – universal jurisdiction and the absence of immunity for crimes against humanity (AI Index: EUR 45/001/99)
- Chile: Torture, an international crime – even one torture victim is one too many (AI Index: AMR 22/010/99)
- Chile: A human rights review based on the International Covenant on Civil and Political Rights (AI Index: AMR 22/013/99).

CHINA
INCLUDING HONG KONG AND MACAO

PEOPLE'S REPUBLIC OF CHINA
Head of state: Jiang Zemin
Head of government: Zhu Rongji
Capital: Beijing
Population: 1.2 billion
Official language: Standard Chinese or Mandarin
Death penalty: retentionist

1999 saw the most serious and wide-ranging crack-down on peaceful dissent in China for a decade. Thousands of people were arbitrarily detained for peacefully exercising their rights to freedom of expression, association or religion. Some were sentenced to long prison terms under draconian national security legislation and after unfair trials; others were assigned without trial to up to three years' detention in "re-education through labour" camps. Torture and ill-treatment of prisoners were widespread. Thousands of people were sentenced to death and many executed. In the autonomous regions of Tibet and Xinjiang those suspected of nationalist activities or sympathies continued to be the targets of particularly harsh repression.

Background
In the year which marked the 50th anniversary of the creation of the People's Republic of China, the serious deterioration in human rights called into question the authorities' sincerity in signing key human rights conventions in the previous two years. It also represented a serious setback for the policy of dialogue on human rights pursued by some governments. Indeed, as the international spotlight faded, the Chinese authorities began to crack down with increased intensity on dissidents and activists. At the UN Commission on Human Rights, China again blocked debate on a draft resolution by using a procedural motion "not to take action".

Crack-down on fundamental freedoms
The human rights situation in China deteriorated sharply during the year. Those targeted in the crack-down included political dissidents, anti-corruption campaigners, labour rights activists, human rights defenders and members of unofficial religious or spiritual groups. Thousands of people were arbitrarily detained by police in apparent attempts to intimidate or silence them. Some were sentenced to long prison terms after unfair trials or sent to forced labour camps. Many were reportedly tortured or ill-treated.
Repression of dissidents
Arrests of members of the China Democratic Party (CDP) continued and more than 20 leading members were sentenced to prison terms during the year. The CDP was founded in Zhejiang province by a group of dissidents. Arrests of its members began in July 1998,

within hours of the first application to register the CDP, and started a chain of protests by other dissidents, many of whom were themselves subsequently harassed, questioned or detained.

A broad range of people were also detained for promoting reforms. Chinese law requires that all independent groups be registered. In October 1998, the same month that China signed the International Covenant on Civil and Political Rights which guarantees the rights to freedom of expression and association, the government revised several laws on the registration of groups which had the effect of increasing the limitations on these rights.

▭ Writer Peng Ming, leader of a grouping of self-styled "moderate" reformers — the China Development Union and the China New Development Strategy Research Institute — was assigned to 18 months' "re-education through labour" in February for allegedly "buying sex" from prostitutes, which he and his family asserted were trumped-up charges. Prior to his arrest he had led weekly discussions in Beijing on reform issues and had been detained more than once and allegedly instructed to dissolve the Institute.

Repression of religious and spiritual groups
The nationwide "anti-superstition" campaign, initiated in 1998, continued. Members of Christian groups were arrested and sentenced to long prison terms. "Unauthorized" temples continued to be demolished and adherents of charismatic or unorthodox religious and millenarian groups were arrested and assigned without trial to terms of "re-education through labour". The death penalty and long prison sentences were imposed on alleged leaders of such groups.

Thousands of members of the *Falun Gong* spiritual movement were arbitrarily detained and put under pressure to renounce their beliefs. Some were reportedly tortured or ill-treated, resulting in at least one death. In July, the day after the Ministry of Civil Affairs announced that the *Falun Gong* movement would be banned for alleged "illegal activities", "promoting superstition" and "jeopardizing public security", at least 97 *Falun Gong* leaders and thousands of practitioners, many of them elderly women gathering for morning exercises, were detained in several cities. Many were released after being taken to stadiums for "education" sessions; some were beaten with electric batons.

Protests against the ban and arrests of practitioners continued over the following months. The crack-down intensified in October when changes to the law were introduced to outlaw cults. According to official sources, by 4 November at least 111 *Falun Gong* followers had been charged with crimes, but dozens more were charged subsequently. Hundreds of other practitioners were reported to have been sent without charge or trial to "re-education through labour" camps. In November, the first publicly reported trial of *Falun Gong* members took place in Hainan province. The four defendants, described as "key members" of the group, were accused of organizing "illegal" gatherings after the ban on the group and sentenced to prison terms ranging from two to 12 years.

Repression of labour activists

Millions of workers were unemployed as a result of the failure of companies in the state sector. There were many demonstrations by unemployed workers protesting at the failure of the state to provide social welfare and against government corruption. Independent trade unions were illegal and the official All China Federation of Trade Unions continued to be controlled by the ruling Communist Party. Activists who attempted to organize independent labour action continued to be detained, imprisoned or subjected to "re-education through labour". They, like other political prisoners, were sometimes singled out for particularly harsh treatment, including beatings and denial of medical care.

Denial of due process

In many cases the authorities continued to show a blatant disregard for the Criminal Procedure Law, revised in 1996 to provide for greater access to legal representation, notification of relatives and public trial. Political defendants were routinely denied their right to due process and their lawyers were often subjected to pressure by the authorities. Political trials continued to fall far short of international standards, with verdicts and sentences being decided by the authorities before the trial, and appeal hearings usually a mere formality.

☐ Lin Hai, a 30-year-old computer software businessman and the first person to be imprisoned for "subversive" use of the Internet, was sentenced in January to two years in prison for "inciting the overthrow of the state". Following his detention in March 1998, he was accused of a variety of offences and finally sentenced in connection with the alleged use of other people's Internet domains to covertly share e-mail addresses with "anti-China" magazines abroad. His trial was closed to the public and he was sentenced more than seven weeks after the trial. His lawyer was reportedly informed of the sentence by telephone. His wife, Xu Hong, who had been actively pursuing all legal avenues for her husband despite threats, intimidation and harassment by the authorities, was reportedly detained at Tianping police station for six hours on the day of the hearing on trumped-up charges of theft. She had not been able to see her husband between his detention in March 1998 and his trial hearing in January 1999. Lin Hai was released in September.

Tiananmen – 10 years on

Many of the thousands killed, injured or arrested by the security forces in the clamp-down on the 1989 pro-democracy movement and protests in Tiananmen Square had still not been accounted for. Most of those imprisoned had been convicted, after unfair trials, of "counter revolutionary" offences which by 1997 were no longer crimes under Chinese law. The authorities however refused to review their cases. Those who had been released had their freedom restricted and were closely monitored by the authorities. As in previous years, restrictions on fundamental freedoms intensified in June as the authorities sought to prevent commemoration of the June 1989 massacre; police

detained pro-democracy campaigners and tried to force them to sign statements promising that they would not attempt to commemorate the victims of the massacre. AI continued to call for an amnesty to be granted to all those still imprisoned in connection with the 1989 protests in view of the summary nature of the trials and the absence of adequate safeguards for defence. It also continued to call on the authorities to account for all those killed in the 1989 massacre.

Death penalty

The death penalty continued to be used extensively, arbitrarily, and frequently as a result of political interference. According to the limited records available to AI at the end of the year, at least 1,720 death sentences were passed and at least 1,077 executions were carried out in 1999, bringing the total number recorded in the 1990s to more than 27,120 death sentences and around 18,000 executions. These were believed to be only a fraction of the true figures as death penalty statistics remained a state secret in China. Execution was by shooting or lethal injection and sometimes occurred within hours of sentencing. Appeals were rarely successful. Mass executions were frequently carried out prior to major events or public holidays, such as the Chinese New Year, when death sentences were sometimes imposed for relatively minor crimes which would not attract such a sentence at other times of the year.

Torture and ill-treatment

Torture and ill-treatment of criminal suspects were common. Police used various methods to torture and intimidate people, including kicking, beating, electric shocks, hanging by the arms, shackling in painful positions, and sleep and food deprivation. Prisoners serving sentences in prisons or labour camps were frequently tortured or ill-treated by guards or by other inmates at the instigation of guards.

☐ Zhang Lin, a pro-democracy and labour rights activist held in Guangzhou No.1 "Re-education Through Labour" Centre in southern China since November 1998, was reported to be in poor health as a result of repeated beatings and torture. He was required to work 14 hours a day while in poor health and was reportedly beaten when he tried to protest. Reports suggested he was tortured at least six times, as a result of which he twice attempted suicide. He was beaten by other inmates acting on orders from the guards, stripped of his clothes and dragged on the ground for long distances, and had his head forced under water. In July he went on hunger strike for six days to protest against his treatment and conditions of detention.

Prison conditions

Prison conditions remained harsh. The routine denial of medical care was a serious problem. Prisoners were also denied family visits, which restricted opportunities for providing food and necessary medication to prisoners.

☐ Lu Yongxiang, a 48-year-old writer serving a five-year prison sentence for instigating "reactionary propaganda", continued to be denied adequate health care despite suffering from serious kidney problems. He was arrested in May 1995 in Guizhou Province after distributing leaflets, including an open letter to the authorities, on the sixth anniversary of the events in Tiananmen Square.

Xinjiang Uighur Autonomous Region (XUAR)

Gross violations of human rights continued in the XUAR amid growing ethnic unrest fuelled by unemployment, discrimination and curbs on fundamental freedoms. The targets of this pattern of arbitrary and summary executions, torture, arbitrary detention and unfair political trials were mainly Uighurs, the majority ethnic group among the predominantly Muslim local population.

Over the years attempts by Uighurs to air their views and grievances and peacefully exercise their most fundamental rights have met with repression. AI has called on the government to establish a special commission to investigate human rights violations and assess economic, social and cultural needs in the region; to suggest remedial measures; and to provide a forum for individuals and groups to voice their grievances.

Many Uighurs were arbitrarily detained for their suspected views, associations or peaceful activities. Others were accused of involvement in clandestine opposition activities, including armed opposition. Most were held without charge for several months, in violation of Chinese law, during which time their families received no news of them.

Political trials were a mere formality as the verdict was usually pre-determined. Few defendants had access to lawyers. Some were taken to "public sentencing rallies" — show trials attended by hundreds or thousands of people.

Torture of political prisoners to extract information or coerce them to sign confessions was frequent and systematic. Some particularly cruel methods of torture not used elsewhere in China were reported in the XUAR, for example, the insertion into the penis of horse hair or of a special wire with small spikes which fold flat when it is inserted but extend when it is pulled out.

Scores of Uighurs, many of them political prisoners, were sentenced to death and executed. The XUAR continued to have the highest ratio of death sentences relative to its population and was the only region where political prisoners were known to have been executed in recent years. Others, including women, were reported to have been extrajudicially executed.

⌧ Zulikar Memet was sentenced to death in July, together with his brother and eight other Uighurs, at least four of whom were executed the following month. He was originally accused of "helping separatists" to hide or escape, but was subsequently tortured and forced to confess to other, unknown, offences. At his trial he denied the accusations against him and stated that he had been tortured to extract a confession. He reportedly showed the court signs of torture, including missing fingernails, but the court ignored his complaint and sentenced him to death. At the end of the year

Zulikar Memet's fate remained unknown.

⌧ Rebiya Kadeer, a well-known Uighur businesswoman, was detained in August for "illegally offering state secrets across the border". She was apparently arrested in connection with her communications to her husband, Sidik Rouzi, a former political prisoner now resident in the USA, and her attempts to meet a visiting group from the US Congressional Research Service. At the end of the year she was believed to be held at Liu Daowan jail in Urumqi.

Tibet Autonomous Region

Gross human rights violations, particularly against Tibetan Buddhists and nationalists, continued. Hundreds of prisoners of conscience, most of them monks and nuns, remained imprisoned. Reports persisted of torture and ill-treatment, harsh prison conditions, and deaths in custody. The "patriotic education" campaign intensified with further closures of monasteries, and ill-treatment and expulsions of monks and nuns deemed "unpatriotic".

Many Tibetan prisoners suffered health problems as a result of inadequate food coupled with poor sanitation and long hours working in unacceptable conditions. Many detainees were tortured and ill-treated. Kidney and liver ailments were common as a result of kicking and beatings by prison guards. Other forms of torture reported included the use of electric shock batons, particularly on sensitive areas such as the mouth or genitals; being forced into painful positions; and the use of ankle, hand and thumb cuffs.

⌧ In July, 16-year-old Phuntsog Legmon, a Tibetan novice monk, was sentenced to three years' imprisonment and two years' deprivation of political rights. The accusation — "plotting or acting to split the country or undermine national unity" — related to an incident in March when he and another young monk, who was also arrested, had shouted slogans such as "Free Tibet" for several minutes in the Tibetan capital Lhasa on the anniversary of the 1959 uprising in Tibet.

Hong Kong Special Administration Region

Controversy over interpretation of the Basic Law — the Region's Constitution — exposed both the limits of the autonomy of the Hong Kong Special Administration Region (HKSAR) and loopholes in the checks, balances and separation of powers which underpin human rights guarantees in the Basic Law.

In January the Court of Final Appeal ruled against the HKSAR government over Basic Law provisions concerning the right of abode in Hong Kong of residents' children born in mainland China. The HKSAR government claimed this would result in an insupportable population increase and its Chief Executive requested that the National People's Congress Standing Committee intervene and interpret the Basic Law's provisions, effectively challenging the authority of the Court. The Committee gave an interpretation which had the effect of reversing the Court's judgment. However, the Basic Law only explicitly provides for the courts to request such interpretations. This expedient also bypassed procedural safeguards governing amendment to the Basic Law. The HKSAR government reassured critics that the move had been "exceptional", but refused to limit its future use.

In April Li Yuhui was executed in Guangdong Province in mainland China after an unfair trial for the alleged murder by poison of five women in Hong Kong. He had been charged under the Chinese criminal code which, under the "one country two systems" policy, should not apply in the HKSAR. Negotiations between the Chinese and HKSAR governments on the return of criminal suspects were continuing at the end of 1999. However, the HKSAR government would not guarantee to abide by either international standards excluding return for political crimes, or not to return suspects to jurisdictions where they could face the death penalty. The HKSAR government was also slow to intervene on behalf of Hong Kong citizens illegally detained elsewhere in China.

In June an estimated 60,000 people joined the annual vigil commemorating the June 1989 Beijing massacre.

In December the Court of Final Appeal upheld the conviction of two activists who desecrated regional and national flags during a peaceful protest. It ruled that relevant laws were consistent with limitations on freedom of expression permitted under the International Covenant on Civil and Political Rights (ICCPR).

Those denied entry to Hong Kong during the year included exiled Chinese dissidents Wang Dan and Wei Jingsheng. Some Hong Kong legislators continued to be barred from mainland China.

In November the UN Human Rights Committee, commenting on the first report submitted by China on the implementation of the ICCPR in Hong Kong, expressed concern that government requests for reinterpretation of the Basic Law could undermine the right to fair trial. It affirmed that deportation procedures should provide effective protection against the risk of imposition of the death penalty.

Macao Special Administrative Region

On 20 December, after four centuries of Portuguese rule, Macao returned to the full sovereignty of the People's Republic of China. The new Macao Special Administrative Region (MSAR) will be governed by a Basic Law which preserves a degree of autonomy for the territory under a "one country two systems" model. While Portugal had previously taken steps to extend several international human rights standards it had ratified to Macao, uncertainties and ambiguities remained about their application after the handover.

In November the UN Human Rights Committee, hearing Portugal's final report on the implementation of the ICCPR in Macao, affirmed that these obligations devolved with the territory to China. It expressed concern about several apparent shortcomings in human rights protection in the MSAR and the risk to prisoners who might be transferred for trial to other jurisdictions in China where they might face the death penalty. No arrangements were agreed between China and the MSAR on continued reporting to the Committee on the MSAR. Chief Executive Edmund Ho Hau-wah stated that he was not seeking to reintroduce the death penalty as part of a crack-down on crime, but there were no formal guarantees that the death penalty would not be reintroduced.

In October the National People's Congress Standing Committee decided which of Macao's existing laws contravened the Basic Law and would not be adopted by the MSAR. These included provisions governing the independence of the Ombudsman. One of the new laws enacted at the handover criminalized any "public insult or failure to respect" state symbols.

AI country reports
- People's Republic of China: Gross violations of human rights in the Xinjiang Uighur Autonomous Region (AI Index: ASA 17/018/99)
- People's Republic of China: Tiananmen – 10 years on – "forgotten prisoners" (AI Index: ASA 17/009/99)
- People's Republic of China: No improvement in human rights – the imprisonment of dissidents in 1998 (AI Index: ASA 17/014/99)
- People's Republic of China: Reports of torture and ill-treatment of followers of the *Falun Gong* (AI Index: ASA 17/054/99)
- Macau: Human rights challenges for transition (AI Index: ASA 27/003/99)

COLOMBIA

REPUBLIC OF COLOMBIA
Head of state and government: Andrés Pastrana Arango
Capital: Santafé de Bogotá
Population: 36.2 million
Official language: Spanish
Death penalty: abolitionist for all crimes
1999 treaty ratifications/signatures: Inter-American Convention to Prevent and Punish Torture

Against a background of a continuing escalation in the long-running armed conflict, serious human rights violations increased. The parties to the conflict intensified their military actions throughout the country leading to widespread violations of human rights and international humanitarian law. The principal victims of political violence continued to be civilians, particularly community leaders, living in areas disputed between government forces and allied paramilitaries, and armed opposition groups. Trade unionists, political and social activists, academics, human rights defenders, judicial officials,

church workers and journalists were among those targeted. More than 3,500 people were victims of politically motivated violence, scores "disappeared" and an estimated 250,000 people were forced to flee their homes. At least 1,000 people were kidnapped by armed opposition groups and paramilitary organizations and held for ransom or for political reasons. Mass kidnappings of civilians by armed opposition groups increased. Torture – often involving mutilation – remained widespread, particularly as a prelude to murder by paramilitary forces. Children suffered serious human rights violations, particularly in the context of the armed conflict. "Death squad"-style killings continued in urban areas. New evidence emerged of collusion between the armed forces and illegal paramilitary groups. Important progress was made in some judicial investigations, but impunity for human rights abuses remained the norm. The government vetoed a bill designed to bring national legislation closer into line with international standards.

Background

In a series of unprecedented demonstrations throughout the country, millions of people peacefully marched to call for an end to political violence and human rights violations. Despite progress made in the peace process, however, no cease-fire was agreed and the armed conflict continued to escalate and to extend to new areas of the country. Regions particularly affected included North Santander, Antioquia and Córdoba in the north, the south of Bolívar department in central Colombia and Valle del Cauca and Putumayo departments in the south. The conflict continued to be characterized by gross and massive violations of human rights and humanitarian law. According to the National Human Rights Ombudsman in 1999, 402 massacres of civilians occurred, a significant increase on the previous year. All parties to the conflict were responsible for serious human rights violations — including massacres — but the majority were carried out by illegal paramilitary groups which systematically targeted the civilian population. AI continued to urge all parties to the conflict to observe basic humanitarian standards.

Peace process

Progress was made in preparing peace talks with the two main armed opposition groups: the *Fuerzas Armadas Revolucionarias de Colombia* (FARC), Revolutionary Armed Forces of Colombia, and the *Ejército de Liberación Nacional* (ELN), National Liberation Army. A third group, the *Ejército Popular de Liberación* (EPL), Popular Liberation Army, also announced its interest in peace talks with the government.

The government extended the temporary demilitarization of five municipalities in Meta and Caquetá departments which remained under the *de facto* control of the FARC. Formal talks between the government and the FARC, originally scheduled to begin in January, finally began in October, although no

substantive talks had taken place by the end of the year.

Growing tensions between the armed forces and the government over the peace strategy came to a head in June with the resignation of the Defence Minister and 17 senior generals. All the generals subsequently withdrew their resignations. A series of contacts between government representatives and the ELN in the second half of the year gave rise to hopes that the long-stalled peace process would be reactivated. However, preconditions for the start of talks had not been agreed by the end of 1999.

Those working for peace continued to face serious dangers; "death lists" containing the names of prominent peace activists and human rights defenders were publicly circulated in September. Several were killed.

▢ Mass demonstrations followed the murder of political humorist Jaime Garzón Forero in August. Jaime Garzón was a member of a commission appointed by the government in an attempt to revive the stalled peace process with the ELN. Shortly before his death Jaime Garzón had told friends that he had been threatened by senior military and paramilitary commanders. Investigations failed to establish responsibility for the murder by the end of 1999.

Paramilitaries

Paramilitary action was characterized by a succession of atrocities against the civilian population during military offensives to expand territorial control. Attacks against non-combatant civilians were routinely justified by claiming victims were "guerrillas in civilian clothing". The attacks continued throughout the year as paramilitary forces opened new fronts of conflict in Valle del Cauca, Casanare and North Santander departments. Guerrilla forces retaliated by targeting civilians considered to be collaborating with the paramilitaries. Repeated paramilitary atrocities drew little or no reaction from the authorities. Despite repeated commitments to create special military task forces to combat paramilitary forces, no such unit was deployed and paramilitary forces continued to act with impunity throughout the country.

▢ More than 150 civilians were killed in January as units attached to the national paramilitary organization *Autodefensas Unidas de Colombia* (AUC), United Self-Defence Groups of Colombia, swept through villages in several regions, torturing and murdering suspected guerrilla collaborators, stealing livestock, burning entire villages and displacing the population.

▢ Nearly 200 civilians were killed between May and September when AUC forces launched an offensive in the Catatumbo region of North Santander department on the border with Venezuela. In an attempt to wrest control of the area from the ELN, FARC and EPL, the AUC carried out a series of massacres of civilians in the towns of La Gabarra, Tibú, the departmental capital Cúcuta, and surrounding communities.

Armed forces

The armed forces carried out disproportionate and indiscriminate attacks resulting in civilian loss of life.

The armed forces were also responsible for the selective killing of people considered to be guerrilla sympathizers or collaborators. According to the National Human Rights Ombudsman, the Colombian army was responsible for five massacres of civilians during the first nine months of 1999.

Further evidence emerged of the active or tacit support of the armed forces for illegal paramilitary groups.

▱ Following the paramilitary massacres of civilians in the region of Catatumbo, North Santander department, the regional army and two regional police commanders were relieved of their posts. Initial investigations established that the police commander of Tibú had given logistical support to the paramilitaries. In August General Alberto Bravo Silva was relieved of his command of the army's 5th Brigade by the Minister of Defence and then sacked three days later by President Andrés Pastrana Arango for having failed in his duty to protect civilians in North Santander from paramilitary attack.

Government orders to the armed forces to combat paramilitary groups generally went unheeded and no action was taken against national paramilitary leaders. However, in an exceptional case in June, the army announced that it had killed paramilitary leader Pedro González Velásquez, accused in judicial investigations of responsibility for a number of massacres.

Armed opposition

Armed opposition groups were responsible for serious violations of international humanitarian law, including indiscriminate attacks against military targets which caused civilian casualties; deliberate and arbitrary killings; and hostage-taking. At least 800 civilians were believed to have been kidnapped by armed opposition groups during 1999.

▱ In April the ELN hijacked an internal Colombian flight and kidnapped the passengers and crew. Although several passengers were released within days, and others during the course of the year, 14 passengers and crew were still held at the end of the year. One passenger died of a heart attack while in captivity.

▱ In May the ELN abducted some 180 churchgoers during a mass in a Catholic church in Cali, Valle del Cauca department. The guerrillas shot and killed the bodyguard of one of the churchgoers before driving the hostages into nearby mountains. Eighty hostages, the majority women and children, were released within hours and others were released in the following months. Relatives of the abducted churchgoers reported that they were forced to pay ransoms. All of the churchgoers had been released by the end of the year.

▱ In August the EPL abducted the Catholic Bishop of Tibú, José de Jesús Quintero, and demanded that an international verification commission visit the Catatumbo region to document human rights violations against the civilian population. Bishop Quintero was released unharmed in mid-September.

Consistent reports emerged of serious violations of international humanitarian law by the FARC in the demilitarized area.

▱ The FARC summarily executed at least six people they accused of being military infiltrators. The whereabouts of a further 12 people remained unknown after they were illegally detained by the FARC in the demilitarized area.

▱ The FARC also acknowledged responsibility for the killing in May of 13 members of a Gnostic community in the municipality of Puerto Rico, Caquetá department.

Children as young as 13 were routinely recruited by the FARC in breach of international standards. In July the UN Children's Fund (UNICEF) reported that more than 6,000 children were fighting with the armed opposition groups or with paramilitary forces.

Displacement

The mounting ferocity of the conflict continued to drive thousands of families from their homes. Some were casual victims caught up in hostilities, but in many cases displacement was a deliberate strategy employed by paramilitary forces to "cleanse" the civilian population from areas of guerrilla influence.

Internally displaced communities who returned to their lands and declared themselves "peace communities" continued to be attacked by paramilitary forces and by armed opposition groups.

The government failed to fulfil its commitments to maintain the security in the area of the peace communities and in other areas where internally displaced people attempted to return to their communities.

Human rights defenders

Human rights defenders continued to face harassment, intimidation and violent assaults. In response to the relentless persecution, the government took some steps to improve the protection of human rights defenders and in September President Pastrana issued a directive recognizing the legitimacy of their work. However, despite these measures, attacks against human rights defenders continued throughout 1999 and little progress was made in identifying and holding accountable those responsible.

▱ Two members of the Committee of Solidarity with Political Prisoners (CSPP) — Everardo de Jesús Puerta and Julio Ernesto González — were killed in January. The two men were shot dead after the bus in which they were travelling was intercepted by two heavily armed men and a woman who picked them out from among the passengers. Following the killings, the CSPP closed all its offices.

▱ Four members of the Popular Training Institute (IPC), including its director Jairo Bedoya, were abducted from the IPC office in Medellín, Antioquia department. The national commander of the AUC, Carlos Castaño Gil, announced they were being held as "prisoners of war" and that his forces would "purge" human rights organizations of "guerrilla infiltrators". Following intense national and international pressure, all four were released in February.

▱ Three US environmental activists taking part in an international campaign to support the U'wa indigenous community in northeastern Colombia — Ingrid Washinawatok, Lahe'ena Gay and Terence Freitas — were abducted by members of the FARC's Eastern Bloc on 25 February. Their bound and blindfolded bodies were found on 4 March over the border in Venezuela. All three had been shot in the head. Although the FARC initially denied involvement, an internal investigation identified a group of FARC combatants responsible for the killings. A judicial arrest warrant was issued against the FARC's regional commander on charges of having ordered the murder of the three US citizens. However, the FARC refused to hand him over to be tried in the national courts. In October FARC commanders told an AI delegation that internal disciplinary proceedings were at a preliminary stage and that three FARC members would face "revolutionary courts martial".

'Social cleansing'

The killing of so-called "disposables" — homosexuals, prostitutes, petty criminals, drug dealers and vagrants — by police-backed "death squads" and urban militias linked to armed opposition groups continued.

◻ In June an association of more than 300 prostitutes wrote to the National Human Rights Ombudsman after 19 prostitutes had allegedly been murdered in three months in Bogotá by a "death squad" calling itself "Clean City". They also reported routine arbitrary detention and ill-treatment by the national police.

Justice and impunity

The vast majority of perpetrators of human rights violations continued to evade accountability. Despite outstanding arrest warrants, no attempt was made by the armed and security forces to capture paramilitary leaders responsible for widespread human rights violations. In October judicial authorities reported that there were more than 300 outstanding arrest warrants against paramilitary members. However, the Attorney General's office made progress in a number of key cases.

◻ Arrest warrants were issued against AUC paramilitary leader Carlos Castaño Gil for the abduction of the four IPC members and Senator Piedad Córdoba; the massacre of 18 civilians in Puerto Alvira, Meta department, in May 1998; the murder in 1990 of Carlos Pizarro León Gómez, leader of the recently demobilized M-19 opposition group; the abduction of the sister and brother of an ELN commander in April 1997; and the massacre of 20 civilians in El Aro, Ituango, in October 1997. Despite these and previously outstanding arrest warrants, no attempt was made by the armed forces to capture Carlos Castaño Gil and other paramilitary leaders.

◻ Colonel Bernando Ruiz Silva, former commander of the army's intelligence brigade, was arrested in April and formally charged in connection with the murder of leading conservative politician Alvaro Gómez Hurtado in November 1995.

◻ General Jaime Humberto Uscátegui was arrested in May, accused of failing to prevent a massacre of up to 30 civilians by paramilitary forces in Mapiripán, Meta department, in July 1997, when he was commander of the 7th Brigade. In August General Uscátegui's case was passed to the military justice system in breach of the 1997 Constitutional Court ruling that excluded serious human rights violations from military jurisdiction. In November a military judge ordered his provisional release. General Uscátegui was dismissed in November following a disciplinary investigation by the Procurator General for failing to support a judicial commission which was attacked by paramilitary forces in San Carlos de Guaroa in 1997; 13 members of the commission died in the attack.

Legislation

In June the regional justice system (also known as the "faceless justice" because of the anonymity of judges) was restructured and renamed the Specialized Justice System. Some of the serious concerns repeatedly expressed by the UN and other international organizations about the regional justice system were addressed in the restructured system. However, the Office of the UN High Commissioner for Human Rights in Colombia said that the new Specialized Justice System still fell short of international standards.

A new Military Penal Code introduced important modifications, including allowing civilians to act as plaintiffs in military penal proceedings and prohibiting commanding officers from sitting as judges in cases involving military personnel under their command. However, the new law failed to restrict military jurisdiction to crimes directly related to "acts of service" as defined by the Constitutional Court or to exclude "due obedience" as a defence plea. Moreover, the bill was not due to come into effect for at least 12 months.

A bill designed to incorporate the crimes of forced disappearance, genocide and forced displacement into the Penal Code was passed by Congress in November. However, in December, President Pastrana vetoed the bill on the grounds that it was "inconvenient and unconstitutional".

UN Commission on Human Rights

AI's concerns about Colombia were addressed in a statement by the Chairman of the UN Commission on Human Rights. The Commission welcomed the extension of the mandate of the permanent Office of the UN High Commissioner for Human Rights in Colombia until April 2000.

AI country reports and visits
Reports
- Colombia: Repression of human rights defenders (AI Index: AMR 23/016/99)
- Colombia: Barrancabermeja — a city under siege (AI Index: AMR 23/036/99)
Visits
AI delegates visited Colombia twice and during a meeting with the Vice-President in October reiterated AI's call to the government to end human rights violations.

CONGO
(DEMOCRATIC REPUBLIC OF THE)

DEMOCRATIC REPUBLIC OF THE CONGO
Head of state and government: Laurent-Désiré Kabila
Capital: Kinshasa
Population: 46.7 million
Official languages: French, Kikongo, Kiswahili, Lingala, Tshiluba
Death penalty: retentionist

The war, which started in August 1998 and involved the forces of at least eight countries and numerous armed groups, continued. Fighting escalated as did unlawful killings and other human rights abuses by combatants. Thousands of unarmed civilians, mainly in the east of the country, were unlawfully killed. Several hundred thousand people fled to neighbouring countries and as many as one million were internally displaced. Ill-treatment and torture, including rape, were widespread. The government and its armed opponents persecuted their critics and clamped down on the rights to freedom of expression and association. Some 200 people were sentenced to death by a government military court; as many as 100 of them were executed.

Background
The armed opposition — composed of the *Rassemblement congolais pour la démocratie* (RCD), Congolese Rally for Democracy, and the *Mouvement pour la libération du Congo* (MLC), Movement for the Liberation of Congo — continued to be supported by forces of the governments of Burundi, Rwanda and Uganda. Democratic Republic of the Congo (DRC) government forces continued to be supported by those of the governments of Angola, Namibia, Zimbabwe and reportedly Sudan. Chad withdrew its forces after signing a peace agreement with the DRC government and Uganda in April. The two other parties to the agreement, which was mediated by Libya, did not implement it.

By the end of the year, the armed opposition and allied foreign forces had captured most of eastern, northern and central DRC from forces loyal to the government. A number of Congolese armed groups known as *mayi-mayi*, as well as others including Rwandese *interahamwe* militia and former Rwandese government forces, continued to attack opposition forces and their foreign backers in eastern DRC after forces loyal to the government were routed. In September, President Laurent-Désiré Kabila appointed several *mayi-mayi* commanders to senior military posts.

RCD factions and their allies carried out widespread unlawful killings and other human rights abuses against unarmed civilians suspected of supporting the government and local armed groups. Their armed opponents also committed abuses.

Early in the year the RCD split into two factions; one supported by Uganda and the other by Rwanda. Disagreements over control of captured territory and the war strategy culminated in several days of fighting in August in the capital of Orientale province. In December, the RCD factions and the MLC announced that they had agreed to form a common front against the government.

All forces involved in the fighting obtained extensive arms and recruited thousands of combatants, including children as young as 10.

Most people in the DRC were victims of either direct attacks by combatants or of hunger and disease. Services such as education and health collapsed. Most ordinary Congolese lost their livelihoods and most government employees were rarely paid, if at all. Whereas foreign forces on both sides of the conflict were reportedly paid, Congolese combatants were generally not paid, and became increasingly undisciplined, living on extortion and looting from already impoverished civilians and humanitarian organizations.

Government-controlled areas
Unlawful killings
Although extrajudicial executions by government forces were far less widespread than in late 1998, many unarmed civilians were killed as a result of direct or indiscriminate attacks. Some of the victims were reportedly killed by government forces who suspected them of supporting armed opposition groups and their allies. Many civilians were reportedly killed when government aircraft indiscriminately bombed areas in which there were high concentrations of unarmed civilians.

□ In January government soldiers reportedly killed several hundred unarmed civilians in the northwestern towns of Zongo and Libenge, which were under attack by MLC and Ugandan troops.

□ From May onwards, dozens of unarmed civilians were reportedly killed when the air forces of the DRC, Zimbabwean and Sudanese governments bombed the towns of Goma, Uvira and Kisangani.

Political prisoners
At the start of 1999 more than 1,000 people were being held for their known or suspected opposition to the government. The majority of the detainees, including members of opposition political parties, journalists, human rights defenders and members of the Tutsi ethnic group, had not used or advocated violence and were considered prisoners of conscience. Most of them were released during the year.

Members of the opposition
As many as 200 members of opposition political parties were detained for periods ranging from a few days to several months because they had failed to abide by a 1997 presidential decree banning opposition political party activity. Most of those detained were members of the *Parti lumumbiste unifié* (PALU), United Lumumbist Party, and of the *Union pour la démocratie et le progrès social* (UDPS), Union for Democracy and Social Progress.

At least 76 members of PALU were arrested during July and held in detention centres around Kinshasa. Seventy-two of them, including 70-year-old Albert Mputucieli, 67-year-old Louis Nkwese, and Alexandre Tata, were held until mid-December when the government released most political prisoners.

Several UDPS leaders in Lubumbashi were arrested because they were linked to documents criticizing the government. Professor Kambaji wa Kambaji, a lecturer in sociology at the University of Lubumbashi, was arrested on 30 July. Tabu Kalala Mwin Dilemb, President of the UDPS for the province of Katanga, and Tshiwadi Shamuyi, were arrested in August. All three were still being held in the central prison in Kinshasa at the end of the year.

Journalists
Dozens of journalists were arrested, intimidated or harassed, often for writing or publishing articles critical of the government or its policies. Most journalists arrested during 1998 and 1999 were released. However, several remained in custody, some after they had been sentenced to prison terms by the Military Order Court.

Mbakulu Pambu Diambu, a journalist with a private television station and President of the local division of the *Union de la presse du Congo*, Congolese Press Union, was still held at the end of 1999; he had not been formally charged with any offence. Mbakulu Pambu Diambu had been arrested by the *Agence nationale de renseignements* (ANR), National Intelligence Agency, in Matadi at the end of November 1998 because he hosted a television program on which representatives of the armed opposition appeared.

Thierry Kyalumba, editor of the newspaper *La Vision*, was sentenced to four years' imprisonment by the Military Order Court for divulging state secrets. He had been arrested in January after his newspaper published an article refuting a government claim that an armed opposition leader was dead. He was repeatedly beaten in custody. He escaped in May while recovering from an operation for appendicitis and left the country.

Human rights defenders
Human rights defenders were targeted by the authorities for demanding respect for the rights of ordinary Congolese citizens.

Sister Antoinette Fari, a Roman Catholic nun and veteran prison humanitarian worker, was arrested by the ANR in Lubumbashi on 5 November. A day earlier, she had been questioned by the ANR for two hours about her work with prisoners at Buluo prison. She was transferred to Kinshasa before being conditionally released on 7 December.

Union and student leaders
Trade unionists and student leaders were subjected to human rights violations for demanding that the government pay salary arrears to government employees or allowances to students.

Celestin Mayala, Malu Tshisongo and at least seven other trade union leaders accused of organizing a workers' strike were arrested on 3 August by members of the Rapid Intervention Police in Kinshasa. They were held at the headquarters of the Kinshasa Provincial Police, where they were reportedly beaten before their release two days later without charge.

Persecution of Tutsi
The government and its supporters continued persecuting members of the Tutsi ethnic group and others who had family or other links with them. They were accused of supporting the RCD and their allies. Several dozen who had been in hiding since late 1998 were arrested and joined hundreds of others arrested soon after the armed conflict started. The government claimed that the Tutsi were being held for their own protection. During the second half of the year, the government succumbed to international pressure and released most of the Tutsi detainees. Several hundred were taken to Rwanda while others were taken to Benin and Cameroon on the understanding that those fulfilling US immigration regulations would be allowed temporary residence in the USA. However, the vetting process had not started by the end of the year.

Torture and ill-treatment
Many people were threatened with or subjected to violence, including torture, at the time of their arrest by members of the security forces. There were reports that women were raped and men had their genitals beaten and pulled in custody. Conditions in detention centres, particularly those run by the security forces, often amounted to cruel, inhuman or degrading treatment.

Clovis Kadda, a journalist, was arrested on 22 September and taken to Kinshasa military headquarters for questioning. After the authorities established that he was a relative of an armed opposition commander, he was severely beaten by members of the security forces, four of whom reportedly administered 57 lashes. He was released the following day and went into hiding. Clovis Kadda was still suffering from his injuries at the end of the year.

Military Order Court
The government increasingly used the Military Order Court as a weapon against its opponents. Although the Court was set up in August 1997 to try soldiers accused of military offences, it also tried civilians accused of political and economic offences. Trials by the Court were fundamentally unfair and contravened international law and standards. The decree setting up the Court specifically denies defendants the right to appeal to a higher jurisdiction. Those convicted could only appeal to the President for clemency, but in some cases the execution of those sentenced to death took place so soon after the trial that it was doubtful that President Kabila had been able to consider appeals for clemency. Opposition political leaders and journalists critical of the government or its policies were among those convicted and sentenced to prison terms by the Court on political charges. In many cases defendants had no access to legal counsel and, when they did, lawyers did not have sufficient time to examine the evidence, interview witnesses and adequately prepare a defence.

Death penalty
As many as 100 civilians and soldiers were executed, virtually all of them in the first half of the year. The victims had been sentenced to death by the Military

Order Court which had found them guilty of criminal offences including armed robbery and murder. Some of them were soldiers convicted of cowardice, desertion or other military offences. In a letter to the UN Secretary-General and in a meeting with AI in July, the Minister for Human Rights said that his government was making plans to abolish the death penalty. However, the Minister said that abolition would occur sooner if the government received material assistance to reform and equip the judiciary and the penal system.

Areas under rebel and foreign control
Unlawful killings
Thousands of unarmed civilians were victims of deliberate and arbitrary killings by armed opposition groups and their allies from Burundi, Rwanda and Uganda. Most of the killings occurred during or soon after armed clashes between RCD and allied forces on one side and *mayi-mayi* and allied armed groups on the other. Most of the victims appeared to be women, children and the elderly who had not been able to flee or had not fled because they did not expect to be targeted by combatants.

☐ Local human rights groups said that as many as 800 unarmed civilians were killed by RCD and allied troops from Burundi and Rwanda at Makobola in South-Kivu province at the beginning of January. The attack was apparently to avenge fellow combatants killed by *mayi-mayi*. A team sent by the RCD to investigate the massacre claimed that only 23 people had been killed, while at the same time calling for another investigation. No such investigation is known to have occurred.

☐ RCD soldiers publicly killed at least 12 women — some of whom were buried alive after being tortured and raped — accused of witchcraft in Mwenga, South-Kivu, between 15 and 20 October.

In Orientale province, many of the killings were carried out by Ugandan and Ugandan-backed RCD troops. These forces reportedly participated in the killing of hundreds of members of the Lendu ethnic group in the context of intercommunal violence between Lendu and members of the Hema ethnic group in Ituri district.

Armed groups opposing the RCD and its allied foreign forces also deliberately killed and abducted unarmed civilians, including many women.

☐ In October at least four women were killed by *mayi-mayi* in Walungu, South-Kivu, accused of helping RCD soldiers.

Political prisoners
Dozens of suspected or known critics of the war waged against the government by RCD and allied forces were arrested and detained by the RCD and their allies for periods ranging from a few days to several months. Many were arrested and held in secret or unofficial detention centres, including private houses, on unsubstantiated accusations that they supported the *mayi-mayi* or the *interahamwe* militia. Some of those arrested were journalists and human rights defenders targeted for denouncing human rights abuses committed by forces opposing President Kabila.

☐ Raphael Wakenge, a member of the human rights organization *Héritiers de la Justice* was arrested on 27 August by the RCD in Bukavu. His arrest was apparently linked to the arrest two days earlier of journalists Mushizi Nfundiko Kizito and Omba Kamengele, accused of using their radio receiver to listen to sensitive military transmissions. Raphael Wakenge had been producing human rights programs on *Radio Maendeleo*, where the two journalists worked before the RCD closed it in July. All three were released on 8 September.

Torture and ill-treatment
Many of those arrested by the RCD and their allies were reportedly subjected to beatings, rape and other forms of torture while in custody.

☐ Francine Ngoy, a 22-year-old woman, was arrested in Goma in May and ill-treated in a military detention centre. She was accused of collaborating with President Kabila's government. In November, she was transferred to Gisenyi, in northwestern Rwanda, where she was still held in military custody at the end of the year.

☐ Several prominent people were arrested and tortured in November by the Ugandan-backed RCD faction in Butembo. On 11 December, just 11 days after their release, one of them, Désiré Lumbu Lumbu, died from a brain haemorrhage believed to have been caused by torture.

International action
Although they resisted pressure from the DRC government to condemn the invasion of its territory by neighbouring countries, the UN, the Organization of African Unity and the European Union called for an end to the armed conflict in the DRC. In April the UN Security Council passed a resolution demanding an end to the conflict and an inquiry into violations of human rights and international humanitarian law as soon as the security situation permitted. These organizations supported mediation between the main parties to the conflict by Zambian President Frederic Chiluba. The mediation culminated in the signing of a cease-fire agreement by the governments of Angola, the DRC, Namibia, Rwanda, Uganda and Zimbabwe in July, and by the armed opposition groups in August. However, fighting continued as the opposing forces accused each other of violating the cease-fire.

In August the UN Security Council authorized the deployment of military liaison officers to prepare for the deployment of a peacekeeping force. The liaison officers visited the countries involved in the conflict, but the peacekeepers required by the cease-fire agreement had not been deployed by the end of the year. A threat by the European Union to suspend aid to countries continuing the fighting was only implemented to any significant degree against the DRC and Zimbabwe.

AI country reports and visits
Public statements
• Scores of executions in the Democratic Republic of Congo (AI Index: AFR 62/015/99)

- Amnesty International urges peace negotiators to place the protection of DRC human rights defenders on the agenda (AI Index: AFR 62/019/99)

Visits

AI delegates visited Tanzania and Zambia in September and interviewed Congolese refugees. Other AI delegates visited parts of the DRC under government control in August and eastern DRC in November.

CONGO
(REPUBLIC OF THE)

REPUBLIC OF THE CONGO
Head of state and government: Denis Sassou Nguesso
Capital: Brazzaville
Population: 2.6 million
Official language: French
Death penalty: abolitionist in practice

Government forces, militias and armed opposition groups carried out widespread human rights abuses in the context of continued armed conflict. Unarmed civilians were victims of extrajudicial executions and deliberate and arbitrary killings, as well as "disappearances". Many arbitrary arrests and detentions were reported. Detainees, including political prisoners, were held for prolonged periods without charge or trial. Some were tortured or ill-treated. A number of political prisoners were released. Critics of the government, including human rights activists and journalists, were harassed and intimidated.

Background

The country continued to be gravely affected by armed conflict, which had flared up again at the end of 1998. Fighting was particularly intense in January and February, in the capital Brazzaville and elsewhere. On the one side were regular government forces and allied "Cobra" militias of President Denis Sassou Nguesso. On the other were armed opposition groups – primarily the "Ninjas" (loyal to former Prime Minister Bernard Kolelas), active in the Pool region, and the "Cocoyes" (loyal to former President Pascal Lissouba), active in Niari, Bouenza and Lekoumou regions. All parties to the conflict took part in widespread fighting, killing and looting.

Insecurity and deliberate violence by both sides against civilians caused massive population displacements and a serious humanitarian crisis. Several thousand fled to neighbouring countries including Gabon and the Democratic Republic of the Congo (DRC). Some internally displaced persons returned to their home areas during 1999, only to face further violence during or upon their return; they were among the victims of serious human rights abuses, including killings, "disappearances" and rape.

Peace initiatives and amnesty

Two cease-fires were signed during 1999: the first in Pointe-Noire in Congo in November; the second in the Gabonese capital, Libreville, in December, when President Omar Bongo of Gabon was appointed as an official mediator. The cease-fires were signed by representatives of the Congolese government and of the Ninjas and the Cocoyes. However, the exiled leaders of these two armed groups – Bernard Kolelas and Pascal Lissouba – disowned the cease-fire. Fighting continued at the end of 1999, despite the cease-fires.

In August the government announced an amnesty for armed opposition combatants who surrendered and handed in their weapons, including those who had carried out grave human rights abuses during armed conflict in previous years.

Killings of unarmed civilians

Many unarmed civilians, including the internally displaced, were killed in the context of the armed conflict, particularly in January after fierce fighting had erupted in December 1998. Several thousand people were estimated to have been killed during this period, including in Brazzaville and in the Pool region.

Some were killed by the Congolese security forces. However, most killings attributed to supporters of the government were carried out by current or former members of the Cobra militia allied to President Sassou Nguesso, some of whom had been reintegrated into the army. Angolan government troops fighting alongside the Congolese security forces were also reported to have killed unarmed civilians. Many people, including civilians, were killed indiscriminately, for example when government forces shelled areas viewed as strongholds of the Ninjas, sometimes with the use of helicopters. Other victims were singled out for execution on the basis that they were supporters of the Ninjas or Cocoyes, in many cases without evidence of links with these groups. Some victims, who included women and children, were extrajudicially executed at point-blank range, without any attempt to arrest them or to undertake any kind of judicial proceeding. The government was not known to have taken measures to prevent extrajudicial executions or to bring those responsible to justice.

In January, five men suspected of being Ninjas because their identity cards indicated that they came from Mindouli in the Pool region – a stronghold of the Ninjas – were extrajudicially executed by police in Pointe-Noire.

Deliberate and arbitrary killings of unarmed civilians were also committed by armed opposition groups. In particular, cases of killings and abductions by the Ninjas were reported. As with the government, leaders of armed opposition groups were not known to have taken any measures to prevent further killings of civilians or to instruct those under their command to respect international humanitarian law.

Arrests and detention

There were many arbitrary arrests and detentions by the security forces, often of people suspected of supporting groups opposed to the government. Detainees included children, such as Frid Mfilou, aged 16, and Herman Mfilou, aged 15, who were arrested with their mother in January by the police in Brazzaville, apparently because the police could not find their father who was accused of training the Ninjas. Government agents frequently extorted money from relatives of detainees in exchange for their release.

Individuals associated with the former government or who had served in the armed forces under former President Lissouba were also targeted. Some detainees were held for months without charge or trial.

Releases of political prisoners

In October, 12 senior military officers who had been arrested in late 1997 and early 1998 on accusations of supporting former President Lissouba and detained for more than a year without trial were released. Former government officials accused of the same offence were also released. Hervé-Ambroise Malonga, president of the Brazzaville Bar Association and a former member of the Constitutional Council, was among those released. He had been detained without trial since November 1998. His health had deteriorated as a result of harsh prison conditions and inadequate access to medical care.

Two other former government officials – Henri Marcellin Dzouma-Nguelet, former law lecturer at Brazzaville university, and Colonel Jean-Michel Ebaka, former prefect of Owando – were also released. They had been detained without charge or trial since February and March 1998 respectively.

Violations of freedom of expression

Several journalists and human rights activists who were perceived as critical of the government or who had publicly denounced the gravity of the situation in Congo were subjected to threats and intimidation.

⬚ Two journalists were arrested at the end of May. Television journalist Maurice-Lemaire Moukouyou was arrested and detained without trial at the *Direction régionale de la surveillance du territoire* (DRST), Regional Directorate of Territory Surveillance, in Pointe-Noire, accused of sending information to supporters of the former government in exile. He was released in October without charge. Hervé Kiminou Missou, a Congolese correspondent for Angola for the regional radio station *Africa No. 1*, was also detained in Pointe-Noire, accused of being a spy for opponents of the government. He was released without charge after eight days. The police who arrested him appeared to have targeted him because he was born in former President Pascal Lissouba's region.

Torture, ill-treatment and harsh prison conditions

A number of detainees were victims of torture and ill-treatment. There were also many cases of rape of women by members of the security forces and militia. Conditions of detention were harsh.

In October, Paul Omoye Kamaro, a medical worker who had been arrested in October 1998, died in the military hospital of Pointe-Noire as a result of tuberculosis contracted in detention. He had been detained without charge for a year, without adequate medical treatment. A period of detention in especially harsh conditions in Impfondo, in the north of the country, was believed to have aggravated his condition.

Judicial reforms

In January the government created a High Court of Justice which it said would be used to try members of the former government and their allies for crimes committed in previous years. No one was known to have been brought to trial before this court during 1999.

In September the authorities announced plans to create military courts in Brazzaville and Pointe-Noire to try government soldiers accused of human rights violations and other crimes.

AI's findings

AI published a report in March entitled *Republic of Congo: An old generation of leaders in new carnage*, based in part on the findings of an AI visit to Congo in 1998. The report documented widespread human rights abuses by all parties to the conflict. The Congolese government responded by acknowledging that its forces may have committed a few violations but blamed almost all human rights abuses on its opponents. The armed opposition rejected allegations that its forces had committed atrocities.

AI country report

• Republic of Congo: An old generation of leaders in new carnage (AI Index: AFR 22/001/99)

CÔTE D'IVOIRE

REPUBLIC OF CÔTE D'IVOIRE
Head of state: General Robert Guei (replaced Henri Konan Bédié in December)
Capital: Yamoussoukro
Population: 15 million
Official language: French
Death penalty: abolitionist in practice

On 24 December a military coup, which began with a mutiny by unpaid soldiers, overthrew the government of President Henri Konan Bédié, who left the country some days later. A National Public Salvation Committee composed of high-ranking soldiers and led by General Robert Guei, former army Chief of Staff, took power. The new head of state invited political parties to nominate potential ministers in a transitional government and promised a democratic presidential election, but did not set any timetable. Earlier in the year, opposition leaders were imprisoned under a law which holds anyone who calls or leads a gathering accountable for any violence that occurs, irrespective of whether they are personally responsible. Student activists were tortured or ill-treated in detention.

Background
Political tension rose at the start of 1999, when it was announced that Alassane Ouattara, leader of the opposition party, the *Rassemblement des Républicains* (RDR), Republican Assembly, would be a candidate in presidential elections originally scheduled for October 2000. The ruling *Parti démocratique de Côte d'Ivoire* (PDCI), Democratic Party of Côte d'Ivoire, headed by President Henri Konan Bédié, stated that Alassane Ouattara was not eligible to run as head of state since his father was of Burkina Faso nationality. This dispute led to ethnic divisions, as the RDR was mostly identified by the authorities with the Muslim northern part of the country.

In October the Minister of Justice annulled a nationality certificate submitted by Alassane Ouattara on the grounds that it was forged. An arrest warrant was issued against him on charges of fraud and forgery. This arrest warrant was lifted some days after the December military coup.

Until the December 1999 military coup, the first in Côte d'Ivoire, the country had been ruled since independence by the PDCI. Sporadic periods of unrest had occurred which had been violently curbed by the security forces. The preceding presidential election in October 1995 had been boycotted by the two main opposition parties, the *Front populaire ivoirien* (FPI), Ivorian Popular Front, and the RDR, and in the ensuing unrest dozens of opposition party supporters, including prisoners of conscience, were held. All were subsequently released, notably after an amnesty granted by President Konan Bédié in December 1998.

RDR leaders imprisoned under unfair law
In November, 16 leaders of the RDR including its Secretary General, Henriette Diabaté, were sentenced to prison terms of one to two years under an anti-riot law passed in 1992. Under this law anyone who calls or leads a gathering is held accountable for any violence that occurs, even if he or she did not personally incite or use violence. The RDR leaders were arrested after a demonstration in October which became violent, but no evidence was produced that the RDR leaders had any personal responsibility for acts of violence. AI considered the 16 to be prisoners of conscience.

Seven members of the local leadership of the RDR in the northern town of Korhogo were arrested in November for public order offences under this same law. All the RDR prisoners were released after the December military coup.

Torture and ill-treatment of students
Scores of student activists belonging to the *Fédération estudiantine et scolaire de Côte d'Ivoire* (FESCI), Ivorian Federation of Students and School Pupils, were detained for weeks. Some were arrested during a series of university strikes in May. A number of FESCI leaders, including its Secretary General, Charles Blé Goudé, were detained under the 1992 anti-riot law. All were released without charge in October. Some of the detainees were tortured and ill-treated in Abidjan, at the Police Academy and the *Direction de la sécurité du territoire* (DST), Internal Security Office. Some students were reportedly handcuffed with their hands behind their backs for 10 days, beaten and forced to drink dirty water. There was no investigation into these allegations.

AI country visit
AI's Secretary General visited Côte d'Ivoire in May and met President Bédié.

CROATIA

REPUBLIC OF CROATIA
Head of state: Vlatko Pavletić (replaced Franjo Tudjman in December)
Head of government: Zlatko Mateša
Capital: Zagreb
Population: 4.8 million
Official language: Croatian
Death penalty: abolitionist for all crimes

There was continued resistance by the Croatian authorities to the return of tens of thousands of Croatian Serbs who fled the country during the armed conflict between 1991 and 1995. There were sporadic violent incidents against Croatian Serbs who remained in the Eastern Slavonia region. Independent journalists and people critical of the government or the ruling political party, the *Hrvatska Demokratska Zajednica* (HDZ), Croatian Democratic Union, continued to face harassment, which could lead to the imprisonment of prisoners of conscience. Reports of ill-treatment and use of excessive force by police increased. The further deterioration in Croatia's cooperation with the International Criminal Tribunal for the former Yugoslavia (the Tribunal) led the Tribunal's President to report Croatia's non-compliance to the UN Security Council in November.

Background
In November Vlatko Pavletić was appointed acting President, owing to the serious illness of President Franjo Tudjman who was hospitalized in November. President Tudjman died on 11 December. General elections, which had first been announced for December, were postponed until 3 January 2000.

Croatian Serbs
Problems with return and reintegration
During 1999, according to Croatian government statistics, nearly 9,000 Croatian Serbs returned to the country, including around 5,000 under the return program adopted by parliament in June 1998. In addition, around 5,000 Croatian Serbs who had been internally displaced in Eastern Slavonia reportedly returned to their pre-war homes elsewhere in Croatia, and some 18,000 Croats returned to their homes in Eastern Slavonia.

However, tens of thousands of Croatian Serbs who had expressed their willingness to return remained refugees in the Federal Republic of Yugoslavia (FRY) and in the Bosnian Serb entity. They had problems establishing their right to citizenship under Croatian law and experienced delays and difficulties in obtaining identification papers through local consular offices. Those who managed to return to Croatia faced further obstacles from local authorities when trying to regain their property.

Eastern Slavonia
Although the security situation for Croatian Serbs apparently improved in Eastern Slavonia and other parts of Croatia, notably the Knin area, sporadic incidents of ethnically motivated violence against them continued to be reported. For example, two Croatian Serbs were killed in villages near Vukovar in Eastern Slavonia in May and August. Although in both cases police arrested a suspect almost immediately, no charges had been brought against either by the end of 1999. In addition, police investigations into the August killing appeared to be inadequate, as police failed to act on information provided by eyewitnesses about a group of people involved in the killing.

Restrictions on freedom of expression
Government officials brought suits for defamation against independent journalists and others who criticized the government or the HDZ party, apparently to silence them. In most cases, private criminal complaints were brought by officials against people criticizing them. In addition, public prosecutors brought charges against people who had published or released information criticizing government officials. Many of the charges brought could result in imprisonment.

In April Orlanda Obad, a journalist with the daily newspaper *Jutarnji list*, was charged with publishing, and unauthorized procurement of, trade secrets. She had written a series of articles in 1998 detailing the financial holdings of President Tudjman's wife in a Zagreb bank. It was alleged that the President had unlawfully failed to declare this as income. If convicted of these charges, she could be imprisoned for up to five years, and would be a prisoner of conscience. No date had been set by the end of 1999 for the case to go to trial.

Ill-treatment by police
There was an increasing number of reports of police ill-treating people in custody or using excessive force in carrying out their duties. In the few instances in which the authorities responded to such allegations, investigations and prosecutions were not pursued promptly and impartially.

In October special police officers in Dubrovnik were reported to have severely ill-treated Nikola Miletić, a bar owner, after he failed to close his bar on time. When one police officer twisted his arm behind his back and he tried to free himself, another officer beat him. Nikola Miletić also claimed that after he was handcuffed, an officer touched the handcuffs with an electro-shock baton. He was detained overnight in the police station. Several hours after his release he lost consciousness and had to undergo hospital treatment. According to his medical records, he had sustained bruising to his head, neck and shoulders as well as to his eye.

In September the retrial started of two members of the Croatian secret police, the SZUP, charged in connection with the death in custody of Šefik Mujkić, a Croatian citizen of Bosnian origin, in September 1995. A forensic expert who testified at the retrial stated that the victim had been seated while being repeatedly beaten with a blunt object on his upper back, arms, legs and soles of his feet. The expert concluded that Šefik Mujkić's death was caused by a combination of the injuries he sustained, psychological stress and an existing heart condition (of which the police officers were allegedly aware). An AI delegate who attended the trial considered that the public prosecutor accepted without questioning the defendants' defence that they were acting in self-defence. In December the two officers were found guilty of extracting a confession by the use of force and of inflicting grievous bodily harm. They were sentenced to 18 months' imprisonment.

Failure to achieve justice for war crimes

Trials continued of people suspected of having committed war crimes, including trials held *in absentia*. Many of these trials violated international standards of fairness. AI urged the Croatian authorities to hand over the relevant case files in all war crimes cases to the Prosecutor of the Tribunal, for an independent review of the evidence against the suspects in order to determine whether it was sufficient to pursue a prosecution.

AI remained concerned that the authorities failed to undertake serious efforts to investigate and prosecute members of the Croatian armed forces or police suspected of war crimes and other human rights violations. In September the Justice Ministry and the Council for Cooperation with the International Court of Justice and International Criminal Court released a "White Paper" which was a comprehensive overview of Croatia's cooperation with the Tribunal as well as of domestic prosecutions related to violations of international humanitarian law since 1991. The White Paper also included the latest official statistics on investigations and prosecutions before Croatian courts for crimes committed against Croatian Serbs in 1995. However, the information provided appeared to be incomplete, out of date and misleading, and contained virtually no detailed recent information on cases which had been brought to the government's attention by domestic and international organizations, including AI.

On 2 November the outgoing Tribunal President wrote to the President of the UN Security Council, denouncing repeated non-compliance with provisions of the Tribunal's Statute by Croatia and the FRY. The Tribunal President criticized Croatia for its failure to recognize the Tribunal's jurisdiction over events relating to the 1995 Croatian government offensives, Operations Flash and Storm, and for its failure to transfer indicted suspects to the Tribunal's custody. She repeated her earlier requests to the FRY authorities to arrest and surrender three Yugoslav citizens indicted for the killings of more than 260 unarmed men in Vukovar in November 1991.

The trial of six members of the Croatian security forces for crimes committed against Croatian Serb civilians in the Pakrafika Poljana area in 1991 and 1992 ended in May. The Zagreb County Court acquitted four of the defendants and sentenced the remaining two to

prison terms of up to 20 months for minor offences. One of the defendants, Miro Bajramović, had confessed in a Croatian newspaper in 1997 to killing more than 70 Serbs. However the indictment contained only one charge of murder and one of attempted murder, as well as crimes of illegal detention and extortion. Local non-governmental organizations expressed concern that the charges were too weak and vague. For example, the deaths of three Serb civilians as a result of their detention were mentioned in the indictment but the role of the defendants in their deaths was not raised. There was further concern that some key prosecution witnesses, all Croatian Serbs who had been detained and ill-treated by the accused, had changed their earlier statements out of fear of reprisals.

In contrast, prosecutions of Croatian Serbs for war crimes were pursued vigorously. In most such cases trials failed to meet international standards of fairness. Five Croatian Serbs from the Eastern Slavonian village of Šodolovci were convicted of war crimes against the civilian population by the Osijek County Court in May and sentenced to long-term imprisonment. They had been charged with indiscriminate shelling of Croatian-held villages in 1991 and 1992 and had been already convicted in 1995 after a trial *in absentia*. AI concluded that the trial court could not be considered an impartial and independent tribunal, and that the defendants' rights to be presumed innocent and to present a full defence had been violated. In November the Supreme Court quashed the lower court's verdict and sent the case back for a further retrial, in recognition of the substantial violations of domestic criminal procedure which had taken place.

The retrial for war crimes of another Serb, Mirko Graorac, was postponed in September after his lawyer had requested that the case be transferred from the Split County Court as he did not consider it to be impartial. Mirko Graorac had been convicted by the Split County Court of war crimes against prisoners of war and against the civilian population in 1996 after a trial which AI considered to be unfair. In March 1998 the Supreme Court quashed the lower court's verdict and sent the case back for retrial, although AI expressed concern that the Supreme Court's revision of the case did not address the violations of a right to fair trial but only sought to clarify the role of certain prosecution witnesses. In November 1999 the Supreme Court refused the defence request.

Missing persons

AI continued to urge the Croatian and FRY authorities to clarify the fate and whereabouts of more than 2,000 people still missing since the armed conflict in Croatia. AI specifically called upon the FRY authorities to provide the Croatian government with information on grave sites reportedly containing the remains of some 300 Croats who had been taken prisoner in late 1991 and transferred to FRY territory.

AI also reminded the Croatian authorities of their obligation to ensure the efficient functioning of the Subcommission for Detained and Missing Persons for the Croatian Danube region (Subcommission), as agreed between the Croatian government and the departing UN Transitional Authority for Eastern Slavonia (UNTAES) in January 1998. According to the Organization for Security and Co-operation in Europe (OSCE), by September 1999 the Subcommission had not been fully established as no Serb delegates had been included. The OSCE further noted that apparently no attempts had been made by the Croatian government to locate Serb missing persons in the region. Organizations representing relatives of Croatian Serbs who had gone missing in the Krajina area after the 1995 offensives told AI that they were not aware of any exhumations of grave sites thought to contain the bodies of Croatian Serbs.

Some progress was made in resolving the approximately 2,000 outstanding cases of mainly Croatian missing persons. According to a government commission, more than 100 bodies were exhumed during 1999 and roughly half of them were identified. The commission stated in November that it was still looking for some 1,900 missing persons.

AI country reports and visits
Reports
• Croatia: Fear for safety – violent attacks against Serbs in Eastern Slavonia (AI Index: EUR 64/004/99)
• Croatia: Shortchanging Justice – The "Šodolovci" group (AI Index: EUR 64/006/99)
Visit
An AI delegate visited Croatia in September and October to conduct research and trial observations.

CUBA

REPUBLIC OF CUBA
Head of state and government: Fidel Castro Ruz
Capital: Havana
Population: 11.2 million
Official language: Spanish
Death penalty: retentionist

Dissidents, who included journalists, political opponents and human rights defenders, suffered severe harassment during the year. Several hundred people remained imprisoned for political offences, some of whom were recognized by AI as prisoners of conscience. Some trials of prisoners of conscience took place which did not conform to international standards. New legislation was introduced to combat dissent and widen the use of the death penalty. At least 13 people were executed and at least nine people remained under sentence of death. There were some reports of ill-treatment. Prisoners were sometimes subjected to cruel, inhuman or degrading treatment.

Background
President Fidel Castro continued as head of state, 40 years after coming to power. His party, the *Partido Comunista de Cuba*, Cuban Communist Party, remained the only legal political party. In April the UN Commission on Human Rights censured Cuba for human rights abuses, calling on the government to respect fundamental freedoms. In November the UN General Assembly overwhelmingly demanded an end to the US embargo against Cuba, for the eighth consecutive year. The mandate of the UN Special Rapporteur on Cuba, which expired in April 1998 without his ever having been granted access to the country, was not renewed.

New legislation
Tough new legislation aimed at combating political dissent and protecting the Cuban economy was approved in February and became effective in March. Law 88, the Law for the Protection of the National Independence and Economy of Cuba, provided a penalty of up to 20 years' imprisonment for a series of offences. These include providing information to the US government; owning, distributing or reproducing material produced by the US government or any other foreign entity; and collaborating, by any means, with foreign radio, television, press or other foreign media, with the purpose of destabilizing the country and destroying the socialist state.

Restrictions on human rights monitoring
Research into human rights violations in Cuba was hampered by restrictions imposed by the government, such as the reported monitoring of telephone calls and mail, the illegality of human rights groups, the absence

of any official data on the prison population, and the difficulties imposed by the authorities on access to the country for independent human rights monitoring.

Prisoners of conscience

Several hundred political prisoners, including a number of prisoners of conscience, were believed to be held in Cuba, most of whom were convicted after unfair trials. By the end of 1999, AI was working on behalf of 19 prisoners of conscience. The absence of official data and the severe restrictions on human rights monitoring made it difficult to confirm information on other possible prisoners of conscience.

Several new prisoners of conscience were convicted and sentenced during 1999.

◻ Jesús Joel Díaz Hernández, executive director of the independent press agency *Cooperativa Avileña de Periodistas Independientes,* Cooperative of Independent Journalists of Ciego de Avila, was detained on 18 January, tried the following day and sentenced to four years' imprisonment for "dangerousness". Jesús Díaz' trial reportedly did not conform to international standards of fairness, particularly since his lawyer had inadequate time to prepare his defence.

◻ In March Félix A. Bonne Carcasés, René Gómez Manzano, Vladimiro Roca Antúnez and Marta Beatriz Roque Cabello, all members of the *Grupo de Trabajo de la Disidencia Interna para el Análisis de la Situación Socio-Económica Cubana*, Internal Dissidents' Working Group for the Analysis of the Cuban Socio-Economic Situation, were tried and convicted of "other acts against State security", in relation to a crime of "sedition". They were sentenced to terms of imprisonment ranging from three and a half to five years. All four had been detained in July 1997 after issuing a critique of a document disseminated for the Fifth Congress of the Cuban Communist Party.

◻ In May the trial took place of Manuel Antonio González Castellanos, a reporter for the independent press agency *Cuba Press*, and three others, Yoanis Caridad Varona González, Leonardo Varona González and Roberto Rodríguez Rodríguez. All four defendants were convicted of "disrespect". Three received prison sentences ranging from 16 to 31 months, and Yoanis Varona was sentenced to 18 months' restricted freedom.

Releases

There were some releases of prisoners of conscience. In March Reinaldo Alfaro García, vice-president of the unofficial *Asociación de Lucha Frente a la Injusticia*, Association for Struggle against Injustice, was released on condition that he left the country. Reinaldo Alfaro, who reportedly remained in Cuba, had completed more than half his three-year sentence for "spreading false news".

All the remaining imprisoned members of the unofficial *Partido Pro Derechos Humanos en Cuba*, Party for Human Rights in Cuba, in Santa Clara, who had been detained in October 1997, were released. They were Daula Carpio Mata, José Antonio Alvarado Almeida, Iván Lema Romero, José Manuel Llera Benítez, Lilian Meneses Martínez and Ileana Peñalver Duque.

Lorenzo Páez Nuñez, president of the unofficial *Centro No Gubernamental para los Derechos Humanos "José de la Luz y Caballero"*, "José de la Luz y Caballero" Non-Governmental Centre for Human Rights, and correspondent for the independent press agency *Libertad* (Freedom) was released in January. He had served an 18-month sentence imposed for "disrespect" and "defamation".

Short-term detentions and harassment

Freedom of expression, association and assembly continued to be severely limited in law and in practice. Those who attempted to organize meetings, express views or form organizations that conflicted with government policy were subjected to punitive measures and harassment. These included short-term detention, interrogation, threats, intimidation, eviction, loss of employment, restrictions on travel, house searches, house arrests, phone bugging and physical and verbal acts of aggression carried out by government supporters.

Short-term detention

Short-term detentions were frequent, and there were several incidents of mass detentions. For example, on 14 January about a dozen people were reportedly detained, allegedly to stop them from participating in a march to commemorate the anniversary of the birth of US civil rights activist Martin Luther King.

Between 22 and 27 January at least a dozen dissidents were detained after members of the *Fundación Lawton de Derechos Humanos,* Lawton Human Rights Foundation, reportedly held a public meeting calling on people to join their peaceful struggle. A pilgrimage was also due to take place on 25 January, to mark the anniversary of a mass that took place on Pope John Paul II's last day in Cuba in 1998, and on 28 January a peaceful human rights demonstration was due to take place in celebration of the birth of Cuban national hero José Martí. All detainees were subsequently released.

In August some two dozen dissidents were temporarily detained to prevent them attending two anti-government protests, one of which was called by the ecological group *Naturpaz* and was to take place in Lenin Park, Havana. The other was to take place in Pedro Betancourt, Matanzas province. One of the detainees, Oscar Elías Biscet González, claimed that he was threatened with imprisonment if he did not leave the country.

In September, seven opposition activists were arrested in Butari Park, Havana, where they were holding an informal class on civil disobedience. The detainees were all taken to a police station and then to the *Departamento Técnico de Investigaciones* (DTI), Technical Investigations Department, in Havana. Five of the detainees were released shortly afterwards, but Marcel Valenzuela Salt and Marlon Cabrera remained in detention for two weeks. Marcel Valenzuela was reportedly hit in the face by a plainclothes policeman when he was arrested.

In October at least a dozen people were detained after congregating at the house of Maritza Lugo Fernández for a meeting called by the *Foro Tercer*

Milenio, the Third Millennium Forum, a group of non-governmental organizations who had written to Ibero-American presidents calling for human rights and democracy in Cuba.

In November and December some 260 dissidents were detained around the time of the Ibero-American Summit in Havana. Many more were placed under house arrest. At the end of 1999, 11 of these people remained in detention, including Oscar Elías Biscet González, president of the *Fundación Lawton de Derechos Humanos,* who was detained on 3 November and charged with "insult to the symbols of the homeland". No date had been set for a trial. He was considered to be a prisoner of conscience.

Eviction

Eviction was another method of repression used by the authorities to suppress dissidence.

🗀 In August, as well as being temporarily detained, opposition activist Ramón Humberto Colás Castillo, was evicted from his home in Las Tunas province, along with his wife, Berta Mexidor Vázquez, and their two children. Ramón Colás and Berta Mexidor, who were both founders of the first independent library in Cuba, had lived in their home for 13 years before being told they were illegal occupants. Other independent librarians were also subjected to threats, short-term detentions and the confiscation of their books.

Restrictions on movement

Some people had restrictions imposed on their movement by the authorities.

🗀 The Reverend Santos Osmani Domínguez Borja was sent to Holguín province, more than 700 kilometres from his home. He and the Reverend Lázaro William Urbina Dupont had both been temporarily detained after formally requesting permission from the government to hold an act of public worship.

Threats

Many people were threatened with imprisonment in order to intimidate them.

🗀 In August Venancio Roberto Rodríguez Martínez of the *Hermanos Fraternales por la Dignidad,* Fraternal Brothers for Dignity, was threatened with imprisonment for being a counter-revolutionary.

Many dissidents were threatened with being tried under the new Law 88. They included Lázaro Estanislao Ramos González of the *Movimiento Cívico Máximo Gómez,* Máximo *Gómez* Civic Movement, Raúl Rivero and Hirán González González, both independent journalists of *Cuba Press,* and Oswaldo Paya Sardiñas of the *Movimiento Cristiano Liberación,* Christian Liberation Movement. Several people who took part in a 40-day fast starting in June were also threatened.

🗀 Leonel Morejón Almagro of *Naturpaz* left the country in October because of the continual harassment and threats to which he was subjected.

Summonses

There were numerous cases of people suspected of anti-government activities being summoned for questioning before local authorities. During interrogation, which sometimes lasted a few hours, many were threatened with imprisonment.

Loss of employment

Several government opponents and their relatives were dismissed from their jobs, reportedly for political reasons.

🗀 Former prisoner of conscience Eduardo Blanco Tolosa was dismissed from his job and then threatened with being returned to prison and charged with "dangerousness" if he did not find new employment.

Death penalty

There was an increase in the use of the death penalty, particularly after the introduction in March of new legislation imposing the death penalty for serious cases of drug trafficking, corruption of minors and armed robbery. At least 13 people were executed and at least nine people reportedly remained on death row.

Ill-treatment

There were several reports of political prisoners being beaten by prison guards and a few reports of beatings of non-prisoners.

🗀 On 14 August human rights activist Oscar Elías Biscet González was arrested in a park where he was to give a talk on civic resistance. On arrest, he was reportedly beaten about the face and neck and his elbow was burned with a cigarette by policemen. He was then reportedly put in a cell, forced to strip naked, beaten and kicked. He was subsequently transferred to the DTI in Havana, where he claimed he was interrogated and threatened with imprisonment if he organized any other dissident activity. He was released on 16 August.

Prison conditions

Prison conditions continued to be poor and in some cases, especially in punishment cells, constituted cruel, inhuman or degrading treatment. Punitive measures reportedly included the withholding of food or medical attention, detention for months at a time in cells with no light or bedding, threats, discrimination, verbal abuse and beatings. Many prisoners reported being ill because of poor nutrition and poor hygiene. The effects of the US embargo on the availability of medicines and equipment contributed to the problem.

AI country reports

• Cuba: Some releases but repression and imprisonment continue (AI Index: AMR 25/005/99)
• Cuba: Prisoners of conscience – Manuel Antonio González Castellanos, Leonardo Varona González and Roberto Rodríguez Rodríguez (AI Index: AMR 25/027/99)
• Cuba: A worrying increase in the use of the death penalty (AI Index: AMR 25/029/99)
• Cuba: Current prisoners of conscience must be released (AI Index: AMR 25/036/99)

CZECH REPUBLIC

CZECH REPUBLIC
Head of state: Václav Havel
Head of government: Miloš Zeman
Capital: Prague
Population: 8.9 million
Official language: Czech
Death penalty: abolitionist for all crimes
1999 treaty ratifications/signatures: Rome Statute of
the International Criminal Court

Roma continued to be vulnerable to racist attacks
and did not receive adequate protection from the
authorities. There were reports of ill-treatment by
police officers.

Background

The issue of discrimination against Roma and their
segregation within Czech society attracted
international attention when in October the town
council of Ústí nad Labem constructed a wall to fence
off Romani tenants from other residents who objected
to them. Following international condemnation and a
late response by the central authorities, who had failed
to respond to the call in March by the UN Committee on
the Elimination of Racial Discrimination for preventive
action, the wall was demolished on 24 November, after
the central authorities paid a grant to the town council.
Large numbers of Czech Roma continued to seek asylum
in Western Europe and Canada.

Attacks on Roma

Reports of attacks and harassment of Roma,
particularly by "skinhead" gangs, continued. Police
officers reportedly often failed to intervene to protect
Roma or to investigate allegations of such violence
seriously. The perpetrators of assaults resulting in
serious injury or death were often only convicted of
lesser or peripheral offences by the courts.
◻ On 27 August, the landlord of some farmhouses in
the village of Dvorek u Ohrazovic, southern Moravia,
reportedly attacked his Romani tenants with the support
of a gang of about 30 "skinheads" wielding guns, bricks,
stones and tear gas. The police initially characterized the
raid as an attack on property, not on people, and failed
to protect the Roma against the threat of further attacks.

In November the authorities appeared to demonstrate
greater resolution in addressing the issue. The Minister
of the Interior considered outlawing some extremist
organizations, and an investigation was initiated into 24
people involved in an attack by a "skinhead" gang
wielding metal bars, stones and handguns on a Romani
gathering in a restaurant in /eské Budějovice.

Ill-treatment by police officers

Some police officers appeared to target young people
who were followers of alternative lifestyle movements,
or who questioned police actions.

In May the Ministry of Justice stated to AI that no
police officers were indicted for alleged ill-treatment of
demonstrators in Prague at the May 1998 "Global Street
Party". However, the Government Commissioner for
Human Rights acknowledged to AI that the police used
force arbitrarily and made arbitrary arrests. He noted
that the report of the Ministry of the Interior's
investigation concluded that several demonstrators
had indeed been brutally beaten by police officers, but
the culpable officers could not be identified or
prosecuted. In the Commissioner's Report on the State
of Human Rights in the Czech Republic, published in
May, he criticized the system for investigating alleged
police abuses, and proposed that it be made
independent of the Ministry of the Interior.
◻ Stanislav Penc, a member of the Czech Human
Rights Committee, was reportedly dragged by his hair,
beaten and briefly detained by police officers on 27
January, after he queried the reasons why police
officers who were wearing black uniforms, balaclavas,
and reportedly no official identification, demanded his
identity document when they raided a Prague
restaurant where he was dining with friends.

AI country report

- Czech Republic: Reported ill-treatment of Stanislav
  Penc by police officers in Prague (AI Index: EUR
  71/002/99)

DJIBOUTI

REPUBLIC OF DJIBOUTI
Head of state: Ismail Omar Guelleh (replaced Hassan Gouled Aptidon in May)
Head of government: Barkat Gourad Hamadou
Capital: Djibouti
Population: 0.6 million
Official languages: French, Arabic
Death penalty: abolitionist for all crimes

There was little change in the human rights situation. Some human rights abuses reported were linked to continued fighting between government forces and the armed wing of the *Front pour la restauration de l'unité et de la démocratie* (FRUD), Front for the Restoration of Unity and Democracy; there were reports that civilians were killed in areas affected by the conflict. Other reported abuses included the repression of peaceful opposition activists and torture of suspected criminals and refugees.

Background
The war between Ethiopia and Eritrea led to Djibouti becoming Ethiopia's port outlet and closer ties developing between Ethiopia and Djibouti.

Presidential elections
Former security director Ismail Omar Guelleh was elected president in April with three quarters of the vote, and inaugurated in May. He replaced his uncle, President Hassan Gouled Aptidon, in power since independence in 1977. Some 200 opposition members were briefly detained at an election rally in February, five opposition leaders imprisoned for six months in 1996 for criticizing the president were barred from standing for election, and a clan chief was arrested immediately after the elections for calling on people to vote against the government; he was still held at the end of the year.

Armed conflict
There was intermittent fighting between government forces and the FRUD armed group. More than 20 people including civilians were killed by landmines, although both sides denied responsibility for them. There were allegations of killings of civilians by government forces.

Prisoners of conscience and unfair trials
People continued to be imprisoned after unfair trials for peacefully exercising their right to freedom of expression. Those targeted included a human rights defender and journalists.
Aref Mohamed Aref, a human rights defender and prisoner of conscience, was convicted of embezzlement in February after an unfair trial and given a six-month prison term, a further 18-month suspended sentence, and a fine. He lost his appeal after a brief and unfair court hearing but was granted an amnesty by the new President in May, along with more than 40 convicted criminals. In November he was questioned by police on a charge of defamation in relation to a television interview with a French reporter who was subsequently deported. At the end of the year he remained barred from legal practice and his passport had not been returned to him.
Three journalists were arrested in September and October over articles claiming a military helicopter crash was the result of a FRUD attack, which the government denied. Daher Ahmed Farah, leader of the *Parti du renouveau démocratique,* Party of Democratic Renewal, and editor of the party's newspaper, *Le Renouveau,* was convicted of spreading false news likely to demoralize the army and sentenced to eight months' imprisonment, reduced on appeal to six months, and a fine. The paper was banned. Ali Meidal Wais, a retired general and editor of *Le Temps,* the party publication of the *Opposition djiboutienne unifiée* (ODU), Unified Djiboutian Opposition, received the same sentence. Moussa Ahmed Idriss, a member of parliament who left the ruling party and stood as opposition candidate for the ODU, was arrested for the same offence in October. During his arrest police killed one person, wounded others and beat several people. Moussa Ahmed Idriss was jailed for four months, together with 19 of his relatives, for violently resisting arrest. In October the Inter-Parliamentary Union criticized his arrest and trial. Daher Ahmed Farah, Ali Meidal Wais and Moussa Ahmed Idriss were freed by presidential pardon in December.

Prison conditions
Forty-three people suspected of membership of FRUD who were detained in Gabode prison in the capital went on hunger strike between February and May in protest at denial of access to doctors and at the death of two co-detainees. They had been detained since they were deported from Ethiopia in 1997; none had been tried by the end of the year. In March the government allowed access to the prisoners to the International Committee of the Red Cross (ICRC) and to an international medical team in May.

Refugees
Djibouti continued to host tens of thousands of refugees from Ethiopia and Somalia. In several round-ups of alleged illegal aliens in the capital, hundreds of Ethiopians were arrested and tortured and ill-treated. Women were reportedly raped in police custody.
Ibrahim Mohamed Osman, chair of the Ethiopian Oromo refugee community, was arrested in May for alleged links with the Oromo Liberation Front (OLF), which was fighting the Ethiopian government. He remained detained without charge or trial throughout the year.

DOMINICAN REPUBLIC

DOMINICAN REPUBLIC
Head of state and government: Leonel Fernández Reyna
Capital: Santo Domingo
Population: 7.5 million
Official language: Spanish
Death penalty: abolitionist for all crimes

Despite progress with some judicial and penal reforms and several measures aimed at improving respect for human rights, serious violations continued. At least 200 people were reportedly killed by police in 1999, many in disputed circumstances; several police officers were charged in connection with killings. Dozens of people were reportedly shot, some fatally, during demonstrations against the deterioration of public services, electricity shortages or rising costs. There were some reports of ill-treatment of demonstrators, criminal suspects and detainees.

Police killings and excessive use of force
According to reports, at least 200 people were killed by the National Police in 1999. Police claimed that many of these deaths occurred during exchanges of gunfire, but this was disputed in many cases by witnesses. Several police officers were charged after evidence emerged indicating that they had carried out extrajudicial executions or used excessive or disproportionate force. The Inter-American Commission on Human Rights expressed concern about this issue in its October report on the Dominican Republic.

☐ Police claims that three suspects had been killed during an exchange of gunfire in Cayetano Germosén, Espaillat province, in July were publicly disproved when television stations broadcast footage of the three handcuffed men being loaded into a police vehicle. Later, officers reportedly admitted summarily executing the three in revenge for the death of a colleague believed to have been killed by the same men. In the subsequent public outcry, President Leonel Fernández Reyna declared that such violations would not be tolerated. A judicial enquiry was opened, but no result had been made public by the end of the year.

☐ After calls for prosecution from the Attorney General, the District Attorney for the capital province and the head of the Commission in Support of Judicial Reform, a police officer accused of killing Gersón Elías Núñez Arias in September appeared before civilian judicial authorities for questioning. The victim had allegedly been shot in the back while trying to break up a fight.

The Attorney General and the Chief of Police signed an agreement on coordination between public prosecutors and the police. An internal investigative unit reviewed alleged police misconduct, and some cases were brought before military or civilian tribunals. However, results of investigations and any subsequent sanctions against officers were not always announced publicly. In October police officials stated that the police force was conducting a purge of its members; it was not known how many of the 400 reported dismissals were connected with human rights violations. Discussions continued about the creation of the post of human rights ombudsman.

Justice and detention
At the end of December the authorities stated that 14,657 people were detained, of whom 73 per cent were in pre-trial detention. Overcrowding reportedly contributed to poor conditions and tension within prisons. Prosecutorial and prison authorities took steps to improve judicial review and to alleviate overcrowding.

During 1999 the General Prison Supervisor investigated several cases of ill-treatment of detainees. The Attorney General and prison authorities published a Manual on Inmate Discipline, aimed at clarifying acceptable procedures.

☐ In December, the Chief of Police announced the arrest of a colonel accused of torturing and ill-treating detainees in his custody; the police investigative unit was said to be reviewing the case against him.

Haitians
There were reports of ill-treatment of Haitians. The Haitian National Migration Office reported that 6,000 people were expelled to Haiti in November in an operation which violated international standards. The Dominican authorities reportedly rounded up suspected Haitians and expelled them *en masse*, sometimes separating children from their parents. In December the two countries signed an agreement to improve treatment during deportation.

Updates
In November a former Dominican air force sergeant was extradited from the USA to face charges in the case of journalist Orlando Martínez Howley, who was allegedly extrajudicially executed in 1975 after printing criticism of the then President, Joaquín Balaguer.

In April a police and military commission set up by President Fernández to investigate the "disappearance" in 1994 of Narciso González reportedly stated that it had been unable to reach a conclusion owing to lack of evidence. Narciso González, a journalist and university lecturer critical of former President Balaguer, "disappeared" after reportedly being arrested by members of the army. A judicial investigation into the case remained active.

In March the Dominican Republic accepted the jurisdiction of the Inter-American Court of Human Rights.

AI country visit
AI delegates visited the Dominican Republic in October.

ECUADOR

REPUBLIC OF ECUADOR
Head of state and government: Jamil Mahuad Witt
Capital: Quito
Population: 11.9 million
Official language: Spanish
Death penalty: abolitionist for all crimes
1999 treaty ratifications/signatures: Inter-American Convention to Prevent and Punish Torture

A state of emergency was imposed and in Guayas province remained in force for much of the year. During the state of emergency, hundreds of people were detained by the police and armed forces for not carrying their identity documents. There were reports of torture and ill-treatment and a number of people were reported to have been killed by the security forces in circumstances which suggested they were extrajudicially executed.

Background
Ecuador experienced an acute social, economic and political crisis in 1999. In March President Jamil Mahuad Witt announced a series of measures to improve the economic situation which led to economic paralysis and widespread protests. In July various sectors of civil society called for a national strike. In response the authorities decreed a national state of emergency which lasted nine days and was lifted after the government reached an agreement with unions which included reducing the price of petrol and other goods.

A state of emergency was declared in January in Guayas province as part of an attempt to control what the government called "a crime wave which puts at risk the life and property of the citizens"; it remained in force for most of the year.

In November the judicial system was brought to a halt when employees of the judiciary called a strike in protest at budgetary cutbacks. Prison employees also went on strike in November demanding higher wages.

Delays in bringing criminal suspects to trial continued. By the end of 1999 more than 500 people detained awaiting trial were released under provisions of the Constitution which allow judges to order the immediate release of all those detained for more than a year who have not been convicted, without prejudice to criminal proceedings against them.

Prison conditions remained harsh. Severe overcrowding and the lack of basic services in many facilities amounted to cruel, inhuman or degrading treatment. Scores of prisoners were killed as a result of violence by fellow inmates.

Violations under the state of emergency
During the state of emergency in Guayas province, hundreds of people were detained by the police and armed forces for not carrying their identity documents.

Most were released after 48 hours on production of their identity documents and the payment of a fine. However, reports indicated that some were held without charge for longer if they were unable to produce their identity papers.

There were reports of torture and ill-treatment and a number of people were reported to have been killed by the security forces in circumstances which suggested they were extrajudicially executed.

▭ Victor Javier Icaza Olmedo was detained on 2 February outside his home in the city of Guayaquil by Navy and National Police officers on suspicion of having carried out a robbery three years earlier. The arrest was carried out without a judicial order. He was kicked and beaten with rifle butts while being taken to the San Eduardo Naval Base, and at the naval base he was struck in the chest and testicles. Two days later a judge ordered his release after the charges against him were dropped. He was released the following day without receiving medical attention.

▭ On 11 January Michael Zambrano Giler was reportedly shot dead by police in a suburb of Guayaquil. He was standing on a street corner with his brother and a group of friends when the police approached in a patrol car and asked them for their identity documents. Michael Zambrano's brother was detained because he could not produce his identity papers. When Michael Zambrano approached the patrol car to speak for his brother, the police apparently hit him in the face and then shot him in the back when he turned away.

Political killings, intimidation and harassment
Opposition and trade union activitsts and human rights defenders were harassed and intimidated; at least three were the victims of political killings.

▭ Three men — Jaime Hurtado Gonzalez and Pablo Vicente Tapia, members of parliament for the opposition Democratic Popular Movement, and Wellington Nazareno Borja, an assistant to Jaime Hurtado Gonzalez — were shot dead on 17 February near the National Congress in Quito. In the days prior to the killings, reports had circulated of a "death list" containing the names of 11 public figures who were apparently among a group of foreign nationals invited to a ceremony marking the opening of a "peace dialogue" in Colombia in January; Jaime Hurtado Gonzalez' name was believed to be on the list. The Ecuadorian government established an independent special commission to investigate the killings. However, the commission faced serious obstacles in conducting its work. For example, it was repeatedly denied access to the three people detained by police on suspicion of involvement in the killings. In November the Supreme Court of Justice ruled that the case should be heard before a civil court and not before a police tribunal, as had been demanded by the President of the Police Justice Court. Hearings had not started by the end of 1999.

▭ Human rights defender Alexis Ponce, whose name was also believed to be on the "death list", received threatening telephone calls the day after the assassination of Jaime Hurtado. He left Quito, but returned briefly in March to meet a National Police officer who reportedly informed him that those on the "death list" were being targeted by Colombian paramilitaries. However Alexis Ponce told the officer that it was possible that those involved in the killings were Ecuadorians rather than Colombians. For several days after this meeting, friends looking after Alexis Ponce's house received anonymous telephone threats and on 12 March his house was broken into.

Police brutality

There was continuing concern about deaths resulting from the use of firearms by the security forces in the context of anti-crime operations in circumstances suggesting the victims may have been extrajudicially executed.

◻ In February Pedro Baque and brothers Carlos and Pedro Jaramillo Mera were stopped by police officers in El Guabito, Portoviejo, Manabi province. Pedro Jaramillo was shot in the face and died instantly. Pedro Baque and Carlos Jaramillo were blindfolded and taken to an area of wasteland where Carlos Jaramillo was forced to confess to having killed a policeman a few days earlier. He was shot in the arm and mouth and his throat was slit. Pedro Baque was left for dead after being shot in the head. However, he survived and was put under military protection in case of retaliation from the police officers. Five policemen were charged with his attempted murder. However, the trial had to be abandoned as Pedro Baque refused to testify before a court in fear of his life.

AI country statement

• Ecuador: State of emergency cannot justify human rights abuses (AI Index: AMR 28/012/99)

EGYPT

ARAB REPUBLIC OF EGYPT
Head of state: Muhammad Hosni Mubarak
Head of government: 'Atif Muhammad 'Ubayd (replaced Kamal Ahmed El-Ganzouri in October)
Capital: Cairo
Population: 62.1 million
Official language: Arabic
Death penalty: retentionist
1999 treaty ratifications/signatures: African Charter on the Rights and Welfare of the Child

Fourteen prisoners of conscience were sentenced to prison terms and five prisoners of conscience sentenced in previous years remained held. While hundreds of suspected supporters of banned Islamist groups were released, thousands of others, including possible prisoners of conscience, remained held without charge or trial, sometimes for years. Others served sentences after grossly unfair trials before military courts. Torture and ill-treatment of detainees continued to be systematic. Prison conditions amounted to cruel, inhuman or degrading treatment. At least 108 people were sentenced to death and at least 16 people were executed.

Background

President Hosni Mubarak, the sole candidate in a presidential referendum held in September, was confirmed for his fourth six-year term in office. In October he appointed a new Prime Minister, 'Atif Muhammad 'Ubayd, who formed a new government. A state of emergency declared in 1981 remained in force.

At the end of December tensions in a village in Upper Egypt led to the worst outbreak of sectarian violence in years. More than 20 people, almost all of them Christians, were killed.

Freedom of expression and association

Civil society institutions, such as political parties, non-governmental organizations (NGOs), professional associations and trade unions, and the news media, continued to face legal restrictions and government control.

In May a new law regulating NGOs came into force, which imposed a wide range of restrictive conditions, including a requirement that NGOs seek prior approval from the authorities for various activities at the international and local level. Breaches of the law carry prison sentences of up to one year.

Scores of prisoners of conscience — including leaders of professional associations, NGO activists and political activists — were detained on charges relating to their non-violent activities.
Human rights defenders
The Egyptian Organization for Human Rights (EOHR) continued to face official investigations into its publications and funding, following a report it issued

on human rights violations in a village in Upper Egypt. The investigations focused on Hafez Abu Sa'ada, General Secretary of the EOHR, who remained on bail following his release from several days' detention in December 1998.

In October Fathi al-Masri, board member of the Centre for Trade Union and Workers' Services, was arrested in the town of al-Mahalla al-Kubra. He was accused of "disturbing public order", because he had distributed leaflets criticizing medical services at a state-owned company. He was released after four weeks, but he and another staff member of the NGO were still under investigation.

Prisoners of conscience
In October, 20 doctors, lawyers and other professionals, most of whom held leading positions in professional bodies, were arrested for alleged membership of the banned Muslim Brothers. In December their trial began before the Supreme Military Court. The defendants included former prisoner of conscience Muhammad Sa'd 'Aliywa al-Sayid Taha, a board member of the Giza branch of the doctors' association, who was sentenced to three years' imprisonment in 1995 by the same court. More than 160 other alleged members of the Muslim Brothers, all possible prisoners of conscience, were held for weeks or months in so-called "preventive detention" before being released. Dozens of them were held for nearly six months, the maximum period after which, according to the Criminal Procedure Code, a decision has to be taken on whether to go to trial.

▭ Five prisoners of conscience, each serving a five-year prison term, remained in Mazra 't Tora Prison at the end of 1999. They were among 54 prisoners of conscience tried and sentenced for membership of the Muslim Brothers in 1995.

▭ In December 1998, 20 people accused of spreading "extremist ideas" regarding a religion were detained for advocating modifying Islamic rules. In July 1999 a State Security Court in al-'Atarein sentenced the leader of the group, Muhammad Ibrahim Mahfouz, and 13 of his followers to prison terms ranging from one to five years.

Detention under emergency legislation
In April more than 1,000 political detainees were released and in December further releases were reported. Dozens of new cases of administrative detention under emergency legislation were reported, which was fewer than in previous years. However, thousands of suspected members or sympathizers of banned Islamist groups arrested in previous years, including possible prisoners of conscience, were still held as administrative detainees without charge or trial. Others were acquitted by military or (Emergency) Supreme State Security Courts but remained in detention.

▭ 'Abd al-Mun'im Gamal al-Din 'Abd al-Mun'im, a freelance journalist, remained in detention. He had been held since February 1993 despite having been acquitted by military courts in separate trials in 1993 and 1999 on charges of belonging to Islamist armed groups.

▭ Hassan al-Gharbawi Shahhata, a lawyer arrested in January 1989, remained in detention at the end of 1999 despite having been acquitted in May 1990. At least 90 lawyers arrested in previous years remained in administrative detention.

▭ A group of 29 young people from al-Kum al-Ahmar, near Cairo, including 17-year-old students, who were arrested in November 1998 and accused of membership of the al-Gama'a al-Islamiya, Islamic Group, were issued with administrative detention orders in August and September, after the prosecution dropped charges against them. They remained in detention in Damanhour Prison and al-Fayoum Prison at the end of 1999.

Prison conditions
Thousands of detainees were held in prisons where conditions amounted to cruel, inhuman or degrading treatment. Scores of Islamist activists in administrative detention were reportedly suffering from illnesses including tuberculosis, skin diseases and paralysis, which were common because of lack of hygiene and medical care, overcrowding and poor food quality. Several prisoners reportedly died as a result of diseases which received little or no treatment.

Thousands of political detainees continued to be denied the right to be visited by lawyers and family members. For several years the Ministry of the Interior has routinely extended a ban on any visits to four prisons holding political detainees. However, in December the Administrative Court at the State Council decided that 14 detainees at prisons where visits continued to be banned should be given permission to receive visitors. They were among dozens of detainees on whose behalf complaints had been filed in a bid to lift the ban.

Unfair trials
Trials of alleged members of armed Islamist groups before military or (Emergency) Supreme State Security courts continued to be grossly unfair.

▭ In April 1999 the Supreme Military Court issued its verdict in a trial of 107 people, 60 in absentia, accused of membership of the Islamist armed group al-Gihad (Holy Struggle). Nine defendants were sentenced to death in absentia, 78 received prison sentences ranging from three years to life imprisonment, and 20 were acquitted. The defendants included more than a dozen people forcibly returned to Egypt from various countries including Albania, Saudi Arabia and the United Arab Emirates. Returned defendants were interrogated over several months while held in unacknowledged incommunicado detention by the State Security Intelligence (SSI), and defence lawyers were not allowed to meet the defendants until they appeared in court in February. Several defendants alleged that they had been tortured, but no independent investigation was apparently carried out.

Torture
Torture continued to be systematic in the headquarters of the SSI in Lazoghly Square in Cairo, SSI branches elsewhere in the country and police stations. Torture of

criminal suspects in police custody continued to be widely reported. The most common methods reported were electric shocks, beatings, suspension by the wrists or ankles and various forms of psychological torture, including death threats and threats of rape or sexual abuse of the detainee or a female relative.

On 20 September, 23-year-old Sami 'Amer Hassan Ahmad was reportedly blindfolded with his hands tied behind his back and beaten with a stick, including on the soles of his feet (falaka), in a police station in the al-Muski district of Cairo. On 22 September he was released and filed a complaint, despite having been threatened by police officers.

Deaths in custody

At least seven people died in police custody in circumstances suggesting that torture and ill-treatment may have caused or contributed to their deaths.

Ahmed Muhammad Mahmoud Tamam, a 19-year-old student, was taken from his home on 19 July to 'Omraniya Police Station in Cairo reportedly following an argument with a neighbour. He told a visiting relative at the police station that police officers were beating him. On 21 July he died in a police vehicle where police officers had reportedly beaten him — including hitting his head against the metal frame of the vehicle.

UN Committee against Torture

Having examined Egypt's third periodic report, the UN Committee against Torture recommended in May 1999 "that Egypt takes effective measures to prevent torture in police and State Security Intelligence custody and that perpetrators are vigorously prosecuted". It also recommended that "effective steps... be taken to protect women [in custody] from sexual abuse... [and] that a proper registry of detainees, both police and State Security Intelligence, which is accessible to members of the public be established and maintained."

Inadequate investigation

Although hundreds of victims of torture have filed complaints with the authorities over the past decade, no prompt and impartial investigations meeting international human rights standards are known to have been conducted.

In August the General Prosecution reopened investigations into allegations of torture in the course of a murder investigation in 1998 in the predominantly Coptic Christian village of al-Kushh, Upper Egypt. The investigation was reopened after the authorities received a list containing the names of hundreds of villagers who alleged that they had been tortured and ill-treated by police officers. Initial investigations into a torture complaint filed on behalf of 14 villagers — including people who had pictures of their injuries widely publicized — were closed in December 1998 on the grounds that forensic examination did not reveal injuries inflicted under torture. The authorities failed to conduct prompt investigations into allegations by other villagers, including women and children, whose testimonies were reported by the media and human rights organizations.

In October 1998 Alexandria Criminal Court referred the investigation into the involvement of 13 police officers in torturing Muhammad Badr al-Din Isma'il in

1996 and 1997 to the Public Prosecution, but at the end of 1999 it had not yet decided how to proceed with the case.

'Disappearances'

In February 1999 the Cairo Court of Appeal ordered the Egyptian Ministry of the Interior to pay Baha al-'Emari compensation for having failed to provide the necessary protection for her husband, Mansour Kikhiya, a prominent Libyan opposition leader and human rights activist who "disappeared" in 1993 in Egypt (see Libya entry). However, on 7 April the Court of Cassation suspended the ruling.

In October the Human Rights Centre for the Assistance of Prisoners, a local human rights organization, stated that relatives had located two detainees who had "disappeared" in previous years. In both cases relatives learned that their family member was detained in a prison where visits are banned, and were able to meet them after they had been transferred to other prisons. However, several other people who reportedly "disappeared" after arrest in previous years remained unaccounted for.

Death penalty

The death penalty continued to be used extensively. Nine people were sentenced to death, all in absentia, by a military court after an unfair trial which allowed no appeal. At least 12 women and 87 men were sentenced to death by criminal courts during 1999, the majority of them on charges of murder. At least three women and 13 men were executed.

Armed groups

Isolated incidents of clashes between security forces and armed Islamist groups were reported. In March the leadership of the main armed Islamist group, al-Gama'a al-Islamiya, reiterated that it had halted its armed operations.

In September four member of an armed Islamist group were killed when security forces raided a flat in Cairo. The circumstances of the incident suggested that the four men may have been extrajudicially executed.

Dr Nasr Hamed Abu-Zeid, subject to a court ruling that he had insulted Islam through his writings, remained under threat of death from the Islamist group al-Gihad. He and his wife, Dr Ibtihal Younis, continued to live abroad fearing for their safety if they returned home.

AI country visit

In October and November AI delegates conducted a research visit to Egypt where they met victims of human rights violations, representatives of human rights organizations, other members of civil society and government officials. In meetings with officials they raised concerns about the lack of proper investigation of and efficient preventive measures against human rights violations in Egypt.

EL SALVADOR

REPUBLIC OF EL SALVADOR
Head of state and government: Francisco Flores
(replaced Armando Calderón Sol in June)
Capital: San Salvador
Population: 5.7 million
Official language: Spanish
Death penalty: abolitionist for ordinary crimes

Prominent human rights defenders were threatened and harassed. Members of the police were responsible for human rights violations, including ill-treatment of detainees, reportedly contributing to deaths in custody in some cases. The Human Rights Procurator apparently failed to fulfil his mandate. A local non-governmental organization made progress in efforts to discover the whereabouts of children who had "disappeared" during the armed conflict.

Background

There was a sense of institutional crisis throughout 1999. The National Civil Police, the Human Rights Procurator's Office and the judicial system, institutions created by the Peace Accords after the end of the armed conflict in 1992, faced serious problems. Their difficulties arose largely from the government's lack of commitment to these institutions and repeated failures in decision-making.

The Attorney General's position remained vacant for many months as the Legislative Assembly could not come to an agreement about whom to appoint. The lack of leadership adversely affected investigations and judicial procedures.

El Salvador continued to face an extremely high level of criminal activity, leading to widespread insecurity among the population, who had little trust in the police. A number of people suspected of involvement in criminal activity were killed by unidentified groups. There was concern that those responsible could be "extermination groups", performing execution-style killings, as victims were often found with their hands tied behind their back and shot in the head.

A Presidential election was held in March with an abstention rate of more than 60 per cent. The ruling *Alianza Republicana Nacionalista* (ARENA), Nationalist Republican Alliance, won and the elected President, Francisco Flores, former president of the Legislative Assembly, took office in June.

Allegations of corruption regarding the use of aid received after natural disasters, such as Hurricane Mitch, were made against the authorities and public officials.

Human rights defenders

Human rights defenders were subjected to harassment, threats and intimidation throughout 1999. People working on behalf of the poor and church human rights workers were among those targeted. A number of

human rights organizations had their premises broken into.

☐ The President of the non-governmental *Comisión de Derechos Humanos de El Salvador* (CDHES), Commission on Human Rights of El Salvador, Miguel Montenegro, was abducted in April by several heavily armed men. He was dragged out of his van on a street in San Salvador. His assailants, travelling in two vehicles with darkened windows, drove Miguel Montenegro around for about two hours and finally released him in the east of San Salvador. They insulted him and threatened him with death. The men warned him not to report the abduction, saying that they knew where he worked and lived and would take retaliatory measures against him and his family if he talked. They also claimed to have contacts within the police force. No investigation had been initiated by the end of 1999.

Sexual minorities

Members of sexual minorities and an organization working on their behalf were targets of intimidation and violence. Members of the National Civil Police were reported to have beaten, insulted and made death threats against six homosexual men. Several gay men were reportedly killed or shot at. These incidents were not apparently investigated thoroughly, and no one was prosecuted in connection with them.

☐ William Hernández, the executive director of the non-governmental organization *Asociación Salvadoreña de Desarrollo Integral para Minorías Sexuales, Entre Amigos,* Salvadoran Association for the Integral Development of Sexual Minorities, Among Friends, received death threats throughout 1999. The Association has spoken out about human rights violations against sexual minorities and the failure of the authorities to investigate such abuses. In March, August and November unidentified people called William Hernández' office and threatened to kill him. AI called on the authorities to investigate these attacks, and those against other human rights defenders, but no steps had been taken by the end of 1999 to identify and punish those responsible.

Police

Several people were victims of human rights violations by the National Civil Police. By 1999, the force had not reached the levels of professionalism outlined in the Peace Accords, even though hundreds of its members were punished for wrongdoing, some with dismissal.

The police force was reportedly responsible for the ill-treatment of people in custody, including beatings and keeping them handcuffed for extended periods of time. In a few cases such ill-treatment reportedly contributed to the death of the detainee.

Human Rights Procurator's Office

Strong criticisms of the Human Rights Procurator, Eduardo Peñate, whose office was created by the Peace Accords with the aim of "safeguarding human rights protection, promotion and education", were made by at least 20 local organizations and hundreds of individual citizens. There were indications that the Office had failed even to meet its constitutional and legal obligations. Civil society groups and individuals asked the Legislative Assembly to set up a special commission to investigate alleged irregularities, evaluate the performance of the Human Rights Procurator and consider his removal from office. Criticisms included a marked decrease in the number of reports and recommendations issued and a fall in the number of cases presented to the Procurator's Office, which was seen as indicating a lack of confidence in the Procurator. In December the Legislative Assembly formed a commission to investigate the Procurator's performance. Proceedings were to continue in 2000.

'Disappeared' children

The non-governmental *Asociación Pro-Búsqueda de Niñas y Niños Desaparecidos* (Pro-Búsqueda), Association *Pro-Búsqueda* for the Search for Disappeared Children, continued its work to find children who had "disappeared" in the course of military operations during the armed conflict. Many were separated from their parents and taken away. Some were adopted by military officials or by civilians, others were taken abroad. By the end of 1999, Pro-Búsqueda had received information about more than 500 cases and had located 92 children.

Updates
Francisco Manzanares

Four members of the *División de Investigación Criminal* (DIC), Criminal Investigation Division, were sentenced to prison terms in connection with the death of Francisco Manzanares: two of them to 15 years and two to 10 years. Francisco Manzanares, a member of the *Frente Farabundo Martí de Liberación Nacional* (FMLN), Farabundo Martí National Liberation Front, was shot dead in 1996 by eight heavily armed men. Shortly before his death he had reported to the police that unidentified men had been watching his house and asking about his activities.

Death penalty

In July the Legislative Assembly decided it would not ratify the constitutional amendment approved in 1996 extending the scope of the death penalty to kidnapping, rape and aggravated homicide.

Extrajudicial executions in 1989

In December the Inter-American Commission on Human Rights issued its decision on the case of six Jesuit priests and two women extrajudicially executed in November 1989. The Inter-American Commission concluded that El Salvador had violated Article 4 (right to life) of the American Convention on Human Rights; that it had failed in its duty to investigate and punish those responsible for the extrajudicial executions, thus maintaining impunity for the crimes; and that the 1993 Amnesty Law contravened the right to justice and the obligations to investigate and bring those responsible to justice, and to provide reparation to the victims. The Inter-American Commission recommended, among other things, that the authorities should take steps to annul the 1993 Amnesty Law.

EQUATORIAL GUINEA

REPUBLIC OF EQUATORIAL GUINEA
Head of state: Teodoro Obiang Nguema Mbasogo
Head of government: Angel Serafin Seriche Dougan
Capital: Malabo
Population: 0.4 million
Official languages: Spanish, French
Death penalty: retentionist

Harassment and intimidation of peaceful political opponents continued throughout the year, peaking at the time of legislative elections in March. Dozens of opposition party candidates were arrested or confined to their villages. The elections, which were reportedly undermined by significant levels of fraud, were won by the ruling *Partido Democrático de Guinea Ecuatorial* (PDGE), Equatorial Guinea Democratic Party. The two main opposition parties, the *Convergencia para la Democracia Social* (CPDS), Convergence for Social Democracy, and the *Unión Popular*, Popular Union, challenged the results and refused to sit in Parliament.

Background

Despite the fact that the government ended one-party rule in 1992, the authorities continued to tolerate no dissenting views. All opposition political activity was systematically repressed, and torture and ill-treatment of opposition party activists were common. Most detained political opponents were arrested for peaceful party activities, such as organizing an unauthorized meeting, criticizing the government or being members of parties which were not legally registered. Despite several requests, the authorities refused to allow the creation of local human rights organizations.

Arrests to undermine free elections

At the time of the March legislative elections there was a wave of arrests of opposition party candidates in a clear attempt to intimidate them and contradict the government's promise of free elections. Dozens of opposition party candidates and members, including women, were arrested or confined to their villages. Some were tortured or ill-treated. The arrests took place mainly in the continental part of the country.

In September Plácido Mikó, the CPDS Secretary General, was detained for one week. The security forces seized his personal computer and apparently tried to implicate him in a coup attempt. He was released without charge but was obliged to present himself every two weeks before a military court.

Three members of the not yet legalized *Fuerza Demócrata Republicana* (FDR), Republican Democratic Force, were arrested in June and tried by a military court in December in Bata. Mariano Oyono Ndong and Antonio Engonga Bibang were sentenced to three years' imprisonment and Carmelo Biko Ngua received a six-month prison sentence.

UN Commission on Human Rights

In April the UN Commission on Human Rights examined the report of the UN Special Rapporteur on Equatorial Guinea who had visited the country in December 1998. The Commission called on the government to implement the recommendations made by the Special Rapporteur, including those aiming to put an end to arbitrary arrests and torture.

Harsh prison conditions

Eighty members of the Bubi ethnic group convicted by a military court after an unfair trial in June 1998 continued to be held throughout the year in very harsh prison conditions. They were held in severely overcrowded cells in Malabo, the capital, on Bioko Island. Nine of them, whose death sentences had been commuted, continued to be held incommunicado. Digno Sepa Tobachi "Elako" died in October as a result of torture and lack of medical care and several others did not receive necessary medical treatment. Many of these prisoners appeared to be prisoners of conscience, arrested solely on account of their ethnic origin.

Impunity

In January AI published a report on human rights violations in Equatorial Guinea. The authorities denied all the information contained in the report and accused AI of supporting those who wanted to destabilize the country. There was no investigation into the allegations of human rights violations described in the report.

AI country report

- Equatorial Guinea: A country subjected to terror and harassment (AI Index: AFR 24/001/99)

ERITREA

ERITREA
Head of state and government: Issayas Afewerki
Capital: Asmara
Population: 3.6 million
Official languages: English, Arabic, Tigrinya
Death penalty: retentionist
1999 treaty ratifications/signatures: African Charter on Human and Peoples' Rights; African Charter on the Rights and Welfare of the Child

1999 was dominated by the border war with Ethiopia which broke out in May 1998. Each side accused the other of human rights abuses and breaches of the Geneva Conventions, but many allegations were difficult to substantiate or verify independently. There were huge casualties on both sides and other disastrous effects on civilians and the economy. Intensive international and regional mediation efforts to obtain a lasting cease-fire and a peace agreement were continually frustrated. Information on human rights violations in Eritrea was difficult to obtain. The government claimed that there were no political detainees and continued to deny allegations of "disappearances" of political opponents.

Background
War with Ethiopia

Heavy fighting between Ethiopia and Eritrea resumed after a three-month lull in February 1999, when Eritrean troops lost the Badme area they had earlier occupied. There was intermittent further fighting in later months on several fronts along the disputed border. More than 250,000 Eritrean troops were deployed. Most were conscripted for national service, which applied to men and women aged between 18 and 45, with no provision for conscientious objection. Tens of thousands of troops on both sides were reported to have been killed, and hundreds captured. Several civilians were killed too, mainly in air strikes which breached a 1998 moratorium, and more than 200,000 Eritreans were displaced from their homes. Eritrea refused to provide details of the prisoners of war it was holding and it denied the International Committee of the Red Cross access to them.

There were numerous unsuccessful mediation attempts by the international community. In July, both sides accepted an Organization of African Unity peace plan and cease-fire, which provided for deployment of peacekeepers and neutral demarcation of the border. However, in December Ethiopia rejected the implementation terms.

Constitutional processes

The processes set up after Eritrea's independence from Ethiopia in 1993 towards creating a constituent assembly, holding elections and creating some form of multi-party democracy were postponed indefinitely because of the war. President Issayas Afewerki's ruling

People's Front for Democracy and Justice continued to be the sole permitted party. A revised penal code was still being drafted.

Eritrean armed opposition

The government continued to face sporadic armed opposition from the Sudan-based Islamic Salvation Movement (formerly known as the Eritrean Islamic *Jihad* Movement), the Eritrean Liberation Front (ELF) and other Eritrean exile opposition groups. Allegations of arbitrary detentions and extrajudicial executions of suspected rebel supporters in the conflict areas bordering Sudan were impossible to verify.

International treaties

Eritrea continued to refuse to ratify the Geneva Conventions. In 1999 Eritrea ratified the African Charter on Human and Peoples' Rights and the African Charter on the Rights and Welfare of the Child.

Ethiopian nationals in Eritrea

More than 3,000 Ethiopians resident in Eritrea returned to Ethiopia in early 1999 through pressure of unemployment or homelessness as a consequence of the war. They did not appear to have been expelled by the government or as a result of government policy. This brought to more than 25,000 the total number of Ethiopians who returned during the war. The Ethiopian government repeatedly accused the Eritrean government of forced expulsions, detentions, torture and extrajudicial executions. In January the government admitted holding six Ethiopians for investigation into alleged espionage, but otherwise AI could not find evidence to substantiate most of Ethiopia's claims.

Detention without trial

Allegations that the authorities had arbitrarily detained government opponents or critics, some accused of links with exiled opposition groups, were difficult to substantiate. Abdulrahim Mohamed Ahmed, a pilot and former ELF activist, was reportedly detained secretly in January. A former ambassador, Ermias Debessai, was reportedly detained in early 1999 for possible trial in a special court dealing mainly with corruption cases. More than 450 people were detained during 1999 for eventual trial by this court, which holds secret trials with no right to legal defence representation or appeal, and where normal judicial procedures are shortened, in contravention of international fair trial standards.

Updates

More than 120 Eritrean officials of the former Ethiopian administration and ruling party, held since 1991 when the Eritrean People's Liberation Front took power, were still serving prison sentences of up to 15 years imposed for human rights abuses. Their trials were secret and unfair.

The government continued to deny responsibility for the "disappearance" of three officials of the Eritrean Liberation Front-Revolutionary Council abducted in Sudan in 1992, and a former Eritrean member of the Ethiopian parliament, Ali Higo.

AI country report and visit

Report

• Ethiopia and Eritrea: Human rights issues in a year of armed conflict (AI Index: AFR 04/003/99)

Visit

In January an AI delegation visited Eritrea for the first time since 1991. It met government ministers and officials, the Committee for Peace in Eritrea (a non-governmental association documenting the deportations of Eritreans from Ethiopia), and others.

ETHIOPIA

FEDERAL DEMOCRATIC REPUBLIC OF ETHIOPIA
Head of state: Negasso Gidada
Head of government: Meles Zenawi
Capital: Addis Ababa
Population: 58.8 million
Official language: Amharic
Death penalty: retentionist

The continuing war with Eritrea dominated events, with each side accusing the other of human rights abuses. Many allegations were difficult to verify independently, but Ethiopia detained and forcibly deported Eritreans in harsh conditions. The war led to huge casualties and massive internal displacement. Ethiopia also faced internal armed opposition, and many human rights violations by government forces were reported. Suspected rebel supporters were detained, tortured or sometimes extrajudicially executed. As many as 10,000 remained in detention at the end of 1999, some of whom had been held for several years without charge or trial. Critics of the government, including journalists, were arrested. Some received unfair trials. The trial for genocide of 46 former government leaders continued and trials of more than 2,000 other officials held since 1991 began.

Background
War with Eritrea

Heavy fighting on the border between Ethiopia and Eritrea resumed in February 1999 after a three-month lull. Ethiopian troops regained the Badme area occupied in May 1998 by Eritrean forces. There was intermittent fighting in later months on several fronts along the 1,000 kilometre disputed border. More than 300,000 Ethiopian troops were reportedly deployed, some of whom were alleged to have been forcibly recruited, including some aged under 18. Tens of thousands of troops on both sides were reported to have been killed and hundreds captured. Several civilians on both sides were killed, mainly in air strikes which violated a 1998 moratorium. More than 200,000 Ethiopians were displaced and living in camps in poor conditions. Ethiopia allowed the International Committee of the Red Cross (ICRC) access to Eritrean prisoners of war.

International and regional mediation efforts to obtain a lasting cease-fire and peace agreement, including UN Security Council resolutions, had not succeeded by the end of 1999. In July both sides accepted an Organization of African Unity peace plan and cease-fire, but outbreaks of fighting continued and in December Ethiopia formally rejected the terms of implementation of the peace plan.

Ethiopia repeatedly accused Eritrea of human rights violations against Ethiopians. More than 3,000 Ethiopians returned to Ethiopia from Eritrea in early 1999, bringing the number of Ethiopians who had returned since the start of the war to more than 25,000. They did not appear to have been expelled by the Eritrean government and most of Ethiopia's claims of abuses against its nationals in Eritrea were not independently substantiated.

In July the African Commission on Human and Peoples' Rights meeting in Rwanda heard submissions from both sides regarding human rights abuses during the war. It reserved judgment but appealed to both sides to observe the cease-fire and halt all propaganda activity against each other.

Other conflicts
The government continued to face armed opposition in several regions. Fighting was reported in the Oromo region by the Oromo Liberation Front (OLF), and in the Somali region by the Ogaden National Liberation Front (ONLF) and *Al-Itihad*, an Islamist group allied to the ONLF.

Ethiopian troops pursued *Al-Itihad* fighters into Somalia's Gedo region, as well as supporting Somali factions in other border regions. Ethiopia promoted peace talks among the Somali factions, and in October apparently agreed to withdraw Ethiopian troops from Somalia in exchange for Somali faction leader Hussein Aideed's agreement to disarm and expel OLF forces in Somalia. More than 300 OLF fighters captured by Ethiopian troops in Somalia in early 1999 were taken to Ethiopia and detained in Ziwai.

Elections
The government announced in August that parliamentary elections would be held in May 2000. Candidates were registered but few opposition parties participated, and most candidates were linked to the ruling Ethiopian People's Revolutionary Democratic Front (EPRDF) coalition headed by Prime Minister Meles Zenawi. Several opposition parties alleged intimidation, harassment, arrests of members and closure of offices. Exiled political groups refused to participate and armed opposition groups were excluded. The government said it would not accept foreign election observers.

Human Rights Commission and Ombudsman
A draft law to establish an official Human Rights Commission and Ombudsman was presented to parliament in mid-1999 but was not finalized during the year.

Expulsions and internment
Ethiopia continued its policy of mass expulsions of Eritreans. In January and February Ethiopia expelled more than 6,300 people of Eritrean origin in cruel, inhuman and degrading conditions and stripped them of Ethiopian citizenship. During 1999, several thousand Eritreans in Ethiopia voluntarily registered with the ICRC to return. In July, 2,350 Eritreans were rounded up and bussed to the border, and 3,000 more were expelled between October and December. They had to pay for the transport but were allowed to take little food and few possessions. Not all had volunteered to leave, and some families were deliberately split up. Some had been in prison for months.

Approximately 1,200 Eritreans detained in Bilate military camp were allowed access to the ICRC, but not family visits. In June they were transferred to Dedessa camp near Dire Dawa, where conditions were harsh. Several died of malaria and other illnesses, and ill-treatment and denial of medical treatment were alleged. Although the Ethiopian authorities reportedly said they would allow them to depart for a third country, few managed to leave. Thirty-eight university students were released in February and returned to Eritrea. Over 40 who went to Malawi in June were forcibly returned and redetained – one was shot dead by Malawian police while allegedly escaping arrest.

Political imprisonment
Hundreds of people were arrested for political reasons, most of whom were detained without charge or trial, some in secret. Some were prisoners of conscience.

Detention without trial
In January, 18 members of the opposition Gambela People's Democratic Congress, including Abula Obang, were arrested in the southwestern Gambela region. They were still held without charge at the end of 1999.

In the Omo district in the southwest, some 500 people of the Wolaita, Mali and Aree ethnic groups were detained without charge in November and December for peacefully opposing government imposition of a newly created language.

Many people were arrested on suspicion of involvement with armed opposition groups, particularly the OLF. Mosissa Duressa, an Ethiopian Red Cross official in Nekemte, was detained for two months from August and was a prisoner of conscience. Tassew Begashew, a doctor arrested in August, was still held at the end of 1999.

In May several government opponents in Sidama region were detained without charge on suspicion of links with the Sidama Liberation Movement. Hundreds of ethnic Somalis were reportedly arrested for alleged links with the ONLF. Iid Dahir Farah, president of the Somali Region Assembly, was arrested in September and was still held without charge at the end of 1999.

Political trials
Trials began of a number of long-term detainees. In April, Wondayehu Kassa and three other officials of the opposition All-Amhara People's Organization (AAPO), and 18 other people, were convicted of conspiracy to armed opposition in connection with an

attack on a prison in 1996. They were sentenced by the High Court in Addis Ababa to prison terms ranging from three to 20 years. Several defendants withdrew confessions, alleging torture, but the judges ignored the torture allegations. The AAPO officials (who were released after serving their sentences) and some other defendants appeared to be prisoners of conscience.

Professor Asrat Woldeyes, the AAPO chairperson who had been the chief defendant in the trial but had been allowed to go abroad for medical treatment in December 1998, died in the USA in May. At his funeral in Addis Ababa, police shot dead one demonstrator and beat and briefly detained several others.

In June Taye Wolde-Semayat, president of the Ethiopian Teachers' Association and a former university lecturer, was convicted in Addis Ababa with four others of armed conspiracy in 1996. He was sentenced to 15 years' imprisonment and appeared to be a prisoner of conscience. Two defendants withdrew confessions allegedly made under torture. A sixth defendant, Kebede Desta, died in detention in April, allegedly as a result of denial of medical treatment.

In October, 12 members of the Somali Region Assembly who had criticized the central government and were arrested in 1997 for alleged corruption and mismanagement, were convicted of armed conspiracy by the High Court in Dire Dawa. They were sentenced to three years' imprisonment after an unfair trial and released in October after serving their sentences.

The trial in Addis Ababa of over 60 Oromos for armed conspiracy with the OLF which began in 1997 continued *in camera*. The defendants included seven human rights defenders and two journalists. Three defendants were provisionally released in April. Several alleged that they had been tortured. At least 10 of the defendants, including Addisu Beyene, secretary general of the Oromo Relief Association, Gabissa Lamessa, an accountant for Save the Children Fund, and Tesfaye Deressa, a journalist, were prisoners of conscience.

Journalists
Government repression of the private press continued. In April, Samson Seyoum, detained in Addis Ababa since 1995, was finally brought to court, convicted under the Press Law for alleged incitement to violence and jailed for four and a half years. He was released on completion of his sentence. Aberra Wogi received a one-year sentence in December. Two other journalists were arrested in 1999 and were awaiting trial.

Torture and ill-treatment
There were continued reports of torture and ill-treatment of political prisoners. Torture took place in police stations and unofficial detention centres where prisoners "disappeared". In cases which went to trial, judges did not investigate complaints of torture. Prison conditions were generally harsh, and some political prisoners were refused adequate medical attention, leading to deaths in custody. There were reports of a secret underground cell in a military police prison in Harar holding more than 150 uncharged detainees in appalling conditions, some of whom had been detained for several years.

Dergue trials
The prosecution case against 46 members of the former military government (known as the *Dergue*) for genocide and other crimes against humanity, which started in 1994, continued. Some trials started of the 2,246 other former officials detained since 1991 and charged with similar offences. Two defendants were convicted of murder and torture and sentenced to prison terms, while two tried *in absentia* were sentenced to death in November. Eighteen former air force pilots were freed in August to join the war.

There were international demands for former President Mengistu Haile-Mariam, who visited South Africa from exile in Zimbabwe, to be tried for massive human rights violations committed during his 17-year rule. AI criticized his apparent impunity in Zimbabwe and pressed for him to be tried but, if returned to Ethiopia, without the use of the death penalty and with respect for fair trial standards.

Extrajudicial executions
Extrajudicial executions of suspected rebel supporters were reported but details were difficult to confirm.

Death penalty
No executions were reported. Several people were sentenced to death for murder in 1999, adding to scores of others sentenced to death since 1991.

Updates
Journalists
Eleven journalists were in prison at the beginning of 1999 on account of their work. Three were released on completion of their sentences.
Detainees
Up to 10,000 people detained in previous years, mostly suspected of supporting Oromo or Somali armed opposition groups, remained in detention without charge or trial but with access to the ICRC. Some were prisoners of conscience. There was no progress in the trial of 285 OLF fighters held in Ziwai since 1992. There were some releases of political detainees, mostly on a provisional basis. Several opponents forcibly returned from Somaliland and Djibouti in 1996 remained in detention.
'Disappearances'
Some people held in secret detention centres "reappeared", but there was little hope for the survival of many government opponents who "disappeared" between 1992 and 1995.

AI country report
- Ethiopia and Eritrea: Human rights issues in a year of armed conflict (AI Index: AFR 04/003/99)

FINLAND

REPUBLIC OF FINLAND
Head of state: Martti Ahtisaari
Head of government: Paavo Lipponen
Capital: Helsinki
Population: 5.1 million
Official languages: Finnish, Swedish
Death penalty: abolitionist for all crimes

Six conscientious objectors were adopted as prisoners of conscience in November. The findings of the European Committee for the Prevention of Torture and Inhuman or Degrading Treatment or Punishment (ECPT), and of the UN Committee against Torture, were made public. There were reports of an increase in racist and xenophobic attitudes, and of discrimination against the Sami people.

Conscientious objectors
Under current legislation, conscientious objectors to military service serve a period which is more than twice as long as that served by approximately 50 per cent of military recruits. AI considers this to be punitive. Under the Military Service Act 19/1998, the length of military service was shortened while alternative civilian service remained unchanged. Although the length of armed service depends on rank, type of service and length of contract, about half the military recruits serve 180 days while all conscientious objectors have to serve 395 days.

AI informed the Minister of Labour in November that it had adopted six conscientious objectors as prisoners of conscience. Most were students who had been sentenced to 197 days' imprisonment for refusing to carry out alternative civilian service.

The Finnish Minister of Labour informed AI in October that a review of the alternative civilian service system had been initiated in July. The review was to take into account human rights and to include a comparative study of systems in other countries. AI replied that it welcomed such a review but stated that until the length of alternative service was reduced, it would adopt as a prisoner of conscience any conscientious objector imprisoned for refusing alternative civilian service.

Ill-treatment
The findings of a visit in June 1998 by the ECPT were published by the Finnish government in May 1999. The Committee found that since its previous visit in 1992 there had been positive action to implement its recommendations. However, it expressed concern that under the Aliens Law people could be detained in local prisons and police stations; that long-term prisoners spent most of the day in their cells; and that prisoners at Riihimäke Central Prison were often left naked in the observation cell.

On 9 November the government responded to the ECPT's report. It stated that the latest Aliens Act of 22 April was addressing detention facilities for aliens and that a working group had been appointed to set them up. The government denied that prisoners were placed naked in the observation cell at Riihimäke Central Prison, except in cases where it was found necessary to strip prisoners, and that they were given clothes once in the cell. It also stated that it aimed to increase the planning of long-term prisoners' activities.

The UN Committee against Torture issued its conclusions and recommendations in November after considering Finland's third periodic report. The Committee recommended that Finland incorporate adequate penal provisions to make torture a punishable offence in line with the Convention against Torture and Other Cruel, Inhuman or Degrading Treatment or Punishment, and that the law governing isolation in pre-trial detention be changed. It expressed satisfaction about legal measures taken by the government to accommodate asylum-seekers in places other than prisons.

FRANCE

FRENCH REPUBLIC
Head of state: Jacques Chirac
Head of government: Lionel Jospin
Capital: Paris
Population: 58.6 million
Official language: French
Death penalty: abolitionist for all crimes

France was found guilty of torture and of excessively lengthy judicial proceedings by the European Court of Human Rights which, in a separate judgment, also found the French authorities had breached international norms on the length of preventive detention. There were allegations of ill-treatment and use of excessive force by law enforcement officers, sometimes resulting in fatal or near-fatal incidents. Prison guards were also accused of ill-treatment and prisons were criticized for cruel, inhuman and degrading treatment. Courts appeared to remain reluctant to convict police officers for crimes of violence or excessive force, or to uphold sentences that attempted to reflect the seriousness of the crime. In some cases prosecutors appeared to play an active part in perpetuating a situation of effective impunity where police officers were concerned.

Torture, ill-treatment and death in police custody

In July the European Court of Human Rights found that France had violated international norms on torture and the length of judicial proceedings in the case of Moroccan and Netherlands national Ahmed Selmouni who had been arrested by judicial police for drug offences and held in custody for three days at Bobigny (Seine-Saint-Denis) in November 1991.

The Court found that Ahmed Selmouni had clearly "endured repeated and sustained assaults over a number of days of questioning". It stated that the physical and mental violence inflicted — such as repeated punchings, kickings, beatings with a baseball bat and truncheon, hair-pulling and other humiliating treatment — "caused 'severe' pain and suffering and was particularly serious and cruel". Ahmed Selmouni also claimed he had been raped but the Court found his allegations were made too late to be proved or disproved by medical evidence.

New complaints of ill-treatment by police officers were lodged with the courts. The number of such complaints — which included claims that a woman had been hit twice in the face at a Toulouse police station, resulting in damage to and loss of teeth, and that a black post-office worker had been subjected to racially motivated harassment and beating in the course of an identity check in the Paris area — focused attention on the continuing need for independent scrutiny of police conduct. Although in January 1998 the government had announced the creation of a body to oversee police conduct, this was still not in place by the end of 1999.

In January the family of Mohamed Ali Saoud, who died after involvement in a struggle with police officers at Toulon in November 1998, joined criminal proceedings as a civil party following concern that the investigation lacked impartiality. Mohamed Ali Saoud, who suffered from a mental disability, died after a violent struggle, in which police officers hit him twice at close range with rubber bullets. Mohamed Ali Saoud then reportedly seized a police weapon while in the throes of a nervous crisis. He allegedly shot one police officer in the foot. Others were slightly injured in the struggle.

The family alleged that, after he was restrained by the feet and wrists and laid on his stomach on a nailed wooden plank, he was repeatedly beaten with truncheon blows to the head and kicks to the stomach and back. An officer then sat astride him while another placed a foot on his arm and a third held his legs. According to a pathologist's report, he had been subjected to "slow positional asphyxia" and an autopsy report stated that "the visceral lesions are compatible with direct trauma to or compression of the torso". The family was concerned that the investigation remained in the hands of the *Inspection générale de la police nationale* (IGPN), a police investigation unit, after it had produced a preliminary report favourable to the police argument of "legitimate defence" and that access to the case file was being continually obstructed. A complaint about the biased nature of the inquiry was filed with the European Court of Human Rights in November.

Police shootings

Judicial inquiries continued into a number of police shootings in disputed circumstances.

In July a police officer was placed under criminal investigation for homicide in connection with the fatal shooting of 16-year-old Abdelkader Bouziane in December 1997. The officer had originally faced a less serious manslaughter charge. In a separate but related case, a police officer reportedly admitted in February, more than a year after the event, that she had shot Mohamed Dries, who was wounded by a bullet in the thigh during the rioting at Dammarie-les-Lys (Seine-et-Marne) that followed the death of Abdelkader Bouziane. At the end of 1999 she was under investigation on a charge of committing violence with a weapon.

In December a former police officer was sentenced by the Rhône Court of Assizes to 12 years' imprisonment for the manslaughter of Fabrice Fernandez in December 1997. The officer had shot Fabrice Fernandez in the head with a pump-action shotgun while the latter was being held at a Lyon police station.

A police officer was placed under criminal investigation for "deliberate assault with a weapon" after a shot was fired from his gun while he and two colleagues were questioning Farad Boukhalfa about an alleged traffic offence at Cormeilles-en-Parisis (Val d'Oise) in September. Police sources reportedly stated that the serious head wound sustained by Farad Boukhalfa was caused by a struggle in which the latter had tried to seize the gun; after it was accidentally fired in the air he had fallen to the ground and hit his head. However, doctors at the Pitié-Salpêtrière Hospital to which Farad Boukhalfa was admitted, informed the Pontoise prosecuting authorities that they had recovered "a metallic fragment" from the head wound. This was later identified as part of a bullet fired from the officer's weapon. The officer, briefly held in custody, was released under judicial control and temporarily suspended from the police force.

Impunity

Several court verdicts highlighted the apparent reluctance of the judicial system to deliver or confirm anything but token sentences on police officers convicted of ill-treatment or using disproportionate force. In some cases prosecutors, often too passive in applying the law, appeared to play an active part in perpetuating a situation of effective impunity.

In February, more than eight years after the event, and just before the case of Ahmed Selmouni opened before the European Court of Human Rights, five officers of the Departmental Judicial Police Service (SDJP), appeared before the criminal court of Versailles (Yvelines) on charges including assault and indecent assault committed collectively and with violence and coercion against him. Finding that the evidence substantiated the claims of Ahmed Selmouni, and another civil party, Abdeljamid Madi, the court delivered "exemplary" sentences. One officer was sentenced to four years' imprisonment and was immediately imprisoned. Three other officers were sentenced to three years' imprisonment and a fifth to two years' imprisonment. All defendants appealed and angry protests and demonstrations were held by police union members. An unusually swift hearing was held before a Versailles appeal court in May and June. Setting aside the conviction for sexual assault, but upholding the gravity of the acts of violence committed, the court commented that the "complete unreliability of the documents drawn up by the investigation [carried out by the SDJP officers] is extremely serious in that the entire functioning of the criminal justice system rests on the reliance that may be placed on the reports of senior police officers and their assistants". Nevertheless, the court cut the "exemplary" four-year sentence to one of 18 months, 15 of which were suspended, allowing for the officer's immediate release; the sentences against the other officers were also reduced. All five remained in or resumed service, pending appeal before the Court of Cassation. The prosecutor had reportedly called for an amnesty should the officers be convicted.

⌷ In May the Court of Assizes in Seine-Saint-Denis acquitted a police officer charged with inflicting violence leading to the death of taxi driver Etienne Leborgne in 1996. Three days before his death, Etienne Leborgne had injured a police officer while trying to escape from a time-clock check at Roissy Airport. Three days later his taxi was stopped by a team of police officers who fired at the car, shooting Etienne Leborgne dead. A section of the Paris Appeal Court had earlier decided that there was sufficient evidence against the officer to warrant a manslaughter charge, stating that the disproportionality of the officer's action had been "incontestable". Despite the judgment's detailed explanation as to why this was so, the prosecutor requested the officer's acquittal for lack of evidence.

Prisons

In July the Minister of Justice announced the creation of a working group on the external control of the penitentiary system. The announcement came at about the same time as a report by seven non-governmental organizations which called for the establishment of an independent body to control prisons. There was concern about the trend towards longer sentences, with consequent overcrowding, and the frequent inability of custodial staff to effectively monitor and protect the safety of inmates — for instance, at the juvenile detention centres of Fleury-Mérogis (Essonne) and Saint-Paul in Lyon. There was also concern at continuing reports of ill-treatment, such as beatings, by prison guards, and allegations about the effects of isolation in prisons.

⌷ There were persistent reports that Georges Cipriani, one of the former members of the armed group *Action directe* held at Ensisheim (Haut-Rhin), had become mentally ill after spending many years in isolation. Although no longer held in isolation he had reportedly become unable to relate to others or to care for his personal hygiene. In a separate development, two other former members of the group, Joëlle Aubron and Nathalie Ménigon, were transferred in October to a prison at Bapaume (Pas-de-Calais), thus ending a 12-year period of special surveillance. In 1998 AI had written to the Minister of Justice to express concern

that they continued to be subjected to especially restrictive measures outside normal prison life and that Nathalie Ménigon, who was suffering from severe depression, had had a heart attack.

Fair trial within a reasonable time

In January, 51 defendants out of a total of 138 who had been denied a fair trial in 1998 were acquitted of the main charge of "criminal association" by the 11th criminal court of Paris. The defendants, detained during mass arrests in 1994 and 1995, were accused of belonging to support networks for Algerian armed opposition groups. Another 87 defendants in the mass trial — known as the "Chalabi" trial — were given prison sentences, a number of them suspended. A total of 22 people remained in prison following the verdict. An appeal was under way at the end of 1999.

In November the European Court of Human Rights found that France had violated international norms on trial within a reasonable time in the case of one of the defendants, Ismael Debboub (also known as Ali Husseini). The Court found that Ismael Debboub, arrested in 1994 and released in 1999, had been questioned by an investigating judge only seven times during the entire period of preventive detention, and castigated the French courts for their lack of diligence.

Expulsions to Spain

Several Spanish Basques imprisoned in France were handed over to the Spanish police after completing prison sentences in France. There was concern that, in the absence of extradition requests, the practice of rearresting Spanish nationals after they were released from prison and delivering them to the Spanish police at the frontier, was becoming almost systematic. Some of those returned in this way were held in detention awaiting trial before the National Court in Madrid for several years, with administrative courts in France belatedly reversing decisions to expel them to Spain.

⌷ Mikel Zarrabe Elkoroiribe, who was not the subject of an extradition request, was expelled to Spain in December 1995 after serving an eight-year prison sentence in France. He was held incommunicado for four days by Spanish police and was then placed in preventive detention for four years before being brought before the National Court in October 1999. Earlier, in May, while upholding the decision to expel Mikel Zarrabe, a French administrative court found that the decision to expel him to Spain was unjustified and the decision was annulled, but too late to take effect.

⌷ In November the UN Committee against Torture decided that the expulsion of Josu Arkauz Arana, a Basque prisoner who had been handed over to the Spanish police at the border in January 1997 without being able to contact his family or lawyer or to appeal to a court, violated Article 3 of the UN Convention against Torture and Other Cruel, Inhuman or Degrading Treatment or Punishment.

AI country report

- Concerns in Europe, January – June 1999: France (AI Index: EUR 01/002/99)

GAMBIA

REPUBLIC OF THE GAMBIA
Head of state and government: Yahya Jammeh
Capital: Banjul
Population: 1.2 million
Official language: English
Death penalty: abolitionist in practice

Freedom of expression and association continued to be restricted. Journalists were harassed, detained briefly and threatened with a new law that would restrict their activities even further. Members of opposition parties also faced harassment and arrest. There were reports of severe ill-treatment of prisoners.

Background
After the Armed Forces Provisional Ruling Council (AFPRC) seized power in a military coup in 1994, AI criticized the suspension of the previous constitution, as well as the new constitution that reintroduced the death penalty and allowed for impunity and derogations of human rights. The former chair of the AFPRC, Colonel Yahya Jammeh, retired from the military and was elected president in controversial elections in September 1996.

Decrees were passed banning politicians in the former government from political activity and granting total immunity from prosecution to those who held power from the military coup in 1994 until the return to civilian rule. These decrees remained in force at the end of 1999.

In the years following the 1994 coup, the Gambian government's international isolation was gradually overcome. Several governments and intergovernmental organizations resumed bilateral aid, although the country's human rights record did not improve.

In February 1999, Gambia sent 120 soldiers to Guinea-Bissau to join a West African peace-keeping force there. The peace-keeping force left Guinea-Bissau in June following a change of government in May.

Press freedom restricted
Police and the security forces continued to intimidate journalists with arbitrary detentions and threats of violence.

The government proposed legislation to create a National Media Commission with judicial powers to fine and jail journalists for six months or more if they refused to be a witness, or if they interrupted, insulted or otherwise disobeyed the Commission. The Commission could also seize a reporter's information or goods in connection with its inquiries. No appeal against the Commission's decision would be allowed. Under the proposed law, no media organization or journalist could work unless licensed by the Commission. AI believed that all these restrictions

unduly limited freedom of expression. The National Assembly still had not debated the proposed law by the end of 1999.

Until March 1999, immigration officers had conducted open surveillance of the largest selling independent daily newspaper, *The Daily Observer*. For almost a year, the identity papers of those entering the newspaper's premises had been checked, in a policy of intimidation aimed at non-Gambian journalists working there. Many foreign journalists were expelled in previous years. A new proprietor, reportedly close to the government, bought the newspaper in May and immediately dismissed the deputy managing director, Theophilus George, and the news editor, Demba Jawo, who is also president of the Gambia Press Union. The dismissals were alleged to be connected to past publication of articles critical of government policy.

The radio station *Citizen fm* remained closed throughout 1999. The government had ordered it to cease operations in February 1998, apparently because of its broadcasts about the government's National Intelligence Agency, which has been connected with serious and persistent human rights violations. The authorities called the broadcasts "irresponsible journalism" and refused to renew the radio station's licence. An appeal was still pending before the High Court at the end of 1999. The government appeared to delay the case, so prolonging the radio station's closure: government lawyers failed to turn up in court and a new magistrate was appointed to hear the case.

🖾 In July, less than three weeks after it opened, the government ordered *The Independent* newspaper to close, citing deficiencies in registration, although its papers were in fact in order. The closure appeared to be linked to an editorial condemning alleged human rights violations since the 1994 military coup. The newspaper reopened after about one week. In July and August agents of the National Intelligence Agency briefly detained three staff members of the newspaper: the editor-in-chief, Baba Galleh Jallow; the managing editor, Yorro Alagi Jallow; and a reporter, N.B. Daffeh. At the end of December, the police Serious Crimes Unit arrested the three men and another reporter, Jalali Walli, on charges of libelling President Jammeh, in connection with an article speculating that President Jammeh had married for a third time.

🖾 In September, the editor-in-chief of *The Daily Observer*, Sheriff Bojang, and a senior reporter, Alieu Badara Sow, were briefly detained and interrogated by National Intelligence Agency officers. They had published reports that a Senegalese helicopter had circled the birthplace of President Jammeh, exchanging gunfire with the presidential guard.

The Brikama Mosque trial
In February the four remaining defendants charged in June 1998 with conspiracy to commit riot and damage to a building in the town of Brikama were acquitted. Originally, the National Intelligence Agency arrested and held incommunicado 10 prisoners of conscience — including members of the United Democratic Party (UDP) and the Imam of Brikama, Alhaji Karamo Touray.

The arrests were in connection with alleged attempts to destroy a wall being erected around the mosque, reportedly by a pro-government youth group trying to prevent the Imam from speaking about political issues. At least one of the detainees was allegedly tortured in custody. After almost nine months of trial, the presiding magistrate discharged the defendants. The state filed an appeal against the judgment.

Opposition parties
Restrictions on opposition political activity continued, despite the 1997 lifting of the ban on multi-party politics. Under a presidential decree, all individuals who had held the office of President, Vice-President or government minister prior to the military coup were prohibited from engaging in political activities. In October President Jammeh dissolved the July 22 Movement, an unofficial organization supporting the ruling Alliance for Patriotic Reorientation and Construction party, and its youth wing, the National Youth Action Group. Members of the July 22 Movement were alleged to have harassed and intimidated opposition party members, journalists and members of the public with impunity.

▱ Opposition politician Syngle Nyassi was held for 26 days in incommunicado detention, during which he said he had been denied food and beaten. Syngle Nyassi had been held without charge, in unacknowledged detention, by the National Intelligence Agency from 25 May, despite a high court order for his release.

▱ Ousainou Darboe, leader of the UDP, accused the government in May of arresting and harassing members of his party. He alleged that three party activists had been arrested, and others held for questioning, in connection with his visit to their village.

Torture
AI received reports that inmates at State Central Prison (Mile 2) were severely beaten and ill-treated by prison officers. Conditions at the prison amounted to cruel, inhuman and degrading treatment with denial of medical attention, insufficient food and unhygienic conditions.

Women's rights
Discrimination and violence against women persisted and, in particular, the practice of female genital mutilation (FGM) remained widespread in rural areas. President Jammeh in January defended the practice of FGM and threatened the lives of those campaigning against the practice, saying: "There is no guarantee that after delivering their speeches they [those opposing FGM] will return to their homes." The President later revised his earlier statements on the issue. In September, the National Assembly ratified a policy to grant women equal access to education, health, appropriate technology and decision-making.

Death penalty
Four men were sentenced to death in June 1997 by the High Court of the Gambia on charges of treason for trying to overthrow the government in an armed attack

on Farafenni military camp in November 1996. The convictions were quashed on appeal in October 1997, but the state appealed and the men remained in custody in 1999.

Three other men were sentenced to death by the High Court in 1999 for the 1997 armed attack on Kartong military post. Two of the accused men claimed that they were tortured during police interrogations.

GEORGIA

GEORGIA
Head of state and government: Eduard Shevardnadze
Capital: Tbilisi
Population: 5.4 million
Official language: Georgian
Death penalty: abolitionist for all crimes
1999 treaty ratifications/signatures: Second Optional Protocol to the International Covenant on Civil and Political Rights, aiming at the abolition of the death penalty; International Convention on the Elimination of All Forms of Racial Discrimination; Convention relating to the Status of Refugees and its 1967 Protocol; European Convention for the Protection of Human Rights and Fundamental Freedoms and its Protocol No. 6 concerning the abolition of the death penalty

Reports of torture and ill-treatment in custody continued during 1999, including one instance in which police allegedly beat a man to death. In the disputed region of Abkhazia, ethnic Georgians continued to allege that they faced arbitrary detention, ill-treatment and robbery at the hands of Abkhazian forces. At least one death in custody in disputed circumstances was reported in Abkhazia. At least one death sentence was passed in Abkhazia, but no executions were carried out. Some 200,000 ethnic Georgians displaced by the conflict faced obstacles to their return.

Background
Georgia was accepted as a full member of the Council of Europe in April. The ruling party retained its parliamentary majority after elections in October. The disputed regions of Abkhazia and South Ossetia remained outside the control of the Georgian authorities, and there was little progress in peace talks. The situation in Abkhazia remained tense, in part due to the activities of irregular armed groups, but there was no major outbreak of hostilities.

Alleged torture and ill-treatment
There were persistent allegations of torture and ill-treatment in custody.

Six men detained after a robbery near the city of Kutaisi were reportedly ill-treated in police custody. Five were named as Temur Khaburzania, Ramaz Khantadze, Kvantaliani, Giorgadze and Lipartiani. The men were said to have been detained in two groups of three on 24 January and taken to Kutaisi regional police station. Ramaz Khantadze reported that police officers slapped him in the face, causing his nose to bleed, beat him on the chest and legs, and dictated a "confession" to him. He was released shortly after this. Another, Kvantaliani, told his lawyer that he had been brutally beaten on the legs and feet by a named police officer. The lawyer said he saw wounds on his client's legs consistent with this allegation. When a Georgian non-governmental organization (NGO) subsequently asked to see those still detained, Kvantaliani was brought to them wearing a hat, scarf and long sleeves. He refused to speak to his lawyer or the NGO representative.

Deaths in custody

At least one man was reported to have died as a result of being beaten by police.

Davit Vashaqmadze and his friend Zaza Buadze were in a stationary car in Tbilisi's Tavisupleba Square when two police officers asked for their documents on the evening of 13 November. Davit Vashaqmadze did not have his documents on him, and the officers reportedly pulled the two men out of the car and started to beat them. Several other police officers also reportedly joined in the beating. Davit Vashaqmadze and Zaza Buadze were then told that they would be taken to Mtatsminda police station, but were instead taken to a district outside the city centre where the beating continued. Davit Vashaqmadze apparently suffered multiple fractures and other serious injuries, and died in hospital two days later. Zaza Buadze was also said to have sustained serious injuries. A criminal investigation was opened by Tbilisi City Procurator's office, and two police officers were reportedly arrested and charged in connection with Davit Vashaqmadze's death.

At least two men also died after allegedly throwing themselves from upper floor windows while in police custody. Ivane Kolbaya died in March after falling from the fifth floor window of the Tbilisi Central Police Department, and Zaza Tsotsolashvili fell to his death in December from the sixth floor window of the Ministry of Internal Affairs building in Tbilisi. Police claimed both deaths were suicides.

However, the head of the Georgian forensic medical centre reportedly said that forensic medical examiners could not determine whether the trauma marks they found on Ivane Kolbaya's body were the result of the fall or were sustained prior to his death, and the head of the parliamentary Human Rights Committee questioned the circumstances of Zaza Tsotsolashvili's death after examining the room from which he is said to have fallen. Zaza Tsotsolashvili's brother was allegedly pressurized by police into refusing an independent autopsy, but four law enforcement officers were suspended pending investigations into this case.

Compulsory military service

Although a law providing a civilian alternative to compulsory military service came into force on 1 January 1998, it was not implemented owing to a failure by the Georgian authorities to enact relevant procedures. Aspects of the law itself also raised concern. It was not clear, for example, that any alternative service would be of a genuinely civilian nature and completely separate from military structures. It also appeared that while those performing alternative service could transfer to military service, there is no corresponding provision for those on military service to transfer to an alternative civilian one. AI sought further information in view of reports that the alternative service would be one year longer than compulsory military service.

Discrimination against women

In June the Committee on the Elimination of Discrimination against Women considered Georgia's first periodic report under the Convention on the Elimination of All Forms of Discrimination against Women. The Committee noted positive aspects such as the establishment within the ombudsperson's office of a confidential hotline for women victims of violence. However, the Committee expressed concern about the lack of a real understanding of discrimination against women; the persistence of a patriarchal culture and the prevalence of gender stereotyping; and the policy of not criminalizing procurement for the purpose of prostitution, which had created an environment in which women and children were not protected from sexual exploitation in sex-tourism, cross-border trafficking and pornography. The Committee's recommendations included comprehensive measures to eliminate gender stereotypes; gender-sensitive training for law enforcement officials and agencies; amending the criminal code to impose severe penalties for sexual violence and abuse of women and girls; and establishing a network of crisis centres and consultative services to assist women victims, especially girls.

Abkhazia

Many reports on events in Abkhazia were extremely polarized and difficult to verify independently. The *de facto* Abkhazian authorities failed to respond to AI's concerns, which meant that AI was unable to reflect their assessment of allegations against forces under their control.

Hostage-taking

In April the crew of a Georgian fishing boat named *Alioni* were detained by Abkhazian border guards. The only female crew member was released around 10 days later, but the rest were taken to Sukhumi. There it was reported that the captain and chief mechanic were to be charged with illegally entering Abkhazian waters, and the remaining crew with fishing illegally in a conservation area. However, Abkhazian officials were quoted as saying that crew members could be released without any further legal proceedings if exchanged for four Abkhazian civilians captured by Georgian irregular armed forces. AI expressed concern that if the crew members were held without formal charge, with their release conditional on an exchange for others, then in effect they were being held as hostages. In August the Abkhazian Supreme Court began hearing the case, but the nine men were released the following month in exchange for three Abkhazians and one Cossack, said to have been held in western Georgia by Georgian irregular forces.

Ill-treatment and death in custody
Allegations of torture and ill-treatment continued, with at least one reported death in custody in disputed circumstances.

An ethnic Georgian named Apollon Markelia was reported to have died following a beating by Abkhazian law enforcement officials. He and another man named Ushangi Todua were said to have been detained in the Gali district, then taken to a preventive detention unit in the town of Ochamchira. On 5 August it was reported that Apollon Markelia had died after being beaten in this unit.

Georgian irregular forces
Abkhazian forces continued to face armed attacks, sometimes leading to fatalities, and Abkhazian civilians and military personnel were said to have been taken hostage by irregular Georgian armed groups. AI continued to approach the Georgian authorities about alleged links between such groups and Georgian officials, and urged them to take all appropriate steps to ensure that anyone within Georgian jurisdiction responsible for human rights violations in Abkhazia was apprehended and brought to justice.

Return of the civilian population
In March the Abkhazian side unilaterally began implementing a "refugee return program" to the Gali district, but this was not supported by the Georgian side or the international community. In a statement in May the UN Security Council demanded that both sides put a stop to the activities of armed groups and establish a climate of confidence allowing refugees and displaced persons to return. The Security Council reaffirmed the right of all those affected by the conflict to return home in secure conditions.

Death penalty
At least one death sentence was passed during the year. Otak Kulaia was sentenced to death on 31 August for heading a terrorist group which caused explosions in the town of Tkvarcheli in 1998. The head of the Commission for Human Rights in Abkhazia reported in November that 14 people had been sentenced to death since the region had declared itself independent. No executions were reported.

AI country report
• Concerns in Europe, January – June 1999: Georgia (AI Index: EUR 01/002/99)

GERMANY

FEDERAL REPUBLIC OF GERMANY
Head of state: Johannes Rau (replaced Roman Herzog in May)
Head of government: Gerhard Schröder
Capital: Berlin
Population: 82.1 million
Official language: German
Death penalty: abolitionist for all crimes

There were reports of ill-treatment by police officers. Most involved foreign nationals and were frequently connected with forced deportations. The authorities attempted to deport people who were at risk of human rights violations in their countries of origin. One person died during a forced deportation and one man was reportedly shot dead by police.

Death during forced deportation
There was concern that the actions of federal border police officers may have contributed to the death of a Sudanese deportee in May by using restraint techniques which impeded breathing. Aamir Ageeb, a 30-year-old Sudanese national, died during his forced deportation from Frankfurt airport to Khartoum via Cairo, Egypt. Federal border police officers reportedly bound Aamir Ageeb's arms and legs and placed a helmet over his head before departure when he resisted deportation. Once on board the airplane, the officers allegedly forced his head between his knees and kept him in this position during take-off. After take-off, Aamir Ageeb stopped struggling and was pushed upright by the officers, who then noticed that he had stopped breathing. The death led to a debate among various professional groups, including doctors and pilots, about their participation in forced deportations. In August the government clarified who had ultimate authority during deportations by announcing that federal border police officers are subordinate to the captain of the airplane during deportations once the airplane doors are shut.

Refugees
In 1999 more than 95,000 people reportedly sought political asylum in Germany. Increasing pressures on national and local administrative structures led to renewed scrutiny of the future of the right to asylum. However, both domestic and international organizations criticized the authorities for deporting individuals who were not medically fit to travel or who had been living in Germany for a long time and for seeking to deport people who were at risk of human rights abuses in their countries of origin.

Fathelrahman Abdallah, a Sudanese national detained in Nuremberg, was repeatedly threatened with deportation to Sudan. He had been an active member of the Democratic Union Party of Sudan and was therefore in serious danger of imprisonment or torture if he were deported. At the end of the year he had been granted leave to remain in Germany, but only until February 2000.

Special flights

There were reports that the authorities used special chartered flights to deport larger numbers of asylum-seekers. In September the German and Austrian authorities announced that they would consider jointly using such arrangements to deport rejected asylum-seekers to common destinations. There were allegations that deportees were subjected to cruel, inhuman and degrading treatment by federal border police officers during special flight deportations.

▢ In March, 15 asylum-seekers were reportedly placed on a special flight at Düsseldorf airport destined for Conakry in Guinea. They were reportedly accompanied by 41 federal border police officers. When they arrived in Conakry, the Guinean authorities refused to recognize the asylum-seekers' travel documents and the chartered airplane was forced to return to Germany with all 15 detainees on board. It was alleged that federal border police officers physically and verbally abused the detainees during the journey. There was particular concern at reports that prior to departure one deportee had a helmet placed over his head and was forced to sit with his head between his knees for 20 minutes during take-off.

Ill-treatment

There were allegations of ill-treatment by police. The majority of complaints involved foreign nationals, particularly members of ethnic minorities and asylum-seekers. Most alleged that they were repeatedly kicked, punched and beaten with truncheons. In some instances police officers allegedly used derogatory and racist language.

▢ Ibrahim Kourouma, a Guinean national, alleged that he was ill-treated by federal border police officers at Schönefeld airport in Berlin on 7 April after he refused to board an airplane. He stated that he was placed in a room furnished with a table approximately one-metre wide and laid on his back across the table with his hands and feet fastened with handcuffs to the table. Ibrahim Kourouma's lower back rested on the edge of the table causing him pain. He was left in this position for around three hours. One officer put a wet T-shirt over his face, causing him breathing difficulties. A doctor who treated him in Berlin on 10 April stated that Ibrahim Kourouma had a number of injuries which were consistent with the events he described.

Places of detention

There were allegations that asylum-seekers were ill-treated by officials in various places of detention. There were also complaints about the physical conditions in which they were detained. In May the European Committee for the Prevention of Torture and Inhuman or Degrading Treatment or Punishment published the findings of its 1998 visit to various detention centres belonging to Frankfurt am Main airport in which asylum-seekers were held. The Committee made a number of recommendations to improve the physical aspects of the detention centres at the airport. In its report to the German government the Committee requested information about the outcomes of a number of investigations into allegations of police ill-treatment which the Committee had received in 1997 and in the first half of 1998. In its response to the Committee, the government stated that either final decisions in the investigations were still pending or insufficient evidence had resulted in the termination of the investigations.

Police shootings

A tourist from Cologne was shot dead by police officers in June. There were fears that his death may have resulted from police negligence. The 62-year-old hill walker was shot dead through the door of his hotel room in Heldrungen in Thuringia state by a group of four plainclothes police officers from Nordhausen. The police had reportedly received a call from a hotel employee claiming that a wanted murderer was staying in the hotel. Although the officers were supposed to establish the identity of the man, it was alleged that none of them knew what he looked like and that after knocking on the hotel door two shots were fired through the door. At the end of the year two police officers were suspended from duty and an investigation into the death was under way.

AI country reports

- Concerns in Europe, January – June 1999: Germany (AI Index: EUR 01/002/99)

GHANA

REPUBLIC OF GHANA
Head of state and government: J.J. Rawlings
Capital: Accra
Population: 18.8 million
Official language: English
Death penalty: retentionist
1999 treaty ratifications/signatures: Rome Statute of
the International Criminal Court

Four people were sentenced to death for treason. In
connection with the same case, a former armed
forces officer was detained by West African peace-
keeping forces in Sierra Leone and handed over to
the Ghanaian authorities. A journalist was
imprisoned after being convicted of libelling the
head of state's wife. Other journalists, and an
opposition member of parliament, were detained.

Background
With the prospect of presidential elections in
December 2000, there was increasing debate about the
succession to President J.J. Rawlings, head of state and
government since a coup in 1981. Since 1993 President
Rawlings had headed elected civilian governments, and
under the 1992 Constitution he was serving his last term
in office.

The government's sensitivity to criticism in the
privately owned news media was reflected in continued
prosecutions and arrests of journalists for alleged
defamation of government officials and associates.

Treason trials
Following a long-running treason trial, four men were
sentenced to death in February by the High Court in
Accra. Sylvester Addai-Dwomoh, Kwame Alexander
Ofei, Kwame Ofori-Appiah and John Kwadwo Owusu-
Boakye had been charged with plotting to overthrow
the government in 1994. A fifth defendant, Emmanuel
Kofi Osei, was acquitted. All five had been imprisoned
since their arrest in September 1994.

Some of the defendants alleged that they had been
beaten and ill-treated to coerce them into making
incriminating statements. The special High Court trying
the case ruled such statements admissible despite
evidence, from prosecution witnesses as well as from
some defendants, that soldiers who later testified for
the state and defendants had been beaten following
their arrest. The defendants lodged an appeal with the
Supreme Court, which has appellate jurisdiction in
treason cases.

In March James William Owu, a former army captain
who had been named as a co-conspirator by the
prosecution in the same treason trial, was charged
before the High Court in Accra with treason. He had
been detained in 1982, shortly after the 1981 coup, but
had escaped in a mass jail break-out in 1983. In early
1999 he was detained in Sierra Leone by forces of the

Economic Community of West African States (ECOWAS)
Cease-fire Monitoring Group, known as ECOMOG. In
February he was flown by the Ghanaian armed forces to
Ghana, where he was handed over to the authorities.
No formal extradition proceedings took place.

The retrial on treason charges of Karim Salifu Adam,
a member of the opposition New Patriotic Party, did
not proceed. He had been sent for retrial in July 1997
because no judgment had been reached in his trial
before one of the judges died, although all the evidence
had been heard. In February 1998 the Supreme Court
rejected a defence application against a retrial. His
allegations that he was tortured while in
incommunicado and illegal detention after his arrest in
May 1994 were not thoroughly and impartially
investigated.

Imprisonment for defamation
Journalists were imprisoned and record fines were
imposed on the privately owned news media in
connection with defamation cases brought by
government officials and their associates.

▭ Ebenezer ("Eben") Quarcoo, former editor of the
Free Press newspaper, was sentenced to 90 days in
prison with hard labour by the Circuit Court in Accra, in
November. He was also fined 1.5 million Cedis (US$600),
or sentenced to two years' imprisonment if he failed to
pay. He was released in December after the fine was
paid. He was convicted of intentionally libelling Nana
Konadu Agyeman Rawlings, wife of President Rawlings,
in an article published in December 1994. Another
outstanding libel suit brought by President Rawlings'
wife against Eben Quarcoo continued. His co-defendant
in both cases, *Free Press* publisher Tommy Thompson,
died in 1998.

▭ In late October, two journalists from *Joy FM* radio,
Samuel Atta Mensah and Mawuko Zormelo, and Yaw
Amfo Kwakye, chief executive of the *Statesman*
newspaper group, were arrested and detained
overnight for questioning by the security police. In
early November armed police surrounded the home of
Ferdinand Ayim, a *Statesman* correspondent, and
arrested him. The *Statesman*'s proprietor, opposition
member of parliament and human rights lawyer Nana
Akufo-Addo, was questioned by police, together with
Samuel Okyere, a receptionist. All were provisionally
charged with making or abetting false reports which
bring the government into disrepute — an offence
punishable by up to 10 years' imprisonment — and
released on bail. The charges were in connection with
the publication and broadcast of a tape recording in
which a man alleged to be a presidential security guard
admitted involvement in the 1985 murder of a Catholic
priest and the 1992 bombing of a hotel belonging to the
family of Nana Akufo-Addo.

Impunity
There were investigations into some incidents in
which protesters and others were killed by security
officials.

▭ In June the government ordered a police officer to
be disciplined and compensation be paid to the families

of two protesters killed by police in Kumasi in March 1997 after an inquiry found that riot control procedures had not been followed.

Local community leaders in Aflao, near the border with Togo, appealed for an independent investigation after Sylvanus Akortsu was shot dead in June by an officer of the police or customs service, and expressed concern about at least 10 other such killings since 1994 which had not been investigated. No information was made known about the outcome of an inquiry which police said in August 1999 had been established.

The son of Kwadwo Agyei Agyepong, a judge widely believed to have been extrajudicially executed with two other judges and a retired army officer in 1982 by government agents, repeatedly called for a "truth and reconciliation commission" to establish the truth about these and other alleged extrajudicial executions. In November President Rawlings acknowledged that injustices had occurred following coups in 1979 and 1981, but expressed the view that such a commission would reopen healed wounds.

Death penalty
The last known execution was in 1993. However, the death sentence remained mandatory for murder and treason, and at least five death sentences were passed by the courts.

In June the High Court in Kumasi sentenced to death Andrew Addai Ampratwum, a farmer, following his conviction for murder.

AI action
AI expressed concern in November at the imprisonment of journalists in connection with libel laws used to protect government officials and their associates.

In May AI launched a report in Ghana about the discriminatory use of the death penalty in the United States of America — *Killing with Prejudice: Race and the Death Penalty in the USA* — on the eve of a meeting of African and US business leaders in Accra.

GREECE

HELLENIC REPUBLIC
Head of state: Konstandinos Stephanopoulos
Head of government: Konstandinos Simitis
Capital: Athens
Population: 10.5 million
Official language: Greek
Death penalty: abolitionist for all crimes

Legal proceedings continued against a member of the Turkish minority, Mehmet Emin Aga, for peacefully exercising his right to freedom of religion and expression. Conscientious objectors who refused to perform alternative civilian service of punitive length continued to face trial. There were further allegations of ill-treatment by law enforcement officers. Conditions in some detention centres and prisons amounted to cruel, inhuman or degrading treatment. Lengthy investigation procedures into past human rights abuses raised serious concerns about impunity.

Freedom of religion and expression
Legal proceedings continued against Mehmet Emin Aga for peacefully exercising his right to freedom of religion and expression. The Supreme Court upheld sentences totalling 28 months' imprisonment imposed following four separate convictions for "usurpation of the function of a Minister of a known religion". Mehmet Emin Aga was allowed to pay a sum of money in lieu of terms of imprisonment. Appeals relating to additional cases remained pending at the end of 1999. Moreover, Mehmet Emin Aga had been charged in 1998 with four similar counts of the same offence, for which he was due to stand trial in 2000. The charges related to Mehmet Emin Aga carrying out "duties which by their nature apply exclusively to the legitimate Mufti" by "sending out to the Muslims of Xanthi written messages of a religious content" to mark religious festivals and signing them as "Mufti of Xanthi, Mehmet Emin Aga". AI takes no position on the procedures to be followed for choosing religious leaders and has no view on who is, or should be, the legitimate Mufti of Xanthi. AI's concern in this case is based solely on its belief that Mehmet Emin Aga was exercising his right to freedom of religion and expression and that if he were imprisoned he would be a prisoner of conscience.

Conscientious objection
Provisions of the law on conscription fell short of international standards, for example, the length of alternative civilian service remained punitive, and its application was discriminatory. Applications for conscientious objector status were rejected in cases where the applicants alleged they were unable to submit their documents in time because the relevant authorities refused to provide them with the certificate requested or because applicants were given

unreasonably short deadlines. Applicants were subsequently charged with insubordination, which carries a sentence of up to four years' imprisonment. In at least 25 cases, conscientious objectors who performed alternative civilian service in health institutions were subjected to punitive measures which included working up to 68 hours a week, no right of leave and threats of revocation of their right to alternative service if they refused to comply with such conditions.

📁 Conscientious objector Lazaros Petromelidis wrote to the Navy Conscription Office in October 1997 stating that he was prepared to perform alternative civilian service. In May 1998, he was arrested for draft evasion while he was trying to obtain the necessary documents to complete his application to carry out civilian service. He was released on bail after five days and summoned to perform alternative civilian service for 30 months. However, Lazaros Petromelidis refused to perform a civilian alternative service which was punitive in length and did not start work at a health institution in Kilkis until January 1999. He subsequently lost his right to perform civilian service and was called up for military service. He refused to respond to the summons and was charged with draft evasion. In April Lazaros Petromelidis was sentenced to four years' imprisonment for insubordination, of which he served about two months before being released pending the outcome of his appeal against the sentence which was still pending at the end of 1999.

Torture and ill-treatment

There were allegations of ill-treatment by police; members of ethnic minority groups such as the Romani community were among the victims.

📁 In September, Nikos Katsaris, a 23-year-old Rom, his father, his 16-year-old brother and his 17-year-old cousin were ill-treated by police in Nafplio. Their car was reportedly stopped by three police officers for a routine check of papers. They were all ordered to get out of the car with their hands up. While they were being searched, Nikos Katsaris and his cousin were reportedly kicked and punched. When the father asked the officers why they were hitting them for no reason, one of the officers grabbed him by the hair and punched him repeatedly. Concerns about the case were raised with the authorities by Network DROM for the Social Rights of Roma and Greek Helsinki Monitor; no response had been received by the end of the year.

📁 In August, two British citizens were arrested by police on Crete. At the police station, they were kicked, punched, slapped, insulted and told in English "you sign and go to jail or you die" by the police, after they had refused to sign statements written in Greek, a language they could neither read nor understand. According to reports, no lawyer was present during their interrogation. One of the men was released on bail four days after his arrest. However, Michael Tonge was transferred to Neapoli prison where he was stripped naked and searched and forced to sleep on a blanket in the corridor. He was also told by a prison guard that he would be killed and would have his throat cut while

asleep. The following day, he was taken to a cell six-metres square which he shared with 16 other detainees. Michael Tonge was then transferred to Korydallos prison, near Athens. He claimed that he remained handcuffed to his seat in the "crucifix position" during the 13-hour journey from Irakleio to Piraeus. While on the boat a police officer started to whip the legs of the prisoners with a rope covered in rubber. Michael Tonge was released pending trial in November.

Impunity

Twenty months after the incident, no progress had been made by the authorities in bringing to justice the police officers suspected of the shooting and killing of Angelos Celal in Partheni in April 1998. In September the authorities stated that the investigation initiated in 1998 was still under way and was under the responsibility of the Ministry of Public Order. Charges of manslaughter, attempted murder and illegally carrying and using weapons had also been brought against the police officers by the prosecutor in 1998. At the end of 1999 a date had still to be set for the examination of the police officers on these charges.

Prison conditions

Conditions in some prisons and detention centres were so poor as to amount to cruel, inhuman and degrading treatment.

📁 A prisoner in Iannena complained that overcrowding was so severe that some detainees were forced to sleep in corridors. He also alleged that the prison had only two toilets and no running water; that the food was insufficient; that prisoners had only restricted access to the exercise yard; and that reported cases of tuberculosis and HIV/AIDS were left without adequate medical care.

📁 In April, 32 detainees went on hunger strike in protest at conditions of detention in Drapetsona where they were held pending deportation to their country of origin. Conditions reported at the centre — which was allegedly used only for non-EU nationals — included severe overcrowding; lack of natural daylight; insufficient sanitary facilities; lack of adequate exercise; restriction on visits; inadequate food; very poor ventilation; severely limited access to doctors or medical treatment; and no access to social services.

AI country report

• Greece: No satisfaction — the failures of alternative civilian service (AI Index: EUR 25/003/99)

GUATEMALA

REPUBLIC OF GUATEMALA
Head of state and government: Álvaro Arzú Irigoyen
Capital: Guatemala City
Population: 11.2 million
Official language: Spanish
Death penalty: retentionist

A commission of enquiry into past human rights violations established under the 1996 Peace Accords published its report in February. It concluded that official forces and their civilian adjuncts had been responsible for the vast majority of the gross abuses committed during Guatemala's bitter civil conflict. All but a handful of those responsible continued to evade justice. Attempts to address impunity for past human rights violations were hampered by the intimidation of victims, witnesses and judicial personnel involved in human rights prosecutions and in the exhumations of mass clandestine graves, and by widespread judicial corruption. A number of abuses which occurred after the Peace Accords also remained unresolved. By the end of 1999, death sentences had been imposed on at least 32 people, including some who reportedly suffered from mental impairment, after trials which fell far short of international standards of due process. No executions were reported. Security officials reportedly used high crime rates as a pretext to harass, intimidate, torture and extrajudicially execute political opponents and to obstruct human rights monitors and others inquiring into past violations. Frustration at crime levels led to an increase in lynchings of suspected petty criminals, some allegedly instigated by the security forces. In 1999, 72 lynchings were officially recorded; the true number was believed to be much higher. The general lawlessness was fuelled by the easy availability of unregistered small arms, allegedly illegally imported and sold by criminal rings which included military and police officials.

Background

The 1996 Peace Accords — negotiated over several years under the aegis of the UN and agreed by the government and the former armed opposition, the National Guatemalan Revolutionary Unity (URNG) — formally ended the civil conflict which had raged over a period of more than three decades. Following the Accords, the armed opposition was largely demobilized and the overall rate of abuses declined significantly. However, there were occasional reports that small groups of genuine or purported former members of armed opposition groups carried out acts of aggression or intimidation in the countryside.

The Accords agreed in principle a number of far-reaching measures, many relevant to human rights protection; the magnitude and complexity of these measures meant that the Accords and the gains attained under them remained vulnerable. In May a number of proposed constitutional reforms, aimed at formalizing key military and judicial reforms agreed in the Accords, were rejected in a national referendum.

In December the UN Mission in Guatemala (MINUGUA) judged that the government's serious shortcomings in implementing the Accords had weakened efforts to ensure respect for the rule of law and citizens' rights. By the end of 1999 the provision in the Accords calling for the disbanding of the Presidential High Command, which serves as the army's high command, had still not taken place, owing to "insufficient funds."

However, other provisions in the Accords were implemented. In December the military announced a new military doctrine which it said reflected its new role in a democratic society at peace, and an Indigenous Women's Defence Agency was inaugurated. Also in December, a law went before Congress to establish a Peace and Harmony Commission, as recommended by the Historical Clarification Commission established under the Accords.

The UN Special Rapporteur on the sale of children, child prostitution and child pornography found in July that child prostitution and trafficking in children were major problems. In November, the Latin American Institute for the Prevention of Crime described violence against women as a grave problem.

Impunity

The Historical Clarification Commission report, the result of 18 months of investigation involving 42,000 victims of human rights violations, was made public in February. The Commission recognized the responsibility of the military and its civilian adjuncts for the vast majority — 93 per cent — of the atrocities committed during the years of civil conflict. It also found that in four specific areas, the army's counter-insurgency campaign had perpetrated genocide against indigenous people, who made up 83 per cent of the victims. The Commission also pointed to the role played by the US Central Intelligence Agency (CIA) in these violations. Data obtained in 1999 by human rights groups under the US Freedom of Information Act confirmed that as early as the 1960s, the USA had formulated, encouraged and helped implement a counter-insurgency strategy which relied on clandestine actions by "death squads", made up of police and military agents but wearing plain clothes in order to maintain "government deniability", to eliminate suspected "subversives". During a visit to Central America in March, US President Bill Clinton made an unprecedented apology for US involvement in "the dark events" of Guatemala's tragic conflict.

Progress in human rights cases

In November the third trial of former civil patrol leader Cándido Noriega resulted in his conviction for human rights violations in the early 1980s against indigenous villagers of Tululché, El Quiché department, including extrajudicial executions, torture and mass rape. His lawyers appealed against the verdict and 220-year sentence. Throughout the proceedings, survivors, witnesses, judicial personnel and staff of the Guatemalan Bishops' Conference (CONFREGUA), involved in the case were intimidated and threatened. In May, indigenous CONFREGUA lay worker Juan Jeremías Tecú who accompanied and interpreted for the indigenous witnesses, was seized for several hours, beaten and threatened with death.

In September, the government finally paid compensation to the family of 13-year-old street child Nahamán Carmona López who died in 1990, after being savagely kicked by four policemen. The officers served only half of their 12-year prison sentences.

In December the Inter-American Court of Human Rights ruled that there was significant evidence that five street youths who "disappeared" from the centre of Guatemala City in 1990 had been seized, tortured and murdered by identified members of the National Police without regard for detention procedures specified in Guatemalan legislation and that the Guatemalan state had not fulfilled its responsibilities to protect the victims and investigate their deaths.

In December in Spain, Nobel Peace Prize winner Rigoberta Menchú filed charges against eight former Guatemalan officials for genocide, state terrorism, torture and extrajudicial executions, carried out while they were in office. Victims included four of her relatives; four Spanish Roman Catholic priests; and 37 others, both Guatemalan and Spanish nationals, who died during an attack on the Spanish embassy by the Guatemalan security services in 1980. Among those named in Rigoberta Menchú's lawsuit was retired General Efraín Ríos Montt, the country's leader during the most brutal phase of the army's counter-insurgency campaign in the early 1980s. He was elected to Congress in the 1999 elections and will serve as its President.

Set-backs in human rights inquiries
Investigations into many past human rights abuses were slow. In the few cases where individuals were convicted, the sentences passed usually failed to reflect the gravity of the offence or were overturned on appeal.

In August, 25 soldiers were convicted in connection with the extrajudicial executions of 11 returned indigenous refugees, including two children, in Xamán, Alta Vera Paz, in 1995. The commanding officer and 10 soldiers in his squad were found guilty of manslaughter and sentenced to five years' imprisonment. Fourteen others convicted of complicity to manslaughter were sentenced to four years' imprisonment. The sentences were commutable to fines of five quetzales (US 5 cents) per day. Fifteen other soldiers involved in the action were acquitted. After appeal, 10 soldiers were sentenced to nine years' imprisonment for homicide and three additional years, commutable at the same rate, for bodily harm. The commanding officer was acquitted and released. A request by the Public Prosecutor that the acquittal decisions be set aside was pending at the end of 1999.

US human rights groups published material which they claimed recorded the activities of a Guatemalan military unit responsible for the kidnapping, torture and execution of suspected left-wing political activists. The document, reportedly sold to them by a low-ranking Guatemalan military official, listed 183 people allegedly seized between 1983 and 1985. According to the published material, several had been released after they agreed to act as army spies. The majority, however, were listed as secretly killed in custody. Much of the information accorded with AI's records for that period, but the Guatemalan military denied the document's authenticity. Some Guatemalan human rights groups initiated legal proceedings based on the document and prosecutors from the Public Ministry were assigned to investigate these cases. Local human rights groups believed some of the victims were clandestinely buried at the old Military Polytechnic, now the new National Civil Police Training Institute. Exhumations began in 1999, but the Institute's director, a police inspector, who requested them received death threats.

Proceedings against several former armed opposition leaders for ordering the killings of former supporters during internal disputes, also remained pending at the end of 1999.

The unsolved murder of Bishop Gerardi
Bishop Juan José Gerardi, Coordinator of the Archbishop's Human Rights Office (ODHA) was brutally beaten to death outside his home in 1998, two days after presiding over the public presentation of the report of the Guatemalan Roman Catholic Church's Inter-Diocesan Recuperation of the Historical Memory Project (REMHI) concerning the civil conflict. Despite a tremendous and sustained public outcry in Guatemala and abroad, the case remained unresolved. Four people and a dog were arrested at various points in connection with the case, but none remained in custody at the end of the year. A number of people involved in the case, including members of ODHA's staff, two former judges, a prosecutor, a witness and a member of the Presidential High Command who accused colleagues of involvement in the murder, fled abroad after death threats.

Possible 'disappearance'
Carlos Coc Rax, an indigenous peasant leader and father of nine, went missing in April in circumstances suggesting he may have "disappeared". He had led local Kekchí villagers in El Estor, Izabal department, in trying to protect their plots of land against encroachment by local landowners and in protesting against the policies of the local subsidiary of a Canadian mining company which held a concession in the area.

Death penalty
At the end of 1999, some 32 people were on death row. Lack of adequate legal representation and lack of respect for international standards of due process were concerns in virtually all of their cases. In several cases, people condemned to death appeared to be suffering from mental impairment.

One of those closest to execution at the end of 1999 was Kekchí-speaking peasant Pedro Rax Cucul, condemned to execution by lethal injection for a homicide carried out in 1996. He was found wandering around the day after the machete murder with the arm of the victim in the bag in which he carried his salt and tortillas. Doctors found him to be suffering from paranoia, and he was being treated in the course of 1999 in a mental hospital. However, the judge handling his case said his behaviour "fell within normal parameters", and that the execution should proceed. An alternative proposal was that he be kept under psychiatric observation until such time as his mental faculties were judged to have been restored, at which point he would be executed.

Administration of justice

In March MINUGUA found that inadequate recruitment, selection and training, exacerbated by a lack of effective internal disciplinary mechanisms and the reintegration of former police and army personnel into the new police force were undoubtedly factors in continuing human rights abuses.

In August the UN Special Rapporteur on the independence of judges and lawyers reported that corruption, lack of resources, threats and intimidation still prevailed in the judicial system. Many prisoners remained in detention without trial for long periods, in overcrowded conditions; corruption and drug-trafficking were rife in prisons and inmates were sometimes the victims of "social cleansing."

AI country reports and visits
Reports
- Guatemala: To the dead we owe the truth (AI Index: AMR 34/007/99)
- Guatemala: Words are not enough (AI Index: AMR 34/008/99)
- Guatemala: Exhuming the truth for justice (AI Index: AMR 34/023/99)
- Guatemala: Making human rights an electoral issue (AI Index AMR 34/035/99)
Visits
AI delegations visited Guatemala in March and June. An AI Guatemala Trial Observers Project sent lawyers to trials arising from 1982 massacres at Tululché and Agua Fría, El Quiché, and Río Negro, Baja Vera Paz.

GUINEA

REPUBLIC OF GUINEA
Head of state: Lansanna Conté
Head of government: Lamine Sidibe (replaced Sidya Touré in March)
Capital: Conakry
Population: 7.4 million
Official language: French
Death penalty: retentionist

Members of the opposition, including Alpha Condé, president of the *Rassemblement du peuple de Guinée* (RPG), Guinean People's Rally, remained in detention without charge or trial. Other members of parliament and local government councillors, as well as other elected officials of the RPG, were sentenced to prison terms in April. Many appeared to be prisoners of conscience. At least 30 soldiers, including possible prisoners of conscience sentenced to prison terms in 1998, remained in detention. Freedom of expression was once again threatened. Three journalists were arrested and detained briefly, and two were expelled from the country.

Background
The presidential election of December 1998, in which President Lansanna Conté was re-elected, was marred by violence and arrests accompanied by torture and ill-treatment. Opposition parties whose leaders were arrested criticized the result as unfair and accused the government of rigging the election by denying their supporters voting cards. President Conté was sworn in for a new five-year term of office in January. In March, President Conté appointed Lamine Sidibe, president of the Supreme Court, as Prime Minister. He replaced Sidya Touré, who had been Prime Minister since July 1996.

Violations arising from the elections
During the presidential poll in 1998, scores of individuals, including opposition members of parliament and local government councillors, were arrested. Some were released after two months without charge. These included Marcel Cros, leader of the *Parti démocratique africain de Guinée*, African Democratic Party of Guinea, who had been accused of illegal possession of firearms. Others, including RPG members of parliament, were tried and sentenced to prison terms.

In March, more than 60 people were tried by a court in Kankan. The charges against them included involvement in an unauthorized march and incitement to violence. In April, some were sentenced to prison terms ranging from four months to five years and a large fine, and two were acquitted. All those sentenced to five years' imprisonment were tried *in absentia* and the court ordered an international arrest warrant to be issued against them. RPG supporters sentenced to four months' imprisonment were released after having served their prison terms. They included members of parliament and at least eight women. AI believed that most of these people, including Koumbafing Keita, El-Hadj Amiata Kaba, Ibahima Kalil Keita and Mamadou Yö Kouyaté, were prisoners of conscience.

Detention without trial

Alpha Condé, president of the RPG, a member of parliament and a candidate in the 1998 presidential election, was arrested with other members of his party in December 1998. The RPG members and Antoine Bogolo Soromou, former mayor of Lola and president of the *Alliance nationale pour la démocratie* (AND), National Alliance for Democracy, also arrested in December 1998, remained in detention without charge throughout 1999. The Guinean authorities accused Alpha Condé of wishing to leave the country illegally and of seeking to recruit troops in order to destabilize the country. In July, before a visit to Guinea by Jacques Chirac, the French President, the authorities announced their intention to try him before the State Security Court in September, but this trial was not held. Alpha Condé and the other detained members of the opposition were held in the Central Prison in Conakry, and denied family visits. Alpha Condé's French lawyer was refused entry to the country.

Following Jacques Chirac's visit to Conakry, at least 12 members of the opposition were arrested and released within a few days.

Possible prisoners of conscience

At least 30 soldiers, including possible prisoners of conscience, remained held. They had been sentenced to prison terms of up to 15 years after an unfair trial in 1998 before the State Security Court, in connection with a mutiny in 1996.

Freedom of expression

Journalists continued to be under attack. In February the authorities expelled Don de Dieu Agoussou, a journalist of Beninese nationality, working for *L'Oeil*, a weekly newspaper. In 1998, he had received threats after writing an article critical of the authorities. In April Jean-Baptiste Kourouma, the associate director and editor-in-chief of *L'Indépendant*, a private weekly, was arrested and detained at Conakry police station after he published an article in which he accused senior state officials of bribery. He was held for three weeks before being released without charge. In December, the owner of *L'Indépendant*, Aboubacar Sylla, and his editor-in chief, Saliou Samb, were arrested and detained without charge. Aboubacar Sylla was released after two days and Saliou Samb was detained for 12 days and then expelled to Ghana.

Torture

Torture was frequently used shortly after arrest and as a punishment during interrogation. During the trial of the RPG supporters in Kankan, most of the detainees stated that they had been tortured in detention. They said that members of the security forces held them on the ground, stamping on their hands and feet before

beating them. Some received up to 50 truncheon blows on the same day. The President of the court apologized but he did not order any investigation into these allegations.

There were no investigations into any allegations of torture in the past or in the course of 1999.

Use of lethal force

In October, two students were killed in a demonstration protesting against high transport fares. The security forces used teargas as well as live bullets to break up the march.

AI appeal

In January, on the eve of President Conté being sworn in for a new term of office as head of state, AI appealed to him to put an end to torture and to release all prisoners of conscience.

GUINEA-BISSAU

REPUBLIC OF GUINEA-BISSAU
Head of state: Malam Bacai Sanhá (replaced João Bernardo Vieira in May)
Head of government: Francisco José Fadul
Capital: Bissau
Population: 1.2 million
Official language: Portuguese
Death Penalty: abolitionist for all crimes

The transitional Government of National Unity, established after a civil war in 1998, promised to end impunity and initiated reforms to increase protection for human rights. There were two further outbreaks of fighting in February and May, during which human rights violations were committed. In May President João Bernardo Vieira was ousted and replaced by the President of the National Assembly, Malam Bacai Sanhá. Hundreds of former government soldiers and some civilian officials were arrested in connection with crimes related to the war, including human rights violations.

Background

The civil war between forces loyal to President Vieira (including troops from Senegal and the Republic of Guinea) and the self-styled *Junta Militar*, Military Junta, ended with a peace agreement in November 1998. However, there was further fighting in Bissau from 31 January to 3 February. Subsequently, the Economic Community of West African States (ECOWAS) completed its deployment of 600 peace-keeping troops and a Government of National Unity, led by Prime Minister Francisco José Fadul, was installed on 20 February.

In early May, there was another outbreak of fighting. Hundreds of soldiers and civilians were killed, including 60 civilians who had sought refuge in a mission school and were killed by shells apparently fired from the navy headquarters in the direction of *Junta Militar* troops. The fighting ended when the *Junta Militar* took control of Bissau and ousted President Vieira, who went to Portugal on the understanding that he would return to Guinea-Bissau for trial. In June the ECOWAS troops left Guinea-Bissau. Following consultations in July, the European Union decided not to impose sanctions on Guinea-Bissau in response to the ousting of President Vieira.

The devastation caused by the war included widespread looting and damage to hospitals. Thousands of landmines were laid, killing and maiming at least 10 people, although none of the parties to the conflict admitted laying them. Approximately 250,000 people were displaced and about 8,000 fled to other countries, most of whom returned during the year.

During the conflict in 1998, parliamentarians, representatives of religious groups and non-governmental organizations, and other community leaders had mediated between the warring parties, physically protected individuals at risk, encouraged international peace-making efforts and lobbied decision-makers to include human rights guarantees in agreements.

The Guinea-Bissau Human Rights League, many of whose members had been exiled during the conflict in 1998, continued to provide information, investigate reports of human rights violations, visit political prisoners and advocate human rights. In August, 300 people, including members of the government, armed forces and civil society organizations, attended a conference on national reconciliation. The conference called for an end to impunity, for those suspected of crimes committed in connection with the war to be tried, for vengeance to be avoided and for freedom of expression to be guaranteed.

In June the UN opened a Post-Conflict Peace-Building Support Office in Guinea-Bissau (UNOGBIS). Its mandate included consolidating the peace agreement and helping to build democracy and the rule of law.

In July the National Assembly approved a constitutional amendment excluding from high office people whose parents were not born in Guinea-Bissau. This was subsequently dropped after widespread opposition.

Measures to increase stability included the initiation of projects to demobilize soldiers and collect the weapons circulating among the civilian population. Soldiers continued to carry out policing functions. Soldiers at roadblocks often demanded money from motorists and pedestrians. In November members of the *Junta Militar* proposed that the military should play an advisory role in government, including in the appointment of senior government officials. This proposal was shelved after parliamentary deputies and members of the public protested. In November and December there were protests by soldiers, whose numbers had increased by

recruitment on both sides during the conflict, demanding payment of salary arrears.

Presidential and parliamentary elections were held in November. The *Partido da Renovação Social* (PRS), Social Renewal Party, won the legislative election, gaining 38 of the 102 National Assembly seats. Its leader, Kumba Ialá, narrowly defeated Malam Bacai Sanhá in the presidential contest but failed to gain the required majority of the vote. A second presidential ballot was subsequently scheduled for January 2000.

Human rights abuses

Most human rights abuses reported during the fighting were carried out in 1998. In 1999 violations were committed at military checkpoints by soldiers loyal to President Vieira. Most incidents involved the arbitrary and excessive use of force. In addition, at least two people suspected of working with the *Junta Militar* were arrested and tortured.

☐ Loyalist soldiers reportedly entered the Simão Mendes hospital in Bissau in early February and removed a wounded *Junta Militar* soldier, saying that he was to be interrogated. The next morning the soldier was returned to hospital with cuts on his chest and back and what appeared to be cigarette burns. He died a few days later, apparently of gangrene in his battle wound.

In March, violence was provoked by government militia who attacked a peaceful march of thousands of people from all over the country. The marchers were calling for an end to the conflict and the withdrawal of foreign troops. In the ensuing scuffles, stones were thrown and several people were hurt. AI delegates saw militia members chase and beat an onlooker. The Prime Minister set up a commission of inquiry into the incident but the results were not published by the end of 1999.

In areas under *Junta Militar* control, police arrested and ill-treated members of President Vieira's *Partido Africano para a Independência da Guiné e Cabo Verde* (PAIGC), African Party for the Independence of Guinea (Bissau) and Cape Verde. Police also ill-treated criminal suspects.

In October the Guinea-Bissau Human Rights League complained that several imprisoned security officials who were alleged to have committed crimes in Bafatá had been brought from Bissau to Bafatá where police made them walk through the streets with their hands tied behind their backs. The police had reportedly paraded the prisoners in order to show the people of Bafatá that there was to be no impunity. The Attorney General declared that action would be taken against the police involved.

Child soldiers

Very young soldiers fought on both sides. A 14-year-old was reported to have been among *Junta Militar* troops. In May, 186 young members of a loyalist militia, including several aged between 15 and 17, were released and returned to their families.

Human rights reforms

The Government of National Unity restructured the state security police, whose members had been responsible for human rights violations, designating it a state information service with no powers of arrest or interrogation. The government also undertook to accede to all international human rights treaties to which Guinea-Bissau was not yet a party.

The Government of National Unity promised donors in May that it intended to put the judicial system into working order; reduce impunity and increase people's knowledge of the law and their rights; and train police and soldiers to respect human rights and the law. In August the Attorney General set up an office to investigate official corruption.

Political prisoners

After the ousting of President Vieira, *Junta Militar* forces detained more than 500 soldiers and police and security officials. The Guinea-Bissau Human Rights League and the International Committee of the Red Cross were given access to the prisoners. None was reported to have been tortured, but prison conditions were reported to be harsh. Subsequently more than 200 prisoners were released. By the end of 1999 the cases of most of the remaining prisoners had been investigated, some of them in connection with alleged violations of human rights and humanitarian law, but none had been brought to trial.

A number of businessmen and former government officials were arrested in August and charged with incitement to war and giving financial support to President Vieira. Manuel dos Santos "Manecas", a former minister and businessman, was tried in August and sentenced to a fine on a charge of obstruction of justice. He remained in detention, accused of crimes connected with the civil war. At least 18 others were released on bail.

Steps against impunity

Government officials and others repeatedly declared that action would be taken to end impunity. However, while various investigations began, few were completed.

Two state security officials suspected of human rights violations during the conflict, including arbitrary arrest, torture and extrajudicial executions, were arrested early in the year but not brought to trial.

There were official investigations into several incidents involving alleged human rights violations but the results had not been published by the end of 1999.

📁 Eighteen-year-old Lai António Lopes Pereira was killed in July 1998 by a security officer who suspected him of robbery. Witnesses said that the security officer kicked in the door of Lai Pereira's house, took out a pistol and fired shots which hit the floor. He left and returned with seven colleagues in camouflage uniforms. The officer punched Lai Pereira's pregnant sister in the stomach before entering the house randomly firing shots. Lai Pereira ran into the pantry where he was gunned down, shot seven times.

📁 In March the body of Júlio Sami was found at a building site. Relatives said that a Senegalese soldier had arrested him in October 1998 after a dispute about placing an artillery piece in Júlio Sami's yard, which was near the front line. Júlio Sami's wrists had been tied together and his head was disfigured. Human rights workers alerted the authorities and the state forensic doctor examined the body.

Four members of the state security police under President Vieira were arrested and charged with the 1993 murder of Jorge Quadros, a Portuguese journalist. Former President Vieira was accused of giving the order to kill the journalist, and his then minister of security was also indicted.

Two mass graves were discovered which apparently contained the bodies of prisoners who had been deliberately killed. One, discovered in a cemetery in Bissau in September, contained the bodies of 14 people believed to have been arrested during the recent conflict and who appeared to have been bound and shot. Another, found in Portogole in October, contained 22 bodies, six of which were thought to be those of people executed in 1986 after being unfairly tried on charges of plotting to overthrow the government.

AI country reports and visits
Reports
- Guinea-Bissau: Protecting human rights – a new era? (AI Index: AFR 30/004/99)
- Guinea-Bissau: Human rights in war and peace (AI Index: AFR 30/007/99)

Visit
AI delegates visited Guinea-Bissau in March, held talks with the Prime Minister and other officials, and interviewed victims of human rights abuses.

GUYANA

REPUBLIC OF GUYANA
Head of state: Bharrat Jagdeo (replaced Janet Jagan in August)
Head of government: Samuel Hinds
Capital: Georgetown
Population: 0.8 million
Official language: English
Death penalty: retentionist

A reservation to the Optional Protocol to the International Covenant on Civil and Political Rights (ICCPR), preventing death-row prisoners from petitioning the Human Rights Committee, came into force in April. There were violent clashes between police and strikers in May and June.

Death penalty

In December 1998 the government denounced the (first) Optional Protocol to the ICCPR and re-acceded with a reservation precluding the UN Human Rights Committee from considering petitions filed by people under sentence of death concerning violation of their right not to be arbitrarily deprived of life. This came into effect in April. AI called on the government to remove this reservation and to respect the rights of all people in Guyana, including those under sentence of death.

⌂ Abdool Saleem Yasseen and Noel Thomas were scheduled to be executed in September. Both men were granted stays of execution to allow the national courts to consider further legal applications. The government issued execution warrants despite a ruling by the Human Rights Committee that the men's rights under the ICCPR had been violated and a recommendation that both should be released. AI reminded the government that it would be a serious breach of international law to execute the men in these circumstances and urged that their death sentences be commuted. In December, following a ruling by Guyana's highest appeal court, Abdool Saleem Yasseen and Noel Thomas received further stays of execution in order that their petitions, originally brought in September, could be heard and determined.

Violence during strike

In May the Guyana Public Service Union declared a strike demanding a pay increase. The strike lasted for 55 days (ending in June), during which time there was social unrest and violent clashes between the authorities and the strikers. There were reports that the government was about to impose a state of emergency when an agreement was reached.

⌂ On 18 May, at least 17 people were injured in Georgetown when police fired pellets and tear gas to disperse a crowd of demonstrators. In July the government established an inquiry to examine this incident and other incidents of violence that occurred during the strike.

Police shootings

There were a number of reports of fatal and non-fatal shootings by the police in disputed circumstances.

Victor Bourne inquest

Victor Bourne was shot and killed by police officers in the bedroom of his house in June 1998. Police stated that they shot him in self-defence. However, witnesses alleged that the police officers executed Victor Bourne in his sleep and then turned on witnesses and beat them. An inquest was held but its findings had not been made public by the end of 1999.

Ill-treatment in police lock-ups

There were reports of ill-treatment in police lock-ups, and of conditions that amounted to cruel, inhuman or degrading treatment. In Brickdam police lock-up, for example, there were no proper sanitary facilities. In December, a nine-year-old child was released from Brickdam lock-up upon the intervention by the Minister for Home Affairs, following allegations that the child had been sodomized over a period of two months by other adult inmates. The Minister for Home Affairs subsequently ordered that no children should be detained with adults at Brickdam police lock-up, and ordered that they be transferred to a separate police station.

HAITI

HAITI
Head of state: René Préval
Head of government: Jacques Edouard Alexis
Capital: Port-au-Prince
Population: 6.6 million
Official languages: French, Creole
Death penalty: abolitionist for all crimes
1999 treaty ratifications/signatures: Rome Statute of the International Criminal Court

The climate of respect for human rights established since Haiti's 1994 emergence from *de facto* military government was dealt a series of blows in 1999. The five-year-old police force, the *Police nationale d'Haïti* (PNH), Haitian National Police, committed relatively few abuses in dealing with protests in the run-up to elections in the year 2000. However, some officers were implicated in killings in disputed circumstances, at times suggesting possible extrajudicial execution, as well as other serious human rights violations. In spite of some efforts to strengthen the justice system, 1999 witnessed a growing backlog of untried cases and accusations of corruption and lack of independence. The body responsible for overseeing the elections was put into place; some electoral officials were subject to what appeared to be politically motivated threats and intimidation. Several public figures were attacked by unidentified armed assailants during 1999.

Background

After nearly two years of political paralysis, dating from 1997 allegations of electoral fraud and the resignation of the then Prime Minister, Parliament appointed Jacques Edouard Alexis as Prime Minister. However, after President René Préval failed to extend the Parliament's mandate when it expired on 11 January, his appointment was never ratified. Without a Parliament, President Préval essentially ruled by decree throughout 1999. In the absence of this key element in Haiti's system of checks and balances, state institutions were perceived as ever more vulnerable to outside interests. Both the police and judiciary came under increasing pressure from external sectors apparently seeking to undermine their independence and impartiality, thereby diminishing their effectiveness during the run-up to elections. There was a marked growth in armed crime, stemming partly from ongoing economic crisis in Haiti, the poorest country in the Americas, and partly from the drug trade and the accompanying increase in accessibility of firearms. The rising crime rate added to the pressure on institutions. As the year ended, the mandates of the UN police mission and the UN/Organization of American States (OAS) human rights mission were extended until mid-March 2000.

Haitian National Police

The PNH was created in 1995 to replace the discredited armed forces, and has been generally commended for professional behaviour in the face of increasing pressures. However, 1999 saw a rise in killings by the police in disputed circumstances, in some cases suggesting that they were extrajudicial executions, as well as ill-treatment of criminal suspects by police during or following arrest. The UN/OAS human rights mission, the International Civilian Mission in Haiti (MICIVIH), reported 66 killings apparently involving police in 1999, up from 31 in 1998. In its final observations in August, the UN Committee on the Elimination of Racial Discrimination expressed concern about violations by the PNH.

On 28 May, 11 residents of the Carrefourfeuilles area of Port-au-Prince were shot dead by police in circumstances suggesting that they were summarily executed. Police claimed that three of them had been killed in a shoot-out, but witnesses testified that police shot the men while they were in custody and lying on the ground. Police then reportedly arrested eight others. Family members and witnesses who saw the bodies in the city morgue stated that 10 of the 11 had been shot once in the head, and one of them in the heart.

The Minister of Justice immediately announced the opening of a three-person commission of inquiry into the killings, and the PNH Inspector General announced

that an internal investigation had been opened as well. By the end of 1999, no findings had been made public but eight police officers suspected of involvement were detained, including the Commissioner of Port-au-Prince following his arrest in the Dominican Republic. Following the arrests, MICIVIH reported that "disappearances", summary executions and police killings, which had reached an unprecedented peak in previous months, decreased.

In July the bodies of eight people were found in Titanyen, outside Port-au-Prince. In what would be the first alleged "disappearance" since the inception of the PNH, the bodies were alleged to be those of eight young criminal suspects last seen in custody of the police. A reported eyewitness was interviewed by the public prosecutor's office, and an internal police investigation was opened. However, no results had been made public by the end of 1999.

External pressures on the police increased markedly in 1999, in part from an apparently politically motivated campaign to undermine the independence and impartiality of the force, culminating in the October resignation of the Secretary of State for Public Security, Robert Manuel. Jean Lamy, a PNH adviser named as a possible replacement, was assassinated the next day; and the head of the Judicial Police charged with investigating the killing himself escaped an attempted shooting shortly thereafter. PNH Director Pierre Denizé was forced to flee the funeral of Jean Lamy on 16 October when protesters claiming to be partisans of *Fanmi Lavalas*, the party of former President Aristide, violently disrupted the ceremony.

The Inspector General continued to investigate alleged abusive behaviour by police, with mixed results. The PNH reported that 145 police officers were dismissed between January and October 1999, seven of them for involvement in human rights violations. Some serious cases remained unpunished. Among these were officers reportedly involved repeatedly in beatings of detainees. Only a handful of cases were prosecuted through the justice system, in most instances apparently because of judicial inaction rather than police resistance.

Judicial system

Five years after the return to constitutional order, the justice system remained largely dysfunctional. Efforts since 1994 to reform the judicial system were generally piecemeal and intermittent, despite widespread recognition of its inadequate independence, strength and resources. Sources in Haiti attributed frequent "popular justice" killings of suspected criminals to lack of faith in the judicial process.

Basic safeguards such as the guarantee of judicial review within 48 hours of arrest were often not respected and the timeframe for judicial decision on cases was systematically flouted. Haitian and UN authorities indicated that four fifths of the roughly 3,800 detainees in Haitian prisons and police stations at the end of 1999 had not been tried; nearly a third of all detainees had been waiting for trial for more than one year.

The judicial system's failings appeared most prevalent in cases with perceived political or state security elements. Particularly in sensitive cases, release orders issued by judges were ignored by public prosecutors, resulting in continued, and illegal, detention. The Minister of Justice named a Commission to address this issue and told AI delegates in October that the Commission had submitted its final report. However, its results were apparently not made public.

The Ministry of Justice undertook a series of short- and medium-term initiatives to improve the situation. After the appointment of a new Minister in March 1999, measures were taken to strengthen the *Ecole de la Magistrature*, judicial training institute; to ensure the attendance of judges; and to fight corruption. The Ministry also set up working groups of donors and Haitian and international legal experts to address issues such as prison overcrowding and the establishment of a legal aid system.

◻ Nine officers of the disbanded armed forces were held for 15 months after protesting against non-payment of their pensions. Although they were charged with state security offences, there was reportedly no evidence substantiating the charges and no record of any investigation into the charges. They were released only after joining a hunger strike begun in September by long-term detainees in the National Penitentiary to press for action on their cases. One of the hunger strikers was Evans François, brother of Michel François, chief of police under the military government. Evans François was imprisoned in April 1996, although there was reportedly no evidence on file and no record of any investigation. He reportedly suffered a stroke during the hunger strike. The public prosecutor released him and 20 other long-term detainees, justifying her decision on humanitarian grounds.

Detention issues
The failings of the justice system contributed to overcrowding within prisons, which are run by the prison administration, *Direction de l'administration pénitentiaire*, a branch of the PNH. Overcrowding contributed to a rise in tension between guards and detainees, increasing the risk of abuses. It also created conditions that in some instances constituted cruel, inhuman and degrading treatment: these included insufficient ventilation and light, acute shortage of beds and mattresses and lack of medical attention. There were numerous cases of serious malnutrition because of food shortages; the prison authorities stated that they lacked resources to provide inmates with the requisite two meals per day.

While there was no indication of systematic ill-treatment, 1999 saw several serious incidents in which prison guards beat detainees, in most cases as punishment. In Les Cayes, two inmates were allegedly beaten by prison guards following an escape attempt in July. This provoked a riot by other inmates, some of whom were reportedly beaten in retribution after their transfer to another prison. In Hinche, detainees reported being teargassed following an escape attempt in September. Those involved in the escape attempt and subsequent aggression against a prison guard were reportedly handcuffed and beaten while lying on the ground, before being transferred.

In June, the prison administration publicly released the internal guidelines for prisons, covering such issues as record-keeping, detention conditions and disciplinary guidelines. Haitian non-governmental organizations (NGOs) set up a prison observation network, to carry out prison monitoring across the country.

Human rights defenders
AI was concerned about the safety of human rights defenders in Haiti, who appeared to be at risk of abuse for denouncing political and other violence and misconduct. A leaflet containing threats against member organizations of the Platform of Haitian Human Rights Organizations was found at the Platform's offices on 1 March. On 8 March Pierre Espérance, director of the National Coalition for Haitian Rights in Port-au-Prince and treasurer of the Platform, was wounded in an attack by unidentified gunmen in Port-au-Prince. In early June leaflets containing threats against specific human rights activists and groups were again delivered to several organizations. The organizations continued to carry out their work and AI took steps through its human rights defenders program to help prevent further incidents.

The *Office de la protection du citoyen*, Human Rights Ombudsman, expanded its presence in 1999, opening its first field office, in Gonaïves.

Impunity
During the coup that deposed President Jean-Bertrand Aristide in 1991, and for the next three years of *de facto* rule, Haitian military and paramilitary forces committed numerous serious human rights violations. Haitian NGOs applied increasing pressure on the government to investigate violations, bring perpetrators to justice, and make reparation to victims or their families. However, an extensive report published by MICIVIH in September pointed to a lack of political will on the part of the state to address impunity. For example, the government had not yet systematically implemented the recommendations of the 1995 report of the *Commission nationale de vérité et justice*, National Truth and Justice Commission.

One exception was the 1994 Raboteau massacre case, which advanced significantly in 1999 with the completion of the examining judge's trial order and the prosecutor's brief. Formal charges were brought against 22 defendants, most of whom appealed. The legal action against eight others arrested for investigation was dismissed. At the end of 1999 the eight were still, illegally, in detention, as were seven defendants against whom the state prosecutor had recommended dropping charges. The state prosecutor responsible for the case was dismissed, to the approval of local victims' groups which had questioned his credibility. Efforts were under way to address the logistical and organizational demands of such a large trial.

Haitian NGOs were preparing for an international conference on impunity in 2000, proposed during the April 1999 visit of Nobel Peace Prize laureate Adolfo Pérez Esquivel.

AI country visit
AI delegates visited Haiti for three weeks in October, meeting a range of government officials, other authorities and members of diverse sectors of civil society.

HONDURAS

REPUBLIC OF HONDURAS
Head of state and government: Carlos Flores Facussé
Capital: Tegucigalpa
Population: 5.7 million
Official language: Spanish
Death penalty: abolitionist for all crimes

Members of indigenous groups continued their efforts to persuade the authorities to investigate killings of members of their communities and to bring those responsible to justice. Police employed excessive use of force against people demonstrating peacefully to promote long-standing demands for land and justice. Children were killed by law enforcement officers in circumstances suggesting that at least one had been extrajudicially executed. Human rights defenders and journalists were threatened and attacked as a result of their work.

Background
The possible existence of "death squads" concerned human rights organizations. They feared that such groups could be behind the deaths of people suspected of involvement in criminal activity and youth gangs. More than 50 youths were reported to have been killed during 1999, but the authorities apparently took no action to investigate the deaths. In August the UN Committee on the Rights of the Child noted the measures taken by the Honduran authorities to investigate cases of police brutality against street children and provide compensation, but concluded that judicial measures needed reinforcement. It recommended that Honduras reinforce its judicial mechanisms to deal with complaints of police brutality, ill-treatment and abuse of children, and that cases of abuse of children be duly investigated in order to avoid impunity for perpetrators.

There were reports of government corruption in the use of international aid donations received following Hurricane Mitch in 1998.

In January the post of Commander in Chief of the Armed Forces was abolished and replaced by a civilian Minister of Defence. Edgardo Dumas Rodríguez was appointed as minister. In July there were widespread fears of a threatened military coup. During the absence of the Minister of Defence, his deputy, Vice-Minister General Roberto Lázarus Lozano, made a number of personnel changes. The Minister overturned these changes when he returned, but his deputy and commanders of military units refused to obey the order. After several hours of escalating tension, President Carlos Flores Facussé dismissed four high-ranking military officers, including the Vice-Minister. Others resigned later. In June, President Flores had warned top military personnel from conspiring against the Minister of Defence and to give up any hopes of seizing power.

In April the National Congress unexpectedly presented and hurriedly approved amendments to the Law of the National Commissioner for the Protection of Human Rights. These amendments limited the Human Rights Commissioner's scope for action and reduced the Commissioner's period of office by two years. They were reportedly put forward in response to a report by the Commissioner containing allegations of government corruption with regard to the management of foreign aid sent to help survivors of Hurricane Mitch. After a wave of national and international protest and condemnation, the amendments were withdrawn.

Indigenous groups
There were further abuses against indigenous people and no investigations into past human rights violations.

Indigenous groups organized demonstrations during 1999, calling for an end to impunity for the deaths of leaders and members of their communities and seeking solutions to their land problems. In October police used teargas, firearms and rubber bullets against peaceful demonstrators, leaving at least 22 people injured. Three policemen were also injured. Twenty-three people were charged with criminal offences. However, in November the government promised to instruct the Minister of Security to drop the charges and to compensate people who had been injured by the police. The demonstration was also against the ratification of an amendment to Article 107 of the Constitution, which would have allowed non-Hondurans to buy coastal lands if they were used for tourism projects, threatening indigenous communities. The Acting President of the National Congress announced at the end of the day of demonstrations that the amendment would not be submitted to Congress for discussion, thereby suspending its ratification.

By the end of 1999 there were no indications that investigations had been initiated into the killings of members of indigenous groups in previous years, including Cándido Amador Recinos, Jesús Álvarez Rochez and 17-year-old Manvil Pinace, all of whom were killed in 1997.

Children
Law enforcement officers were responsible for the deaths of children, which in one case may have amounted to extrajudicial execution. More than 50

minors, including street children and alleged gang members, were killed during 1999 by unidentified people, in circumstances suggesting they were victims of a "social cleansing" campaign. In one case, three children aged 17, 16 and 13 were found dead in an abandoned house. They had been in police custody and were killed shortly after they were released. All three had been shot in the head. Officials frequently asserted that these killings were the result of fights between gangs, but there was little evidence to support such claims.

🗁 Alexander Obando Reyes was shot by a police officer in April. He and a friend were in a park in Tegucigalpa at about 10pm when a police officer came to the park and started an argument with the two youths. He threatened them and shot in the air with his service weapon. The two youngsters ran away but the policeman shot at Alexander, hitting him in the stomach and chest. The policeman then fled. Alexander was taken to hospital but died the following day as a result of damage to his lungs. He was not armed and did not pose a threat to the officer or anyone else. There had been no investigation and the officer had not been arrested or brought to trial by the end of 1999. AI wrote to the Attorney General calling for the suspension of the officer while an investigation and trial were in progress, but received no reply.

Human rights defenders
Human rights defenders were again threatened and harassed. In July Dora Oliva Guifarro, a staff member of the *Comité de Familiares de Detenidos Desaparecidos en Honduras* (COFADEH), Committee of Relatives of the Disappeared in Honduras, was forced into her car at gunpoint by two unidentified young men who abducted her for about two hours and threatened to kill her and harm her children. Members of the *Comité para la Defensa de los Derechos Humanos en Honduras* (CODEH) Committee for the Defence of Human Rights in Honduras, were also targets of death threats in their offices in different parts of the country.

Journalists
Critical coverage of police and military actions brought intimidation and harassment to at least two journalists. Renato Álvarez, a news editor, and Cesar Silva Rosales, a reporter, covered the unrest among the military in mid-1999 and issues related to the police, for a television company. They were harassed and followed around by unidentified men in cars without number plates.

Impunity
Human rights organizations and the Special Human Rights Prosecutor in the Attorney General's Office continued their efforts to put an end to impunity. Several sites were located allegedly containing the bodies of some of those who "disappeared" in the 1980s. However, the courts issued controversial decisions in favour of some military officers charged in connection with those "disappearances", allowing them to go free or reducing the charges or applying amnesty

laws incompatible with Honduras' international obligations to investigate and punish those responsible for human rights violations. Human rights organizations and victims' families deplored those decisions.

AI country reports
- Honduras: Justice fails indigenous people (AI Index: AMR 37/010/99)
- Honduras: Human rights violations against children (AI Index: AMR 37/011/99)

HUNGARY

REPUBLIC OF HUNGARY
Head of State: Árpád Göncz
Head of government: Viktor Orbán
Capital: Budapest
Population: 10.2 million
Official language: Hungarian
Death penalty: abolitionist for all crimes
1999 treaty ratifications/signatures: Rome Statute of the International Criminal Court

Roma were reportedly victims of racially biased policing and ill-treatment by police officers. Some asylum-seekers were deported without being allowed to submit an asylum claim. Many others were detained in poor conditions for long periods, and faced deficiencies in the asylum procedure. Many asylum-seekers went on hunger strike to protest against their detention and against alleged unfair implementation of the asylum procedure.

Background
Roma continued to face multi-faceted discrimination, which has marginalized them socially and economically. The belief that Romani communities are inherently criminal appeared to be widespread among the public and police. The European Commission's annual report on Hungary's progress towards European Union accession was positive, yet identified treatment of Roma as a concern, along with corruption, press freedom, and refugee issues.

Ill-treatment of Roma by police
Reports of ill-treatment of Roma by police officers in Budapest and the eastern town of Hajdúhadház demonstrated a pattern of police violence against Roma.

🗁 In Hajdúhadház on 11 January, two police officers allegedly kicked and beat two Romani youths, Attila Rezes and D.B., with rubber truncheons. The youths were taken to the police station, interrogated about the breaking of a shop window, reportedly beaten further, then released without charge. Attila Rezes fell into a coma the next day, and required an operation. Three police officers and a civilian were subsequently charged in connection with the alleged ill-treatment.

⌴ On 5 September about 30 police officers reportedly beat and verbally abused six young Roma, aged from 13 to 21, in two apartments in a block in north Budapest. They also reportedly beat the mother of one of them. Police officers reportedly continued to beat three of the young Roma males, aged 16, 17 and 21, on the street and then at a police station. All six were released without charge later that day.

Roma who filed complaints or who talked to the media about their alleged ill-treatment by police risked being further ill-treated or intimidated by police officers.

⌴ D.K., a Roma man who was interviewed in Hajdúhadház about the Attila Rezes case by the *Fókusz* TV documentary program in March, was reportedly beaten by a police officer who said he deserved "special treatment" for appearing in the TV program. A few days later the *Fókusz* program secretly filmed another police officer hitting D.K. in the face in a Hajdúhadház bar.

⌴ László Sárközi, a Roma student who was reportedly beaten by police officers in Budapest's Népliget park and at a police station in June, was visited and allegedly insulted and intimidated in his student hostel by police officers after he filed a complaint and appeared on a TV program.

Refugees
Non-admission to the asylum procedure
Border guards often ignored oral requests for asylum. At the eastern border many asylum-seekers were deported to Ukraine. Amendments to the asylum law were introduced in September to improve the special accelerated procedure used at the international airport, by suspending deportations of asylum-seekers whose claims were rejected if they appealed. However, officials reportedly circumvented the new rules.

⌴ In September border guards at the international airport reportedly tried to prevent MEJOK, a Hungarian human rights organization, from gaining access to K.H., an asylum-seeker from the Democratic Republic of the Congo who had arrived from Lebanon. K.H. was deported to Lebanon two days later.
Detention of asylum-seekers
Asylum-seekers, including children, were detained for long periods, despite the Hungarian government's assertion to the UN Committee against Torture in 1998 that it did not detain asylum-seekers. The September amendments to the asylum law limited detention of asylum-seekers to 18 months.
Ill-treatment of detained asylum-seekers
In Szombathely detention centre cases of guards ill-treating detainees and spraying CS gas into their faces or their rooms were reported.

⌴ In Nyirbátor detention centre O.P., a Kurdish Turkish asylum-seeker, was reportedly taken into a room by seven guards, tied to a wall, beaten with rubber batons, and injected against his will with an unknown substance to quell his screaming.
Inadequacies of the asylum procedure
The asylum procedure was often seriously deficient in its implementation. Superficial and inadequate interviews and poor translation often resulted in failure to elicit the substance of an asylum-seeker's fear of persecution. Negative decisions and the reasons for them were not always given in a language asylum-seekers could understand. Detained asylum-seekers' applications were not always passed on to the appropriate authorities by the guards. Access to detained asylum-seekers by lawyers and human rights groups was increasingly restricted.

AI country reports and visits
Report
• Hungary: Alleged ill-treatment of Roma in Hajdúhadház (AI Index: EUR 27/001/99)
Visit
An AI delegate visited Hungary in September for research. Permission to visit Szombathely and Nyirbátor detention centres was denied to AI.

INDIA

REPUBLIC OF INDIA
Head of state: Kocheril Raman Narayanan
Head of government: A.B. Vajpayee
Capital: New Delhi
Population: 967.6 million
Official language: Hindi
Death penalty: retentionist

Human rights violations occurred throughout India against a backdrop of political instability. The socially and economically weaker sections of society continued to be particularly vulnerable to human rights abuses. Attacks, often with the apparent connivance of police and local authorities, on *dalit* communities (disadvantaged groups determined by caste hierarchies) and tribal people were commonplace. Women continued to be particularly vulnerable to abuse in these contexts. Access to justice for these victims of human rights abuses remained problematic and those engaged in protecting the rights of the most vulnerable groups also came under increasing pressure, often themselves becoming the victims of abuses. 1999 saw a rise in communal violence, often attributed to Hindu groups close to the *Bharatiya Janata* Party (BJP). The government's preoccupation with matters of national security led to discussion of new anti-

terrorism legislation at the end of the year. Armed conflicts in northeastern states and in Jammu and Kashmir claimed the lives of hundreds of civilians.

Background

In April the BJP government of A.B. Vajpayee fell following a vote of no confidence. General elections in September resulted in the formation of an alliance government made up of a range of parties — the National Democratic Alliance — with A.B. Vajpayee as Prime Minister.

Attacks on members of religious minorities — most notably Muslims and Christians — continued to increase. There were widespread allegations that attacks were carried out directly by, or in connivance with, right-wing Hindu groups. Much of the violence against Christians centred around deprived areas where Christian groups have traditionally carried out development activities with tribal and *dalit* communities, organizing health and educational services.

The security forces continued to be engaged in operations against armed groups active in states throughout India. A cease-fire in Nagaland was extended. Police were involved in operations against *naxalite* (armed left-wing) groups in Andhra Pradesh and parts of Madhya Pradesh and Orissa. In Bihar, clashes between left-wing Maoist armed groups and private landlord armies continued, resulting in the deaths of scores of people. In May, fighting escalated along the line of control between Pakistan and India. The fighting continued until the end of July when armed groups reportedly agreed to withdraw from the area and return to Pakistan territory.

Human rights defenders

Human rights defenders working on a range of issues including caste discrimination, domestic violence and trade union rights came under attack from both the state and other powerful interests throughout 1999.

⌷ In July, 17 people, including two women and a child, died following police action to suppress a protest march in connection with a wage dispute between tea estate workers and their employers in Tirunelveli in Tamil Nadu. Although the demonstrators had obtained official permission for the march, police reportedly charged the protesters with *lathis* (long wooden sticks), used tear gas and finally fired shots into the air to disperse them. Many of the protesters were chased by police into a nearby river. Eyewitness reports indicated that police continued to beat protesters when they were in the river and prevented them from getting out of the water. The government ordered a Commission of Inquiry which was continuing at the end of the year.

Methods of harassment included the filing of apparently false criminal cases. Section 151 of the Criminal Code of Procedure, which allows police to preventively detain people they suspect may commit a crime, was regularly used to detain human rights defenders and suppress peaceful protests.

Several activists were detained under the 1980 National Security Act (NSA).

⌷ Asish Gupta, Secretary General of the North East Co-ordination Committee on Human Rights, was arrested in June in Assam. The official grounds for his detention under the NSA included reference to a press release issued by the Co-ordination Committee condemning the conflict between India and Pakistan and appealing to the UN and the international community to intervene to allow the Kashmiri people to decide their own future. He was finally released on the orders of the Guwahati High Court on 16 December.

The government imposed increased administrative restrictions on human rights organizations. Several organizations, including those involved in an advertisement campaign at the time of the elections to raise concerns about the gender policies of the BJP, were threatened with having their registration withdrawn. Requests to visit India by UN Special Rapporteurs on torture and on extrajudicial, summary or arbitrary executions, and by the UN Working Group on Enforced or Involuntary Disappearances were not taken up by the authorities.

Impunity

There were continued concerns about the government's failure to implement recommendations made by various commissions of inquiry, by the National Human Rights Commission (NHRC), by state human rights commissions and by other statutory commissions.

⌷ In August the NHRC filed a petition in the Supreme Court indicating that the government was hindering its five-year-long investigation into the shooting of 37 people in October 1993 in Bijbehara, Jammu and Kashmir, by members of the Border Security Forces. The shootings took place during an apparently peaceful protest against an army siege of the Hazratbal shrine. The NHRC asked the Court to order the authorities to hand over certain files which they had refused to release.

⌷ The new state government in Maharashtra announced its intention to reconsider the recommendations of the Srikrishna Commission of Inquiry. The Commission had been set up in 1993 to investigate the circumstances surrounding riots between members of the Hindu and Muslim communities in Mumbai in December 1992 and January 1993 in which 1,788 people died. There had been reports that police had sided with Hindu mobs in the riots which followed the destruction of the mosque at Ayodhya. The Commission's report had pointed to communalism in the police force which led to discrimination against Muslim communities, and incitement to riot by members of the Shiv Sena Party. The Commission's recommendations had been rejected by the former Shiv Sena–BJP alliance in the state.

Human rights commissions

In January the NHRC clarified its role with reference to a 1996 Supreme Court order that the NHRC should investigate human rights violations in Punjab following allegations that hundreds of bodies had been illegally cremated by Punjab police. The NHRC stated that it would restrict itself to awarding monetary compensation only to those families who could prove that their relatives were illegally cremated by police in Amritsar district between 1984 and 1994. In September a petition challenging this — on the grounds that it ignored the wider pattern of "disappearances" and extrajudicial executions in Punjab and the need to provide full redress to victims and their relatives — was dismissed by the Supreme Court. By the end of 1999 the NHRC had reportedly received around 80 claims from individuals in Punjab.

In October an Advisory Committee, established in 1998 by the NHRC to review the 1993 Protection of Human Rights Act, finalized its recommendations. These included amendments to the composition of the NHRC and a proposal that the NHRC should be able to independently investigate allegations of human rights violations by members of the paramilitary forces, but not the armed forces. The NHRC was still considering these recommendations at the end of the year.

In November Justice J.S. Verma took over as Chair of the NHRC which continued to monitor abuses and make recommendations for the promotion and protection of human rights.

No further state human rights commissions were established during 1999.

Special legislation

In December it was learned that the Law Commission of India was considering draft anti-terrorism legislation at the request of the Home Ministry. The Criminal Law Amendment Bill, as recommended by the Law Commission, retained many of the features of the 1987 Terrorist and Disruptive Activities (Prevention) Act (TADA) which lapsed in 1995 and which had been used to detain thousands of political suspects without charge or trial.

The Armed Forces (Special Powers) Act — which gives the security forces powers to shoot to kill and grants them virtual immunity from prosecution — remained in force in areas of the northeast and in Jammu and Kashmir. Human rights organizations in the northeast marked the second anniversary of a Supreme Court judgment upholding the constitutionality of the Act as a "Black Day", although activities were prevented by police in Manipur.

In February the Maharashtra Control of Organized Crime Ordinance was enacted. This gives the police widespread powers to intercept communications and allows for arrest, detention and trial procedures which do not conform fully to international standards.

In May the Tamil Nadu state government withdrew the Prevention of Terrorist Activities Bill. There had been strong objections to the legislation which bore many similarities to the TADA.

The authorities continued to use the lapsed TADA to detain people in Jammu and Kashmir by linking them to ongoing cases filed before 1995. Hundreds of people remained in detention under the TADA despite Supreme Court orders for the review of all cases.

▢ Fifty people, including 12 women, were awaiting trial under the TADA in Karnataka at the end of the year. They had been arrested between 1993 and 1995 by members of the Special Task Force established by the Karnataka and Tamil Nadu state governments to apprehend a notorious smuggler. Almost all testified that they had been tortured after arrest.

Many individuals were detained under the 1978 Jammu and Kashmir Public Safety Act, which allows for widespread preventive detention.

▢ In September and October, 25 members of the All Parties Hurriat conference, including its chairman, Syed Ali Gilani; senior members Mohammad Yasin Malik, Javed Ahmed Mir and Abdul Gani Bhat; and their associates were detained under the Act after they peacefully called for a boycott of elections. Their detention appeared to be punitive in character; the Chief Minister of Jammu and Kashmir publicly stated that he intended to "let them rot in jail". Petitions challenging the legality of their indefinite detention were before the High Court in Srinagar at the end of the year.

Torture

Deaths in custody continued to be widespread throughout all states. Various forms of torture, including rape, continued to be used by the police and security forces. This was acknowledged by government officials, including the Attorney General; senior members of the judiciary; and NHRC officials, at an international symposium on torture held in New Delhi in September.

▢ In September, 21-year-old Devinder Singh died in custody in Punjab, reportedly after being tortured by police. His brother, Sapinder Singh, and fellow villagers Karnail Singh and Inderjit Singh were also tortured. Police claimed they were attempting to locate a rifle belonging to Devinder Singh and that he died of a heart attack on the way to hospital after falling ill while in detention. Doctors failed to record injuries on the bodies of Sapinder Singh, Karnail Singh and Inderjit Singh when they were brought before them. The magistrate also reportedly failed to note their injuries when remanding them to further police custody. A case of murder was subsequently filed against a police sub-inspector in connection with the death of Devinder Singh.

'Disappearances'

Reports of "disappearances" were received from Jammu and Kashmir and from Assam. Attempts by relatives in Jammu and Kashmir to establish the fate of individuals continued to be obstructed by the state, the security forces and an inadequate legal system. No substantive response was received from the government to an AI report on "disappearances", published in February, which referred to between 700 and 800 people whose fate remained unknown.

▢ In Manipur the report of an investigation by a district judge into the "disappearance" of 15-year-old Yumlembam Sanamacha following his arrest by members of the 17th Rajputana Rifles in February 1998 was published. The report found clear evidence that Yumlembam Sanamacha had been arrested by the armed forces and that he had not escaped as they claimed. An official Commission of Inquiry into the "disappearance" also submitted its report to the Manipur state government, but this had not been published by the end of 1999.

Death penalty

At least 18 people were sentenced to death in 1999. At least 35 people remained on death row. It was not known if any executions were carried out. Human rights organizations throughout the country joined in a campaign against the death penalty. However, the Home Minister continued to refer to government plans to extend the use of the death penalty for crimes including rape.

▱ In May the Supreme Court upheld the death sentences against four people tried in connection with the assassination of former Prime Minister Rajiv Gandhi in 1991. The four had been sentenced after what appeared to be unfair trials under the TADA. A clemency petition was under consideration at the end of the year.

Abuses by armed groups

Armed groups operating in many states continued to violate international humanitarian law. Human rights abuses reported included torture, hostage-taking and killings of civilians. In Tripura hostage-taking continued at an alarming level; several children were among those taken hostage. In Jammu and Kashmir armed groups continued to kill civilians; Hindus were particularly targeted for attack.

AI country reports and visits

Reports

- India: "If they are dead tell us" – "Disappearances" in Jammu and Kashmir (AI Index: ASA 20/002/99)
- India: A vital opportunity to end impunity in Punjab (AI Index: ASA 20/024/99)
- India: Appeal against death sentences (AI Index: ASA 20/028/99)

Visits

AI delegates attended a series of four seminars for human rights activists in India. AI delegates visited Uttar Pradesh and West Bengal during May and June to research custodial violence and violence against women.

INDONESIA AND EAST TIMOR

REPUBLIC OF INDONESIA
Head of state and government: Abdurrahman Wahid (replaced B.J. Habibie in October)
Capital: Jakarta
Population: 199.5 million
Official language: Bahasa Indonesia
Death penalty: retentionist
1999 treaty ratifications/signatures: International Convention on the Elimination of All Forms of Racial Discrimination

A UN-sponsored ballot in East Timor, which resulted in Indonesia relinquishing its claim to the territory, was marked by systematic and widespread human rights violations – including extrajudicial executions, rape and forcible expulsions – perpetrated by militia groups acting in concert with the Indonesian National Army (TNI) and the police. Human rights violations continued to be widespread throughout Indonesia, despite some progress towards political and legal reform. Extrajudicial executions and "disappearances" were particularly prevalent in Irian Jaya and Aceh, where demands for independence were forcibly repressed by the security forces. Extrajudicial executions also took place in the context of ethnic and religious conflicts and excessive use of force against demonstrators also led to deaths. Although 29 prisoners of conscience and a number of political prisoners were released, at least six people were on trial or facing trial at the end of the year for political offences. AI believed that some of them would be prisoners of conscience if convicted. Previous cases of "disappearances", extrajudicial executions, torture and other human rights violations remained unresolved.

Background

In June, the first genuine multi-party elections in Indonesia for 44 years were held, in which the ruling *Golkar* party was defeated.

In August the people of East Timor voted overwhelmingly for independence from Indonesia. Following the ratification of the ballot results by the Indonesian Parliament on 19 October, authority for East Timor was transferred to the UN Transitional Administration in East Timor (UNTAET).

In October presidential elections were won by Abdurrahman Wahid who became Indonesia's fourth President. However, economic problems, regional insurgencies, endemic corruption and conflicts between the civilian and military arms of government contributed to ongoing instability.

East Timor

In January the Indonesian government unexpectedly offered to rescind its claim to East Timor if an offer of special autonomy within Indonesia was rejected by the East Timorese people. Agreements were signed by the Indonesian and Portuguese governments and the UN on 5 May which set out the modalities for the popular consultation process on the special autonomy option. The UN Mission in East Timor (UNAMET) was set up to oversee the process.

Indonesia was entrusted under the Agreements with ensuring a secure environment for the popular consultation process. Despite repeated assurances by the Indonesian authorities that it would take steps to improve the security situation, no effective measures were taken to curb the activities of pro-integration militias which were responsible for many human rights violations. Indeed, there was much evidence of official involvement in the establishment of these militias and of the direct and indirect support of the military and police for their activities, including by providing weapons, training and facilities. Members of the TNI and police also participated in militia attacks.

The autonomy option was rejected by 78.5 per cent of voters in the ballot which took place on 30 August. A wave of violence by militias, the TNI and the police followed, forcing most UNAMET personnel to evacuate East Timor. In response, the UN Security Council authorized the establishment of a multinational force which was deployed on 20 September.

Arbitrary detention, torture and killings

Scores of people were extrajudicially executed in East Timor in the months prior to the ballot. Others "disappeared" or were arbitrarily detained. Many of those held by the militias, TNI and police were believed to have been tortured or ill-treated. Among the main targets of the violations prior to the ballot were pro-independence activists and students suspected of being involved in political activities. There was evidence that "death lists" were used to identify victims. A small number of abuses by the pro-independence armed opposition group *Falintil* was also reported.

After the ballot the violence intensified. Many hundreds of people were believed to have been killed, although the exact number was not known. Members of the National Council of Timorese Resistance (CNRT) and students were again specifically targeted, as were members of the Roman Catholic Church and local UNAMET staff. Other killings were more indiscriminate.

◻ Father Hilario Modeira, well known for his vocal opposition to human rights violations, was among three Roman Catholic priests killed in a joint attack on a church compound in Suai by militias, the TNI and the police mobile brigade on 6 September. An unknown number of people displaced by the violence and sheltering in the church were also killed.

◻ Three Roman Catholic priests and two nuns were among nine people who were killed by militias in Los Palos on 25 September.

Reports of violence against women, including rape, were received throughout the year. In some cases women were raped or held in sexual slavery in retaliation for the political activities of their male relatives. There were persistent reports of sexual violence against women in refugee camps in West Timor.

Internally displaced people and refugees

Threats, intimidation and attacks caused the internal displacement of tens of thousands of people in the months preceding the ballot. Internally displaced people were vulnerable to attack, and humanitarian workers and others trying to assist them were also threatened and in some cases attacked.

◻ An attack by militias and the TNI on 6 April on internally displaced people sheltering in a church in Liquica resulted in the killing of at least 30 people.

◻ On 4 July a convoy returning from delivering humanitarian supplies to internally displaced people in Sare was attacked by militias. Several people were injured in the attack including a driver who was badly beaten.

After the ballot, some 75 per cent of the population fled their homes; more than 250,000 people fled, or were forcibly expelled from, East Timor. The majority went to West Timor. East Timorese refugees, particularly those in West Timor, remained at risk of human rights violations by militia groups. Access to the refugees by the UN High Commissioner for Refugees (UNHCR) and humanitarian agencies was restricted by militia activity. The voluntary repatriation program was hampered by threats, intimidation, attacks on refugee convoys and UNHCR representatives, and by misinformation. By the end of 1999 more than 100,000 East Timorese refugees remained in West Timor.

Investigations into abuses

In September a Special Session of the UN Commission on Human Rights adopted a resolution calling for the establishment of an international commission of inquiry to gather information on possible violations of human rights and acts which might constitute breaches of international humanitarian law committed since January 1999. The international commission visited East Timor and Jakarta from 25 November to 8 December, but was denied permission to go to West Timor. It had not published its report by the end of the year.

The visit by the international commission was preceded by a visit to East Timor in November by the UN Special Rapporteurs on extrajudicial, summary and arbitrary executions, on violence against women and on torture. In a joint report, published in December, the Special Rapporteurs recommended further investigative measures and the establishment of an international criminal tribunal if, within a matter of months, the Indonesian government's efforts to investigate proved ineffective.

A separate inquiry team, the Commission for the Investigation of Human Rights Abuses in East Timor (*KPP-HAM*), was established by the Indonesian National Commission on Human Rights (*Komnas HAM*). *KPP-HAM* made two visits to East Timor and several visits to West Timor towards the end of 1999. In December it published an interim report in which it said that it had found evidence that TNI members were involved in, or had prior knowledge of, the terror campaign.

AI's response

AI believed the grave and systematic human rights violations in East Timor amounted to crimes against humanity and war crimes and called for investigations to continue with a view to bringing the perpetrators to justice before an international tribunal. In the lead-up to the ballot and throughout September, AI's international membership responded to the human rights crisis in East Timor by engaging in mass letter-writing campaigns, government lobbying and demonstrations.

Reform in Indonesia

While the reform process begun in May 1998 proceeded, the human rights situation deteriorated in many areas. Among the reforms was the official separation of the police force from the military and the repeal of Anti-subversion Law, which had facilitated the detention and imprisonment of thousands of prisoners of conscience since its promulgation in 1963. However, the separation of the police from the military was incomplete as the police remained under the control of the Minister of Defence, and key provisions of the Anti-subversion Law, which prohibit criticism of the state ideology, *Pancasila*, and ban communist teachings, were incorporated into six new regulations in the Criminal Code. Popular protests against a new law on national security, which would give the military broad powers during a state of emergency, delayed the signing of the bill by the President. The bill had not been signed by the end of the year. Although the number of parliamentary seats assigned to the military was reduced from 75 to 38, it continued to wield considerable political influence and persisted in responding to dissent and disturbances with repression.

Political prisoners and prisoners of conscience

Twenty-nine prisoners of conscience and at least 30 political prisoners were released in a number of separate amnesties during 1999. Among those released were 10 elderly men who had been jailed in connection with an alleged coup attempt by the Communist Party of Indonesia in 1965 and seven members of the People's Democratic Party and its associated organizations, including its chairman Budiman Sudjatmiko, and the labour activist Dita Indah Sari. Acehnese political prisoners and Muslim activists from Lampung were also among those freed.

All remaining East Timorese prisoners of conscience and political prisoners in Indonesia had been released by the end of 1999. Among them were Xanana Gusmão, president of the CNRT, who was released on 8 September.

Unfair political trials continued.

⊏ In Irian Jaya, six people were on trial or facing trial at the end of the year in connection with pro-independence activities. The six had been arrested in 1998 in connection with their involvement in planning pro-independence meetings and demonstrations.

They were believed to have been charged under articles of the Criminal Code which relate to planning to bring the territory under foreign domination and intending to cause a revolution. AI believed that the six men were on trial for their legitimate political activities and that, if convicted, they would be prisoners of conscience.

Killings and violence by the security forces

Hundreds of people were killed in the context of counter-insurgency operations, communal violence and political protest. Counter-insurgency operations in Aceh against the armed opposition group the Free Aceh Movement intensified as demands for independence in the area increased and resulted in scores of extrajudicial executions. The Free Aceh Movement was also responsible for human rights abuses including arbitrary killings.

⊏ On 3 February, at least seven people were shot dead when members of the TNI opened fire on a procession in Idi Cut, East Aceh.

⊏ On 3 May, at least 38 people, including at least six children, were shot dead by the TNI in Dewantara Sub-district, North Aceh District, as they took part in a demonstration against military violence in a neighbouring village.

⊏ On 23 July, at least 45 people were extrajudicially executed at a religious school in Beutong Sub-district, West Aceh.

Extrajudicial executions also took place in Irian Jaya in the context of mounting pressure for independence from the local population.

⊏ Three people participating in pro-independence ceremonies in Sorong in July and September were reportedly killed by the security forces.

Excessive and lethal force characterized the authorities' response to many disturbances and demonstrations, including armed and peaceful opposition movements and civil unrest.

⊏ In Jakarta, at least six people were shot dead during demonstrations in September against the proposed new security law.

⊏ In Maluku killings by the military and police occurred as they tried to restore order in the context of communal violence between Muslims and Christians. The security forces were also accused of bias and there were reports of their supporting one side or the other during the violence which resulted in hundreds of deaths during the year.

⊏ Robby Young was shot dead by a member of the military during a disturbance at Jayapura port, Irian Jaya, in July.

Torture and ill-treatment

There were continuing reports of torture and ill-treatment of both criminal and political suspects.

⊏ In Sorong, Irian Jaya, two men who were among a group of 22 people arrested in connection with a flag-raising ceremony sustained broken legs as a result of torture.

'Disappearances'

Dozens of people "disappeared" in Aceh after being taken into custody by members of the military or the

PPRM, a riot police unit. Some people who "disappeared" were subsequently found dead and were believed to have been killed by the security forces. Others remained unaccounted for.

Death penalty
At least 27 people remained under sentence of death. In September an official at the Directorate General of Correctional Institutions was reported to have said that 16 prisoners could be executed imminently. However, no executions took place during 1999. Draft legislation to establish a human rights court provided for a maximum punishment of death for those convicted of serious human rights violations. The court had not been established by the end of the year.

Impunity
A number of prosecutions of members of the security forces took place during 1999.

In February, five soldiers were sentenced to between two years and six-and-a-half years' imprisonment in connection with the beating to death of five detainees in Lhokseumawe, Aceh, in January. At least 20 other detainees were injured in the incident.

A soldier convicted of killing Robby Young in Irian Jaya was sentenced to five years in jail and dismissed from military service in July.

In July, the Independent Commission for the Investigation of Violence in Aceh was formed. The Commission focused on five specific incidents and recommended that those responsible for the violations be brought to trial. No trials had taken place by the end of the year.

Despite these initiatives a climate of impunity persisted. Prosecutions of members of the security forces for human rights violations continued to be the exception rather than the rule. Those who were brought to trial were generally from the lower ranks and were given light sentences. Many cases of past human rights violations remained unresolved.

AI country reports and visits
Reports
- Indonesia: An audit of human rights reform (AI Index: ASA 21/012/99)
- Indonesia: Thirty-three recommendations to Indonesia's development assistance partners (AI Index: ASA 21/014/99)
- Indonesia: Open letter to President Abdurrahman Wahid from Pierre Sané, Secretary General, Amnesty International (AI Index: ASA 21/198/99)
- East Timor: Paramilitary attacks jeopardise East Timor's future (AI Index: ASA 21/026/99)
- East Timor: Seize the moment (AI Index: ASA 21/049/99)
- East Timor: Violence erodes prospects for stability (AI Index: ASA 21/091/99)
- East Timor: The terror continues (AI Index: ASA 21/163/99)
- East Timor: Demand for justice (AI Index: ASA 21/191/99)

Visits
Research visits were made to Indonesia, including to Jakarta and West Timor. AI delegates also visited East Timor in May, October and November. A temporary research office was established in Darwin, Australia, from September to November to work on the crisis in East Timor.

IRAN

ISLAMIC REPUBLIC OF IRAN
Leader of the Islamic Republic of Iran: Ayatollah Sayed 'Ali Khamenei
President: Hojjatoleslam val Moslemin Sayed Mohammad Khatami
Capital: Tehran
Population: 62.3 million
Official language: Farsi
Death penalty: retentionist

Hundreds of people, including possible prisoners of conscience, were held without charge or trial following student demonstrations in July against the growing restrictions on freedom of expression and the closure of the daily newspaper *Salam*. Most were released within two months, but hundreds remained in detention at the end of the year and at least four people were sentenced to death. Numerous publications were forced to close and scores of journalists faced arrest and interrogation. There were continued reports of torture and ill-treatment, and judicial corporal punishments continued to be imposed. AI recorded 165 executions, although the true number may have been considerably higher. Religious minorities continued to face persecution.

Background
Issues relating to freedom of expression dominated the year. Journalists began to address in print the political, economic and social problems facing Iran and broached issues that had previously been taboo. Political debate centred on the permissible level of freedom for the press, accentuating divisions that already existed between the two broad, but opposing, political factions that had supported and opposed President Mohammad Khatami's 1997 election.

The different policy positions taken by various elements of the two opposing factions were vigorously debated both inside and outside the *Majles* (parliament). This political tension exacerbated the rivalry for power that already existed between different elements of the administration. It was due in part to the *Majles* elections scheduled for February 2000 and led to an increasingly inconsistent and arbitrary application of policy and law. As the year progressed, a pattern of intimidation, harassment and administrative detention emerged as a mechanism for silencing a range of opinion.

The Special Representative of the UN Commission on Human Rights on the situation of human rights in the Islamic Republic of Iran continued to be denied access to the country during the year. A resolution adopted by the UN Commission on Human Rights in April expressed concern at continuing human rights violations in Iran and "the apparent absence of respect for internationally recognized legal safeguards".

Student demonstrations

Widespread student protests in Tehran and other cities in July resulted in serious clashes with the official Law Enforcement Forces (LEF), the *basiji* (mobilization units) and a militant group *Ansar-e Hezbollah*, Partisans of the Party of God. The violence began on 8 July when the students, who had gathered outside their university dormitories in Tehran to protest peacefully against the closure of the daily newspaper *Salam*, were attacked by armed members of *Ansar-e Hezbollah*. Security forces posted at the scene failed to protect the students and some hours later members of *Ansar-e Hezbollah* and the LEF, having fired teargas, forced their way into the student residences. There was one confirmed death and reports of several others. Hundreds were reportedly wounded.

The scale of the demonstrations changed dramatically in the following days and the levels of violence escalated. Demonstrations were officially banned in Tehran, but the unrest continued and spread to provincial cities. Hundreds were arrested throughout the country, most of whom were held without charge or trial. The majority had been released by the end of August, but scores of people remained in detention at the end of 1999, where they continued to be at risk of torture. Four men, whose identities were not disclosed, were reportedly sentenced to death after unfair trials by the Tehran Revolutionary Court, and at least 12 people were sentenced to between three months' and nine years' imprisonment by a Revolutionary Court in Tabriz in September for their role in the protests. One of those sentenced to death was believed to be Akbar Mohammadi, who was reportedly tortured while in detention.

▢ Student activists Manuchehr Mohammadi – the brother of Akbar Mohammadi – Gholamreza Mohajeri-Nezhad and Malous Radnia, also known as Maryam Shansi, were arrested in Tehran on 13 July and initially held in incommunicado detention. Manuchehr Mohammadi was accused of having connections with "a fugitive counter-revolutionary element" and of seeking "to initiate and spread disorder and violence". In July Iranian state television broadcast two separate video recordings of his "confessions", which were thought to have been made under duress, and which resulted in the detention of four members of the *Hezb-e Mellat-e Iran*, Iran Nation Party, on similar charges. Manuchehr Mohammadi was reportedly sentenced to 13 years' imprisonment in October. Gholamreza Mohajeri

Nezhad and Malous Radnia were reportedly released in November, possibly on bail.

Restriction of freedom of expression

Numerous publications were forced to close, particularly those established after President Khatami came to power in 1997. They included the cultural journals *Adineh* and *Zan*, the newspapers *Salam*, *Neshat*, *Khordad*, *Rah-e No*, *Iran-e Farda* and the bi-weekly *Hoveyat-e Khish*. Scores of journalists, editors and publishers were arrested and interrogated, and many were convicted and banned from journalism after unfair trials.

▢ Heshmatollah Tabarzadi, editor of *Hoveyat-e Khish*, was detained in June in connection with articles that were alleged to have insulted "the principles of the Islamic Republic". He was reportedly tortured by having the soles of his feet whipped with cable (see below). He was released on bail in November.

▢ Mohammad Musavi Khoeiniha, publisher of *Salam*, was tried by the Special Court for the Clergy. The jury found him guilty of "publishing classified material" but the judge suspended a prison sentence and punishment of flogging on the grounds that Mohammad Musavi Khoeiniha was a former revolutionary leader. He was banned from journalism for five years.

Unfair trials by special courts

Government critics, including Shi'a clerics, journalists and students, were tried and sentenced after trials in which procedures did not conform to international standards for fair trial. The Special Court for the Clergy, the Press and the Revolutionary Courts followed inconsistent and often summary proceedings. Juries in the Press Court were sometimes dismissed prior to trial and on other occasions their decisions were ignored. Press Court judgments were occasionally issued prior to jury consultation. Defendants were generally tried *in camera* in the Revolutionary Courts and denied legal representation of their choice.

Public criticism of the special courts was unprecedented and they were widely perceived as a mechanism for silencing criticism.

▢ Abdollah Nouri, a former Minister of the Interior and publisher of the daily newspaper *Khordad*, was tried by the SCC in November on 20 charges, including insulting government officials. In his defence he reportedly upheld the constitutional rights of a variety of groups and theologians to present their views in his newspaper; he also claimed that the Special Court for the Clergy was "unlawful and incompetent" to try his case. The judge brought the proceedings to an end on 11 November when he prevented Abdollah Nouri from completing his defence and gave him 10 days to submit a written text of the defence. However, on 17 November the jury reportedly found Abdollah Nouri guilty of 15 of the 20 charges against him. He was sentenced to five years' imprisonment and disqualified from standing in the parliamentary elections in February 2000.

▢ Mashallah Shamsolva'ezin, editor of the daily newspaper *Asr-e Azadegan*, was tried in November on charges of "insulting Islam" in articles printed in the subsequently banned newspaper, *Neshat*. The Press Court judge dismissed the jury prior to the trial and sentenced Mashallah Shamsolva'ezin to three years' imprisonment. Mashallah Shamsolva'ezin questioned the absence of the jury and observed that the Court had "no legal basis".

'Abbas Amir Entezam
Prisoner of conscience and former Deputy Prime Minister 'Abbas Amir Entezam continued to be held in Evin prison despite the 1998 recommendations of a trial judge that he be released on bail. A hearing to answer charges of defamation was held in February, but 'Abbas Amir Entezam was refused permission to appear in court and his lawyers were excluded from the proceedings. He was released on bail for medical treatment in October, but rearrested in December after the authorities claimed that he violated his bail conditions by giving an interview to a journalist. He remained in Evin prison at the end of 1999.

Death penalty
The death penalty continued to be passed routinely in connection with charges of murder, drug trafficking and armed robbery. It was occasionally imposed for affiliation with armed opposition groups. AI recorded 165 executions, although the true number may have been considerably higher. Seventeen-year-old Ebrahim Qorbanzadeh was hanged for murder in October.

◻ In February the Supreme Court reportedly overturned the death sentence against Helmut Hofer, a German businessman who had been convicted of having illicit sex with an Iranian woman, and ordered a retrial. He was rearrested in August and charged with having "links to foreign elements".

Religious minorities
◻ Up to 20 members of the Baha'i religious minority detained in previous years continued to be held, and among them five remained under sentence of death.

◻ Twenty-one people, including 13 members of Jewish communities in the southern cities of Shiraz and Isfahan, were arrested in March. They were thought to include rabbis, religious teachers and community leaders. No official explanation was provided for the arrests, but news reports citing the Iranian authorities stated that they were accused of spying for Israel and the USA and would be tried for espionage before a Revolutionary Court. Most were denied family visits and access to legal counsel. All 13 remained in detention without charge at the end of 1999.

Flogging and amputation
AI recorded 26 cases of flogging and 16 cases of amputation, although the true number may have been considerably higher.

◻ Two women, identified only as Jamileh and Zahra, were convicted of theft and murder by a Tehran court in February and sentenced to the amputation of a hand. Jamileh was also sentenced to death by hanging and Zahra to 15 months' imprisonment.

Torture and ill-treatment
Several defendants facing trial before Revolutionary Courts stated that they were tortured during detention, prior to trial or release on bail. Methods of torture included repeated beatings, flogging on the soles of the feet with metallic cables and being suspended upside-down from a ceiling (see Akbar Mohammadi and Heshmatollah Tabarzadi above).

Investigations into allegations of torture and the 1998 murders
A military court in Tehran tried Brigadier General Gholamreza Naqdi and 10 colleagues on charges of torture in May, after allegations made by 30 Tehran district mayors who were detained in March 1998 on charges of corruption. It was believed to be the first time that charges of torture were brought against a serving officer and military personnel since the establishment of the Islamic Republic of Iran in 1979. All were acquitted of torture, but cautioned for ill-treatment of prisoners in custody.

In February the National Security Council, led by President Khatami, established a committee to investigate the 1998 murders of numerous writers and intellectuals. Initial inquiries led to the identification of suspects within the Ministry of Intelligence. In February the Minister of Intelligence, Qorbanali Dorri-Najafabadi, resigned along with some other senior officials. Sa'id Emami, one of the officials implicated in the murders, was detained in February and died in custody in June, reportedly due to suicide. By the end of 1999 no charges had been laid and no one had been brought to trial.

Communications with the government
AI wrote to the government on nine occasions in 1999. In February it sought details about the composition of the committee investigating the 1998 murders and the terms of reference. It called for the findings to be made public and sought permission to observe any trial proceedings which may result from these investigations. In August AI expressed concern about restraints on freedom of opinion and expression and sought information about a number of the students detained in July. The organization had not received a response to any of its letters by the end of the year. AI was not permitted to visit the country.

IRAQ

REPUBLIC OF IRAQ
Head of state and government: Saddam Hussain
Capital: Baghdad
Population: 22.2 million
Official language: Arabic
Death penalty: retentionist

Violent clashes between the security forces and armed Islamist activists in the predominantly Shi'a south were frequently reported, especially following the killing in suspicious circumstances on 19 February of Ayatollah Sadeq al-Sadr, a prominent Shi'a cleric. Dozens of people from both sides were killed. Hundreds of people, including political prisoners and possible prisoners of conscience, were executed and large-scale arbitrary arrests of suspected political opponents took place. Torture and ill-treatment of prisoners and detainees were widely reported. Hundreds of non-Arab families, mostly Kurds, were forcibly expelled from their homes in the Kirkuk area to Iraqi Kurdistan.

Background

Iraq continued to be subjected to stringent economic sanctions imposed by UN Security Council resolutions after Iraq's invasion of Kuwait in 1990. The sanctions have crippled the country's economic infrastructure and have contributed to a deteriorating economic situation, increased unemployment, rising malnutrition and mortality levels and widespread corruption. In 1999, UNICEF estimated that sanctions had contributed to the deaths of some 500,000 children under the age of five.

In January the UN Security Council established three separate panels on Iraq: the first to examine disarmament and verification issues; the second to assess the humanitarian situation; and the third to investigate the issue of Kuwaiti prisoners of war and Kuwaiti property. The three panels submitted their recommendations two months later. The humanitarian panel recommended the raising of the ceiling on oil sales to create additional revenue, more humanitarian assistance and better distribution of humanitarian supplies to meet pressing humanitarian needs in Iraq. It also recommended that the Iraqi government facilitate the timely distribution of humanitarian goods and address the needs of vulnerable groups.

After months of negotiations, the UN Security Council adopted Resolution 1284 in December. This resolution established a new arms inspection body, the UN Monitoring, Verification and Inspection Commission (UNMOVIC), and raised the possibility of the lifting of sanctions if the government of Iraq allowed arms inspections to start again. The resolution also included some provisions intended to ease the humanitarian impact of the sanctions. However, divisions in the Security Council and Iraq's stated refusal to cooperate with the arms monitoring program left much uncertainty as to the likelihood of any improvement.

In August 'Ezzat Ibrahim al-Duri, Vice-Chairman of Iraq's Revolutionary Command Council, the highest executive body in the country, went to Austria for medical treatment. While he was in hospital a Vienna city councillor filed a complaint against him with the Vienna courts, accusing him of being responsible for the 1990 Iraqi invasion of Kuwait and personally taking part in attacks on Kurds and of committing other atrocities, including torture. A few days later 'Ezzat Ibrahim al-Duri left Austria, reportedly before completing his treatment and despite calls on the Austrian government by the USA, Iraqi opposition groups and human rights groups to investigate or indict him.

In September AI received a communication from the Iraqi authorities about the *Amnesty International Report 1999*, which failed to allay AI's concerns.

Civilians killed in US and UK air attacks

Since the four-day air strikes launched by US and United Kingdom (UK) forces in December 1998, these forces had been carrying out regular strikes on Iraqi targets inside the two air exclusion zones in northern and southern Iraq. These zones, north of the 36th parallel and south of the 33rd parallel, were imposed by allied forces at the end of the Gulf war and were intended to protect Iraq's Kurdish and Shi'a Muslim population. The strikes reportedly resulted in the deaths of dozens of civilians and left many more injured. US military officials often accused Iraq of stationing military equipment near civilian population centres.

⌂ On 30 April a shepherd and six members of his family were killed in their tent in Mosul in the north. A UN humanitarian official who visited the area confirmed the killings.

AI issued worldwide appeals expressing concern about the continuing loss of civilian lives as a result of these air strikes. The organization received responses from UK and US government officials stating that their forces had been acting in self-defence and were making great efforts to avoid civilian casualties. However, the responses did not give any indication as to what steps were being taken to avoid civilian loss of life, although in October US military officials publicly stated that US warplanes were using concrete-filled bombs instead of explosives in attacks on northern Iraq to "minimize the chances of damage to people and property around military targets".

Death penalty

The death penalty continued to be used extensively. Hundreds of people, including possible prisoners of conscience, were executed during 1999. In many cases it was impossible to determine whether the reported executions were judicial or extrajudicial, given the secrecy surrounding them. Most of the victims were Shi'a Muslims suspected of anti-government activities. Also among those executed were a number of senior army officers suspected of having links with the Iraqi opposition outside the country or plotting to overthrow the government.

◻ In March a 36-year-old army officer in the Special Forces, Mohammad Jabbar al-Rubay'i, was executed. He had reportedly been detained in the Military Intelligence Prison for about two years. His body was handed over to his family for burial but without any religious ceremony. He had allegedly been accused of planning to flee the country.

◻ At least 100 people were executed in Abu Ghraib Prison on 12 October 1999. They included 19 political detainees, among them the writer Hamid al-Mukhtar. He had been held for several months after the assassination of Ayatollah al-Sadr in February. He reportedly decided to organize a religious ceremony in his house to commemorate Ayatollah al-Sadr's death. The security forces stormed his house and arrested him and his son. The son was reportedly tortured and released. Hamid al-Mukhtar was executed.

Torture and ill-treatment

Torture and ill-treatment were used systematically against detainees in prisons and detention centres despite its prohibition under the Iraqi Constitution. Political detainees were subjected to severe torture. The most common methods of physical and psychological torture included electric shocks to various parts of the body, pulling out of fingernails, long periods of suspension by the limbs, beating with cables, falaqa (beating on the soles of the feet) cigarette burns, piercing of hands with an electric drill, mock executions and threats of bringing in a female relative of the detainee, especially the wife or the mother, and raping her in front of the detainee.

◻ A 59-year-old doctor was arrested in her clinic in June on suspicion that she had contacts with an Iraqi opposition group, an accusation she strongly denied. She was held incommunicado for a month during which she was tortured. During the first few days she was forced to lie down on the floor and was beaten with a cable on the soles of her feet (falaqa) by a hooded man. She lost consciousness on several occasions. She escaped by bribing a prison officer and fled the country.

Arbitrary arrest and detention

Reports of widespread arbitrary arrests of suspected political opponents, including possible prisoners of conscience, continued throughout 1999. Most of those arrested were Shi'a Muslims suspected of having links with underground Islamist armed groups or simply relatives of people sought by the authorities. Thousands of suspected political opponents arrested in previous years continued to be held at the end of 1999. Generally it was not possible to obtain information on the detainees' fate and whereabouts, because of both the government's control of information and the fear of reprisals. In some cases those arrested were later executed and there was no information as to whether they had been tried and convicted or simply extrajudicially executed.

◻ In January and February, before the assassination of Ayatollah al-Sadr on 19 February, a number of his closest associates were arrested in southern Iraq and in Baghdad; their whereabouts remained unknown at the end of 1999. Among them were al-Shaikh Awus al-Khaffaji, an Imam in al-Nassirya, and al-Shaikh 'As'ad al-Nassiri, a religious scholar in al-Najaf.

◻ Dr Hashem Hassan, a lecturer in journalism at the University of Baghdad, was arrested at the beginning of October and his whereabouts remained unknown at the end of 1999. He was reportedly on his way to Jordan when he was arrested on the Iraqi side of the border by plainclothes security men. Dr Hassan had written numerous articles in newspapers. Before his arrest he had reportedly been stripped of his membership of both the Iraqi Journalists' Union and the Iraqi Writers' Union because he had criticized government policies in his writing.

Iraqi Kurdistan

Since 1997 the human rights situation in Iraqi Kurdistan had gradually improved. A cease-fire declared in 1997 brought an end to large-scale abuses by the ruling parties, their militias and security forces. However, isolated cases of human rights abuses continued to be reported in Iraqi Kurdistan in 1999. These included arbitrary arrests and political killings. The fate of scores of political prisoners and people who had "disappeared" in previous years remained unknown.

The cease-fire declared at the end of 1997 between the Kurdistan Democratic Party (KDP) and the Patriotic Union of Kurdistan (PUK) remained in force during 1999. Further talks between the PUK and KDP were held during 1999 on the implementation of a peace agreement signed in Washington, USA, in September 1998, which included a commitment to elections in areas controlled by the two groups. In October the two parties agreed to exchange all remaining prisoners and to open offices in each other's territories.

◻ In February, two Iranian opposition members, Mehdi Satter-Aloyoub and his brother Massoud Satter-Aloyoub, were arrested in Sulaymania by PUK security forces, a few days after fleeing Iran. They were accused by the PUK of entering Iraqi Kurdistan illegally and attempting to join the People's Mojahedin Organization of Iran, based in Baghdad. At the end of 1999 they were reportedly still held without trial in Sulaymania General Security Directorate.

◻ In October Nabil Khalil Karim, a trade unionist sought by the Iraqi security authorities for suspected anti-government activities, fled from Baghdad. On arriving in Arbil he was arrested, reportedly by the KDP security forces, and his whereabouts remained unknown at the end of 1999.

AI received reports of politically motivated killings during 1999. Armed Islamist activists were reported to have committed some of the killings. Most of those targeted were reported to be secularists, including well-known communist figures. Death threats and harassment, reportedly by Islamist groups, against women members of women's organizations and communist groups continued to be reported.

◻ In April Nicholas Sleight, a New Zealand national and UN mine-clearance worker, was killed by an unidentified gunman near the UN compound of Ain Kawa in Arbil. In May the KDP informed AI that an investigation was under way, the results of which would be made public.

☐ In October Farhad Faraj Amin, a member of the Central Committee of the Organization of Communist Revolutionaries, an opposition group, was shot and killed at his home in Sulaymania by unidentified armed men.

☐ In July the KDP informed AI that judicial investigations were still continuing into the killing of two Assyrian women, Nasreen Hina Shaba and her daughter Larsa Tuma, whose house was bombed in December 1998. According to the KDP, investigations were also continuing into several other attacks on Christian families in Arbil as well as the killing of two Iraqi Workers' Communist Party members in April 1998.

AI country report
• Iraq: Victims of systematic repression (AI Index: MDE 14/010/99)

IRELAND

IRELAND
Head of state: Mary McAleese
Head of government: Bertie Ahern
Capital: Dublin
Population: 3.6 million
Official languages: Irish, English
Death penalty: abolitionist for all crimes

The government participated in negotiations about a future political settlement in Northern Ireland. Various human rights provisions of the 1998 Multi-Party Agreement were under active consideration by the government. The tradition of tolerance towards minorities was eroded during the year – in particular there were many reports of racially motivated physical and verbal abuse against asylum-seekers and travellers.

Human rights provisions
The Multi-Party Agreement of April 1998 concerning the future of Northern Ireland envisaged a continuing role for the Irish and United Kingdom governments, and proposed mechanisms to promote and protect human rights. The government acted on some of these proposals. It put forward draft legislation in July on the creation of a Human Rights Commission with powers of inquiry, monitoring and reviewing, and it considered the incorporation of the European Convention for the Protection of Human Rights and Fundamental Freedoms into domestic law. These provisions were

discussed in a meeting in June between the Minister of Justice and AI representatives. Other issues raised at the same meeting included: asylum legislation; emergency legislation; procedures to examine complaints against the police; inquests; and inquiries into the Dublin and Monaghan bombings and the case of Seamus Ludlow.

The government initiated a thorough review of the Offences against the State Acts. In October AI urged the Review Committee to recommend the disestablishment of the Special Criminal Court and the repeal of provisions including those permitting internment and impinging on the right to silence. AI called for detainees to have the right to free legal assistance during questioning.

Inquiries into alleged collusion
The government appointed the retiring Chief Justice, Liam Hamilton, to carry out a private, but independent, judicial inquiry into the bombings in Dublin and Monaghan in 1974, which killed 33 people and injured hundreds. Members of the Northern Ireland security forces' intelligence units allegedly colluded with the Ulster Volunteer Force, a Loyalist armed group, in the bombings. The inquiry would also examine the police investigation of the bombings, and the bombing of a pub in Dundalk in 1975. By the end of 1999, it was still not decided whether the inquiry would also examine the killing of Seamus Ludlow in 1976, and the alleged subsequent cover-up by both British and Irish authorities. Seamus Ludlow was killed in Ireland, reportedly by a Northern Irish Loyalist group, which included two soldiers.

The government stated that the inquiry's results would be published, and that a subsequent public inquiry remained possible. AI had called for public inquiries into these incidents.

Inquests
In October a High Court judge overturned a coroner's decision to allow police witnesses involved in a fatal shooting to remain anonymous and to give evidence from behind screens, and a further decision to allow the police to limit the family's access to forensic evidence. The decision was taken in the case of John Morris, a member of the Irish National Liberation Army (INLA), who had been shot dead in disputed circumstances in 1997 by police during an attempted robbery. The coroner appealed against the High Court decision.

Refugees
The Immigration Bill 1999 was introduced in order to amend the 1996 Refugee Act, which the government claimed was unworkable, and which had not been enacted in full, leaving gaps in the legal framework for refugee protection. AI was concerned about various parts of the bill, including its failure to recognize the fundamental nature of the right of *non-refoulement*. AI was also concerned about the Illegal Immigrants Trafficking Bill, which failed to make a distinction between professional traffickers and those assisting genuine asylum-seekers.

AI country reports and visits
Report
- Republic of Ireland: Submission to the Committee to Review the Offences Against the State Acts and Other Matters (AI Index: EUR 29/001/99)

Visit
AI delegates visited Ireland in June and met the Minister of Justice.

ISRAEL AND THE OCCUPIED TERRITORIES

STATE OF ISRAEL
Head of state: President Ezer Weizman
Head of government: Ehud Barak (replaced Binyamin Netanyahu in July)
Official languages: Hebrew, Arabic
Death penalty: abolitionist for ordinary crimes

Official permission for torture and ill-treatment ended in September when the High Court ruled that various interrogation techniques used by the General Security Service (GSS) were unlawful. Scores of Palestinian administrative detainees were released during 1999, but 14 Palestinians were still held in administrative detention at the end of the year. Hundreds of Palestinians were tried before military courts whose procedures failed to comply with international standards for fair trial. At the end of 1999 there were about 1,500 Palestinian political prisoners; more than 300 were released during the year under peace agreements. Israeli security forces killed at least eight Palestinians in circumstances suggesting that they were unlawfully killed. On the basis of a policy that discriminated against Palestinians, houses in the West Bank were demolished because their owners had been unable to secure building permits. At least 29 Lebanese nationals were held in Israel, including 16 held in administrative detention. More than 150 Lebanese nationals were held without charge or trial at the end of 1999 in Khiam Detention Centre in Israeli-occupied south Lebanon. Incidents of ill-treatment by members of the security services in Israel and the Occupied Territories were frequently reported. At least six conscientious objectors were imprisoned for refusing to perform military service.

Background
In May Ehud Barak, of the One Israel party, was elected Prime Minister. Parliamentary elections also took place. A coalition government assumed power in July.

After resuming talks in August, Israel and the Palestine Liberation Organization (PLO) signed the Sharm al-Shaykh memorandum in September, agreeing to resume final status negotiations. In accordance with the agreement, in September and October Israel released 309 Palestinian political prisoners and 41 other Arab political prisoners, and redeployed its troops in certain areas of the West Bank. Palestinians' freedom of movement continued to be severely restricted. Israel maintained the border closures between Israel and the West Bank (excluding East Jerusalem) and between Israel and the Gaza Strip. In October Israel opened a safe passage route to facilitate travel by Palestinians between the West Bank and Gaza Strip. Attacks were carried out on Palestinians by armed Israeli settlers and on settlers by armed Palestinians.

The military conflict between the Israel Defence Force (IDF) and the South Lebanon Army (SLA) on the one hand and *Hizbullah* on the other continued. In July the Prime Minister announced Israel's intention to withdraw from Israeli-occupied south Lebanon within one year. The SLA had withdrawn from the Jezzine salient in south Lebanon in May and June.

Israel's large population of migrant workers, including women trafficked for prostitution from the Commonwealth of Independent States, continued to be the target of human rights abuses. Hundreds were held in detention for extended periods pending deportation and there were reports of police brutality against them.

Torture
Torture and ill-treatment continued to be officially permitted and systematically used by the GSS to interrogate security detainees until September, when the High Court of Justice ruled that such interrogation methods were unlawful. The GSS immediately ceased to use the specified techniques, which included *tiltul,* violent shaking; *shabeh,* where detainees were shackled to low sloping chairs in contorted positions for extended periods and forced to listen to loud, distorted music; *gambaz,* where detainees were forced to crouch for extended periods; excessive tightening of handcuffs; and sleep deprivation. In October the ministerial committee overseeing the GSS set up a professional committee to investigate the implications of the Court's decision. In October draft legislation was submitted to the parliament (*Knesset)* to empower the GSS to use physical force during interrogations in certain circumstances.

Ill-treatment
There were many reports of Palestinians being beaten and otherwise ill-treated at checkpoints, during demonstrations or immediately after arrest. There were also reports of beatings of migrant workers by the police and other officials in public places and during searches of their homes.

In May members of the Border Police beat Ziad 'Ali Taamra, a driver aged 21, at a checkpoint near Bethlehem, injuring his legs, stomach and chest. The Israeli army admitted, after an initial investigation, that it appeared that the officers had used "unreasonable force". The Department for Investigation of Police Misconduct recommended their prosecution. No charges had been brought against them by the end of 1999.

An inspector from the Ministry of Trade and Industry beat two illegal migrant workers from China with a metal rod one metre in length in August after he found them trapped in a commercial vehicle in Tel Aviv.

Administrative detention

Scores of Palestinian administrative detainees were released, including Usama Barham, who had been held without charge or trial since 1994. At the end of 1999, 14 Palestinians remained in administrative detention. An additional 16 Lebanese nationals remained in administrative detention. Nine were held beyond the expiry of their prison sentences and seven were held without charge or trial, including two detainees held incommunicado. They were held to exchange for Israeli nationals who had "disappeared" in Lebanon or for information concerning them. The Supreme Court had not ruled on appeals against their continued detention by the end of the year. Five other Lebanese administrative detainees were released in December.

'Abdallah 'Abdallah al-Khatib, a 27-year-old Palestinian, was held in administrative detention at the end of 1999. He had been arrested and placed under administrative detention in July 1998. During appeals neither he nor his lawyer had been allowed to examine the evidence against him.

Ghassan Fares al-Dirani, a Lebanese national aged 30, was held in administrative detention at the end of 1999. He had been detained without charge or trial since his arrest in Lebanon in 1987. He was reported to be in poor physical and mental health.

Unfair trials

Hundreds of Palestinians were arrested and tried in military courts for offences such as membership of illegal organizations and stone-throwing. Many were detained incommunicado for days without being brought before a court. Confessions extracted under torture frequently formed the main evidence against them. In August the military government lowered the age at which Palestinian children could be tried in military courts and imprisoned, from 14 to 12 years. The courts increased the tariff sentence for stone-throwing by children from four weeks' to four months' imprisonment.

Su'ad Hilmi Ghazal, a Palestinian school student from Sebastiya village who was arrested in December 1998 at the age of 15, was still in detention at the end of 1999, pending trial on charges of assaulting an Israeli. She was held with adult prisoners at Neve Tirza Prison.

House demolitions

At least 39 Palestinian houses in the West Bank were demolished because their owners had been unable to obtain building permits from the Israeli authorities. The policy of house demolitions discriminated against Palestinians and appeared to be aimed at stopping Palestinian development in parts of the West Bank under Israeli control.

South Lebanon

During 1999, 23 Lebanese and two Israeli civilians were reportedly killed as a result of the military conflict in south Lebanon. Most civilians were killed as a result of deliberate or indiscriminate attacks.

In June, at least eight Lebanese civilians were killed in Israeli air raids directed against Lebanese infrastructure. The raids were a retaliation for the killing of two Israeli civilians in rocket attacks by *Hizbullah* and were followed by further *Hizbullah* shelling of northern Israel.

As well as at least 29 Lebanese nationals detained in Israel, more than 150 Lebanese nationals, including children, were detained without charge or trial at the end of 1999 in Khiam Detention Centre in Israeli-occupied south Lebanon. Torture and ill-treatment were used routinely at the prison and in other SLA detention centres. Israel continued to deny responsibility for the administration of the prison and maintained that its militia ally, the SLA, was exclusively responsible. In September the IDF admitted that GSS officers visited the prison and had assisted in training SLA interrogators, and that the salaries of prison staff were paid by Israel.

Extrajudicial executions and unlawful killings

Israeli security forces frequently used excessive force or opened fire on Palestinians in circumstances where the lives of the security forces were not apparently in danger. Eight Palestinian civilians were killed in circumstances suggesting that they may have been extrajudicially executed or otherwise unlawfully killed.

In January the Border Police used excessive force when they opened fire in 'Isawiyeh in East Jerusalem on Palestinians demonstrating against house demolitions. Zaki 'Ubayd, aged 28, was killed after a rubber-coated metal bullet fired at close range struck him in the neck. In August the Department for Investigation of Police Misconduct recommended that two Border Police officers be prosecuted in connection with the death, but by the end of 1999 the District Attorney's office had not brought charges against them.

Conscientious objectors

Israel continued to imprison conscientious objectors who refused to perform military service. Military courts sentenced at least six conscientious objectors to imprisonment and nearly all of them served multiple sentences. They were prisoners of conscience.

In June a military court sentenced Walid Muhammad Naffa', a Druze conscientious objector from Beit Jann, to five months' imprisonment for desertion. This was his 11th prison sentence for refusing to serve in the IDF on grounds of conscience. He was released in September and exempted from military service on grounds of "unsuitability".

Impunity

Most members of the security forces who used torture or ill-treatment, carried out unlawful killings or committed other violations enjoyed impunity for their actions. In those cases where members of the security forces were convicted of human rights violations, light sentences were imposed.

▭ In November 1997 an IDF soldier fired in the direction of a group of three children, killing 'Ali Jawarish, aged eight. The soldier's life did not appear to be in danger. In February the Military Advocate General's office concluded that the soldier had behaved appropriately and that no further action would be taken.

Intergovernmental developments

The UN Special Rapporteur, appointed pursuant to Commission on Human Rights Resolution 1993/2A "to investigate Israel's violations of the principles and bases of international law", visited areas under the Palestinian Authority's jurisdiction. Israel continued to refuse to cooperate with the Special Rapporteur. In an oral statement to the UN Commission on Human Rights in March, AI reiterated its concerns that Israel had violated international human rights treaties in the name of "security".

In February the UN General Assembly requested the High Contracting Parties to the Fourth Geneva Convention to hold a conference to discuss enforcement measures against Israel for failure to implement the Convention in the Occupied Territories. The conference took place in July. Israel and the USA did not attend. The conference was adjourned with no date set for its resumption.

AI country reports and visits

Reports
- Israel: The price of principles – imprisonment of conscientious objectors (AI Index: MDE 15/049/99)
- Israel and the Occupied Territories: Demolition and dispossession – the destruction of Palestinian homes (AI Index: MDE 15/059/99)

Visits
AI delegates visited Israel in January to conduct research on conscientious objectors, in April and May to research the trafficking of women from the Commonwealth of Independent States to Israel, and in May and June to investigate house demolitions in the West Bank.

ITALY

ITALIAN REPUBLIC
Head of state: Carlo Azeglio Ciampi (replaced Oscar Luigi Scalfaro in May)
Head of government: Massimo D'Alema
Capital: Rome
Population: 57.5 million
Official language: Italian
Death penalty: abolitionist for all crimes
1999 treaty ratifications/signatures: Rome Statute of the International Criminal Court

There were further allegations of ill-treatment inflicted by law enforcement and prison officers. Conditions in some prisons reportedly amounted to cruel, inhuman or degrading treatment. Criminal proceedings opened into alleged ill-treatment were often subject to lengthy delays. By the end of 1999, no one had been committed for trial as a result of criminal investigations opened into the allegations which came to light in 1997 and 1998 of the ill-treatment, torture and unlawful killing of Somalis by members of the Italian armed forces participating in a multinational peace-keeping operation in Somalia in 1993. Several criminal proceedings were under way in connection with human rights violations committed against Italian citizens by members of the Argentine security forces in the 1970s and 1980s and as a result of past collaboration between the security forces of several South American countries. Three men imprisoned in 1997 following possibly unfair trial proceedings for participation in a politically motivated murder were granted a judicial review. Parliament approved a constitutional amendment introducing, in principle, strengthened fair trial guarantees for defendants in criminal proceedings. Enabling legislation to allow its practical application was still under parliamentary consideration at the end of 1999.

Alleged ill-treatment by law enforcement officers

There were a number of allegations of gratuitous and deliberate violence inflicted on detainees by law enforcement officers; at least one detainee died in disputed circumstances. The allegations concerned both Italian and foreign nationals, but a high proportion of the allegations received by AI continued to concern foreign nationals, many from Africa and a number of Roma. Some were reluctant to make official complaints because they feared repercussions. The government argued that, according to official figures emerging from surveys conducted by one law enforcement agency in previous years, allegations of ill-treatment by foreigners were in fact a small proportion of the total number of such allegations. It stated that "foreign citizens, especially those from outside the Community who are less familiar with the guarantees offered by the Italian legal order and who sometimes find themselves in Italian territory only for a very brief time, are inclined to turn to non-governmental organizations to complain about alleged ill-treatment rather than avail themselves of the ordinary juridical channels". The authorities appeared thus to recognize that the official statistics at their disposal were not a true reflection of the full extent of the phenomenon.

Update

In October, almost three years after two police officers were committed for trial, a court in Catanzaro found them guilty of abusing their powers and causing Grace Patrick Akpan injuries in February 1996. AI had repeatedly expressed concern to the authorities about her allegations of ill-treatment. The officers were put on probation for two months and charged with the expenses of the legal proceedings. The charges against Grace Patrick Akpan, who had been accused of refusing to identify herself to the officers and of insulting, resisting and injuring them, were dismissed.

Alleged ill-treatment in prisons

Allegations of ill-treatment by prison officers emanated from several prisons and there was concern that in some prisons, including several newly established detention centres for aliens, the overall conditions of detention might amount to cruel, inhuman or degrading treatment. Chronic prison overcrowding persisted, despite continuing efforts by the authorities to address the problem. Reports of overcrowding were often accompanied by complaints of inadequate medical assistance, poor sanitation and other connected problems, including high rates of suicide, attempted suicide and self-inflicted injury. Several criminal proceedings against prison officers accused of ill-treatment in previous years were subject to excessive delays and fears were expressed that the failure of the criminal justice system to function swiftly and efficiently in such cases might be creating a climate of impunity.
▢ Criminal proceedings opened in 1993 into the alleged ill-treatment of inmates of Secondigliano prison, Naples, ended in the acquittal of some 60 prison officers. Separate proceedings opened in 1993 against six other officers accused of various offences, including falsifying records and instigating other officers to commit offences, were apparently still under way. In 1997 lawyers in Catania had complained that inmates of Bicocca Prison were regularly subjected to ill-treatment by prison officers and expressed concern that those involved included officers transferred from Secondigliano where they were already under investigation for alleged ill-treatment. In October, following a criminal investigation into further alleged ill-treatment of Secondigliano prisoners between June 1995 and February 1999, 20 prison officers were ordered to stand trial in 2000.

Intergovernmental organizations

In March the UN Committee on the Elimination of Racial Discrimination included in its principal subjects of concern "reports of acts of violence and ill-treatment by police and prison guards against foreigners and members of minorities in detention" and "the apparent lack of appropriate training for law enforcement officials and other public officials regarding the provisions of the Convention" on the Elimination of Racial Discrimination. It recommended that Italy "strengthen its efforts towards preventing and prosecuting incidents of racial intolerance and discrimination against foreigners and Roma people", as well as "ill-treatment of foreigners and Roma in detention".

In May the UN Committee against Torture urged that "the legislative authorities... proceed to incorporate into domestic law the crime of torture as defined in article 1 of the Convention" against Torture and Other Cruel, Inhuman or Degrading Treatment or Punishment "and make provision for an appropriate system of compensation for torture victims".

The Committee highlighted its concern that "the prison system remains overcrowded and lacking in facilities which makes the overall conditions of detention not conducive to the efforts of preventing inhuman or degrading treatment", that reports of ill-treatment continued and that "many of them involved foreigners". It recommended that all prisoners' correspondence addressed to "international procedures of investigation and settlement be excluded from 'censor checks' by prison personnel or other authorities". Regarding the incidents in Somalia, the Committee expressed concern about "lack of training in the field of human rights, in particular the prohibition against torture, given to the troops participating in the peace-keeping operations and the inadequate number of military police accompanying them". The Committee considered these factors "responsible in part" for the incidents and asked that the government inform it of the progress and result of the relevant judicial proceedings.

In April, AI drew the Committee's and the government's attention to a report describing its concerns about alleged torture and ill-treatment.

Violations against Italian citizens in South America

Seven former members of the Argentine armed forces were committed for trial *in absentia* in connection with the abduction and murder of seven Italian citizens and the kidnapping of the child of one of them during the years of military rule in Argentina. The trial, scheduled to open in Rome in October, was postponed until December when, after one day, it was postponed until March 2000. The trial was the result of investigations opened by the Italian judiciary in 1983, following complaints lodged by relatives of "disappeared" Italian citizens. In the intervening years, AI joined relatives and civil rights groups in calling on the Italian authorities to keep the investigations open.

In July the Minister of Justice gave authorization for a criminal prosecution to be pursued against five more Argentine officers accused of the murder of three Italian citizens in a secret detention centre in

Argentina. Several other criminal proceedings, in the early stages of investigation, were under way into complaints of further human rights violations committed against Italian citizens by members of the Argentine security forces and as a result of past collaboration between the security forces of several South American countries.

Adriano Sofri, Giorgio Pietrostefani and Ovidio Bompressi

In March the Brescia Appeal Court ruled on an application which Adriano Sofri, Giorgio Pietrostefani and Ovidio Bompressi — three leading members of the former extra-parliamentary left-wing group *Lotta Continua* (Continuous Struggle) — had lodged in December 1997, requesting a judicial review of a sentence issued by the Milan Appeal Court in 1995. The sentence had resulted in their imprisonment in January 1997, after nine years of judicial proceedings and seven trials, to serve 22-year sentences for participation in the killing of a police commissioner in Milan in 1972. The men's argument that the application contained new witness and technical evidence and that, therefore, the proceedings qualified for review had already been rejected by the Milan Appeal Court in 1998. However, the Supreme Court annulled that decision and returned the case to appeal court level for re-examination.

When the Brescia Appeal Court also ruled the application inadmissible, a further appeal was lodged with the Supreme Court which in May annulled the Brescia decision and referred the application to the Venice Appeal Court. In August the Venice Appeal Court ruled that the application was admissible and that the review should commence in that court in October. It also suspended the men's prison sentences, resulting in the release of Adriano Sofri and Giorgio Pietrostefani; Ovidio Bompressi's sentence had already been temporarily suspended on health grounds in 1998.

The judicial review was still under way at the end of 1999. AI had repeatedly expressed concern at the excessive length and complexity of the proceedings leading to the men's imprisonment. AI also expressed serious doubts about the fairness of the proceedings, including the extent to which the final verdict relied on the uncorroborated evidence of a *pentito* (a person benefiting from remission of sentence in return for collaboration with the judicial authorities) and whose testimony had contained contradictions and inaccuracies.

AI country reports
- Italy: A briefing for the UN Committee against Torture (AI Index: EUR 30/002/99)
- Concerns in Europe, January – June 1999: Italy (AI Index: EUR 01/002/99)

JAMAICA

JAMAICA
Head of state: Queen Elizabeth II, represented by Howard Felix Cooke
Head of government: Percival James Patterson
Capital: Kingston
Population: 2.5 million
Official language: English
Death penalty: retentionist

At least 44 people were on death row. In July the government announced that it would consider withdrawing from the American Convention on Human Rights. Prime Minister P.J. Patterson stated that the government was taking this step because the Convention's monitoring body, the Inter-American Commission on Human Rights (IACHR), was taking too long to consider petitions filed by people under sentence of death. Reports of police brutality and excessive use of force continued.

Death penalty
There were about 44 people on death row at the end of 1999; no executions were carried out. Following the execution of nine men in Trinidad and Tobago in June, the Prime Minister stated publicly that, despite international lobbying, Jamaica would probably follow Trinidad and Tobago and hang its death-row inmates.

Twelve men were scheduled to be hanged in 1999. All were granted stays of execution pending the outcome of legal applications before national courts. The UN Human Rights Committee ruled in six of the cases that the state had violated the men's rights guaranteed by the International Covenant on Civil and Political Rights (ICCPR) and recommended that the government commute their death sentences. The government refused to implement these recommendations and issued execution warrants despite the fact that under international law the government is under an obligation not to execute a person whose rights under the ICCPR have been violated.

One of the 12 men was issued an execution warrant even though the UN Human Rights Committee was still considering his petition. Two others were issued execution warrants despite the fact that the IACHR was still considering their petitions. In June the Jamaican Court of Appeal ruled that instructions issued by the government to the IACHR placing time limits on the IACHR's consideration of cases were unlawful.

Shootings and brutality by police
The government announced measures to address the rise in crime. These included the imposition of curfews, cordons and spot checks of individuals in 15 areas with particularly high levels of crime. The military were called upon to assist the police in maintaining public order. Incidents of shootings, brutality and ill-treatment by police were common. In May the

government announced the establishment of a police unit to investigate shootings and other complaints against the police, under the supervision of the Director of Public Prosecutions. In September the government announced that, in response to civilian complaints, 29 officers had been dismissed for misconduct and more than 1,000 had been otherwise disciplined. By August, 112 people had been killed by police officers. In many cases the circumstances of the shootings were disputed; police officers stated that they had fired in self-defence while witnesses stated that the victims were not posing a threat when they were shot.

▭ During five days of sometimes violent demonstrations against fuel tax rises in April, seven people were shot and killed by police officers, some in circumstances disputed by witnesses. An unspecified number of people were injured.

▭ In one incident in July, up to 35 homeless people were illegally and forcibly removed from Montego Bay by police officers. Some of those removed were sprayed with a chemical thought to be Oleorosin Capsicum spray ("OC" or "pepper" spray) or mace. They were driven to a remote mudlake approximately 80 kilometres away and left there. Reports that some people drowned were rejected by authorities. In October a police inspector and two other men were ordered to stand trial by the Director of Public Prosecutions; the trial was set for February 2000.

▭ On 21 August, Michael Gayle, a paranoid schizophrenic, was beaten severely by members of the armed forces and police after trying to pass through a roadblock near his home after curfew. He was reportedly kicked repeatedly in the stomach and beaten by a number of soldiers after an altercation with one of them. He died as a result of a ruptured abdomen. At the Coroner's inquest, the jury returned a majority verdict that all military and police personnel on duty at the roadblock at that time should be charged with manslaughter.

Police officers convicted of murder

In October, three police officers were convicted of the murder of David Black and sentenced to life imprisonment. David Black had been beaten to death at a Trelawny police station and his body dumped at sea in September 1995.

Children

In July the government removed all those under 18 years of age from police lock-ups. The move was taken after Human Rights Watch published a report showing that children were being subjected to abuse while being held with adults in the detention facilities.

JAPAN

JAPAN
Head of state: Emperor Akihito
Head of government: Obuchi Keizo
Capital: Tokyo
Population: 126.1 million
Official language: Japanese
Death penalty: retentionist
1999 treaty ratifications/signatures: UN Convention against Torture and Other Cruel, Inhuman or Degrading Treatment or Punishment

Five people were executed in 1999 and 99 others remained under sentence of death. Japan acceded to the UN Convention against Torture and other Cruel, Inhuman or Degrading Treatment or Punishment with effect from 29 July. However, it did not make a declaration under Article 22 of the Convention, which would allow private individuals who claim to have been subjected to torture and cruel, inhuman or degrading treatment to bring their cases before the UN Committee against Torture.

Background

On 5 October Prime Minister Obuchi Keizo launched a new conservative coalition government, securing control of both houses of parliament. The economy showed continuing but slow signs of recovery after a decade of large economic rescue packages.

Death penalty

Five people were executed in 1999. One of the five had filed a habeas corpus petition to the court, and another had petitioned for a retrial; the outcomes of the petitions were not known. The authorities continued to carry out executions in secret. There were some 99 prisoners under sentence of death at the end of the year, at least 45 of whom had had their sentences upheld by the Supreme Court. Prisoners under sentence of death can receive visits only from one family member and are held in solitary confinement, sometimes for many years. A prisoner under sentence of death for 15 years reportedly committed suicide in November.

Torture and ill-treatment

Prisoners continued to face cruel and humiliating treatment including the use of instruments of restraint such as leather body belts and metal handcuffs, the imposition of severe penalties for minor infractions of prison regulations, and 24-hour surveillance. Efforts to reform Japan's harsh and highly secretive prisons suffered a setback with the ruling in April by the Asahikawa District Court that solitary confinement was "reasonable" and "necessary for keeping order" in prisons and that decisions on solitary confinement were at the discretion of prison wardens. The ruling had been made in the case of Isoe Yoichi, sentenced to life imprisonment for killing a policeman in 1979, who had filed a suit against the government in December 1987. Isoe Yoichi, who had been in solitary confinement for most of the 13 years he had spent in prison, had sued the government for five million yen for physical and mental pain. He had claimed that solitary confinement had violated the constitutional ban on torture and cruel punishment.

Asylum-seekers

1999 saw a marked increase in the number of asylum-seekers. Fifteen people were granted asylum, at least 177 had their applications rejected and the applications of a further 171 remained pending. The process for determining asylum, which continued to be subject to long delays, lacked transparency. For example, a rule requiring asylum-seekers to lodge their claims within 60 days of arrival was applied inconsistently. The government has never given reasons for its decisions in asylum cases.

In March the Immigration Control and Refugees Recognition Law was revised, making overstaying illegally in the country a separate offence from illegal entry. Foreign nationals found to have stayed three years or more after illegally entering the country cannot be prosecuted for illegal entry owing to the statute of limitation of three years.

Legislation

New laws came into force in December under which groups implicated in serious crimes can be placed under the surveillance of the chief of the Public Security Investigation Agency for up to three years. In addition bankruptcy administrators can take control of assets held before groups are declared bankrupt, even if those assets have been transferred to other entities.

There was concern that a wire-tapping law passed in August could violate constitutionally guaranteed rights to privacy and confidential communication. Human rights organizations raised concerns that such laws may infringe basic human rights. There was concern that these laws could be arbitrarily used by police against peaceful activists.

The Public Security Investigation Agency can launch investigations if it determines that an organization may engage in subversive activities in the future. In previous years the Agency had ordered its eight regional bureaux to monitor the activities of 40 organizations including AI Japan and the Japan Congress of Journalists.

Detention of lawyer and activists

There were concerns that the authorities were seeking to restrict the legitimate activities of human rights defenders and civil society groups.

🗀 Yasuda Yoshihiro, a well-known human rights lawyer and campaigner against the death penalty arrested in December 1998, was detained for 10 months before being released on bail in September. He was kept in solitary confinement under 24-hour video surveillance in a so-called "suicide prevention cell" for more than four months. There was concern that the length of Yasuda Yoshihiro's detention was

disproportionate to the charges against him, which carry a maximum penalty of two years' imprisonment. His prolonged detention also led to him being dismissed as the court-appointed lawyer for the defence of *Aum Shinrikyo* leader Matsumoto Chizuo (also known as Asahara Shoko) who was charged with an offence which could carry a death sentence. There was concern that Matsumoto Chizuo's right to a fair trial may have been jeopardized by Yasuda Yoshihiro's dismissal from the case.

🗀 Three activists belonging to the environmental organization Greenpeace were arrested on 18 March after unfurling a large banner from the side of the Tokyo Big Sight convention centre in protest at the Tokyo Toy Show. They were later fined 100,000 yen (approximately US$830) for trespass and released after 11 days in detention. On 23 March police in Tokyo conducted an unprecedented raid on the Greenpeace offices and on the home of the Executive Director of Greenpeace Japan confiscating campaign reports, accounting records and records of supporters and donations.

JORDAN

HASHEMITE KINGDOM OF JORDAN
Head of state: 'Abdallah bin Hussein (replaced King Hussein bin Talal in February)
Head of government: 'Abd al-Ra'uf Rawabdeh (replaced Fayez Tarawneh in March)
Capital: Amman
Population: 4.5 million
Official language: Arabic
Death penalty: retentionist

Scores of people were arrested for political reasons during the year. Most of those arrested, apparently for opposition to the government or to the peace process, were held for up to two months and then released. Arrested prisoners of conscience included journalists and members of Islamist parties. At least 70 people were arrested and charged with offences involving political violence. Trials of most of those charged with political offences continued to be heard before a State Security Court where procedures did not meet international fair trial standards. Some reports of torture or ill-treatment of detainees by members of the security services were received. More than 20 people were sentenced to death and 12 were executed. Four members of *Hamas*, an Islamist group opposed to the peace process with Israel, were forcibly exiled from Jordan. There were reports of the *refoulement* (forcible return) of Iraqi asylum-seekers.

Background

In January King Hussein bin Talal discharged his brother Hassan from the post of Crown Prince, naming his eldest son, 'Abdallah, as Regent. In February King Hussein died of cancer and was succeeded by his son as King 'Abdallah II. In March 'Abd al-Ra'uf Rawabdeh was named as Prime Minister, succeeding Fayez Tarawneh. Municipal elections, held in July, were dominated by tribal and independent candidates; however, the Islamic Action Front was returned in three towns. A committee, set up in the Press and Publications Department in the Ministry of Information following an appeal by King 'Abdallah for greater openness, removed hundreds of books from censorship. A new Press and Publications Law was passed by parliament in September, abolishing Article 37 of the 1998 Press Law which listed a range of 14 prohibited topics such as news harming national unity or disclosing information on the armed forces. An amendment to repeal Article 340 of the Penal Code, one of whose clauses allows an exemption from penalty for men who kill female relatives discovered in the act of adultery, was rejected by the lower house of parliament but passed by the Senate in December.

Amnesty

At least 25 political prisoners were released in an amnesty of 500 prisoners in March on the occasion of 'Id al-Adha. They included Ata' Abu'l-Rushta and members of the banned Islamist party *Hizb al-Tahrir fi'l-'Urdun,* Liberation Party in Jordan, which seeks to re-establish the Islamic Caliphate, sentenced to one year's imprisonment in 1998 after distributing leaflets and considered probable prisoners of conscience.

Arrests

Scores of people were arrested during the year for political reasons. Most political detainees were arrested and held by the General Intelligence Department (GID) and released after days or weeks in detention, often without charge. At least 70 people were arrested during the year on charges involving violence, such as plotting "terrorist" attacks. Prisoners of conscience included members of the Muslim Brotherhood and journalists arrested after writing critical articles.

🗁 Sinan Shaqdih, the head of the Correspondents' Department of the daily newspaper *Al-Masa'iyeh,* was arrested by the GID in July. He was detained for more than two weeks and charged with harming relations with Syria through articles he had written. He was released, apparently after the intervention of King 'Abdallah, and charges against him were dropped.

🗁 'Abd al-Karim Barghouthi, the editor-in-chief of *al-Bilad,* a weekly newspaper, was arrested in August and detained for five days after 'Isam al-Rawabdeh, the son of the Prime Minister, lodged a complaint of libel. In November he was rearrested and detained once more for two days.

Torture and ill-treatment

Reports of torture or ill-treatment at the hands of the security or prison services continued to be received.

🗁 Salim Ibrahim Marji, aged 73, serving a life sentence at Swaqa Prison, was allegedly abused and beaten while tied by prison guards. Following the beating, Salim Marji suffered a heart attack and was taken to al-Ashraf hospital where he was found to have suffered two fractured tibiae and three fractured fingers. He reportedly showed visible bruising and marks of *falaqa* (beatings on the soles of the feet). He died after a further heart attack in December. A police inquiry was set up into the beating but had not made any report public by the end of the year.

Unfair trials

Trials of political detainees before the State Security Court, a court which almost invariably used panels of military judges, failed to provide adequate safeguards for fair trial.

🗁 In April the State Security Court sentenced nine alleged members of the Reform and Challenge Movement, including three tried *in absentia*, to up to life imprisonment for carrying out "terrorist" acts, including placing bombs in Amman in 1998. They included 'Abd al-Nasser Shehadeh Salim and Samer Muhammad Isma'il 'Amer. Four, including 'Abd al-Nasser Sayyed Hassanayn, were acquitted. Defendants said they were tortured to extract confessions but the judge rejected lawyers' requests for confessions not to be accepted as evidence. He also excluded a confession from another detainee that he, and not the accused, had carried out the explosions.

Death penalty

More than 20 death sentences were imposed and 12 executions were carried out during 1999. Four executions took place during one week in June, immediately after the end of the period of mourning for King Hussein.

🗁 Muhammad 'Abed Hussein was hanged at Swaqa Prison in October. He had been sentenced to death in 1998 after the criminal court found him guilty of murdering his wife. His death sentence had been upheld by the Court of Cassation in June 1999.

Forcible exile

Four leaders of *Hamas*, including Ibrahim Ghosheh and Khaled Mesh'al, who had returned to Jordan in September after arrest warrants had been issued against them, were forcibly exiled by Jordan to Qatar after two months' detention in Jweideh Prison. They had been charged with belonging to an illegal organization and possessing arms. The government denied forcibly exiling them and said they had left of their own accord.

Refugees

There were reports of asylum-seekers being forcibly returned to countries where they were at risk of human rights violations.

🗁 Robar Yahya Latif al-Salihi was arrested in August by Jordanian intelligence after he wrote an article about the kidnapping of his brother. His mother Gulbahar, his brother 'Uma'ed and his sister Joanne were also arrested. They were apparently only saved from forcible return to Iraq by wide media coverage, including public appeals by AI. They were reportedly granted safe passage to Syria. However, other Iraqi asylum-seekers were reportedly forcibly returned at the same time.

KAZAKSTAN

REPUBLIC OF KAZAKSTAN
Head of state: Nursultan Nazarbayev
Head of government: Kasymzhomart Tokayev (replaced Nurlan Balgimbayev in October)
Capital: Astana
Population: 16.6 million
Official language: Kazak
Death penalty: retentionist
1999 treaty ratifications/signatures: Convention relating to the Status of Refugees and its 1967 Protocol

Prison conditions continued to be poor. There were complaints that presidential and parliamentary elections had not been free and fair and that opposition candidates had been barred from taking part. Under pressure from China, Kazakstan forcibly returned at least three ethnic Uighurs to Xinjiang Uighur Autonomous Region (XUAR) to face charges of "ethnic separatism".

Background
Monitoring the parliamentary elections in October, the Organization for Security and Co-operation in Europe (OSCE) concluded that the process had been "severely marred by widespread, pervasive and illegal interference by the executive authorities". Several opposition candidates gained positions in the *Majlis* (lower house of parliament) but most were won by the pro-President parties *Otan* and the Civic Party. The OSCE also criticized the January presidential election, in which the incumbent President Nazarbayev won a landslide victory after banning his main opponent for having allegedly committed minor offences under the electoral system.

Prison conditions
Claims by the government that prison conditions had improved since the adoption of a new criminal code were refuted by released detainees. The President's legal adviser, Igor Rogov, stated in October, "In Kazakstan prisoners lose everything, including their health and lives", and called for alternative punishments to be introduced.
☐ Madel Ismailov, who was released from Petropavlovsk prison camp in February, described it as one of the worst detention centres in the country. He alleged that prisoners were deprived of basic rights, including access to medical treatment, that hygiene facilities were grossly inadequate, and that personal belongings were regularly confiscated by prison personnel. Arbitrary beatings with rubber truncheons were a common punishment. According to Madel Ismailov, prisoners were frightened to complain about their conditions and suicides or attempted suicides were common.

Death penalty
The death sentence imposed on Vladimir Nikolayevich Kardash was commuted in April to 25 years' imprisonment as a result of presidential clemency.
On 2 November the Regional Court in Aktyubinsk sentenced two men to death after convicting them of murdering 10 people during robberies carried out at a summer community outside the city. Six accomplices of the men reportedly received prison terms of between seven and 22 years.

Forcible deportations
AI became increasingly concerned that the authorities were complying with China's request to some Central Asian republics to help China fight what it terms "ethnic separatism" in the XUAR.
☐ Three ethnic Uighurs, Hemit Memet, Kasim Mahpir and Ilyas Zordun, were forcibly returned in February to China. They had been arrested a few months earlier while trying to cross into Kazakstan from China and were subsequently reported to have sought political asylum. Posters had been distributed in the XUAR indicating that they were wanted for separatist political activities. Reports were received in June that they had been transferred to incommunicado detention in Gulja. There was concern that they might be tortured or face the death penalty.

AI country report
• Concerns in Europe, January – June 1999: Kazakstan (AI Index: EUR 01/002/99)

KENYA

REPUBLIC OF KENYA
Head of state and government: Daniel arap Moi
Capital: Nairobi
Population: 28.7 million
Official languages: English, Swahili
Death penalty: retentionist
1999 treaty ratifications/signatures: Rome Statute of the International Criminal Court

Pro-democracy activists, human rights defenders, politicians, journalists and others continued to be harassed, ill-treated or detained for non-violent activities. Torture by security officials was widespread, causing a number of deaths in custody. Excessive force was used by police against peaceful protesters, and in a number of incidents the police made no attempt to stop vigilante groups from attacking peaceful demonstrators. Scores of people were killed by police during the year; some may have been extrajudicially executed. Prison conditions remained harsh. At least 55 people were sentenced to death, and more than 1,000 people were under sentence of death at the end of 1999.

Background
Human rights violations were committed in a context of widespread popular calls for constitutional and legal reform. The promise of constitutional reform, which appeared to be making progress when President Daniel arap Moi signed into law the Constitution of Kenya Review Commission Act in December 1998, delayed all other law reform. The Act provided for a review commission to examine federal and unitary systems of government and to make recommendations on electoral systems (including the composition and functions of the executive, judiciary and legislature). However, in January 1999 the process stalled over the allocation of seats in the commission. In December a parliamentary select committee was established to review the Act. A parallel review process was set up by religious leaders and others who opposed parliament's control of constitutional reform.

In August a judicial commission of inquiry set up in 1998 to investigate the causes of the political violence that has affected Kenya since 1992 submitted its report to President Moi. It had not been made public by the end of 1999.

In September, in an attempt to reduce government spending and tackle corruption, there was a major government reshuffle which resulted in the number of ministries being reduced from 27 to 15, although the number of ministers remained the same.

In November Kenyan women's groups campaigning for the introduction of legislation against domestic violence expressed concern at the increase of violence against women. They said that the majority of cases were not reported, that police records in domestic violence cases were inaccurate and not even available in one of Kenya's eight provinces, and that prosecutions were rare and sentencing lenient.

Impunity
Although human rights violations by security officials continued to be widespread, there were few investigations into alleged violations. In April the then Chief Justice, Zacchaeus Chesoni, stated that investigations into torture allegations were rare despite the fact that one in three suspects brought to court in Kenya alleged that they had been tortured. When investigations were carried out, in many cases the findings were not made public and no further action appeared to have been taken.

⊟ On 23 May members of the Kenyan military, together with police officers, attacked Kenyan herdsmen of the Gabbra community at the Baresa water point in Marsabit District, Eastern Province. More than 70 herdsmen were stripped naked, tortured and threatened with execution. No details of the investigation announced by the Department of Defence into the incident were made public, and the investigation led to no arrests. The military had been sent to the area ostensibly to engage in a mine-clearing exercise. It was not clear who was responsible for planting the landmines, but there had been reports of several skirmishes in the North Eastern and Eastern provinces involving the Kenyan security forces, Ethiopian government forces and the Oromo Liberation Front, an Ethiopian armed opposition group.

Judicial proceedings against law enforcement officers accused of torturing or killing prisoners usually occurred only after sustained pressure, and were subject to long delays.

⊟ Four police officers charged in 1996 with the murder of Rosemary Nyambura, who died in Ruaraka police station in May 1992, had not been brought to court seven years after her death. A post-mortem indicated that she died of ruptured kidneys and spleen.

Torture
Police torture was systematic, primarily for common criminals. At least seven people died in custody apparently as a result of torture.

⊟ In May the Appeal Court ordered the retrial of two police officers sentenced in 1997 to 10 years' imprisonment for torturing a suspect to death in 1994. The third officer convicted with them died in prison.

Killings
Scores of people were killed by police during the year; some may have been extrajudicially executed. Some criminal suspects were shot dead by police even though they appeared to pose no threat. Excessive force continued to be used by riot police. Investigations were rare, prosecutions virtually non-existent.

⊟ In July Antony Mwangi Kamau, a 22-year-old member of the *Mungiki* religious sect, was shot dead when members of the sect began throwing stones at the police who were trying to arrest their leader.

Freedom of expression and association

Meetings organized by government critics, opposition members of parliament, and others were violently disrupted by the police. Meetings held by farmers to complain about agricultural pricing policies and local officials were broken up by the police using tear gas and dogs. On several occasions security guards, vigilante groups and others violently disrupted peaceful meetings or demonstrations while the police present did nothing to stop the violence.

In January Wangari Maathai, a prominent human rights and environmental activist, was hit on the head by security guards while police watched, during a demonstration against the handover of public land to developers in Karura Forest, northern Nairobi. The Attorney General later ordered an investigation, but it was not known if anyone was arrested in connection with the incident.

Journalists reporting political meetings were also targeted by the police.

In May at a rally in Ugunja town, Nyanza province, journalists were charged by riot police while filing their stories from nearby phone booths. The police had declared the rally illegal and had dispersed the crowds using batons and teargas.

On 10 June scores of demonstrators were hurt by police when participants at a rally organized by pro-democracy advocates and church groups decided to march on the Kenyan Parliament. Demonstrators were prevented from reaching parliament by police officers who violently broke up the march using batons, teargas, stun grenades and water cannon — riot control equipment purchased from South Africa. The Reverend Timothy Njoya, who led the march, was attacked by two men, believed to be members of *Jeshi la Mzee* (the Old Man's army), a pro-government group, who used their fists, boots and sticks to beat him to the ground and broke his arm while uniformed police watched. Following a public outcry, one man was later arrested and charged with assaulting Reverend Njoya. The man was released on bail.

In August Tony Gachoka, editor of the *Post on Sunday*, was sentenced to six months' imprisonment for contempt of court after an unfair trial. The trial followed articles in the *Post on Sunday* accusing the Court of Appeal and the Chief Justice of corruption arising from Kenya's biggest corruption scandal, known as "Goldenberg". He was released on 3 November following a presidential pardon.

Refugees

Mass arrests of refugees and asylum-seekers were reported in August and September. Most were from Somalia and Ethiopia. Some were arrested in a refugee camp near Mombasa. There were reports of ill-treatment by the police and threats of forcible return to countries where they would be at risk of serious human rights violations. It is not known if any refugees were forcibly returned to their country of origin.

In November the Kenyan authorities refused to allow 4,700 refugees, including women and children, into Kenya from Ethiopia on the grounds that they did not have Kenyan identification documents. Concern was expressed by the UN refugee agency UNHCR, which had been assisting with their repatriation, that the refugees faced severe food shortages at Moyale trading centre, a border town, where they were being temporarily housed.

Death penalty and prison conditions

The death penalty continued to be imposed frequently and an increasing number of suspects appeared to be being charged with capital offences. At least 55 prisoners were sentenced to death during 1999, the majority after unfair trials at magistrates' courts, where defendants do not have the right to legal aid. Although no one has been executed for more than 10 years, hundreds of prisoners remained under sentence of death, some of them for many years. Prison conditions are life-threatening and in many prisons amount to cruel, inhuman or degrading treatment.

In October a magistrate was so concerned about conditions in Kapsabet prison that he threatened to release all the prisoners. Severe overcrowding and the disconnection of the prison's water supply, forcing prisoners to use untreated water from local rivers, had resulted in an outbreak of infectious diseases.

Intergovernmental organizations

The UN Special Rapporteur on torture visited Kenya in September to investigate allegations of torture. The Rapporteur's report was still pending at the end of the year.

AI country visit

AI delegates visited Kenya in June and met human rights activists, torture victims and their relatives.

KOREA
(DEMOCRATIC PEOPLE'S REPUBLIC OF)

DEMOCRATIC PEOPLE'S REPUBLIC OF KOREA
Head of state: Kim Jong il
Head of government: Hong Song Nam
Capital: P'yongyang
Population: 23.7 million
Official language: Korean
Death penalty: retentionist

Despite some diplomatic steps towards dialogue, access to the Democratic People's Republic of Korea (North Korea) and information about human rights remained tightly controlled.

Food crisis
The food crisis, described by the World Food Programme as "a famine in slow motion", continued to give cause for serious concern. A joint nutrition survey of children under seven years old conducted by UNICEF, the World Food Programme and the European Union (EU) revealed that 16 per cent suffered from acute malnutrition and 62 per cent were affected by stunting (low height for age). In the absence of data concerning other groups, the full extent of the crisis was not known, but the young and the elderly were believed to be especially vulnerable. Officials acknowledged that the mortality rate had increased over the previous four years, indicating that 220,000 more people had died than would be anticipated over that period.

In April 1999 the highest legislative body, the Supreme People's Assembly (SPA), considered the budget, which had lapsed since the death of Kim Il-sung in 1994. The budget itself gave only broad indications, but these revealed that both revenue and expenditure had declined by one-half in the five years since figures were last published.

The persistent crisis resulted in hundreds of people crossing to China in search of food. There were reports of people trying to cross the border being shot at by North Korean security forces. Those caught by border guards or returned by the Chinese authorities were at risk of human rights violations. There were reports of detainees being severely beaten by North Korean security guards and sent to unheated, overcrowded prison camps with little food. (Winters in North Korea are harsh with temperatures dropping to minus 25 degrees centigrade.)

There were also reports of trafficking of women and girls in the border area.

International scrutiny
In August the UN Sub-Commission on the Promotion and Protection of Human Rights encouraged the government to continue to assume its international human rights obligations under the International Covenant on Civil and Political Rights (ICCPR). North Korea had announced in 1997 that it had "withdrawn" from the ICCPR, following a critical UN Sub-Commission resolution. The government announced in 1999 that it would soon present its second periodic report on its implementation of the ICCPR to the UN Human Rights Committee, but to AI's knowledge this had not happened by the end of the year. North Korea submitted its first report in 1984.

International contacts
1999 saw increased diplomatic activity by the authorities, who initiated a number of meetings with several European countries, the EU and Canada, reviewed their relations with Japan, and held high-level talks with the USA. North Korean officials held talks with the EU where it was reported that the discussions would focus on food assistance, human rights and North Korea's missile program. Former US Defense Secretary William Perry visited the country and offered the lifting of further sanctions by the USA in exchange for greater restrictions on North Korea's missile and nuclear weapons programs. Japan sent a delegation under former Prime Minister Tomiichi Murayama in November and December which called for a normalization of relations between the two countries. Some sanctions were lifted and civilian links re-established after Japan lifted a ban on charter flights to North Korea.

Contacts between North and South Korea continued to increase, and about 80,000 South Korean tourists visited Mount Kumkang in North Korea during 1999. However, relations with South Korea fluctuated greatly during the year. In June talks on bilateral issues broke down, and for the first time since the Korean War, the South and North Korean navies fought a brief gun battle. One North Korean boat was sunk and some 80 fatalities were reported. In August a workers' team from the Korean Confederation of Trade Unions was allowed to travel north to play football with their northern counterparts.

KOREA
(REPUBLIC OF)

REPUBLIC OF KOREA
Head of state: Kim Dae-jung
Head of government: Kim Jong-pil
Capital: Seoul
Population: 45.6 million
Official language: Korean
Death penalty: retentionist

Most long-term political prisoners were released in a series of amnesties during 1999. President Kim Dae-jung pledged to carry out further political and judicial reforms including a review of the National Security Law and the enactment of a Human Rights Law, but progress continued to be stalled. The economy showed a remarkable recovery, but the human cost of the economic crisis and the conditions laid down by the International Monetary Fund generated further tensions and conflict between business, labour and government. There was no further progress in the formation of a National Human Rights Commission, amid debate about the proposed institution's independence and powers. There were no executions, although no steps were taken towards abolishing the death penalty.

Prisoner amnesties
There were prisoner amnesties in February, to mark the first anniversary of President Kim's presidency; in August to mark Independence Day; and at the end of the year. The government announced the release of 43 political prisoners, including 19 long-term political prisoners, in February and of 56 political prisoners, including prisoners of conscience, in August.

🗀 Seventy-year-old Woo Yong-gak, who had been in prison for more than 40 years, and Cho Sang-nok and Kang Yong-ju, who had served 21 and 14 years in prison respectively following unfair trials under the National Security Law, were among those released in February.

🗀 Sixty-six-year-old Ahn Jae-ku and 70-year-old Yu Rak-jin, who were serving long sentences imposed under the National Security Law, were released in August.

🗀 Two long-term prisoners who had been arrested on espionage charges under the National Security Law — 70-year-old Son Song-mo and 71-year-old Shin Kwang-soo — were released at the end of the year.

National Security Law
In October the UN Human Rights Committee examined the Republic of Korea's second periodic report on its implementation of the International Covenant on Civil and Political Rights and expressed concern about "the continued existence and application of the National Security Law". It called for the abolition of the "law-abidance oath" imposed on some prisoners, particularly those arrested under the National Security

Law, as a precondition for their release. The Committee also expressed deep concern about "the laws and practices that encourage and reinforce discriminatory attitudes towards women".

By the end of 1999, 111 political prisoners were believed to be held, 82 of whom had been detained under the National Security Law. They included 62 students and 15 labour activists. In August, 115 civic groups formed the National Coalition Against the National Security Law, whose objective was to abolish Article 7 of the Law.

🗀 In December, Hong Kyo-sun, a representative of the Chaekgalpee Publishing Company, was sentenced to one year in prison and one year's suspension of his civil rights for violating Article 7 of the National Security Law which prohibits "praising, encouraging or supporting an anti-state organization or its components". The books he sold on Marxist theory were already prescribed as textbooks in 10 South Korean universities.

🗀 In December legal proceedings concluded against 15 members of the "Youngnam Committee". They had been arrested in July 1998 and charged initially with membership of "an anti-state organization" under Article 3 of the National Security Law. However, they were later convicted of "participating in enemy-benefiting activities" under Article 7 of the National Security Law. One of them, Park Kyung-soon, was sentenced to seven years' imprisonment. Two others, Kim Chang-hyon and Bang Seok-su, were sentenced to two and three years' imprisonment respectively. The detainees were all critics of the government's economic and social policies and many of them had been involved in a local election campaign.

Security Surveillance Law
The Security Surveillance Law continued to be used to track the activities of some former prisoners, including prisoners of conscience. Human rights groups estimated that hundreds of former political prisoners were subject to this law, but the exact number was not publicly available. Under the law, former prisoners are required to report their activities regularly to the local police and are subject to police surveillance. They also face arbitrary restrictions on their activities, such as a ban on meeting other former prisoners or on participating in certain meetings and demonstrations. Often police make regular phone calls to check on former prisoners' whereabouts and ask neighbours and work colleagues to report on their activities.

Trade unions
In a major shift in its policy towards the labour movement, the government recognized a second labour umbrella group, the Korean Confederation of Trade Unions, in December. The Confederation, which had 570,000 members in key industries, had been outlawed for several years. From July onwards teachers were finally permitted to form trade unions and most civil servants, while being prohibited from joining trade unions, were permitted to form workplace associations from January.

The government reacted to strike action by arresting or threatening to arrest trade union leaders it deemed responsible and by deploying large contingents of riot police to break strike action and block demonstrations. Often the police used excessive force which exacerbated tensions and contributed to an outbreak of violence. There were arrests in April and May when the Korean Confederation of Trade Unions organized a series of strikes by public and private sector workers.

⌐ Lee Sang-choon, President of the Korean Health and Medical Workers' Union and the Korean Federation of Hospital Workers' Unions, was arrested on 17 May and charged with "obstruction of business".

⌐ More than 60 trade union leaders of Seoul Subway Union had arrest warrants issued against them in May.

In early December, shortly after the recognition of the Korean Confederation of Trade Unions, tens of labour activists were arrested during a police crackdown on strikes held by the Confederation and by the Federation of Korean Trade Unions.

Prison conditions and ill-treatment
Conditions in prisons and detention centres continued to be harsh and ill-treatment of prisoners was reported. Prison cells were unheated in winter, leading to many cases of frost-bite, and lacked ventilation in summer. Prisons were reported to have become overcrowded as a result of higher crime rates during the economic crisis. Medical facilities in prisons and detention centres were poor. Political prisoners were often held in solitary confinement. Women, who constituted a small percentage of the prison population, suffered discrimination in a system which often failed to address their particular needs. There appeared to be no special provision for the health needs of women prisoners and no separate cells or dietary provisions for pregnant women and women who had recently given birth. There were reports from several prisons and detention centres of prisoners being held in handcuffs and chains and placed in solitary confinement for long periods as punishment for breaking prison rules. Prisoners were also allegedly denied adequate food, beaten and held in disciplinary cells which had no natural light and were too small to lie down in. Other prisoners complained that they were deprived of sleep and forced to sit in the same position for prolonged periods.

⌐ In May, nine political prisoners held in the "Youngnam Committee" case claimed that they were severely beaten by officials at Pusan Detention Centre. The incident occurred several days after the prisoners had started a hunger strike to protest against plans to move some of them to a different prison. Five of the prisoners claimed that they were handcuffed and then punched and kicked repeatedly as they were transported to Pusan Prison. The four who remained in Pusan Detention Centre were also beaten, including Park Kyong-soon who suffered from cirrhosis of the liver.

AI country reports
• Republic of Korea (South Korea): Summary of concerns for 1999 (AI Index: ASA 25/001/99)
• Republic of Korea (South Korea): Workers' rights at a time of economic crisis (AI Index: ASA 25/002/99)
• Republic of Korea (South Korea): Time to reform the National Security Law (AI Index: ASA 25/003/99)

KUWAIT

STATE OF KUWAIT
Head of state: al-Shaikh Jaber al-Ahmad al-Sabah
Head of government: al-Shaikh Sa'ad al-'Abdallah al-Sabah
Capital: Kuwait City
Population: 1.8 million
Official language: Arabic
Death penalty: retentionist

Dozens of political prisoners, including prisoners of conscience, continued to be held; they had been convicted in unfair trials since 1991. The fate of more than 70 people who "disappeared" in custody in 1991 remained unknown. At least 12 people were sentenced to death. In two separate cases, the editor of the newspaper *al-Qabas* and a professor of political science were convicted on charges of insulting Islam.

Background
The Amir, al-Shaikh Jaber al-Ahmad al-Sabah, dissolved parliament in May citing the lack of cooperation between members of parliament and the Cabinet as the reason for his decision. Fresh elections to the National Assembly were held in July. The Amir issued a decree that, subject to ratification by the new parliament, women would be allowed to vote and stand as candidates in parliamentary and municipal elections in the year 2003. However, in November parliament narrowly rejected the decree. Some members of parliament subsequently introduced an equivalent bill on women's voting rights which was also narrowly rejected by parliament in December.

Past human rights abuses
The majority of human rights violations in Kuwait related to the period of Martial Law following the withdrawal of the Iraqi forces in February 1991. Despite having taken some positive steps in a series of political and human rights reforms, the government failed to address many of these violations including the imprisonment of prisoners of conscience, unresolved extrajudicial executions and "disappearances", and political prisoners sentenced after manifestly unfair trials in the Martial Law and State Security Courts. The last eight political prisoners of Jordanian nationality, including at least four prisoners of conscience, were

released following an amnesty granted by the Amir in February. About 30 other political prisoners, mainly of Jordanian nationality, had been released in successive amnesties in the previous three years. However, dozens of men and women of other nationalities, convicted on similar charges of "collaboration" with Iraqi forces, remained imprisoned. One, Khalaf 'Alwan al-Maliki, an Iraqi national who had lived in Kuwait since 1950, died in custody in February.

Bidun (stateless people)
The status of the *Bidun* continued to be discussed in various committees. The Cabinet announced in June that to qualify for citizenship, a *Bidun* must have registered in the 1965 census. Following its consideration of Kuwait's report, the UN Committee on the Elimination of Racial Discrimination expressed concern that, despite its efforts, the government had not found a solution to the problems of the *Bidun*, the majority of whom remained stateless.

Freedom of expression
An appeal court judgment in January overturned a sentence of six months' imprisonment against Muhammad Jassem al-Sagher, editor of *al-Qabas,* for printing a joke which a lower court had found offensive to Islam.

In October Ahmad al-Baghdadi, professor of Political Science at Kuwait University, was convicted on charges of insulting Islam and sentenced to one month in prison. Following increasing pressure for his release, both from within the country and internationally, he was granted an amnesty by the Amir after serving half his sentence.

The government ordered the newspaper *al-Siyassah* to be suspended for five days for publishing a report deemed harmful to the Amir and to the country's interests. The editor said that his newspaper was not to blame as it "only reported the words of the secretary general of an Islamist movement during a symposium, criticizing the Amir's decision to give Kuwaiti women their political rights".

The verdict in the trial of two Kuwaiti women writers, 'Alia Shu'aib and Laila al-'Othman, charged respectively with insulting Islam and offending public decency in their writings, due to be announced in December, was postponed until January 2000. They were sued in early 1997 by a group of four men who alleged that their books promoted moral corruption and were against Islamic traditions. The publisher, Yahya Rubi'yan, was charged with printing and distributing books offending public decency.

Forcible return: risk of torture
In January the security forces arrested a group of 25 Arab men resident in Kuwait and accused them of "subversive acts to destabilize the security and stability of Kuwait". Several days later, 15 men of Egyptian nationality were forcibly returned to Egypt where they were detained incommunicado by the State Security Investigation Department, where they were at risk of torture. They were reportedly interrogated about their alleged membership of a banned Islamist organization. Four of the men, Ahmad Hassan Badi'a, Magdi Fahmi, Youssri Hamad and Muhammad Farag, who had been living in Kuwait with their families for several years, were transferred to a prison near Cairo in April; the other 11 were released.

Death penalty
At least 12 people, including one woman, were sentenced to death following their convictions for murder and drugs offences. No executions were reported.

KYRGYZSTAN

KYRGYZ REPUBLIC
Head of state: Askar Akayev
Head of government: Amangeldy Muraliyev (replaced Jumabek Ibragimov in April)
Capital: Bishkek
Population: 4.6 million
Official language: Kyrgyz
Death penalty: retentionist

Scores of ethnic Uzbek citizens of Kyrgyzstan suspected of supporting the banned Islamic opposition in neighbouring Uzbekistan were reportedly detained by Kyrgyz and Uzbek law enforcement officers, following bomb explosions in the Uzbek capital Tashkent in February. Some people were forcibly deported to Uzbekistan. When armed groups claiming to be members of the banned Islamic opposition in Uzbekistan crossed into Kyrgyz territory in August and took hostages, the authorities' clampdown against suspected supporters of banned Islamic opposition parties intensified. Death sentences continued to be passed by the courts, although a moratorium on executions remained in place.

Background
A series of bomb attacks in February 1999 in Uzbekistan was blamed on violent foreign-trained Islamic groups intent on establishing an Islamist state, and triggered a wave of arrests in Uzbekistan. Alarmed at the possible spread of religious extremism, Kyrgyzstan also clamped down on so-called "extremist" Islamic groups, particularly in the southern regions bordering Uzbekistan, home to a large ethnic Uzbek community.

Kyrgyzstan faced increasing political tension in August, when hundreds of armed men claiming to be members of the banned Islamic opposition in Uzbekistan crossed into Kyrgyz territory from neighbouring Tajikistan, reportedly on their way to Uzbekistan. They took several hostages, including four Japanese nationals, and declared a *jihad* (holy war) on Uzbekistan. After two months of a military stand-off the hostages were released. One hostage was reportedly killed by his abductors.

Detention and abduction on grounds of religion

Uzbek law enforcement officers were reported to have frequently entered Kyrgyz territory and to have arbitrarily detained Kyrgyz citizens of ethnic Uzbek origin whom they accused of having links to banned Islamic opposition parties in Uzbekistan. Dozens of ethnic Uzbek men were abducted to Uzbekistan, where they were at serious risk of human rights violations. Scores of men were detained by Kyrgyz law enforcement officers while distributing leaflets of banned Islamist parties, in particular *Hizb-ut-Tahrir*. In September, during identity checks, the Kyrgyz authorities reportedly rounded up hundreds of foreign citizens predominantly of Asian or Turkish origin, including 200 asylum-seekers, and confined them in temporary detention centres.

In August Yuldashbai Tursunbayev, an ethnic Uzbek Imam of the Bazar-Korgon mosque in Jalal-Abad in the southern Osh region, was abducted. He was reportedly apprehended in the street by two armed men in civilian clothes as he was leaving the mosque after his morning prayers, and forced into a waiting car which drove in the direction of Andizhan Region in Uzbekistan. Imam Tursunbayev had reportedly been detained several times by Uzbek law enforcement officers on Kyrgyz territory in the weeks following the February bombings in Tashkent.

Harassment of human rights defenders

At the end of September 1998, the Ministry of Justice revoked the registration of the Kyrgyz Committee for Human Rights (KCHR), amid allegations that the timing was politically motivated. At the end of March 1999, the KCHR submitted its completed registration documents to the Ministry of Justice. In May, the KCHR was informed that a public association of the same name but under a different chairman had been registered by the Ministry of Justice in April. Members of the original KCHR alleged that the registration of a new organization under the same name was an attempt by the authorities to prevent a well-known human rights organization from carrying out its work. In June, the original KCHR was threatened with confiscation of its office equipment and its chairman faced criminal charges for failing to surrender the property. Following international protests and an intervention by the Organization for Security and Co-operation in Europe (OSCE), the KCHR was finally re-registered in August.

Restrictions on freedom of the press

Despite an amendment to the Constitution guaranteeing freedom of the press, the independent media continued to be harassed by Kyrgyz authorities, including being sued for libel and tax evasion or other administrative offences.

In August tax police raided the offices of the largest independent daily newspaper *Vecherniy Bishkek* (Bishkek Evening News), allegedly without a proper search warrant, and threatened to arrest its editor-in-chief, Aleksandr Kim, whom they accused of tax evasion. This was seen as an attempt by the government to silence any criticism in the run-up to elections. The newspaper had recently published interviews with opposition politicians.

Death penalty

According to a non-governmental source, 20 people were sentenced to death during 1999. By the end of the year, two of these had had their petitions for clemency turned down, and decisions were still pending on the other 18 cases. About 60 people were reported to be on death row at the end of 1999. A moratorium on executions introduced in 1998 remained in place.

LAOS

LAO PEOPLE'S DEMOCRATIC REPUBLIC
Head of state: Khamtay Siphandone
Head of government: Sisavat Keobounphanh
Capital: Vientiane
Population: 5.1 million
Official language: Lao
Death penalty: retentionist

Freedom of expression and association continued to be restricted, and more than 50 people were arrested after planning an anti-government protest in Vientiane in October. Ongoing restrictions on religious expression led to more than 30 people being detained for their beliefs. Three prisoners of conscience and two political prisoners continued to be held in cruel, inhuman and degrading conditions.

Closed government

Restrictions on access to Laos for independent human rights monitors, and the government's tight control over information within Laos, hampered the collection of independent and impartial information about human rights. Neither the international community nor local people were able to monitor the situation adequately, raising concerns that the population remained vulnerable to hidden human rights violations. The government failed to respond positively to international concerns about the human rights situation, and AI's attempts to open a dialogue met with no response.

Freedom of expression

More than 50 people were arrested in October in connection with planning an anti-government protest in Vientiane. They included Thongpaseuth Keuakoun, Kamphouvieng Sisaath, Seng-Aloun Phengphanh, Bouavanh Chanhmanivong and Keochay. Scores of others were reportedly questioned by the authorities and subsequently released. An open letter from the protest organizers, the "Lao Students Movement for Democracy of 26 October 1999", included calls for respect for human rights, the release of political prisoners, a multi-party political system and elections for a new National Assembly.

Persecution on religious grounds

Restrictions on freedom of religious expression continued; people belonging to small church groups outside state control faced imprisonment and forced relocation. More than 30 Christians were arrested between January and July in the provinces of Savannakhet, Attapeu, Champassak, Xieng Khouang and Luang Prabang. Most of the men were rice farmers and day labourers belonging to the Bru ethnic minority group, and several had been arrested previously because of their religious beliefs.

◻ Pa Tood, a rice farmer and local church leader, was among 15 evangelists arrested in March 1999 in Savannakhet province. He was detained in Savannakhet City Prison and accused of "creating social disorder and division", "receiving money from outsiders" and "support from foreigners". A court reportedly dismissed the charges against him on the grounds that there was no evidence to support them, but new charges were formulated by the police. His family was ordered to relocate from their village, despite having received official permission to settle there in 1994; they were reportedly ordered to move on again in July 1999. Pa Tood continued to be held in harsh conditions at the end of the year, despite concerns for his deteriorating health.

◻ Prisoner of conscience Khamtanh Phousy was convicted of "irresponsibility in his work" and corruption, and sentenced to seven years' imprisonment at Prison Camp 7 in Houa Phanh province. He had been arrested in March 1996 after officials became suspicious of his religious activities and his contact with foreigners. AI believed that the charges against him were politically motivated.

Ten prisoners of conscience held since January 1998 on account of their religious activities and their contacts with foreigners were pardoned and released in June.

Ill-treatment

Detainees faced ill-treatment and insanitary conditions; they were reportedly denied adequate food and medical care. Detainees at Prison Camp 7 in Houa Phanh province and in Savannakhet City Prison were reportedly held in stocks for prolonged periods.

◻ Prisoners of conscience Feng Sakchittaphong and Latsami Khamphoui continued to be held in harsh conditions at Prison Camp 7 in a remote area of Houa Phanh province. Both men were suffering from serious medical problems, but they were denied access to medical care and their families were prevented from visiting them on a regular basis. Feng Sakchittaphong and Latsami Khamphoui were serving 14-year prison sentences for state security offences, imposed in November 1992 after unfair trials. However, AI believed that they were detained for advocating peaceful political and economic change.

LATVIA

REPUBLIC OF LATVIA
Head of state: Vaira Vike-Freiberga (replaced Guntis Ulmanis in July)
Head of government: Andris Skele (replaced Vilis Kristopans in July)
Capital: Riga
Population: 2.3 million
Official language: Lettish
Death penalty: abolitionist for ordinary crimes
1999 treaty ratifications/signatures: Rome Statute of the International Criminal Court

Latvia ratified Protocol No.6 to the European Convention for the Protection of Human Rights and Fundamental Freedoms, which provides for the abolition of the death penalty in peacetime, but did not complete the process of abolishing the penalty in Latvian law. Latvian legislation did not allow for conscientious objectors to undertake an alternative civilian service.

Death penalty

After joining the Council of Europe, the parliament (*Saeima*) debated the abolition of the death penalty on a number of occasions but without reaching a consensus. In April a large majority of the members of the recently elected *Saeima* voted for the ratification of Protocol No.6. On 7 May it was officially ratified. In April AI wrote to President Ulmanis welcoming these positive developments and urged the authorities to complete abolition by removing the remaining provisions relating to the death penalty from Latvia's Criminal Code. The organization learned that the *Saeima* introduced a new Criminal Code in April, reportedly containing several clauses relating to the death penalty.

Conscientious objectors

According to AI's information, a law on military service adopted in February 1997 contained no provision for conscientious objectors to undertake an alternative civilian service. In September AI once again urged

Latvia to introduce an alternative civilian service of non-punitive length for conscientious objectors who base their objection on religious, ethical, moral, humanitarian, philosophical or similar grounds. The organization informed the Latvian authorities that it would adopt as a prisoner of conscience anyone imprisoned for refusing to bear arms on grounds of conscience, unless they had access to an alternative civil service, non-punitive in length and of purely civilian character and under civilian control.

◻ Romans Nemiro and Vladimirs Gamajunovs, both Jehovah's Witnesses, objected to serving in the military on grounds of conscience. Their appeals to the Military Conscription Commission were rejected. In March and April they filed appeals against the Commission's decisions to a civil court. No decision on these had been taken by the end of 1999.

LEBANON

LEBANESE REPUBLIC
Head of state: Emile Lahoud
Head of government: Salim al-Huss
Capital: Beirut
Population: 3.1 million
Official language: Arabic
Death penalty: retentionist

Scores of people were arrested on political grounds, including students arrested after demonstrations, who were prisoners of conscience. Dozens of people accused of "collaborating" with Israel received trials which fell short of international fair trial standards. There were reports of torture and ill-treatment. At least 12 people were sentenced to death; no one was executed. Armed opposition groups, such as *Hizbullah* and *al-Takfir wa'l-Hijra*, also killed civilians and took prisoners.

Background
Several officials were arrested as part of President Emile Lahoud's continuing anti-corruption campaign. Four judges were shot inside a court in Sidon in June by unknown gunmen.

The government introduced a number of reform bills, but none had been adopted by the end of the year. Among them was a proposed new Code of Criminal Procedure. AI was concerned that a draft law to reform the judiciary might reduce the independence of the judiciary if adopted. During the year tensions increased between Palestinian refugees and the Lebanese authorities.

A strip of south Lebanon about 15 kilometres wide continued to be occupied by Israel and was policed by Israel's proxy militia, the South Lebanon Army (SLA). Syria continued to maintain a large military and intelligence presence in Lebanon.

Arrests
Scores of people, including prisoners of conscience, were arrested on political charges during the year. Among them were students who were detained for distributing leaflets on behalf of opposition groups; they were usually released after a few hours or days.

Dozens of people were arrested, accused of involvement in armed attacks against Lebanese or Syrian officials or of "collaborating" with Israel.

Freedom of expression
Journalists and artists continued to be charged for exercising their right to freedom of expression.

◻ Three journalists — Melhem Karam, publisher of several journals and Chairman of the Journalists' Association, and Paul Elie Salem and Jamil Jamel Mroué, owner and managing editor respectively of the journal *The Lebanon Report* — were charged in July in connection with the publication of excerpts from and interviews with the author of the book *From Israel to Damascus*. The book contained references to the alleged participation of a former militia leader and government minister in human rights violations during the civil war in Lebanon. The charges were later dropped.

◻ Marcel Khalifeh, a well-known musician, was brought before the Beirut Court of First Instance in November on charges of blasphemy. The charges related to his song entitled "I am Yusuf, my father" which was based on a poem by the famous Palestinian poet Mahmud Darwish and cited a verse from the Qur'an. He was acquitted in December; the judgment stated that the song was sung solemnly and did not insult the Qur'an.

Torture and ill-treatment
There were some reports of torture and ill-treatment, including instances of brutality or excessive use of force by the army and military police against demonstrators.

◻ In February Mahmud Ahmad Jallul, a cameraman for the television station *Tele-Liban*, was pulled out of his car as he was driving to work in Beirut. He and his wife were beaten by men in plain clothes and he was taken away in a car. It was reported that he had been detained by *Hizbullah* who handed him over after two days to Lebanese Military Intelligence who also beat him. He was detained in various detention centres and his family and lawyer did not have access to him for a month. He was found guilty by a military tribunal on charges of collaboration with the enemy, but acquitted on appeal and released in August.

◻ A number of students were detained in October for several hours following a protest organized by Greenpeace against pollution from a chemical fertilizer company in Salata. There were reports that police beat protestors with rifle butts; one protestor was said to have had his arm broken during the demonstration.

◻ A student, Walid Achkar, secretary of the Free Patriotic Movement, which supports former President

Michel 'Aoun, was arrested without warrant by the General Intelligence in Amioun in December and transferred to the Military Intelligence Centre in Kebbeh in Tripoli. There he was reportedly tortured for three hours by being beaten and forced to stand on one leg. He was transferred to Beirut and released without charge after four days' detention.

Unfair trials

Dozens of political prisoners were tried by the Justice Council and the Military Court whose proceedings — such as summary proceedings in the Military Court and the lack of judicial review for the verdicts of the Justice Council — failed to meet international fair trial standards.

▱ In June the Justice Council convicted 12 defendants of the killing of former Prime Minister Rashid Karami in 1987. Among them was Samir Gea'gea', former leader of the banned Lebanese Forces — the main Christian militia during the civil war — who was sentenced to death, later commuted to life imprisonment. Samir Gea'gea' was already serving two other life sentences imposed by the Justice Council in 1995 and 1997. He and about 15 others, mostly former members of the Lebanese Forces, continued to be detained in the Ministry of Defence in cruel, inhuman or degrading conditions; all were said to be held in solitary confinement in damp basement cells with almost no access to exercise or visits.

Jezzine arrests and trials

More than 160 former members of the SLA surrendered to the Lebanese authorities in May after the SLA withdrew from Jezzine. Most were brought to trial in the following months before the Military Court in Beirut charged with "collaboration" with Israel or "contact with the enemy" and were sentenced to up to a year's imprisonment. During their interrogation they were reportedly kept hooded and not allowed access to family or lawyers.

▱ One trial before the Military Court in June of 19 people from Jezzine lasted for six hours before those accused were found guilty solely on the basis of their own confessions and sentenced to up to six months' imprisonment.

Releases

Antoinette Chahin and Jihad Abi Ramia were released in June after five years' imprisonment. They were acquitted by the Criminal Court of Cassation in a retrial. In 1997 Antoinette Chahin had been sentenced to death, commuted to life imprisonment with hard labour, and Jihad Abi Ramia to 12 years' imprisonment, in connection with the politically-motivated killing of Father Sam'an Boutros al-Khoury; the court had based its decision almost entirely on confessions by the two defendants extracted under torture. AI welcomed the acquittal but regretted that the Court had not ordered a proper inquiry into the torture allegations.

Death penalty

More than 12 people were sentenced to death, including at least two women. No one was executed.

South Lebanon

The village of Arnun on the edge of the zone occupied by Israel was disputed between Israel and the SLA, and Lebanon. In February, after being "annexed" by Israel and the SLA, the village was "liberated" by a mass demonstration of Lebanese students. It was reoccupied by Israel in April. In May and June the SLA withdrew from the Jezzine salient.

During the year 23 Lebanese and two Israeli civilians were reportedly killed in the military conflict in south Lebanon, most as a result of deliberate or indiscriminate attacks.

▱ In June, at least eight Lebanese civilians were killed in Israeli air raids. The raids were in retaliation for the killing of two Israeli civilians in a rocket attack by the *Hizbullah* armed group and were followed by further *Hizbullah* shelling of northern Israel.

Khiam detention centre

At least 130 people, including women and children, were held in the Khiam detention centre; some had been held for up to 14 years. The Khiam detention centre was run by the SLA in cooperation with the Israel Defence Force (see Israel and the Occupied Territories entry). Those detained were not charged or tried and had no contact with lawyers, although they were allowed to meet families once every three months. Detainees were routinely tortured and ill-treated in Khiam and in other SLA detention centres.

▱ Suleiman Ramadan and Riyad Kalakesh, arrested in 1985 and 1986 respectively, were still detained in Khiam at the end of 1999.

▱ Fatima Ja'afar, aged 16, was detained overnight in October at the SLA's No.17 Detention Centre. During interrogation she was reportedly struck on the head and knocked unconscious. The next day she was hospitalized in Sidon with multiple fractures of the skull and memory loss. Following her release the SLA also reportedly arrested her parents and detained them overnight. Ten other villagers from 'Ainata were detained in October, apparently in an attempt to find those who sympathized with the resistance to Israeli rule.

▱ In November, 13 detainees including 'Ali Tawbeh and his father Mustafa Tawbeh, arrested in 1997, were released from Khiam Detention Centre. They had both been tortured in Khiam by methods including severe beating all over the body. Mustafa Tawbeh had spent seven months in hospital while imprisoned; 'Ali Tawbeh had been about 15 years old when arrested.

'Disappearances'

Despite repeated calls for investigations by the families of victims, there was no investigation during the year into the fate of more than 17,000 people, including Palestinians, Lebanese and other nationals, abducted by armed groups in Lebanon during the civil war (1975 to 1990).

AI country visit

In November AI delegates met Prime Minister Salim al-Huss and Minister of the Interior Michel al-Murr.

LESOTHO

KINGDOM OF LESOTHO
Head of state: King Letsie III
Head of government: Pakalitha Bethuel Mosisili
Capital: Maseru
Population: 2 million
Official languages: Sesotho, English
Death penalty: retentionist
1999 treaty ratifications/signatures: African Charter
on the Rights and Welfare of the Child

The aftermath of political turbulence in 1998 dominated human rights developments. The court martial of soldiers charged with mutiny continued, amid concerns about the independence and fairness of the proceedings. There were new reports of torture and ill-treatment, as well as harassment of human rights defenders.

Background
Violence in late 1998 over disputed elections and arising from the intervention of South African and Botswanan military forces left political tensions which continued to undermine progress in reforming political institutions. The multi-party Interim Political Authority (IPA), established in December 1998, struggled to reach agreement on a new electoral model and a timetable for elections. However, in December the IPA and the government signed an agreement on a new mixed electoral model, which was guaranteed by President Joaquim Chissano of Mozambique on behalf of the Southern African Development Community and witnessed by representatives of intergovernmental organizations.

South African and Botswanan military forces had largely withdrawn from Lesotho by May. A small contingent remained to conduct a retraining program for the Lesotho Defence Force (LDF). During 1999 relatives of some of the soldiers killed by South African forces in September 1998 sued the Lesotho government, which had invited the South African forces into the country, for civil damages.

Political trials
The court martial of LDF soldiers for the capital offence of mutiny opened in January and had not concluded by the end of 1999, when 38 soldiers remained on trial. The military tribunal convened by the Minister of Defence, who was also Prime Minister, included five LDF officers assisted by a former Chief Justice as Judge Advocate.

Defence counsel unsuccessfully challenged the holding of the trial within the Maximum Security Prison, Maseru, where the accused were held. However, the court martial president agreed to remove a member of the prosecution team and a court official after defence objections. Defence counsel challenged unsuccessfully in the High Court and the Court of Appeal the constitutionality of the proceedings on grounds of lack of independence and failure to provide a fair trial.

In February the Minister of Defence ordered charges against nine of the accused to be withdrawn and the prosecution withdrew charges against three others.

In January AI raised a number of concerns about the fairness of the proceedings, among them that the composition of the tribunal did not meet international standards of independence and impartiality. In his reply the Prime Minister rejected the concerns as unfounded.

In a separate case, at the end of 1999, 31 police officers remained on trial for the capital offence of high treason, as well as sedition and contravention of the 1984 Internal Security Act. The prosecution closed its case in June and withdrew charges against Sergeant Nthabiseng Penesi. The case against a second accused was withdrawn in December. Defence lawyers unsuccessfully applied for an order dismissing the case against the remaining accused, who had been in custody since an uprising at police headquarters in February 1997. The case was postponed until January 2000.

Charges were brought against opposition political party members, including Basotho National Party electoral candidate Thabang Nchai, and Basotholand Congress Party member Thabiso Mahase, in connection with political violence in late 1998. Trial proceedings had not concluded by the end of 1999.

Prison conditions
Fifty of the soldiers on trial for mutiny were involved in a protest in January against inhumane conditions in the Maximum Security Prison. Their protest was suppressed by a combined Lesotho, South African and Botswanan military force. Subsequently the court martial tribunal members visited the cells and noted problems with bedding, ventilation, light and sanitation. In February the High Court ordered improvements and by June, when a High Court judge inspected the cells, some improvements appeared to have been made.

In January AI publicly called on the authorities to improve conditions in the prison and to act on recommendations AI made after its visit to the prison in October 1998.

Human rights defenders
Two defence lawyers for the accused soldiers, Thabang Khauoe and Haae Phoofolo, informed the military tribunal in June that they had received telephoned death threats and appeared to be under surveillance. An LDF official was reportedly investigating the allegations but no results had been reported by the end of 1999.

Journalists attempting to report the court martial proceedings also experienced harassment. In January military police prevented a radio journalist, Candi Ramainoane, from attending the hearings. Officials later said that they had banned him because he had interviewed some of the defendants. In a subsequent incident the Judge Advocate summoned Candi

Ramainoane to apologize to the court martial for stories critical of its conduct and referred the matter to the prosecuting authorities, which had taken no action to charge him by the end of 1999.

In November Tseliso Fosa, a lawyer in Maseru, was allegedly forcibly removed from his law offices, handcuffed and kicked by police attempting to seize confidential documents. He was released from detention but faced charges of obstruction of justice.

Torture and ill-treatment
The newly established police-military Counter Crime Unit (CCU) was alleged to have tortured arrested suspects. In an incident in October, CCU members reportedly beat Teboho Lepoqo Mohale, a resident of Maseru, and tied plastic tubing over his face until he lost consciousness. He was released uncharged two and a half days later.

In November the Lesotho High Court ordered the police to refrain from torturing or ill-treating Maqentso Neko, a 48-year-old mother of three. Subsequently, she was charged with murder and released pending trial. She had been arrested by the police in Teyateyaneng in connection with a murder which occurred in 1993, and had allegedly been subjected to suffocation torture while handcuffed and naked. She had allegedly also been beaten by the police in 1993 when arrested and interrogated about the same murder.

Death penalty
No new death sentences were imposed by the courts in 1999. In September the Lesotho High Court overturned the death sentence on Nkalimeng Mothobi, who had been in custody since 1993. He was originally one of four accused, three of whom were tried separately in 1996 and sentenced to death for the same murder. Two had their sentences reduced on appeal and the third was acquitted and released in 1997.

UN Human Rights Committee
In March AI submitted a memorandum on its concerns in Lesotho to the Human Rights Committee, which was meeting to consider the government's report on its compliance with the International Covenant on Civil and Political Rights.

LIBERIA

REPUBLIC OF LIBERIA
Head of state and government: Charles G. Taylor
Capital: Monrovia
Population: 2.6 million
Official language: English
Death penalty: retentionist

Human rights violations by Liberia's security forces, including torture and possible extrajudicial executions, continued to be reported. There were renewed outbreaks of fighting in Lofa county, during which further human rights abuses were reported, some of which were allegedly committed by members of the security forces. Human rights defenders, including journalists, continued to be at risk from the authorities. No significant effort was made to investigate recent violations nor to bring to justice the perpetrators of massive human rights abuses committed during the civil war which ended in 1997. No significant progress appeared to have been made in the restructuring and retraining of the security forces; many former combatants appear to have been included in security forces and paramilitary bodies without any meaningful attempt to rehabilitate or retrain them.

Background
During the seven-year civil war gross human rights abuses were committed by numerous armed factions including the Armed Forces of Liberia (AFL), the national army which often acted as an armed group outside government control, and the National Patriotic Front of Liberia (NPFL), whose cross-border attack started the war and which at times controlled most of Liberia.

All the warring factions committed serious human rights abuses, including deliberate and arbitrary killings of unarmed civilians, torture and ill-treatment of prisoners, summary executions, rape, hostage-taking and forced displacement of civilians. About 200,000 people were killed. Some 700,000 were forced to become refugees and an estimated 1.4 million people, half the pre-war population, were internally displaced. The UN estimated that some 15,000 to 20,000 children, some as young as six years old, had participated in the conflict.

The Abuja peace agreement which ended the civil war laid down a timetable for disarmament, demobilization and elections.

Disarmament and demobilization were delayed and not fully completed. According to the peace agreement, the Economic Community of West African States (ECOWAS) Cease-fire Monitoring Group (ECOMOG) was in charge of disarmament and the UN in charge of demobilization.

Despite delays, the transition to an elected constitutional civilian government was completed in

1997. Contested elections were won by Charles G. Taylor, former leader of the NPFL, and his party, the National Patriotic Party. The 1985 Constitution was reinstated and the Supreme Court reconstituted.

Once he was in power, President Taylor pressed ECOMOG to hand over responsibility for restructuring the army to him. Many former NPFL combatants were enrolled into the country's security forces without any significant attempt at retraining, which should have included training in international human rights standards. In addition, a number of special security units were created or restructured, largely manned by former NPFL combatants, including the Special Security Service, the Special Security Unit, the Special Operations Division (a special unit within the police), and the Anti-Terrorism Unit. These units have been accused of serious violations of human rights.

By mid-1999, the Liberian operations of ECOMOG had ended at President Taylor's insistence.

In mid-1999 a UN delegation visited Liberia to investigate events surrounding a renewed outbreak of fighting in September 1998 between forces loyal to President Taylor and supporters of Roosevelt Johnson, another former faction leader. The official death toll from the fighting in Monrovia was 52, with 49 people wounded, but independent and credible estimates suggested that the victims, including the dead and injured, ran into several hundred. Some of the killings were apparently extrajudicial executions. The report of the UN delegation had not been made public by the end of 1999.

The government was widely accused of providing arms, ammunition and fighters to the armed opposition in Sierra Leone, in violation of a UN Security Council resolution, before the conclusion of a peace agreement between the government of Sierra Leone and rebel forces in Lomé, Togo, in July 1999. AI urged the Liberian authorities to prevent military supplies for rebel forces from crossing its borders into Sierra Leone.

The National Human Rights Commission, set up by law in 1998, remained inactive. Its five Commissioners were not approved by parliament until late 1999, and its powers were limited. The Commission could not order witnesses to appear nor initiate investigations.

Treason trial

At least 34 people were charged with treason following the fighting in September 1998. Nineteen were arrested, five of whom were released after becoming state witnesses. Among those held and tried were: Bai Gbala, former political adviser to President Taylor; former Senator James Chelly; former Presidential Affairs Minister Charles Breeze; former Transport Minister Armah Youlu; former Deputy Justice Minister David Gbala; and former commander of the State House under President Samuel Doe, Edward Slanger. Others were charged in absentia, including Roosevelt Johnson, former faction leader and subsequently a minister in President Taylor's government. Roosevelt Johnson sought refuge in the US embassy during the fighting in September 1998 and was subsequently flown out of Liberia.

In April, 13 of the defendants were convicted of treason, an offence carrying a sentence of death or life imprisonment. One defendant was acquitted. Those convicted were sentenced to 10 years' imprisonment, and the judge declared that the reason for the lenient sentencing was the "need for genuine reconciliation in the country". Leave to appeal was granted both to the defence, which claimed that the prosecution had failed to prove its case, and to the prosecution, which claimed that the sentences were illegal.

AI sent a delegate to observe the trial and was concerned about the competence of the court and irregularities in the trial proceedings. Some of the defendants told the delegate that they had been ill-treated before and during the trial. Some appeared to have been beaten severely, and at least two had loss of hearing and broken limbs.

Sedition trial

A group of military officers, nine of whom were charged with sedition, was arrested in connection with the fighting in Monrovia of September 1998 and brought to trial during 1999. Their trial was suspended several times by a Court Martial Board amid controversy about the government's reported failure to ensure adequate financial resources for the trial. By the end of 1999, the trial was suspended indefinitely. Concerns were also expressed about the perceived lack of guarantees for a fair trial and about alleged intimidation of defence lawyers. Moreover, the defendants were reportedly ill-treated and held in conditions which might have amounted to cruel, inhuman and degrading treatment. They were reported to have been regularly denied food and medical care. On at least one occasion defendants fainted during the trial proceedings, reportedly because they had been denied food for several days. The prisoners were also repeatedly beaten and flogged in the early days of their detention.

Human rights defenders

Human rights defenders continued to be threatened and harassed because of their work. In March the Justice and Peace Commission of Liberia (JPC), a human rights non-governmental organization, and FOCUS, a children's rights group, were sued by legislators from Sinoe, Maryland, Grand Kru and Bong counties after publishing a report on child slavery. The legislators said reports of forced labour by the JPC and FOCUS damaged the image of their counties, making it difficult to obtain international assistance. The legislators asked for damages of US$10 million. AI urged the government to respect the right of all human rights defenders to carry out their work without harassment or fear of arrest.

In March, and again in December, journalists were detained on charges which were apparently politically motivated. Police briefly detained Isaac Menyongi of *Heritage* newspaper for refusing to disclose the source of his article about a South African businessman's ties to Liberian officials. Also in March, Philip Moore, a reporter with the independent newspaper *The News*, was arrested on charges of "criminal malevolence". He was released a day later after intervention from the

Press Union of Liberia and the JPC. In December, police arrested the news editor of the *Concord Times* newspaper, Sarkilay Kantan, and a reporter on similar charges, following their articles about corruption in government and state-run companies. Four other journalists were also sought for arrest.

☐ In December, police arrested James Torh, the executive director of FOCUS, on charges of sedition in connection with comments he had made in a speech at a high school. James Torh had a record of speaking out about human rights concerns in Liberia and had publicly criticized President Taylor over the issue of a truth commission to investigate past abuses. He was released on bail after three days.

☐ A journalist was arrested and detained in January for four days, apparently because of his investigative work on the involvement of Liberia in the Sierra Leonean conflict. He was allegedly beaten and held naked. He was accused of treason and espionage, but no formal charges were brought against him. The police authorities denied his arrest. His fiancée was briefly detained when she tried to locate him. A few weeks later, he was again seized by plainclothes security officers, and released only after the intercession of senior officials and foreign representatives. He had previously been arrested and reportedly tortured in August 1998.

Violations by the security forces

Human rights violations by the security forces, including rape, were widespread. Incidents of harassment, beatings and serious injuries against civilians continued to be reported with alarming regularity. In March members of the military, searching for a missing man, detained and beat elders in the village of Dambala, Grand Cape Mount county, near the Sierra Leone border. Villagers complained that the soldiers had raped several women and had looted money and goods. The alleged violations followed several hours of shooting in the village. Military authorities admitted that looting had occurred but denied the allegations of violence and rape. The authorities reportedly set up an inquiry into the incident, but by the end of 1999 there had been no investigation.

On 4 August at least one civilian was reported to have died after police reportedly belonging to the Special Operations Division attacked a group of street sellers in the red-light district in Paynesville, Monrovia. It appears that the police intervention was ordered to stop street sellers from trespassing on private land. Officers armed with guns and machine-guns were reported to have violently assaulted and in some cases beaten unarmed sellers, including women and children, and to have arrested about 15 civilians.

Members of the security forces frequently threatened vulnerable individuals and groups in order to extort money, goods and services.

Street children in slum areas of Monrovia were reportedly harassed, intimidated and flogged by members of security forces, including members of the paramilitary Special Security Unit and the Special Operations Division. Although some members of the security forces accused of abuses were reportedly dismissed by the security forces, many of those responsible for human rights violations enjoyed impunity.

Fighting in Lofa county

Relations between Liberia and neighbouring Guinea deteriorated when the Liberian government accused Guinea of allowing armed opposition forces to base themselves across the border and launch attacks into Liberia. Guinea denied the allegations, and accused Liberia of cross-border attacks on Guinean villages. There were several cross-border incidents, and civilians were subject to harassment and violence at the hands of Liberian security forces, especially members of the Mandingo ethnic group, which had opposed Charles Taylor during the civil war.

In March 1999 at least two people were killed, and eight houses and a mosque burned down in the town of Zowudomai, Lofa county, in one of several inter-communal clashes between members of the Lorma and Mandingo ethnic groups.

In April the town of Voinjama was reportedly attacked by a group of armed men. A number of civilians, mostly belonging to the Mandingo ethnic group, were reportedly killed in Voinjama during and after the fighting. Some were alleged to have been deliberately killed by the Liberian security forces. Others, including children, were reportedly detained without charge or trial by the security forces in Voinjama for several weeks after the fighting. Some were reportedly beaten.

In August the Liberian government announced that armed men had crossed the border from Guinea and infiltrated the town of Kolahun and other villages and towns in Lofa county. Fighting was reported to have broken out between the attackers and government security forces. At least six aid workers were abducted by the attackers. Later in August a commission of representatives from the Liberian and Guinean governments and five other ECOWAS countries was created to find a solution to the security problems between the two countries.

However, in September the Guinean authorities announced that 28 villagers had been killed, many injured and property looted by members of Liberian security forces in a cross-border operation in three villages near the town of Macenta. An unknown number of people had reportedly been wounded and property had been looted. At least one Liberian soldier was reported to have been taken prisoner by the Guinean authorities. The Liberian authorities denied the allegations.

Refugees

The assisted voluntary return of refugees from West African countries after the end of the civil war continued at a slow pace. The Liberian Refugee, Repatriation and Resettlement Commission complained that security personnel at checkpoints were harassing returnees.

Up to 9,000 Liberians, most belonging to the Mandingo ethnic group, fled Lofa county and sought refuge in Guinea and other neighbouring countries after the April fighting. Hundreds of others were reported to have left other counties, including Nimba county, for Guinea.

AI country visit
AI visited Liberia in June and July to research human rights violations since the end of the war and to analyse the institutions put in place in Liberia for the protection of human rights.

LIBYA

SOCIALIST PEOPLE'S LIBYAN ARAB JAMAHIRIYA
Head of state: Mu'ammar al-Gaddafi
Capital: Tripoli
Population: 5.6 million
Official language: Arabic
Death penalty: retentionist

Hundreds of political prisoners, including prisoners of conscience, remained in detention. Many of them had been detained for more than a decade without charge or trial. Torture, especially during incommunicado detention, continued to be reported.

Background
Celebrations of the 30th anniversary of the revolution which brought Colonel Mu'ammar al-Gaddafi to power coincided with the holding of an extraordinary summit of the Organization of African Unity (OAU) in September in Libya.

Libya has no independent non-governmental organizations, human rights groups or independent bar association. Libyan law prohibits the formation of political parties and criticism of the political system. The press is strictly controlled by the government.

The Lockerbie bombing
In April the UN Security Council suspended the seven-year international air embargo and other punitive measures against Libya after the Libyan authorities handed over two Libyan nationals suspected of being responsible for an airplane bombing over Lockerbie in Scotland in 1988 in which 270 people were killed. The trial before a Scottish court convened in the Netherlands was expected to open at the beginning of 2000.

Following the handover of the Lockerbie suspects, the Arab League called for a full lifting of the sanctions against Libya. The European Union (EU) decided to suspend sanctions imposed on Libya, but to keep an

arms embargo in place. Libya was given observer status in the Euro-Mediterranean process and invited to accept the terms of the Barcelona Declaration of 1995, which include a commitment to human rights and democracy.

The UTA airliner bombing
In March the Court of Assizes in Paris, France, sentenced six Libyan nationals *in absentia* to life imprisonment for the bombing of a French UTA airliner which exploded in 1989 over Niger killing 170 people. Among those sentenced were high-ranking Libyan officials from the Libyan secret service and diplomatic corps. Libya did not accept responsibility for the incident, but reportedly transferred funds of more than US$30 million to France in order to compensate relatives of the victims of the bombing. However, in October a French high court judge decided to open investigations into the alleged involvement of Colonel al-Gaddafi in the bombing of the airliner.

Political prisoners
In a television speech broadcast on 30 September Colonel al-Gaddafi invited AI and other human rights organizations to come to Libya, claiming that there were no political prisoners in the country. AI wrote to the Libyan government reiterating its concerns about hundreds of political prisoners held without trial or after unfair trials, including prisoners of conscience. AI proposed a research visit and sought assurances that it could be conducted without interference. By the end of the year the organization had not received a reply to its request.

Five prisoners of conscience, who were arrested in 1973 and convicted of membership of the prohibited Islamic Liberation Party, continued to serve life sentences in Abu Salim Prison in Tripoli.

Several people, including possible prisoners of conscience, detained during the year in connection with their political activities or religious beliefs or activities remained in detention.

Scores of professionals, including engineers and university lecturers, who were arrested in June and July 1998 on suspicion of supporting or sympathizing with *al-Jama'a al-Islamiya al-Libiya*, the Libyan Islamic Group, an underground Islamist movement which was not known to have used or advocated violence, remained held at Abu Salim and 'Ain Zara prisons in Tripoli.

Hundreds of political prisoners arrested in previous years, including possible prisoners of conscience, remained held without charge or trial. Many of them have been detained for more than a decade. Scores of other political detainees remained in detention despite having been tried and acquitted by the courts. Others continued to serve prison sentences imposed in previous years after grossly unfair trials.

⌂ Rashid 'Abd al-Hamid al-'Urfia, a law graduate, was reportedly arrested with 20 others in 1982 on suspicion of founding an Islamist opposition group. All those arrested with him were released following a general amnesty in 1988, but he remained in Abu Salim Prison in Tripoli.

Al-Sayyid Mohammad Shabou, a Libyan citizen with refugee status in the United Kingdom, was detained by the Libyan authorities after he and his family were forcibly returned to Libya by the Saudi Arabian authorities in 1998. He continued to be held without charge or trial, reportedly in connection with his Islamist opposition activities.

Prison conditions
Political detainees were reportedly held in cruel, inhuman or degrading conditions and denied adequate medical care, which led to several deaths in custody.

Mohammad 'Ali al-Bakoush, detained since 1989 without charge or trial, died in Abu Salim Prison in August, reportedly as a result of poor conditions of detention.

'Disappearance' of Mansour Kikhiya
Mansour Kikhiya, a prominent Libyan opposition leader and human rights activist, "disappeared" in 1993 in Egypt. In February 1999 the Cairo Court of Appeals ordered the Egyptian Interior Ministry to pay Baha al-'Emari, Mansour Kikhiya's wife, about US$30,000 compensation for having failed to provide the necessary protection for her husband. The court's verdict stated that "according to international law and the Universal Declaration of Human Rights the [Egyptian] State has a responsibility concerning action committed against foreigners on its territory". However, on 7 April the Egyptian Court of Cassation suspended the ruling.

Torture
There were continued reports that political detainees were routinely tortured while held in incommunicado detention. Reported methods of torture included beatings, hanging by the wrists, being suspended from a pole inserted between the knees and elbows, electric shocks, burning with cigarettes and attacks by aggressive dogs causing serious injuries.

In April the UN Committee against Torture examined Libya's implementation of the Convention against Torture and Other Cruel, Inhuman or Degrading Treatment or Punishment and concluded that the Libyan authorities had failed to substantially address concerns and recommendations previously raised by the Committee. The Committee reiterated its concerns that it continued to receive allegations of torture and that "prolonged incommunicado detention in spite of the legal provisions regulating it still seems to create conditions which may lead to violation of the Convention". The Committee's recommendations included that the Libyan authorities should "send a clear message to all its law-enforcement personnel that torture is not permitted under any circumstances".

LITHUANIA

REPUBLIC OF LITHUANIA
Head of state: Valdas Adamkus
Head of government: Andrius Kubilius (replaced Rolandas Paksas in October, who replaced Gediminas Vagnorius in May)
Capital: Vilnius
Population: 3.7 million
Official language: Lithuanian
Death penalty: abolitionist for all crimes
1999 treaty ratifications/signatures: Protocol No. 6 to the European Convention for the Protection of Human Rights and Fundamental Freedoms concerning the abolition of the death penalty

Lithuania abolished the death penalty in 1999 by ratifying Protocol No. 6 to the European Convention for the Protection of Human Rights and Fundamental Freedoms concerning the abolition of the death penalty. The small number of prisoners under sentence of death had their sentences commuted to life imprisonment.

Death penalty
Lithuania abolished the death penalty in June when the parliament (*Seimas*) voted by an overwhelming majority to ratify Protocol No.6, which provides for the abolition of the death penalty except in time of war or the imminent threat of war.

After the ruling of the Constitutional Court of Lithuania on 9 December 1998 that the death penalty was unconstitutional, Lithuania made rapid progress to abolition during peacetime. The Constitutional Court ruled that the death penalty violated the basic human rights to life and protection from cruelty which are enshrined in the country's Constitution. On 21 December 1998 the *Seimas* voted for new legislation which replaced the death sentence with life imprisonment. As a result, nine prisoners under sentence of death were given life sentences. In January 1999 Lithuania signed Protocol No.6. On 22 June the *Seimas* voted overwhelmingly in favour of ratification and for the abolition of the death penalty. On 8 July Lithuania officially ratified Protocol No.6.

MACEDONIA

THE FORMER YUGOSLAV REPUBLIC OF MACEDONIA
Head of state: Boris Trajkovski (replaced Kiro Gligorov in December)
Head of government: Ljubfio Georgievski
Capital: Skopje
Population: 2 million
Official language: Macedonian
Death penalty: abolitionist for all crimes

The Kosovo crisis (see Federal Republic of Yugoslavia entry) dominated events in the country because of the huge influx of refugees and the presence of NATO forces. The failure of the authorities to meet in full their obligations to protect refugees, and ill-treatment by police, were the main human rights concerns. There were reports of ill-treatment by police. At least one conscientious objector to military service was imprisoned.

Background

A coalition government was led by the main Macedonian nationalist party, VMRO-DMPNE, but included ministers from other parties such as the main ethnic Albanian party, the Democratic Party of Albanians. The government came under extreme pressure as hundreds of thousands of Kosovo Albanian refugees fled into Macedonia between April and June. Macedonian members of the government and other Macedonian politicians pointed to the delicate ethnic balance in the country and the threat of destabilization arising from the influx. Tension increased between the ethnic Albanian minority population, which was keen to receive the refugees, and the Macedonian majority who were mostly apprehensive or hostile. Similar divisions prevailed in relation to the NATO presence in the country. The NATO forces were deployed officially in support of international monitoring, humanitarian and peace-keeping efforts. Many Macedonians feared that they would eventually be used as part of a NATO ground invasion of Kosovo or the Federal Republic of Yugoslavia (FRY) if no peace agreement was reached, drawing Macedonia into the conflict.

The mandate of a UN peace-keeping force, UNPREDEP, ended in February. A monitoring mission from the Organization for Security and Co-operation in Europe continued, working within the mandate it was given in 1992.

The Kosovo refugee crisis

The authorities were reluctant to receive the ethnic Albanian refugees fleeing Kosovo and to meet the country's obligations under international refugee law. The border was closed on numerous occasions with the result that thousands of people waited for days in squalid conditions at the border. Families were separated and some refugees were forced back into Kosovo where they risked further human rights violations.

The government insisted that it would give temporary protection to only 20,000 refugees, and that further refugees would be allowed to enter only on condition that they would be evacuated to other countries. In response, the UN refugee agency UNHCR established a "Humanitarian Evacuation Programme" (HEP), under which refugees were flown to other countries according to various quotas and selection criteria. Some 90,000 refugees were flown to other countries under the HEP between April and June.

This program was unprecedented in international refugee law and practice, and AI documented serious flaws in the implementation of the evacuations. AI had concerns about the unclear and varied nature of the protection being offered in host countries to the refugees being evacuated, and about the information made available to refugees. It appeared that some refugees were transferred to other countries, including Albania, against their will. The protection offered in other countries was predominantly temporary in nature, despite the view of UNHCR that the refugees qualified for refugee status under the 1951 Convention relating to the Status of Refugees (Refugee Convention).

AI called on the international community to share responsibility for the refugees and pointed to the failure of other states to assist adequately in the crisis. At the same time AI considered that the Macedonian government failed to meet its obligations under the Refugee Convention by closing its border to refugees and demanding their urgent transfer to other countries.

At the peak of the crisis, there were about 240,000 refugees in Macedonia, but most returned to Kosovo between June and August after the NATO deployment in Kosovo. However, smaller numbers of new refugees arrived from June onwards, mainly Roma and Serbs who were fleeing human rights abuses in Kosovo committed by ethnic Albanians. Some of the new arrivals were obstructed by the authorities. For example, a group of 450 Roma waited one week at the border before they were allowed to enter. At the end of 1999 there were about 20,000 Kosovo refugees remaining who had been given temporary protection until early 2000. Some 8,000 of them were Roma or Serbs.

In April AI appealed to the authorities to ensure that refugees were let into the country and that the government met in full its obligations under the Refugee Convention. In May and June respectively it issued reports which detailed its concerns.

Police ill-treatment

There were allegations of ill-treatment by police, although fewer than in previous years. Some of the allegations related to Kosovo Albanians, including refugees in camps, but the victims included people of all nationalities.

⌂ Xhafer Mustafa, an ethnic Albanian from Kosovo, was beaten by police at a border crossing in July after becoming involved in an argument with police about the long delays at the crossing.

Conscientious objection

There is no purely civilian alternative to military service. Jehovah's Witnesses complained that they were repeatedly prosecuted – receiving fines or short prison sentences as a result – for refusing to serve in the army on grounds of conscience.

⌐ A Jehovah's Witness from Kriva Palanka was imprisoned for three months from October for refusing military service. He expressed his willingness to perform a civilian service outside the armed forces if it were to be offered. In 1996 he was imprisoned for two months for refusing to serve in the army and was fined on two other occasions. A further case against him was in process at the end of 1999.

Releases

In February an amnesty law passed by parliament in December 1998 became law, after a delay resulting from President Kiro Gligorov's refusal to sign it. Some 900 prisoners were released as a result, including political prisoners such as Rufi Osmani and prisoners of conscience such as Refik Dauti, who were both local council officials in Gostivar sentenced to prison terms after a dispute with the central authorities over the display of flags.

AI country reports and visits

Reports

• The former Yugoslav Republic of Macedonia: The protection of Kosovo Albanian refugees (AI Index: EUR 65/003/99)
• The former Yugoslav Republic of Macedonia: Humanitarian evacuation and the international response to the refugees from Kosovo (AI Index: EUR 65/005/99)

Visits

AI delegates maintained a continuous presence between April and July to gather information about human rights in Kosovo and to monitor the treatment of Kosovo refugees.

MALAYSIA

MALAYSIA
Head of state: Sultan Salahuddin Abdul Aziz Shah Alhaj
Head of government: Mahathir Mohamad
Capital: Kuala Lumpur
Population: 21.8 million
Official language: Bahasa Malaysia
Death penalty: retentionist

Political tensions, heightened by the trials of former deputy Prime Minister Anwar Ibrahim, intensified in expectation of general elections, eventually called in November. The authorities continued to apply laws restricting rights to peaceful expression, assembly and association. Malaysia's former police chief was charged with assaulting Anwar Ibrahim in custody, but reports of the ill-treatment of other prisoners of conscience held incommunicado were not adequately investigated. Police used excessive force to disperse peaceful demonstrations amid persistent reports of the ill-treatment of detained protesters. Hundreds of demonstrators were tried on charges of illegal assembly or rioting and dozens were imprisoned or fined. Students involved in the demonstrations were disciplined by university authorities. At least one person was sentenced to death.

Background

Public acceptance of government justifications for the restriction of individual rights and liberties was shaken by events following Anwar Ibrahim's dismissal from office in September 1998. The detention of Anwar Ibrahim and his supporters under the Internal Security Act (ISA), the ill-treatment of detainees in custody, and the use by police of excessive force in dispersing peaceful demonstrators prompted public questioning of state institutions and fuelled calls for *"reformasi"* (reform). In April groups supportive of *reformasi* founded the *Parti Keadilan Nasional* (PKN), National Justice Party, and later formed an electoral alliance with other opposition parties. However, in the November general elections the ruling *Barisan Nasional*, National Front, coalition won a two-thirds parliamentary majority. Divisions in the ethnic Malay community were reflected in significant electoral advances made by the *Parti Islam Sa-Malaysia* (PAS), Islamic Party of Malaysia.

Prisoners of conscience; ill-treatment of detainees

Calls were renewed for the repeal of the ISA, which allows detention without charge for up to two years, renewable indefinitely, of anyone considered a potential threat to national security. At least 27 prisoners of conscience were detained under the ISA from September 1998 to early 1999 in connection with Anwar Ibrahim and the *reformasi* movement. All were released from ISA detention before the end of their 60-day interrogation period, but a number, including Anwar Ibrahim, continued to be detained under separate criminal charges or were rearrested.

In April, after a four-month trial, Anwar Ibrahim was convicted of corrupt practices (using his ministerial office to interfere with a police investigation into alleged sexual misconduct) and sentenced to six years' imprisonment. AI concluded that the charges against him were politically motivated and a pretext to remove him from public life. This conclusion was reinforced by the unfair conduct of his trial, including the public undermining by government leaders of his right to be presumed innocent, the intimidation of his defence team, and procedural decisions during the trial.

In January prisoner of conscience Munawar Anees, a Pakistani academic, was released after serving three months of a six-month sentence imposed after he pleaded guilty in September 1998 to having "allowed himself to be sodomized by Anwar Ibrahim". Sukma Darmawan, Anwar Ibrahim's adopted brother, convicted at the same time after confessing to the same offence, was released on bail in December 1998. New charges of sodomy were brought against Anwar Ibrahim and Sukma Darmawan in April, who went on joint trial in June. The judge ruled that Sukma Darmawan's 1998 confession was admissible as evidence despite his testimony of serious physical and psychological ill-treatment by police. The trial had not been completed at the end of 1999.

AI continued to call for full, open and independent investigations into all reports of ill-treatment of detainees. Although Anwar Ibrahim's claims of assault and his visible facial bruising in September 1998 led to a Royal Commission of Inquiry in February, which found that he had been assaulted by the Inspector General of Police, other credible allegations of ill-treatment, at times amounting to torture, were not properly investigated. Munawar Anees and Sukma Darmawan stated that they had been subjected to severe physical and psychological pressure, including being stripped, sexually humiliated, struck and threatened with indefinite ISA detention. Abdul Malik Hussein, a supporter of Anwar Ibrahim, also stated that he was stripped and beaten, humiliated and forced to drink water tainted with urine after being detained under the ISA in September 1998.The authorities subsequently filed perjury charges against Sukma Darmawan and two other men who had complained of ill-treatment during the course of police investigations into Anwar Ibrahim.

Two other prisoners of conscience were released during the year. Che Kamarulzaman Ismail, the last of seven Shi'a Muslims ordered detained under the ISA for two years in 1998 for allegedly posing a threat to "national security and Muslim unity", was set free, reportedly in May. In August former parliamentarian Lim Guan Eng, imprisoned in 1998 for sedition and "spreading false news" concerning a statutory rape case involving a government minister, was released. As a convicted criminal he was disqualified from his parliamentary seat and prohibited from standing for parliament for five years.

Right of peaceful assembly and association
Periodic demonstrations in support of Anwar Ibrahim and reformasi continued on a reduced scale in Kuala Lumpur. Most of the demonstrations were peaceful, but police repeatedly used excessive force during dispersal operations, including unprovoked assaults on participants, using fists, batons and canes. Additionally there were persistent reports of ill-treatment, including the beating and kicking of protesters, immediately after arrest and in police station detention cells (lock-ups). Many detainees were denied access to legal counsel before their remand hearings.

More than 1,000 people were reportedly arrested between September 1998 and June 1999 for allegedly participating in illegal assemblies or rioting. At least 334 were charged, and the first of eight separate mass trials began in January. Most of the defendants were acquitted, although at least 30 were found guilty of illegal assembly and sentenced to imprisonment or fines. In September, 14 people, including leading members of opposition parties, were arrested after a rally which had led to some violent incidents. Eight were held in custody before being charged with illegal assembly. University and college students accused of participating in illegal assemblies faced suspension or expulsion under legislation prohibiting students from participating in any political activity without permission.

Opposition parties and non-governmental groups continued to complain about the refusal by the authorities to issue permits for public meetings. In April an indoor forum on reformasi to be addressed by academics was cancelled after police refused to issue a permit, and in May a number of planned PKN meetings had their licences revoked at the last minute.

Curbs on freedom of expression
The threat of government prosecutions for allegedly seditious statements, or for printing "false news", continued to curb freedom of expression. In May the Attorney General warned that those who criticized his office for "selective prosecutions" could be charged with sedition. The trial of women's rights activist Irene Fernandez entered its fourth year. She had been charged with maliciously publishing "false news" in a 1995 report detailing allegations of ill-treatment, sexual abuse and denial of medical care in camps holding detained migrant workers.

In May the Bar Council expressed concern at the growing number of civil defamation suits in which plaintiffs demanded or had been awarded unusually high levels of damages. In February the ruling United Malay National Organisation (UMNO) set up an "anti-defamation" committee to study statements by opposition parties and to recommend the filing of defamation suits.

AI expressed concern at the failure of the government and judiciary to abide by the April ruling of the International Court of Justice (ICJ) upholding the immunity from prosecution of the UN Special Rapporteur on the independence of judges and lawyers, Param Cumaraswamy. In 1995, four defamation suits were filed against the Special Rapporteur for comments he made in his official capacity concerning complaints that certain business entities were able to manipulate the Malaysian courts. Proceedings were continuing at the end of 1999.

The use by the judiciary of contempt of court powers also raised concerns. In May Zainur Zakaria, one of Anwar Ibrahim's defence lawyers, was summarily sentenced to three months' imprisonment for filing an affidavit alleging that two public prosecutors had attempted to fabricate evidence. An appeal was lodged. In September the Court of Appeal ordered Canadian journalist Murray Hiebert to be jailed for six weeks for contempt; he had referred to the speed with which a defamation case involving the son of a judge had come to court. AI expressed concern that the right to freedom of expression was not being adequately protected by the courts.

Corporal punishment; death penalty
Caning, a form of cruel, inhuman and degrading punishment, was imposed throughout the year as an additional punishment to imprisonment. At least one person was sentenced to death during the year.

National Human Rights Commission
In July Parliament passed legislation to establish a Human Rights Commission for the protection and promotion of human rights in Malaysia. AI expressed concern that the Commission might fall short of the UN Principles relating to the Status of National Institutions for the Promotion and Protection of Human Rights (Paris Principles). For instance, the Commission's mandate defines human rights primarily as those fundamental liberties enshrined in the Malaysian Constitution, which have been heavily qualified, rather than defining them in terms of international human rights standards.

AI country reports and visits
Report
• Malaysia: Human rights undermined – restrictive laws in a parliamentary democracy (AI Index: ASA 28/006/99)
Visits
AI delegates observed stages of the trials of Anwar Ibrahim and of Sukma Darmawan, and conducted research on arbitrary arrest, detention and ill-treatment in the context of the government's response to the *reformasi* movement.

MALDIVES

REPUBLIC OF MALDIVES
Head of state and government: Maumoon Abdul Gayoom
Capital: Male
Population: 0.3 million
Official language: Maldivian Dhivehi
Death penalty: abolitionist in practice

As in previous years, the government failed to provide credible information about the situation of political prisoners. Despite AI's efforts, there was no contact from the government. There were continued reports of torture and of official cover-ups to protect the perpetrators.

Background
Parliamentary elections were held in November amid reports of suspected irregularities. Political parties were not allowed to function.

Lack of government response
The government remained silent about the situation of Richard Wu Mei De, a Chinese national detained without due process of law since November 1993 at the instigation of a Maldivian national whom he tried to sue for irregularities in a business partnership; government connivance in the detention was suspected. His detention was declared arbitrary by the UN Working Group on Arbitrary Detention.

Political prisoners
Possible prisoners of conscience continued to be held. Among those believed to be held were Hussain Shakir, Ibrahim Nusthafa and Mohamed Rasheed, reportedly detained since early 1996 in connection with a demonstration about electricity price rises on Fubahmulaku Island.

Political prisoners were detained on the prison island of Maafushi, in Dhoonidhoo detention centre and in police stations. They reportedly included a parliamentary candidate detained after an argument with a rival candidate with links to the government.

Ten people from Faafu Magoodhoo were banished, reportedly without being tried or sentenced, for seeking to organize a demonstration against the local Atoll chief.
Health concern
There was continued concern about the health of Ismail Saadiq, a businessman arrested in June 1996 for alleged fraud, who was reportedly denied medical attention. In June, for example, he was transferred to Dhoonidhoo detention centre where he was reportedly held in a small cell, denied appropriate food, and prevented from receiving a scheduled blood transfusion. Three weeks later he was transferred to house arrest, reportedly after he fell ill and after he had signed a declaration that he would not seek contact with the

outside world. Ismail Saadiq continued to claim that his prolonged detention was politically motivated. During his trials, he was reportedly not allowed to appoint a lawyer and was denied adequate time or access to documentation to prepare his defence.

Ill-treatment

Information emerged indicating that many inmates in Gamaadhoo prison were subjected to various forms of ill-treatment after a fire which burned down the prison. According to reports, security guards beat some prisoners who were tied to palm trees. A former detainee at Dhoonidhoo stated that prison guards regularly beat prisoners, at times on orders from the senior warden.

MALI

REPUBLIC OF MALI

Head of state: Alpha Oumar Konaré
Head of government: Ibrahim Boubacar Keita
Capital: Bamako
Population: 9.9 million
Official language: French
Death penalty: abolitionist in practice
1999 treaty ratifications/signatures: UN Convention against Torture and Other Cruel, Inhuman or Degrading Treatment or Punishment

President Alpha Oumar Konaré commuted all death sentences passed in 1998 and in 1999. Former President Moussa Traoré, his wife and his brother-in-law were among those who benefited from this measure. A number of students, some of whom appeared to be prisoners of conscience, were released after a presidential pardon. Opposition supporters detained pending trial since mid-1998 were released provisionally in October.

Background

President Konaré, who was re-elected in 1997, stressed that the Malian Constitution would be respected and that he would not stand for a third term. The Constitution allows for only two presidential terms. In March the Ministry of Justice convened a national forum on the reform of justice, which was attended by participants from Africa, France and Canada. In his opening speech, President Konaré reiterated his opposition to the death penalty. He expressed regret that the Malian judicial system was subject to delays and that the country's prisons held more pre-trial detainees than prisoners sentenced to prison terms. The Justice Minister announced the organization of a debate on the death penalty. There have been no executions in Mali during the past decade. In December Demba Diallo, a lawyer and former President of the *Association malienne des droits de l'homme*, Malian Association for Human Rights, was appointed Mediator of the Republic.

Political prisoners

Former President Moussa Traoré, his wife Mariam, and his brother-in-law were convicted of embezzlement and other economic offences and sentenced to death by the Bamako Assize court in January. The court also sentenced the presidential couple to fines amounting to 300 million francs. Two other former government officials tried on the same charges were acquitted.

Imprisoned students, most of whom were leading members of the *Association des étudiants et élèves du Mali*, Association of Malian Students, were released in July after a presidential pardon. They had been tried in 1998 before the Bamako Assize Court on charges including arson, obstructing a public highway and manslaughter.

Nine opposition supporters, including Adama Koyaté and Dancry Foune Sissoko, who were detained pending trial were released provisionally in October. They were arrested in June 1998 and accused of conspiracy, threatening the safety of the state and illegal possession of arms and ammunition.

AI visit to Mali

In December, an AI delegation led by Pierre Sané, AI's Secretary General, visited Mali. President Konaré was the incoming Chairman of the Economic Community of West African States (ECOWAS) and Mali had been elected to a non-permanent seat on the UN Security Council. AI's delegates met President Konaré and sought to ensure that human rights protection was placed high on the agenda of West African governments. The delegation also met the Prime Minister and other government officials.

During talks with the Minister of Justice, the AI delegation insisted that all allegations of torture should be impartially investigated and those responsible should be brought to justice. The delegates also raised the provisional releases of political prisoners. The Minister of Justice informed the delegation that disciplinary and legal action had been taken against two prison guards responsible for ill-treatment of prisoners at Kayes prison.

Shortly after this visit, the government named a commission of inquiry to investigate allegations of torture and ill-treatment made by opposition party supporters who were arrested in 1997 in Niamakoro. They were alleged to have been tortured by police in the presence of senior police officials.

MAURITANIA

ISLAMIC REPUBLIC OF MAURITANIA
Head of state: Maaouiya Ould Sid 'Ahmed Taya
Head of government: Cheikh El Avia Ould Mohamed Khouna
Capital: Nouakchott
Population: 2.3 million
Official language: Arabic
Death penalty: retentionist

Press freedom and the activities of human rights groups continued to be severely curtailed, making information about human rights difficult to obtain. The Mauritanian authorities took no steps to investigate massive human rights violations committed during the late 1980s and early 1990s, but the French judicial authorities arrested and investigated a Mauritanian army officer in France accused of torture.

Background
Human rights violations, including political killings, "disappearances" and torture, were widespread during the late 1980s and early 1990s. The victims included suspected government opponents from both black and Arab-Berber communities, civil servants and farmers and cattle herders from the south. Between 1989 and 1991 black African villagers, particularly those from the Senegal River Valley, were targeted by the Mauritanian authorities, dominated by Moors and members of the Beidane ethnic group. More than 500 black Mauritanians held in military custody in 1990 and 1991 were allegedly the victims of extrajudicial execution. A variety of torture techniques were used, including electric shocks, burning with hot coals and the "jaguar", which involved suspending the victim upside down from a metal bar and beating the soles of the feet. Tens of thousands of mostly black Mauritanians were expelled or fled to Senegal and other neighbouring countries. The Mauritanian authorities continued to prevent investigations into past human rights violations.

Human rights organizations continued to operate without recognition by the government, leaving human rights activists open to harassment for "administer[ing] associations which are functioning without authorization" according to Mauritanian law. In 1998, a number of prominent human rights defenders were arrested, tried, convicted and sentenced to prison terms under this law.

In October, after Mauritania established full diplomatic ties with Israel, student protests in Nouakchott and in other towns were dispersed by police. Further student protests in November led to the brief arrest of more than a dozen people. A few days later, Mauritanian authorities also banned the opposition *Taliaa* (Vanguard) Party, accusing party leaders of stirring up the unrest. Police detained an official of the Iraqi Ba'th Party, releasing him shortly afterwards but retaining his passport.

Prisoners of conscience
Three opposition activists were held without charge or trial for more than one month. They were: Ahmed Ould Daddah, President of *Le Front des Partis d'Opposition* (FPO), Opposition Parties Front, an umbrella group of opposition parties, and Secretary General of *l'Union des Forces Démocratiques-Ere Nouvelle* (UFD-EN), Union of Democratic Forces-New Era, one of the four parties that make up the FPO; Mohameden Ould Babah, a member of the UFD-EN executive bureau; and Maître Mohameden Ould Ichiddou, a human rights lawyer and a UFD-EN supporter.

The three men were arrested on 16 December 1998 in Nouakchott, apparently after allegations were made at an FPO meeting that the government was planning to accept Israeli nuclear waste for dumping. This allegation had appeared earlier in the Moroccan press. The following day the Minister of the Interior announced that they were to be charged with "attacking the national interest and the country's reputation by making baseless accusations". However, no charges were brought.

The three men were held under armed guard in the town of Boumdeid, more than 500 kilometres from the capital. They were reportedly confined in a room so small that they could not all lie down at the same time. Between 16 December 1998 and 3 January 1999 they were allowed out to exercise only once. After 17 days in incommunicado detention, they were each allowed a visit by one family member, but continued to be denied access to lawyers and the news media.

There were numerous demonstrations in Nouakchott, demanding the release of the three prisoners, which were violently suppressed by the security forces, who reportedly injured several women. The three men were released on 17 January, the end of Ramadan. In March they were tried and acquitted of charges of inciting intolerance and acts likely to breach public order.

International action against impunity
In July, Ely Ould Dah, a Mauritanian army officer, was arrested in Montpellier, southern France, for alleged crimes of torture. He was approached by the French authorities while attending a course run by the French army at a military school in Montpellier, and was detained and questioned by judicial authorities in Montpellier. In September, a French court ordered his provisional release, but required Ely Ould Dah to stay in the region until the completion of the investigation into torture charges.

The authorities intervened after human rights organizations, including the *Fédération internationale des droits de l'homme* (FIDH), International Federation of Human Rights, and the *Ligue des droits de l'homme* (LDH), League of Human Rights, put forward a formal complaint to the police authorities in Montpellier. Ely Ould Dah was accused of having tortured at least two people in a prison near Nouakchott in 1990 and 1991.

The two alleged victims were cooperating with the judicial authorities.

AI welcomed the investigation as a positive step in ensuring justice for the victims of gross human rights abuses committed in Mauritania over the years, and urged the French authorities to consider investigating any Mauritanian official against whom there might be allegations of serious human rights violations and who entered their jurisdiction.

A similar case to the one brought against Ely Ould Dah was earlier brought to the attention of the judicial authorities in Paris. However in that case, Ould Hmeid Salem – a Mauritanian army officer receiving specialist medical care in Paris – was informed of the initiative by the French judicial authorities and fled to the Canary Islands. The French tribunals had declared themselves competent to hear Ould Hmeid Salem's case on the basis of the UN Convention against Torture and Other Cruel, Inhuman or Degrading Treatment or Punishment.

MAURITIUS

REPUBLIC OF MAURITIUS
Head of state: Cassam Uteem
Head of government: Dr Navinchandra Ramgoolam
Capital: Port Louis
Population: 1.1 million
Official language: English
Death penalty: abolitionist for all crimes

The death in police custody of a well-known singer brought into sharp focus an ongoing problem of police brutality, which included the use of torture to extract confessions and the use of excessive force during arrests.

Death in police custody
On 21 February the popular singer known as Kaya (real name Joseph Reginald Topize) died in police custody in the capital Port Louis, three days after his arrest for smoking cannabis. An autopsy obtained by his family revealed signs of beating, contradicting police claims that his injuries had been self-inflicted. An official inquiry into his death had not been completed by the end of 1999.

Police brutality
Kaya's death provoked several days of rioting and protests, fuelled by ethnic tensions, during which another singer, Berger Agathe, was killed after being hit by a rubber bullet during a demonstration on 22 February.

Dozens of criminal suspects were ill-treated in detention throughout the year and some were tortured into making confessions.

AI wrote to the government expressing its concern about continuing police brutality and calling for the findings of the inquiries into the deaths of Berger Agathe and Kaya to be made public. The organization also expressed its dismay that a National Commission on Human Rights, approved by parliament in December 1998, had still not been established by the end of 1999.

MEXICO

UNITED MEXICAN STATES
Head of state and government: Ernesto Zedillo Ponce de León
Capital: Mexico City
Population: 94.3 million
Official language: Spanish
Death penalty: abolitionist for ordinary crimes

Arbitrary detentions, torture, killings and death threats continued to be reported. The victims included peasants, indigenous people, human rights defenders and political activists. In Mexico City students participating in a strike at the National Autonomous University of Mexico were abducted, ill-treated and threatened with death. Inmates in the Cereso de Apodaca Prison, Nuevo León state, claimed they continued to be the victims of human rights abuses by the prison authorities.

Background
The government acknowledged there were still problems with the protection of human rights and claimed it remained committed to reforms and to strengthening the rule of law. In August, the government put forward proposals to reopen peace negotiations with one of the armed opposition groups, the Chiapas-based *Ejército Zapatista de Liberación Nacional* (EZLN), Zapatista National Liberation Army, but by the end of the year the negotiations remained suspended. Critics doubted whether the government's proposals to reopen negotiations with the EZLN were genuine in the face of the increased militarization of Chiapas state. Two other armed opposition groups – the *Ejército Popular Revolucionario*, Revolutionary Popular Army, and the *Ejército Revolucionario del Pueblo Insurgente*, Insurgent People's Revolutionary Army – continued to carry out sporadic attacks in Guerrero and Oaxaca states. Constitutional reforms to ensure the independence of the National Commission for Human Rights, a federal government body, were implemented in September, but had yet to demonstrate their effectiveness.

The UN Special Rapporteur on extrajudicial, summary or arbitrary executions and the UN High

Commissioner for Human Rights visited Mexico in June and November respectively. In the context of an impending free-trade agreement with Mexico, member states of the European Union also maintained a special interest in the government's efforts to strengthen democracy and protect human rights.

Chiapas state
The plight of the indigenous population and the unresolved conflict with the EZLN in Chiapas state remained at the centre of domestic and international attention. Human rights abuses, including killings, the torture and ill-treatment of detainees, and the displacement of indigenous communities, were attributed to the actions of the security forces, or to so-called "paramilitary" or "armed civilian" groups. In addition, indigenous people were also the victims of conflicts between communities and groups with opposing political and religious affiliations.

Acts of intimidation directed at indigenous people by "paramilitary" or "armed civilian" groups were frequently reported. These continued despite a public statement in early 1998 by a former Federal Attorney General that prosecutors had identified 12 "armed civilian" groups operating in Chiapas state and that their funding and source of weapons would be investigated.

In December the Federal Attorney General's Office published a report on criminal proceedings related to the 1997 Acteal massacre in which 45 indigenous men, women and children were killed by a "paramilitary" group known as *Paz y Justicia* (Peace and Justice). By the end of the year, 102 men had been detained in connection with the massacre. Of these, 37 had been sentenced to terms of imprisonment and 65 were still subject to criminal proceedings. Those convicted included 26 civilians sentenced to 35 years' imprisonment on charges of aggravated murder and nine policemen who were sentenced to up to seven years and eight months' imprisonment for illegally transporting weapons intended for exclusively military use. Among the proceedings which were continuing at the end of 1999 were those involving three former Chiapas public security officials charged with murder, and a former Public Ministry official and a former soldier charged with illegally transporting weapons.

Arbitrary detention, torture and ill-treatment
Under Mexican law, no person should be detained without a judicial order or held for more than 48 hours without being brought before a judge; in cases deemed to be "urgent", including those relating to organized crime, this period can be extended to 96 hours. However, there were frequent reports that in practice the security forces arrested suspects and transferred them into custody without complying with these provisions. The suspects were sometimes ill-treated during arrest and tortured while held in custody in the days immediately following their arrest. Several factors contributed to the practice of illegal detention and abuse of detainees by judicial police and public

prosecutors. These included allegations that some judges accepted as evidence confessions obtained under duress. The most frequently reported torture methods included beatings, electric shocks, and death threats.

In June the National Commission for Human Rights published a report following a visit earlier in the year to the Cereso Apodaca Prison in Nuevo León state. The visit was prompted by longstanding complaints that inmates were tortured and ill-treated. In its report, the Commission concluded that there was compelling evidence that numerous prisoners were subjected to a range of abuses, including having their hands and feet manacled, being forced to eat off the floor, and being prevented from going to the toilet for up to five days. The state governor and other authorities rejected the Commission's findings and recommendations.

'Disappearances'
The number of unresolved "disappearances" reported during the year declined for the second year running. Most of the victims were detained in the context of anti-narcotics and counter-insurgency operations and then held in unacknowledged detention for short periods of time before being released. In November clandestine graves were discovered near Ciudad Juárez, Chihuahua state, and close to the border with the United States of America (USA). The Mexican authorities claimed the remains found in the graves could be those of some of the 100 people suspected of having been abducted by drug traffickers operating in the region. However, at the time witnesses had reported that some of the victims had last been seen in the custody of the police. Exhumations and the analysis of the remains, conducted with the assistance of forensic experts from the USA, were still being carried out at the end of 1999.

Despite two bills designed to prohibit enforced disappearances having been submitted to Congress, one of them in 1997, no legislation had been approved to outlaw the crime by the end of 1999.

Impunity and the judicial system
Impunity surrounding gross human rights violations remained the norm. One of the main causes lay in the ineffectiveness of the judicial system. Public prosecutors' offices, the judicial police and the courts were overloaded with work, and their personnel remained inadequately trained and open to corruption. Investigating those suspected of human rights abuses, whether at the federal or state levels, rarely resulted in the full facts being clarified or the suspects being brought to justice and convicted. Public prosecutors' offices lacked independence and remained under the authority of the executive both at federal and state levels. In exceptional cases state agents accused of gross abuses were referred to the courts. However, procedural delays and irregularities opened the way for the accused to either secure acquittal or, if convicted, obtain their release by filing a petition of *amparo* (a mechanism similar to a habeas corpus petition).

The government was accused of failing to tackle the problem of impunity seriously after 15 of the 28 policemen and one public prosecutor accused of homicide in connection with the Aguas Blancas massacre in 1995 were released by judicial order following successful petitions of *amparo*. The judges ordering the releases did so on the grounds of technical irregularities at the trials. In addition, six of the eight high-ranking officials, including a former state governor, found to have been implicated in the massacre by the Supreme Court of Justice had still not been brought to justice by the end of 1999.

Human rights defenders
Human rights defenders faced intimidation and harassment on account of their activities. They were subjected to surveillance, abduction and death threats. Human rights defenders working in remote parts of Chiapas state came under attack from "paramilitary" groups.

◻ Between August and October human rights lawyer Digna Ochoa and other staff of the *Centro de Derechos Humanos Miguel Agustín Pro Juárez* (Prodh), a non-governmental human rights organization based in Mexico City, suffered a series of death threats. Digna Ochoa was abducted twice. The second time, two unidentified men entered her home, bound her to a chair and questioned her about her work. These abuses occurred shortly after she made representations before a court in relation to allegations that members of the army had tortured Rodolfo Montiel Flores and Teodoro Cabrera García, two environmental activists detained in Guerrero state earlier in the year and accused of having links with an armed opposition group. In November the Inter-American Court of Human Rights urged the government to take the necessary measures to protect Digna Ochoa and three other human rights defenders working for the Prodh, to investigate the threats, and bring to justice those responsible.

In July the UN Human Rights Committee recommended to the government that it repeal special visa requirements introduced in 1998 by the Ministry of the Interior for representatives of foreign non-governmental human rights organizations. The requirements made it more difficult to conduct on-site monitoring of the human rights situation in Mexico by restricting visits to 10 days and requesting details about the monitors' program of work, thereby jeopardizing the confidentiality of victims, relatives and witnesses. However, by the end of 1999 the requirements remained in force.

◻ In September the authorities lost their appeal challenging a previous court ruling that the ban imposed on human rights defender Tom Hansen entering Mexico be lifted. Tom Hansen, a US citizen and former director of Pastors for Peace, a non-governmental organization, was detained in Chiapas state and summarily deported in 1998 on the grounds that he was interfering in Mexico's internal affairs.

AI country report
• Mexico: Under the shadow of impunity (AI Index: AMR 41/002/99)

MOLDOVA

REPUBLIC OF MOLDOVA
Head of state: Petru Lucinschi
Head of government: Dumitru Braghiş (replaced Ion Sturza in December, who replaced Ion Ciubuc in March)
Capital: Chişinău
Population: 4.4 million
Official language: Moldovan (Romanian)
Death penalty: abolitionist for all crimes (self-proclaimed Dnestr Moldavian Republic is retentionist)

Arbitrary detention and ill-treatment by police continued. Contributing factors were wide-ranging police powers of administrative detention. Insufficient subordination of law enforcement and national security structures to the rule of law engendered a climate in which police officers allegedly exceeded their already extensive powers of detention in certain cases. At least four political prisoners remained imprisoned in the self-proclaimed Dnestr Moldavian Republic (DMR).

Background
Allegations of corruption, abuse of power, official hindering of investigations, and of links with organized crime exchanged between senior governmental, parliamentary, prosecutorial and law enforcement figures undermined trust in their institutions. The recession, prompted by the 1998 Russian financial crisis, government indebtedness, and an energy crisis continued. Citing a need for strong government, President Petru Lucinschi sought constitutional amendments to concentrate more power in the presidency, a plan which gained guarded approval in a May national referendum, and which caused increasing tension between the President and Parliament. In November the World Bank cut off funding and the government of Ion Sturza fell when Parliament blocked plans to privatize key industries. Talks on regulating the status of the DMR continued inconclusively. Russia made a halting start to the withdrawal of its military stockpiles and forces from the territory.

Ill-treatment and torture
Police officers were reported to have resorted to more frequent use of administrative detention in order to detain suspects arbitrarily for periods of up to one month. There were reports of ill-treatment and torture in order to extract confessions during such periods of administrative detention. Inadequate procedures for registering detainees contributed to difficulties in obtaining access to them. In some cases the authorities failed to acknowledge that detainees were in police custody.

Alleged police 'protection rackets'
There were reports that networks within the senior law enforcement hierarchy exploited the possibilities of

arbitrary detention by the police to target the business community in order to extract "protection money" by the use of torture and threats.

☐ On 14 July Chişinău police detained and allegedly tortured businessman Andrei Roşca for three days before officially acknowledging his detention to his family, at which point the detention was formalized on an administrative ground. During the period of Andrei Roşca's alleged torture, a senior police officer reportedly proposed to him that he personally assume "protection" of the Roşca family's business. On 22 July another senior police officer reportedly tried to obstruct a court decision secured by Andrei Roşca's lawyer, ordering his release. The Roşca family were reportedly intimidated after filing a criminal complaint about his treatment.

Failure to protect from *refoulement*
The Moldovan authorities failed to prevent or properly investigate the arbitrary arrest and transfer of a Kurdish leader to Turkey where he was at risk of torture. On 13 July Cevat Soysal, allegedly a senior leader in the Kurdistan Workers' Party (PKK), was detained in Chişinău by unidentified men and flown to Turkey, where he was reportedly tortured and faced charges which could carry a death sentence. Turkish Prime Minister Bulent Ecevit stated that Turkey acted alone in seizing Cevat Soysal and bringing him to Turkey. However, a Moldovan Ministry of National Security source reportedly admitted its officers' involvement, although the Moldovan authorities strenuously denied this.

Political prisoners in the DMR
Ilie Ilaşcu, Alexandru Leşco, Andrei Ivanţoc and Tudor Petrov-Popa of the so-called "Tiraspol Six" remained in prison. They had been convicted in December 1993 by a court in the DMR of the murder of two DMR officials. Their trial had apparently failed to meet international fair trial standards. Local human rights organizations maintained that the men were prosecuted for political reasons. Alexandru Leşco, Andrei Ivanţoc and Ilie Ilaşcu were reported to be suffering from serious illnesses and not receiving adequate medical care.

MOROCCO/ WESTERN SAHARA

KINGDOM OF MOROCCO
Head of state: King Mohammed VI (replaced King Hassan II in July)
Head of government: Abderrahmane Youssoufi
Capital: Rabat
Population: 27.2 million
Official language: Arabic
Death penalty: retentionist

An arbitration body to decide on compensation for the victims of "disappearance" and arbitrary detention and their families was established in August; more than 3,900 people had submitted their claims by the deadline of 31 December. However, the authorities failed to clarify the fate of some 450 "disappeared", most of them Sahrawis, or to acknowledge the deaths of some 70 Sahrawi "disappeared" in secret detention between the 1970s and early 1990s. Left-wing critic Abraham Serfaty, in forcible exile since 1991, was allowed to return to Morocco. More than 40 political prisoners imprisoned after unfair trials in previous years and at least five prisoners of conscience continued to be detained. Demonstrations in Western Sahara in September were brutally suppressed and were followed by arrests and allegations of torture. Dozens of people were sentenced to terms of imprisonment following trials which failed to conform to international standards for fair trial. Steps were taken to begin the process of judicial reform. However, impunity remained a major concern, with perpetrators of human rights abuses continuing to escape prosecution.

Background
King Hassan II, in power since 1961, died in July and was succeeded by his son, Mohammed VI. Following his enthronement, King Mohammed VI spoke about the importance of human rights, including women's rights. In November he replaced Interior Minister Driss Basri, who had held this position since 1979, and other security officials. The UN Mission for the Referendum in Western Sahara (MINURSO) announced in July that it had registered some 84,000 of the 147,000 people who had applied to vote in a referendum on whether Western Sahara should be independent or should be integrated into Morocco. However, in November it was announced that the referendum, subject to many delays and most recently scheduled for July 2000, would have to be postponed once again in order to process the tens of thousands of appeals lodged by people excluded from the register of electors. In August the Moroccan authorities withdrew permission for AI to hold its International Council Meeting in

Rabat. No official explanation was given for this decision, although AI received different and sometimes contradictory messages from various Moroccan authorities.

'Disappearances'

In April the *Conseil consultatif des droits de l'homme* (CCDH), Human Rights Advisory Council, set up by King Hassan II in 1990, proposed that an arbitration body be established to decide on compensation claims. However, under this proposal the only claims which would be considered were those connected with some of the individuals mentioned in a list of 112 "disappearance" cases published by the CCDH in October 1998.

In August King Mohammed VI ordered the establishment of an arbitration commission to decide on compensation for material and psychological damage suffered by the victims of "disappearance" and arbitrary detention and their families. The commission began its work on 1 September and claimants were required to submit their applications for compensation by 31 December. The commission's internal regulations stated clearly that its decisions were final and admitted no recourse to appeal. At the end of the year the commission announced that it had received more than 3,900 applications and that it had "been able to examine... several dossiers and had completed the examination of a few of these".

The families of the 56 "disappeared" whose deaths had been officially announced by the CCDH in October 1998 received no further information about the date, place or cause of the deaths. By the end of the year the families had not received the bodies for burial nor been told where the bodies were.

By the end of 1999, the fate of some 450 people, the majority of them Sahrawis, who "disappeared" between the mid-1960s and early 1990s, had not been clarified. The deaths between 1976 and 1991 of some 70 Sahrawi "disappeared" in the secret detention centres of Agdz, Qal'at M'gouna and Laayoune had not been acknowledged by the authorities nor had their bodies been returned to their families for burial.

Violent suppression of demonstrations

Non-violent demonstrations continued to be dispersed with excessive force by the security forces, particularly in the form of beatings. As in previous years, it was protesters in Western Sahara who were most seriously affected. Although journalists enjoyed improved access to the territory in 1999, the human rights situation there continued to lag a long way behind that in Morocco itself, particularly with regard to freedom of expression and association.

▭ In September, a peaceful sit-in for socio-economic demands by Sahrawi students, sacked workers and people with disabilities in Laayoune, Western Sahara, was violently broken up by the security forces, as was a march held several days later to protest at the brutal manner in which the sit-in had been dispersed. Dozens of Sahrawis were severely beaten, and many sustained serious injuries, including broken bones. Dozens were arrested and there were reports of torture and ill-treatment in custody.

Unfair trials

Dozens of people were sentenced to prison terms of up to 15 years following trials which failed to conform to international standards for fair trial. These included protesters arrested following demonstrations in Laayoune, Western Sahara, in September and trade unionists arrested while on strike. Allegations that dozens of them had been tortured in detention were not investigated by the courts during the trials.

Prisoners of conscience and political prisoners

More than 40 political prisoners imprisoned after unfair trials in previous years continued to be detained. They included members of Islamist groups sentenced in the 1970s, 1980s and 1990s, and Sahrawis arrested following pro-independence demonstrations in 1998. At least three prisoners of conscience sentenced to up to five years' imprisonment for "insulting the royal family" remained in prison at the end of 1999.

▭ Prisoner of conscience 'Abdessalam Yassine, the spiritual leader of the banned Islamist association *al-'Adl wa'l 'Ihsan,* Justice and Charity, remained under administratively imposed house arrest for the 10th consecutive year. By the end of 1999, neither he nor his lawyer had been shown an order permitting his detention, nor had they been informed of the charges or alleged offence.

Impunity

Investigations were opened into several allegations of torture and ill-treatment and into deaths in custody and in suspicious circumstances which occurred in 1999 and previous years. In several cases, members of the security forces implicated in the violations were arrested and prosecuted, including a police officer who was convicted of torture and sentenced to 10 years' imprisonment. However, in the majority of cases, investigations were either not opened into complaints and allegations of torture and ill-treatment or of deaths in custody and in suspicious circumstances, or were opened but dismissed without adequate investigation. In no case were investigations known to have been carried out to establish responsibility for grave and systematic human rights violations which occurred in the past, and the perpetrators, including those who carried out gross violations over long periods of time, were not brought to justice.

Polisario camps

Freedom of expression, association and movement continued to be restricted in the camps controlled by the *Frente Popular para la Liberación de Saguia el-Hamra y Rio de Oro*, Popular Front for the Liberation of Saguia el-Hamra y Rio de Oro (known as the Polisario Front), near Tindouf in southwestern Algeria. Those responsible for human rights abuses in the camps in previous years continued to enjoy impunity. The Polisario authorities failed to hand over perpetrators still resident in the camps to the Algerian authorities to be brought to justice and the Moroccan authorities failed to bring to justice the perpetrators of abuses in the Polisario camps present on its territory.

International standards
The UN Committee against Torture and the UN Human Rights Committee considered periodic reports on Morocco during the year. Both recognized the positive steps taken by the Moroccan government in the field of human rights. However, in its concluding observations in November, the Human Rights Committee urged Morocco "to intensify investigations into the whereabouts of all persons reportedly missing, to release any such persons who may still be held in detention, to provide lists of prisoners of war to independent observers, to inform families about the location of the graves of disappeared persons known to be dead, to prosecute the persons responsible for the disappearances or deaths, and to provide compensation to victims or their families where rights have been violated."

Communications with the government
In response to its report *Morocco/Western Sahara: 'Turning the page' — achievements and obstacles*, AI received two documents, one from the Moroccan Human Rights Ministry and the other from the CCDH. Both documents commented on cases of torture and ill-treatment and of prisoners of conscience raised in AI's report, addressed aspects of the issue of "disappearance", and outlined proposals for judicial and penal reforms. The Human Rights Ministry and the CCDH argued that AI had not sufficiently recognized the improvements in the human rights situation in the country and took a position on the territorial dispute about the status of Western Sahara. In order to acknowledge and remark on these responses, AI published an addendum to the report.

AI country reports and visits
Reports
- Morocco/Western Sahara: 'Turning the page' — achievements and obstacles (AI Index: MDE 29/001/99)
- Morocco/Western Sahara: Addendum to 'Turning the page' — achievements and obstacles (AI Index: MDE 29/005/99)
Visits
In March and June AI delegates visited Morocco and met government and other officials, victims of human rights violations, representatives of human rights organizations and other members of civil society.

MOZAMBIQUE

REPUBLIC OF MOZAMBIQUE
Head of state: Joaquim Chissano
Head of government: Pascoal Mocumbi
Capital: Maputo
Population: 18.1 million
Official language: Portuguese
Death penalty: abolitionist for all crimes
1999 treaty ratifications/signatures: UN Convention against Torture and Other Cruel, Inhuman or Degrading Treatment or Punishment

Respect for human rights increased, particularly in Maputo, with fewer reports of abuses by police. Efforts to reform the criminal justice system and to retrain the police continued. One journalist detained after reporting a death in police custody was a prisoner of conscience. There were some reports of police brutality, and prisons were severely overcrowded. Elections took place in December. The ruling *Frente para a Libertação de Moçambique* (FRELIMO), Mozambique Liberation Front, continued in power.

Background
Mozambique, which emerged in 1992 from a prolonged civil war between FRELIMO and the *Resistência Nacional Moçambicana* (RENAMO), Mozambique National Resistance, remained one of the poorest countries in the world despite recent economic growth. Crime levels were high, having risen sharply after the 1994 withdrawal of the UN, which had monitored the peace process. The introduction of a free market economy had widened the gap between rich and poor, thousands of demobilized soldiers had increased the already high numbers of unemployed, access to land was limited by the prevalence of landmines, and criminals had easy access to weapons. The President of the Supreme Court stated that 75 per cent of the population had no access to official justice, owing, primarily, to lack of resources.

The draft of an amended Constitution, containing enhanced protection for human rights, was open for public discussion.

The Procurator General announced moves to inspect and monitor the work of judges, in order to prevent corruption. Proposed reforms to the penal code were discussed by members of the judiciary during the year.

In the run-up to presidential and parliamentary elections in December, and afterwards, before results were announced, there were clashes between supporters of FRELIMO and RENAMO. Police intervened and a number of people were injured after incidents, many provoked by FRELIMO. There were also reports of abuses by RENAMO. RENAMO members were reported to have harassed ordinary citizens as well as government officials in villages, and to have assaulted people engaged in civic education.

Reform and retraining of police

Work to restructure and retrain the police continued under a project coordinated by the United Nations Development Programme, with assistance from Spain and the Netherlands. Members of the Spanish *Guardia Civil* helped to train police trainers and to retrain police officers. The syllabus included courses on police ethics and human rights. Originally, the whole police force — more than 18,500 officers — was to be retrained, but the project was scaled down to about 4,500 officers for lack of funding. By the end of 1999 more than 4,100 officers had been retrained.

In areas where retraining had taken place, police wore name badges and patrolled in threes armed with pistols rather than rifles. In addition, police salaries were increased, and police officials said they intended to assign an officer responsible for relations with women and children to each police station.

Although new police laws were developed during the year, little attention was paid to the need to introduce effective complaints and monitoring procedures, and procedures for receiving and processing complaints by members of the public continued to be inadequate.

Abuses by police

There was evidence of improvement in police behaviour, especially in Maputo where detainees are more likely to be brought before a magistrate within the required 48 hours. Although allegations of police brutality were fewer than in previous years, some cases continued to be reported, and information from parts of the country outside Maputo was less readily available.

◻ In January, João Munguambe, a mechanic, was shot dead by police in Maputo as he tested a car he had been working on. His body was taken to the morgue and registered as unknown. One policeman was reportedly arrested in March in connection with his death.

Prisoner of conscience

Fernando Quinova, a journalist, was detained for a second time after reporting the death in police custody of Cabral Manica, a suspected thief. In October 1998 Fernando Quinova was arrested in Chiure, Cabo Delgado province, and held for 23 days. He escaped and submitted a complaint to the provincial police command. He was rearrested on 15 February 1999, when he returned to Chiure, and charged with slandering the police and "leaking information", which is not a criminal offence. He was released on 6 March.

In June Severino Charles, the district police commander who illegally detained Fernando Quinova, was sentenced to three months' imprisonment. It was also announced that a police officer had been charged with homicide in connection with the death of Cabral Manica, and was awaiting trial.

Prison conditions

Prison conditions remained extremely harsh and severely overcrowded, amounting sometimes to cruel, inhuman and degrading treatment. Prisons were old and dilapidated, and sanitation was rudimentary. Food, blankets, mattresses, soap and medicines were in short supply or unavailable and most prisons were having to accommodate three times their capacity.

In addition, in the absence of any juvenile facilities, children were detained in prisons together with adults, in contravention of international standards. In April, six minors aged between 14 and 16 who were held on suspicion of offences such as burglary were released from the high security prison in Tete. They were freed on the orders of the Procurator General after he visited the province.

AI country visit

AI visited Mozambique in July.

MYANMAR

UNION OF MYANMAR
Head of state and government: General Than Shwe
Capital: Yangon
Population: 46.8 million
Official language: Burmese
Death penalty: retentionist

Scores of people were arrested for political reasons and 200 people, some of them prisoners of conscience, were sentenced to long terms of imprisonment. More than 1,200 political prisoners arrested in previous years, including 89 prisoners of conscience and hundreds of possible prisoners of conscience, remained in prison. The International Committee of the Red Cross (ICRC) announced in May that it had begun to visit prisons and other places of detention. The military continued to seize ethnic minority civilians for forced labour duties and to kill members of ethnic minorities not taking an active part in hostilities, during counter-insurgency operations, particularly in the Kayin State. Forcible relocation continued to be reported in the Kayin State, and the effects of massive forcible relocation programs in previous years in the Kayah and Shan States continued to be felt as civilians were still deprived of their land and livelihood and subjected to forced labour and detention by the military.

Background

There was a continuing stand-off between the State Peace and Development Council (SPDC, the military government) and the National League for Democracy (NLD, the main opposition political party which won the 1990 elections). Domestic and international efforts to initiate dialogue between them failed to break the deadlock. The NLD maintained its right to convene parliament and refused to dissolve the 10-member

Committee Representing the People's Parliament (CRPP) in the face of the SPDC's demands to do so before considering dialogue. Although a peaceful civil disobedience campaign was planned by exiled opposition groups in September, the plan did not materialize after the pre-emptive arrest of scores of people by the SPDC. The Myanmar army continued to engage in skirmishes with ethnic minority armed opposition groups — the Karen National Union (KNU), the Karenni National Progressive Party (KNPP), and the Shan State Army-South (SSA-South). The fighting caused further displacement of ethnic minority villagers. Sixteen cease-fire agreements negotiated in previous years between the SPDC and various ethnic minority armed opposition groups were maintained.

Repression and secrecy

The SPDC continued to severely restrict the activities of the NLD and other opposition groups, keeping anyone suspected of opposition to the government under surveillance. Opposition sources reported that the SPDC forced thousands of NLD members to resign in 1999. The SPDC announced that over 34,000 NLD members had resigned. Press censorship continued to be strictly enforced and independent information on human rights violations remained limited. Under a 1996 martial law decree, computer ownership and access to the Internet without government permission was punishable by a prison term of seven to 15 years. The government did not permit indigenous independent non-governmental organizations to function in Myanmar, although there were government-sponsored organizations such as the Myanmar Maternal and Child Welfare Association.

Although the ICRC was allowed to commence prison visits, the government continued to impose restrictions on access to the country by international human rights organizations and foreign journalists. However in July and October, AI delegates held meetings with Myanmar diplomats outside the country.

International initiatives

In March the UN Special Rapporteur on Myanmar submitted his report to the UN Commission on Human Rights. Throughout the year the SPDC continued to deny him access to the country. In April the Commission adopted by consensus its eighth resolution extending the mandate of the UN Special Rapporteur for another year and stating its grave concern "...at the increasingly severe and systematic violations of human rights in Myanmar". A strong resolution was also adopted by consensus at the UN General Assembly in December. In October the Special Envoy of the UN Secretary-General visited Myanmar, in part to encourage dialogue among ethnic minority representatives, the SPDC, and the NLD; however no progress was reported by the end of 1999.

The USA renewed sanctions banning new US investment in Myanmar in May, and in October the European Union (EU) renewed its common position on Myanmar, enacting limited sanctions. The Cooperation Agreement between the EU and the Association of South-East Asian Nations (ASEAN) had been blocked since Myanmar joined ASEAN in July 1997 as a result of EU protests at Myanmar's human rights record. However the EU-ASEAN Joint Committee, a non-ministerial meeting, took place in May, although Myanmar was not allowed to speak. In August the Human Rights Commissioner of Australia visited the country and met with government officials about the possibility of establishing a human rights commission there.

In May the Director-General of the International Labour Organisation (ILO) issued a report which concluded that the Myanmar government had not amended its laws or practice with regard to the military's widespread use of civilian forced labour. At the International Labour Conference in June, the ILO ruled that Myanmar could no longer attend ILO meetings or receive any technical assistance until it complied with ILO Convention No. 29 on forced labour, to which the state became a party in 1955.

Political imprisonment

Prisoners of conscience U Ohn Myint and Dr Ma Thida were released in January and February respectively. Five NLD members of parliament-elect were also released, leaving approximately 40 members of parliament-elect arrested in previous years in prison. At least 1,200 political prisoners, most of them possible prisoners of conscience arrested in previous years, remained behind bars. Fewer than 50 NLD members who were arrested in 1998 after the NLD established the CRPP continued to be detained in government guesthouses and other detention centres without charge or trial. However, in November the NLD announced that 21 members of its youth and women's wings had been released that month. They had been arrested in September 1998 along with hundreds of other NLD members after the party announced the formation of the CRPP.

In May the ICRC announced that it was visiting prisoners and in November it stated that it had visited 19,000 prisoners, 700 of whom were being held for "national security reasons". Prison conditions amounting to cruel, inhuman or degrading treatment continued to be reported, especially in prisons outside Yangon (Rangoon), such as Myitkyina, Kachin State and Thayet Prison. However, some improvements were reported, including better sanitation.

In January, about 200 young political activists arrested in previous years received long prison sentences, including prisoner of conscience Thet Win Aung, who was given a sentence of 59 years. Some 80 people were arrested in the run-up to the civil disobedience campaign planned for September, including 19 people in Bago (Pegu) town, central Myanmar, in July. Three of them, including a three-year-old girl handed over to her family, were released but the status of the others was unknown.

Forced labour

The military continued to seize ethnic minority civilians for forced labour on infrastructure projects and for portering duties in the Shan, Kayin and Kayah States. Children from eight to 15 years were forced on a regular basis to work on a temple construction in Kunhing, Shan State, in January and February. Civilians were taken by the military for portering duties, carrying heavy loads for long periods, and were beaten if they could not keep up with the column. Forced labour was also reported in areas where cease-fires held, including the Mon and Kachin States, where teenaged children often worked on roads. In May the SPDC announced that the military had issued directives for the suspension of legislation which provides for forced labour (the 1907 Towns Act and the 1908 Village Act). It was not known if these directives were enforced. AI called for the legislation to be repealed.

Abuses by armed opposition groups

The KNU was reported to have killed eight to 13 civilian immigration officials in the Kayin State in February. In July the KNPP was believed to have killed two Karenni civilians who were acting as mediators between the SPDC and the KNPP. In November the SSA-South abducted nine Myanmar nationals belonging to the Shan ethnic minority from Thai territory, but released four shortly afterwards. One of the five remaining, said to be an SSA-South defector, was killed for alleged drugs trafficking. In October five armed Myanmar nationals called the Vigorous Burmese Students Warriors seized control of the Myanmar embassy in Thailand for 25 hours, holding over 80 people hostage (see Thailand entry).

AI country reports

- Myanmar: The Kayin (Karen) State, militarization and human rights (AI Index: ASA 16/012/99)
- Myanmar: Update on the Shan State (AI Index: ASA 16/013/99)
- Myanmar: Aftermath – Three years of dislocation in the Kayah State (AI Index: ASA 16/014/99)

NAMIBIA

REPUBLIC OF NAMIBIA
Head of state: Dr Samuel Nujoma
Head of government: Hage Geingob
Capital: Windhoek
Population: 1.6 million
Death penalty: abolitionist for all crimes
1999 treaty ratifications/signatures: African Charter on the Rights and Welfare of the Child

The human rights situation in Namibia deteriorated in 1999. A large number of refugees fled from the northeastern Caprivi province into neighbouring Botswana early in the year. In August the Caprivi Liberation Army (CLA) attacked several government institutions in Caprivi. The government declared a state of emergency that lasted until late August, and conducted a major police and army operation during which torture and arbitrary arrests were frequently reported. In December Namibia allowed Angolan troops to use Namibian territory for their attacks on the Angolan armed opposition. This destabilized the border area, where beatings, rapes and looting by Angolan forces were reported.

Background

Namibia won independence in 1990 following a long war. The South West African People's Organization (SWAPO), which headed the armed struggle, won the country's first elections with a large majority and SWAPO leader Samuel Nujoma won presidential elections. The country adopted a Constitution with strong human rights guarantees. In 1998 Parliament made the first change to the Constitution, to allow President Nujoma to stand for a third term. After this change several leading members of SWAPO left to form a new opposition party, the Congress of Democrats (COD).

On 30 November and 1 December Namibia held presidential and parliamentary elections, in which President Nujoma and SWAPO were re-elected and SWAPO increased its two-thirds majority in Parliament. There were allegations that opposition supporters had suffered intimidation and violence by SWAPO supporters, and that the police had failed to intervene.

Impact of the Angolan war

From November, large numbers of Angolan refugees entered Namibia following major advances by the Angolan army into territory held by the *União Nacional para a Independência Total de Angola* (UNITA), National Union for the Total Independence of Angola, north of Namibia. In early December the Angolan army launched attacks on all major UNITA-held towns along the Namibian border. Several of the attacks were launched from Namibian territory. (See Angola entry.) The Namibian police and defence forces were reported to have participated in the forcible return of Angolan refugees. At least six young men were reported to have been extrajudicially executed by Angolan forces after being forcibly returned to Angola on 12 December. At least 50 Angolan men "disappeared" after arriving in Namibia, while their wives and children arrived at Namibia's only refugee camp in Osire. Namibian police also increased identity checks in Kavango province to search for illegal immigrants, and there were reports of beatings and torture in connection with these checks.

Torture following secessionist attack

A large number of refugees fled from Caprivi province into neighbouring Botswana between late 1998 and April 1999. The formerly unknown CLA launched an attack on four government institutions in Katima Mulilo, district capital of Caprivi, on 2 August. Following the attack more than 300 people were arrested, many of whom were tortured. By the end of 1999, 35 of those released uncharged had filed complaints seeking compensation. Allegations were made that some people were arrested in order to remove members of the Mafwe tribe from senior positions in Caprivi province. At the end of 1999, 115 men were awaiting trial on charges including high treason, of whom 111 were in detention. Most claimed to have been tortured during interrogation following their arrest. Three police officers repeatedly named in the torture allegations remained on active duty.

NEPAL

KINGDOM OF NEPAL
Head of state: King Birendra Bir Bikram Shah Dev
Head of government: Krishna Prasad Bhattarai (replaced Girija Prasad Koirala in May)
Capital: Kathmandu
Population: 21.4 million
Official language: Nepali
Death penalty: abolitionist for all crimes

The political situation turned a corner in May when elections resulted in the establishment of a majority government. While this brought a degree of political stability, there was no parallel improvement in the human rights situation. The new government of Prime Minister Krishna Prasad Bhattarai largely failed to address allegations of widespread extrajudicial executions and torture and an emerging pattern of "disappearances " in the context of the "people's war" declared by the Communist Party of Nepal (CPN) (Maoist) in early 1996. There were worrying signs that the government was pursuing a hardline approach, particularly after it put before Parliament a bill increasing the powers of the police to arrest and

detain suspects and to shoot on sight anyone who "engages in any violent or subversive act", and granting further judicial powers to district administrators rather than the courts. The establishment of the National Human Rights Commission remained stalled despite widespread protests by local human rights organizations.

Possible extrajudicial executions

At least 300 people were reported to have been killed by police in 1999. The police invariably claimed that the killings occurred during exchanges of fire with members of the CPN (Maoist). However, there was evidence that in many cases police officers had used lethal force in situations where such force was unjustified. These included cases where people had been deliberately killed after they were taken prisoner, and others where they had been killed as an alternative to their arrest.

There were various contradictory accounts of the circumstances in which seven young people, including young girls, died at Anekot VDC, Ward No. 1, Kabrepalanchok district, on 19 March. Some newspapers reported that they had died when a bomb which they had tried to hurl at police hit a wall and exploded among them. Others alleged that the police set fire to the house in which the seven people were staying, and shot them one by one as they came out of the house. Fourteen-year-old Manju Kunwor and 15-year-old Shuvadra Sapkota were among the five girls said to have been members of the Cultural Wing of the CPN (Maoist) gathered at the house. No independent investigation was held into the incident.

An emerging pattern of 'disappearances'

A very disturbing pattern of "disappearances" and long-term unacknowledged detention emerged during 1999. There was evidence that police used secret places of detention and vehicles without numberplates. The total number of "disappearances" reported to have occurred during 1999 was 18. Further reports of "disappearances" which occurred during 1998 were received, bringing the total number of such reports for both years to 44.

Bishnu Pukar Shrestha, a schoolteacher and member of a human rights organization, was arrested on 2 September at Satumangal, Kathmandu. Witnesses saw six men in civilian clothes, believed to be police officers, force him into a jeep with black tinted windows. There were unconfirmed reports that he was held at the Maharajgunj Police Training Centre, an unofficial place of detention. Despite action in the Supreme Court, his whereabouts remained unknown at the end of the year.

Torture and death in custody

Torture of political and criminal detainees to extract confessions or intimidate suspects continued to be reported on a regular basis. Many of those arrested in the context of the "people's war" complained of torture. Methods of torture frequently reported included beatings on the soles of the feet and rolling a weighted stick or other object over the thighs of the prisoner (*belana*).

A woman arrested in November in Ilam district reported that she was hung upside down and beaten on the soles of her feet; subjected to *belana*; had pins inserted under the nails of two toes; and had electric current applied to her chest.

Suk Bahadur Lama, a 21-year-old man from Dolakha district, died as a result of torture inflicted for six successive days at the area police office, Nawalpur, Nawalparasi district, in August. A post-mortem found he had multiple burn injuries on both feet, cauterized abrasions on his upper back, and bruises on his back and sides as well as on both his thighs, calves and the soles of the feet. Eight police officers were arrested and charged with his murder. They were released on bail, pending the start of their trial. A case filed under the Torture Compensation Act was withdrawn after police allegedly bribed his family.

Arbitrary arrest and detention

Several hundred people were arrested on suspicion of being members of or sympathetic to the CPN (Maoist) or its front organizations. The total number of political prisoners in custody in mid-November was 1,560. The International Committee of the Red Cross (ICRC) continued its visits to political detainees throughout the year, with access to 42 prisons.

There was widespread abuse of the Public Security Act (PSA) to curtail freedom of expression and imprison government opponents. Scores of political activists suspected of being members of or sympathetic to the CPN (Maoist) or its front organizations were repeatedly arrested and detained under the PSA despite court orders for their release.

Suresh Ale Magar, a lecturer at Kathmandu University and leader of the All Nepal Nationalities Organization, was rearrested immediately after the Supreme Court ordered his release on no less than three occasions. He was released on 23 December and was last seen being driven away in a police van; his whereabouts remained unknown at the end of the year.

More than 400 people were considered under a scheme encouraging CPN (Maoist) activists to surrender. The legal basis for the scheme was unclear.

Total abolition of the death penalty

The death penalty was formally abolished for all crimes at the beginning of May after King Birendra Bir Bikram Shah Dev gave royal assent to two legislative amendments. Although there is no provision for the death penalty in the 1990 Constitution, the death penalty had remained on the statute books in a number of laws passed before 1990, including for acts of high treason. Under the authority of Article 28 of the Constitution, the King repealed these provisions, replacing the death penalty for treason with a maximum term of 25 years' imprisonment and confiscation of assets.

Impunity

Impunity was widespread in relation to extrajudicial executions, "disappearances" and torture. This manifested itself at the constitutional level; the right to life is not explicitly provided for in the Constitution and relatives of people believed to have been killed by the police therefore do not have recourse to the Supreme Court. Habeas corpus petitions filed before Supreme and Appellate courts in the cases of "disappeared" prisoners proved ineffective.

There was a complete lack of accountability for possible extrajudicial executions during so-called "encounters"; the investigations were kept as an entirely internal police matter and the bodies of victims were disposed of without any inquiry. The limited existing legal provisions applicable to the investigation of alleged "encounters" proved inadequate and contributed to the prevailing climate of impunity.

Several cases filed under the Torture Compensation Act of 1996 failed owing to intimidation or corruption by the police.

Abuses by the CPN (Maoist)

There were reports of deliberate killings of civilians judged by the CPN (Maoist) to be "enemies of the revolution", including alleged police informants. "People's courts" were functioning in some parts of the country. Some of the sentences reportedly imposed by these courts, such as beatings, amounted to cruel, inhuman or degrading punishments.

Tek Bahadur Shahi, a journalist and potential Nepali Congress election candidate, was killed by members of the CPN (Maoist) armed with *kukuris* (traditional curved knives) in September in Achham district.

National Human Rights Commission

The long-awaited appointment of the members of the Commission was further delayed, subject to the deliberations of a Task Force set up in November and mandated to draw up internal guidelines for the functioning of the Commission.

AI country reports and visits
Report
• Nepal: Human rights at a turning point? (AI Index: ASA 31/001/99)
Visit
An AI delegation visited Nepal in November.

NEW ZEALAND

NEW ZEALAND
Head of state: Queen Elizabeth II, represented by
Michael Hardie Boys
Head of government: Helen Clark (replaced Jenny
Shipley in November)
Capital: Wellington
Population: 3.7 million
Official language: English
Death penalty: abolitionist for all crimes

There was considerable public debate about human
rights, particularly in the context of new legislation
to detain asylum-seekers and New Zealand's hosting
of the Asia-Pacific Economic Co-operation (APEC)
summit in September, which coincided with calls for
UN intervention in East Timor. In elections in
November, a Labour Party-Alliance minority
government under Prime Minister Helen Clark
replaced a National Party-led government.

Human rights law
In October, amendments to the Human Rights Act 1993
came into effect which gave the government until
December 2001 to resolve inconsistencies between
certain grounds of discrimination prohibited by the Act
and existing legislation, policies and administrative
practices. According to a policy statement, this period
"is intended to provide a reasonable amount of time in
which to consider the complex issues relating to the
extent and scope of Government compliance with the
Act". The amendment requires the Minister of Justice to
report to Parliament at six-monthly intervals on
progress in remedying significant areas of
inconsistency, and on relevant comments by the
national Human Rights Commission. The government
had undertaken to ensure that all new regulations,
policies and practices complied with the provisions of
the Human Rights Act from 1 January 2000, unless an
exemption had been authorized by legislation.

Refugees and asylum-seekers
In October a comprehensive reform package of laws,
policies and regulations on refugees came into force. It
allowed for the indefinite detention in prisons of
people arriving in the country without proper travel
documents, including asylum-seekers.
  ⬚ In September, at least 12 asylum-seekers who
arrived without proper travel documents were
detained on the grounds of security requirements
during the APEC summit in Auckland. Most of them
were not released until December after they
successfully appealed to the High Court and District
Court against their continuing detention.
  ⬚ A group of 16 asylum-seekers held for several
months at Mount Eden Prison, Auckland, were
routinely detained alongside criminal suspects. The
asylum-seekers claimed they were harassed and
assaulted by other prisoners. The 16 were not released
until December after the New Zealand High Court
ordered the government to reconsider its refusal to
grant them conditional bail. An appeal by the
government against the Court's decision was still
pending at the end of 1999.

NICARAGUA

REPUBLIC OF NICARAGUA
Head of state and government: Arnoldo Alemán Lacayo
Capital: Managua
Population: 4.6 million
Official language: Spanish
Death penalty: abolitionist for all crimes
1999 treaty ratifications/signatures: Protocol to the
American Convention on Human Rights to Abolish the
Death Penalty

One student was killed and several were injured
when police fired rubber bullets at students
demonstrating in April. Reports of torture and ill-
treatment in police custody continued.

Background
Allegations of corruption at all levels of government
continued and those who denounced it were
threatened. The economic situation deteriorated
further and was aggravated by natural disasters. Crime
levels continued to rise and government measures to
combat crime led to further police abuses.

Political agreements
The ruling *Partido Liberal Constitucionalista* (PLC),
Constitutionalist Liberal Party, and the *Frente
Sandinista de Liberación Nacional* (FSLN), Sandinista
National Liberation Front, the main opposition party,
came to an agreement in August on more than 30
issues, including possible amendments to the
electoral process, the Constitution and the Supreme
Court of Justice. Implementation of the agreement
could lead to the establishment of a seat-for-life in the
National Assembly for the outgoing President of the
Republic, and the potentially debilitating replacement
of the Comptroller General's post with a five-member
collegiate office. The existing Comptroller General,
Agustín Jarquín, had been instrumental in exposing
some serious corruption cases. He was subsequently
threatened, prompting a request to the Inter-
American Commission on Human Rights to issue
precautionary measures. He was arrested on charges
of fraud in November, but was released on 24
December after the Criminal Court in Managua
dismissed the charges.

In December the National Assembly approved reforms to 16 articles of the Constitution.

President Arnoldo Alemán indicated his intention of calling a constituent assembly to draw up a new Constitution. Some administrative measures were also taken which could curtail freedom of expression. These included taking away the licences of small television companies and proposing that the "discovery and disclosure of secrets" be punished with a prison sentence instead of a fine.

PLC member Benjamín Pérez Fonseca was elected Human Rights Procurator by the National Assembly in June. FSLN member Julián Corrales was appointed Deputy Procurator. Both appointments were widely criticized as political appointments contrary to the spirit of the law. The Procurator's office was still not fully operational at the end of the year.

Police use of rubber bullets

Police fired rubber bullets at students during a peaceful demonstration about university funding inside the Central Bank of Nicaragua in April. Twenty-one-year-old Roberto González Herrera was shot in the chest with a rubber bullet and died instantly. Several other students were injured and dozens were arrested; some were subsequently charged with Roberto González Herrera's murder, as was a member of the National Police.

President Arnoldo Alemán stated in April that an investigation would be carried out. The member of the National Police charged with the killing was acquitted in November. AI wrote to the Attorney General expressing concern at Roberto González Herrera's death and police use of rubber bullets. It had not received a reply by the end of the year.

Torture and ill-treatment by police

Reports of torture and ill-treatment in police custody continued. Detainees were beaten, handcuffed to objects in overcrowded cells and locked up for long periods without food, water or sanitary facilities. Tightly applied handcuffs also caused injury.

▱ In July police fired a rubber bullet at a young man, which wounded him, while he was running away from them. They reportedly kicked him and applied handcuffs tightly after he fell to the ground. The *Centro Nicaragüense de Derechos Humanos* (CENIDH), Nicaraguan Centre for Human Rights, certified the injuries caused by the handcuffs.

NIGER

REPUBLIC OF THE NIGER
Head of state: Mamadou Tandja (replaced Major Daouda Malam Wanké in November, who replaced Ibrahim Baré Maïnassara in April)
Head of government: Ibrahim Assan Mayaki
Capital: Niamey
Population: 9.4 million
Official language: French
Death penalty: abolitionist in practice
1999 treaty ratifications/signatures: UN Convention on the Elimination All Forms of Discrimination against Women

In April President Ibrahim Baré Maïnassara was killed by members of his presidential guard. This was the second military coup in three years, a period which saw a deterioration in the human rights situation in the country. There were reports of human rights violations related to restrictions on freedom of association and expression. The culture of impunity for human rights violations which had characterized Niger throughout the 1990s was reinforced by a new Constitution, adopted in July, which guaranteed impunity to those responsible for the assassination of President Baré and other killings.

Background

The new authorities promised to hand over power to legally elected civilian authorities at the end of a transition period of nine months and to forbid the military from standing in elections. In November Mamadou Tandja, leader of the *Mouvement national pour la société de développement*, National Movement for the Society of Development, was elected president.

Impunity

The new military authorities presented the death of President Baré as the result of an "unfortunate accident", despite confirmation by many eyewitnesses that he had been killed by members of his presidential guard in the presence of Major Daouda Malam Wanké, who succeeded him as head of state.

As a result of increasing demands, at both the national and international level, for an independent inquiry into President Baré's death, the authorities were obliged to entrust investigation of the killing to the national gendarmerie. However, in July the new Constitution granted an amnesty to those involved in both the 1996 and 1999 coups, before the results of the investigation had been published, making it clear that the authorities had no intention of bringing those responsible for the killing to justice.

In September AI published a key testimony on the killing of President Baré. In response, Major Malam Wanké stated that the military had intended to arrest, not to kill, President Baré, who had been hit by bullets as he tried to flee.

Amnesty International Report 2000

Harassment of opponents
The new military authorities sought to intimidate those demanding an inquiry into the killing of President Baré. Several supporters of President Baré who opposed the amnesty were placed under house arrest or forbidden to leave Niamey in May.

In June Yahaya Tounkara, the former Minister of Defence, was placed under house arrest for several days after trying to defy the order forbidding him to leave the capital.

Mass grave
In January a mass grave containing 150 bodies was discovered on the island of Boultoungoure, on Lake Chad in the Diffa region. The grave appeared to contain the remains of people expelled in September 1998 from Nigeria, where they had apparently fled to escape from fighting linked to the Toubou rebellion. The discovery was announced by members of the *Front démocratique révolutionnaire*, Democratic Revolutionary Front, a Toubou movement which led an armed rebellion in the region until a peace accord was signed in August 1998.

The government denied that there had been killings in this region. However, in April, after several months' silence, an information-gathering mission carried out by the High Commissioner for the Restoration of Peace confirmed the existence of a grave containing the bodies of 150 men whose names were published by the press, but no inquiry was initiated.

AI country reports
- Niger: Attacks on journalists threaten freedom of expression (AI Index: AFR 43/001/99)
- Niger: Impunity enshrined in the Constitution (AI Index: AFR 43/002/99)

NIGERIA

FEDERAL REPUBLIC OF NIGERIA
Head of state and government: Olusegun Obasanjo (replaced General Abdulsalami Abubakar in May)
Capital: Abuja
Population: 103.4 million
Official language: English
Death penalty: retentionist

The human rights situation continued to improve, with further releases of political prisoners. Military decrees which provided for administrative detention and unfair political trials were revoked just before the military handed over to an elected civilian government in May. Communal unrest and inter-ethnic killings increased in several parts of the country, particularly in the Niger Delta, where soldiers were alleged to have used excessive and lethal force in dealing with protests and armed groups. The death penalty remained in force but fewer executions were reported.

Return to civilian government
Elections for state assemblies and governors were held in January, followed by national assembly and presidential elections in February. These were further steps in a "transition to civil rule" relaunched by the military government headed by General Abdulsalami Abubakar after the death of General Sani Abacha in June 1998. Retired General Olusegun Obasanjo, military head of state from 1976 to 1979 and a prisoner of conscience from 1995 to 1998, won the presidency and was inaugurated on 29 May 1999. While irregularities seriously marred the elections, the outcome was broadly accepted.

In early May the military government promulgated a new Constitution. This document had remained unpublished after a part-elected Constitutional Conference had made recommendations in 1995 and after further amendments had been made by the military government.

The government announced a review of the Constitution after widespread criticisms of its undemocratic inception, its centralization of powers to the federal government, including over the police and judiciary, and its transfer of jurisdiction in cases involving the government from state-level High Courts to Federal High Courts, which are considerably fewer in number.

In April the UN Commission on Human Rights, which had appointed a Special Rapporteur on Nigeria in 1997, ended its inquiries. The Special Rapporteur reported on the first visit he had been able to make to Nigeria in November 1998 and the improvement in the human rights situation. The Commonwealth, which had suspended Nigeria's membership following the executions in 1995 of Ken Saro-Wiwa and eight Ogoni activists, lifted the suspension in May.

Major legislative changes

Two military decrees were promulgated in late May which revoked 31 military decrees, including those which had suspended human rights provisions of the 1979 Constitution and removed the powers of the courts to challenge actions by the military government. Others were amended to restore jurisdiction to the ordinary courts in criminal cases. Fears were expressed by human rights and other groups after several northern states, led by Zamfara State in October, took steps to extend the jurisdiction of Shari'a (Islamic law) courts and to introduce more severe corporal punishments.

Decrees revoked included the State Security (Detention of Persons) Decree, No. 2 of 1984, which provided for the arbitrary and indefinite detention without charge or trial of any person deemed by the government to be a threat to the security or the economy of the country. It was used to detain hundreds of prisoners of conscience.

Also rescinded were decrees which provided for special courts used to imprison and execute government critics after grossly unfair political trials. The Treason and Other Offences (Special Military Tribunals) Decree, No. 1 of 1986, provided for Special Military Tribunals headed by members of the military government. Between 1986 and 1998, these tribunals held treason trials which failed to meet nearly all standards of fair trial, resulting in a total of 79 executions of armed forces officers and the imprisonment of dozens of prisoners of conscience and possible prisoners of conscience. The Civil Disturbances (Special Tribunals) Decree, No. 2 of 1987, provided for Civil Disturbances Special Tribunals directly appointed by the military. Between 1987 and 1995, such tribunals conducted politically motivated and unfair trials, in 1995 resulting in the execution of nine Ogoni activists.

Other decrees revoked were the Treason and Treasonable Offences Decree, No. 29 of 1993, which broadened the definition of treason, and the retroactive Federal Military Government (Supremacy and Enforcement of Powers) Decree, No. 12 of 1994, which prohibited legal action challenging any government action or decree.

Among the decrees amended to restore the jurisdiction of the ordinary courts was the Robbery and Firearms (Special Provisions) Decree, No. 5 of 1984, which provided the death penalty for armed robbery. Jurisdiction in armed robbery cases was restored to the state-level High Court, with a right of appeal to the Court of Appeal and Supreme Court. More than 2,600 death sentences had been carried out under military governments since 1970, most of which were passed by Robbery and Firearms Tribunals, now effectively abolished.

Impunity

In June the government constituted a judicial commission of inquiry headed by Mr Justice C.A. Oputa, a retired Supreme Court judge, to investigate past human rights violations and make recommendations on redress for victims and preventive measures. Its mandate, to investigate abuses between 1984 and May 1999, was extended in October back to 1966. It received more than 11,000 submissions, many in relation to human rights violations in Ogoniland in the mid-1990s. Hearings had not started by the end of the year.

A number of officials and associates of the previous military government were charged with involvement in human rights violations. In October Mohammed Abacha, a son of former head of state General Abacha, and four others, including senior security officials, were charged in connection with the murder in June 1996 of Kudirat Abiola. She was the wife of Moshood Abiola, the reported winner of the 1993 presidential elections which were annulled by the military, who died in detention in 1998. One of the same security officials and an army doctor were also charged in connection with the suspected murder in custody in December 1997 of retired Major-General Shehu Musa Yar'Adua, a prisoner of conscience and former deputy head of state. In November, five senior armed forces and police officers were charged in connection with the attempted murder in February 1996 of Alex Ibru, a newspaper proprietor and former government minister.

Communal unrest

Hundreds died in inter-communal clashes across the country. Scores of people reportedly died in conflicts between the Ijaw and Itsekiri over land and oil rights in May and June around Warri in the western Niger Delta. Two of Nigeria's three largest ethnic groups, the Yoruba and Hausa, were involved in inter-communal killings in July in Sagamu, southwest Nigeria, followed by reprisal killings in Kano, in the north, and in November in Lagos when more than 100 were reported killed. In the Niger Delta attacks on oil installations grew, as did the hostage-taking of oil workers for ransom; a number were reportedly killed.

The security forces were reported to have used excessive and lethal force against youths protesting against the security forces in the Niger Delta and agitating for a halt to oil production. The armed forces were also reported to have killed defenceless civilians and razed their homes, in reprisal for the killing of police and soldiers by armed groups.

In January soldiers reportedly shot dead up to 20 people in and around the town of Yenagoa, capital of Bayelsa State, after a call by Ijaw groups for the military and the oil companies to leave Ijaw territories.

Wariebi Ajoko, a 14-year-old boy, was among those killed outside his home in Olobiri-Kaiama. Soldiers took the boy's body away and it was not returned to the family. His father was among community elders detained and tortured by the security forces, and forced to drink their own urine after being held for days in the open without food and water.

In September soldiers reportedly carried out reprisal killings in Yenagoa after the killing of at least two soldiers. The government ordered an internal army inquiry.

In November at least 40 people, including soldiers, were reportedly killed in the town of Odi, near

Yenagoa, after an armed group fired on soldiers seeking to arrest them and the armed forces responded by bombarding the town. The armed group had allegedly murdered 12 police officers. A Senate committee which visited a week later reported that the town had been razed and that several corpses remained in the streets. The authorities provided no information about those killed or arrested and no inquiry was instituted.

Releases of political prisoners

The releases of political prisoners which started following the death of General Abacha continued during 1999. In March at least 39 prisoners of conscience and possible prisoners of conscience held in connection with alleged coup plots were released.

Ten soldiers were released who had been imprisoned since a coup attempt in 1990, two of them despite being acquitted by a Special Military Tribunal.

The remaining 17 prisoners convicted of involvement in a fabricated coup plot by a Special Military Tribunal in 1995, all armed forces officers, were released. Civilians convicted in the same 1995 trials had been released in 1998.

Eight armed forces officers and six civilians convicted in April 1998 of involvement in an alleged plot in 1997 were released. Death sentences imposed on six of them, including Lieutenant-General Oladipo Diya, deputy head of state to General Abacha, had been commuted in 1998.

Supporters of the Islamic Movement

Supporters of the Islamic Movement, an Islamist group in northern Nigeria, were released on completion of prison sentences, or on payment of fines in place of their prison sentences. They were reported to have been convicted after politically motivated and unfair trials in 1996 and 1997.

⌷ Mohamed Aminu Ahamed was reported to have died in May as a result of harsh conditions and medical neglect in Lapia prison, Niger State, where two others convicted in the same trials – Abdulkadir Magaji and Mohammed Salisu – had died in 1998.

Journalists

Under military rule, journalists continued to be detained for questioning, usually briefly, after publishing articles critical of the security forces or on the basis of unsubstantiated complaints.

⌷ In February the police in Lagos arrested two employees of The News group of newspapers, Kingsley Uwannah and Kayode Sofuyi, and detained them without charge for a week. Three other employees were detained overnight and also released without charge.

⌷ In October Jerry Needam, an editor of a newspaper produced by the Movement for the Survival of the Ogoni People (MOSOP), was detained incommunicado and without charge or trial for three weeks in Port Harcourt. Police were reportedly seeking the source of a leaked police order which characterized MOSOP and other human rights groups in the Niger Delta as "enemy forces" and which revealed a lack of clarity about when the security forces could use lethal force against protesters. He was released without charge after three weeks.

Ill-treatment

Detainees arrested by police and military were routinely subjected to beatings and detained in harsh and insanitary conditions.

⌷ In April Ugochukwu Agi, a teacher and human rights defender, was arrested with two others, beaten by soldiers and detained for three days with criminal suspects who stripped and also beat him. The reason for his detention appeared to be his involvement in local community protests over an explosion at the Obite gas plant in Rivers State in March which killed five employees, and longstanding community concerns about the gas plant. He was released without charge.

As many as 20 young people, including children aged 14 and 15, were reportedly wounded in nearby Ogbogu when a joint military and paramilitary police anti-robbery unit reportedly fired on protestors.

Death penalty

At least 11 death sentences were passed and three executions carried out. The executions, one in Cross River State in March and two in Osun State in May, were of three men convicted of armed robbery by Robbery and Firearms Tribunals. They were carried out by firing squad. No executions were known to have been carried out after the return to civilian rule.

AI action

In July AI submitted reports detailing hundreds of individual cases of human rights violations to the Oputa investigation panel and made recommendations to the government about the powers and resources which would contribute to the effectiveness of the investigations. AI also raised a number of concerns with the government.

⌷ Moussa Goukouni, a Chadian teacher and former diplomat, was reportedly arrested in Maiduguri, northeastern Nigeria, on suspicion of links with a Chadian armed opposition group, and in August transferred to a military camp near Lake Chad. AI asked the Nigerian authorities about his case, in light of the extrajudicial execution in Chad in 1992 of deportees from Nigeria, and further extrajudicial executions in Chad in 1996.

AI country reports and visits
Report
• Nigeria: Releases of political prisoners – questions remain about past human rights violations (AI Index: AFR 44/001/99)
Visit
AI visited Nigeria in June and July to carry out research and to attend organizational meetings with AI members in Nigeria.

PAKISTAN

ISLAMIC REPUBLIC OF PAKISTAN
Head of state: Mohammad Rafiq Tarar
Head of government: General Parvez Musharraf
(replaced Nawaz Sharif in October)
Capital: Islamabad
Population: 136.2 million
Official languages: English, Urdu
Death penalty: retentionist

Law enforcement personnel carried out arbitrary arrests, torture and extrajudicial executions with impunity. At least 258 people were sentenced to death, most by special courts after unfair trials. Persistent bias against the rights of women on the part of the government, police and judiciary meant that abuses by private individuals, including the honour killings of hundreds of girls and women, were not investigated or punished. The rights of religious minorities, journalists and other human rights defenders continued to come under threat. The new government made some commitments to protect human rights and began to hold people accountable for corruption.

Background
High levels of corruption, disregard for the rule of law and a further weakening of civil institutions resulted in a series of crises, including a protracted confrontation between the government and the press, and the harassment of non-governmental organizations, including human rights and women's rights groups.

Relations with India improved during a visit by Indian Prime Minister A.B. Vajpayee to Lahore in February but experienced a setback when armed groups entered the Kargil area in India in June. At the end of July, they agreed to withdraw to Pakistan territory.

Corruption charges were selectively brought and pursued against members of the opposition. For example, in April, former Prime Minister Benazir Bhutto and her husband Asif Zardari were sentenced to seven years' imprisonment. Both appealed against the conviction. Benazir Bhutto remained outside the country; Asif Zardari continued to be detained on other charges.

In June political tension rose in Sindh when the governor who had ruled the province since October 1998 was replaced by an appointed adviser to Prime Minister Nawaz Sharif.

Mass arrests and false charges were used to stifle protests in June when opposition forces throughout the country joined ranks with the aim of bringing down the government.

On 12 October Prime Minister Nawaz Sharif unexpectedly dismissed the army chief. This subsequently led to a military coup in which General Parvez Musharraf dismissed the government of Nawaz Sharif, suspended national and provincial assemblies,

declared an emergency, suspended the Constitution, and assumed office as Chief Executive. A National Security Council comprising army officers and civilians was set up, assisted by a cabinet to which military personnel, technocrats and members of non-governmental organizations were appointed.

Human rights defenders
In May nearly 2,000 non-governmental organizations in Punjab were closed down. Human rights and women's rights organizations, including the Human Rights Commission of Pakistan, were harassed throughout Pakistan. Journalists faced intimidation, threats and arbitrary arrests.

▭ In January, the owner of the *Jang* group of newspapers was falsely charged and ordered to dismiss outspoken editors and to have articles vetted by the government.

▭ Rehmat Shah Afridi, editor of *The Frontier Post*, was arrested in April and detained throughout the year on apparently trumped-up drug charges.

▭ Najam Sethi of *The Friday Times* was one of several journalists who were harassed after giving interviews to a British Broadcasting Corporation (BBC) team investigating corruption allegations against the government. He was arbitrarily arrested in May and held without charge or trial in incommunicado detention for over three weeks. He continued to be harassed after his release and was refused permission to travel to the United Kingdom to accept the AI Special Award for Journalism under Threat.

Political opponents
As opposition groups intensified their activities against corruption and pervasive lawlessness, increasing numbers of political activists were arrested and detained, often on manifestly unfounded charges. Many were released within a short time.

Special courts with shortened trial periods which denied defendants the right to present a full defence continued to be used to try political opponents and ordinary criminal suspects. In February the Supreme Court declared that special military tribunals set up in 1998 were unconstitutional, and transferred all cases before the military tribunals to special courts set up under the Anti-Terrorism Act (ATA) of 1997. The ATA was amended in April and August to make it applicable to anyone suspected of causing "civil commotion". Opposition politicians and human rights groups feared that legitimate dissent could be criminalized under this provision.

Extrajudicial executions and custodial violence
At least 260 people, both criminal suspects and political prisoners, were reportedly extrajudicially executed. Some observers put the number much higher and claimed that the killings were part of a policy decided at a senior level of government. Police often sought to conceal such killings by claiming they occurred during "encounters" or exchanges of fire with police.

▭ In May officers from the police station in Mangawala, near Sheikhupura, Punjab province, shot dead five young men, claiming that they had acted in self-defence after the men opened fire on the officers during a robbery. A judicial inquiry found that the men had been in custody for a month, that they had been killed by police and that false post-mortem reports had been issued. No action was taken against the police officers.

⌷ Judicial inquiries found that several victims in Sindh belonging to the Muttahida Qaumi Movement had been extrajudicially executed but no action was known to have been taken against the perpetrators. The Sindh Assembly condemned such killings in July and the Senate functional committee on human rights demanded to be informed of inquiry results. However, the killings continued.

Torture in jail and police custody continued to be widespread, leading to at least 52 deaths.

⌷ Arman Danish was arrested on 12 January in Karachi. When his family failed to pay a bribe for his release, his mother was told he would be killed. He later told family members at the magistrates' court that he had been hung upside down and given electric shocks. On 28 January he died of kidney failure. The officer investigating his death was reprimanded for not pursuing it with vigour. No one was held to account.

Religious minorities

The state failed to provide religious minorities with adequate protection. Religiously motivated killings peaked in September when, in one week alone, some 35 people, mostly Shi'a men, women and children, were arbitrarily killed. Prime Minister Nawaz Sharif claimed that the perpetrators had received training in Afghanistan and called on the *Taleban* to close down such training camps in Afghanistan. Shi'a leaders in Karachi were advised to hire private security guards; some police guards were provided for places of worship.

At least 54 Ahmadis were charged under the blasphemy laws; eight of them were charged under a section of the law which carries a mandatory death sentence. In many cases, judicial officers added criminal charges to complaints, after which the cases were tried in anti-terrorism courts which did not provide fair trials. The procedures of such courts, especially the rigid time frame, make a fair trial difficult if not impossible. There is also no bail available for people to be tried by such courts.

⌷ Ghulam Mustafa, who was arrested in December 1998 for preaching his faith and subsequently had additional charges added to the complaint against him, was sentenced to 13 years' imprisonment in March. His case was concluded within a week by an anti-terrorism court.

At the end of the year 30 Ahmadis were prisoners of conscience held solely on account of their conscientiously held beliefs.

⌷ Nazeer Ahmad Baluch was 15 years old when he was arrested in September 1998 in village Chak 4 near Naukot, Mirpurkhas district, Sindh province. He and other Ahmadis had been pulling down a mosque owned by the Ahmadi community in order to rebuild it.

Orthodox Muslims passing the mosque, however, alleged that it belonged to their community and that the Ahmadis were injuring their feelings as Muslims by desecrating the mosque and a Qur'an allegedly lying inside it. This incident led to further attacks on Ahmadi mosques in a nearby town and the arrest of 14 other Ahmadis on similar charges. Nazeer Ahmad Baluch was held throughout the year in Hyderabad Central Jail. An appeal against his trial by an anti-terrorism court was still pending before the Supreme Court of Pakistan at the end of the year.

Death penalty

At least 13 people were executed. At least 258 people were sentenced to death, almost all of them for murder. The vast majority were tried by anti-terrorism courts whose procedures, especially the requirement that trials must conclude within seven days, violate standards for fair trial. More than 3,000 people were on death row at the end of 1999.

Special military tribunals, set up in November 1998, sentenced at least nine people to death. In February the Supreme Court declared that the special military tribunals set up in 1998 were unconstitutional, set aside all death sentences passed by the tribunals and transferred all pending cases to anti-terrorism courts. It said that all sentences executed earlier were "past and closed transactions".

⌷ Rafiuddin Babli was executed on 3 January while petitions were pending in the Supreme Court challenging the constitutionality of the tribunals.

Ignoring the constitutional prohibition of double jeopardy, several people sentenced to death by military tribunals were retried and sentenced to death again.

⌷ Mohammad Saleem, aged around 14 at the time of the alleged offence in June 1998, had been sentenced to death in December 1998 following a trial lasting 12 days. He was acquitted on 7 January and then sentenced to death again on 11 June. The appeal against his conviction was pending at the end of the year.

Government indifference to abuses

Abuses against women, children and other disadvantaged sections of society continued to be widespread, but the government took no effective action to end them. Abuses included child labour, which was known to affect between three and 10 million children; bonded labour; domestic violence, affecting the majority of women and children; and the trafficking of women. Police and judicial officers continued to treat such abuses leniently, contributing to a cycle of impunity and continued abuse. In August the Senate failed to pass a resolution condemning violence against women.

Several hundred girls and women, as well as a large number of men, were killed for allegedly dishonouring their male relatives. Often a mere allegation was sufficient to lead to honour killings. Women's behaviour which was perceived as bringing dishonour included alleged or real sexual relations outside marriage, choosing a marriage partner against parental wishes, or seeking a divorce. Some women were also considered to have dishonoured their community because they had been raped. Defenders of women's rights were sometimes targeted for their work.

⌑ Jameela Mandokhel, a 16-year-old mentally retarded girl, was raped in March. Upon her return to her community in the Kurram Agency, a tribal council decided that she had defiled tribal honour and shot her dead. The government took no action.

⌑ In April Samia Sarwar, a 29-year-old woman who sought a divorce after years of domestic violence, was shot dead in the office of her lawyer in Lahore by a family employee. Her action was perceived as shaming the family. Subsequently, her lawyer was charged with her murder and publicly threatened with death for "misguiding" Samia Sarwar.

Developments since the October coup

On 15 October, following a declaration of emergency, the Chief Executive, General Parvez Musharraf, issued Provisional Constitutional Order No. 1 of 1999 which upheld fundamental rights despite suspension of the Constitution. It also stated that courts were to continue functioning but placed the military takeover and actions of the new administration outside judicial review. On 17 October he issued a policy statement, which included a fight against corruption and protection for religious minorities. On 17 November the National Accountability Bureau Ordinance was promulgated under which a body was set up to investigate corruption among state officials who would then be tried by a special accountability court. In addition to imprisonment, those found guilty would be disqualified from holding public office for 21 years. In December the anti-corruption drive was declared not to apply to members of the judiciary and the army. By the end of 1999, around 60 people had been arrested accused of corruption.

Immediately after the October coup, several members of the dismissed government were arrested and held without charge or trial in military custody. In late November, criminal charges were registered against seven men, including former Prime Minister Nawaz Sharif, accusing them of hijacking, hostage-taking and attempted murder in connection with the alleged attempt to prevent General Musharraf's plane from landing in Karachi on 12 October. They were to be tried by anti-terrorism courts but by the end of the year the court had not finalized the charge sheet necessary to commence the trial.

AI country reports and visits
Reports
- Pakistan: Juveniles sentenced to death (AI Index: ASA 33/008/99)
- Pakistan: Violence against women in the name of honour (AI Index: ASA 33/017/99)
- Pakistan: Open letter to General Parvez Musharraf (AI Index: ASA 33/028/99)
Visits
AI delegates met members of civil society and of political parties to discuss areas of reform benefiting human rights protection after the change in government.

PALESTINIAN AUTHORITY

PALESTINIAN AUTHORITY
President: Yasser 'Arafat
Death penalty: retentionist

More than 350 people were arrested during 1999 for political reasons. At least 90 were prisoners of conscience, including critics of the Palestinian leadership, journalists and members of a legal opposition Islamist party. Most were released, but at least 70 remained in detention at the end of the year. Reports of torture and ill-treatment continued to be received. More than 230 people arrested in previous years remained detained without charge or trial, including suspected members of Islamist opposition groups and people suspected of "collaborating" with the Israeli authorities. The High Court of Justice ordered the release of 52 detainees held without charge or trial, but only four were known to have been released as a result of these judgments by the end of the year. State security and military courts continued to sentence political detainees after unfair trials. One person was executed and four people were sentenced to death after trials before the state security or military courts. Two people were unlawfully killed during a demonstration. The Palestinian Authority (PA) failed to bring those responsible for human rights abuses to justice.

Background
The peace process, which had stalled during the first six months of the year, revived under the government of Ehud Barak. In September and November there were further Israeli withdrawals from parts of the West Bank. By the end of 1999, Israel remained in full control of 64 per cent of the West Bank (Area C); 10 per cent of the West Bank was under the security control of the PA (Area A); and 26 per cent was under the security control of Israel and the civil control of the PA (Area B). In October a safe passage was inaugurated to facilitate travel by Palestinians between the West Bank and Gaza Strip.

There was increasing concern at the failure of the PA to follow decisions made by the judiciary. President Yasser 'Arafat ordered a review of the administration of justice following the publication in May of a report, *Rule of Law Development in the West Bank and Gaza Strip*, by the Office of the Special Coordinator in the Occupied Territories. In May and June President 'Arafat appointed a new Chief Justice and Attorney General; the posts had been vacant for more than a year. However, many judicial decisions continued to be ignored by the security services and no review of the administration of justice had been made public by the end of the year.

Arrests

At least 350 people were arrested in 1999 for political reasons; they included journalists, critics of the PA leadership, and supporters of Islamist opposition groups such as *Hamas* and Islamic *Jihad*. At least 90 were prisoners of conscience. Some suspected members of Islamist groups were arrested after pressure from the Israeli authorities to round up those who might be connected with violent attacks against Israel; others were detained because of opposition to or criticism of the PA leadership. At least 70 suspected Islamist activists remained held without charge or trial at the end of 1999.

▭ Members of a group calling itself the "Free Officers" who issued a communiqué accusing the PA leadership of corruption were arrested in June; they were reportedly released before the end of the year.

▭ Nine of the 20 prominent Palestinians who signed a statement criticizing the PA leadership in November were detained for up to 39 days.

▭ Members of *Hizb al-Khalas,* a legal Islamist political party which has stated its opposition to violence, were arrested in February and August after criticizing the PA leadership and held for up to several months without charge or trial.

▭ Mahmud al-Zahhar, a political leader of *Hamas* in the Gaza Strip, was arrested in February, apparently because he provided medical treatment for one of the people suspected of involvement in the shooting of Rif'at Jawdeh — a member of the security forces — and two children during an attempt to arrest four suspected *Hamas* members. He was released without charge in March.

▭ In September the Preventive Security Service (PSS) arrested Maher al-Dasuqi, a television presenter, after a prisoner's mother criticized the PA leadership on his program. He was detained at a PSS investigation centre in Ramallah, where for three days he was reportedly hooded, deprived of sleep and made to stand almost the entire time. His wife and lawyer were only allowed to visit him after eight days. He was released without charge after 19 days' detention.

Torture

Reports of torture and ill-treatment continued to be received. Prolonged incommunicado detention in the period immediately after arrest facilitated torture. The authorities failed to investigate complaints of torture and to bring those responsible to justice.

▭ In August Sami Nawfel, a leading member of *Hizb al-Khalas,* was arrested by General Intelligence and detained for eight days before being released without charge. While detained he was reportedly subjected to *falaqa* (beating on the soles of the feet), *shabeh* (standing or sitting in painful positions) and sleep deprivation. A medical report confirmed injuries consistent with these allegations.

Detention without trial

At least 300 people were detained without charge or trial. They included more than 100 detainees suspected of "collaborating" with Israel and at least 200 people detained on suspicion of belonging to Islamist or leftist groups opposed to the peace process. The detention of suspected supporters of *Hamas* was frequently linked to pressure from Israel and the USA to arrest individuals suspected of "terrorism". Many detainees, particularly those accused of "collaboration", were tortured after arrest. Palestinian human rights organizations continued to raise the cases of many of those detained without trial before the Palestinian High Court of Justice. The Court ordered the release of 52 detainees, but only four were known to have been released as a result of these judgments by the end of the year. In January there were demonstrations against the continuing detention without trial of political detainees and the Palestinian Legislative Council passed a resolution calling for the release of political detainees; 38 detainees were released.

▭ In February the Palestinian High Court of Justice ordered the release of Wa'el Farraj, detained without charge or trial since April 1996. He had not been released by the end of 1999.

Unfair trials

State Security Courts continued to hold grossly unfair trials. In October President 'Arafat appointed Khaled al-Qidreh as Attorney General of State Security Courts. Khaled al-Qidreh had been Attorney General in 1995 when the State Security Courts were introduced, but had been dismissed in 1997. Civilians were also tried by military courts whose procedures fell short of international fair trial standards.

▭ In May 'Usama Hamad and Karima Hamad, who had been detained since 1996, were tried by a military court in Gaza City. 'Usama Hamad was reportedly charged with unintentionally causing the death of Yahya 'Ayyash, a *Hamas* member said to have made suicide bombs to kill Israeli civilians, in January 1996 by negligence or recklessness. Karima Hamad was accused of aiding her uncle, Kamal Hamad, who was tried *in absentia,* in causing Yahya 'Ayyash's death with a mobile telephone booby-trapped by the Israeli General Security Service. Lawyers representing 'Usama Hamad and Karima Hamad withdrew before the trial opened and the court appointed lawyers for them. The trial was adjourned after one session and had not resumed by the end of the year.

Death penalty

Four people were sentenced to death during 1999 and one person was executed. All trials which resulted in the imposition of death sentences took place in state security or military courts and failed to meet international fair trial standards.

▭ Colonel Ahmad Abu Mustafa was executed in Gaza in March one day after being found guilty of raping a 10-year-old boy and of "inciting the masses against the Palestinian Authority". The summary trial before a military court was grossly unfair. It took place the day after Colonel Abu Mustafa's arrest. No forensic tests were carried out on the rape victim. Colonel Abu Mustafa, who pleaded not guilty, was not allowed to call witnesses who he said could provide him with an alibi. There was no right of appeal.

🗅 Ra'ed al-'Attar, a supporter of *Hamas*, was sentenced to death by a military court in March for the death of a Palestinian policeman during a police chase in Rafah. Ra'ed al-'Attar denied the charge. No forensic tests were carried out. Two co-defendants were sentenced to life imprisonment. President 'Arafat agreed to reconsider the death sentence after demonstrations and riots in Rafah during which two people were killed, reportedly by the Palestinian security forces, and 80 others injured.

Impunity
The PA failed to bring to justice members of the security services responsible for human rights abuses such as torture or unlawful killings.

🗅 In November 'Abd al-Latif 'Abd al-Fattah, a Palestinian General Intelligence officer, sentenced to seven years' imprisonment by a military court in 1998 for "mistreatment and negligence" in connection with the death of Walid al-Qawasmeh in Jericho General Intelligence Centre, was appointed as a General Prosecutor in the Attorney General's Office.

AI country reports and visits
Report
• Palestinian Authority: Defying the rule of law — political detainees held without charge or trial (AI Index: MDE 21/003/99)
Visits
AI delegates visited areas under the jurisdiction of the PA in January, April, May and June.

PAPUA NEW GUINEA

PAPUA NEW GUINEA
Head of state: Queen Elizabeth II, represented by Silas Atopare
Head of government: Mekere Morauta (replaced Bill Skate in July)
Capital: Port Moresby
Population: 4.5 million
Official languages: English, Papua New Guinea Pidgin
Death penalty: abolitionist in practice

There were ongoing concerns about human rights violations by police officers and in the prison system, including suspected extrajudicial executions and ill-treatment. Government neglect of the prison system led to mass escapes and hunger strikes by prisoners in protest at conditions amounting to cruel, inhuman or degrading punishment.

Background
Sir Mekere Morauta was elected Prime Minister in July. Lack of funding for the justice system stifled initiatives to revitalize village court systems. The National Commission on Human Rights, announced by the government in 1997, had still not been established by the end of 1999. The government acknowledged problems with the implementation of the Convention on the Rights of the Child. There were signs of an increasing awareness of human rights in civil society, with more victims of human rights violations prepared to assert their rights in court. In July, the National Court found that the actions of heavily armed police conducting a search of a family home in the presence of journalists had been cruel and in breach of constitutional human rights provisions on privacy and the inherent dignity of the human person.

Bougainville
Despite setbacks, there was gradual progress towards a political settlement to the secessionist conflict on the island of Bougainville. A constituent assembly was formed in Bougainville in January. In May John Kabui was elected President of the Bougainville People's Congress to lead negotiations with the national government on a political settlement. The new government of Prime Minister Morauta ruled out a referendum on independence for Bougainville, which had been offered in July by the previous administration. In August, the national government established a Bougainville Peace and Restoration office under the Prime Minister's control. Formal cease-fire agreements continued to hold and Australia announced its intention to negotiate a withdrawal of the international Peace Monitoring Group from Bougainville.

Police shootings

There were serious concerns about shootings by police officers in circumstances suggesting extrajudicial execution. The shootings occurred in the context of the increasing use of high-powered firearms, both against the police and in local inter-ethnic conflicts. The lack of prompt, independent and impartial investigations into the circumstances of several disputed fatal police shootings heightened concerns about impunity. In October the Chief Justice of the Supreme Court criticized the police for human rights violations and for taking the law into their own hands.

At least 17 criminal suspects were reportedly shot dead and more injured by police in Eastern Highland Province alone, some in disputed circumstances. There were reports of indiscriminate shootings of unarmed villagers by police.

▭ In December, police in Port Moresby shot down a helicopter which had been hijacked by five heavily armed bank robbers. All the hijackers were shot dead by police, including two who were shot while reportedly trying to flee unarmed. The incident raised questions about the alleged "shoot to kill" policy of the new Commissioner of Police.

Ill-treatment and prison conditions

Prisoners were held in severely overcrowded conditions and given inadequate food. There were reports of ill-treatment by police and by prison guards.

▭ Nathan Geno, a prisoner awaiting trial at Buimo Prison near Lae, Morobe Province, died in November after being recaptured by guards following his escape with 17 other prisoners. Prisoners claimed they witnessed Nathan Geno being beaten by guards with iron bars, bottles, batons and a piece of timber. Police investigating the death reportedly failed to question the witnesses and declined to give details of a police report for a coroner's inquest due to be held in 2000. Nathan Geno's death followed at least two hunger strikes by Buimo prisoners in protest at severe delays in court proceedings and overcrowding. A week before Nathan Geno's death, the Lae National Court criticized the government for inadequate prison funding.

PARAGUAY

REPUBLIC OF PARAGUAY
Head of state and government: Luis Ángel González Macchi (replaced Raúl Cubas Grau in March)
Capital: Asunción
Population: 5 million
Official languages: Spanish, Guaraní
Death penalty: abolitionist for all crimes
1999 treaty ratifications/signatures: Protocol to the American Convention on Human Rights to Abolish the Death Penalty

Paraguay's longstanding political crisis culminated in March with the assassination of Vice-President Luis María Argaña and the killing of at least seven demonstrators. There were reports that judicial investigations into the killings were obstructed by police, and concerns regarding the fairness of the judicial proceedings against a number of individuals. As in previous years there were reports of ill-treatment or torture of criminal suspects, of excessive use of force by the security forces in land evictions, of illegal conscription of minors into the armed forces, and of unexplained deaths of military conscripts.

Background

President Raúl Cubas Grau resigned following public outrage at the assassination of Vice-President Luis María Argaña and the killing of at least seven demonstrators in March. Luis Ángel González Macchi was sworn in as President at the head of a coalition government.

The institutional crisis which culminated in the March events dated from 1998 when an extraordinary military court sentenced former army commander and presidential candidate Lino Oviedo to 10 years' imprisonment for an attempted coup in 1996. The presidential elections were won by Lino Oviedo's vice-presidential running mate, Raúl Cubas, who immediately ordered Lino Oviedo's release. However, the Supreme Court ruled this action unconstitutional and ordered Lino Oviedo's rearrest; President Cubas refused to comply with the ruling. A coalition of opposition parties and a section of the ruling Colorado Party, headed by Vice-President Argaña, initiated impeachment proceedings against President Cubas. In early 1999 the political climate rapidly deteriorated as preparation of these proceedings progressed. There were numerous reports that Lino Oviedo was planning to seize power by force.

The March killings

On 23 March Vice-President Argaña and his bodyguard were shot and killed by gunmen in Asunción. In the ensuing crisis, the congressional impeachment hearing against President Cubas was brought forward. On 26 and 27 March supporters of Lino Oviedo, who were seeking to prevent the impeachment hearing, opened fire on people demonstrating in support of Congress and calling for the resignation of President Cubas. At least seven demonstrators were killed and more than 100 others injured. There were eyewitness accounts that police officers assisted the attackers and that some police officers fired on protesters.

President Cubas resigned and fled to Brazil. Lino Oviedo, who was accused of ordering the violence, sought asylum in Argentina. In December Lino Oviedo went into hiding when the new Argentine government promised to revoke his asylum status.

Investigations into the March killings
There were separate investigations into the assassination of Vice-President Argaña and into the killings outside Congress. The investigation into the assassination of Vice-President Argaña and his bodyguard resulted in a number of arrests and produced intense public controversy, particularly with regard to the reliability of witness testimony. There were widespread allegations of manipulation of the case by the media and politicians. By November a number of those originally accused of the murders had been released on bail and the judicial authorities were seeking the detention of newly identified suspects.

In the aftermath of the shootings outside Congress, scores of people were arrested, including the Chief of National Police. Police reportedly hampered the investigation by failing to examine the crime scene effectively or to register victims properly, and by mislaying ballistics reports.

A judicial process was also initiated against more than 20 politicians and journalists who had supported Lino Oviedo or President Cubas, for allegedly inciting the March violence and violating the Constitution. Many of the accused were initially held in pre-trial detention and later placed under house arrest. There was concern at the apparent lack of evidence against a number of the accused, particularly former senator Miguel Ángel González Casabianca and former Vice-President Ángel Roberto Seifart.

Bicameral Commission of Investigation
The two houses of parliament created a commission to investigate the March events. The inquiry, which did not have judicial status, issued a report in October condemning Lino Oviedo and his supporters. There was concern at the apparent bias of the report and its possible negative impact on continuing judicial proceedings against the accused, and at the manner in which it contributed to a climate of political persecution against those who had shown support for Lino Oviedo or President Cubas.

Torture and ill-treatment
As in previous years, there were reports of torture and ill-treatment of criminal suspects, including minors, in prisons and police stations.
☐ In late December criminal investigations were initiated after 23 inmates of Ciudad del Este men's prison filed a criminal complaint against the director of the prison for torture and ill-treatment; he had reportedly ordered prison guards to beat the inmates over a half-hour period. The director of Emboscada prison, where the inmates were immediately transferred after the incident, reportedly confirmed that men showed signs of severe ill-treatment.

Land disputes
There were numerous reports of harassment, intimidation and attacks on peasant farmers in the context of land disputes. There was no information regarding investigations or efforts by the authorities to bring to justice those responsible.
☐ In April Arnaldo Delvalle, a peasant farmer in Puerto Indio, Alto Paraná department, was reportedly tortured and then shot dead on the orders of a local landowner acting with the support of the local police.
☐ In November, during the violent eviction of over 1,000 peasant farmers occupying land in the General Resquín district of San Pedro department, police were reportedly responsible for shooting dead Crescencio González and injuring nine other peasant farmers.

Conscripts
There were fewer reports than in previous years of the illegal forced and arbitrary recruitment of youths, including minors, into the armed forces. However, the conscription of minors by coercive means continued to be the predominant method of recruitment, violating both national legislation and international standards. There were frequent reports of ill-treatment of conscripts. Four conscripts died in unexplained circumstances in 1999. The authorities continued to fail to carry out proper investigations into such cases.
☐ In April Marcial Torres, a 17-year-old conscript in the National Police, reportedly died as a result of a beating by his superior.

Inter-American Commission on Human Rights
The authorities failed to carry out two explicit commitments made to the Inter-American Commission on Human Rights (IACHR). Firstly, to transfer those held in the Panchito López juvenile correction centre to new premises — minors continued to be detained there in conditions amounting to cruel, inhuman and degrading treatment. Secondly, Congress failed once again to fulfil its longstanding obligation to appoint a People's Ombudsman. In July the IACHR issued a press release containing wide-ranging recommendations following a visit to Paraguay.

AI country reports and visits
Public statement
• Paraguay: The new government must end impunity (AI Index: AMR 45/002/99)
Visit
AI delegates visited Paraguay in October and met state officials, including the President.

PERU

REPUBLIC OF PERU
Head of state and government: Alberto Fujimori
Capital: Lima
Population: 24.4 million
Official languages: Spanish, Quechua, Aymara
Death penalty: abolitionist for ordinary crimes

Peru withdrew from the jurisdiction of the Inter-American Court of Human Rights in July 1999. Hundreds of prisoners falsely charged with terrorism-related offences remained incarcerated. Journalists, opposition leaders and human rights defenders received threats in what appeared to be a pattern of systematic intimidation against those critical of the authorities. Torture and ill-treatment remained widespread. Civilians continued to be tried by military courts for the terrorism-related offences of "treason" and "aggravated terrorism".

Background

1999 was the last year of President Alberto Fujimori's second five-year term in office. In the run-up to elections scheduled for April 2000, the human rights situation became critical.

In July 1999 the government decided to withdraw with immediate effect from the jurisdiction of the Inter-American Court of Human Rights, leaving victims of past and present human rights violations without the possibility of redress from an international tribunal. Thousands of unresolved cases of human rights violations perpetrated by members of the security forces between 1980 and 1995 had already been definitively closed by the 1995 amnesty law. Peru withdrew from the Inter-American Court in the wake of the Court's decision to order the Peruvian state to retry four Chilean citizens convicted of treason by military courts in 1994. However, critics maintained that Peru had in fact withdrawn from the Inter-American Court because the Court was about to review two crucial cases: the case of three judges dismissed from the Constitutional Tribunal in 1997 for having ruled that it was unconstitutional for President Fujimori to run for a third term in office; and the case of Baruch Ivcher, the Israeli-born owner of a television station who was stripped of his Peruvian nationality and forced to relinquish his station in 1997 for having revealed gross human rights violations by the intelligence services.

Harassment and intimidation of journalists through anonymous threats and court action became so commonplace that the international community expressed concern over the interference with freedom of the press.

Concern persisted about the judiciary's lack of independence from the executive. The Constitutional Tribunal, which rules on the constitutionality of congressional legislation and government action, continued to be paralysed. The three judges ousted in

1997 had not yet been replaced, so the Tribunal did not have a quorum and was unable to rule on any constitutional issues. More than half the country's judges had provisional or temporary status, leaving them susceptible to outside pressures.

Human rights defenders called for the establishment of a Truth Commission to clarify human rights violations committed in the country during the internal armed conflict.

The fraction of the armed opposition group Shining Path which rejected a 1992 peace accord was weakened by the capture of its leader in July. However, Shining Path remained active, mainly in the Alto Huallaga region in Huánuco and San Martín departments, in Satipo province, Junín department, and in the provinces of Huanta and La Mar in Ayacucho department.

Prisoners of conscience

More than 200 prisoners of conscience and possible prisoners of conscience, all falsely charged with terrorism-related offences, remained imprisoned. In February AI wrote to President Fujimori expressing concern that he had not been pardoning prisoners as recommended by the *Ad Hoc* Commission to review cases of people falsely charged with terrorism-related offences. According to reports, the files of 60 people whom the *Ad Hoc* Commission considered were falsely imprisoned were handed to the President, but he had not yet pardoned them by the end of 1999.

The *Ad Hoc* Commission's mandate ended in December. Since August 1996, when it was set up, the Commission had reviewed more than 3,000 cases. Of these, 469 prisoners were pardoned and released. At least a further 900 prisoners were absolved by the courts during the same period. However, hundreds of women and men remained falsely imprisoned for terrorism-related offences.

▭ Nancy Ruiz Nano was detained on 12 September 1992 and sentenced by a military tribunal to life imprisonment for the terrorism-related offence of "treason". The only evidence that the police presented against her was that she used to work as a maid in a house whose occupants were Shining Path supporters.

Risk of detention

Thousands of women and men accused of terrorism-related offences faced detention. Warrants for their arrest were issued against them although the majority were reported to have had no links with armed opposition groups. They were at risk of being falsely charged and imprisoned, especially given the unfair trial procedures to which they would be subjected. Whole communities faced these warrants and lived in fear of being detained.

▭ In October, 50 peasants from the community of Andarapa, Apurimac department, were finally acquitted. Their ordeal began at the beginning of the 1980s when they were charged with terrorism-related offences. They were absolved by the courts and returned to their communities. However, unknown to them, the police included them in another investigation for the same crimes and issued further arrest warrants. Two of the peasants were detained and sentenced to three and five years' imprisonment in 1996. They were subsequently pardoned by the President for having been falsely imprisoned. The rest had to wait until October 1999 to have their names cleared. Ten members of the community, representing the whole group, appeared before a special court which travelled to the community and acquitted all 50.

☐ Ninety peasants from the district of Chungui, La Mar province, Ayacucho department, who faced arrest warrants sent five representatives to appear before a special court in April. The court acquitted the five who appeared, but ruled that the remaining 85 had to be tried before their cases could be decided.

Unfair trials

Civilians continued to be tried by military courts for the terrorism-related crime of "treason". Intergovernmental bodies such as the UN Committee against Torture and the Inter-American Court of Human Rights reiterated their concern at the use of military courts to try civilians. However, there were no signs of Congress modifying the anti-terrorism legislation and abolishing the use of military courts which are neither independent nor impartial. According to reports, 1,897 people charged with the terrorism-related crime of "treason" were tried by military courts between 1992 and 1999. Of these, 823 were sentenced to prison terms of between 10 years and life imprisonment.

In 1998 a new law to combat crimes committed by gangs of youths came into effect. The law defines these crimes as "aggravated terrorism", and specifies that their trials fall within the military justice system. In November President Fujimori publicly stated that those charged with "aggravated terrorism" should be tried by civilian courts. In late December Congress passed a law which modified the 1998 law, defining crimes committed by youth gangs as "special terrorism" and specifying that these cases should be tried by civilian courts.

Torture and ill-treatment

Reports of torture and ill-treatment by the armed forces and the police remained widespread. Both the 1992 anti-terrorism legislation to combat armed opposition groups, and the 1998 law against "aggravated terrorism", undermine safeguards designed to prevent torture and ill-treatment. Both laws grant extensive powers to the police during the investigation phase. The police have the power to detain a suspect without a judicial warrant or a warrant from the Public Ministry, but have to inform them of the detention within 24 hours. The police are also in charge of the pre-trial investigation. This investigation can be extended for up to 15 days, and for the terrorism-related crime of treason the period can be extended for a further 15 days. During this period the detainee is under the exclusive control of the police, who may request incommunicado detention for up to 10 days. In addition, those convicted have to spend their first year of imprisonment in solitary confinement.

Investigations of alleged torture and ill-treatment by members of the security forces, including cases of death in custody, were opened under 1998 legislation which criminalized torture. However, only in two cases were the perpetrators convicted and sentenced to imprisonment.

In November the UN Committee against Torture reviewed Peru's third periodic report. The Committee expressed concern about "the use of military courts to try civilians; the period of incommunicado pre-trial detention [...] for persons suspected of acts of terrorism; and the special prison regime applicable to convicted terrorists and in particular to convicted terrorist leaders".

☐ Lucas Huamán Cruz was beaten and forced to confess to theft at the police station in the town of San Francisco, La Mar province, Ayacucho department, in September 1998. Four hours later he was released. He died the following day in his home. One policeman was detained and in May 1999 the provincial attorney in charge of the case stated that there was evidence that the accused was responsible for the crime of torture. However, in October, the suspect was acquitted. The judge claimed that there was insufficient evidence to assume that Lucas Huamán had been tortured.

☐ Raúl Miguel Andahua was detained in December 1998 by members of the navy in Aguaytía, Ucayali department. He was reportedly beaten and lost consciousness after a stick was inserted into his anus. When he recovered he found himself in a cell, naked and wet. The following day officers allegedly applied electric shocks to his back and forced him to sign a statement confessing to crimes of terrorism. He was also threatened with death if he refused to state that his injuries were the result of a motorcycle accident. He was released without charge. Seven naval officers were charged with torture. However, a military judge asked for the case to be transferred to the military justice system, arguing that the officers had committed a military offence. By the end of 1999 the case was before the Supreme Court of Justice, for a ruling on whether to try the accused before a military or a civilian court.

Harsh prison conditions

Prison conditions remained harsh and in some circumstances amounted to cruel, inhuman and degrading punishment.

☐ In September, three leaders of the *Movimiento Revolucionario Túpac Amaru* (MRTA), Túpac Amaru Revolutionary Movement, held in a prison in the Callao Naval Base near Lima, went on a 30-day hunger strike. Víctor Polay Campos, Miguel Rincón Rincón and Peter Cárdenas Schulte were protesting against the prison conditions they had endured for six years. They were held in solitary confinement in underground cells and had no direct contact with their relatives during their monthly visits. Over 50 MRTA inmates at the high security prison of Yanamayo, in Puno department, joined the hunger strike for two weeks.

☐ In November and December, inmates of the Challapalca prison went on hunger strike to protest against conditions there. The prison, in Puno department, is more than 4,600 metres above sea level, and is extremely cold. The inaccessibility of the prison seriously limits the prisoners' right to maintain contact with the outside world, including with relatives, lawyers and doctors.

Intimidation and death threats

Human rights defenders, journalists and opposition leaders faced a rising number of incidents of intimidation, harassment and death threats. There were allegations that the National Intelligence Service was behind the incidents.

◻ In May an issue of the satirical version of the national newspaper *La República* called *"Repúdica"* accused Gustavo Mohme, Congressman and editor of the newspaper, of sympathizing with the armed opposition. The issue also contained death threats directed at *La República* journalists, apparently linked to various articles in *La República* about corruption in Peru and to Gustavo Mohme's efforts to unite the opposition for the April 2000 elections.

◻ In June a box containing what appeared to be a bomb was left in the premises of the *Comisión de Derechos Humanos* (COMISEDH), Human Rights Commission. COMISEDH's work includes helping torture victims to obtain redress through the courts, and seeking to ensure that the perpetrators are brought to justice.

Women's rights

In February the Latin American and Caribbean Committee for the Defense of Women's Rights (CLADEM) and the Centre for Reproductive Law and Policy published *Silence and Complicity*. The report detailed cases of rape, humiliating verbal abuse and forced birth control. The vast majority of women who experienced these abuses were young, poor or from rural or marginalized urban areas.

In May the government approved a law allowing courts to prosecute offenders implicated in sexual assault cases without the victim filing charges. Courts were also to assume the costs of the trial under the new law. Women's rights groups applauded the measure, arguing that most women in Peru did not file charges against rapists for fear of retaliation, distrust of a male-dominated judicial system or a lack of money.

AI country reports

- Peru: Amnesty International urges President Fujimori to release "innocent prisoners" (AI Index: AMR 46/006/99)
- Peru: Raúl Teobaldo Miguel Andahua – Another victim of torture (AI Index: AMR 46/012/99)
- Peru: Legislation is not enough – torture must be abolished in practice (AI Index: AMR 46/017/99)

PHILIPPINES

REPUBLIC OF THE PHILIPPINES
Head of state and government: Joseph Estrada
Capital: Manila
Population: 71.5 million
Official languages: Pilipino, English
Death penalty: retentionist

Six people were executed by lethal injection in 1999, the first executions in the Philippines for 23 years. At least 350 people were sentenced to death, bringing the number of death sentences imposed since Congress restored capital punishment in late 1993 to at least 1,200. There were serious concerns at apparent grave defects in the administration of justice – particularly allegations of the torture of criminal suspects to coerce confessions. Peace talks between the government and the National Democratic Front (NDF) broke down in May and moves towards peace talks with the Moro Islamic Liberation Front (MILF) faltered amid repeated outbreaks of fighting. Human rights violations, including extrajudicial executions and the torture or ill-treatment of suspected members of armed opposition groups by security personnel, were reported. Abuses by opposition groups were also reported.

Death penalty

In January, a few hours before the scheduled execution of Leo Echegaray, the Supreme Court granted a temporary stay of execution to allow Congress to consider a resolution to review the death penalty law. Despite vocal opposition from the Roman Catholic Church and human rights groups, Congress voted not to review the death penalty law. Leo Echegaray, who had been found guilty in 1994 of raping his step-daughter, was executed in February.

Concerns that the risk of unfair trials and judicial errors could lead to the execution of innocent people intensified as the government apparently failed to investigate allegations of ill-treatment and torture by police of criminal suspects in pre-trial detention to coerce confessions. Although presidential reprieve and commutation powers were exercised during 1999, there was continuing concern at the apparently arbitrary and inconsistent nature of the Executive Review Procedure.

◻ In June Eduardo Agbayani, who had been convicted of rape, was executed after President Joseph Estrada failed to get through by telephone to the execution chamber in time to grant a reprieve.

◻ Dante Piandong, Jesus Morallos and Archie Bulan were executed in July. They had been found guilty of killing a police officer during an armed robbery. Dante Piandong had alleged that while being interrogated by police in 1997 he had been given electric shocks to his genitals, and had been handcuffed and forced to lie flat while water was dripped on a cloth held over his face.

No investigation was known to have been carried out into these allegations.

☐ In July the Supreme Court overturned its 1997 decision confirming the death sentence of Marlon Parazo and ordered a retrial after medical tests confirmed that he was deaf and mute and had been unable to fully understand the rape and homicide charges on which he had been convicted.

Abuses in the context of armed conflict

In June, Vicente Ladlad, peace talks consultant for the NDF which represents the Communist Party of the Philippines (CPP) and its armed wing the New People's Army (NPA), was arrested without a valid warrant; a court subsequently ordered his release. The number of armed confrontations between the security forces and the NPA increased in at least eight provinces. Within the context of anti-insurgency operations, there were reports of at least 14 possible extrajudicial executions and at least eight incidents of torture or ill-treatment of suspected members of armed opposition groups by the armed forces or militia units.

☐ In August, four suspected NPA members were arrested at a military checkpoint in northeast Mindanao and later reportedly extrajudicially executed, allegedly while trying to escape from a military vehicle.

Periodic aerial bombardment of villages suspected of harbouring members of armed opposition groups led to mass displacements of civilians, especially in Mindanao. With the end of the peace talks, the pace of the amnesty program for former members of armed opposition groups slowed still further, and at least 150 political prisoners, including some possible prisoners of conscience, remained in detention at the end of 1999. Most of the political detainees were held on criminal charges, particularly illegal possession of firearms, robbery and murder.

Armed opposition groups

Members of Muslim armed groups, including the MILF, *Abu Sayyaf* and renegade members of the Moro National Liberation Front, continued to take civilian hostages and to carry out deliberate and arbitrary killings. The MILF's Shari'a courts sentenced suspected criminals to death. In February an NPA unit in Bataan province executed a man accused of raping his two daughters.

Impunity

Concerns increased that a climate of impunity reportedly protecting police and other officials from effective prosecution for alleged human rights violations was becoming further entrenched.

☐ In March a court dismissed charges against 27 police officers allegedly involved in the extrajudicial execution of 11 bank robbers while in police custody in 1995. Key prosecution witnesses, including former police officers, had withdrawn their affidavits. In November one of the former accused, General Panfilo Lacson, was appointed head of the Philippine National Police (PNP).

Incidents of alleged extrajudicial executions by police of suspected criminals were reported in Manila,

Davao and other provincial towns during 1999.

☐ In July PNP Colonel Alfredo Siwa was tried and convicted of killing a suspected criminal in a hospital in Nueva Ecija province in March. The victim had earlier been wounded and four other suspected criminals killed in an operation allegedly led by Colonel Siwa.

One possible "disappearance", allegedly carried out by security personnel, was reported during 1999. At least 1,600 "disappearances" reported since the early 1970s remained unresolved. Attempts by relatives of the victims to discover the truth and to seek justice continued to be unsuccessful.

☐ In a rare test case the family of Jose Sumapad, who "disappeared" in southwest Mindanao in 1986 and whose remains were exhumed in 1996, filed a case in a local court in January. No hearings had taken place by the end of the year, and there were reports that family members and potential witnesses had been threatened by the alleged perpetrators.

Human rights and economic development

Instances of ill-treatment, use of excessive force and possible extrajudicial executions by police and other law enforcement officials were reported within the context of labour or land disputes, and the forced eviction of poor urban residential areas and rural indigenous communities. Some human rights abuses, including deliberate and arbitrary killings, were carried out by private security guards with the apparent connivance of local officials and police.

☐ In May farmer Sani Wahab and his wife Lala Wahab were killed when unidentified men fired at their house in southwestern Mindanao, reportedly after the couple had refused to sell their land. Sources claimed that the perpetrators included security guards from a local logging company and members of the armed forces.

AI country reports and visits
Report

- Philippines: The resumption of executions in the Philippines – An open letter to President Estrada (AI Index: ASA 35/025/99)

Visit

AI delegates visited the National Penitentiary on the day scheduled for Leo Echegaray's execution.

POLAND

REPUBLIC OF POLAND
Head of state: Aleksander Kwasniewski
Head of government: Jerzy Buzek
Capital: Warsaw
Population: 38.8 million
Official language: Polish
Death penalty: abolitionist for all crimes
1999 treaty ratifications/signatures: Protocol No. 6 to the European Convention for the Protection of Human Rights and Fundamental Freedoms concerning the abolition of the death penalty; Rome Statute of the International Criminal Court

At least one conscientious objector to military service was imprisoned in 1999.

International organizations
In July the UN Human Rights Committee considered Poland's fourth periodic report on fulfilment of its obligations under the International Covenant on Civil and Political Rights. The Committee expressed concern about numerous forms of discrimination against women, including discriminatory restrictions on women's access to reproductive health care. The Committee also expressed concern at the lack of an independent system of supervision to address abuses of human rights by police and prison officers, and to monitor prison conditions. The Committee called on the authorities to adopt firm measures to eradicate the abuse and humiliation of new recruits to the army.

Conscientious objection
The law governing conscientious objection was amended in May. However, several of the new provisions were at variance with internationally recognized principles on conscientious objection. The amended law set the length of alternative civilian service at nearly twice the length of military service and limited the time period in which applications for alternative civilian service can be made to "the time of receiving a call-up order for military service".
🗁 Marcin Petke, a conscientious objector to military service, was imprisoned on 29 January for six months for evasion of military service. The judge of the Garrison Court of Gdynia reportedly offered Marcin Petke "alternative" service in an army office, which he refused.

AI country report
• Poland: Draft law concerning alternative service is at variance with internationally recognized principles on conscientious objection to military service (AI Index: EUR 37/004/99)

PORTUGAL

PORTUGUESE REPUBLIC
Head of state: Jorge Fernando Branco de Sampaio
Head of government: Antonio Manuel de Oliveira Guterres
Capital: Lisbon
Population: 9.9 million
Official language: Portuguese
Death penalty: abolitionist for all crimes

Prisoners continued to face cruel, inhuman and degrading conditions, and frequent acts of violence by prison staff, as well as other inmates, were reported. Allegations were made about ill-treatment and illegal detention by law enforcement officers and judicial inquiries were opened, or continued, in relation to a number of ill-treatment cases.

Prisons: a continuing 'scandal'
Although investment in prisons increased and steps were taken to renovate some buildings and improve benefits and facilities, prisoners claimed conditions continued to constitute what President Jorge Sampaio had called a "real national scandal" the previous year. The allegations referred to severe overcrowding, poor standards of hygiene and medical neglect; continuing proliferation, in some places, of cockroaches, fleas and rats; the spread and fear of contagious diseases such as tuberculosis; an escalation in the numbers of prisoners with HIV and AIDS; and widespread drug addiction.
After a new inspection, the Ombudsman for Justice recognized that the authorities had made an "appreciable" effort to improve living and hygiene conditions during the previous two years, but stated that the general situation remained "as black or blacker than in 1996", the year of his critical prison report, largely owing to the pressures caused by drug dependency and the rise in infectious diseases.
Some prisoners claimed they had been ill-treated by prison guards. Allegations were made by prisoners at Linhó (Sintra) that the prison governor and head of custodial staff seemed powerless to prevent beatings of inmates by guards "almost every day". The prison authorities rejected the accusations, stressing the existence of "organized violence" by prisoners. In July, after one prisoner was transferred to a security wing and allegedly beaten by guards, about 200 prisoners in wing B of Linhó protested by refusing to eat. In another incident at Linhó, prisoners demanded to inspect the security wing after an inmate held for 30 days in a disciplinary cell had reportedly been subdued with baton beatings and tear gas; a visit was authorized. There were also allegations of ill-treatment of prisoners at Pinheiro da Cruz and Angra do Heroísmo prisons. A group of prisoners had earlier signed an open letter in which they described a climate of fear and ill-treatment at Pinheiro da Cruz. This was denied by the General Directorate of Prison Services.

▢ António Palma, a prisoner at Pinheiro da Cruz, who was undergoing psychiatric treatment, was allegedly ill-treated in August when he refused to be locked into his cell at the end of the day. A group of between eight and 10 guards, accompanied by two dogs and armed with batons and a riot shield, reportedly beat him to the ground, leaving weals and abrasions across his back. He was taken to the prison infirmary and injected with medication, apparently against his will. Concern was expressed that the number of guards and the dogs and equipment brought in to subdue the prisoner was a use of disproportionate force. An inquiry was opened.

National Republican Guard unit accused of ill-treatment

Allegations of ill-treatment by law enforcement officers were reported both before and after May, when the Regulations on the Material Conditions of Detention in Police Establishments came into force. Introducing the regulations, the Minister of Internal Administration expressed the belief that, while conditions for suspects in police custody had been a "frequent object of criticism by international and human rights institutions and organizations", the situation had improved in recent years and "it is now important to ensure that it does not deteriorate". The regulations, which affect both the Public Security Police (PSP) and the National Republican Guard (GNR), set out a large number of detailed requirements for improving conditions in police custody. They stipulate that all detainees must be treated with humanity and dignity and all arrests must be registered at the police station or command post.

▢ A GNR infantry sergeant claimed in August that, despite the new regulations, ill-treatment of detainees was "virtually systematic" between May and July at a post in Anadia (Aveiro) which he had commanded for almost 18 years. He claimed that, after reporting ill-treatment to his immediate superior, as required by the new regulations, he had been transferred from the post and an inquiry had been opened into allegations that he had committed "illegal acts". He described four cases in which he claimed detainees had been illegally detained or ill-treated at the post by a three-officer Criminal Investigation Unit (NIC). The sergeant claimed that no food or medical care had been provided to detainees, one of whom was suffering from eye, wrist, arm and back injuries as a result of beatings, and that other arrests had not been registered.

In November the General Inspectorate of Internal Administration (IGAI) stated that it had opened an inquiry into the sergeant's specific allegations as well as into the general functioning of the NIC, owing to reports that the NIC had ill-treated and illegally arrested suspects. However, IGAI stated that the disciplinary proceedings being taken against the sergeant were in no way connected with the allegations he had made against the NIC.

▢ Jorge Manuel da Conceição Simões, a former drug addict undergoing rehabilitation, complained that in May he was taken to the Anadia post after being arrested on suspicion of possessing drugs and beaten about the head and chest when he refused to sign a confession. He was later treated for his injuries at Anadia District Hospital. He claimed he had not taken drugs since February 1998 but that the GNR officers visited his workplace after he refused to sign the confession and reported that he had stolen to feed a drug habit. As a result he lost his job.

Alleged ill-treatment by PSP officers

There was concern that in some cases PSP officers had not only failed to register an arrest at the police station but had driven detainees to remote places in order to carry out ill-treatment.

▢ Marco Fernandes, also called Marco Filipe, was known to police as a petty criminal. He claimed that one early morning in September, as he was standing with friends in a street in Funchal, Madeira, he saw two police officers from the Câmara de Lobos station. He attempted to flee but was caught and beaten about the head with a police radio. He was bundled into a car and driven to Cape Girão, several hundred feet above sea level. His head was covered and the officers held him at the top of the cliff, threatening to throw him over. He was then forced to crawl back to the car. While being driven away, his head, which was bleeding, was held out of the door and he was made to undress and clean away the blood at a well. He alleged he was almost strangled with a piece of iron and kicked in the mouth and stomach before being left to find his own way home. A piece of iron and a police radio were reportedly found later, the latter broken. Marco Fernandes received treatment for his injuries at the Hospital Cruz de Carvalho. He and his mother lodged a judicial complaint against the officers and judicial and disciplinary proceedings were opened. Now 19 years old, Marco Fernandes was one of the children from poor areas of the city, such as Câmara de Lobos, who were abused in 1991 by members of a paedophile ring. Since then a large number of inquiries into crimes of child abuse and paedophilia against street children have taken place in Madeira and have led to prosecutions, but an inquiry into police ill-treatment of the children was never pursued by the public prosecutor, despite confirmation by the Ombudsman's Office that ill-treatment had occurred.

Update

An inquiry by the criminal investigation department of the Lisbon public prosecutor's office concluded without being able to establish that the death of Olívio Almada, whose body was discovered in the Tagus river in 1996, was directly connected with his arrest by PSP officers. However, it found that the officers, who had driven him away in a car without taking him to the police station or registering his arrest, had acted illegally, and they were committed for trial in November. Disciplinary procedures ordered against the officers by the PSP General Command were continuing.

QATAR

STATE OF QATAR
Head of state: al-Shaikh Hamad Ibn Khalifa Al-Thani
Head of government: al-Shaikh Abdullah Ibn Khalifa
Al-Thani
Capital: Doha
Population: 0.6 million
Official language: Arabic
Death penalty: retentionist

More than 100 people continued to stand trial for their alleged involvement in the failed coup attempt of 1996, and at least four people who were being tried *in absentia* were arrested. A central municipal council was elected under universal suffrage for the first time in March.

Coup trial

The trial of more than 100 people accused of involvement in the failed coup attempt of 1996 continued. Some 30 defendants were being tried *in absentia,* but at least four were arrested to stand trial during the course of the year including Shaikh Hamad bin Jassim bin Hamad Al-Thani. The former cabinet minister and member of the Qatar ruling family, widely believed to be the main suspect in the coup attempt, was arrested in July when his private aircraft was reportedly diverted to Doha by Qatar undercover agents. He reportedly denied the prosecution's assertions that he had confessed before a judge to the charges against him.

The government failed to investigate allegations raised in previous years that some of the accused had been tortured in police custody, and did not respond to AI's request for assurances that two of the defendants arrested in July were being humanely treated. Many of the defendants faced capital charges.

Elections

A central municipal council was elected by universal suffrage for the first time on 8 March. More than 200 candidates stood for the 29-seat council, and all Qatar citizens over 18 years old, excluding members of the police and armed forces, were entitled to vote. None of the six women candidates were successful.

In July al-Shaikh Hamad Ibn Khalifa Al-Thani, Amir of Qatar, reportedly established a committee to draft the country's first permanent Constitution, stipulating the establishment of a parliament elected by universal suffrage. The provisional Constitution, adopted in 1970, does not refer to an elected parliament.

Proposed human rights initiatives

There were reports that a group, including prominent lawyers and academics, had plans to establish two non-governmental human rights groups: an international committee for the defence of intellectual liberties and freedom of expression, and a committee for the defence of human rights.

'Abd al-Rahman bin 'Amir al-Na'imi

The government failed to respond to AI's request for clarification of the legal status of 'Abd al-Rahman bin 'Amir al-Na'imi, who has been detained since June 1998, apparently on account of his political activities.

ROMANIA

ROMANIA
Head of state: Emil Constantinescu
Head of government: Mugur Isărescu (replaced Radu Vasile in December)
Capital: Bucharest
Population: 22.6 million
Official language: Romanian
Death penalty: abolitionist for all crimes
1999 treaty ratifications/signatures: Rome Statute of the International Criminal Court

Reports of torture and ill-treatment by police continued, and at least one man died after he was shot by police. Inadequate and slow investigations into these allegations, resulting in few prosecutions, continued to provide relative impunity for police officers. A broad package of legal reforms proposed by the authorities in September had not been implemented by the end of the year. It included proposals to repeal the discriminatory legislation that criminalized homosexuals.

Background

The government's attempts to restructure the economy exacerbated hardship in an already fragile situation, as support for large-scale commercial and industrial enterprises ceased. Coal miners marched on Bucharest in January, threatening their fifth violent invasion (*mineriada*) since 1989. It was averted when the authorities negotiated an agreement with the miners' leader Miron Cozma; he was subsequently sentenced to 18 years' imprisonment for his role in a 1991 *mineriada*. Mass strikes and demonstrations by workers in many sectors of the economy took place through the year.

Ill-treatment

Reports of torture and ill-treatment by police officers continued. Detainees were frequently denied access to a doctor or a lawyer, which facilitated ill-treatment. Police officers were sometimes reported to use torture to force suspects to sign "confessions".
◻ Petrie Ilie, Gheorghe Nedelcu and Victor Gheorghe voluntarily went to Buftea police station in March to give statements denying their involvement in the theft of a coffee consignment. Officers from Ilfov County Police Inspectorate arrived and reportedly beat the three men,

breaking some of their teeth. The officers reportedly tore up the original statements and dictated new statements, in which the men confessed to the robbery.

Investigations into these complaints were rarely prompt or impartial. The authorities frequently failed to account for injuries suffered by the complainant, even when they were documented by forensic medical experts, and some official explanations strained credulity. Police officers sometimes responded to complaints of ill-treatment with a counter-charge.

◻ In May AI received information from the authorities that injuries sustained by Adrian Matei when he was arrested in January 1997 were self-inflicted. He supposedly hit himself against a police car several times and threw himself to the ground intentionally, despite being restrained by six police officers and two civilian guards.

Roma continued to face ill-treatment at the hands of law enforcement officials. They were reportedly targeted because of their ethnic identity, rather than solely on the basis of reported crimes of which they were suspected.

Shootings by police

Domestic legislation continued to permit police officers to shoot criminal suspects even if they did not present any immediate danger. This was incompatible with international standards, such as the UN Basic Principles on the Use of Force and Firearms by Law Enforcement Officials, which allow the use of firearms only in self-defence, or the defence of those facing imminent threat of death or serious injury.

◻ Police officers seeking to arrest a group of suspected cigarette smugglers in Bucharest shot and killed Radu Marian, a 40-year-old Roma, and wounded two of his companions, as they attempted to flee.

Freedom of expression

Journalists continued to face imprisonment or heavy fines, on charges of insult, libel, and "offence to authority", for reporting alleged corruption involving public officials.

◻ Prisoner of conscience Cornel Sabou was released from prison in February under a presidential pardon. He had been imprisoned in 1998 on a charge of libel initiated by a judge in Baia Mare county for having reported allegations that the judge and her mother had dishonestly obtained title to land rightfully belonging to a group of local villagers.

Proposed reforms

In September the government proposed a broad package of legal reforms to the Penal Code, the Penal Procedure Code, and other laws regulating the police and prisons, but it had not been implemented by the end of the year. Although welcome, the package went only some way towards meeting recommendations from intergovernmental and non-governmental organizations.

The proposed reforms included the abolition of a Penal Code article stipulating prison sentences for those convicted of verbal "outrage" against public officials, which had sometimes been used to harass those complaining of ill-treatment in police custody, and the complete de-militarization of the police. The package also included the abolition of Article 200 of the Penal Code, which prohibited homosexual relations between consenting adults "if the act was committed in public or has produced public scandal" and condemned anyone enticing or seducing a person to practise same-sex acts, or anyone who publicly promoted homosexuality or formed associations for that purpose, to a maximum prison sentence of five years.

Proposed changes to Penal Code Articles 205, 206 and 238 governing freedom of expression were half-hearted. The crime of "offence to authority" would be abolished and the penalty for "insult" would be reduced from a prison sentence to a fine. The penalty of a fine or a prison sentence, albeit reduced from the previous maximum of three years, would be retained for libel offences. The UN Human Rights Committee had called for the repeal or modification of all three articles.

Proposed amendments to legislation governing arrest and detention procedures failed to address concerns about the practice of obtaining forced "confessions". The amendments did not meet the UN Human Rights Committee's recommendations that the authorities should assume the burden of proving that confessions obtained in police custody were made voluntarily, and invalidating those obtained by unlawful means. However, the proposals did attempt to bring the system of authorizing pre-trial detention into accord with the International Covenant on Civil and Political Rights (ICCPR), which stipulates that a judge or judicial officer should perform this role. The existing function of prosecutors in ordering pre-trial detention of up to 30 days would be assumed by examining magistrates.

Suggested reforms to the regulations governing police use of firearms failed to bring domestic law into line with international standards, despite the UN Human Rights Committee's concern that police officers were reportedly over-using firearms, particularly against children involved in petty offences, and its call for police use of firearms to be closely regulated.

Intergovernmental organizations

The UN Human Rights Committee considered Romania's fourth periodic report on its fulfilment of obligations under the ICCPR in July. The Committee expressed concern about the plight of street children and abandoned children, the discrimination faced by Roma and women, the lack of accountability of the security forces, and excessive powers of the executive which posed a threat to the independence of the judiciary.

The UN Committee on the Elimination of Racial Discrimination discussed Romania's 12th to 15th periodic reports in August. The Committee noted the establishment of a National Office for Roma in 1997, but expressed concern about the continuing disadvantaged situation of Roma. It also expressed concern about the inadequate nature of legislation used to punish and prohibit racial discrimination, the act of forming or belonging to racist organizations, and continuing expressions of xenophobic attitudes and racial prejudice in the mass media, which have been directed against the Roma minority in particular.

The UN Working Group on Arbitrary Detention released the report of its 1998 visit to investigate the situation of immigrants and asylum-seekers held in prolonged administrative detention. The report expressed serious reservations about both domestic law and official practice which affected the treatment of refugees and asylum-seekers, and the decision to grant asylum. It described the conditions in Giurgiu detention centre as "degrading".

The UN Special Rapporteur on torture published a report in November on his April visit to Romania to inspect police lock-ups and prisons. He concluded that there were "persistent, albeit sporadic, cases of police abuse", that ill-treatment by police was a more serious problem in rural communities, and that Roma were at a higher risk than others. He noted that most reported ill-treatment occurred in the first 24 hours in detention and proposed additional controls to protect detainees during this period. He called for urgent measures to reduce "gross overcrowding" in prisons and commented that "no State has the right to subject persons to these conditions".

In its annual progress report on countries seeking accession to the European Union (EU), issued in October, the European Commission urged Romania to end discrimination against Roma and to establish better protection for the estimated 100,000 children in institutional care. Increased budgetary provision to meet the second aim and the establishment of a central child protection agency were set as preconditions for accession negotiations. In December Romania was invited to begin negotiations for EU accession.

AI country reports
- Romania: Alleged ill-treatment by police officers in Teleorman County (AI Index: EUR 39/001/99)
- Romania: Deaths in suspicious circumstances of Toader Elinoiu and Ion Puțoi (AI Index: EUR 39/005/99)
- Romania: The reported ill-treatment of Dănuț Iordache (AI Index: EUR 39/008/99)
- Romania: The reported ill-treatment and shooting of Nicu Olteanu (AI Index: EUR 39/010/99)

RUSSIAN FEDERATION

RUSSIAN FEDERATION
Head of state: Vladimir Putin (Acting President) (replaced Boris Yeltsin in December)
Head of government: Vladimir Putin (replaced Sergey Stepashin in August, who replaced Evgeny Primakov in May)
Capital: Moscow
Population: 147.2 million
Official language: Russian
Death penalty: retentionist

There were serious and widespread human rights violations, both during peacetime and in the context of the renewed conflict in the Chechen Republic (Chechnya). Throughout the Russian Federation torture and ill-treatment in police custody, in prisons and in the armed forces continued; prison conditions were cruel, inhuman or degrading; prisoners of conscience were detained; refugees, asylum-seekers and internally displaced people were not given adequate protection; and conscientious objectors to military service continued to face imprisonment. In Chechnya civilians were the victims of indiscriminate killings, direct attacks, torture and extrajudicial execution by Russian federal forces; there were few, if any, investigations into these violations, and no prosecutions of those responsible were known to have taken place in 1999.

Background
1999 was dominated by political and economic instability, a general disregard for the rule of law and large-scale corruption at all levels of government. Massive unemployment and dysfunctional industries left thousands of people without a salary for several months. Political chaos and the lack of consistent political leadership led to a strengthening of Russian nationalism. In August Vladimir Putin was appointed as Prime Minister, the fifth in two years. In December President Boris Yeltsin announced his resignation; presidential elections were scheduled for March 2000.

The Chechen conflict
Bombings in Moscow and two other Russian cities in September, which killed at least 292 people, were followed by a Russian military offensive in Chechnya and an intensified campaign of intimidation against Chechens in Moscow and elsewhere. Although no group claimed responsibility for the bombings, the Russian authorities blamed Islamic groups from Chechnya. The apparent disregard for international humanitarian law by Russian forces, and the discriminatory manner in which Chechens were targeted by the authorities in Moscow and elsewhere,

suggested that the government was involved in a campaign to punish an entire ethnic group.

Abuses in armed conflict

No journalists or independent monitors were officially allowed by the Russian border guards through the only open border crossing between Chechnya and Ingushetia. However, eyewitnesses and victims reported that Russian forces directly attacked civilian targets including hospitals, medical personnel and vehicles clearly marked with the Red Cross emblem, causing high civilian casualties. Russian forces were also allegedly responsible for indiscriminate attacks. A number of incidents were reported in which civilian convoys carrying people fleeing the conflict, especially those travelling on the main road out of Chechnya towards Ingushetia, were subjected to bombing from the air or artillery shelling.

⌂ On 21 October a series of explosions in the central market, a mosque and the only working maternity hospital in Grozny reportedly left at least 137 civilians dead and about 400 wounded in what appeared to be an indiscriminate attack by Russian forces. The dead included 13 mothers and 15 new-born babies.

According to reports women and men were separated from each other and their identity documents were checked by Russian troops at the border crossing with Ingushetia. A number of men were reportedly detained following such checks. They were usually held for a short time at the checkpoint before being taken to undisclosed detention facilities, or so-called "filtration camps". The whereabouts of many of those believed held in "filtration camps" remained unknown at the end of the year.

There were allegations of human rights abuses by Chechen armed groups. Abuses reported included that Chechen armed groups were preventing people from leaving their villages, using civilians as "human shields", attacking villages which refused to allow them in, and killing prisoners of war.

Internally displaced people

Some 200,000 people fled the fighting in Chechnya, about 168,000 of whom sought refuge in neighbouring Ingushetia. However, there were reports that a large number of the civilians attempting to seek safety outside the areas affected by the conflict were prevented from doing so, placing their lives at risk.

⌂ According to reports at least 40 civilians fleeing Grozny, the Chechen capital, were killed by Russian special detachment ("*spetsnaz*") troops on 3 December. According to seven survivors interviewed in a hospital in Ingushetia, a convoy of seven cars and a bus, all marked with white flags, heading towards the border with Ingushetia was stopped at a Russian checkpoint near the village of Goity, a few kilometres south of Grozny. Russian troops wearing masks and camouflage uniforms checked the cars and then opened fire at point-blank range. The bus caught fire and more than 40 passengers were killed.

Persecution of Chechens

Chechens and other people from the Caucasus reported that they were arbitrarily detained, ill-treated and tortured in Moscow and other parts of the Russian Federation. There were allegations that in some cases police fabricated criminal charges against them and planted drugs or weapons on them.

In September law enforcement officials and local authorities in Moscow and other big cities launched what appeared to be a massive intimidation campaign mainly targeting Chechens. The so-called *propiska* (residence permit) system, although legally abolished in 1991 in national law, continued to be enforced by the authorities in Moscow, St Petersburg and other large cities. Migrants, internally displaced people or asylum-seekers who did not have residence permits were subjected to arbitrary detention and forcible expulsion by law enforcement officials. Verifying possession of a residence permit or registration appeared to be used by the authorities as a pretext to stop any person who appeared to be from the Caucasus and detain them. Reports suggested that in Moscow in September alone up to 20,000 non-Muscovites were rounded up by police and some 10,000 expelled from the city. There were reports that Moscow law enforcement officials, including those working with the passport and visa department, had received verbal orders to detain and refuse registration to ethnic Chechens. There were a number of reports of torture and ill-treatment of Chechens and other people from the Caucasus by police.

⌂ Rezvan (not his real name), an ethnic Chechen and a resident of Ingushetia, had been undergoing medical treatment for two months at a Moscow hospital. In September he left the hospital to spend a weekend with relatives. Police officers arrived at the relatives' apartment and took Rezvan and a male relative to Police Department No. 38, where the two men were put into different cells. Police officers reportedly confiscated and destroyed all Rezvan's medicines. Rezvan was then handcuffed with his arms behind his back and hung from the ceiling by the handcuffs, while reportedly being beaten by two police officers. Following his release, a medical examination concluded that two of Rezvan's ribs were broken, but the doctors refused to give him a medical certificate because he was not registered in Moscow.

Prisoners of conscience

Prisoners of conscience continued to be detained and to face trials.

⌂ Grigory Pasko, a journalist and Russian naval captain, was released on 20 July after the Russian Pacific Fleet military court in Vladivostok found that there was insufficient evidence to support the charges against him of espionage and revealing state secrets. However, he was found guilty of "abuse of office" and sentenced to three years' imprisonment; he was immediately released under the provisions of an amnesty law adopted in June. There were concerns about the fairness of his trial, which took place in closed session in January. Grigory Pasko had been detained in November 1997 for reporting on the navy's illegal dumping of nuclear waste in the Sea of Japan in 1993. He was subsequently held in prolonged solitary confinement and denied proper medical treatment despite fears that he may have contracted tuberculosis.

In July former prisoner of conscience Aleksandr Nikitin was indicted for the eighth time for espionage and revealing state secrets, charges which carry a prison sentence of up to 20 years. He had initially been arrested in February 1996 after writing articles on the risks of radioactive pollution from Russia's North Fleet. In February 1999 the Supreme Court had upheld the ruling of the St Petersburg City Court that the previous indictment, almost identical to the one issued in July, was unclear and based on evidence unacceptable to the court. He was acquitted in December by the St Petersburg City Court which ruled that his activities did not amount to a crime.

Conscientious objectors

There was still no civilian alternative to military service. Young men who claimed conscientious objection to military service based on their religious beliefs and membership of banned organizations, such as the Jehovah's Witnesses, were often not considered to be legitimate conscientious objectors by the courts. Conscientious objectors continued to face imprisonment.

Torture and ill-treatment

Torture and ill-treatment by law enforcement officers to extract confessions continued to be reported. Detainees were threatened with death; beaten, sometimes to the point of losing consciousness; tied in painful positions; scalded with boiling water; almost asphyxiated by having plastic bags placed over their heads or by being forced to wear gas masks with the supply of oxygen repeatedly cut or restricted; and denied food and medical care. The authorities failed to investigate most allegations and there were serious delays and deficiencies in those investigations which did take place.

Armed forces

Reports of ill-treatment and torture in the armed forces continued to be received. Efforts by Major General Vasiliy Kulakov, appointed in 1998 to oversee action to eradicate bullying in the army, appeared to have little impact on the number of reports of torture and ill-treatment or on the high rate of suicide among conscripts.

In April AI was informed that a criminal investigation into the circumstances of the death of Dmitry Kaloshin had been opened by the Office of the Procurator of Volgograd Region. A preliminary investigation into the case, carried out by the Procurator of the Dzerzhinskiy District in Volgograd, had not resulted in charges. Dmitry Kaloshin, who was found dead on 16 November 1996, had allegedly suffered a catalogue of abuse and ill-treatment by superior officers.

Conditions of detention

Conditions in penitentiaries and pre-trial detention centres, which held more than a million people, did not improve and continued to amount to cruel, inhuman or degrading treatment. Hundreds of thousands of people awaiting trial continued to be held in grossly overcrowded conditions. Thousands had to sleep in shifts, often without bedding. Many cells were filthy and pest-ridden, with inadequate light and ventilation. Food and medical treatment were often inadequate. Tuberculosis and skin diseases were widespread. In June a new law designed to grant amnesty to around 100,000 detainees and prisoners was adopted, but it was not clear how many people were freed under the amnesty. It was reported that the law would apply only to up to 18,000 of the 350,000 detainees in pre-trial detention, where the conditions were known to be the worst.

Children's rights

The UN Committee on the Rights of the Child reviewed Russia's report in September. It expressed concern at the continuing and widespread practice of torture and ill-treatment of juveniles in police custody and the harsh conditions of detention for juveniles awaiting trial. The Committee also raised concerns about the use of child soldiers, and the alleged extrajudicial execution, "disappearance", arbitrary detention, torture and ill-treatment of juveniles during the previous Chechen conflict. The Committee also recommended revision of the provisions for the imposition of the death penalty and corporal punishment on children by Chechen Shari'a courts.

Politically motivated killings

Three men were convicted in the Republic of Kalmykia in November in connection with the murder in June 1998 of Larisa Yudina, a journalist and editor of an opposition newspaper in Kalmykia. Two of the men, who included a former aide of Kalmykian President Kirsan Ilyumzhinov, were sentenced to 21 years in prison; the third was sentenced to six years' imprisonment for concealing information about the murder. Before her death, Larisa Yudina had been repeatedly warned to stop her critical reporting on President Ilyumzhinov, whom she accused of corruption. The names of those who ordered the killing remained unknown.

In October Latvian police detained a Russian former officer of the special police forces in connection with the assassination of Russian reform politician and member of parliament Galina Starovoitova. She had been shot outside her home in St Petersburg in November 1998 in what appeared to be a politically motivated killing.

Death penalty

In February a ruling of the Constitutional Court banned all ordinary court judges from imposing death sentences until the jury trial system had been introduced throughout the Russian Federation; jury trials were available in only nine of the Federation's 89 regions. The ruling constituted the *de facto* abolition of the death penalty. However, despite the undertaking given to the Council of Europe in 1996, the authorities failed to fully abolish the death penalty. In June President Yeltsin commuted the sentences of all the more than 700 people under sentence of death.

Executions continued to be carried out in Chechnya under the provisions of the Chechen Shari'a Criminal Code. In June Chechen President Aslan Maskhadov revealed that 11 people were executed during the first six months of 1999. According to reports, two more people were executed in Grozny on 11 March, after being sentenced to death by the Supreme Shari'a Court; the executions of Lema Bakayev and Grigory Kryuchkovskiy were shown repeatedly on television in Grozny.

Asylum-seekers

Legal provisions for asylum-seekers remained inadequate. Many people were at risk of *refoulement* (forcible return) to countries where they could face grave human rights violations.

In July Bakhadir Ruzmetov was returned to Uzbekistan. He was believed to have been suspected of involvement in explosions in the Uzbek capital, Tashkent, in February. There was concern that Bakhadir Ruzmetov would be at risk of torture and ill-treatment in detention and that he could face execution after an unfair trial; six death sentences were handed down by a Uzbek court in June for involvement in the bombings after a trial characterized by human rights observers as "biassed and shoddy".

AI country reports and visits
Reports
- Russian Federation: Grigory Pasko – prisoner of conscience (AI Index: EUR 46/007/99)
- Russian Federation: Chechen Republic – Humanity is indivisible – Open letter to the United Nations from the Secretary General of Amnesty International (AI Index: EUR 46/038/99)
- Russian Federation: Chechnya – For the Motherland (AI Index: EUR 46/046/99)

Visits
In June AI delegates attended a conference in Moscow focusing on the abolition of the death penalty. In July and November AI visited the country to research violations of children's and women's rights within the criminal justice system, and to interview people affected by the Chechen conflict.

RWANDA

RWANDESE REPUBLIC
Head of state: Pasteur Bizimungu
Head of government: Pierre-Célestin Rwigema
Capital: Kigali
Population: 7.7 million
Official languages: Kinyarwanda, French, English
Death penalty: retentionist

The number of killings inside Rwanda decreased compared to 1998, but killings of unarmed civilians and "disappearances" were still reported throughout 1999. Meanwhile, thousands of unarmed civilians were killed across the border, in the Democratic Republic of the Congo (DRC), in an armed conflict involving several governments, including Rwanda, as well as various armed opposition groups, including Rwandese *interahamwe* militia and soldiers of the former Rwandese armed forces. Around 125,000 people were detained in prisons and detention centres across Rwanda, most accused of participation in the 1994 genocide. Many were held without charge or trial for prolonged periods in conditions amounting to cruel, inhuman and degrading treatment. Arbitrary arrests were reported. Detainees in local detention centres and in military custody were ill-treated. At least 1,420 people were tried for participation in the 1994 genocide. At least 180 were sentenced to death. A number of detainees who were released were rearrested, including several who had been tried and acquitted. Journalists perceived as critical of the government and opposition politicians were subjected to various forms of harassment, including arrest.

Background
As government troops regained control of the northwest, the armed conflict abated and the level of violence decreased. However, the situation remained tense and the peace fragile. In many respects, the armed conflict during which thousands of civilians had been killed in Rwanda in 1998 continued over the border in the DRC. The presence of armed groups continued to be reported sporadically in Rwanda near the DRC border and the Rwandese Patriotic Army (RPA) carried out military operations in this area. Local defence forces were constituted by the authorities throughout Rwanda, ostensibly to ensure the security of the population; they were made up of civilians who were provided with arms and brief training.

The government implemented a national policy which required many people to abandon their homes in order to be housed in new "villages" or settlements known locally as *imidugudu*. In the northwestern *préfectures* of Gisenyi and Ruhengeri, in particular, families were forced to move, sometimes under threat and intimidation. Some were made to destroy their old homes but were not provided with assistance to construct new ones. The policy was officially designed to improve security and ensure greater facilities and infrastructure, but by the end of 1999 living conditions for hundreds of thousands — especially in the northwest — remained very poor.

In July the National Assembly approved a four-year extension of the transitional government, which had already been in place for five years.

Conflict in Democratic Republic of the Congo

Thousands of RPA troops fought in the DRC alongside the *Rassemblement congolais pour la démocratie* (RCD), Congolese Rally for Democracy, against the Congolese armed forces of President Laurent-Désiré Kabila and various armed groups, including the *interahamwe* militia who were responsible for massacres during the 1994 genocide in Rwanda. Throughout 1999, the RPA continued to send reinforcements to the DRC, including child soldiers, some of whom had been forcibly recruited. RCD and RPA forces carried out widespread human rights abuses in the DRC, including massacres of thousands of unarmed civilians. Deliberate and arbitrary killings of civilians were also carried out by *interahamwe* militia. (See DRC entry.)

Killings of civilians

The level of killings in Rwanda decreased compared to the previous two years. However, a number of unarmed civilians were killed, some by members of the Rwandese security forces, others by armed opposition groups, others by unidentified assailants. Members of local defence forces were also responsible for killings and other abuses, especially in the northwest, sometimes in conjunction with RPA soldiers.

In May, 49 people — including men, women and children — were reportedly killed by RPA soldiers as they were returning from the DRC through the *Parc national des volcans*, National Volcano Park, in northwestern Rwanda.

In August, a judge, Jean Bahizi, was shot dead near his home in Taba *commune*, Gitarama *préfecture*. The identity of the perpetrators remained unknown.

In November, RPA soldiers killed shopkeeper Jean-Damascène Nsanzurwimo, and another trader, Mudeyi, in Mukungu trading centre in Mwendo *commune*, Kibuye *préfecture*.

During the night of 23 December, in the village of Tamira, in Mutura *commune*, Gisenyi *préfecture*, 31 civilians were killed in an attack by an armed opposition group. The victims, at least half of whom were children under 16, were killed in their homes.

'Disappearances'

Cases of "disappearances" continued to be reported, especially in the northwest. Among the "disappeared" were people arrested in eastern DRC and transferred to Rwanda. Some of those reported to have "disappeared" in 1998 reappeared in custody. For example in June, it was revealed that Ignace Kanyabugoyi, who was reported to have "disappeared" in August 1998, was held in Mulindi military detention centre in Kigali.

The vast majority of the hundreds of "disappearances" which had occurred in 1997 and 1998 remained uninvestigated.

Detention in military custody

An unknown number of detainees, including civilians, were held in military detention centres, sometimes in military camps, at other times in unofficial sites. In most cases it was impossible to verify the identity of detainees in military custody, as the military authorities denied access to relatives and to human rights and humanitarian organizations.

Emile Mutanga, a doctor from the DRC who was passing through Rwanda on his way back to Kinshasa, was arrested in June and detained in a military camp in Gikongoro, southern Rwanda, for more than five months, on suspicion of being a spy for the DRC government. His whereabouts were not confirmed until he was released in October.

Ill-treatment was reported in military detention centres. Cases of rape of women by RPA soldiers were also reported.

In September, six workers at the Nyabihu tea factory in Karago *commune*, Gisenyi *préfecture*, were arrested by an RPA soldier on suspicion of theft. They were detained at Mukamira military camp where they were severely beaten. One was released after two days but the other five were detained for a month, until 25 October. On 11 November one of them, Frodouald Ngaboyisonga, a driver and mechanic in his late thirties, died as a result of injuries inflicted in detention.

Genocide trials

At least 1,420 people were tried in Rwandese courts on charges of participation in the 1994 genocide. At least 180 people were sentenced to death. There were no judicial executions. One of the most prominent trials was that of Augustin Misago, Roman Catholic Bishop of Gikongoro, arrested in April after President Pasteur Bizimungu had denounced him in a public meeting. His trial began in August and was not concluded by the end of the year.

The quality and conduct of trials varied. Some trials were unfair. Some prosecution and defence witnesses were subjected to pressure and intimidation. In some cases, false testimonies were delivered in court. Some trials were repeatedly postponed; the process for hearing appeals was often especially lengthy.

Tens of thousands of genocide suspects remained in detention without trial. In December the law was amended to extend once again the period of preventive detention for a further 18 months. This effectively legalized detention without charge or trial for up to seven years for those detained since 1994. The government set out proposals for transferring all but the "Category 1" genocide cases (those accused of playing a leading role in the genocide) to a system known as *gacaca*, loosely based on a traditional system of justice and involving the local population. While the use of the new *gacaca* system might go some way towards alleviating the huge burden on the courts, there were concerns that aspects would not conform to international standards of fairness, particularly regarding the lack of professional training of those trying the defendants and the right to legal defence.

International Criminal Tribunal

Trials continued at the International Criminal Tribunal for Rwanda (ICTR) in Arusha, Tanzania. By the end of 1999, 38 people were detained in Arusha. Clément Kayishema, former prefect of Kibuye, and Georges Rutaganda, second vice-president of the *interahamwe* militia, were sentenced to life imprisonment. Omar Serushago, a leader of the *interahamwe*, and Obed Ruzindana, a businessman, were sentenced to 15 and 25 years' imprisonment respectively.

In November, in a highly controversial ruling, the ICTR's Appeal Chamber ordered the release of Jean-Bosco Barayagwiza, a founding member of the *Radio télévision libre des Mille Collines*, a radio station that incited ethnic hatred, and of the *Coalition pour la défense de la République*, an extremist party whose supporters participated actively in the genocide. The Appeal Chamber ruled that procedural irregularities during his pre-trial detention violated his rights to a fair trial. AI expressed concern that his release was ordered without any assurance that the serious charges against him would be considered by a national court.

In April, in the first trial of its kind in the national jurisdiction of a foreign country, Fulgence Niyonteze, former *bourgmestre* (local government official) of Mushubati in Gitarama, was sentenced to life imprisonment by a military court in Lausanne, Switzerland, for murder, incitement to murder and war crimes during the genocide (see Switzerland entry).

Releases and rearrests

In 1998 the government had announced that 10,000 detainees would be released, primarily those without a case file. By the end of 1999, around 5,700 were estimated to have been released, most of them provisionally. A number were rearrested, in some cases within days of their release and without substantial new evidence against them.

Several detainees who had been tried and acquitted were rearrested, including Théodore Munyangabe, a former *sous-préfet* (local government official) in Cyangugu, and Pierre Rwakayigamba, vice-governor of the National Bank of Rwanda and an official in the former government. Déogratias Bazabazwa, a schoolteacher from Cyangugu who had been acquitted by the high court and released in 1998, was sentenced to death *in absentia* by the court of appeal and rearrested in October 1999.

Restrictions on freedom of expression

There were continued violations of the right to freedom of expression, particularly directed towards critics of the government and political opponents.

In February, Bonaventure Ubalijoro, former leader of the *Mouvement démocratique républicain* (MDR), Democratic Republican Movement, and an outspoken critic of the government, was arrested. He was detained and accused of several offences ranging from supporting the armed opposition to embezzlement. At the end of 1999, he was still detained at Kimironko prison in Kigali awaiting trial.

In March, several MDR members of parliament who had been critical of government policies were suspended from the National Assembly. One of them, Eustache Nkerinka, was held under house arrest for six months; he was released in September. Another, Jean-Léonard Bizimana, was arrested in June and accused of participation in the genocide.

Journalist John Mugabi, news editor of the newspaper *The Newsline*, was arrested in February, accused of libel, after writing an article alleging corruption by a senior Ministry of Defence official. He was provisionally released in May. Amiel Nkuliza, editor of the newspaper *Le Partisan*, who had been detained without charge or trial since May 1997 in connection with articles published in his newspaper, was provisionally released in August. Both journalists were still awaiting trial at the end of 1999.

Arbitrary arrests and detention without charge or trial

Arbitrary arrests and detentions were reported. Unsubstantiated accusations of participation in the genocide were frequently used as a way of settling scores or to prevent property owners from reclaiming illegally occupied property. Such patterns of arbitrary arrests have occurred in Rwanda since July 1994; many of those arrested arbitrarily or unlawfully remained in detention for several months or even several years without charge or trial.

Ill-treatment and harsh prison conditions

Conditions in prisons and detention centres remained harsh, in many cases constituting cruel, inhuman and degrading treatment, especially in local detention centres. The most urgent problems were serious overcrowding, inadequate hygiene facilities and insufficient food. In many local detention centres, food was not provided by the state and detainees had to rely on their families to bring them food, or share the food of other detainees. Ill-treatment was reported in local detention centres and in some gendarmerie detention centres, usually in the form of beatings.

In August, Félicien Gasana, a 35-year-old worker at a construction company, died as a result of ill-treatment at the gendarmerie of Nyamirambo, in Kigali. His wife Epiphanie Uwitakiye was also beaten.

Intergovernmental organizations

In December the UN Secretary-General published the report of an independent inquiry into the actions of the UN during the 1994 genocide in Rwanda. The report highlighted the failure of the UN to prevent and stop the genocide and attributed responsibility for this failure to the UN system as a whole, to different individuals and bodies within the UN, and to member states. It identified as the primary causes of failure a lack of political commitment to stop the genocide and a lack of resources.

The Organization of African Unity's International Panel of Eminent Persons, set up to investigate the genocide, carried out its investigations. Its report was due to be finalized in 2000.

AI country reports and visits
Reports
• AI published several news releases and initiated numerous membership actions during 1999.
Visits
AI delegates visited Rwanda in October and November 1999, to carry out research, meet government officials and attend a conference organized by the National Human Rights Commission.

SAUDI ARABIA

KINGDOM OF SAUDI ARABIA
Head of state and government: King Fahd bin 'Abdul-'Aziz
Capital: Riyadh
Population: 19 million
Official language: Arabic
Death penalty: retentionist

Criminal judicial procedures fell far short of the most basic international standards, with detainees held incommunicado and defendants denied the right of access to a lawyer, the right to a defence, and the right to appeal. In some cases such unfair trials led to execution, amputation or flogging. Political prisoners, including possible prisoners of conscience, were arrested during 1999, and others arrested in previous years continued to be held without trial. There were continuing reports of torture and ill-treatment, including cruel judicial punishments such as flogging and amputation. More than 100 people were reportedly executed and the true figure might have been far higher.

Background
The government continued to enforce a ban on political parties and trade unions. Press censorship also continued to be strictly enforced. Information on human rights violations remained severely limited. There is no independent Bar Association to oversee the activities of lawyers. The government continued to impose restrictions on access to the country by international human rights organizations.

The lack of independent judicial supervision over arrest and detention procedures meant that detainees, including those suspected of being political or religious opponents of the government, could be detained for long periods without charge or trial. They could be held

in incommunicado detention, at risk of torture. Those who came to trial were denied the most basic safeguards for fair trial. The independence of the judiciary in Saudi Arabia is recognized in principle by law. However, in practice the judiciary was subordinated to the executive authority, in particular the Ministers of Justice and the Interior.

In October it was reported that Minister of Justice 'Abdullah bin Muhammad bin Ibrahim al-Sheikh had announced plans to introduce a code of practice for lawyers. However, no further details were available.

Women
There was growing debate during 1999, reported in the Saudi Arabian media, about the rights of women. In April Crown Prince 'Abdullah bin 'Abdel 'Aziz referred to women's "effective role in the service of their religion and nation", sparking media speculation that the ban on women driving could be lifted. However, in May Minister of the Interior Nayef bin 'Abdel-'Aziz told the media that the driving ban was not to be lifted. In October a group of about 20 women were permitted to observe a session of the Consultative Council, a group of 90 appointed male advisers to the government. The move followed a statement by the head of the Council in which he reportedly said, "There is absolutely nothing that prevents the council from being enlightened by the views of women". In November the Deputy Interior Minister was reported as saying that female Saudi Arabian citizens would be issued with their own identity cards for the first time. However, no further details were reported.

Prisoners of conscience and political prisoners
Dozens of people were arrested on political or religious grounds, including possible prisoners of conscience.
▢ Muhammad Al-Farraj, a lecturer at the Imam Mohamed bin Sa 'ud Islamic University in Riyadh, was reportedly arrested at his home in Riyadh by *al-Mabahith al-'Amma* (General Investigations) in August 1999. At the end of the year he was understood to be in al-Ha'ir prison in Riyadh. Reports indicated that he was arrested because of a poem he wrote and publicized about a week before his arrest. The poem was about two former political prisoners, Sheikh Salman bin Fahd al-'Awda and Sheikh Safr 'Abdul-Rahman al-Hawali.
▢ Ishaq al-Sheikh Yaqub, a 70-year-old journalist was arrested in April upon his return to Saudi Arabia from Bahrain. AI did not know the reasons for his arrest, but reports suggested that he might have been detained for his activities as a journalist. He was reportedly released without charge in October.

Dozens of Christians were arrested during 1999, reportedly for the non-violent expression of their religious beliefs. All the Christians known to have been arrested were foreign nationals who were released and deported after a short period. They included a group of 13 individuals, all Philippine nationals, who were arrested in October, reportedly while participating in a Christian service in a private home. They were held incommunicado for nearly three weeks before being released and deported.

A number of Shi'a clerics were also arrested during 1999, most reportedly because they were suspected political or religious opponents of the government. Those arrested included al-Sayyid Munir al-Sayyid 'Adnan al-Khabaz, a cleric from al-Qutaif. He was reportedly arrested in December at Jeddah airport, on his return from studying in the city of Qom, Iran.

Political prisoners, including possible prisoners of conscience, arrested in previous years continued to be held without trial. They were believed to number between 100 and 200. According to AI's information, some of the detainees were held as suspects in connection with violent activities such as the bombing of a US military base in 1996. Other political detainees were reported to be held primarily for their political views and criticism of the state.

▭ Hani al-Sayegh, a 30-year-old Saudi Arabian who was seeking asylum in the USA, was forcibly returned to Saudi Arabia in October. He was detained immediately on arrival as a suspect in connection with the bombing of a US military complex at al-Khobar in 1996, an offence punishable by death. At the end of 1999 he was still held without access to lawyers and remained at risk of torture, unfair trial and possible death sentence. The US government stated that it had received assurances from the Saudi Arabian government that Hani al-Sayegh would not be tortured, but no details of the assurances were made public. Shortly after Hani al-Sayegh's forcible return to Saudi Arabia, AI announced that it proposed to send a delegation to observe trial proceedings against the detainee. However by the end of 1999, no response had been received concerning visa applications by the proposed delegates.

▭ Dr Sa'id bin Zua'ir, head of the Department of Information at Imam Mohamed bin Sa'ud Islamic University, was arrested in early 1995 at his home in Riyadh by members of al-Mabahith al-'Amma. He was believed to have been denied any visits by his relatives and to have been pressured to sign an undertaking to cease political activities in exchange for his release. He continued to be held in al-Ha'ir prison. To AI's knowledge, he and other political detainees were not charged with any recognizably criminal offence and were denied the right to challenge the legality of their detention.

Releases
A number of political prisoners, including possible prisoners of conscience, arrested in previous years were released. They included Kamil 'Abbas al-Ahmad, a possible prisoner of conscience, who was released in May. Kamil 'Abbas al-Ahmad was arrested in July 1996 and held in the al-Mabahith al-'Amma headquarters in Dammam without trial and possibly without charge. Kamil 'Abbas al-Ahmad is a member of the Shi'a religious community in Saudi Arabia.

Sheikh Salman Bin Fahd al-'Awda and Sheikh Safr 'Abdul-Rahman al-Hawali, both political prisoners, were released in June. Sheikh Salman bin Fahd al-'Awda and Sheikh Safr 'Abdul-Rahman al-Hawali were both prominent religious figures and critics of the system of the government in Saudi Arabia. They were arrested on 13 September 1994 and 17 September 1994 respectively,

after giving public lectures criticizing the government. They were both held in al-Ha'ir prison without charge or trial.

Torture and cruel, inhuman or degrading treatment or punishment
There were continuing reports of torture and cruel, inhuman or degrading treatment or punishment.

▭ Phil Lomax, a UK national who worked in Saudi Arabia, was arrested and beaten at night in May. He said that seven mutawa'een (religious police) and two government policemen entered his flat and kicked him, both before and after handcuffing him behind his back. They refused to tell him why they were there and destroyed personal effects including photographs and videos.

To AI's knowledge there was no investigation into the case of Ahmad bin Ahmad Mulablib, a prayer leader from al-Jufer village in al-Ihsa, who reportedly died in custody in November 1998.

New information came to light during 1999 concerning torture which had reportedly taken place in previous years.

▭ Roger Cortez, a Philippine national, who was released from prison in Riyadh in October 1999, was allegedly tortured when first arrested in 1997. His interrogators slapped him on his ears and pushed his face against the wall. He was beaten and kicked while wearing handcuffs and shackles, making it difficult to maintain his balance when hit or kicked, and for him to stand up again when he fell over. He was also threatened with a baseball bat. Roger Cortez was arrested in connection with a murder, but the precise nature of the charges against him, and his sentence, were unclear. He was released in October 1999, after receiving 250 lashes.

Judicial corporal punishments
Flogging and amputations continued to be imposed, although information about court cases and the carrying out of such punishments was limited.

▭ In May, two Philippine women were reportedly sentenced to 700 lashes each and two years' imprisonment for carrying out illegal abortions. However, no further details were available.

▭ In December a Ministry of the Interior statement, published in the local press, stated that Nuwiga' bin Faraj bin Hadar al-'Amiri and 'Ali bin 'Aeed bin Maful al-'Amiri each had a hand and a foot amputated. The men had reportedly been found guilty of highway robbery. The amputations were reported to have taken place in the city of Tabuk.

Death penalty
At least 103 executions were carried out during 1999. However, AI fears that the true number of people executed may have been much higher. Executions carried out were for various crimes including murder, rape, and drug smuggling. Of those that were announced, 64 were of foreign nationals. They included 15 individuals from Pakistan and 10 from Nigeria, as well as people from Afghanistan, India, Jordan, the Philippines, Indonesia, Ethiopia, Chad, Yemen, Syria and Thailand. At least three women were

executed, reportedly after being found guilty of drug smuggling. They were Hawa Faruk, Aishah Sa'adah Qasim and Safira Ounbiyi Salami, all Nigerian nationals.

A number of people sentenced to death were reportedly pardoned. They included Mohammad bin Abdullah al-Hajji, sentenced to death for murder. In October he was reportedly pardoned by the relatives of the victim just minutes before he was due to be executed.

The exact number of prisoners under sentence of death at the end of 1999 was not known as the government continued to keep such information secret. AI sought information from the government on scores of individuals understood to be sentenced to death or arrested in connection with capital offences in previous years.

Those sentenced to death included Sarah Dematera, a Philippine domestic worker who was convicted of murdering her employer in 1992.

Government communications

The government failed to respond to any letters from AI, including visa applications to attend the trial of Hani al-Sayegh. In September AI received a letter from the adviser to Saudi Arabia's ambassador to the UK. The letter indicated that Saudi Arabia was planning to ratify the International Covenant on Civil and Political Rights, the Convention on the Elimination of All Forms of Discrimination against Women and the International Covenant on Economic, Social and Cultural Rights. The letter also indicated that the government had plans to establish a national commission for human rights, a number of units concerned with human rights within specific ministries, and a non-governmental commission concerned with human rights. The letter did not give further details nor did it address a range of concerns that AI had brought to the government's attention. AI wrote to the ambassador seeking more details of the new initiatives.

Intergovernmental organizations

AI submitted information on Saudi Arabia for review by the UN Commission on Human Rights (CHR) under a procedure established by UN Economic and Social Council Resolutions 728F/1503 for confidential consideration of communications about human rights violations. AI's submission followed the CHR's decision, in 1998, to discontinue consideration of an earlier submission under the procedure.

SENEGAL

REPUBLIC OF SENEGAL
Head of state: Abdou Diouf
Head of government: Mamadou Lamine Loum
Capital: Dakar
Population: 9.4 million
Official language: French
Death penalty: abolitionist in practice
1999 treaty ratifications/signatures: Rome Statute of the International Criminal Court

Despite attempts to find a peaceful solution to the 17-year-old conflict in the Casamance region, tension remained high. Suspected supporters of the *Mouvement des forces démocratiques de Casamance* (MFDC), Democratic Forces of Casamance Movement, an armed opposition group claiming independence for Casamance, were detained without trial; many appeared to be prisoners of conscience. The security forces in Casamance were responsible for torture, "disappearances" and extrajudicial executions. Torture and ill-treatment by police were also reported in northern Senegal.

Background

There were several attempts during 1999 to open negotiations between the Senegalese government and the MFDC. In January President Abdou Diouf met the Secretary General of the MFDC, Father Augustin Diamacoune Senghor, for the first time. Although Father Diamacoune was under house arrest, he was authorized to travel to the Gambia on several occasions to consult MFDC members with a view to reaching a joint position, which would provide a starting point for negotiations with the Senegalese government. Finally in December, a first round of peace talks between the Senegalese authorities and the MFDC took place in Banjul, Gambia, and the opposing sides agreed to honour a 1993 cease-fire that had collapsed.

Political tension increased as the February 2000 elections grew nearer. The main opposition parties challenged the impartiality of the Minister of the Interior, General Lamine Cissé, who was responsible for organizing these elections. In July General Amadou Abdoulaye Dieng resigned from the presidency of the *Observatoire national des élections* (ONEL), National Observatory of Elections, after being accused by some opposition parties of being a supporter of President Diouf. There were also allegations of fraud in connection with national identity cards necessary for voting.

Detention without trial

Scores of suspected MFDC sympathizers remained in prison without trial throughout 1999. Most of these detainees appeared to be prisoners of conscience, arbitrarily arrested because they were members of the

Diola community. They were charged with "threatening state security" but no evidence was ever produced as to their individual responsibility for acts of violence. In February and December some 160 detainees who had been detained since 1995 were released after years of detention without trial.

There were new arrests in Casamance throughout 1999 and, at the end of the year, at least 30 people were held without trial in the prisons of Dakar and Ziguinchor.

Torture

Many Casamance civilians arrested by the security forces were tortured during the 10 days' incommunicado detention allowed by law before they had to be presented before a court. A number of them were reported to have been burned with petrol-filled plastic bottles set alight. None of these allegations were investigated.

Torture and ill-treatment were also reported in northern Senegal. In April about 40 people were arrested in Tamba after demonstrations against electricity cuts. Most were severely ill-treated and some were reportedly shaved with pieces of broken bottles. The police authorities denied these allegations, but no independent inquiry was opened.

In June, police broke up a peaceful demonstration which had been banned by the government. The demonstration had been called by 14 opposition parties to request transparency in the electoral process. A leader of an opposition party, Samir Abourzik, was hit on the head by a policeman and suffered a broken nose. Some days later, a formal complaint was lodged and an investigation was opened, but it had not concluded by the end of 1999.

Extrajudicial executions and 'disappearances'

As in previous years, the security forces in Casamance were responsible for dozens of extrajudicial executions and "disappearances". Most of the victims appeared to be civilians arrested in roadblock checkpoints or denounced by neighbours as supporters of the MFDC.

◻ In April, Moro Sadio, a 17-year-old schoolboy, was shot by a soldier in Thionck Essyl. The soldiers wanted to arrest his uncle, suspected of harbouring armed members of the MFDC.

◻ In August, several men wearing military clothes arrested Jean Diandy at his home. A friend who was arrested with him and released shortly later said that Jean Diandy was taken to the military camp of Ziguinchor. He then "disappeared". His family lodged a formal complaint in September and an investigation was opened, but had not concluded by the end of 1999.

Ziguinchor shelled

In April the town of Ziguinchor, the regional capital, was shelled for the first time, reportedly by armed elements within the MFDC. These shellings, which were carried out on three occasions, resulted in at least six dead and dozens of wounded among the civilian population. They were forcefully denounced by Father Diamacoune, and appeared to have been carried out by armed groups within the MFDC opposed to peace negotiations or feeling excluded from the decision-making process.

AI country reports and visits
Report
• Senegal: Casamance civilians shelled by the *Mouvement des forces démocratiques de Casamance* (MFDC), Democratic Forces of Casamance Movement (AI Index: AFR 49/005/99)
Visit
AI delegates visited Senegal in November to conduct research. The delegates met the Minister of Justice and the Secretary General of the MFDC. They visited Casamance to investigate human rights abuses.

SIERRA LEONE

REPUBLIC OF SIERRA LEONE
Head of state and government: Ahmad Tejan Kabbah
Capital: Freetown
Population: 4.4 million
Official language: English
Death penalty: retentionist

The political and human rights crisis deepened as rebel forces attacked Freetown in January 1999. Thousands of unarmed civilians were deliberately and arbitrarily killed, mutilated, raped or abducted. Although conclusion of a peace agreement in July provided opportunities to end human rights abuses, the political and security situation remained precarious and human rights abuses against civilians continued. The peace agreement included a general amnesty which provided impunity for human rights abuses, including war crimes and crimes against humanity, committed during the conflict.

Background

Rebel forces of the Revolutionary United Front (RUF) and the Armed Forces Revolutionary Council (AFRC) attacked Freetown on 6 January and committed large-scale atrocities against civilians. Extensive destruction of property made as many as 200,000 people homeless. Although rebel forces were forced to retreat by forces of the Economic Community of West African States (ECOWAS) Cease-fire Monitoring Group (ECOMOG), fighting continued in other parts of the country and some towns, including Makeni in Northern Province, remained under rebel control. Liberia was widely accused of providing military support to rebel forces, in violation of a UN Security Council resolution.

A cease-fire was agreed in May, and a peace agreement — signed in Lomé, Togo, in July — provided for an immediate cessation of hostilities and disarmament and demobilization of former combatants. RUF and AFRC members were appointed to ministerial positions in a government of national unity in October and the RUF became a political party. RUF leader Foday Sankoh, with the status of vice-president, chaired a commission to manage mineral resources and post-conflict reconstruction, and Johnny Paul Koroma, leader of the AFRC, a commission to oversee implementation of the peace process.

Implementation of key provisions of the peace agreement, including disarmament and demobilization, release of captured civilians and unhindered humanitarian access, was, however, limited. Full deployment of a UN peace-keeping force to monitor the cease-fire and assist with disarmament and demobilization was delayed. By the end of 1999 only some 3,500 of an estimated 45,000 combatants had been disarmed and demobilized. Despite the appointment of their leaders to official positions, political rivalry between AFRC and RUF forces resulted in heavy fighting, in particular in Makeni and Lunsar in October. Rifts also emerged between Foday Sankoh and other rebel leaders who had yet to disarm, and doubts remained about the commitment of the RUF to the peace process. Parts of the north and east of the country, including strategic diamond-mining areas, remained inaccessible.

Abuses by rebel forces
RUF and AFRC forces committed gross human rights abuses on a large scale. AI repeatedly called for an end to abuses and to transfers of arms, ammunition and combatants to rebel forces.

Despite improvement after the signing of the peace agreement, there was a marked increase in attacks on civilians from October in areas west of the Occra Hills and in Northern Province, in particular around Makeni, Lunsar, Port Loko, Kambia and Kabala, and a pattern of deliberate intimidation and terrorizing of civilians re-emerged. From November such attacks, often during raids for food, money and other goods, occurred almost daily in Northern Province.
Deliberate and arbitrary killings
Although it was impossible to ascertain the exact number of deaths during the rebel incursion into Freetown, an estimated 5,000 people, at least 2,000 of them civilians, were killed. Medical authorities subsequently put the figure at over 6,000. Although most killings were arbitrary, some individuals and groups — including government officials, journalists, lawyers, human rights activists, prison officials and police officers — were deliberately targeted. For example, more than 200 police officers and eight journalists were reported to have been killed.

After being forced from Freetown, rebel forces continued to commit atrocities. In Masiaka, east of Freetown, civilians accused of sympathizing with government forces were killed or mutilated. In one incident in a village between Masiaka and Mile 38, several babies and young children were reported to have been killed. Deliberate and arbitrary killings of

civilians continued after the peace agreement, particularly in Northern Province.
Torture, including mutilation and rape
As rebel forces retreated from Freetown, they mutilated civilians by cutting off limbs, most frequently hands and arms. In February reports indicated that some 500 victims of mutilation who required surgery were being treated in Freetown hospitals. Among the youngest recorded victims was a six-year-old girl whose left arm had been severed. It was probable that many other victims failed to reach medical help and died from their injuries.

Amputations and others forms of torture continued to be reported after rebel forces retreated from Freetown, although on a lesser scale. In May boys and young men in the area around Masiaka were seen with the letters RUF carved across their chests. In an attack on a village near Port Loko in October there were cases of attempted amputation of limbs, and burns inflicted by molten plastic.

Rape and other forms of sexual abuse of women and girls were systematic and widespread. During the rebel incursion into Freetown, women and girls were rounded up and gang-raped, often in public. More than 90 per cent of women and girls abducted and held captive were believed to have been raped: many were forced to submit to rape or be killed. Many girls subsequently released were pregnant, had given birth or had contracted sexually transmitted diseases. Rape of women and girls caught up in the fighting between AFRC and RUF forces in Makeni and Lunsar in October was common.
Abduction of civilians
Rebel forces abducted several thousand civilians, including children, from Freetown in January. Some of those abducted were subsequently killed. Some were selected for training as fighters, others used as porters to carry looted goods. Abducted women and girls were forced into sexual slavery and retained to cook and undertake other tasks. Up to 4,000 children were reported missing from Freetown, most of them abducted.

A small number of prominent Sierra Leoneans, including the Roman Catholic Archbishop of Freetown, and foreign nationals, including priests and nuns, were also abducted. At least eight were killed and two others seriously injured. Others, including the archbishop, either escaped or were released.

Although the peace agreement provided for the release of captured civilians, only some 1,000 adults and children, a comparatively small number, had been freed by December. Many of those released suffered from malnutrition and disease. The release of girls and young women was particularly difficult to secure. Some 2,400 children, most of them girls, abducted from Freetown remained missing.

As attacks against civilians increased from October, the number of civilians being abducted exceeded those released.
Hostage-taking
AFRC forces captured more than 30 UN military and civilian personnel who had gone to the Occra Hills in August with an ECOMOG escort to supervise the release

of abducted civilians. Their captors claimed that Johnny Paul Koroma was held under duress by RUF forces and that the peace agreement disadvantaged AFRC forces. All were released after six days.

In December RUF forces captured two foreign nationals working for an international humanitarian organization, *Médecins sans frontières* (MSF-France), in Kailahun District, Eastern Province, and held them hostage for 10 days in protest against disarmament and demobilization being supervised by UN peace-keeping forces and ECOMOG troops.

ECOMOG and Civil Defence Forces

ECOMOG forces were commended by the international community for their role in Sierra Leone. They and the civilian militia supporting President Ahmad Tejan Kabbah, the Civil Defence Forces (CDF), however, also committed human rights violations.

During the rebel incursion into Freetown, large numbers of captured or suspected rebels were extrajudicially executed by ECOMOG and the CDF, often without any real attempt to establish guilt or innocence. Children, including an eight-year-old boy caught in possession of a gun, were among the victims. Ill-treatment, including beatings, whippings and public humiliation, was common at ECOMOG and CDF checkpoints.

At least 10 Sierra Leonean staff of humanitarian organizations and the International Committee of the Red Cross were detained by ECOMOG forces in January; most were beaten. Although accused of cooperating with rebel forces, these allegations were unfounded.

Indiscriminate aerial bombardments on densely populated areas of Freetown during the rebel incursion resulted in large numbers of civilian casualties.

AI called for strict compliance by ECOMOG forces with international human rights and humanitarian law. In April the ECOWAS Executive Secretary called for an investigation into extrajudicial executions by ECOMOG forces but none took place. A committee subsequently established to monitor relations between ECOMOG forces and the civilian population failed to function effectively.

Reports of harassment and ill-treatment by ECOMOG forces continued in the months which followed. Detainees held by ECOMOG forces and the CDF were ill-treated, including by being beaten and having arms and hands tied extremely tightly. Civilians and humanitarian convoys travelling along major roads were frequently harassed.

Child combatants

Several thousand children under the age of 18 fought with rebel and CDF forces. An estimated 10 per cent of rebel forces who attacked Freetown were children, many of them previously abducted and frequently under the influence of drugs. Some were responsible for killings and mutilations.

Before the peace agreement, widespread recruitment of children by the CDF in Southern and Eastern Provinces continued. The peace agreement specified that particular attention be given to the issue of child combatants and the government made repeated commitments to end recruitment of children. Although the CDF subsequently demobilized some child combatants, it admitted in November that some 200 children aged between 15 and 18 were in its forces in the Kabala region and that there had been no effort to demobilize them.

In September the UN estimated that 5,400 child combatants were awaiting disarmament and demobilization; the real number, however, was likely to be much higher. Child combatants, including those who had been abducted, were still engaged in combat; in October a number of boys were among those injured in fighting between rebel forces.

AI called for priority to be given to disarmament, demobilization and reintegration of child soldiers and for adequate resources for agencies, including UNICEF, specifically helping them.

Refugees and internally displaced people

More than a million people were internally displaced and half a million were refugees, most of them in Guinea. Often still at risk of human rights abuses, they also suffered acute hardship including shortage of food and basic health care. In some areas up to 80 per cent of internally displaced people were reported to be children, many unaccompanied.

Delays in disarmament and demobilization, continuing insecurity and lack of access to parts of the country limited the return of internally displaced people and refugees.

Intergovernmental organizations

Human rights abuses and violations of the peace agreement by rebel forces were repeatedly condemned by the international community which took major initiatives to establish peace and security. An international contact group bringing together intergovernmental organizations and key governments met in April and July. AI called on the international community, including the UN and the World Bank, for protection and respect of human rights to be at the centre of efforts to resolve the political crisis and during post-conflict reconstruction.

A Human Rights Manifesto for Sierra Leone was adopted during a visit by the UN High Commissioner for Human Rights in June. It included commitments to promote children's rights and to raising the age of military recruitment to 18 years. It also pledged UN support for a Truth and Reconciliation Commission and a National Human Rights Commission, both subsequently included in the peace agreement.

In September, after visiting Sierra Leone, the Special Representative of the UN Secretary-General for Children and Armed Conflict proposed specific measures to meet the needs of children affected by the conflict.

In October the UN Security Council authorized the deployment of an international peace-keeping force of 6,000 troops as part of the UN Mission in Sierra Leone (UNAMSIL). The force, to include a substantial number of troops from ECOWAS countries, was to be deployed for an initial period of six months to help implement the peace agreement, in particular monitoring the cease-fire and the disarmament and demobilization of former combatants. The full complement of troops, however, had not been deployed by the end of 1999. A reduced ECOMOG force was to remain to maintain security and help implement the peace agreement with UNAMSIL. Subsequent plans to withdraw ECOMOG troops, however, prompted a recommendation by the UN Secretary-General in late December for a substantial increase in UNAMSIL troops. The UN peace-keeping force was mandated to protect civilians under imminent threat of physical violence, within its capabilities and areas of deployment.

Following the peace agreement, the UN Security Council agreed to expand the human rights section of UNAMSIL, including by appointing advisers on child protection. The human rights section monitored and reported abuses and promoted respect and protection of human rights. It was actively involved in securing the release of prisoners and captured civilians and in assisting in the establishment of the Truth and Reconciliation Commission and the National Human Rights Commission. It also provided human rights training for police and UN military observers and support for Sierra Leonean human rights groups. AI called for the human rights section to receive full political support and adequate resources.

In November the African Commission on Human and Peoples' Rights decided to send a delegation to Sierra Leone in early 2000.

Impunity
The peace agreement provided for a general amnesty for all acts undertaken in pursuit of the conflict. The Special Representative of the UN Secretary-General for Sierra Leone, signing the peace agreement as a moral guarantor, added a disclaimer that the UN did not recognize the amnesty as applying to genocide, crimes against humanity, war crimes, and other serious violations of international humanitarian law. It remained unclear, however, how impunity for such abuses would be addressed. While the Truth and Reconciliation Commission provided by the peace agreement could examine human rights abuses committed during the conflict, it could not alone establish full accountability because of the amnesty.

Shortly after the peace agreement was signed, the UN High Commissioner for Human Rights called for an international investigation into human rights abuses during the conflict and the UN Secretary-General acknowledged that the amnesty was difficult to reconcile with the goal of ending impunity. He suggested to the UN Security Council that it consider measures to ensure accountability for serious violations of human rights and humanitarian law, including the establishment of an international commission of inquiry. While noting the views of the Secretary-General, the Security Council neither explicitly supported nor endorsed such a commission, judging that insistence on accountability for human rights abuses at that stage would undermine the peace process.

In a letter to the Security Council in July, AI urged that it recommend an effective international mechanism for investigating human rights abuses and for bringing those responsible to justice. Although the High Commissioner's Office established a study on the possible relationship between the Truth and Reconciliation Commission and an international commission of inquiry, no recommendations were known to have been made by the end of the year.

AI country reports
- Sierra Leone: Escalating human rights crisis requires urgent action (AI Index: AFR 51/001/99)
- Sierra Leone: UN human rights presence reduced as abuses worsen (AI Index: AFR 51/003/99)
- Sierra Leone: Recommendations to the international contact group on Sierra Leone, New York, 19 April 1999 (AI Index: AFR 51/005/99)
- Sierra Leone: Mary Robinson's visit to Freetown – placing human rights centre stage (AI Index: AFR 51/006/99)
- Sierra Leone: A peace agreement but no justice (AI Index: AFR 51/007/99)
- Sierra Leone: The Security Council should clarify the United Nations' position on impunity (AI Index: AFR 51/010/99)
- Sierra Leone: Amnesty International's recommendations to the Commonwealth Heads of Government Meeting, Durban, South Africa, 12–15 November 1999 (AI Index: AFR 51/011/99)
- Sierra Leone: Escalating human rights abuses against civilians (AI Index: AFR 51/013/99)

SINGAPORE

REPUBLIC OF SINGAPORE

Head of state: S.R. Nathan (replaced Ong Teng Cheong in September)
Head of government: Goh Chok Tong
Capital: Singapore City
Population: 3.1 million
Official languages: Chinese, Malay, Tamil, English
Death penalty: retentionist

Freedom of expression continued to be curbed by an array of restrictive legislation and by the use of civil defamation suits against political opponents. Two members of an opposition party and at least 32 Jehovah's Witnesses were imprisoned during the year. The death penalty continued to be imposed but it was not known how many executions were carried out. Criminal offenders were also sentenced to caning.

Background

The ruling People's Action Party (PAP), in power since 1959, continued to dominate the political scene, with 80 of 83 elected seats in parliament. In September S.R. Nathan was sworn in as the new President of Singapore. Backed by the government, he was elected unopposed after several other potential contenders were declared ineligible. Only those who have served as a cabinet minister, chief justice, senior civil servant or as head of a large company are eligible to stand for the presidency.

There was continued concern that, while no new civil defamation suits were filed, this practice continued to be misused by government leaders to curb the right to freedom of expression and the right of political opponents to participate freely in public life. An array of restrictive legislation remained in place, further undermining the right to freedom of expression and engendering a climate of self-censorship.

Restrictions on freedom of expression

Dr Chee Soon Juan, Secretary-General of the opposition Singapore Democratic Party, was jailed twice in February for giving two speeches in public without a licence. For both convictions he was fined a total of 3,900 Singapore dollars (approximately US$2,340), but chose instead to serve two prison terms of seven and 12 days respectively. The Party's Assistant Secretary-General, Wong Hong Toy, was also imprisoned for 12 days after refusing to pay a fine for adjusting Dr Chee Soon Juan's microphone and the volume of the speaker. Both men were prisoners of conscience. They were also disqualified automatically from participating in elections for five years. However, in May their fines were reduced on appeal, allowing them to stand for elections in future.

Dr Chee Soon Juan was also fined in March for selling, without a permit, his book about the persecution of several prominent Asian dissidents. He had pleaded not guilty to the charge, claiming that book stores and vendors had refused to sell his books out of fear of prosecution. In August the police were reported to have refused him permission to hold two public rallies on "the need for political openness in Singapore".

In July Prime Minister Goh Chok Tong withdrew his petition to make J.B. Jeyaretnam, leader of the opposition Workers' Party, bankrupt. The petition stemmed from a civil defamation suit lodged by the Prime Minister against J.B. Jeyaretnam for allegedly defaming him at an election rally in 1997. J.B. Jeyaretnam, who lost the suit, had been unable to pay the full amount of damages awarded to the Prime Minister. AI had expressed concern at the high level of damages which appeared to be designed to bankrupt J.B. Jeyaretnam, thereby disqualifying him from parliament and curtailing his participation in public life.

In May the Court of Appeal dismissed an appeal by J.B. Jeyaretnam and the Workers' Party against a large defamation award for allegedly defaming a PAP parliamentarian and nine other members of the ethnic Tamil community in an article published in a Workers' Party newsletter in 1995. Although proceedings were suspended, J.B. Jeyaretnam continued to face bankruptcy and disqualification from parliament, and the Workers' Party faced closure, if they were unable to pay the award, amounting to 511,000 Singapore dollars (approximately US$307,000) including costs.

Conscientious objectors to military service

At least 32 conscientious objectors to military service were imprisoned during the year. All were members of the Jehovah's Witnesses, a religious group which has been banned in Singapore since 1972. The men refused to perform military service on religious grounds and were considered to be prisoners of conscience. There is no alternative civilian service for conscientious objectors to military service in Singapore.

Death penalty

The death penalty remained a mandatory punishment for drug trafficking, murder, treason and certain firearms offences. At least three death sentences were reported to have been passed during the year for drug trafficking or murder. The true number was believed to be higher.

It was difficult to obtain information about the number of death sentences passed and executions carried out during the year as the government does not publish statistics. However, newspapers reported that 11 executions by hanging were carried out between January and March alone. AI has recorded at least 190 executions since 1994, which means that in proportion to its population, Singapore has possibly one of the highest rates of executions in the world. The majority of executions are believed to have been for drug trafficking.

Cruel judicial punishment

Caning, which constitutes cruel, inhuman or degrading punishment, remained mandatory for some 30 crimes, including attempted murder, rape, armed robbery, drug trafficking, illegal immigration offences and vandalism. Drug addicts also face a mandatory caning sentence and imprisonment if they have been admitted more than twice to a drug rehabilitation centre. Caning may also be imposed for a number of other crimes, including extortion, kidnapping and causing grievous injury. It was not known how many sentences were carried out during the year. Juvenile offenders may be caned as a punishment.

▢ In October a 14-year-old boy, described in court by the prosecution as a "social monster", was sentenced to 10 strokes of the cane and five years' imprisonment for attacking and robbing an elderly man.

SLOVAKIA

SLOVAK REPUBLIC
Head of state: Rudolf Schuster (elected in May)
Head of government: Mikuláš Dzurinda
Capital: Bratislava
Population: 5.4 million
Official language: Slovak
Death penalty: abolitionist for all crimes
1999 treaty ratifications/signatures: Second Optional Protocol to the International Covenant on Civil and Political Rights, aiming at the abolition of the death penalty

There were reports of ill-treatment of Roma at the hands of law enforcement officials. One Rom died after he was shot during interrogation in police custody. A pattern of large-scale police operations which appeared to target entire Romani communities reportedly continued. Conscientious objectors to military service faced prosecution and imprisonment.

Roma
Large numbers of Slovak Roma, economically disadvantaged by social exclusion and discrimination and reportedly subject to racially motivated attacks by "skinheads", continued to seek asylum throughout Western Europe and Scandinavia. The authorities responded to international pressure over the treatment of Roma with a September strategy paper detailing a package of measures to improve their situation.

Roma continued to face ill-treatment at the hands of law enforcement officials, but the authorities failed to carry out prompt, impartial and thorough investigations into allegations of ill-treatment.

▢ Ľubomír ˇarisk˝ died in August after he was shot in the abdomen during interrogation while in police custody in Poprad.

A pattern of large-scale police operations, which appeared to target entire Romani communities instead of focusing on the arrest of individual criminal suspects, reportedly continued.

▢ Nearly 100 police, equipped with guns and dogs, arrived in the Romani settlement of Zehra at 6am on 2 December and ordered hundreds of people to stand outside their apartments under guard. Some police officers allegedly shouted racist abuse. They entered some apartments, reportedly damaging doors, windows and contents. They allegedly forced male occupants who were left inside to lie on the floor and beat them. A 14-year-old boy was injured by a rubber bullet and several Roma were refused treatment for their injuries by local doctors; this prompted allegations that doctors had been instructed by the police.

Conscientious objection
Milan Kobolka, a conscientious objector to military service, faced a possible maximum sentence of five years' imprisonment. The authorities continued to deny him the opportunity to perform alternative civilian service, justifying their refusal on the grounds that the 1995 Law on Civilian Service only permits such applications within 30 days of call-up. In a letter to the authorities in December, AI expressed concern about the intended prosecution of Milan Kobolka. It stressed that their actions contravened internationally recognized principles on conscientious objection and called for a judicial review.

AI country report
• Slovak Republic: Reported ill-treatment of Roma by police officers (AI Index: EUR 72/001/99)

SOLOMON ISLANDS

SOLOMON ISLANDS
Head of state: Queen Elizabeth II, represented by Moses Pitakaka
Head of government: Bartholomew Ulufa'alu
Capital: Honiara
Population: 0.4 million
Official languages: Melanesian Pidgin, English
Death penalty: abolitionist for all crimes

Throughout the year, violent inter-ethnic conflict in the context of land disputes led to widespread human rights abuses and suffering among thousands of displaced civilians. Emergency laws restricted public reporting about alleged human rights abuses, including deliberate killings and indiscriminate shootings of civilians, by both police and armed militant groups. The failure to investigate abuses and to bring those responsible to justice fuelled mistrust between ethnic groups and undermined peace initiatives.

Background

Long-running disputes escalated into widespread violence between islanders from Guadalcanal and local settlers from other provinces, mostly from Malaita. During the year, an estimated 32,000 people — almost a quarter of Guadalcanal's population — fled their homes because of police shootings and actual or threatened violence by organized armed groups known as "militants". In June, police roadblocks in Honiara temporarily prevented humanitarian supplies from reaching villagers. Hundreds of homes were burned down or looted. During the height of the conflict, government restrictions on information hampered adequate monitoring of the human rights situation by the international community. Fundamental rights and media reporting were limited by laws enacted under a four-month state of emergency which ended in October.

Shootings and brutality

There were reports of deliberate killings of civilians, by both militant groups and police; of police brutality during arrests; and of police indiscriminately shooting at village huts containing women and children. At least 13 people were reported killed and scores injured, although the real figures were believed to be much higher. There were reports that at least seven people were killed by police, some in suspicious circumstances. There were no impartial inquiries into these abuses. The trial of a police officer charged with the fatal shooting of a suspected militant in 1998 was continuing at the end of the year.

In early September a 16-year-old boy, who was reportedly unarmed, was confronted by police who shot him in the back and killed him as he ran away near Suaghi village, northeast of Honiara.

Kidnappings

Up to 20 people were reported missing, presumed kidnapped by rival ethnic groups. At least four were freed by police, released or found alive.

Prison conditions

Suspected members of militant groups and other prisoners were held in an overcrowded prison block lacking basic sanitation. Prison conditions amounted to cruel, inhuman and degrading treatment. Juvenile inmates were not held separately from adult prisoners and convicted prisoners were held together with those awaiting trial. Work on new prison buildings was halted for financial reasons.

Intergovernmental organizations

Commonwealth Special Envoy, former Prime Minister of Fiji Sitiveni Rabuka, negotiated two peace agreements, and the UN sent two humanitarian missions to the Solomon Islands. The mandate of an international Peace Monitoring Force — set up in October under the auspices of the Commonwealth and comprising Fijian and Vanuatu police officers supported by Australia and New Zealand — was extended into 2000. In November, the UN Committee on Economic, Social and Cultural Rights considered the situation in an extraordinary session with international agencies and non-governmental organizations.

AI country visit

AI delegates visited Guadalcanal and Malaita provinces in September to conduct research and meet government and community leaders.

SOMALIA

SOMALIA
Head of state and government: Somalia has no
functioning government
Capital: Mogadishu
Population: 6.9 million
Official language: Somali
Death penalty: retentionist

Somalia continued to witness widespread abuses of
human rights by the armed militias of clan-based
factions, who operated with impunity. Somalia has
had no judiciary or functioning court system since
the central government collapsed in 1991. Islamic
(Shari'a) courts formed militias and were themselves
involved in human rights abuses. They condemned to
death several prisoners who were subsequently
executed. Scores of deliberate and arbitrary killings
of unarmed civilians were carried out by clan-based
militias. Human rights abuses included abductions
and hostage-taking. Forced recruitment of child
soldiers and rape were widespread.

Background
Armed conflict
Continued fighting, especially in the south of the
country, imperilled hundreds of thousands of people
already at risk of famine.
Regional involvement
Eritrea and Ethiopia were directly involved in the inter-
factional fighting, with Ethiopia supplying troops,
hardware and humanitarian support to the Rahenweyn
Resistance Army (RRA) in Bay and Bakol. The RRA used
its increased military power to contain the advances of
Hussein Aideed's forces. Ethiopia also reportedly
supported the Somali Salvation Democratic Front
which had formed a government in the self-proclaimed
Puntland State, and a faction of the United Somali
Congress—Peace Movement.

Eritrea and Yemen provided arms to the Somali
National Alliance (SNA) militias of Hussein Aideed.
Around 200 fighters from the Ethiopian armed
opposition group the Oromo Liberation Front (OLF),
supported by Eritrea, were also involved in the Somali
conflict on the side of the SNA. Hussein Aideed
attended a series of meetings on peace and
reconciliation with Ethiopian government officials in
October. His forces subsequently disarmed a group of
OLF fighters in their base in Mogadishu.
Reconciliation
A national reconciliation plan proposed by Djibouti
President Ismael Omar Guelleh was endorsed by the Inter-
Governmental Authority on Development (IGAD) summit
in December and further discussions were due to take
place in Djibouti early in 2000. Ethiopia held discussions in
Addis Ababa and played a role as a mediator to the various
factions, despite being a party to the conflict. No
agreement emerged out of negotiations in Addis Ababa.

Somaliland Republic and Puntland State
The Somaliland Republic in the northwest, which
proclaimed its independence in 1991, continued to seek
international recognition. It enjoyed relative stability
and a functioning administration. Regular police and
militia were in place, but the judicial system faced
serious problems and did not function well.

Similarly, in the self-proclaimed Puntland Regional
State, some administrative structures were in place, but
the judicial system, largely based on clan courts, failed
to meet international standards.

Protection of civilians in conflict
Scores of unarmed civilians were killed in inter-
factional fighting during 1999. None of the factions
respected the principles of international
humanitarian law, which regulate the conduct of
armed conflict and protect civilians. The
International Committee of the Red Cross distributed
copies of the Geneva Conventions among the clan
militias, but unarmed civilians continued to be killed
indiscriminately. Civilians were neither warned nor
evacuated before areas were attacked, and were not
spared in the fighting. In fighting in the south,
factions did not differentiate between combatants,
civilians and wounded soldiers. Hospitals were
raided and patients, both civilians and wounded
soldiers, were killed. Civilians were also abducted
and taken as hostages. Rape was widespread in
villages under militia control and the forced
recruitment of children less than 15 years old into
combat was common.
☐ During fighting in Lower Juba region at least 47
people were killed and more than 60 wounded in
September. Entire villages were destroyed.

Killings of aid workers
There was a pattern of killings of local and
international staff working for humanitarian aid and
relief agencies. More than 10 people died in attacks on
relief agency vehicles and a number of aid workers
were targeted and killed.
☐ In September Dr Ayub Yarrow Abdiyow, a Somali
doctor working for UNICEF, was killed by gunmen who
ambushed his car between Afgoi and Jowhar town.
☐ Deena Umbarger, a US national consultant for the
Methodist Committee on Relief (UMCOR), was shot and
killed on March 20 as she was taking tea with town
elders, allegedly by the militia *al Itihad.*

Absence of rule of law
In the absence of a national police force or judiciary,
various clan-based militias established their own
courts and took over responsibility for policing and
judicial functions. Islamic and clan courts condemned
to death several prisoners who were subsequently
executed.
☐ In October Islamic court militias seized port
facilities, the police headquarters and the prison at
Merca. They claimed that they did so in order to
establish law and order. Nine people died during the
battle.

In December the militia of the Islamic Court in Mogadishu detained and beat the head of the editorial board of the *Qaran* newspaper. They accused him of undermining their efforts to restore peace in Somalia.

Somaliland
Freedom of expression came under threat in Somaliland. In October a reporter was detained on the orders of the Criminal Investigation Department, after publishing a report about malpractices by customs officials at Berbera.

Puntland Regional State
In November Colonel Abdullahi Yusuf, the leader of the Puntland Regional State, which proclaimed its autonomy in 1998, outlawed the carrying and possession of arms, except for the police and the administration's special forces.

In August, three journalists were arrested in Puntland after publishing reports critical of the authorities.

AI country report
• Human rights in Somaliland – Awareness and action, Report of a workshop held in Hargeisa, Somaliland, organized by AI and International Cooperation for Development (AI Index: AFR 52/001/99)

SOUTH AFRICA

REPUBLIC OF SOUTH AFRICA
Head of state and government: Thabo Mbeki (replaced Nelson Mandela in June)
Capital: Pretoria
Population: 42.4 million
Official languages: Afrikaans, English, Ndebele, Pedi, Sotho, Swazi, Tsonga, Tswana, Venda, Xhosa, Zulu
Death penalty: abolitionist for all crimes

There were frequent reports of police torture and ill-treatment and unjustified use of lethal force while investigating crime. Asylum-seekers and suspected illegal immigrants were also victims of official ill-treatment or racially motivated attacks. Politically motivated violence continued in parts of the country. Trial proceedings began against the former head of the Chemical and Biological Warfare program in connection with killings of opponents of the former apartheid government.

Background
In June a new government under President Thabo Mbeki was elected into office after largely peaceful elections.

Public anger and international concern over high rates of violent crime, allegations of police corruption and a spate of fatal bombings in Western Cape province placed pressure on the government to protect communities against crime. The increasing number of vigilante assaults and killings underscored public loss of faith in the criminal justice system.

The government established a new national priority crime investigation unit, the "Scorpions", under the authority of the National Director of Public Prosecutions (NDPP). President Mbeki's government introduced legislation to tighten controls over gun ownership, but delayed implementing the 1998 amendment to the Criminal Procedure Act. This would restrict the police use of lethal force unless proportionate to the threat posed to life. The government also requested the Law Commission to review the period allowed for interrogation of suspects without charge.

Human rights violations by the security forces
There were reports of torture, ill-treatment and unjustified use of lethal force by the security forces, including specialized police squads such as the Murder and Robbery, Firearms and Dog Units; the Municipal Police; and the South African National Defence Force stationed in Gauteng and KwaZulu Natal provinces. The Independent Complaints Directorate (ICD), responsible for investigating deaths in custody or as a result of police action and other serious alleged violations, received reports of 363 deaths as a result of police action, 153 deaths in police custody and 28 alleged incidents of torture between April and December 1999.

There were other cases of torture during crime investigation.

In February, in the Johannesburg area of Townsview, members of a security firm, BBR, beat and kicked 19-year-old Archie Ngubalane, whom they had handcuffed to a railing and accused of an attempted stabbing. They threatened to shoot a relative who tried to intervene. Police failed to arrest the BBR members for assault, but arrested Archie Ngubalane and detained him at Booysens police station, where he was denied proper medical care. He was subsequently charged with attempted murder, denied bail and transferred to Diepkloof Prison, where he was again denied proper medical care, including for epilepsy. He was released on bail in August and acquitted of the charge in September. No progress had been made in the police investigation of his complaint against BBR for assault.

In August police at Bayview station in Durban arrested and severely assaulted four teenage boys in connection with a robbery. One died within 24 hours of his arrest. The police allegedly hit them with broom handles and kicked and punched them in the station parking lot, before transferring them to Chatsworth police station where they were locked in a freezing, filthy cell. Although the detainees pleaded for medical treatment, the police allegedly refused.

Certain police units were frequently linked to allegations of torture, including the Brixton Murder and

Robbery Unit in Johannesburg. In October government lawyers conceded that Unit members had tortured 54-year-old Lucy Themba and 24-year-old Charlotte Pharamela in June 1996. Both women, who were being interrogated about the whereabouts of Lucy Themba's son, had been assaulted during arrest and subjected to electric shocks and suffocation torture while tied by their arms and legs to chairs.

Shaheed Cajee was arrested in October in connection with possession of stolen goods and was allegedly subjected to electric shocks and smothered with a wet bag while tied naked and blindfolded to a chair at Unit headquarters. He signed a statement under duress and was transferred to Diepkloof prison pending his trial.

The Director of Public Prosecutions (DPP) declined to prosecute most of the police officers investigated for involvement in beatings, inflicting cigarette burns, and setting police dogs on arrested criminal suspects. The incidents, which had been filmed by a television journalist, had been publicly broadcast in April. However, the DPP ordered two officers from the Brixton Flying Squad to be prosecuted for assault with intent to do grievous bodily harm.

Excessive use of lethal force by police emerged in a number of cases where evidence suggested that criminal suspects had been deliberately killed by police when they posed no threat to life. In May the ICD arrested a Hout Bay police officer after he had allegedly shot dead suspected robber Dumisane Zwane while he was lying injured on the ground. The DPP ordered the officer, who had been released on bail in June, to be prosecuted for murder and defeating the ends of justice. Three other officers from Hout Bay police station were also charged as accessories.

Political killings

Government officials accused the anti-crime vigilante group People Against Gangs and Drugs (PAGAD) of politically motivated terrorism after a series of bomb attacks on Cape Town police stations and the Wynberg regional court, and attacks on police officers investigating crimes linked to PAGAD. Some Muslim critics of PAGAD tactics had their homes bombed or were victims of "drive-by" shootings. During 1999 independent investigations indicated that there may have been police and intelligence agency involvement in certain bombing incidents blamed on PAGAD.

On 8 January, 22-year-old Yusuf Jacobs was shot by police who were attempting to disperse a demonstration by Muslim organizations against the visit to Cape Town by the British Prime Minister. A number of others were injured, including a journalist. Yusuf Jacobs, who was dragged from the scene by the police, died in hospital four days later. The ICD had not concluded its investigation by the end of 1999. In the wake of Yusuf Jacobs' death PAGAD officials reportedly denounced the government and threatened to kill police officers in revenge.

On 14 January, Captain Benny Lategan, who was leading an investigation into PAGAD-linked crimes, was shot dead in a drive-by shooting. In the following days police raided homes of PAGAD members and allegedly assaulted them with fists, gun butts and other objects.

Political tensions and violence continued in KwaZulu Natal, including in the volatile Richmond area. The assassination on 23 January of Sifiso Nkabinde, General Secretary of the United Democratic Movement, was followed by other acts of violence and killings in Richmond. Eleven members of one African National Congress (ANC) supporting household in Maswazini, Richmond, were shot dead in their sleep on 23 January. On the same night a military patrol shot and killed Mbongoleni Mtolo, one of Sifiso Nkabinde's bodyguards, in disputed circumstances. He was due to appear in court charged in connection with the July 1998 Richmond "tavern massacre". In November the trial of seven men in connection with Sifiso Nkabinde's murder began in the Pietermaritzburg High Court amid concerns for the safety of witnesses, investigators and lawyers involved. In the same month police arrested suspects in the Maswazini massacre, including four members of an infantry battalion involved in patrolling the Richmond area earlier in the year.

Impunity

The Amnesty Committee of the Truth and Reconciliation Commission (TRC) continued hearings on hundreds of remaining amnesty applications. The Committee announced in December that it had granted amnesty to some 560 applicants and refused it to nearly 10 times that number. Among other decisions made public in 1999, the Committee refused amnesty to three former security police officers in connection with the 1977 death in custody of Black Consciousness leader Steve Biko and to Janusz Walus and Clive Derby-Lewis convicted for the 1993 assassination of former ANC military leader Chris Hani. The Committee granted amnesty to, among others, a serving police officer, Jeffrey Benzien, for "politically motivated" acts of torture of apartheid government opponents, and to six former members of a covert military "hit squad" responsible for scores of assassinations in KwaZulu Natal in the early 1990s.

The NDPP established a unit to investigate possible prosecutions of perpetrators of past human rights violations who had failed to receive amnesty or to cooperate with the TRC.

The former head of the apartheid-era Chemical and Biological Warfare (CBW) program, Dr Wouter Basson, appeared in the Pretoria High Court in October, to face a range of charges including multiple counts of murder and attempted murder of opponents of the apartheid government. However, shortly after the trial began the presiding judge set aside six conspiracy to murder charges relating to planned or actual murders in the 1980s of former government opponents abroad, including the murder of about 200 imprisoned members of the South West African People's Organization (SWAPO). The judge ruled that South African courts did not have the jurisdiction to try these crimes. In October survivors of past human rights violations publicly protested against the government's failure to implement the TRC's recommendations for financial and other reparations to thousands of victims.

Human rights defenders

Human rights activists, lawyers and members of official investigation bodies were subjected to malicious prosecutions, death threats or physical attacks as a result of their work.

⌐ Members of the Violence Investigation Unit (VIU), responsible for investigating politically motivated violence in northern KwaZulu Natal, came under sustained gunfire on 14 April when trying to recover the body of Vasi Ntuli. He had been shot and abducted on 29 March by men linked to a local councillor and "warlord", acting with the complicity of the local police. A member of the VIU was injured and their vehicle damaged.

⌐ In May Brixton Murder and Robbery Unit police arrested two human rights lawyers who had been gathering evidence near the police station in corroboration of alleged torture by Unit members of two security guards in April. The police seized a camera, notepad and mobile phone from them and locked the lawyers in a cell, before charging them under the 1959 Correctional Services Act which prohibits the photographing of prisons and police stations. They were released provisionally. The charges were withdrawn in October.

Refugee concerns

Violations of the rights of refugees and migrants were detailed in a report published in March by the South African Human Rights Commission in collaboration with non-governmental organizations from the National Consortium on Refugee Affairs. The report documented a pattern of arbitrary arrest, extortion, degrading verbal abuse and assault targeted at people of "foreign appearance". It also described a pattern of prolonged, unlawful detentions at the Lindela Repatriation Facility and found that a number of people had been returned to their country of origin in spite of having a *prima facie* claim for refugee status.

In November the Commission obtained a High Court ruling ordering Lindela to release 41 named detainees who had been held for many months longer than the permitted 30-day period.

⌐ A police officer from Brixton police station verbally abused, assaulted and unlawfully detained Dr Frank Nyame, a Ghanaian research scientist, claiming that he was an "illegal immigrant". On 18 April Dr Nyame was accosted in the street by two white men in plain clothes, one of whom demanded to see his immigration papers and attempted to force him into a nearby police vehicle. When he later complained at Brixton police station, one of the two men, now in police uniform, told him he was under arrest and knocked him unconscious. After he had recovered consciousness he was locked in a cell and, despite repeated requests to see a doctor, was given no medical treatment. He was released after some hours.

⌐ On 10 April an asylum-seeker from Burundi, Charles Manirakiza, was attacked and killed by a number of white men in the Sunnyside area of Pretoria. During the attack neighbours and friends tried to obtain police assistance, but the police allegedly refused to intervene. He died while police were at the scene. A post-mortem indicated that he had been strangled to death. His body also had multiple abrasions and bruising. Three suspects were charged in the Pretoria magistrate's court with murder and were released on bail in May. Some witnesses were forced to move away from the area because of intimidation and threats.

The courts ruled in a number of cases that the police had acted unlawfully. In October an inquest magistrate ruled that the Cape Town police were *prima facie* responsible for the death in June 1997 of Jean-Pierre Kanyangwa, a Burundian asylum-seeker, by negligently failing to take him to hospital. In the same month a Zimbabwean citizen, Thabani Ndlodlo, was awarded damages after the state conceded that two police officers had unlawfully assaulted him and shot him in the legs, had maliciously prosecuted him on criminal charges and had wrongfully detained him for 446 days. The Randburg regional court had acquitted him on all charges in May 1999 after finding the police had lied to the court.

AI country reports and visits
Reports and public statements
- South Africa: Human Rights Day – preserving human rights gains (AI Index: AFR 53/002/99)
- South Africa: Torture and misuse of lethal force by security forces must end (AI Index: AFR 53/005/99)
- South Africa: Establishing a culture of accountability for human rights violations (AI Index: AFR 53/006/99)
- South Africa: No impunity for perpetrators of human rights abuses (AI Index: AFR 53/010/99)
- South Africa: Mengistu – the opportunity for justice must not be lost (AI Index: AFR 53/012/99)
- South Africa: Mengistu – failure to respect international human rights obligations (AI Index: AFR 53/013/99)
- Forensic Medicine and Ethics: A workshop on the application of forensic skills to the detection and documentation of human rights violations, Durban, July 1998 (AI Index: ACT 75/012/99)

Visits
An AI delegate visited South Africa in April and August to conduct research into developments affecting human rights.

SPAIN

KINGDOM OF SPAIN
Head of state: King Juan Carlos I de Borbón
Head of government: José María Aznar López
Capital: Madrid
Population: 39.3 million
Death penalty: abolitionist for all crimes

In November the Basque armed group *Euskadi Ta Askatasuna* (ETA), Basque Homeland and Freedom, announced that it was ending its indefinite cease-fire. The Basque peace process had survived more than a year, although troubled by serious and persistent "street violence" by some nationalist groups and allegations that law enforcement officers continued to torture suspected ETA members. Judges pursued investigations into the 1980s "dirty war" waged against ETA by the *Grupos Antiterroristas de Liberación* (GAL), Anti-terrorist Liberation Groups, which included officers of the security forces and hired gunmen linked at the highest levels with the former Spanish administration. In December, 16 years after the abduction of two suspected ETA members, José Antonio Lasa and José Ignacio Zabala, the trial opened before the National Court of suspected GAL members, including a former Civil Guard general, a former civil governor of Guipúzcoa, two former Civil Guard officers, and a former secretary of state for security. Charges included murder of the two men, belonging to an armed band, and illegal detention. There were allegations of ill-treatment in police custody and many prisoners alleged ill-treatment by custodial staff. Excessive force was attributed to Civil Guards in cases of shootings of unarmed civilians, and police officers were criticized for disproportionate action against demonstrators in various parts of Spain. Effective impunity continued to be enjoyed by law enforcement officers charged with or convicted of acts of torture and ill-treatment. As thousands of immigrants, including some children, attempted to cross from North Africa to Spain in tiny boats and rubber dinghies, many perishing in the Straits of Gibraltar, there were growing concerns about racist attacks on sub-Saharan and North African immigrants in various parts of Spain.

Basque peace process

In June, a year after the last killing carried out by ETA, AI published a report stressing the belief that respect for human rights is vital to the future of peace in Spain and the Basque Country. The report urged the Spanish authorities to revoke immediately the laws under which terrorism suspects can be held incommunicado for up to five days with access only to officially appointed lawyers, subject to special restrictions. It also recommended abandoning the practice of incommunicado detention and that of blindfolding and

hooding detainees. It called for interrogations to be recorded on video both as a safeguard for detainees and as a means of protecting Civil Guards and police officers from false accusations. The report welcomed the introduction of a law awarding compensation to victims of "terrorist acts" since 1968, but stressed the need for a review of all cases since that time involving conviction of public officials for torture or serious injury and ill-treatment, to ensure that those victims too received fair compensation. The authorities were urged to ensure that the GAL suspects — most of whose trials were still pending — were tried in accordance with international norms, free of any taint of impunity. AI recommended that the authorities reverse the practice of dispersing Basque prisoners throughout the Spanish peninsula, islands and the Spanish North African enclaves of Ceuta and Melilla.

AI separately called on ETA to put an immediate and definitive end to killings, kidnappings and hostage-taking, and to cease committing violent and intimidatory acts, such as arson, bombings and death threats, which had continued against political representatives, companies, newspapers, judicial figures, law enforcement officers and others since the beginning of the cease-fire.

In October the Spanish Interior Ministry replied that it was satisfied that the security forces and courts were rigorous custodians of the constitutional rights of all detainees and defendants. It also stated that, in September, it had decided to transfer 105 ETA prisoners to prisons closer to their homes, including in the Basque Country.

In November, after ETA declared the end of the cease-fire, AI again appealed to the group to respect human rights, irrespective of the existence of a peace process, and stated that human rights were never negotiable.

Alleged torture, ill-treatment and excessive force

Individual ETA suspects continued to allege that acts of torture or ill-treatment were inflicted upon them by Civil Guards or national police officers at time of arrest, during transit to police stations or Civil Guard premises, and while being held incommunicado. There were persistent references to asphyxiation by the placing of a plastic bag over the head and to repeated beatings and forced exercises during interrogation. Some suspects alleged they had been sexually abused.

Complaints of ill-treatment, including beatings with truncheons, punches, kicks and slaps, were also made by people detained in various parts of Spain by local police, national police, Civil Guards and the Basque autonomous police, *Ertzaintza*.

In January a baton charge by national police officers against students demonstrating at the *Universidad Autónoma de Barcelona* (UAB), Autonomous University of Barcelona, reportedly resulted in injuries to 19 people, including five officers. In September the High Court of Justice of Catalonia ruled that the police action was "disproportionate", obstructing the students' right to freedom of expression and assembly. Other reports referred to excessive use of force by police against North African immigrants queuing for work in Jaen in January and against demonstrators, mainly of North African origin, seeking compensation for flood damage in Ceuta in October, when up to 17 people were reportedly injured. Violent attacks on immigrants by neo-Nazi groups and others in Catalonia, Andalusia and the Canary Islands were being investigated by the police and Civil Guard.

☐ ETA suspect Nekane Txarpartegi was arrested in Tolosa (Guipúzcoa) in March by Civil Guards. She was reportedly held incommunicado for five days. She alleged that, before being taken for interrogation in Madrid, she was driven to a wood near Etxegarate. During the journey she was hit on the head and shoulder. She was forced to get out of the car and kneel and a gun was pointed at her head in a simulation of execution. Insulating tape was placed round her hands and legs, her hands were cuffed, her legs tied with a cord and her head covered with a plastic bag (practice known as "la bolsa"). She was then beaten again. She claimed that throughout the days of interrogation by Civil Guards at Tres Cantos, Madrid, she was held under restraint and beaten mainly by "protected" hands on her head and shoulder, continually subjected to the bolsa, sexually abused, with fingers inserted in her vagina, threatened with rape, and kicked each time she fell to the ground. She later received treatment at the Hospital Gregorio Marañon. A medical report from the prison of Soto del Real (Madrid) referred to a number of injuries.

Alleged ill-treatment in prisons

Reports were received of ill-treatment by custodial staff, as well as of poor conditions and medical neglect, involving prisoners from Villabona (Asturias), Ponent Lleida (Barcelona), Badajoz, Soto del Real (Madrid), Villanubla (Valladolid), Dueñas (Palencia), Jaen II and elsewhere. There were complaints that punishment of prisoners included shackling them to a bed for many hours or even days. In some instances a single case of suspected ill-treatment appeared to set off a chain reaction among prisoners who, after protesting about ill-treatment of other inmates, were themselves ill-treated. Often counter-complaints were lodged against prisoners by guards. The non-governmental human rights association Asociación Pro Derechos Humanos de España investigated conditions in 24 prisons. Its report, partly funded by the prison administration service, referred to ill-treatment, overcrowding, medical neglect, poor food, lack of activities and a general failure to individualize treatment.

☐ Jesús Amador del Val, imprisoned at La Moraleja (Dueñas-Palencia), claimed that in March he was beaten by eight guards in an exercise yard after he had accidentally stumbled against a guard while passing through a metal detector. He alleged that he was shackled to a bed by arms and feet for 18 hours before a doctor arrived. Two other prisoners, José Quilis Iniesta and Daniel Ramírez Córdoba, in an adjacent yard, claimed they heard Jesús Amador del Val, who has AIDS,

shouting for his medication and then being beaten. They alleged that, after making a protest, they were themselves beaten, while restrained, by up to 15 guards, both in the yard and later in their cells. After the beating they too were shackled to their beds with their arms crossed for 18 hours, without food or water. Hearing the beating, a fourth prisoner, José Martínez Camino, reportedly set fire to his cell in an attempt to raise the alarm, and was then in his turn beaten and placed for several days in an isolation cell. Judicial complaints were lodged by Jesús Amador del Val, Daniel Ramírez and José Quilis and by the latter's mother, María Dolores Iniesta Martínez, who said she had seen her son covered with bruises. Some prison guards reportedly also lodged complaints of assault against the prisoners.

Civil Guard shootings

There were several reports of Civil Guard shootings, some fatal, of unarmed civilians. They appeared to involve excessive use of force and judicial inquiries were conducted during the year. According to law, arms may only be used where there is a reasonably serious risk to the life or physical integrity of an officer or to that of third persons. The death of a woman in Seville in April focused attention on a number of other serious incidents.

☐ In April Miriam Gómez Cuadrado, a passenger in a friend's car attempting to escape a breathalyzer test, died after being shot by a Civil Guard in Seville. Two officers pursued the car for four kilometres before one, a shooting instructor, aimed his gun at the car. A bullet pierced the left rear door and struck the frame of the driver's seat before entering Miriam Gómez' left lung and heart and lodging in the pelvis. The officer, who reportedly maintained he had, in legitimate defence, fired at a back tyre to stop the car, was suspended from work and remained at conditional liberty pending the result of a judicial inquiry. An internal Civil Guard inquiry reportedly questioned whether there could be "well-founded reasons" for deploying a weapon in such circumstances, even though the driver had made "risky manoeuvres".

Effective impunity of law enforcement officers

In September the Interior Minister withdrew the award of a medal to a lieutenant-colonel of the Civil Guard suspected of involvement in two GAL crimes. In addition, the Defence Ministry reportedly froze the promotion to colonel of another Civil Guard officer, allegedly involved in the murder in 1984 by GAL of Santiago Brouard, a leading member of the Basque nationalist coalition party, Herri Batasuna. However, lengthy judicial proceedings, token sentences and the availability of pardons continued to cast doubt on the will of the courts and authorities to eliminate torture and ill-treatment by public officials. In July, three Civil Guards convicted of the illegal detention and torture of ETA member Kepa Urra Guridi were partially pardoned by the Council of Ministers. This ensured that, despite a September 1998 Supreme Court ruling that the officers had indeed committed acts of torture, they would remain in service. Another concern was the refusal of police officers to provide evidence against fellow officers charged with a crime and the consequent avoidance of conviction.

⬁ In April the Supreme Court severely criticized the fact that it was forced to confirm the acquittal of three national police officers charged with the beating and rape of Rita Margarete R., a Brazilian woman, while in custody in Bilbao in 1995. In 1998 the Provincial Court of Vizcaya accepted that she had been beaten and raped at the police station, but acquitted the officers charged because of lack of evidence identifying those responsible. The Supreme Court was reported as saying that it was incompatible with the democratic rule of law that an "extremely serious and proven case of rape" remained unpunished because of "archaic corporativist ideas or false camaraderie". Two officers were subsequently suspended from duty pending further inquiries.

AI country report
• Spain: A briefing on human rights concerns in relation to the Basque peace process (AI Index: EUR 41/001/99)

SRI LANKA

DEMOCRATIC SOCIALIST REPUBLIC OF SRI LANKA
Head of state and government: Chandrika Bandaranaike Kumaratunga
Capital: Colombo
Population: 18 million
Official languages: Sinhala, Tamil, English
Death penalty: abolitionist in practice

Grave human rights abuses were reported in the context of the protracted armed conflict between the security forces and the Liberation Tigers of Tamil Eelam (LTTE), the main armed opposition group fighting for an independent state, Eelam, in the north and east of the country. Hundreds of thousands of civilians were displaced as a result of the conflict. Both the government and the LTTE manipulated their freedom of movement and their access to food and medicine. The government took some steps to address past human rights violations by the security forces, including exhuming the remains of 15 people who were reported to have "disappeared" in mid-1996. Members of the LTTE were responsible for deliberate and arbitrary killings of civilians, torture, hostage-taking and abductions. The government announced an end to the practice of automatic commutation of death sentences in force since 1976.

Background
A state of emergency remained in force throughout the country. Press censorship declared under the state of emergency in mid-1998 also remained in force. There were several reports of attacks on journalists.

There were various initiatives within civil society aimed at resolving the conflict, including by the business community and relatives of security forces personnel missing in action. On the other hand, several groups within the Sinhalese community became more vociferous in their campaign against negotiations with the LTTE. Government efforts to introduce constitutional reforms to solve the ethnic conflict remained deadlocked, and talks with the LTTE which had broken down in 1995 did not resume.

President Chandrika Bandaranaike Kumaratunga was re-elected in December.

Impunity
While some important steps were taken to address past human rights violations by the security forces, the longstanding problem of impunity remained a major concern. A school principal and six army personnel were convicted and sentenced to 10 years' imprisonment in connection with the "disappearance" of a group of young people at Embilipitiya in late 1989 and early 1990. Two members of the security forces, including the son of the principal, were acquitted at the trial, which ended in February. Both the state and the defendants appealed against the judgment.

The Criminal Investigation Department and the Attorney General's department proceeded with investigations and prosecutions in cases recommended by three presidential commissions of inquiry into involuntary removal and disappearances. By the end of the year, 213 such cases had been filed in High Courts. A fourth presidential commission of inquiry, set up in May 1998 to investigate complaints which the three earlier commissions had not examined, continued its work.

In June and September, the bodies of 15 people who "disappeared" in 1996 were recovered from shallow graves in the Chemmani area of Jaffna. International forensic experts, including from AI, observed the exhumations. Criminal investigations to identify those responsible continued, but by the end of 1999 no one had been arrested.

By the end of 1999, no one had been convicted in relation to the crime of torture in Sri Lanka. However, early in the year, there were press reports that a number of police officers had been charged under Sri Lanka's Convention against Torture and Other Cruel, Inhuman or Degrading Treatment or Punishment Act of November 1994. The cases were reportedly those in which the Supreme Court had found police officers responsible for torture, awarded compensation and recommended further investigation with a view to prosecution.

Political prisoners
Thousands of Tamil political prisoners, including possible prisoners of conscience, were arrested under the Emergency Regulations and the Prevention of

Terrorism Act, which allow for long-term detention without charge or trial. As of early September, 764 detainees were held without charge or trial at Kalutara prison and scores more were held at other places.

There were reports of secret detention, particularly in small army camps in Jaffna and camps run by the People's Liberation Organization of Tamil Eelam (PLOTE), an armed Tamil group operating alongside the security forces in Vavuniya.

☐ Sivam Ashokumar, who was secretly held by PLOTE for 39 days, reported that he was held in chains for 26 days and badly beaten on his chest, legs and hands with a pole and electric wire.

Torture

Torture, including rape, remained common, both in the context of the armed conflict and during routine policing operations. Reports of torture of people arrested on suspicion of involvement with the LTTE were received from all parts of the north and east.

☐ In Colombo, police at Mirihana police station tortured three students arrested on 25 August by hanging them by their wrists and beating them all over their bodies.

☐ Anthonipillai Binoth Vimalraj, was tortured during interrogation at Kotahena police station. Police allegedly beat him all over his body, inserted pins under his fingernails and an iron rod into his anus.

'Disappearances'

There were reports of "disappearances" from Batticaloa (five), Vavuniya, Killinochchi, Colombo and Mannar districts. During a visit in October, the UN Working Group on Enforced or Involuntary Disappearances examined the implementation of recommendations for the prevention and investigation of "disappearances" made during previous visits in 1991 and 1992. It urged the government to establish an independent investigation into the estimated 540 "disappearances" reported from Jaffna district in 1996.

☐ Among those reported "disappeared" from Batticaloa district were 50-year-old Eliyathamby Narayanapillai and 47-year-old Poopalapillai Thiagarajah, two farmers from Mandur who had reported to the local police station on 14 January. Police claimed they were released, but they failed to return home. It is feared that they died under interrogation. Their "disappearance" was investigated by the Human Rights Commission and the Committee against Undue Arrest and Harassment but they failed to establish their fate or whereabouts. No action was initiated against the police.

Violations of international humanitarian principles

The armed conflict has been described as a "no mercy war", given the number of combatants on both sides who appeared to have been deliberately killed on the battlefield instead of being arrested. This practice appeared to continue throughout 1999.

There was heightened concern about violations of international humanitarian principles by both sides. The killing of 23 civilians in a bombing raid by the Air Force in the Puthukkudiyiruppu area of Mullaitivu district in September indicated a lack of precautions to avoid harming civilians. The government claimed it had hit an LTTE camp, whereas independent sources confirmed that all those killed were civilians. The government later stated that the attack had been a "mistake".

In November, 40 displaced civilians were killed when at least three shells hit Madhu church. The exact circumstances of the shelling were difficult to establish, but it was clear that both the security forces and the LTTE were aware that civilians were sheltering in the church. Neither side took all necessary measures to prevent civilian casualties.

Human rights abuses by the LTTE

There were ominous signs that the LTTE might be returning to large-scale deliberate attacks on civilians in Colombo and areas bordering the north and east, a practice from which it had largely refrained over the last three years. More than 50 Sinhalese civilians were killed in a pre-dawn raid on three villages in Amparai district. The deliberate targeting of members of parliament and local councillors belonging to Tamil political parties represented in parliament also became more pronounced.

☐ On 29 July, a prominent member of parliament and member of the Tamil United Liberation Front, Dr Neelan Thiruchelvam, was killed on his way to work by a suicide bomber. In Jaffna, the total number of local councillors killed for not complying with orders by the LTTE to resign from their post rose to 11. Among those killed was 50-year-old Bandari Kandasamy, of the Eelam People's Democratic Party, who was shot dead on his way home from church in February.

☐ In two attacks on election rallies in and near Colombo on 18 December, at least 25 civilians were killed. Numerous others, including President Chandrika Bandaranaike Kumaratunga and four ministers, were injured.

Child soldiers

Throughout the year the LTTE continued to recruit children as combatants. There was little sign of the commitment given by the LTTE leadership to the UN Secretary General's Special Representative for Children and Armed Conflict in May 1998 that it would not use children below 18 years of age in combat, and would not recruit under 17 years. AI obtained a copy of a pamphlet dated 3 June 1999 circulated by LTTE leaders in Batticaloa district to school principals, appealing for people to "join in thousands". The pamphlet did not refer to any age limit.

☐ A 13-year-old boy from the Muttur area in Trincomalee who had been recruited by the LTTE in February and had twice managed to escape from their camp, was on each occasion forcibly taken back. The second time, he was beaten as a punishment.

Death penalty

In March, amid reports of rising crime, the government announced that death sentences would no longer be automatically commuted when they come before the

President. Instead a policy was put in place whereby the President would refrain from commutation if the judge in the case, the Attorney General and the Minister of Justice unanimously recommended execution. AI expressed concern about this retrograde step for Sri Lanka after 23 years of being a *de facto* abolitionist state.

AI country report
• Sri Lanka: Torture in custody (AI Index: ASA 37/010/99)

SUDAN

REPUBLIC OF THE SUDAN
Head of state and government: Omar Hassan Ahmad al-Bashir
Capital: Khartoum
Population: 32.6 million
Official language: Arabic
Death penalty: retentionist

The war dominated Sudan in 1999 and the human rights situation deteriorated significantly. People taking no active part in the hostilities faced gross human rights abuses by all parties to the conflict, massive internal displacement and widespread disruptions to food supplies. Human rights abuses in contested areas included indiscriminate bombing, abductions and enslavement, and deliberate and arbitrary killings of civilians. The activities of oil companies in the southern region resulted in further suffering for people who had already endured over 16 years of conflict. During 1999 more than 200,000 civilians were forced to flee because of the fighting. In cities under government control, restrictions on the rights to freedom of expression and association persisted. In January the government announced the Political Association Act (*Tawali*), allowing political parties to register, but it continued to enforce a ban on political opposition parties and trade unions. Lawyers, journalists and human rights activists remained at risk of arrest, imprisonment, beatings, torture and "disappearances". In December President Omar al-Bashir declared a three-month state of emergency and dissolved parliament.

Background
Despite a cease-fire agreement, the civil war continued in the south and east between regular government forces, the government's paramilitary Popular Defence Forces (PDF) and informal militia groups known as the *murahaleen* on the one side, and various forces allied to the opposition Sudan People's Liberation Army (SPLA) on the other.

Aided by external interest in its oil reserves, the government was largely successful in efforts to overcome its previous isolation from the international community.

In May fighting broke out in the western part of the oil-rich state of Upper Nile between different pro-government forces over the issue of who was in charge of securing oil fields. The Southern Sudan Defence Force (SSDF), led by Riek Machar who signed a peace agreement with the government in 1997, was attacked by the government-allied forces of Paulino Matip. The fighting caused internal displacement and a halt to oil exploration in various locations. Two commanders subsequently defected from the forces of Paulino Matip and formed the South Sudan Liberation Movement (SSLM).

The oil companies took no responsibility for human rights abuses linked to the forces they used to protect their oil fields. According to a report by the UN Special Rapporteur on Sudan the government deployed its military to clear a large area around the oilfields as a safe zone for exploration. At the time of the first shipment of 30,000 barrels of oil in September, local people testified that helicopter gunships had been widely used in the area and that civilian targets had been indiscriminately bombarded from a high altitude.

Kerubino Kuanyin Bol, a key war leader and military commander in Bahr el Ghazal who had defected from the government back to the SPLA in 1998, was shot dead in an ambush in western Upper Nile in September.

On 13 December President al-Bashir declared a three-month state of emergency and dissolved the parliament. The influential Speaker of the Parliament and leader of the National Islamic Front, Hassan al-Turabi, was deprived of power.

Internal displacement
There were almost 4.5 million internally displaced people within Sudan, while more than 350,000 Sudanese were refugees abroad. More than two million people displaced from the war-torn south lived in camps around Khartoum. There were plans to forcibly relocate more than 200,000 of these people further away from Khartoum, to an area with no access to safe water, firewood, shelter or education.

In areas of oil exploration, mainly in western Upper Nile and Southern Kordofan, tens of thousands more people were forced to leave their homes during 1999, abandoning their land, livestock and relatives, after raids by government forces or allied militias. Many of the internally displaced had no access to humanitarian aid, because of the unstable military situation. In July the government imposed a ban on flights to western Upper Nile. An estimated 150,000 people in western Upper Nile were at risk of famine because of displacement and the consequent failure to cultivate.

Abuses in war zones
On all war fronts — in the eastern part of Sudan, the Nuba Mountains and Ingessana Hills, as well as in the south — hundreds of civilians were extrajudicially executed by regular soldiers, PDF forces and irregular militias.

Scores of people were deliberately and arbitrarily killed by the SPLA and its allies, who also looted villages and diverted humanitarian aid. In March, three government employees and one staff member of the Red Crescent were abducted by the SPLA and subsequently killed while held captive.

Bahr el Ghazal

During 1999, hundreds of women and children were abducted, scores of women were raped and scores were killed by pro-government forces. Thousands of women and children abducted from Bahr el Ghazal in previous years, and allegedly held as domestic slaves, remained unaccounted for.

Despite the extension of the cease-fire, there were aerial bombardments and attacks by government forces on civilian targets. In May government troops attacked Rumbek and Yirol from their bases in Wau, northern Bahr el Ghazal. Villages near the railway were attacked by PDF forces and *murahaleen* militias escorting the government supply train which crosses the area one to three times a month. Aid agency staff were evacuated, causing access problems for humanitarian aid.

Equatoria

Government warplanes bombarded hospitals throughout 1999, apparently targeting them deliberately. There was heavy fighting around the towns of Chukudum and New Cush, and the SPLA unlawfully killed a number of people. The SPLA reportedly planted anti-personnel mines around Chukudum, putting hundreds of people at risk.

Western Darfur

In January the local population of Western Darfur, predominantly the Masaalit, were involved in conflict with militias allegedly backed by government helicopter gunships and armed vehicles. Thousands of people died and tens of thousands fled to Chad. In early February, President al-Bashir issued an emergency decree suspending the Western Darfur state authority with regard to security and public order. In mid-March the attacks resumed, carried out by government-backed militias assembled from members of the ruling party (the National Islamic Front), people from Arab ethnic groups, and non-Sudanese.

At least eight Masaalit men were sentenced to death by hanging, cross amputation (one hand and the opposite foot) and crucifixion, for involvement in "tribal clashes".

Eastern Sudan

In January the government attacked the Northern Blue Nile area, partly controlled by the Sudan Allied Forces (SAF), the military wing of some of the parties in the opposition National Democratic Alliance (NDA). Several civilian targets were destroyed. Civilians were displaced and hospitals were targeted in Menza.

In May aerial bombardment and artillery shelling in Telkouk killed at least 17 civilians and hundreds were wounded.

In August government forces attacked the village of Khor Adar, about 140km south of Damarzin. Villagers were allegedly attacked in the mosque and 20 people extrajudicially executed.

The north

Clashes between the military garrison in Wadi Halfa and the people of the northern part of Sudan were reported in July. At least 10 civilians were injured.

Torture and ill-treatment

Torture and ill-treatment continued to be reported, mainly in government-held towns but also in SPLA-held territories.

⌂ Khamis Adlan Idris, a lorry driver from Sinja Town in Blue Nile, originally from the Nuba Mountains, was seized at his home by military intelligence officers in July. He was held incommunicado and interrogated about involvement with the SPLA, which he denied. According to his testimony, his hands and legs were cuffed, he was stretched out on a table and was whipped. His captors poured a salt-like substance on his back and resumed the whipping. They melted plastic and poured it on his back, arms and chest. He did not receive any medical treatment for 11 days and the wounds became infected. Before being admitted to hospital in Sinar, the incident was reported to the police, but after three months in hospital Khamis Adlan Idris learned that the security forces had confiscated the police report. He subsequently left the country.

Restrictions on freedom of expression

Parallel to the increasing war efforts in the south and east, the government arrested and detained without charge scores of suspected opponents, including journalists, lawyers and members of banned political parties. There was a marked rise in arrests and harassment in Khartoum. Newspapers were banned or suspended for days at a time. At least three newspapers were suspended on approximately 10 different occasions during 1999 for publishing articles criticizing the government.

Journalists

As well as suppressing the publication of newspapers, the authorities arrested journalists.

⌂ Mohamed Abd Al-Seed, Maha Hassan Ali and Abdelgadir Hafiz, all journalists, were arrested by security officers in Khartoum in mid-April. They were not charged or taken to court within the period stipulated by law, and their whereabouts were kept secret. They were reportedly accused of spying for a foreign power. Mohamed Abd Al-Seed was released without charge or trial in May and required medical treatment for infected wounds on his arms and legs as a result of being tortured in detention.

Lawyers

There was a pattern of police and security force harassment directed against lawyers. At least eight were arrested during 1999, and at least two were abducted by the security forces and detained without charge or trial.

⌂ Gazhi Suleiman, a lawyer and human rights defender was arrested at least six times during 1999. He was banned from the Sudanese Bar Association and meetings in his office were raided by the police. In November he organized a press conference with the SPLA leader, John Garang de Mabior, speaking via a telephone link. Police raided the press conference, cut the telephone line, and beat, kicked and stabbed participants. Gazhi Suleiman had been arrested in July together with Toby Madut, the leader of a southern Sudanese political party. AI wrote to the government in April about the pattern of harassment directed against Gazhi Suleiman.

Human rights defenders
In May UNICEF published a report on slavery in Wau county, documenting cases of government soldiers and members of the PDF raping women and abducting women and children. In July 1999 security officers arrested UNICEF Programme Officer Hamid El-Basher Ibrahim at his home in Khartoum after searching it and taking his fax, telephone and computer. He was detained without charge and subsequently released.

Students
Students were also targeted for arrest, detention and torture.

▭ Adam Issa Mohamed, a fourth-year economics student at the Islamic University in Omdurman, and Al-Waseela Ahmed Eizeldin Malaa, a second-year law student were abducted at the main gate of the university and allegedly taken to a secret detention centre known as a "ghost house". They were reportedly tortured by having their nails extracted, having chemicals poured on their thighs and being burned on sensitive parts of their bodies.

Forced recruitment
Government officials resorted to "hate speech" and to promoting the war as a *jihad* (holy war) to boost the number of recruits into the armed forces. There was also forced recruitment by both the government and SPLA. There were many reports of the security forces rounding up young men on the streets and buses of Khartoum and other cities in the north for recruitment. In government-controlled garrison towns in southern Sudan, boys as young as 14 were reported to have been forcibly recruited into the PDF.

Despite SPLA assurances that it would not recruit children, various reports from SPLA-held territory indicated that boys below the age of 18, even below the age of 15, were taken by the SPLA to their training camps. According to testimonies from village leaders and relatives, SPLA forces rounded up young men and boys in villages at night, and took away those singled out by chiefs, or took them indiscriminately. Various groups, such as forces led by Paulino Matip and Peter Gadet, reportedly used child soldiers well below the age of 18 in combat.

Women's rights
Violations of women's rights were prevalent. In central Sudan, especially in Khartoum, women faced severe restrictions on their freedom of movement. The Public Order Act of Khartoum, 1992, prohibited women traders from appearing in public places before 5am and after 5pm. No such restriction applied to men. Visas for women wishing to travel abroad were issued only with the written permission of a male guardian. Control over women's bodies, their children and their property was in the hands of their male guardians. Violence against women within the family took place with virtual impunity.

▭ On 14 June, 24 students were arrested and convicted by the Public Order Court on charges of committing indecent or immoral acts and wearing clothes which upset public feelings. The students were arrested at a picnic held with the permission of the University. They were convicted on the grounds that the female students were wearing shirts, trousers and T-shirts and that men and women were holding hands in the traditional Nubian dance they were performing. They were sentenced to up to 40 lashes each, and fined.

AI country reports and visits
Reports
- Sudan: serious risk of human rights abuses after cease-fire ends (AI Index: AFR 54/002/99)
- Sudan: Justice? The trial of Father Hillary Boma and 25 others — an update (AI Index: AFR 54/003/99)

Visit
AI delegates visited Bahr el Ghazal and western Upper Nile in October.

SWEDEN

KINGDOM OF SWEDEN
Head of state: King Carl XVI Gustaf
Head of government: Goran Persson
Capital: Stockholm
Population: 8.9 million
Official language: Swedish
Death penalty: abolitionist for all crimes

Osmo Vallo
Various inquiries into the death in police custody of Osmo Vallo in 1995 had still not resulted in clarification of the full circumstances.

Osmo Vallo died in May 1995 after police officers reportedly kicked him, allowed a police dog to bite him repeatedly, and stamped on his back as he lay handcuffed on the ground. Although he sustained 39 injuries to his body, forensic pathologists had not been able to agree on a cause of death. The findings of the third post-mortem examination, which stated that the use of violence by the police contributed to Osmo Vallo's death, had been sent for comment to the Legal Council of the National Board of Health and Welfare in 1998. On the basis of the Legal Council's assessment, the prosecutor in charge of the case decided to close the case in May. However, the Prosecutor General announced he was reviewing this decision. No decision had been reached by the end of the year.

AI continued to be concerned that responsibility for Osmo Vallo's death had not been determined by a court and about the integrity of most of the investigations into this death.

SWITZERLAND

SWISS CONFEDERATION
Head of state and government: Ruth Dreifuss
Capital: Bern
Population: 7.1 million
Official languages: German, French, Italian
Death penalty: abolitionist for all crimes

There were further allegations of ill-treatment of criminal suspects by police officers, and some foreign nationals were subjected to cruel and dangerous methods of restraint during their forcible deportation. One man died during deportation. The trial of a Rwandese national for war crimes set a historic precedent, although accompanied by concerns that the anonymity of witnesses was inadequately protected. A national referendum, launched by non-governmental organizations campaigning for refugees' human rights, voted in favour of a new asylum law already approved by parliament. There was concern that it restricted access to refugee determination procedures and that some of its provisions were open to restrictive interpretation and might result in the *refoulement* (forcible repatriation) of people at risk of serious human rights violations. A new Federal Constitution, updating the 1874 Constitution, was also approved by national referendum. It was expected to come into force in 2000 or 2001 and paved the way for proposed reforms in the area of civil rights and justice, including the eventual unification of the existing 26 cantonal codes of penal procedure and the three federal laws on penal procedure.

Alleged ill-treatment
Further allegations of police ill-treatment of criminal suspects were reported. There was continued concern that certain fundamental safeguards against ill-treatment in police custody, such as the right to inform relatives of arrest and to have immediate access to a lawyer, had still not been introduced in all cantons, as recommended by intergovernmental bodies in previous years.

▭ Investigations were opened into an administrative complaint which the parents of a 14-year-old boy from the Kosovo province of Yugoslavia lodged against three Geneva police officers in October. The boy had been detained for several hours following a street disturbance. He said that he was an innocent bystander, but that an officer ordered a police dog to attack him and that it bit his right thigh. He claimed that police forced him to the ground, handcuffed him, and insulted his parents and nationality. He said that at the police station he was hit on the back of the neck with a bottle of water, that officers stood on his feet, crushing them, and squeezed him so tightly around the neck that he had difficulty in breathing and feared he would die. The police called in a doctor to examine the dog-bite and a medical report by the boy's own doctor recorded physical injuries compatible with his allegations, as well as psychological trauma.

Restraint methods during deportation
At the end of October the Federal Office for Refugees stated that 6,449 rejected asylum-seekers and illegal immigrants had been deported from Zurich-Kloten airport during 1999, that in 41 cases a two-man police escort and light restraints such as handcuffs were required to execute the deportation, and that in 25 cases — so-called "Level 3" deportations — heavier restraints were necessary.

According to Zurich airport police, Level 3 restraints could be employed in cases where a deportation attempt had already failed because of the individual's physical resistance. However, there were claims that they were also used in some cases where the deportee had not resisted. Some of the restraint procedures used were cruel, degrading or dangerous.

During the first half of 1999 deportees reported having breathing difficulties as a result of adhesive tape being placed across their mouths and a helmet, described as being similar to a motorcycle helmet, placed over their heads, while more adhesive tape was wrapped over and around the helmet, forcing closed their jaws. They said that they were handcuffed, had their feet shackled and were bound by belts to a wheelchair. A Lebanese deported in January claimed that he was left alone in a room in this condition for several hours before his flight, unable to see because he was blindfolded and experiencing difficulties in breathing and hearing. This detainee and others also reported being deprived of food, liquid and access to a lavatory for many hours until they reached their destination. Once in the plane, they were strapped to a seat, still bound hand and foot.

▭ In March Khaled Abu Zarifeh, a Palestinian, died at Zurich-Kloten airport during a deportation operation. The Zurich cantonal authorities subsequently confirmed that adhesive tape had been placed over his mouth and that he had been strapped into a wheelchair. A judicial investigation into his death had not concluded by the end of 1999.

▭ In May, while preparing a man for forcible deportation to the Democratic Republic of the Congo, police officers noticed that he had difficulty in breathing through his nose but nevertheless taped his mouth, inserting a small breathing tube through the tape. He said he continued to suffer breathing difficulties during the flight.

AI sought information and clarification from relevant Zurich and federal authorities about the methods of restraint officially authorized for use and about the three individual cases mentioned above. Basing its position on the expert opinion of internationally recognized forensic pathologists, AI explained its opposition to the use of any materials or methods of restraint which could block the airways of a deportee, such as covering the mouth with adhesive tape. Such practices are highly dangerous and can result in fatalities. AI requested copies of any written guidelines issued to police officers on the use of restraints during forcible deportations and clarification of aspects of police training. AI asked whether detainees automatically received a medical examination before forcible deportation and the use of restraints.

In response Zurich Cantonal Department for Security provided copies of two written answers the cantonal government had given to questions raised in Zurich's cantonal parliament. In one, issued in August, the government stated that adhesive tape would no longer be used to cover the mouth during deportations, and that a new type of open-faced helmet was in use, described as "a light rubber helmet, as used in boxing". A so-called "chin-cup" was attached, to force the jaws together, and a cover which could be placed across the mouth, with a small aperture for a breathing tube. The authorities stated that the cover was to be removed "as soon as the person calms down or there are signs of a deterioration in his health" and that while it was in use the person should be kept under permanent observation. Despite several requests, by the end of the year the Zurich cantonal authorities had not supplied AI with copies of any written guidelines issued to police officers. However, they indicated that by then a standard practice had been introduced for police officers to obtain a medical certificate from a medically qualified person before carrying out a forcible deportation.

Trial of Fulgence Niyonteze
In April a military court in Lausanne found Fulgence Niyonteze, a former local government official in Rwanda, guilty of a number of crimes, including murder, incitement to murder and war crimes, in the context of the 1994 genocide in Rwanda. His appeal against the sentence of life imprisonment was pending at the end of 1999.

Fulgence Niyonteze had been living in Switzerland since October 1994. His trial set a historic precedent. Previously, trials of those accused of crimes connected with the 1994 genocide had taken place either in Rwandese courts, or at the International Criminal Tribunal for Rwanda (ICTR) set up by the UN in Arusha, Tanzania. Although several individuals believed to have played a leading role in the genocide were known to be living in countries in Europe, North America and Africa, none had been tried in any other foreign country by the end of 1999.

AI encourages governments of countries where individuals suspected of participation in the genocide are residing to investigate allegations against them and, if sufficient evidence is found, to bring them to justice, in accordance with international standards for fair trial and without recourse to the death penalty. It welcomed, therefore, the precedent set by Switzerland. However, there were serious concerns that the anonymity of witnesses, many of whom asked to testify anonymously for their own security, was not adequately protected during the trial.

AI country reports
- Switzerland: Alleged ill-treatment by Geneva police – The case of "Visar" and Clement Nwankwo (AI Index: 1EUR 43/003/99)
- Concerns in Europe, January – June 1999: Switzerland (AI Index: EUR 01/002/99)

SYRIA

SYRIAN ARAB REPUBLIC
Head of state: Hafez al-Assad
Head of government: Mahmud al-Zu'bi
Capital: Damascus
Population: 15 million
Official language: Arabic
Death penalty: retentionist

A general amnesty issued by President Hafez al-Assad in July resulted in the release of an unspecified number of political prisoners (although the main beneficiaries were prisoners charged with economic offences). Restrictions imposed on the travel of Syrian nationals were relaxed during the year, but AI remained concerned about continued infringement of the rights of former political prisoners, including their right to freedom of movement and travel. Hundreds of people, including foreign nationals, were arrested on political grounds. Hundreds of political detainees, including prisoners of conscience, remained in detention, some held without charge or trial and others serving long sentences passed after unfair trials before the Supreme State Security Court (SSSC). There were reports of torture and ill-treatment and a number of sick detainees remained held without access to adequate medical care. At least one person "disappeared" during 1999, and scores of "disappearances" from previous years remained unresolved. The death in custody of a Lebanese detainee was reported. At least two people were sentenced to death and executed.

Background
President Hafez al-Assad was re-elected in a national referendum in February for a further five years in office. Since 1973, he has presided over a government led by the National Progressive Front, an alliance of the

Arab Socialist Ba'th Party and other smaller parties. During 1999 there were violent clashes between the authorities and supporters of Rifa't al-Assad, brother of President Hafez al-Assad and former Vice-President, in the coastal city of Latakia. At least two people were killed and scores of Rifa't al-Assad supporters were rounded up and questioned.

Opposition activities remained outlawed and members of unauthorized political parties were at risk of detention. A state of emergency, with attendant legislative and security measures leading to grave and continuing human rights violations, remained in place; it had been in force since 1963.

Arrests

Hundreds of people were arrested and detained during 1999, apparently for political reasons. They included members of the unauthorized Islamist groups *al-Ikhwan al-Muslimun*, Muslim Brotherhood, and *Hizb al-Tahrir*, [Islamic] Liberation Party, and foreign nationals from other Arab states.

More than 500 members of *al-Ikhwan al-Muslimun* and *Hizb al-Tahrir* were rounded up in a wave of arrests in December when Syrian security forces raided homes of suspected members of these groups in the cities of Homs, Damascus and Aleppo. They were reportedly held in incommunicado detention in Damascus and there were fears that they might be tortured or ill-treated. Also in December, the former Deputy Controller General of *al-Ikhwan al-Muslimun*, Amin Yakun, was shot dead by unidentified gunmen.

Foreign nationals arrested during the year were reportedly held incommunicado, mostly in two detention centres: *Far' Falastin*, Palestine Branch, and *Far' al-Tahqiq al-'Askari*, Military Interrogation Branch. Among the detainees were 'Abdallah Ahmad Muhammad, a 71-year-old Iraqi Kurd arrested in July, and Ali Hussein Muhaimid, an Iraqi arrested in August. Both men were reportedly arrested at Damascus airport, and taken to *Far' Falastin*. Muhammad Himo, a Syrian, the owner of a Kurdish bookshop in Aleppo, was reportedly arrested in October. There were fears that these detainees were at risk of torture or ill-treatment, while held in prolonged incommunicado detention.

Releases

At least a dozen political prisoners, including prisoners of conscience, were released during 1999. Most had served long sentences of up to 15 years imposed by the SSSC after unfair trials. They included Doha 'Ashur al-'Askari, and Ratib Sha'bu, who had been held beyond the expiry of long sentences handed down for their involvement with the unauthorized *Hizb al-'Amal al-Shuyu'i* (PCA), Party for Communist Action. Doha 'Ashur al-'Askari staged a hunger strike in protest against her detention beyond the expiry of a six-year sentence.

After the general amnesty in July, an unspecified number of Jordanian and Palestinian political prisoners were reportedly transferred to *Far' al-Tahqiq al-'Askari*, apparently pending release. They included 'Adnan 'Abd al-Rahman al-Dabak, and Nail Isma'il 'Izzat, both detained since 1985 in connection with

alleged involvement with the Palestine Liberation Organization (PLO). They had not been released by the end of 1999.

Prisoners of conscience

Scores of prisoners of conscience remained in detention serving long sentences imposed in previous years by the SSSC after unfair trials. Dozens of prisoners of conscience detained for alleged membership of the PCA continued to serve sentences of up to 22 years. They included Muhammad Ghanim, a doctor, and Faysal 'Allush, a former university student of mechanical engineering, both serving 15 years' imprisonment with hard labour.

At least five prisoners of conscience detained for their involvement with the PCA continued to be held beyond the expiry of long sentences. They included Basel Hurani and 'Abd al-Halim Rumieh, both former students of electrical engineering at Damascus University.

The precise number of prisoners of conscience held on charges of involvement with *al-Hizb al-Shuyu'i al-Maktab al-Siyassi* (CPPB), Communist Party–Political Bureau, was not known. At least one, 'Umar al-Hayek, remained in detention at Tadmur Military Prison, serving a 15-year sentence handed down after an unfair trial. 'Abdalla Qabbara, a lawyer sentenced to 15 years' imprisonment in 1994 in connection with his involvement with the CPPB, was released from Tadmur Military Prison during 1999. He had reportedly been tortured during the interrogation stage of his detention and was suffering from chronic diabetes.

Human rights defenders

The work of human rights groups remained unauthorized in Syria. Five prisoners of conscience remained in detention serving up to 10 years' imprisonment for their involvement in the distribution of a leaflet to mark the anniversary of the Universal Declaration of Human Rights. The leaflet was produced in 1992 by an unauthorized human rights group, the Committees for the Defence of Democratic Freedoms and Human Rights in Syria (CDF). The prisoners of conscience were Nizar Nayyuf, Muhammad 'Ali Habib, 'Afif Muzhir, Bassam al-Sheikh and Thabit Murad. Aktham Nu'aysa, a leading member of the CDF released in 1998, continued to have his civil liberties restricted and was barred from travelling abroad to seek medical treatment.

Long-term political detainees

Hundreds of political prisoners and possible prisoners of conscience, including foreign nationals, remained held. Some were detained incommunicado without charge or trial, others were serving sentences passed after grossly unfair trials.

Hundreds of political prisoners held in connection with activities related to *al-Ikhwan al-Muslimun* remained in incommunicado detention, mostly without charge or trial. They included 'Aziza Jallud, arrested in 1979 in lieu of her husband who was sought by the Syrian authorities, reportedly in connection with a bombing incident. An unspecified number of political prisoners held in connection with *al-Ikhwan al-Muslimun* were reportedly released following the July amnesty. Scores of Lebanese nationals held since the 1980s and 1990s remained in Syrian prisons. Most had been arrested by the Syrian intelligence forces in Lebanon and transferred to Syria where they were mostly held in incommunicado detention.

◻ 'Isam 'Uthman al-Mistrah, a Lebanese carpenter born in 1961, was taken by Syrian forces from Beirut on 8 August 1992 and transferred to Syria. The Syrian authorities acknowledged his detention after nine months' incommunicado detention, and allowed his family monthly visits. He was reportedly tried and sentenced to 20 years' imprisonment on charges of being "an agent" of the intelligence service of former Lebanese army General 'Aoun.

Scores of Palestinian and Jordanian political detainees, most of whom were held in connection with Palestinian political movements, remained in detention without charge or serving long sentences passed after grossly unfair trials.

◻ Tawfiq Yunis 'Abd al-Rahman al-Ashqar, a Jordanian contractor born in 1948, married with six children, was arrested in early 1982 at Dara' on the Jordanian-Syrian border. He was reportedly held in incommunicado detention in Tadmur Military Prison for alleged involvement with an Islamist group. He was reportedly acquitted by a court before his transfer to Tadmur Military Prison, but was never released.

Torture
Torture and ill-treatment of detainees continued to be routine, especially during the initial stage of detention and interrogation and in Tadmur Military Prison, notorious for its harsh conditions. There were also fears that prisoners of conscience transferred to this prison in 1998, including Nu'man 'Ali 'Abdu, may have been tortured and ill-treated as a form of punishment. New cases of torture and ill-treatment were reported during 1999, especially of political detainees held at *Far' Falastin* in Damascus.

◻ Fa'iq Ibrahim al-Yasseri and Khalil Ibrahim Hussain, two Iraqi nationals released in March after being held from November 1998 to March 1999 at *Far' Falastin*, were reportedly tortured or ill-treated, apparently for their involvement with the Damascus-based Iraqi Centre for Humanitarian Activities. They had been held incommunicado for six weeks in an underground cell and were repeatedly beaten by the interrogating officers.

Death in custody
The death in custody during 1999 of a Lebanese detainee gave cause for grave concern, especially given the failure of the Syrian authorities to improve prison conditions and investigate dozens of deaths in custody of political prisoners in previous years.

◻ 'Adel Khalaf Ajjuri, a Lebanese political prisoner detained since 1990, died in custody on 22 September in Sednaya Prison, reportedly after being denied access to specialist medical care. No autopsy was performed on

his body by either the Syrian or Lebanese authorities. His family was not informed until almost a month after his death and were forced to collect his body from Syria themselves. The death certificate issued by the Syrian authorities indicated that the cause of death was heart failure.

Cruel and inhuman prison conditions
Dozens of political prisoners, including prisoners of conscience, continued to be held without adequate medical care in prisons where conditions fell seriously short of international standards. They included prisoner of conscience Wajih Ghanim, serving 15 years' imprisonment on charges of membership of the PCA, who suffered severe strain on the neck affecting the spine apparently caused by torture. 'Abd al-Majid Nimer Zaghmout, a Palestinian political prisoner, remained in detention despite an order by the Minister of Defence for him to be released. 'Abd al-Majid Nimer Zaghmout, held since an unfair trial more than 30 years earlier in 1966, suffered from advanced cancer and was held at Teshrin Military Hospital in Damascus.

'Disappearances'
At least one person "disappeared" during 1999, after reportedly being taken by the Syrian security forces from his home in April following years of residence abroad. Scores of previous "disappearance" cases remained unresolved.

◻ Khadija Yahya Bukhari, a Lebanese national, was arrested by Syrian forces at Beirut airport on 28 April 1992 along with her son and daughter and taken to the Syrian Intelligence centre near the Beau Rivage Hotel in Beirut. They were then transferred to *Far' al-Tahqiq al-'Askari* and *Far' Falastin* in Syria. Both her son and daughter were subsequently released, but the fate and whereabouts of Khadija Bukhari remained unknown. She and her husband, a Syrian officer, were apparently suspected of "collaboration" with Israel.

Death penalty
The death penalty continued to be applied and at least two people were sentenced to death for murder and executed during 1999.

◻ Haytham Sa'id Yaghi, aged 21, and Firaz bin Qassem Yaghi, aged 19, two Syrian nationals from the same family, were executed in June in a public square within a week of being convicted of murder.

Government communications
AI received some responses from the Syrian authorities on cases raised by the organization.

AI country reports
- Syria: Caught in a regional conflict – Lebanese, Palestinian and Jordanian political detainees in Syria (AI Index: MDE 24/001/99)
- Syria: Double Injustice – prisoners of conscience held beyond the expiry of their sentences (AI Index: MDE 24/010/99)

TAIWAN

TAIWAN
President: Lee Teng-hui
Head of government: Vincent Siew
Capital: Taipei
Population: 21.6 million
Official language: Mandarin Chinese
Death penalty: retentionist

The government demonstrated its commitment to improving human rights protection and advancing social welfare by introducing several new laws and reforming existing legislation. However, the authorities made increasing use of the death penalty, claiming that they were responding to public concern about levels of crime. At least 24 people were executed during 1999.

Background
A major earthquake in September claimed the lives of more than 2,000 people and left 100,000 people homeless. The authorities continued to seek international recognition, a policy which perpetuated hostile relations with the People's Republic of China. Taiwan's application for UN membership was unsuccessful, but the authorities anticipated joining the World Trade Organization in 2000.

Death penalty
At least 24 people were executed during 1999. Grave doubts continued to surround the conviction of the "Hsinchu Trio" who were sentenced to death in February 1992. There was widespread concern that there was a lack of evidence against Su Chien-ho, Liu Bin-lang and Chuang Lin-hsun, and that they had been convicted solely on the basis of confessions extracted under torture. The Ministry of Justice advised AI in August that it had reviewed the evidence and referred the case of the three men to the prosecutor general to reconsider a fourth extraordinary appeal. AI urged President Lee Teng-hui in October to ensure that the convictions were reviewed.

Legal reforms
In January the authorities repealed legislation which had been used to control the media during the 40-year period of martial law (1947-1987). In February the Council of Grand Justices (CGJ) ruled that compensation for breaches of civic rights should be extended to cover those detained without indictment during the martial law period.

Amendments to the Criminal Code in February made rape an indictable offence and empowered prosecutors to press charges against alleged rapists without the victim's consent. The amendments also covered sexual harassment, the use of threats or coercion to obtain sexual favours, and the use of drugs to render others defenceless for sexual purposes; they were applicable to men and women in heterosexual or same-sex relationships.

The National Police Administration submitted an amended version of the Assembly and Parade Law to the Ministry of the Interior in April which would decriminalize the acts of advocating a communist system of government for Taiwan or calling for formal independence from China.

The Child and Youth Sexual Transaction Prevention Act was amended in May to allow maximum prison terms of 10 years for people convicted of paying to have sex with children under the age of 14, and shorter prison terms for those convicted of having sex with minors under the age of 18.

The Domestic Violence Prevention Act, introduced in June, established protection for victims of domestic violence. The new law allowed judges to issue restraining orders and provided for those acting on behalf of victims of domestic violence, such as police officers, social workers and prosecutors, to seek court orders. It also required local government to establish domestic violence prevention centres.

Military reforms
It was announced in January 1999 that men reporting for their compulsory two years of national service could apply to serve outside the military. From January 2000 conscripts would have the option of applying to spend their two-year period of service in the police force or the fire service, as workers participating in environmental projects, or as carers to the elderly and the handicapped. The issue of exemption from compulsory national service on religious grounds was still under consideration by the Ministry of National Defence (MND) at the end of 1999.

The MND established a military human rights protection commission in March, in response to the demands of the families of conscripts who died in military accidents. The MND also agreed to form a special military accident investigation committee to ensure impartiality and transparency in investigations into the causes of the accidents.

Proposed amendments to the Military Tribunal Law were submitted to the legislature in May. Under the amendments officers and servicemen would be granted the right to be tried not only in a military court but also in the Taiwan High Court or Supreme Court. Capital cases, or cases of life imprisonment, would be reviewed by the Supreme Court.

Asylum-seeking and immigration
Laws and procedures governing asylum-seeking and immigration continued to lack transparency. A new Immigration Law, passed in May, enabled the foreign spouses and children of Taiwan nationals to apply for residency status, provided they could prove that they had lived in Taiwan for a certain length of time. The new legislation established entry requirements for people of Chinese descent, mainly from Burma (Myanmar), Indonesia and Thailand, who were not covered under previous immigration laws. It also lifted restrictions on Taiwan nationals wishing to travel abroad.

TAJIKISTAN

REPUBLIC OF TAJIKISTAN
Head of state: Imomali Rakhmonov
Head of government: Akil Akilov (replaced Yakhyo Azimov in December)
Capital: Dushanbe
Population: 6 million
Official language: Tajik
Death penalty: retentionist
1999 treaty ratifications/signatures: International Covenant on Civil and Political Rights and its (first) Optional Protocol; International Covenant on Economic, Social and Cultural Rights

Members of opposition parties were harassed and intimidated by the authorities. The death penalty continued to be imposed. At least 15 death sentences and two executions came to light, although the true figures were believed to be far higher.

Background

A constitutional referendum was held in September which increased the powers of the president and allowed religion-based political parties to operate.

Presidential elections were held in November, after a last-minute compromise with the opposition United Tajik Opposition (UTO). President Imomali Rakhmonov was re-elected with a massive majority, although opposition parties claimed widespread voter fraud. Of the initial three opposition candidates, two were excluded from the ballot by the Supreme Court in October. The third, Davlat Usmon of the Islamic Renaissance Party, asked for his name to be withdrawn, but it appeared on the ballot paper despite his refusal to run.

After the October Supreme Court ruling denying Saifiddin Turaev of the Party of Justice and Sulton Kuvvatov of the Democratic Party (Tehran Platform) registration as presidential candidates, the UTO withdrew from the National Reconciliation Commission (NRC), the body responsible for implementing the 1997 peace accord between the government and the UTO which formally ended more than five years of civil war in Tajikistan. This withdrawal effectively suspended the peace process. Hours before the election took place, opposition leader Sayed Abdullo Nuri lifted his movement's boycott of the election in exchange for the release of 93 prisoners held since the civil war and key concessions ahead of parliamentary elections scheduled for 2000. The UTO rejoined the NRC and at least 18 UTO supporters on the list of 93 were released before the end of 1999.

The work of opposition political parties was impeded and obstructed throughout 1999. The Agrarian Party and the National Unity Party were banned, and other political parties were denied registration. Members of political parties were charged by the government with breaches of the Law on Political Parties, and reportedly faced threats and harassment by the authorities.

Restrictions on the news media continued. Independent journalists suffered harassment, intimidation and violence. Independent newspapers faced arbitrary refusals to print by government-owned printing presses, and no independent radio stations were licensed to operate.

Political violence, including abductions and killings, continued at a high rate throughout 1999. Among those killed in 1999, apparently for political reasons, were Tolib Boboev, former deputy procurator general, Safarali Kenjaev, chairman of the Socialist Party of Tajikistan and chairman of the Supreme Council Committee for Legislation and Human Rights, and Jumakhona Khotami, an official of the Ministry of the Interior.

Death penalty

The death penalty continued to be imposed. The Criminal Code of the former Soviet Republic of Tajikistan contains 15 offences which carry a possible death sentence.

Death sentences

At least 15 people were sentenced to death during 1999.

On 26 March the Supreme Court sentenced three members of the UTO to death for the murder of three members of the UN Mission of Observers to Tajikistan (UNMOT) in July 1998. The UN Secretary-General appealed for the death sentences to be commuted.

On 22 June the Supreme Court sentenced to death two former politicians accused of having participated in a coup attempt in August 1997 led by the former Popular Front commander and warlord Makhmud Khudoyberdiyev. It was feared that former parliamentary deputy Sherali Mirzoyev and former deputy governor of Khatlon province Kosym Babayev had been sentenced to death without right of appeal.

Makhmud Nadzhmiddinov, Abdumannon Kholmudminov and Yurabek Ravshanov were sentenced to death in late December by Khatlon Regional Court for crimes which included terrorism, murder and smuggling of weapons. Davlatali Husenov and J. Khojayev were also sentenced to death by the Khatlon Regional Court after they were convicted of organizing an illegal armed group and other crimes which included murder, robbery and rape. They were reportedly followers of Makhmud Khudoyberdiyev and were convicted of involvement in acts of political violence that took place in November 1998 in Qurghonteppa, the regional centre of the southern Khatlon Region, and in the northern Leninabad Region.

Executions

Two executions came to light in 1999, although the true figure was believed to be higher. News of these executions seemed to confirm that a reported *de facto* moratorium on executions was no longer in place in Tajikistan.

Unofficial sources reported that Bakhrom Sodirov, the brother of warlord Rezvon Sodirov, was executed at the end of January 1999. Bakhrom Sodirov was sentenced to death in October 1998 for organizing the kidnapping of members of UNMOT in December 1996 and in February 1997. Although the execution was not publicly confirmed by the Tajik authorities, AI was informed that the prosecutor general acknowledged in March that he had sent a written account of the execution to the President.

🗀 Unofficial sources reported in April that Abdulkhafiz Abdullayev, the younger brother of the former Prime Minister and leader of the Khujand-based opposition National Revival Bloc, Abdumalik Abdullojonov, had been executed at the end of November 1998, despite earlier reports that his petition for clemency was rejected only at the end of December 1998. Abdulkhafiz Abdullayev was sentenced to death in March 1998 after a reportedly unfair trial for his alleged involvement in an attempt to assassinate President Rakhmonov in April 1997. Abdulkhafiz Abdullayev was suffering from terminal cancer and there was widespread concern that he was denied adequate medical care in detention.

TANZANIA

UNITED REPUBLIC OF TANZANIA
Head of state: Benjamin Mkapa
Head of government: Frederick Sumaye
Capital: Dar es Salaam
Population: 29.4 million
Official languages: Kiswahili, English
Death penalty: retentionist

Steps were taken towards ending the political crisis on the semi-autonomous island of Zanzibar, but 18 opposition leaders and their supporters remained in prison awaiting trial on treason charges. Debate continued about constitutional and judicial reform in Tanzania, and there was a proposal to establish a national human rights commission. Former President Julius Nyerere, who had been acting as facilitator in peace negotiations between the government of Burundi and Burundian armed opposition groups, died in October.

Zanzibar

The opposition Civic United Front (CUF) signed a far-reaching agreement on reconciliation and democratic reform with the ruling *Chama cha Mapinduzi* (CCM), Party of the Revolution, in April, bringing an end to a political crisis which had been running since the disputed 1995 elections. The CUF stopped its boycott of parliamentary proceedings and agreed to recognize the government of President Salmin Amour.

🗀 Eighteen CUF leaders and members were finally committed for trial in March after spending more than a year in prison. The 16 men and two women were charged with conspiracy to overthrow the Zanzibar government and would face the death penalty if

convicted, but the trial had not started by the end of the year. They included Juma Duni Haji, a former opposition candidate for the Tanzanian vice-presidency, three other members of the Zanzibar House of Representatives (parliament) and several senior civil servants. All 18 strongly denied the charges against them. AI feared that they would not receive a fair trial and called for their immediate and unconditional release on the grounds that they were prisoners of conscience who had been imprisoned on account of their non-violent political activities.

Refugees

Tanzania continued to give protection to more than 800,000 refugees from Burundi, the Democratic Republic of the Congo and Rwanda, accepting tens of thousands of new arrivals during 1999. On several occasions police arrested Burundian refugees, including children, who had been recruited from the refugee camps by Burundian armed opposition groups. In January police arrested more than 220 refugees, including 70 children. They were taken to court and the convicted adults were imprisoned; the children were caned.

Freedom of opinion

Almost 200 people belonging to rival factions of the National Convention for Construction and Reform, an opposition party, were arrested in Dar es Salaam in April for holding an illegal meeting. They were released a few days later on bail. In July more than 200 Muslim men and women were arrested during an illegal demonstration in Dar es Salaam against a ban on women wearing the *hijab* (veil) and other matters considered discriminatory to Muslims. All the detainees were released on bail, and the government subsequently withdrew the ban on the *hijab*. Several independent newspapers were threatened with legal action after they published articles criticizing the government. Several laws remained in force allowing for the imprisonment of those convicted for publishing or expressing non-violent opinions.

🗀 Several government critics were arrested in November for alleged sedition. The Reverend Christopher Mkitila of the Democratic Party was held for three weeks for defaming the late President Nyerere in a recorded cassette; he was released on bail. Two weeks later he was convicted of sedition for defaming government officials in 1997, and was jailed for a year. Augustine Mrema, a prominent opposition politician from the Tanzania Labour Party, was arrested with six others for alleged sedition during local election campaigning in Moshi, but released on bail.

Extradition request

Bernard Ntuyahaga, a former Rwandese army officer charged with genocide, was released by the Tanzania-based International Criminal Tribunal for Rwanda in March. He was immediately rearrested by the Tanzanian authorities and he faced an extradition request to Rwanda. AI called on the government to refuse the request for Bernard Ntuyahaga's extradition on the grounds that he would possibly face an unfair trial and the death penalty, if convicted. His case was still being heard by a court in Dar es Salaam at the end of the year. The Tanzanian authorities had previously refused a request for his extradition to Belgium to face trial for the murder of Belgian UN soldiers.

'Witchcraft murders'

The murders of elderly women accused of witchcraft continued in the west of the country, predominantly among the Sukuma ethnic group. More than 100 alleged witches were killed in 1999, bringing the total killed in the past three years to around 400. They were murdered and their bodies mutilated by gangs reportedly hired by supposed victims of witchcraft. Government officials criticized the practice, calling it a "national catastrophe", but they took little or no action to prevent the killings or bring those responsible to justice.

Other concerns

Courts imposed several death sentences but, for the fifth successive year, no one was executed. Prison conditions were harsh and there were reports of ill-treatment in police custody. AI campaigned through public educational activities against female genital mutilation which, although illegal, continued to be practised widely.

Update

In April the government replied to AI's 1998 memorandum about the alleged deaths of small-scale gold-miners in Bulyanhulu in Shinyanga region in 1996. The government denied there had been any deaths and rejected AI's call to open an independent judicial inquiry. AI maintained its criticism of local officials who had violated a court injunction by ordering the mines to be filled, but it was unable to substantiate the allegations of deaths.

AI country visits

AI delegates visited refugee camps in Tanzania in August to interview refugees about human rights violations in Burundi, the Democratic Republic of the Congo and Rwanda, and their treatment in the camps in Tanzania.

THAILAND

KINGDOM OF THAILAND
Head of state: Bhumibol Adulyadej
Head of government: Chuan Leekpai
Capital: Bangkok
Population: 60.6 million
Official language: Thai
Death penalty: retentionist
1999 treaty ratifications/signatures: International Covenant on Economic, Social and Cultural Rights

Seventeen people were executed in 1999, the largest number since Thailand resumed executions in 1996. More than 100 people remained on death row. Prison conditions, particularly for Africans and non-Thai Asians, were poor and in some cases amounted to cruel, inhuman or degrading treatment. New legislation established an 11-member National Human Rights Commission designated as a government agency attached to Parliament. More than 14,000 asylum-seekers from Myanmar entered Thailand; most of them were admitted to refugee camps which housed more than 105,000 people by the end of the year.

Death penalty

Seventeen people were executed in Bangkwang Prison by machine-gun fire. For the first time since executions were resumed, a woman was executed; she had been convicted of drug trafficking. The other 16 men had been convicted of murder. Although more than 100 people were believed to be under sentence of death, the government did not publish statistics or names, nor did it announce when executions were scheduled to take place. In December, to mark King Bhumibol Adulyadej's birthday, 30 death sentences were commuted to life imprisonment.

Impunity

In June the government released a summary of a Ministry of Defence report on the military's violent suppression of the May 1992 pro-democracy demonstrations in Bangkok in which more than 52 people were killed and nearly 700 others injured. However, despite appeals from the victims' families and others, the government refused to release the report itself. The fate and whereabouts of dozens of people who went missing during the demonstrations have never been revealed.

Prison conditions

Prolonged shackling of prisoners continued to be reported at Bangkwang Maximum Security Prison and at Chonburi Central Prison. Severe overcrowding was reported throughout the prison system — especially at Lard Yao Prison and Bang Khen Women's Prison — and in immigration detention centres. African and non-Thai Asian prisoners were most at risk of ill-treatment. In

July a Burmese migrant worker was severely beaten by immigration police at Mae Sot Immigration Detention Centre, Tak Province.

Hostage-taking at the Myanmar embassy

In October, five heavily armed Myanmar nationals calling themselves the Vigorous Burmese Students Warriors forced their way into the Myanmar embassy in Bangkok and took 89 people hostage for 25 hours. The five men initially demanded the release of all political prisoners and the restoration of democracy in Myanmar. The hostages were released without casualties when the Thai government acceded to their demands for a helicopter to take them to an area reportedly held by an armed opposition group in the Myanmar border area. The Myanmar government closed the border for seven weeks and stated that they would not resume normal relations with Thailand until the five men were arrested by the Thai authorities. The Thai government subsequently issued arrest warrants for the men; however, none had been arrested by the end of the year.

Refugees and migrant workers from Myanmar

The population of Myanmar nationals living in Thailand was made up of three broad overlapping groups. Members of the Karen and Karenni ethnic groups, who were considered to be "displaced people" by the Thai authorities; migrant workers from all ethnic groups — but particularly the Shan people, some 100,000 of whom had fled human rights violations in Myanmar — who were considered to be "illegal immigrants" and were at risk of arrest and deportation; and Burmese political activists, who were required to register with the UN High Commissioner for Refugees (UNHCR).

During 1999, 14,000 Myanmar asylum-seekers from the Karen and Karenni ethnic groups arrived in Thailand, fleeing forcible relocations, forced labour and other human rights violations. However, thousands more Karen asylum-seekers were prevented from entering by the Thai army. The authorities, the UNHCR, and non-governmental organizations moved two refugee camps, which had been attacked by armed opposition groups from Myanmar in previous years, further inside Thailand for security reasons.

Following the hostage-taking at the Myanmar embassy, the government announced that all young political activists from Myanmar must register with the UNHCR and that those recognized by the UNHCR must enter the Maneloy Safe Area, Raatchburi Province, to await resettlement to third countries. By November 750 people had reportedly registered with the UNHCR. Also in November the police arrested over 20 Burmese political activists, some of whom were recognized by UNHCR, and held them in the Immigration Detention Centre in Bangkok.

In November the immigration authorities arrested thousands of Burmese migrant workers and deported them to the Myanmar-Thai border. Those who had enough money to bribe Thai officials were often allowed to remain on the Thai side of the border.

However, many others with well-founded fears of persecution in Myanmar were returned with no opportunity to claim asylum.

In July a member of the Thai Rangers, a paramilitary unit of the army, raped two Shan female migrant workers from Myanmar in Chiang Mai Province and in November the Border Patrol Police raped a female migrant worker from Myanmar near Mae Sot, Tak Province. No disciplinary action was known to have taken place in either of these cases.

Legal developments

Thailand's report to the UN Human Rights Committee on its implementation of the International Covenant on Civil and Political Rights had not been submitted by the end of the year.

In January, the Committee on the Elimination of Discrimination against Women considered Thailand's combined second and third periodic reports. The Committee expressed concern at the lack of effective law enforcement mechanisms and the lack of cases filed by women in the courts on the basis of constitutional guarantees.

AI country reports and visits

Report

- Thailand: A human rights review based on the International Covenant on Civil and Political Rights (AI Index: ASA 39/001/99)

Visits

AI delegates visited the country between January and March.

TOGO

TOGOLESE REPUBLIC
Head of state: Gnassingbé Eyadéma
Head of government: Eugène Koffi Adoboli
Capital: Lomé
Population: 4.7 million
Official language: French
Death penalty: abolitionist in practice

The Togolese authorities, whose security forces have committed human rights violations for three decades, did nothing to bring those responsible to justice and continued to enjoy impunity. Instead, after AI published a report in May detailing extrajudicial executions, "disappearances" and torture, the authorities took reprisals against human rights defenders suspected of passing information to AI. At least three leading members of Togolese human rights organizations were arrested, detained for several weeks and charged with false accusation and slander. Two members of AI were arrested, beaten and threatened with death while in detention. Other human rights defenders were forced into hiding or to flee the country with their families. A Nigerian member of AI was detained and tortured. Extrajudicial executions, "disappearances" and torture in detention continued to be reported. Opposition supporters were arrested around the time of elections in March.

Background

President Gnassingbé Eyadéma has ruled Togo since 1967, first as a military ruler, and then as a civilian elected President, having been forced to introduce a multi-party system in 1991 after widespread popular protests. Transitional institutions established in 1991 were repeatedly defied by the security forces and the President, who maintained his hold on power after the country's multi-party elections in 1994, even though opposition parties won a majority of seats in the National Assembly. Presidential elections in June 1998 were marred by violence; hundreds of people were alleged to have been extrajudicially executed and dozens of civilians, including opposition activists, were arrested and tortured. The elections were denounced as unfair by international observers, including those from the European Union (EU).

Legislative elections in March 1999 were boycotted by the opposition. The ruling *Rassemblement du peuple togolais* (RPT), Assembly of Togolese People, won 79 of the 81 seats. The EU took the view that the newly elected National Assembly could not accurately reflect the political will of the Togolese people.

In July a political agreement was signed in Togo by both opposition parties as well as those supporting the President. This document, known as the Lomé Framework Agreement, aimed to break the political deadlock which had paralysed the country since the disputed elections of June 1998. The agreement was reached with the mediation of international facilitators from organizations including the EU and the Francophonie. The Lomé Framework Agreement focuses on holding new elections in Togo and does not contain any concrete measures aimed at ending impunity, preventing further human rights abuses or promoting respect for human rights. The agreement does not challenge the 1994 amnesty law which, while allowing some prisoners of conscience to be released, also granted impunity to perpetrators of human rights violations. AI was also concerned that although the signatories of the agreement committed themselves to ensuring that refugees and displaced people could return promptly to Togo, there was no reference to the security criteria which would allow such return to take place.

In September, the European Parliament passed a resolution condemning "all forms of violence and human rights abuses committed in Togo" and called for independent inquiries into cases of torture and extrajudicial executions so that those responsible might be brought to justice.

Proceedings against AI

On 5 May 1999 AI published a report entitled *Togo: Rule of terror*, based on the findings of a fact-finding visit to Togo in November and December 1998. The report described a persistent pattern of extrajudicial executions, "disappearances", arbitrary arrests and detentions followed by torture and ill-treatment, sometimes leading to death, and harsh conditions of detention which amounted to cruel, inhuman and degrading treatment. In particular, it alleged that hundreds of people had been killed by the security forces around the time of the June 1998 elections, and that bodies had been dumped at sea by military aircraft. By July independent journalists and another human rights organization, the *Ligue pour la défense des droits de l'homme*, League for Human Rights, based in Benin, had confirmed AI's findings.

The authorities reacted to AI's report by calling the document "a tissue of untrue statements, false allegations and bias, inspired by the bad faith of its authors", and warned the local press not to report it. A four-person delegation, led by AI Secretary General Pierre Sané, was prevented from entering the country on 21 May, although the delegates held valid visas and sought dialogue with President Eyadéma. Instead of investigating the allegations raised by AI, the Togolese authorities decided to start legal proceedings against AI, and issued a summons to Pierre Sané to appear before an investigating magistrate of the High Court in Lomé for "a possible indictment for contempt, incitement to revolt, dissemination of false news and conspiracy against the external security of the State".

In July, as President Jacques Chirac of France prepared to visit Togo, AI published an open letter urging him to use his influence to persuade the Togolese authorities to invite UN human rights experts (the Special Rapporteurs on torture and on extrajudicial, summary or arbitrary executions, and the

Working Group on Enforced or Involuntary Disappearances) to investigate past crimes, and to bring an end to reprisals against and harassment of human rights defenders in Togo.

On 20 July AI published *Togo: Time for accountability – more than three decades of human rights abuse*, a compilation of AI reports published from 1986 to 1999. The reports provided evidence of the persistence of human rights violations in Togo, and of the climate of impunity in which they flourished. AI called on all members of the international community to take action to end that impunity, by taking steps to bring to justice any Togolese officials in their jurisdiction suspected of crimes of torture and "disappearances". It repeated its call on the French President to bring his influence to bear, and called on Togolese citizens in exile to lodge complaints against Togolese officials responsible for acts of torture.

On 23 July AI rejected categorically a statement made by President Chirac that AI's May 1999 report had been the result of "manipulation", and again called for an end to impunity. AI called on all states which were party to the UN Convention against Torture and Other Cruel, Inhuman or Degrading Treatment or Punishment, where Togolese officials suspected of torture and "disappearances" were present, to take steps to bring them to justice.

In October AI met the Togolese ambassador to the USA, after sending an open letter to the Togolese authorities stressing that AI remained open to dialogue but that human rights are not negotiable.

Commission of inquiry

In August, the UN Sub-Commission on the Promotion and Protection of Human Rights announced the establishment of a commission of inquiry to investigate allegations of extrajudicial executions in Togo in 1998 and noted the government's undertaking to cooperate fully with the international commission of inquiry. In October, the Togolese government issued an invitation to the UN and Organization of African Unity to establish the international commission of inquiry. The commission of inquiry had not been established by the end of 1999.

Attacks on human rights defenders

Human rights defenders continued to be arbitrarily arrested and detained. At least two were known to have been tortured in custody. Members of AI Togo were subjected to surveillance.

☐ Around the time of the publication of AI's report in May, leading members of the *Association togolaise pour la défense et la promotion des droits de l'homme*, Togolese Association for the Defence and Promotion of Human Rights, were arrested: Tengue Nestor, Gayibor François and Brice Sant'anna were all charged with "false accusation and defamation" and held for more than a month. They continued to face criminal charges.

☐ On 14 May Koffi Antoine Nadjombe, a philosophy teacher and member of AI Togo, was arrested together with his wife Adjoa. She was released two days later, but her husband was held for more than a month, first in a police building, the *Sûreté*, and then in the civil prison. While in detention he was beaten and threatened with lethal injections. He was released provisionally in June, but continued to face criminal charges.

☐ On 26 May Arsène Bolouvi and Benjamin Adjoh, members of the Togolese section of *L'Action des Chrétiens pour l'abolition de la torture*, Christian Action for the Abolition of Torture, narrowly escaped arrest and were forced to seek refuge abroad.

☐ On 19 May Ameen Ayodele, a member of AI Nigeria who was returning from Ghana to Nigeria, was arrested at the Togolese border. He was held incommunicado for more than a week in a tiny cell with neither food nor clothing. He was beaten every day and taken to a beach, where police held a gun to his head and threatened to execute him and dump his body in the sea. He was released without charge after nine days.

☐ In December, five leaders of a students' union and members of teachers' unions were detained briefly. They were beaten at the time of arrest and while in custody.

Restrictions on press freedom

Attacks on press freedom continued.

☐ Romain Koudjodji, editor of *Le Reporter,* was arrested in April after the publication of an article on a case of torture by security forces. He was charged with propagation of false news and received a two-month suspended sentence. He was released two months later.

☐ In December, Roland Kpagli Comlan, director of *L'Aurore,* a weekly independent newspaper, was arrested for reporting incorrect information about the death of a secondary-school pupil during a student gathering which was suppressed by the Togolese security forces. This information had been made public during a press conference by a teachers' union. At the end of 1999 he was still in detention.

Killings by security forces

There were further reports of extrajudicial executions by the security forces.

On 23 January 1999, three individuals, who had received permission to cross the frontier post at Avéshivé between Togo and Ghana, were killed by members of the *Forces armées togolaises* (FAT), Togolese Armed Forces. The following day, Koffi Agbassa, a Togolese refugee returning from Ghana, was killed at the same place. When the victim's brother claimed his body at a military camp in Lomé, not far from the border, he was arrested and held without charge for a week.

'Disappearances'

No steps were taken by the authorities to clarify the fate of more than 12 people who had "disappeared" since 1994. There were further reports of "disappearances".

☐ Kokou Akakpo was arrested on 7 February 1999 in Casablanca, a district of Lomé, and taken to the gendarmerie. He then "disappeared". Kokou Akakpo had been a refugee in Ghana in 1993, and was apparently suspected of a criminal offence.

Torture and ill-treatment

The security forces routinely beat and assaulted criminal suspects at the time of arrest, when suspects were transferred to a detention centre, or during interrogation at a gendarmerie, to extract information or confessions. Political activists were also tortured to stifle dissent. As well as being beaten with rifle butts, batons, belts and other implements, kickings and prolonged periods in contorted positions, detainees were often taken from the police station or gendarmerie and subjected to mock executions. Detainees were mainly tortured during the period of *garde à vue* (incommunicado) detention. Criminal investigators forced detainees to sign confessions, without revealing their contents, which were later used as evidence in court.

Impunity

The authorities did virtually nothing to investigate or bring to justice those responsible for human rights violations. The only case to have been pursued, under pressure from the German authorities, was that of a German national killed by members of the FAT in 1996. Although compensation was paid to the relatives of three victims of extrajudicial executions, no legal action was taken to investigate their deaths, or those of the hundreds of other people killed by the security forces. Nor was anything done to change or forbid the procedures and practices that led to widespread and persistent violations of human rights.

Prison conditions

Prison conditions throughout the country, and particularly in Lomé civil prison, were extremely harsh and amounted to cruel, inhuman or degrading treatment. Deficiencies in food, sanitation, and medical care resulted in numerous deaths in custody.

AI country reports and visits
Reports
- Togo: Rule of terror (AI Index: AFR 57/001/99)
- Togo: Time for accountability – Tavio Amorin, Human Rights Defender, executed 23 July 1992 (AI Index: AFR 57/020/99)
- Togo: Time for accountability – More than three decades of human rights abuse (AI Index: AFR 57/022/99)
- Togo: Time for accountability – Komlan Edoh and Kodjo Kouni: two "disappeared" youths (AI Index: AFR 57/031/99)
- Togo: Human rights defenders under attack (AI Index: AFR 57/032/99)
- Togo: Time for accountability – The pressing case for an international commission of inquiry (AI Index: AFR 57/037/99)
- Togo: No political stability without respect for human rights (AI Index: 57/038/99)
Visit
An AI delegation was refused permission to enter Togo in May, despite having valid visas.

TRINIDAD AND TOBAGO

REPUBLIC OF TRINIDAD AND TOBAGO
Head of state: Arthur Napoleon Raymond Robinson
Head of government: Basdeo Panday
Capital: Port-of-Spain
Population: 1.3 million
Official language: English
Death penalty: retentionist
1999 treaty ratifications/signatures: Rome Statute of the International Criminal Court

Ten men were hanged in the first executions in the country for five years. In May the government's withdrawal from the American Convention on Human Rights came into effect with the result that the people of Trinidad and Tobago no longer have the protection of many of the fundamental human rights contained in the Convention. Despite repeated calls for the government to reverse this decision, the authorities maintained that it was justified on the grounds that the Convention had prevented the state from implementing the death penalty and that this withdrawal would facilitate executions. Conditions of detention continued to cause grave concern.

Death penalty

Ten men were hanged, the first executions for five years. Nine of the men were hanged over three days in June, despite appeals to the government for their sentences to be commuted. The 10th man was hanged in July in violation of an order of the Inter-American Court of Human Rights not to execute him until "such time as the court has considered the matter". There were approximately 80 people on death row at the end of 1999.

⬚ Three men were released from death row in April after Trinidad and Tobago's Supreme Court ruled that their confession had been coerced. This overturned the ruling of the trial judge that allowed parts of the confession to be used as evidence, despite an acknowledgement that the men were beaten by police and that one of the confessions had been coerced.

⬚ Russell Sankerali was one of the nine men hanged in June. After his execution it was discovered that on the eve of the execution the Attorney-General had received previously undisclosed evidence about the case. The new evidence cast serious doubt on Russell Sankerali's guilt and on the fairness of his trial. However, the Attorney-General failed to stay the execution in order to allow the courts to decide on the relevance of the evidence. Instead, he convened a meeting of the Prime Minister, the Minister of National Security and the Director of Public Prosecutions who decided, although it was not within their competence to make such a decision, that the evidence did not affect

Russell Sankerali's conviction and that the execution should proceed. AI called on the Attorney-General to establish an independent inquiry to examine why this evidence had not been disclosed to Russell Sankerali's lawyers at the trial and why the Attorney-General did not bring this evidence before the courts once it had been brought to his attention.

⌒ Indravani Pamela Ramjattan's murder conviction was reduced to manslaughter in October. The Court of Appeal decided to reduce the conviction on the basis of a psychiatrist's report which showed that Indravani Pamela Ramjattan was suffering from Battered Women's Syndrome when the murder of her abusive common-law husband took place in 1995. The Court, however, sentenced her to serve another five years in prison, bringing the total to 13 years.

Inter-American Commission on Human Rights
In 1998 the government issued execution warrants to 11 men, even though they had petitions pending before the Inter-American Commission on Human Rights. All 11 executions were stayed pending a decision by the national courts on whether it was constitutional to proceed. In January the Judicial Committee of the Privy Council in the United Kingdom, Trinidad and Tobago's highest court of appeal, ruled that the execution warrants were issued unlawfully and ordered the government to stay all executions while the cases were still pending before the Inter-American Commission on Human Rights.

UN Human Rights Committee
In November the UN Human Rights Committee ruled in the case of Rawle Kennedy that Trinidad and Tobago's reservation to the (first) Optional Protocol to the International Covenant on Civil and Political Rights (ICCPR), denying condemned prisoners the right to file complaints of violations of their rights under the ICCPR, was not permissible. The Committee stated that it "cannot accept a reservation which singles out a certain group of individuals for lesser procedural protection than that which is enjoyed by the rest of the population. In the view of the Committee, this constitutes a discrimination which runs counter to some of the basic principles embodied in the Covenant and its Protocols".

Corporal punishment
In July the Law Commission of Trinidad and Tobago recommended the use of corporal punishment on those convicted of rape or drug trafficking. In December, the Sexual Offences Amendment Bill proposed judicial corporal punishment of 20 strokes with the cat-o'-nine-tails (whip with nine knotted lashes) and life imprisonment for serial rapists.

At least one person was sentenced to corporal punishment. The government failed to supply information on how many people were sentenced to corporal punishment or on how many of the sentences were carried out during 1999.

Prison conditions
Prison conditions were so insanitary and overcrowded as to amount to cruel, inhuman and degrading treatment. The UN Human Rights Committee confirmed this finding in six cases and recommended that the men involved be released because conditions were so deplorable. In April the Attorney-General addressed the UN Human Rights Committee and dismissed the recommendations as unreasonable.

⌒ Between July and September, 10 men died in Port-of-Spain State Prison from unconfirmed diseases. The Prison Commissioner confirmed that up to 12 men were housed in cells designed for three people. Cases of tuberculosis and meningitis were reported in the prison.

Police brutality
There were a number of reported incidents of police brutality.

⌒ In June Dave Rodriguez, a television cameraman, was allegedly beaten by several officers in police custody and sustained a fractured skull as a result.

Inquest
The inquest into the deaths of three men shot by police on 5 August 1997 began in July. Lawyers for the deceased claimed that the men had been extrajudicially executed.

Intimidation and abuse of journalists
The government continued to criticize the press. Following such comments, members of the press were attacked. In May, Prime Minister Basdeo Panday refused to sign the 1994 Inter-American Press Association Declaration of Chapultepec, which outlines principles to promote freedom of expression and the press.

⌒ In May, two journalists were beaten by the police while reporting on a demonstration. Constitutional motions were filed and remained pending at the end of the year.

Gay men and lesbians
The government drafted an Equal Opportunities Bill to protect people from discrimination; however, it contained a clause excluding discrimination on the basis of sexual orientation or sexual preferences. Sexual acts between consenting people of the same sex remained illegal and gay and lesbian people were regularly subjected to discrimination and intimidation.

Domestic violence
In August an Amendment to the Domestic Violence Act was passed by parliament. This provides greater measures for the protection of victims and increases police powers in this area. However, despite this new legislation, there was little evidence of any decrease during the year in the extremely high occurrence of incidents of domestic violence.

TUNISIA

REPUBLIC OF TUNISIA
Head of state: Zine El 'Abidine Ben 'Ali
Head of government: Mohamed Ghannouchi (replaced Hamed Karoui in November)
Capital: Tunis
Population: 9.5 million
Official language: Arabic
Death penalty: retentionist

Hundreds of political prisoners, most of them prisoners of conscience, were released in November. Human rights defenders and their families were increasingly targeted, as were other activists such as trade unionists and journalists, and government opponents and critics from across the political spectrum. Scores were arrested and others were subjected to harassment and intimidation, prevented from leaving the country and had their communication lines intercepted and disrupted. Political trials grossly violated minimum standards for fairness. Reports of torture and ill-treatment during secret detention and in prisons continued to be received. At least one detainee was reported to have died in custody as a result of ill-treatment. No executions were reported.

Background

In October presidential and legislative elections took place. According to official statements, President Zine El 'Abidine Ben 'Ali was re-elected with 99.44 per cent of the votes. The six legal opposition parties were allocated 34 of the 182 seats in Parliament, regardless of their performances at the legislative elections.

Thousands of former political detainees and prisoners, mainly supporters of the unauthorized Islamist group *al-Nahda* (Renaissance), continued to be subjected to restrictions and intimidation. Although hundreds were released in November, up to 1,000 political prisoners continued to be detained in poor conditions and many were denied medical care. Scores had been sentenced more than once on similar charges. Former prisoners continued to be subjected to administrative surveillance and harassment and so prevented from working or resuming a normal life. The circle of repression continued to widen. Human rights defenders, government opponents and critics continued to be falsely accused of "subversive activities" both within Tunisia and abroad. Foreign media and publications critical of the government continued to be banned in Tunisia.

Releases

Between June and September, six prisoners of conscience, four of them women, were released. Khemais Ksila, vice-president of the *Ligue tunisienne des droits de l'homme* (LTDH), Tunisian Human Rights League, was among those freed.

On 7 November, on the 12th anniversary of President Ben 'Ali's accession to power, about 600 political prisoners, most of them prisoners of conscience, were conditionally released. They were mainly alleged supporters of *al-Nahda* but included six alleged supporters of the unauthorized *Parti communiste des ouvriers tunisiens* (PCOT), Tunisian Workers' Communist Party.

Human rights defenders

Human rights defenders continued to be increasingly targeted. Human rights defenders were subjected to surveillance, restrictions on movement, intimidation, and disconnection and interception of their telephone and fax lines and mail. Many human rights defenders and their relatives were refused passports. They included Anouar Kousri, Secretary General of the Bizerte Section of the LTDH, Jamaleddine Bida, LTDH vice-president Khemais Ksila and his wife, and human rights lawyer Radhia Nasraoui's children.

The Tunisian section of AI came under more pressure. Its office, as well as those of the LTDH and the *Association tunisienne des femmes démocrates* (ATDH), Tunisian Association of Democratic Women, was under surveillance, its members were followed and intimidated by the authorities and its communication lines were intercepted and disrupted.

In March the *Conseil national pour les libertés en Tunisie* (CNLT), National Council for Liberties in Tunisia, an association created in December 1998, was refused authorization by the authorities. The CNLT's secretary general and its spokesman, Omar Mestiri and Moncef Marzouki, were arrested in May and June respectively, and charged with maintaining an unauthorized association. From May onwards Moncef Marzouki was charged three times with maintaining an unauthorized association. The leader of the *Forum démocratique pour le travail et les libertés,* Democratic Forum for Labour and Liberties, cardiologist Mustapha Benjaafar, was charged with similar offences in November. All three were awaiting trial at the end of 1999.

Further restrictions on freedom of expression

Further restrictions were imposed on civil society. In May, 10 trade unionists, all senior members of the *Union générale des travailleurs tunisiens* (UGTT), Tunisian Workers' General Union, were detained for two days after they condemned the authorities' increased interference in the UGTT's affairs. In December several trade unionists were beaten with clubs by police officers who intervened to prevent a peaceful march organized by the UGTT in the capital.

Taoufik Ben Brik, an outspoken journalist who published many articles highly critical of the authorities in foreign publications, was under constant surveillance. In May he was arrested and interrogated for several hours; in the preceding weeks he had been attacked outside his home in Tunis in broad daylight by three individuals armed with chains whom he recognized as being security agents.

In November Mohamed Mouadda, a former leader of

the opposition *Mouvement des démocrates socialistes*, Movement of Democratic Socialists, was placed under house arrest for almost a month after he announced as a symbolic gesture his intention to stand for the presidency.

In December, the offices of Sihem Ben Sedrine, a journalist trying to set up an independent newspaper, were ransacked on three occasions. All the computer equipment was taken. Members of the security forces reportedly threatened two employees of the publishing house with being tried on fabricated charges if they refused to provide information on Sihem Ben Sedrine.

Increasing restrictions on the Internet
Throughout 1999, access from Tunisia to human rights organizations' websites, including AI's, was blocked. Access to free e-mail providers was also blocked after human rights defenders set up accounts on these sites. In February AI launched a website entitled "Rhetoric Versus Reality" in order to counteract a website which used Amnesty as part of its name and contained Tunisian government material. In September several university students were detained and questioned about the use they had made of Internet accounts provided during an internship within a governmental body.

Unfair trials
Political trials fell far short of international standards for fairness. Examining magistrates and courts refused to investigate allegations of torture or to call defence witnesses. Lawyers were denied access to their clients' files until just before the hearing. Some defendants detained in connection with other cases were tried and sentenced without being present in court.

☐ At the trial in July of Radhia Nasraoui and her 20 co-accused, most of them students accused of links with the PCOT, the court refused to investigate defendants' allegations of torture or to order medical examinations of the defendants who still bore physical traces of torture. Testimonies about torture were systematically omitted from the court's summary of proceedings. The trial lasted about 20 hours, indicating the determination of the court to conclude the trial in a single session. During the pleadings, the judge prevented one of the lawyers from continuing his arguments, prompting the other defence lawyers to withdraw. Seventeen of the accused were sentenced to terms of imprisonment ranging from 15 months to four years. Radhia Nasraoui was sentenced to a suspended six-month prison term and the other three defendants, including Radhia Nasraoui's husband, were sentenced to nine years and three months' imprisonment *in absentia*.

Torture and ill-treatment
Among those allegedly tortured were Abdelmoumen Belanes and Fahem Boukaddous, both arrested in February on charges of links with the PCOT. No investigation was carried out into their complaints.

☐ At least one detainee died in secret detention, reportedly as a result of torture and ill-treatment. Tahar Ben Bechir Jlasi was arrested in Slimane on 23 July after an argument with a shopkeeper. He was reportedly beaten at night in Slimane police station before being transferred to Grombalia prison, where he died the following morning. His family was informed of the death on 26 July but was not given the body for burial. No investigation was known to have been carried out.

New laws
In July, following recommendations made by the UN Committee against Torture in 1998, a new law was passed making torture a crime punishable by eight years' imprisonment. However, the definition of torture is more restrictive than that required by the UN Convention against Torture and Other Cruel, Inhuman or Degrading Treatment or Punishment. According to the new law, only those who torture are punishable, whereas those who give the order to torture and those who supervise it cannot be prosecuted. The Penal Procedure Code was also modified to increase safeguards during, and reduce the length of, incommunicado detention to six days.

Security force brutality
In February scores of high-school students involved in demonstrations in Sidi Bou Zid and Gafsa against a reform of the examination system were reportedly beaten and otherwise ill-treated both during the demonstrations and after arrest by the security forces. No independent investigation was carried out into any of these incidents.

In June the security forces intervened to break up a fight in Beja football stadium involving supporters of competing teams and reportedly beat and otherwise ill-treated supporters of the local team who shouted slogans against the rival team of a relative of President Ben 'Ali. According to official figures, four people died in the incident but according to other sources the number of deaths was higher.

Intergovernmental action
In August the UN Working Group on Arbitrary Detention announced that it considered Khemais Ksila to be arbitrarily detained and called for his release.

In August the UN Sub-Commission on the Promotion and Protection of Human Rights expressed concerns about the case of Radhia Nasraoui.

In November the UN Committee against Torture strongly condemned the Tunisian judiciary for failing to investigate the circumstances surrounding the death of Faysal Barakat, who died in custody in October 1991 as a result of torture.

In December the UN Special Rapporteur on the promotion and protection of the right to freedom of opinion and expression visited Tunisia.

AI country visit
AI sent three observers to the trial of Radhia Nasraoui and her co-defendants. An AI researcher continued to be banned from Tunisia, and AI received no response to the communications it sent to the Tunisian government.

TURKEY

REPUBLIC OF TURKEY

Head of state: Süleyman Demirel
Head of government: Bülent Ecevit (replaced Mesut Y lmaz in January)
Capital: Ankara
Population: 63.5 million
Official language: Turkish
Death penalty: abolitionist in practice

Abdullah Öcalan, leader of the armed opposition group Kurdistan Workers' Party (PKK), was arrested and tried on charges of treason and separatism. He was sentenced to death in June, after an unfair trial, raising fears that Turkey might resume executions after a 15-year *de facto* moratorium. Hopes for a continuing moratorium and the abolition of the death penalty were, however, revived with Turkey's acceptance as a candidate for European Union (EU) membership. Protests against Abdullah Öcalan's arrest resulted in mass detentions. There were regular reports of torture from all over the country, and several people reportedly died as a result of torture. Ten political prisoners were killed by security officers in Ankara Closed Prison in September in disputed circumstances. Harassment of human rights defenders continued throughout 1999. The president of the Human Rights Association (IHD) was imprisoned. A change in the law led to the release of several writers and broadcasters and prevented some from being imprisoned. Other prisoners of conscience remained imprisoned or were tried for peacefully exercising their right to freedom of expression.

Background

Armed conflict between Turkish security forces and the PKK has continued since 1984 in the southeast of Turkey, which is mainly inhabited by Kurds. Both sides were responsible for human rights abuses during the conflict, in which an estimated 4,500 civilians were killed, around 3,000 settlements evacuated or burned down and up to three million people internally displaced. In mid-1999, Abdullah Öcalan reiterated the PKK's unilateral cease-fire, and urged the PKK to withdraw from Turkish territory.

Bülent Ecevit's centre-left Democratic Left Party (DSP) won general elections in April and formed a coalition government with the extreme right-wing Nationalist Action Party (MHP) and the centre-right Motherland Party (ANAP).

The pro-Kurdish People's Democracy Party (HADEP) and the Islamist Virtue Party (FP) were threatened by a ban. State of emergency legislation remained in force in five provinces and in a sixth was lifted only in December.

In December, Turkey was accepted as a candidate for EU membership. Accession negotiations were to start once certain criteria were met, including improved guarantees for respect of human rights. In the meantime, the human rights situation would be monitored and assessed and Turkish laws screened for compliance with EU standards.

The trial of Abdullah Öcalan

Abdullah Öcalan was taken into the custody of Turkish security forces on 15 February in Kenya. He was brought to Turkey and detained under special security measures on the island of Imral in the Marmara Sea. His main trial before a State Security Court on Imral started on 31 May. Abdullah Öcalan was held responsible for the deaths of 29,000 people (civilians, soldiers and PKK militants) who lost their lives in the conflict.

National law and international fair trial standards were violated throughout the pre-trial detention period and the trial. AI considered that Abdullah Öcalan's rights were violated, including the right to be brought promptly before a judge, the right to defend oneself in person or through legal counsel, and the right to a fair hearing before an independent and impartial tribunal. Abdullah Öcalan's lawyers were harassed, attacked and threatened both by angry crowds and by police officers. During the trial, a Constitutional amendment in response to decisions of the European Court of Human Rights and international scrutiny of the trial led to the replacement of the military judge hearing the case by a civilian judge.

Death penalty

On 29 June Abdullah Öcalan was convicted of "treason and separatism" under Article 125 of the Penal Code and sentenced to death. The death sentence was upheld by the Appeal Court in November, giving rise to fears that Turkey might resume executions after a 15-year *de facto* moratorium. At least 48 other death sentences had been upheld by the Appeal Court and could be carried out if confirmed by parliament. However, at the end of 1999 there were signs that Turkey might abolish the death penalty.

Torture and impunity

Torture continued to be widespread. After the arrest of Abdullah Öcalan, the number of reports of torture increased compared to the previous two years. Torture mainly occurred in police or gendarmerie custody in the days following arrest.

People suspected of offences under the jurisdiction of State Security Courts may be held incommunicado for up to four days, and in practice this period was often extended. Procedures laid down in the Criminal Procedure Code for the registration of detainees and for notification of families were often ignored, facilitating "disappearances" and torture.

Torture methods included severe beatings, being stripped naked and blindfolded, hosing with pressurized ice-cold water, hanging by the arms or wrists bound behind the victim's back, electro-shock torture, beating the soles of the feet, death threats, and sexual assaults including rape. Among the victims were children, women and elderly people, villagers, political activists and the socially disadvantaged.

Several people reportedly died as a result of torture. Among them was at least one non-political detainee, Alpaslan Yelden. Ten police officers were prosecuted in connection with his death in Izmir.

◻ On 5 March Süleyman Yeter, a trade unionist, and four other people were taken into custody at the Anti-Terror Branch of Istanbul Police Headquarters. The following morning Süleyman Yeter told another detainee that he had been stripped naked, severely beaten, sprayed with cold water and forced to lie on ice. He could not move his arms. On 7 March, an official confirmed that Süleyman Yeter had died in custody. His lawyers saw marks on his body that they believed to be evidence of torture. Immediately before his detention in March 1999, Süleyman Yeter had been invited to identify police officers who were on trial for having tortured him and 14 other detainees in early 1997. In late November, three police officers went on trial in connection with Süleyman Yeter's death in custody.

◻ Two Kurdish girls,16-year-old N.C.S. and 19-year-old Fatma Deniz Polattaş, were detained and reportedly tortured for several days at the Anti-Terror Branch of Police Headquarters in Iskenderun in early March. They were held blindfolded and naked. N.C.S. was exposed to verbal and sexual harassment. Fatma Deniz Polattaş was anally raped. A formal complaint was lodged, but the prosecutor decided not to prosecute the police officers.

Impunity

AI campaigned against impunity for torturers in Turkey with a report issued in April which detailed cases in which complaints of serious human rights violations were not pursued by the authorities. Detainees frequently could not identify their torturers because they were almost invariably blindfolded during interrogation. Medical evidence of torture was frequently suppressed. Medical officers who falsified reports have been promoted, and doctors who scrupulously carried out their duties have been put on trial or imprisoned.

Prosecutors were reluctant to investigate security officers. Judges failed to investigate allegations of torture. This also contributed to unfair trials. Statements allegedly elicited under torture were frequently admitted as evidence in trials. In the rare cases in which security officers were convicted, sentences were light.

A new Law on the Prosecution of Civil Servants came into effect on 5 December, but still required the permission of a senior official for the prosecution of suspected human rights abusers. AI recommended that the decision whether or not to prosecute security officers for human rights violations should be taken only by the judicial authorities.

AI welcomed a new law for the prevention of torture, which increased the penalties for torture and ill-treatment and penalized health personnel who conceal torture.

Killings in disputed circumstances

On 26 September, 10 prisoners from left-wing organizations, two of them members of the Central Committee of the Turkey Communist Workers' Party

(TKIP), were killed in Ankara Closed Prison, and dozens were wounded by security officers. The circumstances were disputed and the lawyers and relatives of the dead were excluded from the autopsy. The lawyers filed a complaint against 49 security officers.

Pressure on human rights defenders

The risk of attacks on officials and members of Turkey's largest human rights organization, the Human Rights Association (IHD), increased when the Office of the Chief of the General Staff issued a press statement on 25 February, shortly after Abdullah Öcalan's detention, linking human rights organizations to the PKK. On the same day, members of the IHD in Istanbul and in Ankara received death threats by telephone.

After repeated harassment and a series of detentions, the weekly vigil held by the "Saturday Mothers" for the "disappeared" had to be ended after nearly four years.

Branches of the IHD and the Islamic-oriented association *Mazlum Der* were closed temporarily. Ten executive members of the IHD Diyarbak r branch, on trial since October 1998 under the Anti-Terror Law on charges of producing propaganda for the PKK, were acquitted in May 1999. However, the court did not rule on the IHD's request to reopen the Diyarbak r branch, an important source of information on human rights violations in the southeast of Turkey. The branch was closed in May 1997.

◻ Ak n Birdal, then President of the IHD, was imprisoned on 3 June only a year after barely surviving an assassination attempt and in clear violation of his right to freedom of expression. Despite concerns about his health, he was made to serve two one-year prison sentences under Article 312(2) of the Penal Code. He had called for a peaceful approach to the Kurdish issue and had used the phrase "the Kurdish people" in speeches in 1995 and 1996. Ak n Birdal faced numerous pending prosecutions for his public statements and activities as IHD President. AI feared that his imprisonment was part of the government's effort to discredit and hinder the work of human rights defenders. In April, AI's German Section awarded Ak n Birdal a special human rights prize. In September he was released from prison for six months on medical grounds – a welcome but insufficient step. He continued to be banned from political activities and from leaving the country.

Prisoners of conscience

Writers, publishers, trade unionists, teachers, local and national politicians, human rights defenders and many others continued to be imprisoned or tried after they exercised their right to freedom of expression. Those particularly targeted had expressed opinions on issues related to the Kurdish question or the role of Islam in politics. For example, Recep Tayy p Erdoğan, elected Mayor of Istanbul in 1994 and a leading figure of the Islamist Virtue Party, was imprisoned from 26 March to 25 July because of a speech he delivered in December 1997.

In August a change in the law suspended sentences, trials and investigations related to offences committed through the media, on condition the offence was not repeated within three years. As a result at least 22 prisoners were conditionally released in early September. Human rights defenders such as Eren Keskin, Zeynep Baran and Şanar Yurdatapan, who were due to be imprisoned, also benefited from the measure. Other prisoners of conscience, who had not expressed their opinions through the media, remained imprisoned.

📁 A 54-year-old blind lawyer, Eşber Yağmurdereli, faced more than 17 years' imprisonment after challenging the government over the status of the Kurdish population. He was arrested in Ankara in June 1998 and sentenced to 10 months' imprisonment for a speech he made in 1991, plus the remainder of a life sentence he received in 1978. This sentence, imposed after an unfair trial, was suspended in 1991 on condition that he commit no more offences of a political nature.

Other concerns
A number of possible extrajudicial executions were reported. Seventeen-year-old Necmettin Kahraman was shot in K z Itepe, in Mardin province, when the security forces fired on a non-violent demonstration on 19 February calling for independent monitoring of Abdullah Öcalan's trial. In September, AI was informed that no investigation had yet been opened into his death. Thirteen-year-old Şaban Çad roğlu, a peddler, was reportedly beaten to death by police officers in Van on 16 August. Erdinç Aslan, allegedly a radical leftist, was shot on 5 October in his home in Adana. Police had previously broken into the flat of his neighbour, Murat Bektaş, and shot him in front of his wife and young son. A trial was opened against six police officers, one of whom was held in custody, on 1 December.

At least 29 deliberate and arbitrary killings were attributed to armed opposition groups. The PKK was held responsible for bombings and attacks after the arrest of Abdullah Öcalan. The armed groups DHKP-C and TIKKO reportedly killed alleged informers. The police stated that 13 people were killed in clashes between two wings of the *Hizbullah*.

AI campaigned against the forcible repatriation of Iranian refugees. The organization expressed regret when Rustam Mamatkulov and Zeyniddin Askarov were forcibly returned to Uzbekistan from Turkey on 26 March 1999 despite a formal request from the European Court of Human Rights not to deport them.

AI country reports and visits
Reports
- Turkey: "Creating a silent society" – Turkish Government prepares to imprison leading human rights defender (AI Index: EUR 44/005/99)
- Turkey: Abdullah Öcalan's detention and trial must conform with international standards (AI Index: EUR 44/018/99)
- Turkey: The duty to supervise, investigate and prosecute (AI Index: EUR 44/024/99)
- Turkey: Death sentence after unfair trial – The case of Abdullah Öcalan (AI Index: EUR 44/040/99)

Visits
AI delegates visited Turkey in March and November to research human rights violations. In February, April, October, November and December delegates observed sessions of trials including the IHD Diyarbak r branch trial; trials of police officers in connection with the torture of Süleyman Yeter and others in 1997, and his death in custody in 1999; the death in custody of Alpaslan Yelden; and the retrial of police officers charged with torture of children in Manisa. AI sent a delegate twice to trials of Abdullah Öcalan. He observed the trial in Ankara in April, but was not admitted to Imral◊in June.

TURKMENISTAN

TURKMENISTAN
Head of state and government: Saparmurad Niyazov
Capital: Ashgabat
Population: 4.7 million
Official language: Turkmen
Death penalty: abolitionist for all crimes
1999 treaty ratifications/signatures: UN Convention against Torture and Other Cruel, Inhuman or Degrading Treatment or Punishment

The government restricted access to Turkmenistan and banned several foreign human rights monitors, making monitoring of the human rights situation increasingly difficult. Members of unregistered religious denominations reported frequent harassment by the authorities, including short-term arrest. Fears for the safety of political prisoners heightened after the death in custody of possible prisoner of conscience Khoshali Garayev. The death penalty was abolished in December.

Background
Parliamentary elections were held in December, but the Organization for Security and Co-operation in Europe (OSCE) decided not to deploy any election monitors, on the grounds that even the minimum level of pluralism for competitive elections was absent. Virtually no political activity was allowed, and candidates for the 50-seat *Majlis* (parliament) were reportedly selected by the President. President Saparmurad Niyazov, head of the Democratic Party (formerly the Turkmen Communist Party) since 1985, was made President for life in December.

According to the President's 10-year democratization plan, Turkmenistan was moving gradually towards a multi-party system, with increased powers to be granted to the *Majlis* at the end of 1999, and the creation of opposition political parties to be allowed by 2008 or 2009.

The death penalty was abolished on 29 December 1999. In December 1998 Turkmenistan had announced a moratorium on the death penalty. In previous years, hundreds of death sentences had been imposed, mostly for drug-related offences.

Deportations

Several foreign human rights monitors and journalists were deported from Turkmenistan during 1999.

⌒ On 3 February Aleksandr Petrov, part of a Human Rights Watch delegation in Turkmenistan on a fact-finding mission at the invitation of the government, was deported. He was detained on 2 February by officers of the Committee for National Security (KNB) and accused of possessing materials threatening the security of Turkmenistan. According to Aleksandr Petrov, these materials were reports on the human rights situation in Turkmenistan. He was held incommunicado and not allowed to inform his colleague that he was being forcibly deported.

Repression of religious minorities

Only the Russian Orthodox Church and the officially sanctioned Sunni Muslims were able to gain re-registration for their congregations after re-registration of religious organizations was made compulsory in early 1997.

There was a wave of police raids on Protestant churches in the second half of the year. Adventist and Baptist services were disrupted, congregations dispersed and pastors fined, and sometimes beaten.

⌒ In March Shagildy Atakov, an ethnic Turkmen member of a Baptist congregation in Turkmenbashi (formerly Krasnovodsk), was sentenced to two years in a labour camp and a fine by Kopetdag District Court in Ashgabat after being found guilty of swindling. The charge reportedly related to Shagildy Atakov's car business. Supporters of Shagildy Atakov, however, alleged that the real reason for his sentence was his religious affiliation. The prosecution appealed against his sentence on the grounds that it was too lenient, and in August, Shagildy Atakov was tried again. At the second trial he was sentenced to four years' imprisonment and a fine equivalent to US$12,000. Shagildy Atakov was reportedly beaten severely in prison. In April Shagildy Atakov's brother Chariyar was stopped at a police checkpoint on the Ashgabat-Dashkhovuz highway. He was reportedly beaten at the KNB offices in Dashkhovuz when he refused to give information about the Baptist church.

Short-term detention

Short-term detention was used to harass and intimidate perceived critics of the government and members of unauthorized religious groups.

⌒ Vyacheslav Mamedov, a leading member of the Russian community in Turkmenistan, was reportedly detained by the KNB on 21 January and taken to the KNB investigation-isolation prison in the city of Nebit-Dag. He had described the work of the Russian community in Turkmenistan in the field of emigration in a brief interview given to a Russian radio station in December

1998. According to reports, the following day President Niyazov publicly accused Vyacheslav Mamedov of slandering Turkmenistan and of encouraging emigration among the Russian-speaking population. Vyacheslav Mamedov was released on 3 February after he signed a statement agreeing not to leave the country and to refrain from any political activity.

Death in custody

Khoshali Garayev, a possible prisoner of conscience, died in September in the maximum security prison of Turkmenbashi. He was convicted in 1995 of anti-state crimes, including "attempted terrorism", and sentenced to 12 years' imprisonment. There was compelling evidence that the case against Khoshali Garayev and his co-defendant Mukhametkuli Aymuradov was fabricated solely to punish them for their association with exiled opponents of the government. In December 1998 both men were sentenced to an additional 18 years' imprisonment in connection with an alleged prison escape attempt.

Khoshali Garayev's family were informed of his death on 10 September. They received no death certificate and no official written explanation of his sudden death, and were apparently allowed neither to view the body nor to have an autopsy conducted. According to the prison authorities Khoshali Garayev hanged himself, but in a recent letter he had appeared hopeful that he would benefit from an upcoming presidential amnesty and that he would be back with his family in the year 2000.

Conscientious objectors

Conscientious objectors to military service continued to be sentenced to prison terms; they were prisoners of conscience. Prisoners sentenced in previous years continued to be held.

⌒ Kurban Zakirov, from the city of Chardzhev near the Uzbek border, was sentenced in April to two years' imprisonment for "evading regular call-up to active military service". Kurban Zakirov, a Jehovah's Witness born in 1980, was detained by police for 30 days on charges of participating in an illegal religious meeting after discussing the Bible at the home of some friends in Chardzhev. Following his release in February, he was called to the Military Commissariat where he stated his conscientious objection to compulsory military service. He was charged under Article 219 of the Turkmen Criminal Code and placed in pre-trial detention.

Political prisoners

⌒ Gulgeldi Annanyyazov and Gurbanmurat Mammetnazarov, the last two of a group of political prisoners known as the "Ashgabat Eight", sentenced to long prison terms after an anti-government protest in Ashgabat in July 1995, were released in January. On 3 February, following his release, Turkmen television reportedly showed Gulgeldi Annanyyazov repenting his alleged crimes.

⌒ Pirimkuli Tangrykuliev, a prominent doctor, was arrested on 29 June and detained in a KNB facility in Ashgabat. Dr Tangrykuliev was reportedly sentenced to eight years' imprisonment in August on charges of stealing government property and misusing his government position. The real reasons for his prosecution appeared to be that he wrote a letter in May criticizing the health care system, and that he had expressed an interest in participating in the December elections.

UGANDA

REPUBLIC OF UGANDA
Head of state: Yoweri Museveni
Head of government: Apollo Nsibambi
Capital: Kampala
Population: 20.3 million
Official language: English
Death penalty: retentionist
1999 treaty ratifications/signatures: Rome Statute of the International Criminal Court

Hundreds of political prisoners, including a number of prisoners of conscience, were arrested during 1999. Some were held in illegal detention centres. Prisoners continued to be held without trial on serious charges that preclude bail for statutory periods. Many prisoners were held beyond the statutory period. More than 500 prisoners charged with treason in 1997 were released after trial. There were reports of torture and possible extrajudicial executions by members of the security forces, and at least one person died as a result of torture. Human rights abuses by armed opposition groups continued throughout 1999. Hundreds of civilians were displaced because of the threat of abduction, rape and deliberate and arbitrary killing. Courts continued to impose the cruel, inhuman and degrading punishment of caning. Prison conditions were harsh. The death penalty was used extensively: 28 people were executed in April and at least 62 people were sentenced to death, including one woman. A total of 269 people were under sentence of death at the end of 1999.

Background
Human rights abuses were committed in the context of warfare in northern and western Uganda between the government's Ugandan People's Defence Forces (UPDF) and armed opposition groups supported by the government of Sudan. Bomb attacks in Kampala brought the conflict to the capital in the first part of the year. In December an Amnesty Act was passed, offering an amnesty to all rebel fighters who gave themselves up and handed in their weapons. The legislation raised concerns regarding impunity for armed opposition groups who have been responsible for serious human

rights abuses. The day after the Act was passed, Sudan and Uganda signed an agreement to disband and disarm armed opposition groups based in their respective countries.

There were reports of extrajudicial executions and other human rights violations by the UPDF in the Democratic Republic of the Congo (DRC). Ugandan forces have been fighting in the DRC in support of a rebellion by the *Mouvement pour la libération du Congo*, Movement for the Liberation of Congo, and a faction of the Congolese armed opposition group the *Rassemblement congolais pour la démocratie*, the Congolese Rally for Democracy, since August 1998.

In July and September, in the eastern Moroto district, cattle raids between the Mathenikos and the Bokoras, sub-clans of the Karamojong, resulted in hundreds of people being killed, many of them women and children. In August a senior army officer stated that Karamojong warriors found with guns along the main highway would be shot on sight. The directive followed a series of incidents in which armed Karamojong had shot at vehicles on the road.

In July a Referendum Act was passed, providing for a referendum in 2000 on whether Uganda should change its political system from the current "movement" system which does not allow political parties to contest elections, in preparation for presidential and parliamentary elections in 2001. Critics of the government expressed concern that restrictions on freedom of association and expression unfairly inhibited proponents of a multi-party system. A number of political parties threatened to boycott the forthcoming elections and there were allegations by the government that pro-democracy groups opposed to the referendum had turned to armed opposition. In July a leading government opponent was killed, reportedly in a shoot-out with the UPDF in Apac district, and a number of others were arrested and accused of belonging to an alleged armed opposition group, the Citizens Army for Multiparty Politics. In December a Bill was passed – the Other Political Systems Bill – which provided the legal framework for alternatives to the "movement" to be set up.

In November the Ugandan Human Rights Commission opened an office in Gulu, northern Uganda, the first of six regional offices, and began hearing cases of human rights violations by security officers.

Abuses by armed opposition groups
Human rights abuses by the Allied Democratic Front (ADF), based in the DRC, intensified during 1999. There were reports of deliberate and arbitrary killings, abductions and rape of civilians during attacks on schools, villages and camps for the people displaced by the fighting. More than 100,000 people have been displaced in Bundibugyo and Kasese districts, western Uganda, since ADF attacks began in 1997.

Human rights abuses by the Lord's Resistance Army (LRA) continued during 1999, although to a lesser extent than in previous years following a significant drop in incursions from Sudan into northern Uganda. However, in December more than 150 supporters of the LRA moved into Uganda from Sudan after the agreement between Uganda and Sudan was signed and a number of attacks on civilians were reported. In December, two senior LRA commanders responsible for serious human rights abuses were executed in Sudan reportedly on the orders of Joseph Kony, leader of the LRA.

Rwandese members of the *interahamwe* militia were believed to be responsible for attacks on civilians in Uganda during the year.

In March members of the *interahamwe* attacked a tourist camp in Bwindi Impenetrable National Park, southwest Uganda, killing the local conservation officer, John Ross Wagaba, and abducting 14 tourists. Eight of the tourists were killed and the remaining six released.

Human rights violations by the security forces

There were reports of detention without trial, torture and possible extrajudicial executions by the security services.

Political prisoners

Hundreds of political prisoners were arrested during 1999, many of whom were held without charge beyond the legal limit of 48 hours, some in illegal detention centres. In February the Minister of Internal Affairs, Major Tom Butime, acknowledged in Parliament that the government had been using illegal detention centres to detain suspects and stated that in future special cells in police stations would be used to detain people suspected of terrorist offences. However, illegal detention centres were reportedly still being used in October.

More than 60 suspected government opponents were charged with treason, which precludes bail for at least 360 days.

Five hundred prisoners were released during 1999 after they were tried and acquitted of treason. More than 400 political prisoners remained in custody, held on treason charges, three years after their arrest.

In December, 30 prisoners rioted in Central Police Station claiming that they had been held for six months without charge.

Torture and killings

In January the Acting Inspector General of Police, John Kisembo, criticized police officers for torture, excessive use of force and unlawful arrests. He said that those involved would be punished. However, there continued to be reports of torture throughout 1999 and at least one person died as a result of torture.

In February, two teenage girls were raped while in police custody. The girls, who were under arrest at Kabujogera Police Post, Kabarole, had been handed over to two members of the Local Defence Unit by a police constable for money. Two of these three men were later arrested.

In October, Yusuf Waiswa died shortly after he was released from Buwenge Police Post where he had reportedly been tortured. Following his funeral, hundreds of people rioted and were beaten and shot at by police. Several bystanders received gunshot wounds. A police constable was arrested, charged with the murder of Yusuf Waiswa and released on bail.

There were reports of killings by the security forces during 1999; some may have been extrajudicial executions.

In February, two UPDF soldiers killed five suspected criminals including Julius Sabiiti who was 13 years old. According to eyewitnesses they had been disarmed, made to lie down and then shot. The soldiers were arrested and charged with murder.

Freedom of association and expression

Constitutional restrictions on political activity prevented political parties from meeting.

In November police prevented the launch of the Federal Multi-party (FeParty), stating that the ban on political parties remained. FeParty was finally launched in December.

Journalists continued to be harassed and arrested for their reporting and three faced charges of sedition at the end of the year. In November journalists demonstrated in Kampala against the laws on sedition and criminal libel.

Detention because of sexual orientation

In September, following reports in the Ugandan press of a wedding between two men, President Museveni directed the police to arrest and charge all homosexuals. Homosexuality is a crime in Uganda and carries a penalty of life imprisonment. There followed reports of harassment of people for their sexual orientation.

In October, five people were reportedly arrested at a meeting by army and police officers, accused of being homosexual and held illegally for up to two weeks in illegal detention centres, army barracks and police stations before being released without charge. A number of Ugandans fled the country fearing arrest. In November President Museveni stated that homosexuals could live in Uganda as long as they kept their sexual orientation secret.

Death penalty

In April, 28 men were executed, the largest group of prisoners executed for many years and the first executions since 1996. In December the Ugandan Cabinet rejected recommendations by the Law Reform Commission to end the death penalty for rapists and defilers. There were 269 prisoners on death row, including 150 soldiers, at the end of 1999. Forty-four were apparently facing imminent execution.

Prison conditions

Prison conditions were harsh, with severe overcrowding, and disease was rife.

In November Kakiika prison, Mbarara, originally built for 130 prisoners, was holding 819 inmates and had converted three pit latrines into cells. More than 120 prisoners were in the sick bay suffering from scabies and syphilis.

AI country reports and visits
Report
• Uganda: Breaking the circle – protecting human rights in the northern war zone (AI Index: AFR 59/001/99)

Visit

AI delegates visited Uganda in March to launch the report on human rights in the northern war zone. The report documented a pattern of human rights violations by government forces in northern Uganda and urged the government to implement a coordinated program of action to address human rights violations and end impunity. It also called on the LRA to end child abductions and other human rights abuses and on the Sudanese government to stop providing assistance to the LRA. The delegates met government officials, human rights activists and others.

UKRAINE

UKRAINE
Head of state: Leonid Kuchma
Head of government: Viktor Yushchenko (replaced Valery Pustovoytenko in December)
Capital: Kiev
Population: 50.7 million
Official language: Ukrainian
Death penalty: abolitionist for all crimes

Ukraine abolished the death penalty following persistent pressure from the Council of Europe. There were a significant number of allegations of police ill-treatment and torture of detainees, which in certain cases had resulted in death. People at risk of serious human rights violations in their country of origin were deported, in breach of international standards. AI received information about a number of possible prisoners of conscience.

Background

Ukrainian citizens voted the incumbent President, Leonid Kuchma, back into office in two rounds of presidential elections in October and November. The elections were marred by sporadic violence, violations of election procedure and accusations that President Kuchma received unfair access to the media.

Death penalty

Ukraine came under increasing pressure from the Council of Europe to fulfil its commitment, originally made upon entry to the Council of Europe in November 1995, to abolish the death penalty. In June 1999, the Parliamentary Assembly of the Council of Europe gave Ukraine until its next session in January 2000 to make substantial progress towards reforms aimed at improving human rights or it would commence the procedure for the annulment of the credentials of the Ukrainian delegation at the Council of Europe. During the debate in the Parliamentary Assembly, members

cited as reasons for the January 2000 deadline the forthcoming presidential elections, the need to support democratic forces in the country and the need to engage in constructive rather than punitive criticism.

On 5 August the head of the Supreme Court of Ukraine, Vitaliy Bokyo, stated in a news conference that 35 people had been sentenced to death in the first six months of 1999. However, other unconfirmed sources suggested that the real figure was nearly twice as high for the same period.

In December the Constitutional Court ruled that the death penalty was unconstitutional since it violated the principle of the right to life which is enshrined in the country's Constitution, and contravened the constitutional provision that no one should be subjected to torture or to cruel, inhuman or degrading treatment or punishment. The Ukrainian parliament was charged with the task of removing the death penalty from the Ukrainian Criminal Code as soon as possible.

In a live television broadcast during the presidential election campaign, President Kuchma suggested that he might ignore the existing moratorium on executions in the case of Anatoly Onuprienko. This was not the first time that President Kuchma had spoken out in favour of executing the prisoner, who was convicted of serial murder by a court in the town of Zhytomyr in Western Ukraine on 1 April.

Forced deportations

People at risk of serious human rights violations if returned to their countries of origin were deported, in breach of international standards. The forced deportations were believed to be part of a joint operation between Ukrainian and Uzbek law enforcement agencies against suspected opponents of the President of Uzbekistan.

Four men were deported from Ukraine on 18 March. Two of them — Muhammad Bekzhon and Yusif Ruzimuradov — were prominent members of the banned Uzbek opposition party *Erk*. Both men had lived in Kiev since 1994 after they fled from Uzbekistan to escape arrest during an official clampdown on *Erk*.

Ill-treatment and torture

Ill-treatment and torture of detainees by law enforcement officials were relatively widespread. In July a delegation of the Council of Europe Committee for the Prevention of Torture and Inhuman or Degrading Treatment or Punishment (ECPT) carried out a nine-day visit to Ukraine.

AI received allegations that Sergey Ostapenko died from gangrene on 10 May after being tortured by police officers from the Cherkassy branch of the Directorate Against Organized Crime. Police officers allegedly hung him for several hours by his handcuffed hands so that his feet did not touch the floor. According to reports, he developed gangrene because the flow of blood to his hands was stopped, and he was not given adequate medical care until the gangrene was in an advanced state.

Possible prisoners of conscience

During 1999 AI learned of several individuals who appeared to have been arrested for exercising their right to freedom of expression.

☐ Dr Sergey Piontkovski, an academic at the Institute of Biology of the Southern Seas based in Sevastopol, was arrested by the Security Service of Ukraine (SBU, the former KGB) on 17 October. He was charged with passing on scientific data collected in the Soviet era to several Western universities. He was also charged with receiving grants in hard currency for research purposes, as part of international research in the field of marine biology. Although he was released shortly after his arrest, the charges against him remained in place. A number of other academics at the institute were also reportedly under investigation.

☐ The *Nash Mir* (Our World) Gay and Lesbian Centre was refused official registration as an official public organization by the Lugansk Regional Department of Justice in April rendering illegal any further activities by the organization and exposing active members to possible imprisonment. AI learned that the authorities later reversed their decision, officially registering *Nash Mir* on 30 November.

Prison conditions

Conditions in prisons and pre-trial detention centres continued to fall below international minimum standards, and amounted to cruel, inhuman or degrading treatment. AI received reports that people were sometimes detained for long periods of time before coming to trial.

AI country reports

- Ukraine should abolish the death penalty by January 2000 (AI Index: EUR 50/005/99)
- Concerns in Europe, January – June 1999: Ukraine (AI Index: EUR 01/002/99)

UNITED ARAB EMIRATES

UNITED ARAB EMIRATES
Head of state: Al-Sheikh Zayed bin Sultan Al-Nahyan
Head of government: Al-Sheikh Maktum bin Rashid al-Maktum
Capital: Abu Dhabi
Population: 2.6 million
Official language: Arabic
Death penalty: retentionist

During 1999, at least eight people were sentenced to death and two people were executed. At least five death sentences passed in previous years were commuted. The number of crimes punishable by death was also increased.

Background

The United Arab Emirates (UAE) is a federation of seven emirates: Abu Dhabi, Dubai, Sharjah, Ras al-Khaimah, Umm al-Qaiwain, 'Ajman and Fujairah. There have been no elections and no political parties have been authorized. The main policy-making body is the Supreme Council of Rulers, composed of the rulers of the seven Emirates, who appoint the members of a Federal National Council, which is responsible for reviewing and amending legislation.

Executions

Muhammad Arshad, a Pakistan national, was executed in 'Ajman in June for the murder of a young woman in 1993. Gamini Perera, a Sri Lankan national, was executed in Dubai in November for the murder of an 18-year-old youth. He had been sentenced to death by a Dubai court in 1998. The sentence was upheld by the Court of Appeal in February, and by the Supreme Court in October.

Death sentences

At least eight people were sentenced to death during 1999. Seven were foreign nationals. Six of the eight were reportedly sentenced to death on drug-related charges.

Commutation of death sentences

The death sentences on Rabi' Ghassan Taraf, a Lebanese national, and Ryan Dominic Mahoney, a Canadian national, both of whom were charged with drug-related offences, were commuted to life imprisonment during 1999, after a retrial. Ryan Dominic Mahoney was reportedly released on 31 October.

The death sentences on two Russian nationals charged with murder – Anton Samoilenkov and Ruslan Gerbekov – were commuted in June by an appeal court in 'Ajman to 10 years' imprisonment and an order to pay approximately $US 20,000 "blood money" (compensation) to the victim's relatives. The third Russian national involved in the case, Ivan Tziberkine, had his death sentence quashed.

In September, the death sentence on Malullah Bakkar Fayruz, an Omani national convicted of a drug-related offence, was commuted to life imprisonment by the Court of Appeal. In November, the death sentence on a national of the UAE convicted of rape was commuted to 10 years' imprisonment, 200 lashes and a fine, by the Court of Appeal in Ras al-Khaimah. By the end of 1999, it was not known whether the flogging sentence had been carried out.

In January it was reported that John Aquino, a Philippine national sentenced to death in 1990 for murder, might have had his sentence commuted after the family of the victim reportedly submitted affidavits to the Supreme Court granting him clemency. The Supreme Court in Abu Dhabi had previously allowed John Aquino's lawyers time to seek clemency from the victim's family.

Changes in law
In October a new Federal Environment Law was issued by the President. Article 62(2) of this law states that anyone found storing or dumping nuclear waste and polluting the environment would be subject to either the death penalty or life imprisonment, and a large fine.

Cruel judicial punishments
Sentences of cruel, inhuman and degrading punishments such as flogging were reportedly passed during 1999. In October a Shari'a court in Fujairah reportedly sentenced a number of foreign nationals to flogging for sexual offences. They included a Sri Lankan woman and an Indian man who were sentenced to 15 months' imprisonment and 100 lashes each, to be followed by deportation. The court reportedly also sentenced two Bangladesh nationals to one year's imprisonment and 100 lashes, again to be followed by deportation. An Indian national was also reportedly sentenced to flogging for sexual offences and for using a house as a brothel.

UNITED KINGDOM

UNITED KINGDOM OF GREAT BRITAIN AND NORTHERN IRELAND
Head of state: Queen Elizabeth II
Head of government: Tony Blair
Capital: London
Population: 59 million
Official language: English
Death penalty: abolitionist for all crimes
1999 treaty ratifications/signatures: Second Optional Protocol to the International Covenant on Civil and Political Rights, aiming at the abolition of the death penalty; Protocol No. 6 to the European Convention for the Protection of Human Rights and Fundamental Freedoms concerning the abolition of the death penalty

Negotiations over the implementation of the Multi-Party Agreement in Northern Ireland continued throughout 1999, but sectarian killings and attacks continued. A human rights lawyer was killed in Northern Ireland, further undermining the rule of law. At least two black people died in police custody. Detainees and prisoners were subjected to ill-treatment and racist abuse. An inquiry into police handling of the racist killing of Stephen Lawrence found institutional racism within the police service.

Background
Negotiations over the implementation of the Multi-Party Agreement in Northern Ireland culminated in the establishment of the Executive of the Northern Ireland Assembly in December. Other aspects of the agreement were also implemented. However, the human rights situation in Northern Ireland still gave cause for concern and some areas appeared to have become more polarized, in particular during the marching season.

In May representatives were elected to new devolved institutions: a Scottish Parliament and a Welsh National Assembly.

AI was concerned by proposed new legislation, including the Terrorism Bill and the Freedom of Information Bill, which appeared to restrict further the rights to freedom of expression and association.

General Augusto Pinochet remained under house arrest, pending his extradition to Spain on charges of torture (see pages 14 to 17).

Northern Ireland
Human rights aspects of the Multi-Party Agreement
In March a Human Rights Commission was formed. During 1999 the Commission began consultation on a bill of rights for Northern Ireland.

The Independent Commission on Policing for Northern Ireland published its report in October. AI welcomed many recommendations, including the integration of human rights in all aspects of policing, a new human rights-based oath, and proposals for greater accountability and transparency. However, AI also identified several omissions. It urged the government to address past abusive practices by the Royal Ulster Constabulary (RUC) and to establish further mechanisms to ensure accountability. In particular, AI called for units within the RUC associated with patterns of human rights violations to be disbanded. AI also urged a thorough review of covert operations and the establishment of a civilian body to oversee intelligence agencies and covert operations.

The Independent Commission on Policing echoed recommendations made previously by UN treaty bodies for the closure of special interrogation centres. In December the RUC announced the imminent closure of Castlereagh Holding Centre.

In May AI submitted comments to the Criminal Justice Review. AI called for international human rights standards to be incorporated into all aspects of the criminal justice system, raised concerns about the failure to prosecute members of the security forces involved in killings or assaults, and urged reforms in procedures for appointing the judiciary.

Rosemary Nelson

Human rights lawyer Rosemary Nelson was killed by a car bomb in Lurgan on 15 March; Loyalist paramilitaries claimed responsibility. In recent years she had suffered a campaign of intimidation, harassment and threats by members of the RUC and the army and had received anonymous death threats. AI was concerned that the police team appointed to investigate the killing was not sufficiently independent of the RUC, and that police investigations into complaints made by Rosemary Nelson of intimidation and harassment by the RUC had not been thorough and impartial. In December AI joined five other human rights organizations in urging the authorities to establish an independent inquiry into all the circumstances of her death.

A memorial for Rosemary Nelson was held in Geneva, Switzerland, during the 55th session of the UN Commission on Human Rights, which was addressed by Mary Robinson, the UN High Commissioner for Human Rights. A briefing sponsored by AI and other international human rights organizations was addressed by Geraldine Finucane, the wife of Patrick Finucane.

The Independent Commission for Police Complaints, in its annual report, noted that in 1998 it had received 36 complaints alleging police misconduct against 15 solicitors.

Patrick Finucane

On the 10th anniversary of the killing of lawyer Patrick Finucane in February, a human rights group submitted evidence to the government of active collusion in his killing and in others by members of the RUC and of army intelligence with Loyalist paramilitaries. The RUC asked a senior London police officer to investigate, which resulted in the arrest in June of a former Special Branch (police intelligence) agent, Alfred Stobie. Alfred Stobie, a former member of the Ulster Defence Association, stated that he had informed Special Branch before the murder that someone was to be killed, and told them about the movement of weapons used in the murder.

AI continued to urge the government to institute an independent judicial inquiry into the killing of Patrick Finucane.

Robert Hamill

Of six people charged in connection with the death of Robert Hamill, who died in 1997 after being beaten by a crowd, Marc Hobson was the only one brought to trial. In March he was acquitted of murder and sentenced to four years' imprisonment for affray. The Director of Public Prosecutions decided not to prosecute four RUC officers who were at the scene but reportedly failed to take any action.

Impunity

The new inquiry into the killing of 13 unarmed people by the army on "Bloody Sunday" was delayed by arguments over whether security force witnesses would be allowed to remain anonymous. The inquiry judges continued to collect and process large amounts of evidence.

The establishment of the inquiry, coupled with the cease-fires, raised hopes of resolving hundreds of past cases. In some, victims' families wanted the facts about how their relative was killed; in others, victims of miscarriages of justice were trying to establish their innocence. The Independent Commission on Policing failed to recommend a mechanism to deal with the legacy of past human rights abuses.

Abuses by armed political groups

AI delegates spent three days in Portadown in May, talking to community groups, church leaders, police officials, the Orange Order, politicians and others. The situation in Portadown reflected the human rights issues at the heart of the conflict, including a deeply polarized community and a large number of sectarian attacks. Elizabeth O'Neill, a Catholic woman, was killed by Loyalists in Portadown when a pipe bomb exploded in her home in June.

During 1999 there were seven killings; 73 "punishment" shootings (26 by Republicans and 47 by Loyalists); and 133 "punishment" beatings (42 by Republicans and 91 by Loyalists). Some beatings were of children under the age of 16; children's limbs and fingers were broken after being beaten with baseball bats or hammers.

Deaths in custody

At least three people, two of whom were black, died in police custody in disputed circumstances during 1999. Three died in north London: Roger Sylvester died in January after being restrained; Sarah Thomas, a young black woman, died in August after being arrested; and police shot dead Harry Stanley in September.

Prompted by the deaths in custody of Nathan Delahunty and Roger Sylvester, the London Metropolitan Police announced plans in January for rapid response medical units. An inquest in January decided that the death of Nathan Delahunty in July 1998 had been partly caused by his being restrained by police with his hands behind his back while under the influence of cocaine. Roger Sylvester died eight days after being restrained on 11 January. The eight police officers who restrained him were moved to non-operational duties during an inquiry. In

November, the police file was submitted to the prosecution authorities.

Updates

Five police officers were charged in October in connection with the death of Christopher Alder, who died in April 1998 in Hull.

The Prison Service was criticized in March by the Parliamentary Ombudsman for its conduct in the case of Kenneth Severin, who died in November 1995 after being restrained face-down on the floor by prison officers. Among the shortcomings highlighted were the Prison Service's failure to train its staff adequately and its failure to disclose details of its internal inquiry to his family.

In April a police officer was charged with murder and manslaughter after shooting dead James Ashley during a raid in January 1998. James Ashley was naked, unarmed and in bed with his girlfriend when 30 officers raided his flat, although it subsequently emerged that police were acting on inaccurate intelligence reports. Other officers were charged with misfeasance (neglect of duty or abuse of power) or received disciplinary notices.

After a six-week trial, three police officers were acquitted of the manslaughter of Richard O'Brien who died in custody in 1994.

An inquiry into deaths in custody, carried out by a retired judge, reported in August and made recommendations concerning the role of the prosecution authorities in such cases.

Police handling of racist killings

The judicial inquiry into the police investigation of the racist killing of Stephen Lawrence in 1993 issued its report in February. Sir William MacPherson, a retired judge who led the inquiry, found that the investigation had been fundamentally flawed "by a combination of professional incompetence, institutional racism and a failure of leadership by senior officers". The report made 70 recommendations. However, the subsequent government response to the report was described by civil rights activists as inadequate.

Michael Menson died after being set on fire in a racist attack in January 1997. The police treated the case as suicide for almost two years, despite statements about the attack that Michael Menson made before he died. Following a new investigation by the race and violent crimes task force, three men were charged in March with his murder. Two were convicted of manslaughter and the third of murder.

Ricky Reel died in October 1997 after drowning in the Thames river. The police failed to carry out a thorough and impartial investigation, and the Police Complaints Authority found three officers guilty of neglect of duty. An inquest jury in November returned an open verdict; the family believe he died as a result of a racist attack.

Ill-treatment in prisons

Reports of ill-treatment and racist abuse were received from prisoners in various prisons, including Wandsworth, Frankland, Swaleside and Durham. Reports were also received of neck holds being used on teenagers in Medway Secure Training Centre, and of ill-treatment of teenagers in Portland, Dorset, and in Lisnevin, Northern Ireland.

The criminal investigation into alleged torture and ill-treatment of prisoners at Wormwood Scrubs Prison in London resulted in criminal charges against at least 27 prison officers. The police investigation continued. A report on the prison by the Chief Inspector of Prisons, published in June, was severely critical of the prison, including the attitudes of prison officers and widespread racism and bullying.

Refugees

In November, the government enacted the Immigration and Asylum Act 1999. Although some measures were welcome, the overall impact of the Act was severely detrimental to refugee rights. AI made a series of representations, focusing on three main issues: the extension of pre-entry controls; the need for effective judicial oversight of the detention of asylum-seekers; and the need to ensure access to high-quality legal advice if asylum-seekers were dispersed around the UK.

The High Court decided in July that the practice of prosecuting and imprisoning those using false travel documents to transit the UK was contrary to international refugee law.

In May AI UK published a report on the treatment of unaccompanied refugee children which made a series of recommendations on child asylum-seekers.

Scotland

Human Rights Act

Certain provisions of the Human Rights Act, which came under the responsibility of the Scottish Executive, came into force in Scotland in May 1999. AI was concerned that there was no independent body to monitor the implementation of the new legislation, and urged the establishment of a human rights commission for Scotland.

Two cases were brought, challenging the rule under which the police were allowed six hours in which to interview a suspect before contacting a defence lawyer.

Racism

The case of Gulbar Chokrar Singh highlighted institutionalized racism within the police force and procurator fiscal service. The Scottish Executive announced that it would counter institutionalized racism by making the eight Scottish police forces accountable to HM Inspectorate of Constabulary on their race policy. The Executive also accepted that the Race Relations Act should apply to all police officers. AI urged the Executive to introduce an independent police complaints body for Scotland.

Detention of minors

AI was concerned that juveniles under the age of 18 were detained in adult prisons and detention centres. According to reports, 30 girls under the age of 18 were detained at Cornton Vale prison.

AI country reports and visits

Reports

- Northern Ireland: The killing of human rights defender Rosemary Nelson (AI Index: EUR 45/022/99)

- Northern Ireland: Submission by Amnesty International to the Criminal Justice Review (AI Index: EUR 45/023/99)
- Northern Ireland: End impunity for ill-treatment – the David Adams case (AI Index: EUR 45/045/99)
- Northern Ireland: The sectarian killing of Robert Hamill (AI Index: EUR 45/031/99)
- Northern Ireland: Response to "A New Beginning: policing in Northern Ireland" (AI Index: EUR 45/048/99)

Visits

AI delegates visited Northern Ireland in February, March and October to gather information. In July, a representative monitored the policing of parades in Northern Ireland. A four-person AI delegation visited Northern Ireland in May and had a series of meetings with political leaders, police representatives, government officials, victims and families, and non-governmental organizations. AI delegates also met the Northern Ireland Secretary of State in March to discuss the killing of Rosemary Nelson and in May to discuss issues arising out of the delegation's visit earlier in the month.

UNITED STATES OF AMERICA

UNITED STATES OF AMERICA
Head of state and government: William Jefferson Clinton
Capital: Washington, D.C.
Population: 267.8 million
Official language: English
Death penalty: retentionist

More prisoners were executed in 1999 than in any year since 1951. Police brutality, deaths in custody and ill-treatment in prisons and jails were reported. In October the US submitted its initial report to the UN Committee against Torture, five years after ratifying the Convention against Torture and Other Cruel, Inhuman or Degrading Treatment or Punishment. The report acknowledged there were areas of concern but stated that torture did not occur except "in aberrational situations and never as a matter of policy". US authorities continued to violate international standards protecting children. AI's year-long worldwide campaign against human rights violations in the USA continued throughout most of the year. It called on the authorities at local, state and federal level to take action on a wide range of human rights concerns including the death penalty, police brutality, prison and jail conditions and the treatment of refugees, and called on the government to ratify international human rights treaties.

Death penalty

In 1999, 98 prisoners were executed in 20 states, bringing to 598 the total number executed since the end of a moratorium on the death penalty in 1977. The USA continued to violate international standards such as the prohibition on the use of the death penalty for crimes committed by children under 18 years of age. In October the government urged the Supreme Court not to examine US obligations relating to this ban in connection with an appeal by Michael Domingues who was on death row in Nevada for a crime committed when he was 16. The Supreme Court announced in November that it would not consider the appeal.

Sean Sellers was executed in Oklahoma in February for murders committed when he was 16 years old.

There was continued concern about racism in application of the death penalty.

In June, Brian Baldwin was executed by electric chair in Alabama despite appeals from 26 members of the Congressional Black Caucus in Washington, DC, calling for a stay of execution in view of the "clear pattern of racial discrimination in his case".

Trials for capital offences continued to fall below international standards. Eight prisoners under sentence of death were released from death row in 1999 after evidence of their wrongful conviction emerged, bringing to 84 the number of inmates released after being sentenced to death since 1973.

David Junior Brown was executed in North Carolina in November despite serious questions surrounding his conviction.

Foreign nationals charged with capital offences continued to be denied their right to seek assistance from their consulates, in violation of international standards.

The day before German national Walter LaGrand was due to be executed in Arizona, Germany filed a request for "provisional measures" at the International Court of Justice (ICJ). The ICJ issued an order for the execution to be halted. However, despite a recommendation from the Arizona parole board for a stay to allow the ICJ time to examine the appeal, Walter LaGrand was executed in the gas chamber on 3 March. The German government decided to pursue its legal claim against the USA in the ICJ.

Police brutality

Police brutality — including misuse of pepper spray and police dogs, and deaths from dangerous restraint holds — and shootings by police in disputed circumstances, continued to be widely reported. Systematic human rights abuses were uncovered in several police departments. Several police departments, including the New York Police Department (NYPD), were reportedly under federal investigation, under a 1994 law which allows the Justice Department to sue police agencies accused of a "pattern or practice" of abuses.

Many of the unarmed suspects shot by police were members of ethnic minority groups; some were shot while fleeing the scenes of minor crimes or during routine traffic stops. There was widespread concern that many police forces unfairly targeted motorists who were members of minority groups for stops and searches, a practice known as "racial profiling". A bill requiring the US Attorney General to keep national statistics on race and police traffic stops was reintroduced into Congress but had not passed into law by the end of the year. Meanwhile, some individual states passed their own legislation to outlaw "racial profiling" and some police agencies set up their own monitoring systems. There was also concern at several cases involving mentally or emotionally disturbed individuals who were shot in circumstances suggesting that they could have been subdued by non-lethal means.

Although few police officers were prosecuted for ill-treating suspects, trials were pending in several high-profile cases.

There were reports that police ill-treated demonstrators protesting during the World Trade Organization talks in Seattle (Washington) in December. There were allegations that police used pepper spray and tear gas indiscriminately against non-violent protesters, unresisting residents and bystanders. There were also reported incidents of excessive use of force by police against people held in King County jail after arrest. The allegations were being investigated by local civil rights groups and a Seattle city council panel at the end of the year.

Allegations that Los Angeles Police Department (LAPD) officers from Rampart Station beat and shot unarmed suspects, planted evidence and lied to cover up their actions were being investigated by a special board of inquiry at the end of the year; more than a dozen officers had been fired or suspended. The scandal, which came to light through the testimony of a police officer arrested on unrelated charges, raised concern about the effectiveness of the LAPD's monitoring mechanisms, despite reforms over the past few years.

In April the US Justice Department filed a federal lawsuit against the New Jersey State Police for an alleged "pattern and practice" of discriminatory traffic stops. Similar lawsuits filed by civil rights groups against various state or local police departments were pending in a number of states including Colorado, Illinois, Maryland, Michigan, Oklahoma and Pennsylvania.

In October the Justice Department sued the Columbus (Ohio) Police Department for tolerating a pattern of civil rights abuses, including excessive use of force, false arrests and improper searches.

Margaret Laverne Mitchell, a frail, mentally ill African American woman in her fifties, was shot dead by a Los Angeles police officer in June after she tried to lunge at officers with a screwdriver. An initial LAPD internal review ruled the shooting to be within policy, although the officers were criticized for using "faulty tactics". Following the fatal shooting by an LAPD officer of Felix Valenzuela, who was 16 years old, unarmed, naked and bleeding, in November, the LAPD established a task force to review its procedures for dealing with disturbed individuals.

In December an NYPD officer was sentenced to 30 years' imprisonment for the torture of Haitian immigrant Abner Louima in 1997. The officer had beaten and kicked Abner Louima and thrust a broken stick into his rectum, causing serious injuries to his small intestine and bladder. A second police officer found guilty of taking part in the assault was awaiting sentencing at the end of the year. Two other NYPD officers were charged with second degree murder for killing Amadou Diallo, an unarmed West African immigrant who was shot at 41 times outside his home in February after officers apparently mistook him for a criminal suspect.

In June the Justice Department held a national summit on police brutality attended by community, police and civil rights representatives. This was one of several government initiatives aimed at increasing police accountability and improving relations between communities and the police.

In September and October AI held hearings on police brutality in Los Angeles, Chicago and Pittsburgh and was working with local organizations to draw up further recommendations at the end of the year.

Ill-treatment in prisons and jails

Ill-treatment in prisons and jails, including physical and sexual abuse and abusive use of electro-shock weapons, continued to be reported. Several prisoners died, some reportedly as a result of beatings by guards. Many reported abuses took place in isolation units in high-security prisons.

There were continued concerns about conditions in so-called "supermaximum security" segregation units, where growing numbers of prisoners were kept in long-term isolation in small, sometimes windowless cells, in conditions of reduced sensory stimulation. In March a federal district judge ruled that the "extreme deprivations and repressive conditions of confinement" in segregation units in Texas prisons violated the US constitutional prohibition of cruel and unusual punishment. A state appeal against the ruling, which dealt with a range of Texas prison conditions, was pending at the end of the year.

There were continued concerns about the use of electro-shock equipment including remote control electro-shock stun belts, stun shields, stun guns and tasers (a device which fires darts connected to wires through which an electric shock is transmitted). AI urged federal, state and local law enforcement and correctional authorities to ban stun belts and suspend the use of all other electro-shock equipment pending a rigorous, independent inquiry into the use and effects of such equipment.

In January a federal court issued a preliminary injunction in the case of Ronnie Hawkins banning the use of stun belts in Los Angeles County courtrooms on the grounds that the "chilling effect" of the fear of the pain inflicted through its activation could deter defendants forced to wear such belts from properly participating in their defence. A judge had ordered the stun belt worn by Ronnie Hawkins to be activated during a court hearing in June 1998 after he had repeatedly interrupted the proceedings verbally. An appeal by the county against the ruling was pending at the end of the year.

⌕ On 15 April, the stun belt that Jeffrey Weaver was wearing during his capital trial in Florida was activated.

⌕ Federal and state investigations opened in July into allegations of systematic beatings by guards of prisoners in X Wing in Florida State Prison, a punitive isolation unit. One prisoner, Frank Valdez, died of injuries sustained while he was being "extracted" (forcibly removed) from his cell in July; all his ribs were broken and his body showed imprints of boot marks. Earlier beatings, which guards had tried to cover up, came to light after prisoners wrote to a newspaper about their plight. Nine guards were suspended and one was charged in November with aggravated assault in connection with Frank Valdez' death. Inquiries were continuing at the end of the year.

⌕ Serious human rights abuses, including racist abuse and misuse of stun weapons, were reported in Red Onion and Wallen Ridge state prisons, two new "supermaximum security" facilities in Virginia. AI called for an immediate ban on use of electro-shock weapons in Virginia prisons. In Red Onion State Prison it was alleged that shackled inmates, most of whom were black, were routinely made to wear stun belts and were arbitrarily shocked; had painful rubber pellets fired at them; and were subjected to racist slurs. Alleged abuses at Wallen Ridge included prisoners being beaten, shocked with stun guns while in restraints, verbally racially abused and deprived of sleep and medical attention.

Children in custody

A federal juvenile justice bill was under consideration which threatened to allow more children to be incarcerated with adult prisoners, in violation of international standards which stipulate that they should be held separately. The bill had not come before Congress by the end of 1999. There were continued reports of ill-treatment of children in custody.

Refugees

There were concerns regarding the treatment of asylum-seekers, many of whom were locked up on arrival and detained indefinitely, often together with criminal prisoners and in inhumane conditions, without knowing if or when they would be released.

Women in prison

There were many reports of ill-treatment of women inmates; the number of women held in US prisons and jails had tripled since 1989. Abuses included the use of restraints on sick or pregnant prisoners and inadequate medical care. Sexual abuse of women prisoners by male staff continued to be reported in various jurisdictions. AI called for female inmates to be guarded only by female officers, in line with international standards but contrary to common practice in the USA; for measures to protect inmates who report abuses from retaliation; and for a ban on the routine shackling of pregnant women.

In March the UN Special Rapporteur on violence against women, its causes and consequences, issued a report of her 1998 visit to the USA in which she cited concerns about widespread sexual abuse and the cruel use of restraints on pregnant prisoners and detained asylum-seekers. In calling for a series of reforms, she recommended that certain posts in women's prisons — such as those responsible for guarding housing units and body searches — should be restricted to female staff.

⌕ In April AI published its findings following a visit to Valley State Prison for Women in California in November 1998. AI detailed concerns including harsh conditions in the prison's Security Housing Unit where women, some of them mentally ill, were held in punitive isolation, sometimes for comparatively minor infractions.

The Californian authorities later informed AI that they had tightened procedures for investigating allegations of sexual misconduct in Californian prisons. However, no changes to the Security Housing Unit conditions were reported. In September more than 40 prison staff were reported to be under investigation for sexual misconduct in several women's prisons in California.

⌕ In October, a state inquiry was announced into complaints of widespread sexual abuse by guards at the Fluvanna Correctional Center for Women in Virginia. Complaints ranged from officers giving gifts to inmates in return for sexual favours, to rape. Inmates reported that most prisoners were afraid to report abuse because they feared reprisals from guards.

Six states — Massachussetts, Montana, Nebraska, Virginia, Washington and West Virginia — introduced laws in 1999 criminalizing all sexual contact between prison staff and inmates, bringing to 43 the number of states in which such legislation was in force by the end of 1999.

In July Illinois passed legislation ending the practice of using shackles on pregnant women in prisons and county jails while being transported to hospital, during labour and after giving birth.

Other concerns

AI called for the release of Leonard Peltier, based on its longstanding concerns about the fairness of the proceedings leading to his conviction. Leonard Peltier, leader of the American Indian Movement, had been convicted in 1977 of the murder of two Federal Bureau of Investigation agents and sentenced to two sentences of life imprisonment.

In September President Clinton granted conditional clemency allowing the immediate release on parole of 11 Puerto Rican independence supporters serving long sentences for politically motivated offences.

Intergovernmental organizations

In May the Inter-American Commission on Human Rights found that the incommunicado detention by US forces of 17 Grenadians for between six and nine days following US military action in Grenada in 1983 had failed to comply with US obligations under the American Declaration of the Rights and Duties of Man to prevent arbitrary detention. The case had been filed against the US government in 1991 by the 17 former detainees, most of whom were members of the Grenadian government or military who were subsequently convicted of responsibility for the murder in October 1983 of former Grenadian Prime Minister Maurice Bishop.

AI country reports and visits
Reports
- USA: "Not part of my sentence" – violations of the human rights of women in custody (AI Index: AMR 51/001/99)
- USA: Lost in the labyrinth – detention of asylum-seekers (AI Index: AMR 51/051/99)
- USA: Killing with prejudice – race and the death penalty in the USA (AI Index: AMR 51/052/99)
- USA: The findings of a visit to Valley State Prison for Women, California (AI Index: AMR 51/053/99)
- USA: Cruelty in Control? The stun belt and other electro-shock equipment in law enforcement (AI Index: AMR 51/054/99)
- USA: Killing without mercy – clemency procedures in Texas (AI Index: AMR 51/085/99)
- USA: Speaking out – voices against death (AI Index: AMR 51/128/99)
- USA: Race, Rights and Police Brutality (AI Index: AMR 51/147/99)
- USA: California – update on police brutality (AI Index: AMR 51/150/99)
- USA: Summary of AI's concerns on police abuse in Chicago (AI Index: AMR 51/168/99)
- USA: Shame in the 21st Century – three child offenders scheduled for execution in January 2000 (AI Index: AMR 51/189/99)

Visits
In August AI delegates visited Colorado State Penitentiary, a supermaximum security prison; concerns included the lack of outdoor exercise facilities and the extended periods during which some prisoners remained in isolation for relatively minor infractions.
AI delegates attended police brutality hearings in Los Angeles, Chicago and Pittsburgh in September and October.

URUGUAY

EASTERN REPUBLIC OF URUGUAY
Head of state and government: Julio María Sanguinetti
Capital: Montevideo
Population: 3.2 million
Official language: Spanish
Death penalty: abolitionist for all crimes

Past human rights violations remained unclarified, and there were continued reports that detainees had been ill-treated. AI used the opportunity presented by the presidential elections in November to raise the issue of human rights and urged the candidates to address impunity if successfully elected.

Impunity
Some 34 people "disappeared" and thousands were tortured under military governments between 1973 and 1985. The democratic government which took power in 1985 was urged to clarify the victims' fate, but in December 1986 parliament approved the Expiry Law granting exemption from punishment to all police and military personnel who committed human rights violations for political motives, or to fulfil orders, before 1 March 1985. The Expiry Law was retained after a national referendum in April 1989.

In 1995 Uruguay ratified the Inter-American Convention on Forced Disappearance of Persons thereby acknowledging "disappearances" as continuous or permanent offences "as long as the fate or whereabouts of the victim has not been determined". However, these crimes remained unresolved.

María Claudia García Irureta Goyena, an Argentine citizen, was six months' pregnant when she "disappeared" in Argentina with her husband, Marcelo Gelman, in August 1976. Her husband's body was discovered in 1989, but in May 1999 it emerged that María Claudia García might have given birth to her baby at the Military Hospital of Montevideo. According to information gathered by Marcelo Gelman's father, María Claudia García and her baby were last seen in December 1976 when they left the Third Division of the Defence Information Service escorted by two army officers. Marcelo Gelman's father called on President Julio María Sanguinetti to investigate the allegations, but the President's reply stated that he was unable to corroborate the allegations.

Ill-treatment
There were continued reports that detainees were ill-treated by police and prison guards in 1999.
Inmates at the *Libertad* prison in San José department reportedly went on hunger strike after they had been ill-treated by prison guards in February.

Presidential elections

AI wrote to all presidential candidates running for election in November, calling on them to put human rights issues high on their political agenda and urging them to address impunity if successfully elected. It suggested that the establishment of an independent body, such as an ombudsman, would be a step forward in the protection and promotion of human rights. AI also suggested that torture and "disappearances" should be incorporated into the Penal Code as a way of sending a clear message to the security forces that these crimes would not be tolerated. AI expressed concern that Uruguay had neither signed nor ratified the Statute of the International Criminal Court, which was adopted by the international community in 1998. Jorge Battle, who was elected in November, was due to take office in March 2000.

Carlos and Federico Fasano

Former prisoners of conscience Federico Fasano, director of *La República* newspaper, and Carlos Fasano, the editor of *La República*, were absolved by the Supreme Court of Justice in October 1999. They had been sentenced to two years' imprisonment in May 1996, after they published articles about the alleged corruption of the then President of Paraguay, but conditionally released two weeks later.

UZBEKISTAN

REPUBLIC OF UZBEKISTAN
Head of state: Islam Karimov
Head of government: Otkir Sultanov
Capital: Tashkent
Population: 23.7 million
Official language: Uzbek
Death penalty: retentionist

A series of bomb attacks in Tashkent in February, in which at least 13 people died and more than 100 were injured, triggered a wave of arbitrary arrests of supposed conspirators. These included members of independent Islamic congregations or followers of independent imams (Islamic leaders), supporters of banned political opposition parties and movements and their families. The authorities blamed the bombings on violent foreign-trained Islamic groups intent on establishing an Islamist state, which were operating in concert with the exiled, secular, democratic opposition. Heavy custodial sentences and death sentences were handed down after trials whose conduct gave serious cause for concern and during which the defendants made credible allegations of torture. Arrests and harassment of human rights defenders continued throughout the year. Some unforeseen releases of Christian believers took place ahead of two major international reports on religious tolerance. The death penalty continued to be imposed despite official statements towards abolition.

Background

Although a large turn-out was reported in the parliamentary elections held in December, the first since 1991, there were concerns that their conduct was not free and fair. Five parties competed for the 250 seats in the *Oliy Majlis* (parliament), all of which supported the government. The two opposition parties, *Erk* and *Birlik*, were banned. The Organization for Security and Co-operation in Europe (OSCE) did not send an official monitoring team to the elections, saying that the campaign process did not meet democratic standards. Some OSCE representatives were present and reported a number of problems, including interference by local authorities and the process of nominating candidates which was said to be neither unbiased nor independent. The results of the elections were due in January 2000.

AI received a growing number of reports of ill-treatment and torture by law enforcement officials of members of independent Islamic congregations or followers of independent imams. Hundreds of these so-called "Wahhabists" were sentenced to long terms of imprisonment after trials that fell far short of international fair trial standards. Those reported to have been arrested, ill-treated and tortured included suspected supporters of the banned political opposition parties *Erk* and *Birlik*, including family members and independent human rights monitors, as well as alleged supporters of banned Islamic opposition parties and movements, such as *Hizb-ut-Tahrir*. Concern was heightened in February when hundreds of men and women were detained following bomb explosions in Tashkent.

On 15 March President Karimov publicly named the exiled leader of the banned opposition *Erk* party, Muhammad Salih, as one of the organizers of the February bomb explosions and called for his arrest and extradition to Uzbekistan. On 18 March Muhammad Bekzhon, Yusif Ruzimuradov, Kobil Diyarov and Negmat Sharipov were forcibly deported from Ukraine following a joint Uzbek/Ukrainian police raid on their apartments. All were associates of *Erk*; Muhammad Bekzhon is also a brother of Muhammad Salih. A third brother, Rashid Bekzhon, was sentenced in August to 12 years' imprisonment after being convicted of terrorism. AI received a written statement signed by Rashid Bekzhon and five co-defendants alleging that they were tortured and ill-treated in pre-trial detention in order to force them to incriminate Muhammad Salih. Their appeals against their sentences were turned down in October.

Torture

Uzbekistan acceded to the UN Convention against Torture and Other Cruel, Inhuman or Degrading Treatment or Punishment in 1995. However, AI remained concerned that Uzbekistan failed to implement its treaty obligations. For example, it failed to ensure that all acts of torture were offences under its criminal law and that such offences were punishable by appropriate penalties. AI prepared a briefing for the November meeting of the UN Committee against Torture which was scheduled to review Uzbekistan's initial report on measures taken to implement its obligations under the Convention against Torture and Other Cruel, Inhuman or Degrading Treatment or Punishment.

AI was disturbed by public statements by Uzbek officials, including the President, in the wake of the Tashkent bombings which could be perceived to condone the use of torture and ill-treatment by state agents against certain sections of the population. In April President Karimov stated publicly that he was "prepared to rip off the heads of 200 people, to sacrifice their lives, in order to save peace and calm in the republic".

🗇 On 18 August Tashkent Regional Court sentenced Batyr Khalilov, his brother Farikh Khalilov, Ashrafkhodzha Mashradkhodzhayev, Ubaydullo Rakhmatullayev and Shukhrat Sharafuddinov to prison terms ranging from 16 to 18 years on charges including forming an illegal religious organization, inciting religious hatred and attempting to overthrow the constitutional order. The five members of *Hizb-ut-Tahrir* were reportedly tortured in order to force them to "confess". The methods included near-suffocation with a plastic bag, being hung upside down, having needles stuck under finger- and toe-nails, having their hands and feet burned and having electric shocks administered via a device fitted to the head ("electric cap").

Unofficial prison camps

AI received reports that the authorities were running prison camps in remote areas of Uzbekistan where the overwhelming majority of prisoners were reported to be members of independent Islamic congregations accused of supporting the banned Islamic opposition. The existence of two camps in former Soviet army barracks in the Republic of Karakalpakstan was independently confirmed. Conditions were said to be cruel, inhuman and degrading with prisoners denied adequate rations of drinking water while doing forced labour. There was concern that the camps are situated in chemically or biologically contaminated areas.

Harassment of human rights defenders

Intimidation and harassment continued during 1999 of members of the unregistered Independent Human Rights Organization of Uzbekistan (NOPCHU). In June its Chairman, Mikhail Ardzinov, was seriously injured during a search of his home by officers from the Tashkent City Department of Internal Affairs (GUVD). His injuries included two broken ribs, concussion and bruised kidneys, as well as cuts and bruises. After the search Mikhail Ardzinov was taken to the GUVD where he was reportedly beaten again and questioned before being driven back to his home. AI was concerned that his detention and ill-treatment were related to his outspoken and public criticism of the sweeping arrests of individuals and groups following the Tashkent bombings.

In September Ismail Adylov, a member of NOPCHU and *Birlik*, was sentenced to six years' imprisonment on charges of attempting to overthrow the constitutional order, sabotage and possessing material constituting a threat to public security and order. The charges related to documents allegedly found during a search of his home, but which Ismail Adylov said were planted there. On 26 October Ismail Adylov's appeal against his sentence was turned down by the Syrdarinsky Regional Court.

Akhmadkhon Turakhanov, a 51-year-old NOPCHU member, died in Tashkent prison in June. The cause of death may have been either diabetes, from which he suffered, or tuberculosis which he was believed to have contracted while in prison. He had been sentenced in March to six years' imprisonment for "hooliganism... committed at a mass gathering" and "attempting to overthrow the state". These charges were based on his having interrupted a meeting in a school hall by loudly criticizing the local authorities for failing to deal with such problems as the gas and water supply. The verdict states that he also expressed his discontent with the government, called for an Islamic state, and propagandized "Wahhabism" in local mosques. Akhmadkhon Turakhanov admitted speaking critically, but denied ever having called for the overthrow of the state or supporting "Wahhabism".

🗇 NOPCHU member and prisoner of conscience Makhbuba Kasymova was sentenced in July to five years' imprisonment for "concealing a crime" and "misappropriation of funds" after a grossly unfair three-hour trial described by human rights monitors as a "farce". Plainclothes officers had entered her flat when she was not there and questioned her family and Ravshan Khamidov, who was staying at her home. Ravshan Khamidov was detained after a hand grenade and a small quantity of drugs were allegedly planted on him by the officers. Makhbuba Kasymova, a mother of six and a former teacher, had no prior notice that her trial was taking place, and it was conducted without defence witnesses or a lawyer of her choosing. By the end of 1999 Ravshan Khamidov had not been tried for the crime which Makhbuba Kasymova was convicted of concealing.

Harassment of women

Reports of harassment of women by the authorities were received. On 21 February Munira Nasriddinova, the wife of Obidkhon Nazarov, an independent imam, and her mother-in-law were reportedly taken from their home in Tashkent to a local police station where they were allegedly beaten. The mother-in-law was reportedly released after eight hours, but Munira Nasriddinova was tried and sentenced to 10 days' administrative detention for "hooliganism". She was released on 3 March. While in detention she was reportedly questioned about her husband and imam Tulkin Ergashev. A warrant for the arrest of the two imams, for promoting "Wahhabism", preaching illegally and trying to set up an Islamist state, had been issued in March 1998.

Shahzoda Ergasheva, the wife of Tulkin Ergashev, was also detained on 21 February. She was reportedly held overnight in the cellar of the Ministry of Internal Affairs and questioned about the whereabouts of her husband. Over the next days she was moved to different locations before being transferred to a women's detention centre. She was reportedly beaten up by other prisoners. Her physical condition deteriorated and after her release on 8 March she was admitted to hospital where she remained for more than a month.

Arrests of Christians

Three members of the Full Gospel Church in Nukus, Republic of Karakalpakstan, were sentenced in June to terms of imprisonment on drugs-related charges. Pastor Rashid Turibayev received a 15-year sentence, and church members Parhad Yangibayev and Issed Tanishiyev each received a 10-year sentence. Pastor Tirubayev, who had been trying since 1995 to register the Full Gospel Church with the authorities in Nukus, was accused of holding illegal religious meetings and of converting Muslims. During a search of the homes of the three men, police allegedly discovered small quantities of drugs as well as items of Christian literature, video and audio tapes. All three men denied possession of narcotics and supporters claimed that the drugs had been planted.

Releases of religious followers

In August, five Christian prisoners and one Jehovah's Witness were unexpectedly released, all under presidential decrees. Among them were three members of the Full Gospel Church in the city of Nukus, Karakalpakstan Autonomous Republic. Pastor Rashid Turibayev and church members Parhad Yangibayev and Issed Tanishiyev had been sentenced to long terms of imprisonment on drugs-related charges. Rashid Turibayev had also been charged with participating in illegal religious activity. Supporters claimed the drugs had been planted in order to fabricate a criminal case against the men to punish their religious activity. In addition it was announced that a fine on a Pentecostal leader had been revoked.

The releases took place before two important events: the planned hearing on Uzbekistan by the US Commission on Security and Co-operation in Europe, at which freedom of religion was to be a major concern, and the 1 September deadline for the US State Department to present its report to Congress on religious liberty worldwide. Between August and December 1999 the government registered at least eight religious communities.

AI welcomed the release in September of Abdurauf Gafurov, who had been detained in November 1993 and sentenced to three years' imprisonment in 1994. AI believed that he was a possible prisoner of conscience, detained solely as a consequence of his activity in unregistered Islamic congregations and for the non-violent expression of his religious beliefs.

'Disappearance' in custody

Komil Bekzhon, younger brother of Muhammad Salih, "disappeared" in July while in state custody. Komil Bekzhon was serving a sentence of 10 years' imprisonment for possession of drugs and weapons, a charge which human rights monitors believed was fabricated solely on account of his brother's political activities.

Death penalty

There were serious concerns that the death penalty continued to be carried out despite official statements moving towards abolition. This concern was heightened by the fact that a substantial number of men sentenced to death alleged that they were tortured in pre-trial detention. AI learned of 37 death sentences and at least six executions during the year.

On 28 June the Supreme Court sentenced six men to death for their part in the February bombings in Tashkent. Sixteen co-defendants received prison sentences ranging from 10 to 20 years. All were accused of being members of extremist religious organizations which advocated a *jihad* (holy war) to overthrow the constitutional order and the assassination of President Karimov. There were reports that the defendants had been beaten or otherwise ill-treated in pre-trial detention and forced under duress to give false evidence, and human rights monitors expressed concern that fair trial standards, although promised by the authorities, had not been respected. Conditions on death row have been described by former prisoners as particularly cruel.

☐ Arsen Albertovich Arutyunyan and Danis Vladimirovich Sirazhev were sentenced to death in

November for murder. They were believed to be in danger of imminent execution. There were serious concerns that their confessions had been extracted under duress.

AI country reports
- Uzbekistan: Makhbuba Kasymova, prisoner of conscience (AI Index: EUR 62/022/99)
- Uzbekistan: Ismail Adylov, prisoner of conscience (AI Index: EUR 62/024/99)
- Uzbekistan: Summary of concerns on torture and ill-treatment – Briefing for the United Nations Committee on Torture (AI Index: EUR 62/027/99)
- Uzbekistan: Arsen Albertovich Arutyunyan and Danis Vladimirovich Sirazhev (AI Index: EUR 62/029/99)

VENEZUELA

BOLIVARIAN REPUBLIC OF VENEZUELA
Head of state and government: Colonel Hugo Chávez Frías
Capital: Caracas
Population: 22.8 million
Official language: Spanish
Death penalty: abolitionist for all crimes
1999 treaty ratifications/signatures: Inter-American Convention on Forced Disappearance of Persons

The human rights situation in Venezuela remained poor throughout 1999. The new government, which came to office in February, repeatedly stated its commitment to the protection of human rights. Progressive constitutional and other reforms favouring the protection of human rights had yet to be translated into effective administrative and practical steps. Criminal suspects continued to be arbitrarily arrested and ill-treated; some were tortured or extrajudicially executed. Chronic inefficiency in the administration of justice resulted in continuing prison overcrowding and conditions which amounted to cruel, inhuman and degrading treatment, a long-standing institutional feature of the penal system. At least 400 prison inmates were killed in prison violence. Some 3,700 asylum-seekers fleeing political violence in neighbouring Colombia were returned to the country without being given access to full and fair asylum determination procedures.

Background
In February Colonel Hugo Chávez Frías, leader of a failed military coup in 1992, became President following democratic elections in December 1998. His government — which came to office against a background of serious economic problems, and dissatisfaction with traditional political parties and official corruption — promised radical reforms. A new Constitution, approved by a significant majority of the electorate in December, was brought into effect the same month. Congress failed to approve long-awaited legislation in favour of strengthening indigenous rights and prohibiting torture. The suspension of at least 120 judges was explained by the government as one of the initial steps to reform a judiciary widely regarded as notoriously inefficient and subject to political influence. Between 20,000 and 50,000 people were reported to have died as a result of flooding and landslides in the northern state of Vargas following torrential rainfall in mid-December.

The new Constitution
In November, following several months of consultation with political parties and organizations representing different sectors of civil society, the National Constituent Assembly finalized the drafting of the new Constitution. The Constitution contained provisions to strengthen the protection of human rights. These included the recognition of international human rights treaties, the exclusion of human rights cases from the jurisdiction of the military justice system, and the outlawing of enforced disappearances. Non-governmental human rights organizations characterized these and other provisions as markedly progressive, but warned that they were at risk of being undermined as a result of other constitutional provisions which increased the political power of the armed forces. The Constitution did not prohibit the armed forces from intervening in political affairs.

Killings by the security forces
At least 100 people — the majority suspected of criminal offences — were reported to have been killed by members of the police and armed forces. This figure represented a decrease over past years. Most of the victims were killed by the police, but at least 15 were killed by members of the army. Some 50 of the victims died in circumstances suggesting that they were the victims of extrajudicial executions.

Torture and ill-treatment
Cases of torture and ill-treatment continued to be reported despite legal guarantees protecting the right to personal integrity. The most commonly reported abuses consisted of the police beating detainees on arrest or during interrogation. Many of the victims and their families did not file complaints before the authorities because they feared reprisals. Those cases in which a complaint was filed were rarely investigated independently, and the ineffectiveness of the judiciary meant that cases of torture rarely resulted in convictions.

Prison conditions
The crisis in the penal system continued despite marked reductions in overcrowding and in the proportion of prisoners being held without trial.

Prisoners continued to face endemic violence. At least 400 prisoners were killed in 1999, the majority as a result of violence by fellow prisoners, but some as a result of attacks by guards. The number of deaths led some observers to comment that the authorities had virtually lost control of the penal system. The physical conditions and lack of basic services suffered by prisoners amounted in many cases to cruel, inhuman and degrading treatment. Scores of prisoners were reported to have died as a result of inadequate sanitary conditions and medical care.

In September, and again in November, government officials once again publicly recognized the poor conditions prevailing in Venezuela's prisons and added that the new administration was intent on resolving the problem.

Impunity

Recent reforms to the administration of justice, including ensuring that prosecutors and judges independently and rigorously apply provisions contained in the new Organic Code of Criminal Procedures, had yet to show positive results in combating the impunity enjoyed by those responsible for torture and extrajudicial executions.

In November, in the context of the government's declared commitment to respect human rights, Venezuela announced before the Inter-American Court of Human Rights that it had assumed responsibility for the deaths of 37 people, the enforced disappearance of four others, and beatings inflicted on a further three. All 44 had been the victims of abuses by the security forces during a week of demonstrations and looting in February 1989 in response to economic measures introduced by the government of the then President, Carlos Andrés Pérez. The Inter-American Court had not determined the reparations and damages to be paid by the government to the victims' families by the end of 1999.

Asylum-seekers

The authorities failed to give some 3,700 Colombians, who fled from political violence across the border into Venezuela, access to a full and fair asylum procedure to identify those at risk if returned to Colombia. They had fled in four separate waves, following the start of counter-insurgency offensives by Colombian security forces and paramilitaries. All were returned to Colombia, the majority apparently voluntarily. However, at least 100 of the asylum-seekers were forcibly returned after requesting assistance from Venezuelan human rights organizations in applying for asylum.

VIET NAM

SOCIALIST REPUBLIC OF VIET NAM
Head of state: Tran Duc Luong
Head of government: Phan Van Khai
Capital: Hanoi
Population: 75.1 million
Official language: Vietnamese
Death penalty: retentionist

Dozens of prisoners of conscience remained in prison throughout 1999, and restrictions on recently released prisoners became increasingly harsh. Political dissidents and religious critics of the government were subjected to surveillance, harassment and denial of basic freedoms, including freedom of expression. More than 20 possible prisoners of conscience were sentenced to prison terms. The government continued to prevent independent human rights monitors from visiting the country, and sharply criticized a UN report on lack of religious freedom in Viet Nam. Following a debate over the use of the death penalty, amendments to the Criminal Code approved in December cut the number of crimes for which it could be imposed. Scores of people were sentenced to death; executions by firing squad took place in public.

Background

The leadership of the ruling Vietnamese Communist Party appeared to be increasingly concerned about criticism of the party and the state. Following the publication in January of a letter from a very senior party figure, General Tran Do, criticizing government policies and calling for reform, restrictions on all known and suspected government critics were tightened. After scandals over local officials' corruption, especially in Thai Binh province, the Communist Party launched a two-year self-criticism initiative for members, but announced it was disappointed with the early results. The National Assembly continued with its program of law reform. However, there was no progress on reforming key elements of the Criminal Code which restrict the basic human rights of Vietnamese people.

Denial of access

Government restrictions on access and information hampered the collection of independent and impartial information about the human rights situation. Domestic human rights monitoring was not permitted, and international human rights monitors were denied access, raising concerns that the population remained vulnerable to hidden human rights violations. Following the publication in March of the report of the UN Special Rapporteur on religious intolerance on his October 1998 visit to Viet Nam, which raised serious concerns, a Vietnamese government spokesperson stated: "Individuals or organizations which come to Viet

Nam to conduct activities concerning human rights or religion and interfere with the internal affairs of the country will no longer be accepted."

Prisoners of conscience

The detention of dozens of prisoners of conscience and possible prisoners of conscience continued. Some were very old and in poor health.

▱ Professor Nguyen Dinh Huy, the 67-year-old founder and president of the "Movement to Unite the People and Build Democracy", continued to be detained in a prison camp where conditions were known to be harsh. He had been arrested in November 1993 and sentenced to 15 years' imprisonment in August 1995 for his peaceful political activities, which the authorities claimed were designed "to overthrow the people's government". He had previously been detained without trial between 1975 and 1992.

Unfair trials

Trials in Viet Nam were routinely unfair, with defence lawyers often appointed only at the time of trial, and permitted to do little more than plead for clemency on their clients' behalf.

▱ In September, 24 people were sentenced to prison terms of up to 20 years for "illegal entry into Viet Nam and subversive activities against the Vietnamese state." Most of the group belonged to the overseas-based People's Action Party and had been illegally expelled from Cambodia to Viet Nam in December 1996, since when they had been detained without trial. All were possible prisoners of conscience, and there were concerns that their trial fell far short of international standards for fairness.

Harassment of government critics

The treatment of political dissidents and religious critics of the government became increasingly harsh during 1999. Several prominent former prisoners who had been released in an official amnesty in 1998 were targeted.

▱ Dr Nguyen Dan Que, a doctor imprisoned for 18 of the last 20 years who continued to make public his peaceful political views after his release in August 1998, was officially isolated by the authorities. His telephone line was cut and his access to the Internet terminated. Incoming and outgoing mail was intercepted, and family members were called in by the local police for questioning about Dr Nguyen Dan Que's activities.

Death penalty

Following some public debate early in the year over the widespread use of the death penalty, amendments to the Criminal Code approved by the National Assembly in December reduced the number of capital offences. In January Prime Minister Phan Van Khai was reported to have said that he favoured a reduction in executions, and that he disliked the use of firing squads. This view was also reportedly shared by President Tran Duc Luong. However, nearly 200 people were sentenced to death and eight executed during 1999; the true numbers were believed to be much higher. Executions were carried out in public, by firing squad, with victims blindfolded and tied to wooden stakes, and sometimes gagged with lemons in their mouths. Relatives were not informed beforehand, but were asked to collect executed prisoners' belongings two to three days later. Concerns about the use of the death penalty were compounded by the routine unfairness of trials, which could lead to irreversible miscarriages of justice.

AI country reports and visits

Report

• Socialist Republic of Viet Nam: New debate on the death penalty? (AI Index: ASA 41/004/99)

Visits

Written requests to the Vietnamese authorities for permission to visit the country received no response. AI representatives met an official Vietnamese delegation visiting Sweden in January.

YEMEN

REPUBLIC OF YEMEN
Head of state: `Ali `Abdullah Saleh
Head of government: `Abd al-Karim `Ali al-Iryani
Capital: Sanaa
Population: 16.5 million
Official language: Arabic
Death penalty: retentionist

A number of prisoners of conscience and possible prisoners of conscience, mainly journalists, were arrested and detained for short periods during 1999. Detainees suspected of politically motivated acts of violence were held in incommunicado detention, denied access to lawyers, and were often not informed of the reason for their arrest. Torture continued to be reported. In one case of death in circumstances suggesting torture was the main or a contributory factor, three security officials were tried and sentenced to prison terms. The death penalty continued to be imposed and the cruel judicial punishment of flogging was a regular occurrence.

Background

President 'Ali 'Abdullah Saleh was re-elected in Yemen's first presidential election in September, winning 96.3 per cent of the vote, according to official sources, based on universal suffrage. Najib Qahtan al-Sha'bi, a member of the President's General People's Congress party, who stood as an independent, was the only other candidate. Candidates required 10 per cent of parliamentary deputies to endorse their candidacy and no candidates from opposition parties were endorsed, partly because of their low level of representation in parliament, following their boycott of the 1997 parliamentary elections.

Explosions continued to occur throughout the country. Some were reported to be politically motivated. Approximately 22 people were killed and 60 injured. The Aden-Abyan Islamic Army claimed responsibility for some bombings. This group had claimed responsibility for the December 1998 abduction of 16 tourists, four of whom were later killed in shooting between the abductors and security forces. The group made several threats throughout 1999 to carry out further campaigns of violence, including threats of retaliation in response to the execution of its leader.

Approximately 30 people were reportedly killed in security incidents including armed skirmishes between heavily armed tribes, and clashes between tribes and security forces.

A total of 30 people were reported to have been abducted in nine incidents. In most cases the abductors' demands were for improvement of local services and amenities. None of the reported abductions in 1999 resulted in injuries or fatalities.

In October the government announced the establishment of special courts to hear cases involving abductions of foreigners, explosions targeted at oil pipelines, car theft and acts of sabotage. The government also announced the establishment of a prosecution service to focus specifically on such cases. The move followed the 1998 introduction of the death penalty for abduction. Just days after announcing the new courts, the Interior Minister announced that 46 people accused of such crimes would be immediately referred to the new courts.

Harassment of journalists

Several leading journalists and newspaper editors were arrested and detained for short periods of time, during which they were prisoners of conscience. Most were detained and questioned in association with particular articles they had written or published. During 1999 a number of newspapers, including al-Haq and al-Shura, were suspended.

🗁 'Ali Haitham al-Gharib, lawyer and writer with both al-Ayyam and al-Tariq newspapers, was arrested in early March after publishing articles reportedly deemed a threat to national security. He was released after five days. Also in March Hisham Basharahil, publisher and editor-in-chief of al-Ayyam was detained for questioning for two hours then released. After several court hearings the two men were found guilty of charges which included "harming national unity". They were both sentenced to suspended sentences and Hisham Basharahil was ordered to pay a fine.

Irregularities in arrest and detention procedures

The bombings and explosions were sometimes followed by arrests and detentions which breached Yemen's own laws or international standards by which Yemen is bound, such as the International Covenant on Civil and Political Rights (ICCPR). Detainees were held in incommunicado detention and denied access to family and to lawyers.

🗁 Omar Ibrahim Dagah, for example, was arrested in August in association with an explosion in the Tuwahi area of Aden. He was held in incommunicado detention, and denied access to his family and to a lawyer. On one occasion, several days after his arrest, security officials brought him to his house in order to carry out a search. His family said that Omar Ibrahim Dagah appeared weak and exhausted and was wearing shackles. He was still in incommunicado detention at the end of 1999.

Political trials

Several individuals were tried, in front of ordinary courts, in association with alleged "terrorist" activities, including bombings and abductions. Trials sometimes failed to meet international standards of fairness: some failed to investigate allegations of torture; statements were issued to the press which prejudiced the defendant's right to be presumed innocent until proved guilty; there were irregularities in arrest and detention procedures, such as the use of incommunicado detention; and the defence faced obstacles such as denial of the right of lawyers to have private consultations with their clients or access to relevant documentation.

🗁 Zein al-'Abideen al-Mehdar, also known as Abu al-Hassan, leader of the Aden-Abyan Islamic Army, was executed in October for his role in the December 1998 abduction of a group of tourists and the subsequent killing of four of them. AI did not have precise details of court proceedings but expressed concern to the government that after his arrest in December 1998 Zein al-'Abideen al-Mehdar was ill-treated, was held in incommunicado detention and was denied access to lawyers. Statements made to the press by security officials about the case may have also been prejudicial to his right to be presumed innocent until proved guilty. AI called on the government to ensure that Zein al-'Abideen al-Mehdar was afforded all guarantees for a fair trial but did not receive a response.

🗁 A group of 10 individuals, including Algerian and UK nationals, charged with forming an armed gang and possession of weapons, was sentenced in August to prison terms which ranged from seven months to seven years. Several of the defendants were arrested in late December 1998. They were held in incommunicado detention for two weeks, during which time they were allegedly tortured and ill-treated in order to force them to confess. They were not informed of any charges against them and were denied access to lawyers for approximately three weeks. During the trial proceedings, their access to lawyers was restricted and the right to private consultations at times denied. Although at least some of the defendants were examined by doctors, there was no independent, impartial investigation into the allegations of torture. The prosecution lodged an appeal calling for harsher sentences while the defence appealed against the verdict. In September both appeals were disallowed on the grounds that they had been submitted too late. After the appeals were rejected, three prisoners who had already completed their sentences were released. At the end of 1999 the case was before the Supreme Court.

Torture

Torture and cruel, inhuman and degrading treatment continued to be reported. Methods reported during 1999 included beatings while tied up, beatings on the soles of the feet, sleep deprivation, denial of food, threats of torture and the use of shackles. Torture appeared to take place mostly in incommunicado detention. Most incidents of torture remained uninvestigated.

Mohammed al-Kowkabani was arrested in March on suspicion of theft and died a week later in custody in circumstances suggesting torture was the main or a contributory factor. In July, one police officer and two soldiers were sentenced to prison terms for their part in the torture.

Wadi' al-Sheibani died in the custody of the political security police in 1997. Despite repeated calls for a thorough investigation into the cause of his death from his family and local and international non-governmental organizations, including AI, to AI's knowledge his death remained uninvestigated throughout 1999.

Death penalty

The death penalty continued to be imposed, sometimes after trials which failed to meet international standards for fair trial. AI recorded 35 executions during 1999, including that of Zein al-'Abideen al-Mehdar. Dozens, possibly hundreds, of people were believed to have been under sentence of death or facing trial for capital offences.

Other concerns

Flogging

Local lawyers and journalists reported that flogging was imposed as a judicial punishment on a regular basis, and in some areas was a weekly occurrence. Flogging is prescribed for certain offences of a sexual nature, for the consumption of alcohol and for slander.

'Disappearances'

There were no new reported cases of "disappearance". However, AI continued to seek clarification of the cases of hundreds of people who "disappeared" in Yemen from the late 1960s onwards. In 1996 the government undertook to investigate "disappearances" which had occurred since 1994. AI repeatedly sought information from the government on 27 such cases, but none was received. In 1998 the UN Working Group on Enforced or Involuntary Disappearances (WGEID) visited Yemen and issued a report which recommended that the government "recognises and regrets the events which led to the disappearances and death of hundreds of human beings" and that the government should establish a task force "for the purpose of settling the remaining legal issues in connection with the 1986

disappearances". The government was due to submit a final report on steps taken to WGEID by 31 October 1999.

Intergovernmental mechanisms

In January the UN Committee on the Rights of the Child considered Yemen's second periodic report. The Committee expressed concern at the use of physical punishment, including flogging, and torture in detention centres.

AI's memorandum to the government

In April AI submitted a substantial memorandum to the government detailing many of its concerns. It included an appendix containing five cases of people executed after unfair trials; nine cases of people sentenced to death; 11 examples of people alleged to have been tortured; eight examples of women or children reportedly detained beyond expiry of sentence; and two possible extrajudicial executions. The memorandum asked for clarification of the cases and information as to steps the government had taken to implement commitments made to AI in 1996. It informed the government of AI's plans to publish its concerns in a report, and stated that AI was prepared to reflect the government's response concerning the issues raised. However, none was forthcoming.

AI country report

• Yemen: Empty promises – Government commitments and the state of human rights in Yemen (AI Index: MDE 31/004/99)

YUGOSLAVIA
(FEDERAL REPUBLIC OF)

FEDERAL REPUBLIC OF YUGOSLAVIA
Head of state: Slobodan Milošević
Head of government: Momir Bulatović
Capital: Belgrade
Population: 10.6 million
Official language: Serbian
Death penalty: retentionist

The armed conflict between the Serbian and Yugoslav forces, and armed ethnic Albanians of the Kosovo Liberation Army (KLA) reached its climax between March and June after NATO intervened with air attacks against the Federal Republic of Yugoslavia (FRY). Gross human rights violations on a large scale by Serbian police and paramilitary units and by the Yugoslav army drove around 850,000 ethnic Albanians out of Kosovo, creating a regional refugee crisis. Extrajudicial executions, "disappearances", arbitrary detention, torture, ill-treatment, forcible expulsions and the deliberate destruction of homes were widespread and systematic. There were also reports of rape or other sexual violence against ethnic Albanian women. According to independent estimates, at least 500 civilians were killed by NATO. There were concerns as to whether NATO took sufficient precautions in selecting targets and executing its attacks so as to minimize civilian casualties; AI considered that NATO forces may have violated international humanitarian law. After the withdrawal of Serbian and Yugoslav forces from Kosovo in June, there were widespread human rights abuses by armed ethnic Albanians, many of them belonging to, or representing themselves as members of, the KLA. The victims were Serbs, Roma and ethnic Albanians accused of "collaboration" with the Serbian authorities, or activists in moderate political parties. Hundreds of people were unlawfully killed or abducted and, partly as a result of these attacks, more than half of the non-Albanian population had fled Kosovo by the end of 1999. Human rights violations occurred throughout the rest of the FRY. Hundreds of anti-government demonstrators were beaten by police. Opposition activists, independent journalists and conscientious objectors were arrested and imprisoned.

The Kosovo crisis
For many years demands, expressed largely through peaceful means by ethnic Albanians, for autonomy and independence for Kosovo had been met with routine torture or ill-treatment by police and the incarceration of prisoners of conscience. In the 1990s, frustration with the political situation led to the formation of the KLA, which sought Kosovo's secession through force. By early 1998 the situation had deteriorated into armed conflict. At the beginning of 1999 a cease-fire was in place, but

was growing steadily weaker. Small-scale attacks on Serbian targets by the KLA continued to be met with excessive force by the Serbian police. The killing of 45 ethnic Albanians at Rafiak village by police at the end of January led to intense diplomatic pressure and renewed threats of armed intervention by NATO. Citing violence by the Serbian and Yugoslav forces and the FRY's refusal to sign up to a peace plan, NATO ordered air strikes against the FRY which commenced on 24 March.

Mass expulsions during the NATO bombing campaign
The Yugoslav leadership responded to the NATO action with an upsurge in violence against the civilian ethnic Albanian population in Kosovo and new offensives against the KLA. The Yugoslav army took part in the actions in Kosovo, but human rights violations were perpetrated primarily by Serbian police and paramilitaries who operated alongside them. A systematic program to expel the civilian population began in the first days of the NATO campaign. Extrajudicial executions, arbitrary detention, "disappearances", beatings, rape, and the burning of houses and shops were used to terrorize the population into flight. Serbian forces systematically directed people from western and northern Kosovo towards the Albanian or Macedonian borders, allowing them through or stopping them at will.

Extrajudicial executions
Thousands of ethnic Albanian civilians were killed by police, paramilitaries or soldiers between 24 March and 10 June. The victims appeared to have been targeted for suspected connections with the KLA, for their political activities, or for links with international organizations. Men of military age were widely regarded as suspects and many were killed shortly after coming under the control of Serbian police or paramilitaries.
  ▱ Prominent lawyer and human rights activist Bajram Kelmendi and his two sons, one of whom was only 16 years old, were taken from their house in Pri tina by police on the night of 24/25 March. They were found shot dead two days later.
  ▱ On 27 March Serbian forces overran KLA fighters defending the village of Kladernica, near Srbica (Skënderaj); ethnic Albanian civilians fled into the surrounding hills. Witnesses described the killings of around 30 civilians by Serbian forces. In the nearby village of Izbica, most men of military age had fled before Serbian forces moved into the village the following day. Houses in the village were set on fire and several bodies, apparently of elderly people who had been unable to flee, were later found in the ruins. Witnesses described how scores of men, including the young and elderly, were separated from the women and shot. Some 150 people were believed to have been killed, although it was impossible to confirm whether all were non-combatants.

'Disappearances'
At least 2,000, perhaps many more, ethnic Albanians, the majority of whom were believed to have fallen into the hands of Serbian police or paramilitaries between March and June, were unaccounted for at the end of

1999. Relatives and witnesses of the "disappeared" feared that some had been killed shortly after their arrest. Subsequent discoveries of bodies and exhumations of mass graves confirmed these fears in a number of cases.

◻ In the town of Djakovica (Gjakovë) police arrested large numbers of ethnic Albanian men in house-to-house searches. Most were taken to places of detention where many were tortured or ill-treated. Although some were released or later confirmed to be held in prison, hundreds of people from the area remained unaccounted for at the end of 1999.

Sexual violence against ethnic Albanian women
There were allegations of rape and sexual violence by Serbian police or paramilitaries against ethnic Albanian women. The need to protect victims and witnesses meant that the full extent of the abuses could not be determined.

◻ In April Serbian forces took a village near Suva Reka (Suhareka); only women, children and older men remained in the village. The elderly men "disappeared" amid fears that they were killed. The women and children were kept in three houses from which women were taken out repeatedly over several days. Three women testified that they had been raped, while statements from others indicated that there were many more victims.

NATO's bombing campaign
Despite NATO claims that it mounted the "most accurate bombing campaign in history", AI had serious concerns about several attacks which may have breached international law.

NATO gave only general assurances that every effort had been made to avoid civilian casualties and did not provide substantive answers to AI's questions on specific incidents, nor any indication of whether investigations were being conducted. Despite repeated requests, NATO failed to provide details of the rules of engagement and other relevant instructions, which AI requested in order to allow an assessment of whether they complied with international humanitarian law.

◻ On 12 April a train carrying civilian passengers was twice hit by missiles launched by a NATO airplane during an attack on a railway bridge at Grdelica, reportedly killing at least 12 people. The incident called into question whether the pilot adhered to fundamental principles of humanitarian law which state that an attack should be cancelled or suspended if it becomes clear that the objective is not a military one or may cause disproportionate loss of civilian life.

◻ On 23 April NATO bombed the Serbian state television building in Belgrade killing 15 people, all of them apparently civilians. NATO justified the attack in the context of its policy to "disrupt the national command network and to degrade the Federal Republic of Yugoslavia's propaganda apparatus". However, even if the station could have been considered a military target — which NATO failed to demonstrate — serious questions remained as to why precautions were not taken or warnings given to avoid killing civilians.

Trials and imprisonment of ethnic Albanians
In June the FRY authorities acknowledged that they were holding some 2,000 people, mostly ethnic Albanians on "terrorism"-related charges; some were prisoners of conscience. The majority had been detained in Kosovo and moved to prisons in Serbia. Most had either been sentenced following unfair trials or were under investigation in a new series of trials. There was evidence that they had been tortured or ill-treated in order to extract confessions and that for this and other reasons, they were not receiving fair trials. There were further concerns about the welfare of the prisoners, including complaints of inadequate food and healthcare for prisoners with medical problems. Some 300 prisoners were released between July and December after the charges against them were dropped.

◻ Flora Brovina, a doctor from Pri tina, was sentenced to 12 years' imprisonment by a court in Ni in December. Reports of her trial indicated that it was seriously flawed and that charges of her having been involved in "terrorism" were not substantiated. She was a prisoner of conscience.

Abuses in Kosovo after the withdrawal of Serbian and Yugoslav forces
In mid-June huge numbers of non-Albanians fled Kosovo with the withdrawing Serbian and Yugoslav forces. KLA members and other armed ethnic Albanians, who frequently claimed KLA membership, commenced widespread and almost daily attacks on Serbs, Roma and ethnic Albanians accused of "collaboration" who remained. Houses were burned to force occupants to leave and to discourage their return. People were abducted and questioned; ill-treatment and torture of detainees were routine.

Hundreds of people who were believed to have been abducted remained unaccounted for at the end of 1999. A few of those abducted were later found dead. There were also reports of Serbian or Romani women being raped by ethnic Albanians. According to UN estimates, which were generally regarded as optimistic, 50 per cent of the non-Albanian population had fled Kosovo by the end of 1999.

Kosovo policing and the judicial system
The NATO-led KFOR peacekeeping force struggled to maintain law and order. The UN interim police force, which was to take over policing from KFOR until the formation of a new local force, was desperately short-staffed since less than 1,900 of the promised 6,000 officers had been seconded by governments by the end of the year.

Policing, which like most aspects of civilian administration in Kosovo was the responsibility of the UN Interim Administration Mission in Kosovo (UNMIK), therefore continued to rely heavily on KFOR. UNMIK was also responsible for re-establishing the judicial system, but it was hampered by lack of resources, political pressure on judges, and the strain of trying to re-establish a multi-ethnic judiciary.

Refugees and displaced persons

Between April and June, some 500,000 Albanian refugees were forcibly expelled from Kosovo to Albania, about 350,000 to Macedonia and a smaller number to Montenegro. On several occasions thousands of asylum-seekers had their journeys blocked when the Macedonian authorities closed the border. The Macedonian authorities used closures and restrictions at the border to maintain pressure on other governments, particularly NATO members, to accept refugees. Governments were generally reluctant to share responsibility for the Kosovo refugees, who were given only temporary protection in most countries. The majority of the ethnic Albanian refugees in neighbouring countries had returned to Kosovo by the end of August.

Serbs and Roma who fled or were expelled into Serbia as a result of the actions of the KLA or other armed Albanians found themselves blocked by the Serbian authorities who tried to restrict their movements and prevent them from reaching Belgrade. A Kosovo Serb who succeeded in reaching Belgrade was imprisoned for 30 days after he demonstrated about the plight of displaced Kosovo Serbs.

Arrests for violations of international humanitarian law

KFOR troops in Kosovo arrested Serbs and Roma whom they suspected of involvement in the unlawful killing of ethnic Albanian civilians or other violations of international humanitarian law between March and June. The investigation of the suspects was taken over by investigating magistrates and prosecutors of the interim judicial system which was established in Kosovo from July onwards. Around 30 people were under investigation at the end of 1999.

The federal and Serbian governments failed to cooperate with the UN International Criminal Tribunal for the former Yugoslavia. The Tribunal issued an indictment in May accusing the Federal President, Slobodan Milošević, and four members of the Serbian and federal governments of murder, persecution and deportation perpetrated by forces under their control between January and May 1999.

State of emergency

On 25 March the federal authorities declared a state of emergency as a result of NATO's attack. The declaration, and decrees issued in conjunction with it, widened police powers and restricted the right to freedom of assembly. The penalties for avoiding call-up and desertion were automatically increased to a maximum of 20 years' imprisonment. Most of the emergency decrees were lifted in June.

Conscientious objectors

Thousands of men, including conscientious objectors, who failed to comply with call-up regulations while the state of emergency was in force, were prosecuted and faced the increased penalties. Despite propaganda from NATO encouraging these men not to fight, after the conflict they had difficulty in obtaining protection as refugees in other countries.

Independent journalists and opposition activists

In the aftermath of the Yugoslav withdrawal from Kosovo, opposition party supporters, trade unionists and students demonstrated in towns throughout Serbia calling for the resignation of President Slobodan Milošević. The demonstrations became more frequent from September onwards and were often allowed by the authorities. However, on several occasions police used truncheons to break up what started as peaceful demonstrations. Hundreds of demonstrators were beaten in the course of several such incidents. Independent or opposition publications or printing houses were often given huge fines which threatened their viability. Several journalists were prosecuted for exercising their right to freedom of expression.

Bogoljub Arsenijević, an opposition activist from Valjevo, was severely beaten in police custody following his arrest in August. In October he went on hunger strike in protest at inadequate medical treatment.

Newspaper editor Slavko Ćuruvija and two of his journalists were sentenced to five months' imprisonment in March for "spreading false information" after being accused of associating a Serbian government minister with a murder in an article. Slavko Ćuruvija was murdered in April amid claims that the killing had been ordered by the authorities. No one had been charged with his murder by the end of the year. The two other journalists were called to serve their sentences in July, but reportedly went into hiding. If imprisoned they would be prisoners of conscience.

AI's actions

AI issued a series of appeals, statements and reports on human rights abuses in Kosovo. Researchers in the field carried out interviews with refugees, other victims and witnesses, lawyers, and representatives of the local and international organizations. AI issued recommendations and lobbied governments connected to or influential in the Kosovo crisis.

AI country reports

- Federal Republic of Yugoslavia: A decade of unheeded warnings — Amnesty International's concerns in Kosovo, May 1989 to March 1999, volumes 1 and 2 (AI Index: EUR 70/039/99 and EUR 70/040/99)
- Federal Republic of Yugoslavia: Amnesty International memorandum to the UN Security Council (AI Index: EUR 70/049/99)
- Federal Republic of Yugoslavia: Amnesty International's concerns relating to NATO bombings (AI Index: EUR 70/069/99)
- Federal Republic of Yugoslavia (Kosovo): Killings in the Izbica area (AI Index: EUR 70/079/99)
- Federal Republic of Yugoslavia (Kosovo): After tragedy, justice? (AI Index: EUR 70/080/99)
- Federal Republic of Yugoslavia: Amnesty International's recommendations for the protection of human rights in post-conflict peace building and reconstruction in Kosovo (AI Index: EUR 70/091/99)

- Federal Republic of Yugoslavia: A broken circle —
  "disappeared" and abducted in Kosovo province (AI
  Index: 70/106/99)
- Federal Republic of Yugoslavia (Kosovo): Smrekovnica
  prison — a regime of torture and ill-treatment leaves
  hundreds unaccounted for (AI Index: EUR
  70/107/99)
- Federal Republic of Yugoslavia: The forgotten resisters
  — the plight of conscientious objectors to military
  service after the conflict in Kosovo (AI Index: EUR
  70/111/99)
- Federal Republic of Yugoslavia: Amnesty International
  urges KLA leader to stop human rights abuses (AI
  Index: EUR 70/112/99)

ZAMBIA

REPUBLIC OF ZAMBIA
Head of state and government: Frederick Chiluba
Capital: Lusaka
Population: 9.3 million
Official language: English
Death penalty: retentionist

The treason trial of those accused of involvement in
the 1997 attempted coup ended with the High Court
passing 59 death sentences, bringing the number of
people on death row in Zambia to more than 220.
The police force continued to shoot and kill criminal
suspects as an alternative to arrest, and to torture
criminal suspects with impunity. The government
harassed the independent press through the courts.

Background
In 1991 Zambia became the first country in southern
Africa to transform itself from a one-party state to a
multi-party democracy. When the Movement for
Multiparty Democracy won the elections, expectations
were raised among human rights activists both in the
country and internationally. However, these
expectations were not met. In the run-up to the
second multi-party elections the government used
various tactics to prevent opposition politicians from
standing, including calling into question their
citizenship. Among those stripped of their citizenship
was former president Kenneth Kaunda. Several
members of his party were deported to Malawi,
regardless of whether Malawi accepted them as
Malawian citizens. This led to a partial boycott of the
1996 elections, which international and national
election monitors judged not to have been free and
fair. In a period of growing international isolation,
army officers staged an unsuccessful coup attempt in
October 1997.

The government tried to convince the international
community that it was back on the right track on human
rights issues by producing a document which it
presented to donors at a meeting at the World Bank in
May 1999. AI contacted the Zambian authorities several
times without being able to obtain a copy.

The treason trial
A total of 104 people were arrested in connection with
the October 1997 coup attempt, including leading
opposition politicians. The High Court ruled on various
occasions that some of the detentions were politically
motivated and unlawful. Nine of those arrested were
tortured, according to the government's Permanent
Human Rights Commission.

Of the 104 people originally charged in connection
with the coup attempt, 68 defendants remained at the
close of trial. Of these, 59 were convicted of treason on
17 September 1999 and sentenced to death. One was
convicted of failing to notify the authorities of the plot
and sentenced to 21 years' imprisonment. The
remaining eight were acquitted.

Freedom of expression
Zambia has a vibrant independent press. The
independent newspaper, *The Post*, plays a leading role
and has been repeatedly targeted by the government
for several years. During 1999 its journalists were
charged with a number of criminal offences, the most
serious being espionage, following an article citing
army fears that Zambia's army would not be able to
resist a possible attack from neighbouring Angola. This
article appeared on 9 March. On 10 March, six
journalists were arrested and held for two days. Two
more journalists were arrested on 20 March, and the
editor, Fred M'membe, was arrested on 22 March. All
were released on bail, but their case was still pending in
the courts at the end of 1999.

Secessionist fears
There is an unresolved dispute, dating back to
independence in 1964, over the status of the former
Barotseland Protectorate in Western Province. Fighting
in the neighbouring Caprivi province of Namibia in
August raised fears in Zambia of similar secessionist
violence in Western Province, since the Lozi people of
western Zambia belong to the same ethnic group as the
Caprivi secessionists. The leader of the Barotseland
Patriotic Front, Imasiku Mutangelwa, took refuge in the
house of the South African High Commissioner after
expressing concern about the situation in Caprivi and
urging the government to allow an open debate on the
self-determination of Barotseland. His house was
searched and he was detained and later charged with
minor offences. He was released on bail, but his court
case remained pending at the end of 1999.

In September Zambia returned six Namibians
with refugee status in Botswana to Namibia, in
breach of fundamental principles of international
refugee protection. Upon arrival in Namibia the six
were imprisoned, and charged with high treason
and sedition.

Freedom of association

Towards the end of 1998 a group of people tried to form an organization called Lesbians, Gays and Transsexuals of Zambia (LEGATRA). The government refused to allow the organization to register. AI considered this a breach of the rights to freedom of association and freedom of expression.

African Commission rules against Zambia

The African Commission on Human and Peoples' Rights considered a complaint filed by AI on behalf of William Banda and the late John Chinula in April. The African Commission found that the forcible deportation of the two men from Zambia to Malawi violated various provisions of the African Charter on Human and Peoples' Rights, including the right to freedom of expression and the right to free association. The African Commission also stated that their deportation was politically motivated. Despite this ruling by the African Commission, the Zambian government continued to deny William Banda, an opposition politician forcibly exiled to Malawi in 1994, the right to return to Zambia.

Death penalty

At least 66 people were sentenced to death during 1999, including those sentenced in the treason trial, bringing the total number of people on death row to more than 220. As far as AI was aware, no executions had been carried out in Zambia since 1997. Public debate on the death penalty was growing in Zambia, and major opposition politicians and non-governmental organizations called for its abolition.

AI country reports and visits
Report
• Zambia: Applying the law fairly or fatally? Police violation of human rights (AI Index: AFR 63/001/99)
Visits
An AI delegate visited Zambia in late July and early August and met AI members and representatives of human rights organizations. AI delegates also visited Zambia in September 1999, mainly to investigate conditions for refugees and to interview refugees from the Democratic Republic of the Congo (DRC) and Burundi about the war in the DRC.

ZIMBABWE

REPUBLIC OF ZIMBABWE
Head of state and government: Robert Mugabe
Capital: Harare
Population: 11.4 million
Official language: English
Death penalty: retentionist

During 1999 the human rights situation deteriorated. In January politically motivated torture was reported for the first time since the late 1980s. Harassment of political opponents increased. The President intensified verbal attacks on the opposition, the judiciary and the press as well as "outside" forces (especially the United Kingdom and the USA) and Zimbabwe's white minority. The death of Vice-President Joshua Nkomo reopened the discussion on atrocities committed in Matabeleland in the 1980s.

Background

Social tensions in Zimbabwe, which led to food riots in 1998 in which several people were tortured and killed by police, persisted. The economy continued to be in a critical state, suffering from the country's heavy involvement in the war in the Democratic Republic of the Congo (DRC) and a high level of corruption, leading several foreign donors to reduce or stop funding. The huge inequality between rich and poor showed no sign of narrowing. The government program to redistribute land from white commercial farmers allegedly benefited people associated with the ruling party rather than the landless poor.

Independence in 1980 followed an armed struggle waged against a minority white government that had declared unilateral independence in 1965 from the United Kingdom. There followed, from 1980 to 1987, armed conflict between the two main parties: the ruling Zimbabwe African National Union–Patriotic Front (ZANU-PF), dominated by people of Shona origin, led by Robert Mugabe, and the Zimbabwe African People's Union (ZAPU), dominated by Ndebeles, led by Joshua Nkomo. During this war government forces led by the Fifth Brigade committed serious atrocities.

The process of redrafting the Constitution, which started in May, led to a more open atmosphere of discussion.

Torture and ill-treatment

Torture of criminal suspects by the police was widespread during 1999, despite government training schemes for police recruits, including human rights training with the involvement of a local non-governmental organization (NGO). There were two high profile cases in which the police and the military tortured and ill-treated the accused. Three US citizens charged with illegal possession and transportation of weapons were tortured during police interrogation in March. There were also reports that an air force pilot was arrested and tortured when he returned from the DRC war in August.

⊟ In January Mark Chavunduka, editor of the *Standard* newspaper, and Ray Choto, senior reporter with the *Standard*, were arrested and charged with "publishing a false story capable of causing alarm and despondency", following an article by Ray Choto about an alleged military coup attempt. They were tortured in military detention. Under Zimbabwean law the military has no powers to arrest or detain civilians. After their release they filed complaints against the state for compensation and challenged the constitutionality of the Law and Order Maintenance Act under which they were charged. The cases and counter-cases were pending at the end of 1999.

Independence of the judiciary
The High Court ordered the release of the *Standard* journalists on three separate occasions, but Defence Ministry officials ignored the rulings. When four judges asked President Mugabe to reaffirm his commitment to the rule of law, the President called upon them to resign and said that judges had no right to give instructions to the President. Similarly, in the case of the US nationals, court orders to ease their prison conditions were ignored by prison officials, allegedly following instructions from the executive.

Freedom of expression
Zimbabwe's vibrant independent press came under pressure. In addition to the torture of *Standard* journalists, there were anonymous death threats against journalists, including Ray Choto of the *Standard*, Basildon Peta of the *Financial Gazette* and Dr Ibbo Mandaza, a newspaper publisher.

Impunity
In April, two NGOs, the Legal Resources Foundation and the Catholic Commission for Justice and Peace, issued a summary of the report, *Breaking the silence, building true peace*, about atrocities committed in Matabeleland during the armed conflict that followed Zimbabwe's independence in 1980. *Breaking the silence, building true peace* was the first major report to document human rights violations in the years between 1980 and 1988. The summary was translated into Shona and Ndebele and was the first description of the atrocities to be published in local languages. The publication of the summary led to some discussion of compensation for victims and victims' families, but little debate on bringing the perpetrators to justice.

Forty-two people shot or tortured during and after food riots in 1998 filed complaints. Most of their cases were still pending, but in two cases out-of-court agreements gave victims compensation.

Zimbabwe continued to provide refuge to former President of Ethiopia Mengistu Haile-Mariam, who was responsible for massive human rights violations during his rule from 1974 to 1991 (see Ethiopia entry).

Women
In April the Supreme Court upheld a customary court ruling that unmarried women have the status of minors. This ruling led to protests by women's groups and human rights activists in Zimbabwe, who called for customary law and practices to be brought in line with the Constitution's anti-discrimination clause.

Gays and lesbians
President Mugabe continued his "hate speech" campaign against lesbians and gays, justifying discrimination. Several members of Gays and Lesbians of Zimbabwe (GALZ) suffered harassment and violence following speeches by the President. GALZ also reported an increase in blackmail attempts against gay men. Criminal charges against the program director of GALZ, which carried a maximum penalty of seven years' imprisonment, were still pending at the end of 1999.

The constitutional debate afforded GALZ members some respite from attacks and some members were interviewed for the first time on state television and radio. There was extensive coverage in the media of lesbian and gay issues.

Death penalty
At least three death sentences were passed during 1999, but no executions were reported.

AI country visit
An AI delegate visited Zimbabwe in June to work on human rights cases and to update AI on the constitutional debate.

AI REPORT 2000
PART 3

WHAT IS AI?

Amnesty International (AI) is a worldwide voluntary activist movement working for human rights. It is independent of any government, political persuasion or religious creed. It does not support or oppose any government or political system, nor does it support or oppose the views of the victims whose rights it seeks to protect. It is concerned solely with the impartial protection of human rights.

AI mobilizes volunteer activists — people who give freely of their time and energy in solidarity with the victims of human rights violations. There are more than 1,000,000 AI members and subscribers in over 140 countries and territories. AI members come from many different backgrounds, with widely different political and religious beliefs, united by a determination to work for a world where everyone enjoys human rights.

Many AI members are organized into groups: there are more than 7,500 local groups, youth and student groups and other specialist groups in nearly 100 countries and territories. Thousands of other members are involved in networks working on particular countries or themes. In 55 countries and territories, the work of AI members is coordinated by sections, whose addresses are given below. In another 22 countries and territories, AI has pre-section coordinating structures, which are also listed below.

What does AI do?

AI works independently and impartially to promote respect for all the human rights set out in the Universal Declaration of Human Rights. AI believes that human rights are interdependent and indivisible — all human rights should be enjoyed by all people at all times, and no one set of rights can be enjoyed at the expense of other rights.

AI contributes to building respect for the Universal Declaration of Human Rights by promoting knowledge and understanding of all human rights and by taking action against specific violations of people's fundamental civil and political rights. The main focus of its campaigning is to:
- Free all prisoners of conscience. According to AI's Statute, these are people detained for their political, religious or other conscientiously held beliefs or because of their ethnic origin, sex, colour, language, national or social origin, economic status, birth or other status — who have not used or advocated violence;
- Ensure fair and prompt trials for all political prisoners;
- Abolish the death penalty, torture and other ill-treatment of prisoners;
- End political killings and "disappearances";
- Ensure that governments refrain from unlawful killings in armed conflict.

AI also works to:
- Oppose abuses by armed political groups such as the detention of prisoners of conscience, hostage-taking, torture and unlawful killings;
- Assist asylum-seekers who are at risk of being returned to a country where they might suffer violations of their fundamental human rights;
- Cooperate with other non-governmental organizations, the UN and regional intergovernmental organizations to further human rights;
- Ensure control of international military, security and police relations in order to protect human rights;
- Organize human rights education and awareness raising programs.

AI: a democratic movement

AI is a democratic, self-governing movement. Major policy decisions are taken by an International Council made up of representatives from all national sections. The Council meets every two years, and has the power to amend the Statute which governs AI's work and methods. Copies of the Statute are available from the International Secretariat.

The Council elects an International Executive Committee of volunteers which carries out its decisions and appoints the movement's Secretary General, who also heads up the International Secretariat.

The movement's Secretary General is Pierre Sané (Senegal), and the members of its International Executive Committee are Mahmoud Ben Romdhane (Tunisia), Colm Ó Cuanacháin (Ireland), Mary Gray (USA), Samuel Zan Akologo (Ghana), Margaret Bedggood (New Zealand), Paul Hoffman (USA), Jaap Rosen Jacobson (Netherlands), Hans Landolt (Peru) and Pierre Robert (International Secretariat).

Finances

AI's national sections and local volunteer groups are primarily responsible for funding the movement. No funds are sought or accepted from governments for AI's work investigating and campaigning against human rights violations. The donations that sustain this work come from the organization's members and the public. The international budget adopted by AI for the financial year April 1999 to March 2000 was £18,106,000. This sum represents approximately one quarter of the estimated income likely to be raised during the year by the movement's national sections to finance their campaigning and other activities.

AI's ultimate goal is to end human rights violations, but so long as they continue AI tries to provide practical help to the victims. Relief (financial assistance) is an important aspect of this work. Sometimes AI provides financial assistance directly to individuals. At other times, it works through local bodies such as local and national human rights organizations so as to ensure that resources are used as effectively as possible for those in most need.

During the financial year April 1999 to March 2000, the International Secretariat of AI distributed an estimated £220,000 in relief to victims of human rights violations such as prisoners of conscience and recently released prisoners of conscience and their dependants, and for the medical treatment of torture victims. In addition, the organization's sections and groups distributed a further substantial amount, much of it in the form of modest payments by local groups to their adopted prisoners of conscience and dependent families.

Information about AI is available from national section offices (see below) and from: International Secretariat, 1 Easton Street, London WC1X 0DW, United Kingdom.

AI Online

AI Online is dedicated to providing AI's human rights resources on the web in English (http://www.amnesty.org). It contains nearly 10,000 files and receives an average 4.5 million hits a month. It holds most AI reports published since 1996 and all the latest news releases detailing AI's concerns about human rights stories around the world. Additionally, there is information on the latest campaigns and appeals for action to help protect human rights. You will also find contact details for AI's offices around the world, links to hundreds of websites with a human rights theme and an online order form for publications.

There are also AI international sites in French (http://www.ifrance.com/EFAI/) and Spanish (http://www.edai.org/), and plans for an Arabic-language site.

AI sections

Algeria Amnesty International, BP 377, Alger, RP 16004
Argentina Amnistía Internacional, Av. Rivadavia 2206 - P4A, C1032ACO Ciudad de Buenos Aires
E-mail: info@amnesty.org.ar
http://www.amnesty.org.ar
Australia Amnesty International, Private Bag 23, Broadway, New South Wales 2007
E-mail: adminaia@amnesty.org.au
http://www.amnesty.org.au
Austria amnesty international austria, Moeringgasse 10, A-1150 Wien
E-mail: info@amnesty.at
http://www.amnesty.at
Bangladesh Amnesty International, 28 Kabi Jasimuddin Road, 1st Floor, North Kamalapur, Dhaka - 1217
E-mail: admin-bd@amnesty.org
Belgium Amnesty International (AI Vlaanderen), Kerkstraat 156, 2060 Antwerpen
E-mail: amnesty@aivl.be
http://www.aivl.be
Belgium Amnesty International (francophone), rue Berckmans 9, 1060 Bruxelles
E-mail: aibf@aibf.be
http://www.aibf.be
Benin Amnesty International, BP 01-3536, Cotonou
E-mail: aibenin@nakayo.leland.bj
Bermuda Amnesty International, PO Box HM 2136, Hamilton HM JX
E-mail: aibda@ibl.bm
Brazil Anistia Internacional, Rua Jacinto Gomes 573, CEP 90040-270, Porto Alegre - RS
E-mail: aibrasil@conex.com.br
http://www.anistia.org.br

Canada Amnesty International, 214 Montreal Road, 4th Floor, Vanier, Ontario, K1L 1A4
E-mail: info@amnesty.ca
http://www.amnesty.ca
Canada Amnistie Internationale (francophone), 6250 boulevard Monk, Montréal, Québec H4E 3H7
E-mail: info@amnistie.qc.ca
http://www.amnistie.qc.ca
Chile Señores, Casilla 4062, Santiago
Costa Rica Amnistía Internacional, 75 metros al norte de la Iglesia de Fatima, los Yoses, San Pedro, San José
Côte d'Ivoire Amnesty International, 04 BP 895, Abidjan 04
Denmark Amnesty International, Dyrkoeb 3, 1166 Copenhagen K
E-mail: amnesty@amnesty.dk
Ecuador Amnistía Internacional, Casilla 17-15-240-C, Quito
Faroe Islands Amnesty International, PO Box 1075, FR-110, Tórshavn
Finland Amnesty International, Ruoholahdenkatu 24, D 00180 Helsinki
E-mail: amnesty@amnesty.fi
http://www.amnesty.fi
France Amnesty International, 76 blvd. de La Villette, 75940 Paris cedex 19
E-mail: admin-fr@amnesty.asso.fr
http://www.amnesty.asso.fr
Germany Amnesty International, 53108 Bonn
E-mail: admin-de@amnesty.de
http://www.amnesty.de
Ghana Amnesty International, Private Mail Bag, Kokomlemle, Accra - North
E-mail: amnesty@ighmail.com
Greece Amnesty International, 30 Sina Street, 106 72 Athens
E-mail: info@amnesty.gr
http://www.amnesty.gr
Guyana Amnesty International, PO Box 10720, Georgetown
Hong Kong Amnesty International, Unit C3, Best-O-Best Commercial Centre, 32-36 Ferry Street, Kowloon
E-mail: admin-hk@amnesty.org
Iceland Amnesty International, PO Box 618, 121 Reykjavík
Ireland Amnesty International, Sean MacBride House, 48 Fleet Street, Dublin 2
E-mail: info@amnesty.iol.ie
http://www.amnesty.ie
Israel Amnesty International, PO Box 14179, Tel Aviv 61141
http://www.amnesty.org.il
Italy Amnesty International, Via Giovanni Battista De Rossi 10, 00161 Roma
E-mail: info@amnesty.it
http://www.amnesty.it
Japan Amnesty International, Sky Esta 2F, 2-18-23 Nishi Waseda, Shinjuku-ku, Tokyo 169
E-mail: amnesty@mri.biglobe.ne.jp
Korea (Republic of) Amnesty International, Kyeong Buk RCO Box 36, Daegu 706-600
E-mail: admin-ko@amnesty.org

Luxembourg Amnesty International,
Boîte Postale 1914, 1019 Luxembourg
Mauritius Amnesty International, BP 69, Rose-Hill
E-mail: amnesty@intnet.mu
Mexico Amnistía Internacional, Calle Patricio Sanz
No. 1104, Depto. 8, Col. del Valle, CP 03100, México DF
Nepal Amnesty International, PO Box 135, Bagbazar,
Kathmandu
E-mail: ain@ccsl.com.np
Netherlands Amnesty International, PO Box 1968,
1000 BZ, Amsterdam
E-mail: amnesty@amnesty.nl
http://www.amnesty.nl
New Zealand Amnesty International, PO Box 793,
Wellington
E-mail: campaign@amnesty.org.nz
http://www.amnesty.org.nz
Nigeria Amnesty International, PMB 3061, Suru Lere,
Lagos
E-mail: amnestynigeria@churchgate.com
Norway Amnesty International, PO Box 702 Sentrum,
0106 Oslo
E-mail: info@amnesty.no
http://www.amnesty.no
Peru Señores, Casilla 659, Lima 18
Philippines Amnesty International, Room 602,
FMSG Building, 9 Balete Drive corner 3rd Street,
New Manila, 1103 Quezon City
E-mail: amnesty@info.com.ph
Portugal Amnistia Internacional, Rua Fialho de
Almeida 13-1, PT-1070-128 Lisboa
E-mail: aisp@ip.pt
http://www.amnistia-internacional.pt
Puerto Rico Amnistía Internacional, Calle El Roble
No. 54-Altos, Oficina 11, Río Piedras, Puerto Rico 00925
Senegal Amnesty International, BP 21910, Dakar
E-mail: aisenegal@metissacana.sn
Sierra Leone Amnesty International, PMB 1021,
Freetown
Slovenia Amnesty International, Komenskega 7,
1000 Ljubljana
E-mail: amnesty.slo@guest.arnes.si
http://www.ljudmila.org/ai-slo
Spain Amnistía Internacional, Apdo 50318,
28080 Madrid
E-mail: amnistia.internacional@a-i.es
http://ww.a-i.es
Sweden Amnesty International, PO Box 23400,
SE-10435 Stockholm
E-mail: info@amnesty.se
http://www.amnesty.se
Switzerland Amnesty International, Postfach CH-3001,
Bern
E-mail: info@amnesty.ch
http://www.amnesty.ch
Taiwan Amnesty International, Room 525, No.2,
Section 1, Chung-shan North Road, 100 Taipei
Tanzania Amnesty International, Luther House,
3rd Floor, PO Box 4331, Dar es Salaam
E-mail: amnesty_tanzania@notes.interliant.com

Togo CCNP, BP 20013, Lomé
Tunisia Amnesty International, 67 rue Oum Kalthoum,
3ème étage, Escalier B, 1000 Tunis
E-mail: admin-tn@amnesty.org
United Kingdom Amnesty International, 99-119
Rosebery Avenue, London EC1R 4RE
E-mail: info@amnesty.org.uk
http://www.amnesty.org.uk
United States of America Amnesty International,
322 8th Ave, New York, NY 10001
http://www.amnestyusa.org
Uruguay Amnistía Internacional, Tristan Narvaja 1624,
Ap 1, CP 11200, Montevideo
Venezuela Amnistía Internacional,
Apartado Postal 5110, Carmelitas, 1010 A Caracas
E-mail: admin-ve@amnesty.org

AI coordinating structures
Bolivia Amnistía Internacional, Casilla 10607,
La Paz
Burkina Faso Amnesty International, 08 BP 11344,
Ouagadougou
E-mail: Contact.buro@cenatrin.bf
Caribbean Regional Office Amnesty International
C.R.O., PO Box 1912, Grenada, West Indies
Croatia Amnesty International, Martifieva 24,
10000 Zagreb
E-mail: admin@amnesty.hr
Cyprus Amnesty International, PO Box 2497, 1011
Nicosia
E-mail: amnesty@spidernet.com.cy
Czech Republic Amnesty International, Palackého 9,
110 00 Praha 1
E-mail: amnesty@ecn.cz
http://www.globe.cz
Gambia Amnesty International, PO Box 1935, Banjul
E-mail: amnesty@gamtel.gm
Hungary Amnesty International, 1399 Budapest,
PF 701/343
E-mail: amnesty.hun@mail.matav.hu
Malaysia Amnesty International, Pro-tem Committee,
29 Jalan SS 15/5D, Subang Jaya 47500
E-mail: amnesty@tm.net.my
Mali Amnesty International, BP E 3885, Bamako
E-mail: amnesty-mli@spider.toolnet.org
Mongolia Amnesty International, Ulaanbaatar 21 0648,
PO Box 180
E-mail: aimncc@magicnet.mn
Morocco Amnesty International, Place d'Angleterre,
Rue Souissra, Immeuble No. 11, Appt No. 1,
Rabat - l'Océan
E-mail: admin-ma@amnesty.org
Pakistan Amnesty International, Amber Medical
Centre, Room 210, 4th Floor M.A., Jinnah Road,
Karachi 74400
E-mail: amnesty@cyber.net.pk
Palestinian Authority Amnesty International,
PO Box 543, Khalaf Building, Racheed Street, Gaza City,
South Remal via Israel
E-mail: admin-pa@amnesty.org

Paraguay Amnistía Internacional, Vice-Presidente
Sanchez No. 310, esq. Mcal. Estigarribia, Asunción
E-mail: ai-info@amnistia.org.py
http://www.amnistia.org.py
Poland Amnesty International, ul. Jaśkowa Dolina 4,
80-252 Gdańsk
E-mail: amnesty@logonet.pl
http://www.ai.kampania.sprint.pl
Slovakia Amnesty International, Staromestská 6,
811 03 Bratislava
E-mail: amnesty@internet.sk
http://www.internet.sk/amnesty
South Africa Amnesty International, PO Box 29083,
Sunnyside 0132, Pretoria, Gauteng
E-mail: info@amnesty.org.za
Thailand Amnesty International, 61/9 Park Ploenchit
Tower, Soi Sukhumvit 1, Sukhumvit Road, Klongtoey,
Wattana, Bangkok 10110
E-mail: admin-th@amnesty.org
http://www.thailand.amnesty.com
Ukraine Amnesty International, Maydan Rynok 6,
Drohobych, 293 720 Lvivska obl
E-mail: officeai@dr.lv.ukrtel.net
Zambia Amnesty International, Private Bag 3, Kitwe
Main PO, Kitwe
E-mail: nkandol@mufnet.zccm.zm
Zimbabwe Amnesty International, PO Box 3951, Harare
E-mail: zimright@samara.co.zw (attn AI)

AI groups

There are also AI groups in:
Albania, Aruba, Azerbaijan, Bahamas, Barbados,
Belarus, Bosnia-Herzegovina, Botswana, Cameroon,
Chad, Curaçao, Dominican Republic, Egypt, Grenada,
Jamaica, Jordan, Kazakstan, Kuwait, Kyrgyzstan,
Lebanon, Liberia, Lithuania, Macao, Macedonia, Malta,
Moldova, Romania, Russian Federation, Turkey,
Uganda, Yemen

AI IN ACTION

"The voices of those who have been murdered for political reasons, of those who have 'disappeared' forever – as well as the voices of their families and friends left to mourn their absence – call for perpetrators to be brought to justice. We must honour that fundamental demand."

Pierre Sané, Secretary General of AI

AI members around the world continued to work on behalf of people whose fundamental human rights were threatened or abused.

AI's campaigning activities are based on meticulous research. During 1999 AI delegates visited more than 70 countries and territories to talk with victims of human rights violations, observe trials, and interview local human rights activists and officials.

The facts are gathered in order to generate action. AI members, supporters and staff around the world mobilize public pressure on governments and others with influence to stop human rights abuses. AI makes it possible for any interested person to send messages of concern directly to those who can change the situation.

Activities range from public demonstrations to letter-writing, from human rights education to fundraising concerts, from targeted appeals on a single individual to global campaigns on a specific country or issue, from approaches to local authorities to lobbying intergovernmental organizations.

AI confronts governments with its findings, by issuing detailed reports and by publicizing its concerns in leaflets, posters, advertisements, newsletters and on the Internet; AI information is available on more than 250 websites worldwide.

AI campaigns to change government attitudes and unjust laws. One of the ways it does this is by feeding a constant stream of information to the media, to governments and to the UN, urging them to take action.

AI also strives to promote awareness and strengthen the protection of human rights. It appeals to international organizations to intervene when a crisis appears likely to develop. It seeks the protection of refugees fleeing from persecution and it works with local human rights workers who are under threat of harassment or attack.

Long and medium-term actions

During 1999 AI's local groups worked on behalf of more than 4,500 named individuals, including prisoners of conscience and victims of other human rights violations, whose cases had been assigned to them as long-term Action Files or as medium-term actions through a Regional Action Network (RAN). Action Files and RAN actions were also issued in support of individual human rights defenders and organizations under threat.

There were 23 RAN networks involving around 1,800 groups covering human rights abuses in every country of the world. During the year, groups worked on more than 1,900 Action Files and RAN actions — of which 317 were launched during the year — on behalf of victims of human rights violations in more than 100 countries and territories. AI was able to close more than 212 group assignments on the detention of prisoners of conscience and possible prisoners of conscience.

Urgent actions

If urgent action is needed on behalf of people in imminent danger of gross human rights violations, volunteers around the world are alerted, and thousands of letters, faxes and e-mails are sent within days.

During 1999 AI initiated 538 such appeals from the Urgent Action network. There were also 421 follow-ups; 169 asking for no further action and 252 asking for further appeals to be sent. These actions were issued on behalf of people in 86 countries and territories, who were either at risk or had been the victims of torture or ill-treatment; "disappearances"; political killings and death threats; judicial executions; unfair trials; deaths in custody; or *refoulement* (forcible return) of asylum-seekers.

Crisis response

In addition to its ongoing and consistent work, AI responded to the escalation of human rights violations in Kosovo and East Timor.

Kosovo

In late March the human rights disaster in Kosovo — which AI had been warning about and had worked so hard to prevent — reached its peak.

AI responded by establishing teams of researchers in Albania and Macedonia to interview ethnic Albanian refugees about abuses they had suffered or witnessed. Refugee specialists in the research teams focused on assessing the quality of protection provided to refugees. This work was supplemented by AI sections in countries hosting the refugees.

On the basis of this research AI moved quickly to identify practical steps to help protect human rights, despite the disruption of communication links with Yugoslavia which deprived AI of opportunities for its traditional forms of action.

AI members worldwide called on their governments to give absolute priority to bringing to justice the perpetrators of violations in Kosovo and to providing unrestricted protection for Kosovar refugees.

AI pressed NATO to abide fully by international humanitarian law and continued to lobby for human rights protection to be given the highest priority in any peace agreement, focusing on a set of key post-conflict recommendations to the UN. When AI was again able to approach the Yugoslav authorities directly, it called for an end to restrictions on freedom of expression and assembly and clarification of the fate of Kosovar political prisoners transferred to Serbia.

In October AI established a six-month field mission in Kosovo. The mission addressed the increasing abuses against Serbs and Roma by ethnic Albanians, the role of the international presence in protecting human rights, and efforts to prosecute those responsible for past violations.

AI's mission also provided the movement with new avenues for campaigning — from action to end impunity and clarify the fate of Kosovo's many "disappeared" and "missing", to continuing work on refugee issues and the establishment of a durable human rights future for all of Kosovo's communities.

East Timor

In September, following a UN-organized ballot in which the overwhelming majority voted for independence from Indonesia, international attention turned to the worsening human rights crisis in East Timor. The human rights violations which had characterized the months preceding the ballot intensified.

Hundreds of thousands of people were forced to flee their homes and many were forcibly expelled from East Timor to Indonesia. Unlawful killings, rape and torture were carried out by pro-Indonesian militias acting with the direct and indirect support of the Indonesian military and police.

AI mobilized its membership to take action to stop the killings. AI sections all over the world initiated embassy vigils, mass e-mail appeals, petitions, government lobbying, fundraising actions and much more.

Members in Bangladesh, Nepal, Pakistan and Thailand took part in demonstrations and embassy visits and lobbies, highlighting the particularly important role of AI members in the region in showing solidarity with the people of East Timor, in subjecting the Indonesian government to Asian pressure and in urging regional governments to do more.

AI members in countries with large investments in or military links with Indonesia — including the USA, the United Kingdom (UK), the Netherlands, Japan, Australia, Germany and France — were mobilized to put pressure on their governments. AI called on donor governments to ensure that human rights considerations were central to discussions on donor assistance and to stop the supply of military equipment and expertise which could be used for the abuse of human rights.

As a result of public protest, the USA, Australia and the European Union (EU) imposed arms embargoes and suspended military training to Indonesia.

After a multinational force was sent to East Timor on 20 September and refugees began to return, AI's campaigning turned its focus on three main areas: protecting refugees; ensuring that those responsible for crimes against humanity and war crimes were brought to justice; and helping non-governmental human rights organizations to re-establish themselves. Supporting their work is a vital element in ensuring that people in East Timor and throughout Indonesia will not suffer mass human rights violations in the future.

AI's 24th International Council Meeting

In August some 400 people, representing AI sections in more than 50 countries and territories, took part in the International Council Meeting (ICM), AI's supreme governing body, in Tróia, Portugal. The ICM aims to reach decisions on a range of policy and strategy areas, by consensus where possible.

The 1999 ICM adopted more than 30 major policy decisions during its week-long discussions.

One of the principal themes was ending the impunity enjoyed by senior officials who order human rights violations, as well as bringing to justice those who carry out those orders.

Methods of achieving this aim discussed at the ICM included worldwide campaigns to ensure countries adopt national legislation to prosecute human rights abusers; campaigning against amnesty laws that allow those responsible for "disappearances", political killings or other grave human rights abuses to go free; and establishing strategies on how to support and cooperate with the proposed International Criminal Court.

ICM delegates agreed to strengthen AI's programs of work to end abuses targeted against women and children and to increase the organization's efforts to support the rights of refugees and asylum-seekers. They also discussed action to sensitize large corporations to their human rights responsibilities and resolved to increase AI's support to human rights defenders facing persecution for their activism.

Human rights defenders

Human rights defenders play a vital role in holding states to account in respect of their promises and obligations to protect the rights of their citizens. In Latin America, where for many years those who defend human rights have faced systematic repression, protection of human rights activists continued to be a high priority for AI.

In June AI published a report, *More protection, less persecution: Human rights defenders in Latin America* (AI Index: AMR 01/002/99), which documented human rights violations against human rights defenders in Latin America between 1996 and 1999. In the 1990s, hundreds of human rights activists were assassinated, arbitrarily detained, harassed, forced into exile or "disappeared" for investigating and exposing state violence and human rights violations. The report concluded with a set of 11 recommendations to Latin American governments outlining comprehensive measures to protect defenders.

Throughout 1999, AI continued to report the killing and abduction of human rights defenders, as well as the harassment and obstacles they faced in carrying out their legitimate activities. At the end of the year AI wrote to presidents in the Americas calling on them to ensure that governmental human rights initiatives and agendas gave the highest priority to ensuring protection for human rights defenders.

AI continued to develop its special program, in collaboration with local and international organizations, of protection mechanisms for human rights defenders at risk. In 1999 these primarily benefited Colombian human rights defenders. Its electronic Human Rights Defenders Network for Latin America, made up of members of AI and of human rights organizations in the region, set up to share information among defenders and generate immediate action for defenders on the front line, now involves more than 100 organizations.

In 1999, Network members contributed to improving protection by taking special action on cases involving more than 100 human rights defenders from Argentina, Brazil, Bolivia, Colombia, Chile, Ecuador, Guatemala, Haiti, Honduras, Mexico, Peru and Venezuela.

Worldwide campaigns

AI's worldwide campaign against human rights violations in the USA, *Rights for All*, launched in October 1998, continued for most of the year. The campaign focused on police brutality, ill-treatment of prisoners, detention of asylum-seekers, the death penalty and the USA's failure to uphold international law at home and abroad. Many of the issues highlighted during the campaign found increasing resonance within the country; authorities responded to AI's concerns and the media gave systematic coverage to the campaign, both within and outside the country. In 1999 this campaign was linked with AI's International Women's Day Action (see below).

AI's other concerted campaigns during the year covered human rights abuses in countries such as Afghanistan, Brazil, China, the Democratic Republic of the Congo, Iraq, Israel and the Occupied Territories, the Russian Federation, Togo, Tunisia and Turkey.

AI members also lobbied around the International Labour Conference, the Organization of African Unity Ministerial Conference on Human Rights, the Association of Southeast Asian Nations (ASEAN) Regional Forum, the General Assembly of the Organization of American States, Asia-Pacific Economic Co-operation (APEC) and the Commonwealth Heads of Government Meeting.

Areas of increased priority in AI's work during the year included its work on identity based human rights violations; on the control of international military, security and police transfers; and on companies and human rights.

Children's rights

In 1999 AI's Children's Rights Action centred on celebrating the 10th anniversary of the Convention on the Rights of the Child (CRC) and on lobbying governments for its effective implementation. The three broad themes of the campaign were: children in custody; children in the community and family; and children in conflict.

The campaign was launched during the 22nd Session of the UN Committee on the Rights of the Child in September and lasted several months. In line with AI's ongoing efforts to bring its work on children into the heart of its activities, the broad themes of the campaign were integrated with ongoing campaigns and projects.

AI's lobbying focused on four main areas: implementation of the CRC, the drafting of an Optional Protocol to the CRC raising the minimum age of recruitment into the armed forces and participation in hostilities from 15 to 18 years; implementation of commitments made in regional and international forums to stop the use of child soldiers; and ratification of the CRC by the USA, one of only two states in the world who have not so far ratified it.

AI members around the world undertook a variety of initiatives including a "children's petition", a human rights educational kit for primary school children, and encouraging children to write appeal letters to US President Bill Clinton on behalf of juvenile offenders on death row.

AI continued to call on governments to agree to a total ban on the deployment of under-18s in armed conflict situations. The International Non-governmental Organization Coalition to Stop the Use of Child Soldiers, of which AI is a member, organized regional conferences in Africa, the Americas and Europe during 1999 which brought together governments, regional and international non-governmental organizations and intergovernmental organizations to address this pressing issue.

Women's rights

AI sought to integrate actions on human rights abuses against women and gender-specific recommendations into its ongoing work on individual countries, as well as its thematic and country campaigns.

In many AI sections, the capacity of the women's coordinators has been strengthened and, through their efforts, the Inter-sectional Women's Network has become an important actor for change; some 30 sections were part of the Network, which was established in 1992.

Together with AI's allies within the women's movement and other parts of civil society in countries across all regions, AI tried to provide a voice to women in prisons in the USA.

Amid mounting international pressure on the US government to address the issue of human rights violations against women, AI's International Women's Day Action in 1999 was linked to the *USA: Rights for All* campaign. In March a report on women in US prisons, *USA: "Not part of my sentence" – violations of the human rights of women in custody* (AI Index: AMR 51/001/99), was launched with a series of press conferences across the USA.

The action pushed for a set of specific improvements, including restrictions on and regulation of the role of male staff with regard to female inmates and a ban on the use of restraints on pregnant women prisoners. AI members petitioned US Attorney General Janet Reno and the governors of the 14 states which had not criminalized sexual contact between correctional staff and inmates.

By the end of the year legislation had been approved in Massachusetts, Montana, Nebraska, Virginia, and Washington state which made sexual contact between male guards and women prisoners a criminal offence. In West Virginia, however, new legislation criminalized not only the guard but also the inmate; AI members responded by campaigning to have this part of the law revised.

In September AI launched a campaign against "honour killings" in Pakistan with the publication of a ground-breaking report, *Pakistan: Violence against women in the name of honour* (AI Index: ASA 33/017/99).

The threat of violence permeates every aspect of women's lives in Pakistan. The flimsiest of suspicions can lead to murder. A woman can face death by shooting, burning or slaughter with axes just for being suspected of having shamed her family in some way. She can be killed for having a supposed "illicit" relationship, for attempting to marry a man of her choice, or for divorcing an abusive husband.

In recent years, the number of honour killings has been on the rise as the perception of what constitutes honour — and what damages it — has widened and as more murders have taken on the guise of honour killings on the correct assumption that they are rarely punished. The number of honour killings has also risen parallel to women's increasing awareness and tentative assertion of their rights.

AI's campaign urged the Pakistan government to live up to its obligations under international law to protect women. It called on the government to review judicial practice and criminal laws which allow men to escape criminal prosecution for murdering their female relatives, and to make all forms of domestic violence a criminal offence. The other main themes of the campaign were the need to ensure all reports of honour killings were investigated and prosecuted; to initiate a wide-ranging and sustained public awareness program on women's equal rights; and to train law enforcement and judicial personnel to address impartially complaints of violence committed in the name of honour.

Lesbian, gay, bisexual and transgender rights

The AI network of lesbian and gay rights activists continued to expand, encompassing almost 30 sections. The network not only led campaigning against abuses based on sexual orientation, but also sought to integrate these concerns into the mainstream of human rights activism.

In March the first inter-sectional meeting of members of AI's Lesbian, Gay, Bisexual and Transgender (LGBT) Network took place in London, hosted by AIUK, with representatives from 26 countries. The meeting generated a great deal of enthusiasm for and commitment to LGBT campaigning. It also showed the importance of thematic networks in building links with the vibrant social movements that have developed throughout the world in the past 20 years.

Among the initiatives undertaken by members of AI's LGBT Network, was the decision by AI Philippines to take part in the Gay Pride Parade in June. They chanted that gay rights are human rights in recognition of the need to counter the tendency to neglect human rights abuses against gays and lesbians or to relegate them to the fringes of human rights campaigning.

In July a handbook on campaigning for LGBT rights was issued to enable AI members, groups and networks to get involved in promoting and defending LGBT rights. It looked at ways in which AI can contribute to and cooperate with the wider movement for lesbian and gay rights.

Military, security and police transfers

In 1999 more than 20 AI sections worldwide were engaged in campaigning work to oppose specific transfers of military, security and police (MSP) equipment, weaponry, training or personnel to countries where they were likely to facilitate human rights violations or breaches of humanitarian law.

Such MSP research and campaigning has become a key focus of AI's work — increasing the pressure on those directly responsible for human rights violations and highlighting the responsibility of supplier governments.

During the year, MSP activists campaigned to halt a wide range of arms transfers including the sale of attack helicopters to Turkey; the supply of small arms, light weapons, military training and assistance to combatants in the Democratic Republic of the Congo (DRC) conflict; and the provision of light strike aircraft, armoured personnel carriers, sub-machine guns, assault rifles and related military and security equipment and weaponry to the Indonesian military and security forces.

AI activists have also been involved in lobbying for the development and implementation of stringent controls on MSP transfers at the national, regional and global level.

A particular area of emphasis has been around the control of small arms and light weapons. In May 1999, AI joined more than 200 human rights organizations, development agencies, arms control watchdogs, church groups, grassroots women's organizations and medical associations to launch the International Action Network on Small Arms (IANSA).

The Network seeks to combat the global scourge of unregulated proliferation and misuse of small arms by tackling the problem from both the supply side — lobbying for stringent arms export controls in arms producing states — and from the demand side, using human rights education initiatives, arms destruction operations and ex-combatant demobilization schemes.

Companies

More than 20 AI sections had contact people working on approaches to companies in 1999. AI business groups continued to develop their contacts with companies based in their countries through seminars, round-table discussions and smaller bilateral meetings, at which AI promoted the responsibility of companies to adhere to human rights principles throughout their practices. AI groups held discussions with major oil companies and AI representatives spoke at national and international conferences on issues related to corporate conduct and human rights.

Human rights education

AI supports programs that help people understand and learn about human rights and how to defend them.

During 1999 AI sections in more than 50 countries continued to develop their programs and materials for human rights education. They lobbied governments to ensure that human rights were incorporated into official training and educational curricula in institutions ranging from schools and universities to military and police academies. In several countries, such as Guyana, Israel, Mauritius and Nepal, AI members worked closely with other non-governmental organizations and the relevant authorities to provide advice on the contents of teaching or training curricula.

AI members organized individual workshops and human rights training programs aimed at different target groups, such as teachers, women's groups and journalists.

For example, in April Moroccan AI groups held a workshop attended by 40 primary schoolteachers which was organized in cooperation with the Ministry of Education. AI groups and the Ministry of Secondary and Technical Education subsequently signed an agreement committing themselves to cooperate with each other on human rights education.

AI Nepal secured funding for a three-day training program for police trainers at 10 different locations in Nepal.

AI Senegal organized a successful training seminar for journalists which recommended that human rights should be formally included as part of the curriculum in the National School of Journalism.

AI Paraguay had meetings with the Ministry of Justice which was preparing to sign an agreement to distribute the recommendations in AI's 12-point guide for good practice in the training and education for human rights of government officials.

The Portuguese Minister of Education gave a commitment to introduce human rights into school curricula at a National Congress on Human Rights Education organized by AI Portugal, the National Commission for the Commemoration of the 50th Anniversary of the Universal Declaration of Human Rights, and the UN Decade for Human Rights Education. The Congress was attended by groups including school and college teachers, students, lawyers, journalists, non-governmental organizations and education authorities.

The first ever meeting of AI's Human Rights Education Coordinators took place in Cincinnati, USA, in November. Representatives of AI sections from 35 countries took part in this meeting. An international Coordinating Committee was elected and a four-year program was discussed and adopted. Participants particularly welcomed the rare opportunity the meeting afforded to exchange experiences and information about their work.

Refugees

AI sections around the world continued to intervene in hundreds of cases where asylum-seekers were at risk of being returned to countries where they could face serious human rights violations.

This work included providing information to the authorities and to asylum-seekers' legal representatives about human rights abuses in the countries from which asylum-seekers had fled; raising AI's concerns about legislation and practice which inhibit access to asylum procedures or otherwise put at risk asylum-seekers in need of protection; and campaigning for fair and satisfactory asylum procedures and for the provision of effective and durable protection against *refoulement* (forcible return). On an exceptional basis, AI intervened to resettle or evacuate asylum-seekers at imminent risk of human rights abuses in the countries where they had fled.

AI was increasingly concerned at the use of prolonged and sometimes arbitrary detention of asylum-seekers. AI intervened in a number of cases and jurisdictions. AIUSA launched a comprehensive report calling on the US government to comply with basic international human rights standards. AI Australia continued to campaign against the mandatory detention by the authorities of asylum-seekers who arrived without visas, a procedure which is in breach of international standards. Following lobbying by AI Australia and other non-governmental organizations about some particular individual cases which raised grave concerns, the Australian Senate initiated an inquiry into deportations and refugee determination. AI made submissions to the Senate urging the government to strengthen its refugee protection system, to incorporate international standards into domestic law, and to improve its methods of analysing the risks facing asylum-seekers if returned to the countries they had fled.

In May AIUK issued a report on unaccompanied refugee children in the UK. The report recommended, among other things, that the UK remove its reservation to Article 22 of the UN Convention on the Rights of the Child, which places limitations on the scope of protection afforded to child asylum-seekers. The report also called for information about countries of origin used in refugee determinations to include information about human rights violations against children, for all children to receive good quality legal representation at all stages of the asylum process, and for a total ban on the detention of unaccompanied refugee children.

AI Germany raised concerns with the German authorities about the restrictive refugee definition followed by the German courts and government which requires that, in order to be recognized as a refugee, a person must be at risk of persecution by a state or a "state-like body". As a result, asylum-seekers from countries such as Afghanistan and Somalia were not granted refugee status, despite the grave risk of human rights abuses that such individuals would face if returned.

The 1997 Treaty of Amsterdam — which transfers asylum matters to the competence of the European Community rather than individual member states —

came into force. AI sections in European Union (EU) member states called on heads of state and government at the European Council meeting in Tampere, Finland, to reaffirm their commitment to the 1951 Convention relating to the Status of Refugees. They urged the heads of state and government to interpret and apply the Convention in the light of the UN High Commissioner for Refugees (UNHCR) Handbook on Procedures and Criteria for Determining Refugee Status, and of the Conclusions of the Executive Committee of the UNHCR. In the context of plans by the High Level Working Group on Asylum and Migration of the Council of the EU to take action aimed at controlling migratory flows to the EU, AI sections in the EU called on EU member states to ensure that these measures were based on principles of human rights protection.

INTERNATIONAL AND REGIONAL ORGANIZATIONS

Intergovernmental organizations play an important role in the protection and promotion of human rights worldwide. Throughout 1999 AI continued its efforts to further its human rights work by seeking to influence international and regional organizations both in terms of campaigning against ongoing human rights abuses and in promoting international standards for the protection of human rights.

UN General Assembly
At the 54th session of the General Assembly, AI's priorities were to ensure the smooth endorsement of the Optional Protocol to the Convention on the Elimination of All Forms of Discrimination against Women (the Women's Convention), which would allow for the examination of complaints of violations of the human rights of women, and to ensure that as many states as possible signed the Protocol during the session and committed themselves to its speedy ratification.

AI also pushed for the adoption of a strong resolution on the death penalty following an initiative by the European Union introducing a resolution on this issue, although consideration of the resolution was later deferred.

In addition, AI worked on resolutions on Afghanistan, Cambodia, the Democratic Republic of the Congo, East Timor, Kosovo, Myanmar and Rwanda, as well as on thematic issues relating to the human rights of children and of women.

UN Security Council
Throughout 1999, AI continued to address the UN Security Council and make recommendations on a number of country situations, including Afghanistan, Angola, East Timor, the Great Lakes region of Central Africa, Kosovo and Sierra Leone, as well as on thematic concerns including the protection of civilians in armed conflict, the impact of arms transfers on conflicts, protection for refugees and internally displaced people, child soldiers, impunity and respect for international humanitarian and human rights law.

AI continued to urge the Security Council to recognize the human rights causes of all the situations on its agenda, and called on the Council to take into account human rights information and analysis to better prevent conflicts and so fulfil its responsibility for the maintenance of international peace and security.

AI also urged the Council to tackle the impact of human rights violations during conflict and to recognize the need to make human rights and the rule of law the basis on which shattered societies should be rebuilt to ensure a lasting peace.

AI issued Open Letters to the Security Council to challenge it into action on East Timor and Kosovo. Faced with the Council's inaction in Chechnya, in December AI issued a public statement calling on the Council to fulfil its responsibility and implement its own resolution on the protection of civilians in armed conflicts.

UN Secretariat
AI continued to follow closely the work of UN agencies in their "mainstreaming" of human rights, as called for in the UN reform proposals of the Secretary-General. This included lobbying on specific country operations where the UN played a major role, particularly East Timor and Kosovo, for which two of the most comprehensive mandates ever were approved by the Security Council.

AI also urged the UN to integrate human rights into all spheres of its work including development, humanitarian action, women, children and cooperation with business.

AI Secretary General Pierre Sané met with UN Secretary-General Kofi Annan twice to discuss a number of AI's priority concerns. AI also provided comments to the UN Secretary-General's Report on the Protection of Civilians in Conflict, which was issued in August. This report made a number of important recommendations on the role of the UN Security Council in protecting human rights.

UN High Commissioner for Human Rights
AI welcomed the repeated calls by the UN High Commissioner for Human Rights for the total abolition of the death penalty.

In several cases, she called on the USA not to execute juvenile offenders sentenced to death, and urged the USA to review the case of a foreign national sentenced to death after an unfair trial. The US authorities disregarded these requests.

AI also welcomed her speaking out in favour of the activities of human rights defenders in Colombia, and her strong condemnation of the murder of three of them in March, and of the murder in Northern Ireland of the lawyer Rosemary Nelson.

UN treaty bodies
AI provided information to the Committee against Torture and the Human Rights Committee on several countries under review by those bodies. These included Austria, Azerbaijan, Cambodia, Cameroon, Chile, Egypt, Hong Kong, Italy, Lesotho, Libya, Macao, Malta, Mexico, Morocco, Peru, the Republic of Korea, Romania, Uzbekistan and Venezuela.

In addition, AI presented information to the Committee on the Elimination of Discrimination against Women about violations of women's rights in Azerbaijan and Nepal.

AI also briefed members of the Committee on the Rights of the Child on the situation of children's rights in the Russian Federation. AI welcomed the detailed recommendations issued by the Committee to the government of the Russian Federation; these will act as a clear benchmark against which to measure improvements in the future.

AI also presented information to the Committee on Economic, Social and Cultural Rights on the Solomon Islands, and to the Committee on the Elimination of Racial Discrimination on Australia.

UN Commission on Human Rights
At the 1999 session of the Commission on Human Rights, AI raised concerns about and made specific recommendations regarding the human rights situations in Algeria, Cambodia, Turkey, the Great Lakes region of Central Africa, and the USA.

AI also focused on the issue of child soldiers and the draft optional protocol to the Convention against Torture and other Cruel, Inhuman or Degrading Treatment or Punishment (Convention against Torture).

AI pressed for the establishment of a Special Rapporteur on human rights defenders, but Commission members chose to delay any move in this direction.

AI also lobbied intensely for a resolution on the death penalty, and welcomed the adoption by the Commission — with even greater support than in 1998 — of a strong and innovative resolution calling for a moratorium on the death penalty.

AI was very active at the special session of the Commission, only the fourth in its history, which was devoted to the human rights situation in East Timor.

UN thematic mechanisms
AI continued to send information regularly to the UN mechanisms that deal with specific themes or countries.

AI also briefed the Working Group on Enforced or Involuntary Disappearances before its visit to Sri Lanka and the Special Rapporteur on extrajudicial, summary or arbitrary executions before she visited Mexico.

AI welcomed the joint mission to East Timor by three Special Rapporteurs, and expressed regret to the Working Group on Enforced or Involuntary Disappearances that the Working Group did not participate in that mission, when "disappearances" had been a particular problem in East Timor.

AI sent a joint letter to the UN Secretary-General in light of Malaysia's non-compliance with the Advisory Opinion of the International Court of Justice which stated that the Special Rapporteur on the independence of judges and lawyers was indeed entitled to immunity from the defamation suits against him in Malaysia.

World Bank
AI made recommendations and sent information to the World Bank concerning the situation in East Timor, Sierra Leone and Chechnya and emphasized the importance of integrating human rights into its programs and policies in these countries.

Organization of American States (OAS)
In its first ever audience with the Permanent Council of the OAS in March, AI raised concerns about torture in Brazil and Venezuela; enforced disappearance in Colombia and Mexico; measures facilitating the death penalty in Jamaica, Guyana, and Trinidad and Tobago; the increasing number of executions in the USA; and the vulnerable situation of human rights defenders.

AI raised similar concerns in a meeting with the Inter-American Commission on Human Rights, at which AI also requested that the Commission consider establishing a Special Rapporteur to deal specifically with the rights of human rights defenders.

AI welcomed the adoption by the OAS General Assembly in June of a resolution on human rights defenders, a development AI had actively supported.

AI denounced Peru's attempt to withdraw from the jurisdiction of the Inter-American Court of Human Rights in two cases, and welcomed the Court's finding that the withdrawal was inadmissible.

AI filed a follow-up *amicus curiae* brief with the Court providing an analysis of the law on the right to information on consular assistance. AI welcomed the Court's Advisory Opinion that the failure to provide such information has an impact on due process and, in the case of the imposition of the death penalty, constitutes a violation of the right not to be arbitrarily deprived of life.

AI also submitted an *amicus curiae* brief to the Commission on conscientious objection to military service.

Organization of African Unity (OAU)
The OAU held its first ever Ministerial Conference on Human and Peoples' Rights in Mauritius from 12 to 16 April — a joint initiative of the OAU, the Office of the UN High Commissioner for Human Rights and the African Commission on Human and Peoples' Rights. In preparation for the Ministerial Conference, AI issued a report with recommendations on the integration of human rights into the work of the OAU, and another report urging OAU member states to ratify the African Charter on the Rights and Welfare of the Child.

AI participated in a three-day non-governmental meeting held in Nairobi, Kenya, which preceded the Ministerial Conference. The Ministerial Conference adopted "The Grand Bay Declaration and Plan of Action", which included a call for the integration of human rights into all OAU activities and the evaluation of the functioning of the African Commission on Human and Peoples' Rights.

Inter-Parliamentary Union (IPU)
AI attended the 102nd IPU Conference in Berlin in October and monitored one of the main themes of the session, the "Contribution of parliaments to ensuring respect for and promoting international humanitarian law on the occasion of the 50th anniversary of the Geneva Conventions". The IPU made an important declaration on the International Criminal Court, calling for cooperation with the tribunals for the former Yugoslavia and Rwanda, encouraging states to

promptly sign and ratify the Rome Statute of the International Criminal Court and recommending the revision of domestic legislation in order to conform to the requirements of the Rome Statute.

International Labour Organisation (ILO)
As in previous years, AI sent a representative to observe the discussions of the Committee on the Application of Standards of the International Labour Conference on governments' effective implementation of international labour standards. AI raised concerns about the situation in Myanmar under ILO Convention 29 on forced labour, and about Colombia and Myanmar under ILO Convention 87 on freedom of association. Under ILO Convention 107, AI reported on continuing human rights violations against indigenous people in Brazil in the context of disputes over land rights.

Standard-setting
Women's Convention – Optional Protocol
AI participated closely in the negotiations for and drafting of an Optional Protocol to the Women's Convention, to strengthen the protection of women's human rights under the Convention by allowing individuals the right to bring complaints of a violation, and by authorizing an inquiry by the committee which monitors implementation of the Convention when information is received indicating grave or systematic violations.

On 6 October the UN General Assembly adopted the Optional Protocol and AI began a worldwide campaign for its speedy ratification and entry into force.
Convention against Torture – draft optional protocol
AI participated in the open-ended working group on the draft optional protocol to the Convention against Torture. By the end of this meeting several issues remained unresolved. Some governments were concerned that references to international standards would convert those standards into obligations through their inclusion in a treaty. Some states feared any suggestion that members of the inspection sub-committee might be able to visit any place where prisoners might be held lest this include private homes or places where military secrets were kept. Some states insisted that there must be reference to national legislation in the optional protocol to ensure that such legislation is respected. A group of governments introduced a proposal which suggested a regime of "prior consent" for visits to places of detention.
Draft international convention on 'disappearances'
In an effort to move forward the drafting and adoption by the UN of an international convention dealing specifically with protection against enforced disappearance, AI and other non-governmental organizations asked the Commission on Human Rights to establish an inter-sessional working group to study the draft international convention.

Although several member states expressed their support for such an initiative, the Commission instead

requested states and intergovernmental and non-governmental organizations to submit comments on the draft with a view to examining it in its next session in 2000. At its session in August, the Sub-Commission on the Promotion and Protection of Human Rights (formerly the Sub-Commission on Prevention of Discrimination and Protection of Minorities) urged the Commission on Human Rights to examine the draft international convention as a priority in its next session.
Principles to combat impunity
AI continued its support for the drafting of a set of principles against impunity. Although the Draft Set of Principles for the Protection and Promotion of Human Rights through Action to Combat Impunity was adopted in 1997 by the Sub-Commission on Prevention of Discrimination and Protection of Minorities and submitted to the Commission on Human Rights for its examination, the Commission had not adopted the Principles by the end of 1999. Since AI considers the drawing up of these Principles to be an important advance in the protection of human rights, it urged the UN to adopt them as a new international instrument.
Principles on the right to reparation
Although the UN Expert on the right to reparation was mandated to present the Commission on Human Rights with a new revised version of the draft Basic Principles and Guidelines on the Right to Reparation for Victims of Violation of Human Rights and International Humanitarian Law, he did not do so.

AI and others pressed the Commission to urge the UN Expert on the right to reparation to present it with the definitive version at its session in the year 2000, which the Commission did.
Child soldiers
AI campaigned actively for a minimum age of 18 years to be set for participation in armed conflicts and recruitment into armed forces ("straight 18s"). To strengthen support for this position, the Coalition to Stop the Use of Child Soldiers, of which AI is a founder member, organized a series of regional conferences during 1999 hosted by the governments of Mozambique, Uruguay and Germany. All three regional conferences adopted declarations supporting a strong and effective Optional Protocol to the Convention on the Rights of the Child.

AI welcomed the statement in September by the UN Secretary-General in which he "urge[d] Member States to support the proposal to raise the minimum age for recruitment and participation in hostilities to 18".

AI campaigned, in close cooperation with the Coalition to Stop the Use of Child Soldiers, for the explicit inclusion of child soldiering in ILO Convention 182 on the worst forms of child labour. This new treaty, which was adopted unanimously by the 174 member states of the ILO on 16 June, provides that the worst forms of child labour include "forced or compulsory recruitment of children for use in armed conflict".

This was the first time that an 18-year minimum age limit had been set in relation to child soldiering in an international convention, and was also the first specific, legal recognition of child soldiering as a form of child labour.

International Criminal Court

In 1999 AI continued its work to establish a just, fair and effective International Criminal Court on two fronts.

First, it participated in the Preparatory Commissions drafting the Rules of Procedure and Evidence as well as the Elements of Crimes, which will define the crimes within the Court's jurisdiction.

Second, it participated in a global campaign involving the more than 800 members of the Coalition for an International Criminal Court and launched by AI's Secretary General on 13 May at the Hague Appeal for Peace, to persuade states to sign and ratify the Rome Statute and to enact the necessary implementing legislation.

Ratifications by 60 states are needed to establish the Court. By the end of 1999, six had ratified it, and 92 states had taken the first step towards ratification by signing it.

Rome Statute of the International Criminal Court

1999 ratifications
Fiji	Ghana
Italy	San Marino
Senegal	Trinidad and Tobago

1999 signatures
Argentina	Armenia
Bangladesh	Benin
Bulgaria	Burundi
Central African Republic	Chad
Czech Republic	Estonia
Fiji	Haiti
Hungary	Kenya
Latvia	Malawi
Poland	Romania
Saint Lucia	Uganda

Selected international human rights treaties
(AT 31 DECEMBER 1999)

States which have ratified or acceded to a convention are party to the treaty and are bound to observe its provisions. States which have signed but not yet ratified have expressed their intention to become a party at some future date; meanwhile they are obliged to refrain from acts which would defeat the object and purpose of the treaty.

The **UN Convention on the Rights of the Child** has been ratified by all UN member states with the exceptions of Somalia (which has no functioning government) and the United States of America.

Key:
- ● became a state party in 1999
- ○ state is a party
- ◗ signed in 1999
- D signed but not yet ratified
- [22] Countries making a declaration under Article 22 recognize the competence of the Committee against Torture to consider individual complaints
- [28] Countries making a reservation under Article 28 do not recognize the competence of the Committee against Torture to undertake confidential inquiries into allegations of systematic torture if warranted

	International Covenant on Civil and Political Rights (ICCPR)	(first) Optional Protocol to the ICCPR	Second Optional Protocol to the ICCPR, aiming at the abolition of the death penalty	International Covenant on Economic, Social and Cultural Rights	Convention on the Elimination of All Forms of Discrimination against Women	International Convention on the Elimination of All Forms of Racial Discrimination	Convention relating to the Status of Refugees (1951)	Protocol relating to the Status of Refugees	Convention against Torture and Other Cruel, Inhuman or Degrading Treatment or Punishment
Afghanistan	○			○	D	○			○ [28]
Albania	○			○	○	○	○	○	○
Algeria	○	○		○	○	○	○	○	[22] ○
Andorra					○				
Angola	○	○		○	○		○	○	
Antigua and Barbuda					○	○	○	○	○
Argentina	○	○		○	○	○	○	○	[22] ○
Armenia	○	○		○	○	○	○	○	○
Australia	○	○	○	○	○	○	○	○	[22] ○
Austria	○	○	○	○	○	○	○	○	[22] ○
Azerbaijan	○		●	○	○	○	○	○	○
Bahamas					○	○	○	○	
Bahrain							○		○
Bangladesh					○				○
Barbados	○	○		○	○	○			
Belarus	○	○		○	○	○			○ [28]
Belgium	○	○	○	○	○	○	○	○	[22] ●
Belize	○				○		○	○	○
Benin	○	○		○	○	D	○	○	○
Bhutan					○	D			
Bolivia	○	○		○	○	○	○	○	●
Bosnia and Herzegovina	○	○		○	○	○	○	○	○
Botswana					○	○	○	○	
Brazil	○			○	○	○	○	○	○
Brunei Darussalam									
Bulgaria	○	○	●	○	○	○	○	○	[22] ○ [28]
Burkina Faso	●	●		●	○	○	○	○	●
Burundi	○			○	○	○	○	○	○
Cambodia	○			○	○	○	○	○	○
Cameroon	○	○		○	○	○	○	○	○
Canada	○	○		○	○	○	○	○	[22] ○
Cape Verde	○			○	○	○			○
Central African Republic	○	○		○	○	○	○	○	
Chad	○	○		○	○	○	○	○	
Chile	○	○		○	○	○	○	○	○
China	D			D	○	○	○	○	○ [28]
Colombia	○	○	○	○	○	○	○	○	○
Comoros					○				
Congo (Democratic Republic of the)	○	○		○	○	○	○	○	○
Congo (Republic of the)	○	○		○	○	○	○	○	
Costa Rica	○	○	○	○	○	○	○	○	○
Côte d' Ivoire	○	○		○	○	○	○	○	○

SELECTED INTERNATIONAL HUMAN RIGHTS TREATIES

	International Covenant on Civil and Political Rights (ICCPR)	(first) Optional Protocol to the ICCPR	Second Optional Protocol to the ICCPR, aiming at the abolition of the death penalty	International Covenant on Economic, Social and Cultural Rights	Convention on the Elimination of All Forms of Discrimination against Women	International Convention on the Elimination of All Forms of Racial Discrimination	Convention relating to the Status of Refugees (1951)	Protocol relating to the Status of Refugees	Convention against Torture and Other Cruel, Inhuman or Degrading Treatment or Punishment
Croatia	○	○	○	○	○	○	○	○	22 ○
Cuba					○	○			○
Cyprus	○	○	●	○	○	○	○	○	22 ○
Czech Republic	○	○		○	○	○	○	○	22 ○
Denmark	○	○	○	○	○	○	○	○	22 ○
Djibouti					○		○	○	
Dominica	○			○	○		○	○	
Dominican Republic	○	○		○	○	○	○	○	D
Ecuador	○	○	○	○	○	○	○	○	22 ○
Egypt	○			○	○	○	○	○	○
El Salvador	○	○		○	○	○	○	○	○
Equatorial Guinea	○	○		○	○	○	○	○	
Eritrea					○				
Estonia	○	○		○	○	○	○	○	○
Ethiopia	○			○	○	○	○	○	
Fiji					○	○	○	○	
Finland	○	○	○	○	○	○	○	○	22 ○
France	○	○		○	○	○	○	○	22 ○
Gabon	○			○	○	○	○	○	D
Gambia	○	○		○	○	○	○	○	D
Georgia	○	○	●	○	○	●	●	●	○
Germany	○	○	○	○	○	○	○	○	○
Ghana					○	○	○	○	
Greece	○	○	○	○	○	○	○	○	22 ○
Grenada	○			○	○	○	D		
Guatemala	○			○	○	○	○	○	○
Guinea	○	○		○	○	○	○	○	○
Guinea-Bissau					○	○	○	○	
Guyana	○	○		○	○	○			○
Haiti	○				○	○	○	○	
Holy See							○	○	
Honduras	○	D	D	○	○				○
Hungary	○	○	○	○	○	○	○	○	22 ○
Iceland	○	○	○	○	○	○	○	○	22 ○
India	○			○	○	○			D
Indonesia					○	●			○
Iran (Islamic Republic of)	○			○		○	○	○	
Iraq	○			○	○	○			
Ireland	○	○	○	○	○	D	○	○	D
Israel	○			○	○	○	○	○	○ 28
Italy	○	○	○	○	○	○	○	○	22 ○
Jamaica	○	○		○	○	○	○	○	
Japan	○			○	○	○	○	○	●
Jordan	○			○	○	○			○
Kazakstan					○	○	●	●	○
Kenya	○			○	○		○	○	○
Kiribati									
Korea (Democratic People's Republic of)	○			○					
Korea (Republic of)	○	○		○	○	○	○	○	○
Kuwait				○	○	○			○
Kyrgyzstan	○	○		○	○	○	○	○	○
Lao People's Democratic Republic					○	○			

Legend:

● became a state party in 1999

○ state is a party

◗ signed in 1999

D signed but not yet ratified

22 Countries making a declaration under Article 22 recognize the competence of the Committee against Torture to consider individual complaints

28 Countries making a reservation under Article 28 do not recognize the competence of the Committee against Torture to undertake confidential inquiries into allegations of systematic torture if warranted

Legend:

- ● became a state party in 1999
- ○ state is a party
- ◗ signed in 1999
- D signed but not yet ratified
- 22 Countries making a declaration under Article 22 recognize the competence of the Committee against Torture to consider individual complaints
- 28 Countries making a reservation under Article 28 do not recognize the competence of the Committee against Torture to undertake confidential inquiries into allegations of systematic torture if warranted

Country	International Covenant on Civil and Political Rights (ICCPR)	(first) Optional Protocol to the ICCPR	Second Optional Protocol to the ICCPR, aiming at the abolition of the death penalty	International Covenant on Economic, Social and Cultural Rights	Convention on the Elimination of All Forms of Discrimination against Women	International Convention on the Elimination of All Forms of Racial Discrimination	Convention relating to the Status of Refugees (1951)	Protocol relating to the Status of Refugees	Convention against Torture and Other Cruel, Inhuman or Degrading Treatment or Punishment
Latvia	○	○		○	○	○	○	○	○
Lebanon	○			○	○	○			
Lesotho	○			○	○	○	○	○	
Liberia	D			D	○	○	○	○	
Libyan Arab Jamahiriya	○	○		○	○	○			○
Liechtenstein	○	○	○	○	○		○	○	[22] ○
Lithuania	○	○		○	○	○	○	○	○
Luxembourg	○	○	○	○	○	○	○	○	[22] ○
Macedonia (former Yugoslav Republic of)	○	○	○	○	○	○	○	○	○
Madagascar	○	○		○	○	○	○		
Malawi	○	○		○	○	○	○	○	○
Malaysia					○				
Maldives					○	○			
Mali	○			○	○	○	○	○	●
Malta	○	○	○	○	○	○	○	○	[22] ○
Marshall Islands									
Mauritania						○	○	○	
Mauritius	○	○		○	○	○			○
Mexico	○			○	○	○			○
Micronesia (Federated States of)									
Moldova	○			○	○	○			○
Monaco	○			○		○	○		[22] ○
Mongolia	○	○		○	○	○			
Morocco	○			○	○	○	○	○	○ [28]
Mozambique	○		○		○	○	○	○	●
Myanmar					○				
Namibia	○	○	○	○	○	○	○		○
Nauru									
Nepal	○	○	○	○	○	○			○
Netherlands	○	○	○	○	○	○	○	○	[22] ○
New Zealand	○	○	○	○	○	○	○	○	[22] ○
Nicaragua	○	○	D	○	○	○	○	○	D
Niger	○	○		○	●	○	○	○	○
Nigeria	○			○	○	○	○	○	D
Norway	○	○	○	○	○	○	○	○	[22] ○
Oman									
Pakistan					○	○			
Palau									
Panama	○	○	○	○	○	○	○	○	○
Papua New Guinea					○	○	○	○	
Paraguay	○	○		○	○		○	○	○
Peru	○	○		○	○	○	○	○	○
Philippines	○	○		○	○	○	○	○	○
Poland	○	○		○	○	○	○	○	[22] ○
Portugal	○	○	○	○	○	○	○	○	[22] ○
Qatar						○			
Romania	○	○	○	○	○	○	○	○	○
Russian Federation	○	○		○	○	○	○	○	[22] ○
Rwanda	○			○	○	○	○	○	
Saint Kitts and Nevis					○				
Saint Lucia					○	○			
Saint Vincent and the Grenadines	○	○		○	○	○	○		

	International Covenant on Civil and Political Rights (ICCPR)	(first) Optional Protocol to the ICCPR	Second Optional Protocol to the ICCPR, aiming at the abolition of the death penalty	International Covenant on Economic, Social and Cultural Rights	Convention on the Elimination of All Forms of Discrimination against Women	International Convention on the Elimination of All Forms of Racial Discrimination	Convention relating to the Status of Refugees (1951)	Protocol relating to the Status of Refugees	Convention against Torture and Other Cruel, Inhuman or Degrading Treatment or Punishment
Samoa					○		○	○	
San Marino	○	○		○					
Sao Tome and Principe	D			D	○		○	○	
Saudi Arabia						○			○
Senegal	○	○		○	○	○	○	○	22 ○
Seychelles	○	○	○	○	○	○	○	○	○
Sierra Leone	○	○		○	○	D	○	○	D
Singapore					○				
Slovakia	○	○	●	○	○	○	○	○	22 ○
Slovenia	○	○	○	○	○	○	○	○	22 ○
Solomon Islands				○		○	○	○	
Somalia	○	○		○		○	○	○	○
South Africa	○			D	○	○	○	○	22 ○
Spain	○	○	○	○	○	○	○	○	22 ○
Sri Lanka	○	○		○	○	○			○
Sudan	○			○		○	○	○	D
Suriname	○	○		○	○	○	○	○	
Swaziland							○	○	
Sweden	○	○	○	○	○	○	○	○	22 ○
Switzerland	○		○	○	○	○	○	○	22 ○
Syrian Arab Republic	○			○		○			
Tajikistan	●	●		●	○	○	○	○	○
Tanzania	○			○	○	○	○	○	
Thailand	○			●	○				
Togo	○	○		○	○	○	○	○	22 ○
Tonga						○			
Trinidad and Tobago	○	○		○	○	○			
Tunisia	○			○	○	D	○	○	22 ○
Turkey					○	D	○	○	22 ○
Turkmenistan	○	○		○	○	○	○	○	●
Tuvalu					●		○	○	
Uganda	○	○		○	○	○	○	○	○
Ukraine	○	○		○	○	○			○ 28
United Arab Emirates						○			
United Kingdom	○		●	○	○	○	○	○	○
United States of America	○			D	D	○		○	○
Uruguay	○	○	○	○	○	○	○	○	22 ○
Uzbekistan	○	○		○	○	○			○
Vanuatu					○				
Venezuela	○	○	○	○	○	○		○	22 ○
Viet Nam	○			○	○	○			
Yemen	○			○	○	○	○	○	○
Yugoslavia (Federal Republic of)	○	D		○	○	○	○	○	22 ○
Zambia	○	○		○	○	○	○	○	○
Zimbabwe	○			○	○	○	○	○	

● became a state party in 1999

○ state is a party

▶ signed in 1999

D signed but not yet ratified

22 Countries making a declaration under Article 22 recognize the competence of the Committee against Torture to consider individual complaints

28 Countries making a reservation under Article 28 do not recognize the competence of the Committee against Torture to undertake confidential inquiries into allegations of systematic torture if warranted

Selected regional human rights treaties

(AT 31 DECEMBER 1999)

Organization of African Unity (OAU)

States which have ratified or acceded to a convention are party to the treaty and are bound to observe its provisions. States which have signed but not yet ratified have expressed their intention to become a party at some future date; meanwhile they are obliged to refrain from acts which would defeat the object and purpose of the treaty.

This chart lists countries which were members of the OAU at the end of 1999.

● became a state party in 1999

○ state is a party

◗ signed in 1999

◖ signed but not yet ratified

	African Charter on Human and Peoples' Rights (1981)	African Charter on the Rights and Welfare of the Child
Algeria	○	◗
Angola	○	●
Benin	○	○
Botswana	○	
Burkina Faso	○	○
Burundi	○	
Cameroon	○	●
Cape Verde	○	○
Central African Republic	○	
Chad	○	
Comoros	○	
Congo (Democratic Republic of the)	○	
Congo (Republic of the)	○	◖
Côte d' Ivoire	○	
Djibouti	○	◖
Egypt	○	◗
Equatorial Guinea	○	
Eritrea	●	●
Ethiopia	○	
Gabon	○	◖
Gambia	○	
Ghana	○	◖
Guinea	○	◖
Guinea-Bissau	○	
Kenya	○	
Lesotho	○	●
Liberia	○	◖
Libya	○	◖
Madagascar	○	◖
Malawi	○	●
Mali	○	○
Mauritania	○	
Mauritius	○	○
Mozambique	○	○
Namibia	○	◗
Niger	○	○
Nigeria	○	
Rwanda	○	◖
Saharawi Arab Democratic Republic	○	◖
Sao Tome and Principe	○	
Senegal	○	○

	African Charter on Human and Peoples' Rights (1981)	African Charter on the Rights and Welfare of the Child
Seychelles	○	○
Sierra Leone	○	D
Somalia	○	D
South Africa	○	D
Sudan	○	
Swaziland	○	D
Tanzania	○	D
Togo	○	○
Tunisia	○	D
Uganda	○	○
Zambia	○	D
Zimbabwe	○	○

● became a state party in 1999

○ state is a party

▶ signed in 1999

D signed but not yet ratified

Organization of American States (OAS)

States which have ratified or acceded to a convention are party to the treaty and are bound to observe its provisions. States which have signed but not yet ratified have expressed their intention to become a party at some future date; meanwhile they are obliged to refrain from acts which would defeat the object and purpose of the treaty.

This chart lists countries which were members of the OAS at the end of 1999.

Legend:

- ● became a state party in 1999
- ○ state is a party
- ◗ signed in 1999
- D signed but not yet ratified
- 62 Countries making a Declaration under Article 62 recognize as binding the jurisdiction of the Inter-American Court of Human Rights (on all matters relating to the interpretation or application of the American Convention)

	American Convention on Human Rights (1969)	Protocol to the American Convention on Human Rights to Abolish the Death Penalty	Inter-American Convention to Prevent and Punish Torture (1985)	Inter-American Convention on Forced Disappearance of Persons (1994)
Antigua and Barbuda				
Argentina	○ 62		○	○
Bahamas				
Barbados	○			
Belize				
Bolivia	○ 62		D	●
Brazil	○ 62	○	○	D
Canada				
Chile	○ 62		○	D
Colombia	○ 62		●	D
Costa Rica	○ 62	○	D	○
Cuba*				
Dominica	○			
Dominican Republic	○ 62		○	
Ecuador	○ 62	○	●	
El Salvador	○ 62		○	
Grenada	○			
Guatemala	○ 62		○	D
Guyana				
Haiti	○ 62		D	
Honduras	○ 62		D	D
Jamaica	○			
Mexico	○ 62		○	
Nicaragua	○ 62	●	D	D
Panama	○ 62	○	○	○
Paraguay	○ 62	◗	○	○
Peru	○		○	
Saint Kitts and Nevis				
Saint Lucia				
Saint Vincent and the Grenadines				
Suriname	○ 62		○	
Trinidad and Tobago				
United States of America	D			
Uruguay	○ 62	○	○	○
Venezuela	○ 62	○	○	●

* In 1962 the VIII Meeting of Consultation of Ministers of Foreign Affairs decided to exclude Cuba from participating in the Inter-American system

Council of Europe

States which have ratified or acceded to a convention are party to the treaty and are bound to observe its provisions. States which have signed but not yet ratified have expressed their intention to become a party at some future date; meanwhile they are obliged to refrain from acts which would defeat the object and purpose of the treaty.

This chart lists countries which were members of the Council of Europe at the end of 1999.

	European Convention for the Protection of Human Rights and Fundamental Freedoms (1950)	Protocol No. 6*	European Convention for the Prevention of Torture and Inhuman or Degrading Treatment or Punishment (1987)
Albania	25 ○ 46		○
Andorra	25 ○ 46	○	○
Austria	25 ○ 46	○	○
Belgium	25 ○ 46	○	○
Bulgaria	25 ○ 46	●	○
Croatia	25 ○ 46	○	○
Cyprus	25 ○ 46	▶	○
Czech Republic	25 ○ 46	○	○
Denmark	25 ○ 46	○	○
Estonia	25 ○ 46	○	○
Finland	25 ○ 46	○	○
France	25 ○ 46	○	○
Georgia	●	▶	
Germany	25 ○ 46	○	○
Greece	25 ○ 46	○	○
Hungary	25 ○ 46	○	○
Iceland	25 ○ 46	○	○
Ireland	25 ○ 46	○	○
Italy	25 ○ 46	○	○
Latvia	25 ○ 46	D	○
Liechtenstein	25 ○ 46	○	○
Lithuania	25 ○ 46	●	○
Luxembourg	25 ○ 46	○	○
Macedonia	25 ○ 46	○	○
Malta	25 ○ 46	○	○
Moldova	25 ○ 46	○	○
Netherlands	25 ○ 46	○	○
Norway	25 ○ 46	○	○
Poland	25 ○ 46	▶	○
Portugal	25 ○ 46	○	○
Romania	25 ○ 46	○	○
Russian Federation	25 ○ 46	D	○
San Marino	25 ○ 46	○	○
Slovakia	25 ○ 46	○	○
Slovenia	25 ○ 46	○	○
Spain	25 ○ 46	○	○
Sweden	25 ○ 46	○	○
Switzerland	25 ○ 46	○	○
Turkey	25 ○ 46		○
Ukraine	25 ○ 46	D	○
United Kingdom	25 ○ 46	●	○

● became a state party in 1999

○ state is a party

▶ signed in 1999

D signed but not yet ratified

25 Countries making a declaration under Article 25 recognize the competence of the European Commission of Human Rights to consider individual complaints of violations of the Convention

46 Countries making a declaration under Article 46 recognize as compulsory the jurisdiction of the European Court of Human Rights in all matters concerning interpretation and application of the European Convention

* Protocol No. 6 to the European Convention for the Protection of Human Rights and Fundamental Freedoms concerning the abolition of the death penalty (1983)

For more information on Amnesty International's work, particularly in the United States and Canadian sections, or a complete listing of A.I. publications with dollar prices, write to:

USA:
Amnesty International USA
National Office
Publications
322 Eighth Ave
New York, NY 10001

Canada:
Amnesty International
Canadian Section
(English Speaking)
214 Montreal Road
Suite 401
Vanier, Ontario K1L 1A4

Amniste Internationale
Section Canadienne
(Francophone)
6250 boulevard Monk
Montreal, Quebec H4E 3H7